Willmington's

COMPLETE GUIDE TO
BIBLE KNOWLEDGE

V O L U M E 1
Old Testament People

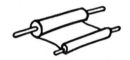

Volume One • Old Testament People

Willmington's
Complete
GUIDE
to
BIBLE
KNOWLEDGE

HAROLD L. WILLMINGTON

Tyndale House Publishers, Inc.

WHEATON, ILLINOIS

This book, the first volume in the series
Willmington's Complete Guide to Bible Knowledge,
is affectionately dedicated
to my brother and two sisters:

GORDON WILLMINGTON
MARY WILLMINGTON HARTFIEL
JUNE WILLMINGTON SMITH

Front cover photo by V. Gilbert Beers

Library of Congress Catalog Card Number: 90-70187
ISBN 0-8423-8161-9
Printed in the United States of America

96 95 94 93 92 91 90
9 8 7 6 5 4 3 2 1

Aaron

CHRONOLOGICAL SUMMARY

I. His service

A. For Moses

1. Aaron was a spokesman for Moses in Egypt.
   a. He was officially appointed by God (Exod. 4:16).
   b. At the time of his calling he was 83 (Exod. 7:6-7).
   c. He accompanied Moses to Egypt (Exod. 4:27-28).
   d. He met with the enslaved Israelites (Exod. 4:29).
   e. He met with Pharaoh (Exod. 5:1).
   f. He was criticized by the Israelites, who accused him of giving them a killing work burden (Exod. 5:20-21).
   g. He cast down his staff in front of Pharaoh, and it became a serpent (Exod. 7:10).
   h. He saw his serpent swallow up the serpents produced by Pharaoh's magicians (Exod. 7:12).
   i. He raised up his staff and struck the Nile, causing it to be turned into blood (Exod. 7:20).
   j. He raised his staff over the waters, bringing in the plague of frogs (Exod. 8:6).
   k. He raised his staff and struck the dust of the ground, introducing the plague of gnats (Exod. 8:17).

2. Aaron was Moses' supporter at Rephidim. He and Hur helped lift up Moses' hands in prayer during Joshua's battle with the Amalekites (Exod. 17:12).

3. Aaron was a spectator with Moses on Mt. Sinai.
   a. He accompanied Moses to the base of Sinai (Exod. 19:24; 24:1).
   b. He saw God's glory on Sinai (Exod. 24:9-11).

B. For God

1. Aaron's appointment
   a. He was formally ordained as Israel's first high priest (Lev. 8:1-36).
   b. He was washed with water, dressed in the garb of the high priest, anointed with oil, and sprinkled with animal blood (Exod. 29:1-21; 40:12-13).
   c. He began his high priestly ministry (Lev. 9).

2. Aaron's assignments
   a. He was commanded to pray for Israel (Exod. 28:9-38).
   b. He was appointed to supervise the tabernacle (Num. 18:5-9).
   c. He was to burn incense on the altar every morning and evening and to tend the lamps (Exod. 30:7-8).
   d. He was to make an annual atonement for Israel (Exod. 30:10).

e. He was given the rules for offering a bull on the Day of Atonement (Lev. 16:11-14, 18-19, 27-28).

f. He was given the rules for selecting the scapegoat for that day (Lev. 16:8-9, 15, 18-19, 27-28).

g. He was given orders concerning the burnt, grain, sin, guilt, trespass, and peace offerings (Lev. 6:9-30; 7:1-27).

h. He determined who was a leper (Lev. 13:1-45).

i. His tribe was to have no land inheritance in Canaan. Instead, they were to receive tithes from all the other tribes (Num. 18:30-31).

j. With Moses, he was in charge of the census taken at Mt. Sinai (Num. 1:1-19).

II. His sins

A. Against the people of God—constructing an idol

1. He gave in to the pressure of the Israelite crowd and constructed a golden calf for them while Moses was on Mt. Sinai (Exod. 32:1-5).

2. He lied to Moses with a pitiful excuse for doing this (Exod. 32:22-24).

3. He was saved from death at God's hand by Moses' prayer (Deut. 9:20).

B. Against the prophet of God—criticizing his brother

1. The cause for this criticism—Both he and his sister, Miriam, criticized Moses over two matters (Num. 12:1-2).

a. Moses' wife (12:1)

b. Moses' leadership (12:2)

2. The consequences of this criticism (Num. 12:4-15)

a. Both Aaron and Miriam were rebuked by God for this (12:5-8).

b. Miriam (the ringleader) was punished with a divine plague of leprosy (12:10).

c. Aaron confessed his sin and begged Moses to ask God to heal her. This was done and Miriam was healed (12:11-15).

III. His sorrow

A. Aaron's two dead sons—These men, Nadab and Abihu, were killed by God for offering strange fire upon the altar. Aaron was commanded by God not to mourn over the deaths of these young apostates (Lev. 10:1-7).

B. Aaron's two remaining sons—After a misunderstanding, Aaron justified the actions of Eleazar and Ithamar before Moses (Lev. 10:16-20).

IV. His staff

A. Aaron's rightful office as high priest was defended by Moses during Korah's rebellion (Num. 16:9-11).

B. Aaron's rightful office as high priest was demonstrated by God after Korah's rebellion by the supernatural blossoming of his wooden staff (Num. 17:1-9).

V. His successor

A. Aaron had his leadership taken from him and given to Eleazar his son on Mt. Hor (Num. 20:23-28).

B. Unbelief and rebellion prevented him from entering Canaan (Num. 20:12, 24).

C. He died (and was buried) on Mt. Hor (Num. 20:27–28).

D. Israel mourned for him 30 days (Num. 20:29).

E. He was 123 at the time of his death (Num. 33:39).

THEOLOGICAL SUMMARY

I. His name was mentioned in a special spiritual contract signed by those who loved God in the days of Nehemiah (Neh. 10:38).

II. His name is referred to several times in Psalms.

A. How God used Aaron and Moses to lead Israel (77:20)

B. How God heard their prayers (99:6)
C. How God worked miracles through them (105:26-27)
D. How Israel rebelled against them (106:16)
E. How God loves unity among his people, comparing it to the precious oil poured on Aaron's head which ran down on his beard and robe (133:2)
III. Micah the prophet mentioned Aaron when reminding Israel of God's faithfulness in the past (Mic. 6:4).
IV. Stephen referred to Aaron during his address before the Sanhedrin just prior to his martyrdom (Acts 7:40).
V. He is mentioned in Hebrews.
A. His priesthood is compared with that of Christ (5:4-5).
B. His priesthood is compared with that of Melchizedek (7:11).

STATISTICS

Father: Amram (Num. 26:59)
Mother: Jochebed (Num. 26:59)
Wife: Elisheba (Exod. 6:23)
Sons: Nadab, Abihu, Eleazar, Ithamar (Exod. 6:23; Num. 3:2-4)
Brother: Moses (Num. 26:59)
Sister: Miriam (Num. 26:59)
Significant ancestor: Levi (Num. 26:59)
Significant descendants: Ezra (Ezra 7:5), Zacharias and Elisabeth (Luke 1:5)
First mention: Exodus 4:14
Final mention: Hebrews 9:4
Meaning of his name: "Enlightened, illumined"
Frequency of his name: Referred to 339 times
Biblical books mentioning him: 16 books (Exodus, Leviticus, Numbers, Deuteronomy, Joshua, Judges, 1 Samuel, 1 Chronicles, 2 Chronicles, Ezra, Nehemiah, Psalms, Mark, Luke, Acts, Hebrews)
Occupation: Israel's first high priest (Exod. 28:1)
Place of birth: Egypt (Num. 26:59)
Place of death: Mt. Hor (Num. 20:27-28)
Age at death: 123 (Num. 33:39)
Important fact about his life: He was Moses'

older brother and Israel's first high priest (Num. 26:59; Exod. 28:1).

✐ Abednego

CHRONOLOGICAL SUMMARY

I. Abednego and the king's food (Dan. 1:1-20)
A. His resolve
1. He was one of four named Jewish youths among those taken from Judah to Babylon by King Nebuchadnezzar in 606 B.C. (Dan. 1:1-7).
2. He was also called Azariah (Dan. 1:7). The names of his three friends were:
a. Daniel, also called Belteshazzar (1:7)
b. Hananiah, also called Shadrach (1:7)
c. Mishael, also called Meshach (1:7)
3. Abednego determined along with his three friends not to defile his body with the king's food and wine. He participated in Daniel's request for a special, simple diet (Dan. 1:8-14).
B. His reward
1. God honored Abednego's decision and gave him great ability to master all the literature and science he was taught in Nebuchadnezzar's school (Dan. 1:17).
2. Upon completion of his three-year training program, Abednego was found by the king to possess 10 times the knowledge and wisdom of those who had remained on the royal diet (Dan. 1:18-20).
II. Abednego and the king's frustration (Dan. 2:1-19)
A. Nebuchadnezzar had dreamed a dream which he could not understand (2:1-3).
B. Nebuchadnezzar threatened to kill all

the wise men if they could not tell him both his dream and its interpretation (2:5).

C. Abednego joined Daniel and his friends in asking God to reveal the content and meaning of Nebuchadnezzar's dream (2:17-19).

D. God answered their request that very night (2:19).

E. Abednego, with Shadrach and Meshach, was promoted in the kingdom at Daniel's request (2:49).

III. Abednego and the king's furnace (Dan. 3:1-30)

A. His resolve

1. Abednego, along with Shadrach and Meshach, refused to bow down and worship a golden pagan statue Nebuchadnezzar had built (3:12).

2. After rejecting the king's final offer (he had given them a second chance), the three Hebrew youths were bound and cast into a fiery furnace (3:15-21).

B. His reward

1. Christ himself joined his three faithful servants in the fire, protecting them from all harm (3:24-25).

2. The three men stepped from the fire without even the smell of smoke upon them (3:26-27).

3. Abednego received another promotion from Nebuchadnezzar and prospered greatly (3:30).

STATISTICS

First mention: Daniel 1:7 (Jewish name was Azariah)

Final mention: Daniel 3:30

Meaning of his name: "Servant of Nego"

Frequency of his name: Referred to 20 times

Biblical books mentioning him: One book (Daniel)

Occupation: Political leader (Dan. 3:30)

Place of birth: Judah (Dan. 1:1-6)

Place of death: Babylon

Important fact about his life: He was preserved in the fiery furnace by Christ himself (Dan. 3:23-25).

 *Abel*

CHRONOLOGICAL SUMMARY

I. Offering a sacrifice to God

A. He presented to God the firstlings of his flock (Gen. 4:4).

B. His offering was accepted by God (Gen. 4:4).

II. Becoming a sacrifice for God—Abel was killed by his jealous brother Cain, whose grain offering had not been accepted by God (Gen. 4:5-8).

THEOLOGICAL SUMMARY

I. Christ referred to Abel's martyrdom when condemning the wicked Pharisees (Matt. 23:35).

II. Hebrews refers to the faith Abel demonstrated when he brought the right sacrifice to God, which serves as an object lesson for us today (Heb. 11:4).

III. Hebrews contrasts the blood of Christ with the blood of Abel (Heb. 12:24).

A. Abel's blood cried out for vengeance (Gen. 4:10).

B. Christ's blood cries out for forgiveness (Matt. 26:28).

IV. John wrote that Satan prompted Cain to kill Abel out of envy (1 John 3:12).

STATISTICS

Father: Adam (Gen. 4:2)

Mother: Eve (Gen. 4:2)

Brothers: Cain and Seth named (Gen. 4:1, 25) (See Gen. 5:4)

First mention: Genesis 4:2

Final mention: 1 John 3:12

Meaning of his name: "Transitory"

Frequency of his name: Referred to 12 times

Biblical books mentioning him: Five books (Genesis, Matthew, Luke, Hebrews, 1 John)

Occupation: Shepherd (Gen. 4:2)

Place of birth: Outside the Garden of Eden (Gen. 3:23–4:2)

Place of death: Field outside of the Garden of Eden (Gen. 4:8)

Circumstances of death: He was killed by his brother Cain (Gen. 4:8).

Important fact about his life: He was the world's first martyr.

Abiathar

CHRONOLOGICAL SUMMARY
I. Abiathar's activities in David's time
   A. He ministered to David during Saul's reign.
      1. He alone escaped Saul's massacre of the priests at Nob (1 Sam. 22:18-20).
      2. He brought the ephod to David on two occasions:
         a. In the city of Keilah (1 Sam. 23:6, 9)
         b. In the city of Ziklag (1 Sam. 30:1, 7)
   B. He ministered to David during Absalom's rebellion.
      1. He carried the Ark of Judah to David during the rebellion (2 Sam. 15:24-29).
      2. He convinced the elders of Judah to receive David after the rebellion (2 Sam. 19:11).
II. Abiathar's activities in Solomon's time
   A. He sided with Adonijah, Solomon's half brother, who led an unsuccessful coup against the king (1 Kings 1:7, 19, 25).
   B. Because of his loyalty to David, Solomon did not execute him but removed from him the office of high priest (1 Kings 2:26-27).

THEOLOGICAL SUMMARY
I. Jesus refers to an event that occurred when Abiathar was high priest to defend his right in plucking grain on the Sabbath (Mark 2:25).
II. Jesus reminded the Pharisees of how David was given food by the priest when he was hungry (Mark 2:26).

STATISTICS
Father: Ahimelech (1 Sam. 22:20)
Son: Jonathan (2 Sam. 15:27, 36)

Significant Ancestor: Aaron (Exod. 6:23; 1 Sam. 22:20; 1 Chron. 24:3)
First mention: 1 Samuel 22:20
Final mention: Mark 2:26
Meaning of his name: "Father of plenty"
Frequency of his name: Referred to 31 times
Biblical books mentioning him: Four books (1 Samuel, 2 Samuel, 1 Kings, Mark)
Occupation: High priest (1 Chron. 15:11)
Important fact about his life: He was a co-high priest with Zadok (1 Chron. 15:11).

Abigail

CHRONOLOGICAL SUMMARY
I. Her life as the wife of Nabal
   A. She was a very intelligent and beautiful woman (1 Sam. 25:3).
   B. She persuaded David not to kill her stupid husband (1 Sam. 25:23-31).
   C. David agreed and praised her for her courage (1 Sam. 25:32-33).
II. Her life as the wife of David
   A. After Nabal's death, Abigail became David's third wife (1 Sam. 25:40-42).
   B. She was briefly taken hostage by some enemy Amalekites from the city of Ziklag (1 Sam. 30:1-5).
   C. She was soon, however, rescued by David (1 Sam. 30:18).
   D. She later moved to Hebron with David (2 Sam. 2:2).

STATISTICS
Spouses: Nabal and David (1 Sam. 25:3; 25:40-42)
Son: Chileab, also called Daniel (2 Sam. 3:3; 1 Chron. 3:1)
First mention: 1 Samuel 25:3
Final mention: 1 Chronicles 3:1
Meaning of her name: "Source of delight"
Frequency of her name: Referred to 14 times
Biblical books mentioning her: Three books (1 Samuel, 2 Samuel, 1 Chronicles)
Important fact about her life: She was David's second wife. (NIV makes it appear in 1 Sam. 25:43 that Abigail was David's third wife. KJV is ambiguous.)

✍*Abihu*

CHRONOLOGICAL SUMMARY

I. He saw God's glory.
   A. He was appointed by God himself to be a priest (Exod. 28:1).
   B. He accompanied Moses, Aaron (his father), Nadab (his brother), and 70 Israelite elders partway up Mt. Sinai (Exod. 24:1).
   C. He was given a view of God's majesty: "They saw the God of Israel: and there was under his feet as it were a paved work of a sapphire stone, and as it were the body of heaven in his clearness" (Exod. 24:10).

II. He scorned God's glory: Abihu and Nadab were killed by the Lord (Lev. 10:1-11).
   A. The method of his death—Fire fell from heaven and consumed him (Lev. 10:2).
   B. The reasons for his death—The context suggests (see Lev. 10:9) that he may actually have been drunk when he "offered strange fire before the LORD" (Lev. 10:1).
   C. The lesson from his death—It served to illustrate God's holiness (Lev. 10:3, 10).
   D. The remembrance of his death—It is mentioned on two later occasions (Num. 3:4; 26:61).

STATISTICS

Father: Aaron (Exod. 6:23)
Mother: Elisheba (Exod. 6:23)
Brothers: Nadab, Eleazar, and Ithamar (Exod. 6:23)
First mention: Exodus 6:23
Final mention: 1 Chronicles 24:2
Meaning of his name: "He is my father"
Frequency of his name: Referred to 12 times
Biblical books mentioning him: Four books (Exodus, Leviticus, Numbers, 1 Chronicles)
Occupation: Priest (Exod. 28:1)
Place of death: Tabernacle at Kadesh-barnea

Circumstances of death: He was killed by God (Lev. 10:2).
Important fact about his life: He offered pagan fire to God in the tabernacle (Lev. 10:1).

✍*Abijam*

CHRONOLOGICAL SUMMARY

I. His background
   A. He was the second king of Judah.
   B. He ruled for three years (1 Kings 15:2).
   C. He was also called Abijah (1 Kings 14:31).
   D. He was an evil king (1 Kings 15:3).
   E. He was, however, well prepared to be king, having previously served as a chief prince in Israel (2 Chron. 11:23).
   F. He married 14 wives, through which he bore 22 sons and 16 daughters (2 Chron. 13:21).

II. His battles
   A. Abijam constantly fought with Jeroboam, king of Northern Israel (1 Kings 15:7).
   B. On one occasion Abijam attacked Jeroboam with 400,000 troops. However, Jeroboam was able to counterattack with 800,000 men (2 Chron. 13:3).
      1. Just prior to the battle, Abijam addressed the enemy soldiers (2 Chron. 13:4-12).
         a. The contents of the speech
            (1) He reminded them that God had once forever given the entire 12-tribe Israelite kingdom to his great grandfather David (13:5).
            (2) He denounced Jeroboam and his rebellion against David's kingdom and God (13:6-9).
            (3) He described the daily worship services the Northern troops were missing in the beautiful Jerusalem temple (13:10-11).
            (4) He warned them that to

fight against him was to
b. The consequences of the speech—During Abijam's lengthy address, he was secretly outflanked by the crafty Jeroboam (2 Chron. 13:13).
2. His salvation during the battle
a. Realizing he was surrounded, Abijam cried out in prayer, resulting in God's delivering Judah from Jeroboam (1 Kings 13:14-16).
b. There were 500,000 casualties inflicted upon Jeroboam's army by Abijam's soldiers (1 Kings 13:17).
c. Following the battle, Abijam grew stronger while Jeroboam grew weaker (1 Kings 13:20-21).

STATISTICS

Father: Rehoboam (1 Kings 14:31)
Mother: Maachah (1 Kings 15:2)
Son: Asa (1 Kings 15:8)
First mention: 1 Kings 14:31
Final mention: Matthew 1:7
Meaning of his name: "Father of light"
Frequency of his name: Referred to 20 times
Biblical books mentioning him: Three books (1 Kings, 2 Chronicles, Matthew)
Occupation: King of Judah (1 Kings 15:1)
Place of birth: Probably Jerusalem
Important fact about his life: He was saved from total defeat on the battlefield from his Northern Israel enemy, Jeroboam I, by crying out to God (2 Chron. 13).

✏️*Abimelech (1)*

CHRONOLOGICAL SUMMARY

I. Abimelech and Abraham
A. The travesty by Abraham
1. Abraham lied to Abimelech, telling him Sarah was really his sister (Gen. 20:2).
2. Abimelech decided to marry her (Gen. 20:2).

3. In a vision God warned him not to do this (Gen. 20:3-7).
4. He then returned Sarah to Abraham with a rebuke and gifts (Gen. 20:8-16).
5. A divine curse of closed wombs was then lifted by God (Gen. 20:17-18).
B. The treaty with Abraham—Abimelech later signed a peace treaty with Abraham at Beer-sheba (Gen. 21:22-32).
II. Abimelech and Isaac
A. The travesty by Isaac
1. Isaac (as his father had once done) lied to Abimelech, telling him Rebekah was really his sister (Gen. 26:7).
2. Abimelech discovered the truth, however, in an embarrassing moment for Isaac (Gen. 26:8).
3. Abimelech warned his people not to harm Isaac or Rebekah (Gen. 26:11).
B. The treaty with Isaac
1. Later, Abimelech asked Isaac to move out of Gerar (Gen. 26:16-17).
2. After Isaac continued to prosper, Abimelech made a treaty with him (Gen. 26:26-31).

STATISTICS

First mention: Genesis 20:2
Final mention: Genesis 26:26
Meaning of his name: "Father of the king"
Frequency of his name: Referred to 24 times
Biblical books mentioning him: One book (Genesis)
Occupation: King of Gerar (Gen. 20:2)
Important fact about his life: He attempted to marry Sarah (Gen. 20:2-6).

✏️*Abimelech (2)*

CHRONOLOGICAL SUMMARY

I. First part of his bloody reign
A. The declaration

1. At Shechem, Abimelech declared himself king (Judg. 9:1-3).
2. He was then given money by the citizens of Shechem, which he used to hire a gang of thugs (Judg. 9:4).

B. The deaths
  1. He went to Ophrah, home of Gideon his father, and tried to murder his 70 half brothers on one stone (Judg. 9:5).
  2. However, the youngest of Gideon's sons, Jotham, escaped (Judg. 9:5).
  3. Abimelech was then officially "crowned" king over all Israel by the citizens of Shechem and Beth-Millo (Judg. 9:6).

C. The derision—He was rebuked and ridiculed by Jotham from the top of Mt. Gerizim as the youngest half brother related the parable of the thornbush king (Judg. 9:7-20).

II. Final part of his bloody reign
  A. His difficulties
    1. After three years, God used an evil spirit to cause dissension between Abimelech and the citizens of Shechem to punish him for murdering his half brothers (Judg. 9:23-25).
    2. He was then plotted against by a disgruntled citizen of Shechem named Gaal (Judg. 9:26-38).
    3. Gaal led an army of Shechem citizens against him (Judg. 9:39).
    4. Abimelech, however, won the battle, capturing the city and murdering all its citizens (Judg. 9:40-49).
    5. He then occupied Thebez, another city which had rebelled against him (Judg. 9:50).
  B. His death
    1. Some of the people of Thebez took refuge inside the strong tower of their city (Judg. 9:51).

2. Abimelech surrounded it, planning to burn it (Judg. 9:52).
3. A woman from the top of the tower dropped a piece of a millstone on his head, which cracked his skull (Judg. 9:53).
4. He then ordered his armor bearer to kill him, lest it be said a woman killed him (Judg. 9:54).
5. His followers quickly dispersed, and the reign of the thornbush king ended (Judg. 9:55-57).

THEOLOGICAL SUMMARY
Joab referred to Abimelech in his report to David following a battle. He instructed his messenger: "If so be that the king's wrath arise, and he say unto thee, Wherefore approached ye so nigh unto the city when ye did fight? knew ye not that they would shoot from the wall? Who smote Abimelech the son of Jerubbesheth? did not a woman cast a piece of millstone upon him from the wall, that he died in Thebez? why went ye nigh the wall? then say thou, Thy servant Uriah the Hittite is dead also" (2 Sam. 11:20-21).

STATISTICS
Father: Gideon (Judg. 8:31)
Brothers: He had 71 half brothers. Jotham is the only one named (Judg. 9:5). (Note: It appears from Judg. 8:30-31 and 9:5 that there were 70 half brothers, of which 69 were killed. Also see "Gideon.")
First mention: Judges 8:31
Final mention: 2 Samuel 11:21
Meaning of his name: "Father of the king"
Frequency of his name: Referred to 40 times
Biblical books mentioning him: Two books (Judges, 2 Samuel)
Occupation: Outlaw; would-be king
Place of birth: Shechem (Judg. 8:31)
Place of death: Base of a tower in the city of Thebez (Judg. 9:50-54)
Circumstances of death: His skull was crushed by a falling stone (Judg. 9:53).
Important fact about his life: He killed his brothers (Judg. 9:5). (See note above.)

✐Abishai

CHRONOLOGICAL SUMMARY

I. Serving David during Saul's reign—He accompanied David into Saul's camp when David took from the sleeping king his spear and water jug (1 Sam. 26:6-12).

II. Serving David during David's reign
A. He became chief among three ranking generals in David's army (2 Sam. 23:18).
B. He later helped Joab kill Abner (Saul's general) for previously killing their younger brother Asahel (2 Sam. 3:30).
C. On two occasions David refused his request to kill Shimei (a relative of Saul) who had cursed the king during Absalom's rebellion (2 Sam. 16:5, 9-11; 19:21-23).
D. He helped his brother Joab put down the rebellion of Sheba following Absalom's revolt (2 Sam. 20:6, 10).
E. He once saved David from a giant Philistine warrior named Ishbi-benob (2 Sam. 21:15-17).
F. He slew 300 enemy troops on one occasion (2 Sam. 23:18).

STATISTICS

Mother: Zeruiah (2 Sam. 2:18)
Brothers: Joab and Asahel (2 Sam. 2:18)
First mention: 1 Samuel 26:6
Final mention: 1 Chronicles 19:15
Meaning of his name: "Source of wealth"
Frequency of his name: Referred to 24 times
Biblical books mentioning him: Three books (1 Samuel, 2 Samuel, 1 Chronicles)
Occupation: Military leader (1 Chron. 18:12; 19:15)
Important fact about his life: He was one of David's 30 brave warriors (2 Sam. 23:18).

✐Abner

CHRONOLOGICAL SUMMARY

I. Abner and Saul
A. Abner was related to Saul, being the son of Saul's uncle (1 Sam. 14:50).
B. He became the commander of Saul's army (1 Sam. 14:50).
C. He introduced David to Saul after the youth had killed Goliath (1 Sam. 17:55-57).
D. He sat at Saul's dinner table next to the king (1 Sam. 20:25).
E. He was rebuked by David for sleeping on duty, thus allowing Saul's spear and water jug to be taken (1 Sam. 26:14-16).

II. Abner and Ish-bosheth
A. He appointed Saul's son Ish-bosheth to reign over Israel after the death of the king (2 Sam. 2:8-9).
B. He proposed a bloody contest at the pool of Gibeon, pitting 12 warriors of David against 12 of his own. This resulted in the stabbing deaths of all 24 (2 Sam. 2:12-16).
C. His men were then defeated by Joab (captain of David's army) in battle (2 Sam. 2:17).
D. He was pursued by Asahel (Joab's youngest brother) and forced to kill him (2 Sam. 2:18-23).
E. He temporarily convinced Joab of the futility of doing battle with each other (2 Sam. 2:26-28).
F. He was accused by Ish-bosheth of sleeping with Rizpah, a former concubine of Saul. Abner angrily denied it and swore to turn the kingdom to David (2 Sam. 3:6-11).

III. Abner and David
A. Abner sent out peace messengers to David's camp (2 Sam. 3:12).
B. He then urged the elders of Israel to accept David as their king (2 Sam. 3:17-18).
C. He met with David and pledged his support (2 Sam. 3:19-21).

IV. Abner and Joab
  A. Abner was murdered by Joab (2 Sam. 3:22-27).
    1. To revenge the death of Asahel (3:30)
    2. To remove a potential rival
  B. His death was lamented by David (2 Sam. 3:31-39).
  C. David later charged Solomon to punish Joab for killing Abner (1 Kings 2:5-6).

STATISTICS
Father: Ner (1 Sam. 14:50)
First mention: 1 Samuel 14:50
Final mention: 1 Chronicles 27:21
Meaning of his name: "Father of light"
Frequency of his name: Referred to 61 times
Biblical books mentioning him: Three books (1 Samuel, 2 Samuel, 1 Chronicles)
Occupation: Military commander (1 Sam. 14:50)
Place of death: Near the main gate of Hebron (2 Sam. 3:27)
Circumstances of death: He was murdered by Joab (2 Sam. 3:27).
Important fact about his life: He was Saul's military commander (1 Sam. 14:50).

✍Abraham

CHRONOLOGICAL SUMMARY
  I. His conversion
    A. He was born and raised in Ur of the Chaldees, a city located in the land of Mesopotamia (Gen. 11:27-29; Acts 7:2-4).
    B. Prior to his conversion, Abraham was a worshiper of idols (Josh. 24:2).
    C. God appeared to him, and Abraham became a believer (Acts 7:2).
  II. His calling—He was commanded by God to leave Mesopotamia for a new land that God had promised to show him (Gen. 12:1; Acts 7:3).
  III. His commission—At age 75 (Sarah his wife was 65), Abraham received from God the sevenfold features of the Abrahamic Covenant (Gen. 12:2-3).
    A. "I will make of thee a great nation" (12:2).
    B. "I will bless thee" (12:2).
    C. "I will . . . make thy name great" (12:2).
    D. "Thou shalt be a blessing" (12:2).
    E. "I will bless them that bless thee" (12:3).
    F. "I will . . . curse him that curseth thee" (12:3).
    G. "In thee shall all families of the earth be blessed" (12:3).
  IV. His complacency
    A. He was to leave his father's house, but allowed both his father, Terah, and his nephew Lot to accompany him (Gen. 11:31-32; Acts 7:4).
    B. For awhile Abraham and his father settled down at a city called Haran (Gen. 11:31).
    C. After the death of his father, Abraham went to Canaan (Acts 7:4).
  V. His Canaan (Gen. 12:5-9)
    A. Abraham at Shechem (Gen. 12:5-7)
      1. Traveling through Canaan, he set up camp beside the plain at Moreh.
      2. God appeared to him there, promising to give the land to Abraham and his descendants.
      3. Abraham built his first recorded altar at this time and worshiped God.
    B. Abraham at Beth-el (Gen. 12:7-8)
      1. He camped between Beth-el and Ai.
      2. He constructed his second altar and called on God.
    C. Abraham at Hebron or Beer-sheba (Gen. 12:9) (He apparently settled down for awhile at one of these two locations in the southern part of Canaan.)
  VI. His carnality—There were two recorded occasions in his life when Abraham lied about his wife Sarah.
    A. His deception in Egypt (Gen. 12:10-20)

1. During a famine in Canaan, Abraham left the land and went to Egypt.
2. He persuaded Sarah to pretend she was his sister, fearing Pharaoh would kill him in order to marry her.
3. To Abraham's distress, Pharaoh did determine to make Sarah his wife.
4. God, however, plagued Pharaoh's household for his proposed action.
5. Upon learning the truth, the Egyptian king soundly rebuked Abraham for deceiving him about Sarah and sent both of them back to Canaan.

B. His deception in Philistia (Gen. 20:1-18)
1. Some years later during another famine, Abraham again left Canaan, this time going to Philistia.
2. For the second time, out of fear, Abraham lied, claiming Sarah was his sister.
3. Abimelech, king of Philistia, determined to marry Sarah.
4. At this point God stepped into the picture.
   a. He plagued the household of Abimelech.
   b. He warned the king not to marry Sarah.
   c. He warned the king not to harm Abraham.
5. Upon being rebuked by Abimelech for his deceit, Abraham offered a twofold defense:
   a. He had done this out of fear.
   b. He said his claim was partly true, for both he and Sarah had the same father, but different mothers, thus making them half brother and sister.
6. Abimelech then bestowed lavish gifts upon both Sarah and Abraham.
7. Abraham prayed for Abimelech, and God healed the barren wombs of Abimelech's household.

VII. His condescension
A. The argument (Gen. 13:1-7)
1. Shortly after returning from Egypt, Abraham settled in Beth-el and became a very wealthy man.
2. An argument broke out between the herdsmen of Lot, Abraham's nephew, and his own herdsmen concerning grazing rights.
B. The agreement (Gen. 13:8-13)
1. Unwilling to allow this to come between them, Abraham graciously invited Lot to take first choice of the land.
2. The young man foolishly chose the land area near Sodom, a notoriously wicked city.
C. The assurance (Gen. 13:14-17)—After their separation, God appeared to Abraham and reaffirmed a twofold promise, concerning both soil and seed.
1. The assurance concerning soil— God promised to give to Abraham and his offspring all the land he could see.
2. The assurance concerning seed— God promised to make Abraham's offspring like the dust of the earth.
D. The altars—Abraham built two altars during this period in his life.
1. The altar at Beth-el (Gen. 13:3-4)
2. The altar at Hebron (Gen. 13:18)

VIII. His courage
A. The villain—A Mesopotamian king named Chedorlaomer attacked and defeated the city of Sodom, carrying off many of its citizens into captivity (Gen. 14:1-11).
B. The victim—Among those enslaved was Lot, Abraham's nephew (14:12).
C. The victory—Upon learning of this, with 318 trained household men Abraham attacked and totally routed Chedorlaomer's army, setting Lot free (14:13-16).

IX. His communion—En route home from his great victory, Abraham was met by two kings.

A. Bera, the godless and perverted king of Sodom (Gen. 14:17, 21-24)

1. He requested that Abraham simply return the freed hostages to Sodom and keep the spoils of war for himself.

2. Abraham refused, lest it be said that the patriarch of God was made rich by this immoral monarch of Sodom.

B. Melchizedek, the godly and priestly king of Salem (Gen. 14:18-20)

1. The blessing Abraham received from Melchizedek—This godly king of Salem (first mention of Jerusalem in the Bible) shared bread and wine with Abraham and blessed him as follows: "Blessed be Abram of the most high God, possessor of heaven and earth . . . which hath delivered thine enemies into thy hand" (Gen.14:19-20).

2. The bounty Abraham remitted to Melchizedek—"And he [Abraham] gave him [Melchizedek] tithes of all" (Gen. 14:20).

X. His covenant

A. Abraham's unwise plan (Gen. 15:1-3)

1. God again appeared to Abraham, reassuring him he was the patriarch's shield and reward.

2. At this meeting Abraham proposed a plan to God.

a. He still had no children.

b. He proposed that he adopt a servant lad named Eliezer and consider this boy as the promised heir of the covenant.

B. God's all-wise plan (Gen. 15:4-21)

1. The features in God's plan—The Lord quickly rejected Abraham's plan in favor of his own divine plan, which was:

a. That a son coming from Abraham's own body would be his heir.

b. That Abraham's offspring would be as the stars in the heavens.

c. That both Abraham and his seed would inherit the land of Canaan.

2. The response to God's plan—"And he believed in the LORD; and he [God] counted it to him [Abraham] for righteousness" (Gen. 15:6).

3. The ratification of God's plan

a. God officially ratified his covenant with Abraham by a blood agreement.

b. At the Lord's command, Abraham sacrificed a heifer, a goat, and a ram, cutting them in two and arranging the halves opposite each other. He also sacrificed whole a turtledove and a young pigeon.

c. The Lord then caused a deep sleep to fall upon Abraham.

d. When the sun had set and darkness had fallen, God himself— in the form of a smoking fire pot with a blazing torch— passed through the pieces, indicating the immutability of the covenant.

4. The prophecy accompanying God's plan—The Lord now gave Abraham a sixfold prophecy:

a. His descendants would be strangers in a foreign land.

b. There they would be enslaved and mistreated for 400 years.

c. The nation that mistreated and enslaved them would be punished by God.

d. Abraham's descendants would then come out with great possessions.

e. In the fourth generation, his descendants would return to Canaan.

f. None of this would directly apply to Abraham, however, for he would live out his life in peace and be buried at a good old age.

XI. His compromise

A. The reason for his compromise (Gen. 16:1-2)
1. Abraham's wife Sarah had given up all hope of having children.
2. Sarah urged her husband to marry Hagar, her handmaid, saying: "I pray thee, go in unto my maid; it may be that I may obtain children by her" (Gen. 16:2).

B. The results of his compromise (Gen. 16:3-16)
1. Abraham married Hagar, who soon became pregnant.
2. Hagar, however, began to look down upon Sarah.
3. In a fit of anger, Sarah drove the pregnant girl into the desert.
4. The angel of the Lord appeared to Hagar, instructing her to return and submit to Sarah.
5. Hagar did this and gave birth to Ishmael, Abraham's first son.
6. The old patriarch was 86 at the time.

XII. His circumcision—When Abraham was 99, God again appeared to him and reconfirmed the Abrahamic Covenant, this time giving additional information concerning its features. Abraham acted according to this new agreement (Gen. 17:1-27).

A. The sign of the covenant—"This is my covenant, which ye shall keep, between me and you and thy seed after thee; Every man child among you shall be circumcised. And ye shall circumcise the flesh of your foreskin; and it shall be a token of the covenant betwixt me and you" (Gen. 17:10-11).

B. The stewards of the covenant
1. Abraham—His name was changed by God from Abram, meaning "exalted father," to that of Abraham, meaning "father of a multitude" (Gen. 17:5-6).
2. Sarah—Her name was changed from Sarai, meaning "contentious," to Sarah, meaning "princess" (Gen. 17:15-16).
3. Ishmael—Although Ishmael would not play an official role in the covenant, he would nevertheless greatly benefit from it. "As for Ishmael . . . behold, I have blessed him, and will make him fruitful, and will multiply him exceedingly; twelve princes shall he beget, and I will make him a great nation" (Gen. 17:20).
4. Isaac—For the first time, God revealed two facts about the long-awaited heir.
   a. What his name would be: "Thou shalt call his name Isaac" (Gen. 17:19).
   b. When his birth would occur: "Sarah shall bear . . . at this set time in the next year" (Gen. 17:21).

XIII. His compassion—The Lord and two angels appeared to Abraham "in the plains" of Mamre with some tremendous news and some tragic news.

A. The tremendous news (Gen. 18:1-15)
1. The reassurance—Once again, as he had previously done (Gen. 17:21), God reminded Abraham and Sarah concerning the birth of their son, saying: "I will certainly return unto thee according to the time of life; and, lo, Sarah thy wife shall have a son" (Gen. 18:10).
2. The reluctance—Upon overhearing God's words to Abraham as she stood inside the tent, Sarah's initial reaction was anything but positive. "Therefore Sarah laughed within herself, saying, After I am waxed old shall I have pleasure, my lord being old also?" (Gen. 18:12).
3. The rebuke—"The LORD said unto Abraham, Wherefore did Sarah laugh, saying, Shall I of a surety bear a child, which am old? Is any

thing too hard for the LORD? At the time appointed I will return unto thee, according to the time of life, and Sarah shall have a son. Then Sarah denied, saying, I laughed not; for she was afraid. And he said, Nay; but thou didst laugh" (Gen. 18:13-15).

B. The tragic news (Gen. 18:16-33)
1. God's indictment of Sodom
   a. Abraham learned the Lord was planning to destroy the notoriously wicked city of Sodom.
   b. Even at that moment the two angels who had previously met with Abraham were hurrying toward the city to make final preparations for its destruction.
2. Abraham's intercession for Sodom—Realizing his nephew Lot was living there, Abraham began praying for this city. He asked God:
   a. Would the city be spared if but 50 righteous people could be found in it? The answer was yes.
   b. Would it be spared for 45? Again, the answer was yes.
   c. What about 40 people? Yes.
   d. What about 30 people? Yes.
   e. What about 20 people? Yes.
   f. What if only 10 could be found? Yes. "And the LORD went his way, as soon as he had left communing with Abraham: and Abraham returned unto his place" (Gen. 18:33).

XIV. His celebration
A. The feast (Gen. 21:1-8)
1. As God had promised, Abraham fathered a son through Sarah.
2. Abraham named him Isaac and circumcised him on the eighth day.
3. He was 100 and Sarah was 90 at this time.
4. On the day Isaac was weaned, Abraham held a great feast to celebrate the occasion.
B. The flaunting—An event occurred

which greatly distressed Abraham on that otherwise glorious day. Sarah saw Ishmael, Hagar's son, mocking and ridiculing Isaac (Gen. 21:9).

C. The fury—An angry Sarah demanded that her husband banish Hagar. "Cast out this bondwoman and her son: for the son of this bondwoman shall not be heir with my son, even with Isaac" (Gen. 21:10).

D. The farewell—God instructed Abraham to follow Sarah's demand, reassuring the reluctant patriarch that both Ishmael and Hagar would be supernaturally provided for (Gen. 21:11-13).

E. The furnishing—Hagar was divinely provided for in the desert, and God fulfilled his promise concerning Ishmael (Gen. 21:14-21).

XV. His contract
A. We read of a *divine covenant* given *to* Abraham (Gen. 15:1-21).
B. We read of a *human contract* made *by* Abraham: Realizing God's hand was upon Abraham, the Philistine king Abimelech proposed to enter into a treaty with the old patriarch (Gen. 21:22-34).
1. The problem involved—"Abraham reproved Abimelech because of a well of water, which Abimelech's servants had violently taken away" (Gen. 21:25).
2. The particulars involved
   a. Abimelech expressed his ignorance of this (Gen. 21:26).
   b. Abraham gave him seven ewe lambs, "That they may be a witness unto me, that I have digged this well" (Gen. 21:30).
   c. Both men then agreed to show mutual kindness to each other and their descendants.
3. The place involved—All this was done at Beer-sheba, which means, "well of oaths" (Gen. 21:31).

XVI. His Calvary (Gen. 22:1-19)
A. Abraham's sorrow (Gen. 22:1-5)
1. The order—Abraham was tested

by God, who ordered him to offer up Isaac as a burnt sacrifice on Mt. Moriah.

2. The obedience—Displaying great obedience, Abraham prepared to carry out this command.
3. The ordeal
   a. Taking two servants and Isaac, he started for Mt. Moriah.
   b. Upon arriving, he instructed the servants to remain at the base of the mountain.
4. The optimism
   a. In spite of his pain, Abraham showed great faith in his final words to the servants: "Abraham said unto his young men, Abide ye here with the ass; and I and the lad will go yonder and worship, and come again to you" (Gen. 22:5).
   b. By these words the servants understood that both he and his son would return from the mountain.
   c. The book of Hebrews explains the reason for this optimism. "By faith Abraham, when he was tried, offered up Isaac: and he that had received the promises offered up his only begotten son . . . Accounting that God was able to raise him up, even from the dead; from whence also he received him in a figure" (Heb. 11:17, 19).

B. Isaac's submission (Gen. 22:6-9)
   1. During the climb, Isaac, not yet realizing he was to be the sacrifice, asked Abraham: "Behold the fire and the wood: but where is the lamb for a burnt offering?" (Gen. 22:7).
   2. Doubtless with breaking heart, Abraham replied: "My son, God will provide himself a lamb for a burnt offering" (Gen. 22:8).
   3. Upon reaching the top and learning the true story, Isaac willingly

allowed himself to be bound to the altar (Gen. 22:9).
   C. God's substitute—"Abraham stretched forth his hand, and took the knife to slay his son. And the angel of the LORD called unto him out of heaven, and said, Abraham, Abraham: and he said, Here am I. And he said, Lay not thine hand upon the lad, neither do thou any thing unto him: for now I know that thou fearest God, seeing thou hast not withheld thy son, thine only son from me. And Abraham lifted up his eyes, and looked, and behold behind him a ram caught in a thicket by his horns: and Abraham went and took the ram, and offered him up for a burnt offering in the stead of his son. And Abraham called the name of that place Jehovah-jireh: as it is said to this day, in the mount of the LORD it shall be seen" (Gen. 22:10-14).

XVII. His cave
   A. Abraham's tears—"Sarah was a hundred and seven and twenty years old: these were the years of the life of Sarah. And Sarah died in Kirjath-arba; the same is Hebron in the land of Canaan: and Abraham came to mourn for Sarah, and to weep for her" (Gen. 23:1-2).
   B. Abraham's transaction
      1. The place he bought—He purchased from Ephron the Hittite a cave called Machpelah located near Hebron where he buried Sarah (Gen. 23:3-16).
      2. The price he paid—Abraham gave Ephron 400 shekels of silver for the cave (Gen. 23:16).
      3. The purpose established—The field and cave became the family burial plot (Gen. 23:17-20).

XVIII. His command (Gen. 24:1-9)
   A. The problem involved—Abraham did not want his son Isaac to marry one of the pagan Canaanite women (Gen. 24:3).

B. The party involved—He called for his
trusted servant (probably Eliezer) to
help him (Gen. 24:1-4).

C. The plan involved (Gen. 24:5-9)

1. Eliezer was to visit Nahor in
northwestern Mesopotamia where
some of Abraham's relatives still
lived.

2. From this group he was to select a
bride for Isaac.

3. Under no circumstances was Eliezer to take Isaac out of the land of
Canaan.

D. The promise involved—"Abraham
said unto his eldest servant of his
house, that ruled over all that he
had, Put, I pray thee, thy hand under my thigh: . . . And the servant
put his hand under the thigh of
Abraham his master, and sware to
him concerning that matter" (Gen.
24:2, 9).

XIX. His Keturah (Gen. 25:1-6)

A. His final spouse—"Then again Abraham took a wife, and her name was
Keturah" (Gen. 25:1).

B. His final sons—"She bare him Zim-
ran, and Jokshan, and Medan, and
Midian, and Ishbak, and Shuah"
(Gen. 25:2).

C. His final settlement—Abraham gave
gifts to his sons and sent them away
from Isaac, to whom he gave all his
possessions (Gen. 25:5-6).

XX. His city

A. His earthly life ended. "These are the
days of the years of Abraham's life
which he lived, a hundred threescore
and fifteen years. Then Abraham
gave up the ghost, and died in a
good old age, an old man, and full of
years; and was gathered to his people" (Gen. 25:7-8).

B. His eternal life began. "He looked for
a city which hath foundations, whose
builder and maker is God" (Heb.
11:10).

THEOLOGICAL SUMMARY

I. His titles

A. He is called "the friend of God"
(2 Chron. 20:7; Isa. 41:8; James 2:23).

B. He is the acknowledged "father of the
Hebrew nation"(Ps. 47:9; 105:6; Isa.
41:8; 51:2).

C. The abode of departed believers prior
to Calvary was named after him,
known as "Abraham's bosom" (Luke
16:22). From this abode Abraham
himself carried on a conversation
with a rich man who had died
unsaved (Luke 16:24-31).

1. The man, being tormented by
flames, asked Abraham for relief.

2. Abraham told him this could not
be done.

3. The man then asked Abraham to
send Lazarus (a poor beggar who
had died saved) back to earth that
he might witness to the rich
man's five lost brothers.

4. Again, Abraham refused, pointing
out that they had had ample opportunity to hear the prophets.

5. If his brothers did not heed their
message, they would not listen
even if someone were to be raised
from the dead.

II. His example

A. He was referred to by John the Baptist to rebuke the unbelieving Pharisees and Sadducees (Matt. 3:7-9).

B. Abraham was often referred to by
Christ.

1. In distinguishing between Abraham's physical and spiritual seed
(Matt. 8:11-12; Luke 13:28-29; John
8:39)

2. To prove that God is the God of
the living and not of the dead
(Matt. 22:32)

3. To contrast himself with
Abraham—"Jesus said unto them,
Verily, verily, I say unto you,
Before Abraham was, I am" (John
8:58).

4. To testify that Abraham enjoyed
the blessings of the preincarnate

Christ—"Your father Abraham rejoiced to see my day: and he saw it, and was glad" (John 8:56).

C. Peter mentioned Abraham on two occasions during his sermon at the Jerusalem gate called Beautiful.
1. "The God of Abraham, and of Isaac, and of Jacob, the God of our fathers, hath glorified his Son Jesus; whom ye delivered up, and denied him in the presence of Pilate, when he was determined to let him go" (Acts 3:13).
2. "Ye are the children of the prophets, and of the covenant which God made with our fathers, saying unto Abraham, And in thy seed shall all the kindreds of the earth be blessed" (Acts 3:25).

D. Stephen referred to Abraham on five occasions during his defense before the Jewish high priest (Acts 7:2, 8, 16-17, 32). Stephen pointed out the following:
1. The God of glory had appeared to Abraham in Mesopotamia.
2. God gave him the seal of circumcision.
3. Abraham had purchased the cave of Machpelah as a burial ground.
4. God had promised Abraham that he would someday deliver his descendants from Egyptian bondage.
5. God invoked the name of Abraham during his call to Moses.

E. Paul mentioned Abraham.
1. During his first recorded sermon (Acts 13:26)
2. To illustrate four great truths
a. The meaning of and need for justification (Rom. 4:1-3, 11-12, 16; Gal. 3:16-18)
b. The true identity of Abraham's spiritual seed, namely, saved Jews and Gentiles, and not merely physical Jews (Rom. 4:11-12, 16; Gal. 3:6-9, 14, 29)
c. The sovereignty of God (Rom. 9:6-9)

d. The wisdom of God (Rom. 11:1)
F. God himself on three occasions reminded various individuals that he was Abraham's God.
1. He reminded Isaac (Gen. 26:24).
2. He reminded Jacob (Gen. 28:13).
3. He reminded Moses (Exod. 3:6).
G. At least 10 individuals referred to Abraham in their prayers or admonitions.
1. Jacob (Gen. 32:9-12)
2. Moses (Exod. 32:13)
3. David (1 Chron. 16:15)
4. Elijah (1 Kings 18:36)
5. Jehoshaphat (2 Chron. 29:7)
6. Hezekiah (2 Chron. 30:6)
7. The Levites in Nehemiah's time (Neh. 9:7)
8. Micah (Mic. 7:20)
9. Mary (Luke 1:55)
10. Zachariah (Luke 1:73)

III. His legacy
A. God often spared Israel and delivered that nation because of his covenant with Abraham. This occurred:
1. In the days of the Egyptian captivity (Exod. 2:24)
2. During the Exodus (Ps. 105:42)
3. During the reign of King Jehoash (2 Kings 13:22-25)
B. At least 18 events from Abraham's life are mentioned in the New Testament.
1. His early life in Mesopotamia (Acts 7:2)
2. His belief (Acts 7:2; Rom. 4:3; Gal. 3:6; James 2:23)
3. His receiving of the Abrahamic Covenant (Luke 1:73; Acts 3:25; Heb. 6:13-14)
4. His call to Canaan (Heb. 11:8)
5. His sojourn in Haran [Charran, KJV] (Acts 7:4)
6. His nomadic life in Canaan (Heb. 11:9)
7. His victory over Chedorlaomer (Heb. 7:1)
8. His meeting with Melchizedek (Heb. 7:1)
9. His (and Sarah's) faith in God's

promise concerning the birth of Isaac (Rom. 4:18-21; Heb. 11:11)

10. His circumcision (Acts 7:8; Rom. 4:11)
11. His marriage to Hagar and the birth of Ishmael (Gal. 4:22-24)
12. His meeting with God, just prior to Isaac's birth (Rom. 9:9)
13. His circumcising of Isaac (Acts 7:8)
14. His offering up of Isaac (Heb. 11:17; James 2:21)
15. His belief that, if necessary, God would raise up Isaac from the dead (Heb. 11:19)
16. His submissive wife, Sarah (1 Pet. 3:6)
17. His purchase of a sepulcher for Sarah (Acts 7:16)
18. His anticipation of that heavenly city (Heb. 11:10)

STATISTICS

Father: Terah (Gen. 11:26)
Spouses: Sarah, Hagar, and Keturah (Gen. 11:29; 16:3; 25:1)
Sons: From Hagar: Ishmael (Gen. 16:15-16). From Sarah: Isaac (Gen. 21:2-3). From Keturah: Zimran, Jokshan, Medan, Midian, Ishbak, and Shuah (Gen. 25:2)
Brothers: Nahor and Haran (Gen. 11:26)
Sisters: Half sister was Sarah (Gen. 20:12)
First mention: Genesis 11:26
Final mention: 1 Peter 3:6
Meaning of his name: "Father of a multitude"
Frequency of his name: Referred to 307 times
Biblical books mentioning him: 27 books (Genesis, Exodus, Leviticus, Numbers, Deuteronomy, Joshua, 1 Kings, 2 Kings, 1 Chronicles, 2 Chronicles, Nehemiah, Psalms, Isaiah, Jeremiah, Ezekiel, Micah, Matthew, Mark, Luke, John, Acts, Romans, 2 Corinthians, Galatians, Hebrews, James, 1 Peter)
Occupation: Patriarch
Place of birth: Ur of the Chaldees (Gen. 11:31)
Place of death: Near Hebron in Canaan (Gen. 23:19; 25:9)
Age at death: 175 (Gen. 25:7)

Important fact about his life: He was the father of the Hebrew nation and the ultimate role model for faith (Gen. 12:1-3; 1 Chron. 1:34; 2:1-2; Heb. 11:8-10).

 # Absalom

CHRONOLOGICAL SUMMARY

I. His revenge
   A. He had his half brother Amnon killed for raping Tamar, Absalom's full sister (2 Sam. 13:28-29).
   B. He then fled to the land of Geshur for three years (2 Sam. 13:37-38).
   C. After this time David was tricked by Joab into bringing Absalom back to Israel (2 Sam. 14:1-23).
   D. It was an additional two years, however, before David would agree to meet with his son Absalom (2 Sam. 14:24, 28-33).

II. His revolt
   A. His characteristics
      1. Absalom was extremely handsome (2 Sam. 14:25).
      2. He had fast-growing and heavy hair (2 Sam. 14:26).
   B. His craftiness
      1. He built himself up by parading around in a beautiful horse-drawn chariot, hiring 50 men to run ahead of him (2 Sam. 15:1).
      2. He stood by the road leading to the main gate in Jerusalem, met the people, listened to their needs, and stole their hearts (2 Sam. 15:2-6).
      3. After four years of this he made final plans for the revolt by receiving David's permission to visit Hebron under the pretext of fulfilling a vow (2 Sam. 15:7-9).
   C. His call to arms
      1. Upon reaching Hebron, he sent out trumpeters and messengers to announce he was Israel's new king (2 Sam. 15:10-11).
      2. At this time, he was joined by

David's counselor, Ahithophel
(2 Sam. 15:12).
3. Absalom forced David from Jerusalem and entered the city
(2 Sam. 15:13–37). David wrote
Psalm 3 on this occasion.
4. He lay with his father's concubines (2 Sam. 16:22).
5. Absalom was offered both wise
and foolish advice on attacking
David.
  a. The wise advice was given by
Ahithophel, namely, "Attack
immediately!" (2 Sam. 17:1-4).
  b. The foolish advice was given by
Hushai, a spy planted there by
David, namely, "Delay the attack" (and thus give David time
to prepare) (2 Sam. 17:5-14).
6. Absalom listened to Hushai, selected Amasa to lead his troops,
and wasted valuable time in preparing for the attack (2 Sam.
17:25).
7. Absalom's army was utterly
crushed during the battle in the
forest of Ephraim, losing 20,000 of
its troops (2 Sam. 18:6-7).
8. In fleeing from the battle on his
mule, Absalom's head was caught
by the thick branches of a large
oak tree, leaving him hanging in
midair (2 Sam. 18:9).
9. Joab found him and plunged
three javelins into his heart. Then
10 of Joab's men made sure Absalom was dead (2 Sam. 18:14-15).
10. His lifeless body was thrown into
a forest pit and covered by some
rocks (2 Sam. 18:16).
11. He was not buried in the pillar he
had previously prepared for himself in the King's Valley in Jerusalem (2 Sam. 18:18).
12. Absalom was mourned by David
(2 Sam. 18:33).

STATISTICS
Father: David (2 Sam. 3:3)
Mother: Maacah (2 Sam. 3:3)

Sons: Three unnamed sons (2 Sam. 14:27)
Daughter: Tamar (2 Sam. 14:27)
Brothers: 18 half brothers are named
(1 Chron. 3:1-8). The three most important were Amnon, Adonijah, and Solomon (2 Sam. 3:2-4; 12:24).
Sister: Tamar (2 Sam. 13:1)
First mention: 2 Samuel 3:3
Final mention: Psalm 3 (in the introduction)
Meaning of his name: "Father of peace"
Frequency of his name: Referred to 108 times
Biblical books mentioning him: Five books
(2 Samuel, 1 Kings, 1 Chronicles,
2 Chronicles, Psalms)
Place of birth: Hebron (2 Sam. 3:2-3)
Place of death: In the forest of Ephraim
(2 Sam. 18:6, 14)
Circumstances of death: He was stabbed to
death by Joab (2 Sam. 18:14).
Important fact about his life: He attempted to
steal the throne from his father David
(2 Sam. 15-18).

✍ Achan

CHRONOLOGICAL SUMMARY
I. The circumstances leading to his sin
  A. Although strictly forbidden to do so,
  Achan stole a Babylonian robe, 200
  shekels of silver, and a 50-shekel
  wedge of gold during the plunder of
  Jericho (Josh. 6:18-19; 7:20-21).
  B. He then buried these items in his tent
  (Josh. 7:21).
II. The consequences resulting from his sin
  A. His sin led to Israel's defeat (Josh.
  7:4-13).
  B. His sin led to his death.
    1. He was found out by a divinely
    conducted manhunt among the 12
    tribes (Josh. 7:14-19).
    2. He was then stoned to death
    (Josh. 7:25).

STATISTICS
Father: Carmi (Josh. 7:1)
First mention: Joshua 7:1
Final mention: 1 Chronicles 2:7

Meaning of his name: "Trouble"

Frequency of his name: Referred to seven times

Biblical books mentioning him: Two books (Joshua, 1 Chronicles)

Place of death: Valley of Achor, near Jericho (Josh. 7:26)

Circumstances of death: He was killed by stoning (Josh. 7:25).

Important fact about his life: His sin caused Israel to lose a battle (Josh. 7:11-12).

 # Adam

CHRONOLOGICAL SUMMARY

I. Inside the Garden of Eden
   A. His divinity
      1. He was created directly by God (Gen. 1:27).
      2. He was made in God's image (Gen. 1:26-27).
      3. He was formed from the dust of the ground (Gen. 2:7).
   B. His duties
      1. He was placed in Eden by God (Gen. 2:8-14).
      2. He was commanded to work and take care of Eden (Gen. 2:15).
      3. He was given dominion over all creatures (Gen. 1:26, 28).
      4. He was commanded to increase in number (Gen. 1:28).
      5. He named all the animals (Gen. 2:19-20).
      6. He was the source for Eve's creation (Gen. 2:21).
      7. He was allowed to eat of any tree in the Garden except one (Gen. 1:29; 2:16-17).
      8. He was forbidden to eat of the tree of the knowledge of good and evil (Gen. 2:17).
   C. His disobedience—He disobeyed God and ate of the forbidden tree (Gen. 3:6).
   D. His despair
      1. Adam realized his spiritual nakedness and tried to hide it from God by sewing fig leaves together (Gen. 3:7).
      2. He was judged by God (Gen. 3:17-19).
         a. A curse was placed upon the ground.
         b. By sweat and sorrow he would till the ground.
         c. At the end, he would return to the ground.
   E. His deliverance
      1. He was promised a future Savior (Gen. 3:15).
      2. He was forgiven and clothed with animal skins by God himself (Gen. 3:21).
      3. He named his wife Eve, meaning "mother of all living."
   F. His departure—Adam was driven from Eden, lest he eat of the tree of life and live forever in his sin (Gen. 3:22-23).

II. Outside the Garden of Eden
   A. He fathered another son, Seth, in addition to several unnamed sons and daughters (Gen. 4:25; 5:4)
   B. He was 130 at the birth of Seth (Gen. 5:3).
   C. He died at the age of 930 (Gen. 5:5).

THEOLOGICAL SUMMARY

I. Job assured God he was not attempting to hide his sin as Adam once had (Job 31:33).

II. Luke traced the genealogy of Christ back to Adam (Luke 3:38).

III. Paul contrasted the person and work of Adam with the person and work of Christ (Rom. 5:12-21; 1 Cor. 15:20-23, 45-50).
   A. Adam came from the dust of the earth and possessed a natural, corruptible body.
   B. Christ came from above and possessed a supernatural, incorruptible body.
   C. Adam introduced sin and death into the world because he disobeyed God. This he passed on to all his descendants.

D. Christ introduced righteousness and life into the world because he obeyed God. This he passes on to all who believe in him.

E. To remain in Adam is to die.

F. To be joined to Christ is to live.

IV. Paul used Adam to explain why he placed the man to be head of the woman (1 Tim. 2:12-14).

A. The chronological reason—Adam was created before Eve.

B. The theological reason—Adam was not deceived when he sinned, as was Eve.

STATISTICS

Father: God (Gen. 1:27; 2:7)

Mother: God (Gen. 1:27; 2:7)

Spouse: Eve (Gen. 2:21)

Sons: Cain, Abel, Seth, and unnamed sons (Gen. 4:1-2, 25; 5:4)

Daughters: Several unnamed daughters (Gen. 5:4)

First mention: Genesis 2:19

Final mention: Jude 1:14

Meaning of his name: "Of the ground, dust"

Frequency of his name: Referred to 30 times

Biblical books mentioning him: Nine books (Genesis, Deuteronomy, 1 Chronicles, Job, Luke, Romans, 1 Corinthians, 1 Timothy, Jude)

Occupation: Tiller of the ground (Gen. 3:17-19, 23)

Place of birth: Inside the Garden of Eden (See Gen. 2:7–8.)

Place of death: Outside Garden of Eden (Gen. 3:23-24)

Age at death: 930 (Gen. 5:5)

Important fact about his life: He was the world's first human being (Gen. 1:27; 2:7).

✍️*Adonijah*

CHRONOLOGICAL SUMMARY

I. His public attempt to steal Solomon's throne

A. His characteristics

1. He was very handsome (1 Kings 1:6).

2. Like his half brother Absalom, he was never disciplined by David (1 Kings 1:6).

B. His craftiness

1. He instigated a rebellion against his half brother Solomon while David was on his deathbed (1 Kings 1:5).

2. He secured the support of Joab, David's general, and Abiathar, one of the two high priests (1 Kings 1:7).

C. His consternation

1. The dying David was told of this rebellion by Solomon's mother, Bath-sheba, and Nathan the prophet (1 Kings 1:18-27).

2. David quickly responded by ordering Solomon to be publicly declared king (1 Kings 1:28-40).

3. Upon hearing of this, the terrified Adonijah sought refuge in the temple (1 Kings 1:50).

4. He was spared by Solomon on the condition that he behave himself (1 Kings 1:51-53).

II. His private attempt to steal Solomon's throne (1 Kings 2:13-25)

A. The plan—He asked Bath-sheba to obtain permission from Solomon to marry Abishag, David's last concubine.

B. The penalty—Upon hearing of this request, Solomon ordered Adonijah to be put to death.

STATISTICS

Father: David (2 Sam. 3:4)

Mother: Haggith (2 Sam. 3:4)

Brothers: 18 half brothers are named (1 Chron. 3:1-8). The three most important were Absalom, Amnon, and Solomon (2 Sam. 3:2-4; 12:24).

First mention: 2 Samuel 3:4

Final mention: 1 Chronicles 3:8

Meaning of his name: "Jehovah is my Lord"

Frequency of his name: Referred to 24 times
Biblical books mentioning him: Three books
  (2 Samuel, 1 Kings, 1 Chronicles)
Place of birth: Hebron (2 Sam. 3:2, 4)
Place of death: Jerusalem (1 Kings 2:13-25)
Circumstances of death: He was executed by
  order of King Solomon (1 Kings 2:25).
Important fact about his life: He attempted to
  steal the throne from his half brother Sol-
  omon (1 Kings 1:5-53).

✍*Ahab*

CHRONOLOGICAL SUMMARY
  I. His accomplishments
    A. He was able to put Moab to tribute
      (2 Kings 3:4-5).
    B. Jericho was rebuilt during his time
      (1 Kings 16:34).
    C. He built a palace in Samaria and in-
      laid it with ivory (1 Kings 22:39).
    D. He defeated the Syrians on two occa-
      sions (1 Kings 20:13-21, 29-30).
    E. He was the seventh ruler of Northern
      Israel.
    F. He ruled for 22 years (1 Kings 16:29).
 II. His apostasy
    A. He was the most wicked king of
      Northern Israel up to his time
      (1 Kings 16:30, 33; 21:35).
    B. He married beautiful but wicked Jeze-
      bel, a Phoenician and fanatical Baal
      worshiper (1 Kings 16:31).
    C. He soon began personally worshiping
      Baal (1 Kings 16:31).
    D. He built a temple and an altar for
      Baal in Samaria (1 Kings 16:32).
    E. His daughter was Athaliah, who later
      became the most brutal and bloody
      queen in the entire Bible (2 Kings
      8:18, 26; 11:1-3).
    F. To punish him for all this, God later
      ordered Jehu to destroy the entire dy-
      nasty of Ahab, including his 70 sons
      (2 Kings 9:6-10; 10:1).
    G. Ahab's wickedness was referred to

years later by the prophet Micah
  (Mic. 6:16).
III. His associates
    A. Ahab and Elijah
      1. Their meeting at the palace—
        Elijah told Ahab God planned to
        punish the sinful king by sending
        a terrible famine upon the land.
        In the New Testament James
        wrote that the famine lasted three
        and a half years (1 Kings 17:1;
        James 5:17).
      2. Their meeting on a mountain
        (1 Kings 18:20–19:2)
        a. At the end of the famine the
          men met again at the base of
          Mt. Carmel. Ahab attempted to
          blame Elijah for Israel's suffer-
          ing, but Elijah reminded him it
          was due to the king's sin
          (1 Kings 18:17-18).
        b. Elijah challenged Ahab to a
          contest on Mt. Carmel between
          himself and two large groups of
          false prophets (1 Kings 18:19).
          (1) The 450 prophets of Baal
          (2) The 400 prophets of Ashe-
            rah
        c. Upon winning the contest, Eli-
          jah told Ahab the drought
          would end and the rains would
          come (1 Kings 18:41).
        d. Ahab told Jezebel Elijah had
          killed all her prophets. She
          vowed revenge (1 Kings
          19:1-2).
      3. Their meeting in a vineyard
        (1 Kings 21:15-23; 27-29)
        a. Elijah condemned Ahab for
          having murdered Naboth,
          the owner of the vineyard, in
          order to seize his choice
          property.
        b. The prophecy condemning
          Ahab was twofold:
          (1) The dogs would lick Ahab's
            blood at the very spot where
            Naboth was murdered.
          (2) Ahab's wife, Jezebel, would

later be eaten by the wild
dogs of Jezreel.

  c. The king displayed a somewhat
shallow and brief repentance
upon hearing these words.

B. Ahab and Ben-hadad

  1. The vexation (1 Kings 20:1-12)

    a. Ahab's capital city of Samaria
was surrounded by the Syrian
Ben-Hadad and his allies.

    b. Ahab paid the original demand
of the enemy, who wanted the
king's gold, silver, and the best
of his wives and children.

    c. However, war broke out when
Ahab refused the second demand, namely, the wealth of
the entire city.

  2. The victories (1 Kings 20:13-21,
28-30)

    a. With but a small force of 7,000
soldiers, Ahab attacked and defeated Ben-hadad.

    b. The next spring Ben-hadad at-
tacked Ahab, but was again
soundly defeated, this time suffering 127,000 casualties.

    c. A prophet told Ahab he had
been allowed to win those two
victories to prove that Israel's
God was not simply a god of
the hills as Ben-hadad had sup-
posed.

  3. The violation (1 Kings 20:31-43)

    a. Ahab was condemned by a
prophet for sparing Ben-
hadad's life after defeating him
in battle.

    b. After hearing the prophet pro-
nounce the death penalty upon
him, the sullen king returned to
his palace in Samaria.

C. Ahab and Naboth (1 Kings 21:1-14)

  1. The request to Naboth—Ahab attempted to buy from its owner,
Naboth, a vineyard in Jezreel located near the palace.

  2. The reply by Naboth—Naboth
refused, saying: "The LORD forbid

it me, that I should give the inheritance of my fathers unto thee"
(1 Kings 21:3).

  3. The reprisal against Naboth—
Jezebel thereupon plotted his
death by having Naboth falsely
accused of blasphemy and treason, resulting in the death by
stoning of the vineyard owner.

D. Ahab and Jehoshaphat (1 Kings 22:2-
27)

  1. Ahab's recommendation

    a. Ahab convinced Jehoshaphat,
King of Judah, to join him in a
military alliance against Syria.

    b. In reality, God had allowed a
lying demon to deceive Ahab
into going to battle, for the
Lord was determined that he
should die.

  2. Ahab's reassurance—The king's
false prophets, led by Zedekiah,
assured both Ahab and Jehoshaphat that they would be victorious
over the Syrians.

  3. Ahab's reluctance

    a. Jehoshaphat, however, wanted
more assurance.

    b. A reluctant Ahab then called
for Micaiah, a true prophet of
God whom he had imprisoned.

    c. Micaiah appeared and predicted
both the defeat and death of
Ahab in battle.

  4. Ahab's rage—The furious king
sent Micaiah back to prison with a
diet of bread and water.

E. Ahab and a Syrian soldier (1 Kings
22:30-37)

  1. The king entered the battle disguised as a regular soldier.

  2. A Syrian soldier drew his bow
and shot an arrow at random; it
struck Ahab, mortally wounding
him.

  3. Soon the battle was lost, and the
dying king was carried home,
where he died.

  4. The dogs licked his blood from

the chariot near Samaria just as Elijah had predicted.

STATISTICS

Father: Omri (1 Kings 16:28)
Spouse: Jezebel (1 Kings 16:31)
Sons: Ahaziah and Jehoram (1 Kings 22:51; 2 Kings 3:1)
Daughter: Athaliah (2 Kings 8:18, 26)
First mention: 1 Kings 16:28
Final mention: Micah 6:16
Meaning of his name: "Father's brother"
Frequency of his name: Referred to 90 times
Biblical books mentioning him: Four books (1 Kings, 2 Kings, 2 Chronicles, Micah)
Occupation: King of Northern Israel (1 Kings 16:29)
Place of death: On a battlefield (1 Kings 22:34-35)
Circumstances of death: He was shot by an archer (1 Kings 22:34).
Important fact about his life: He allowed his wife Jezebel to turn him into one of Israel's worst kings (1 Kings 16:31-33).

Ahasuerus

CHRONOLOGICAL SUMMARY

I. Scene One: A Divorce Court
   A. The rejection by Vashti (Esther 1:1–2:1)
      1. Ahasuerus was the Persian king who ruled from the city of Shushan over 127 provinces, stretching from India to the Upper Nile.
      2. He had made Vashti his queen.
      3. During the third year of his reign the king hosted a 180-day celebration for his nobles and officials.
      4. This was followed by a seven-day banquet.
      5. On the seventh day of the feast when he was drunk, Ahasuerus ordered Vashti to parade herself before his drunken cronies.
      6. Vashti refused to do so.
   B. The rejection of Vashti
      1. The king was furious, and upon the advice of his intoxicated officials, he divorced her.
      2. Upon sobering up, he repented of his hasty action, but could not rescind his original command under Persian law.

II. Scene Two: A Marriage Altar (Esther 2:2-23)
   A. The search—To appease the king, a kingdom–wide search was conducted to find a new queen.
   B. The star
      1. A beautiful Jewish maiden, Esther, whose name means "star," won the beauty contest and became the new queen.
      2. She did not, however, reveal her Jewish background to the king at this time.
      3. Shortly after the wedding, Mordecai, Esther's cousin who had raised her, discovered and reported a plot against the king's life. The two would-be assassins were promptly arrested and hanged.

III. Scene Three: A Den of Iniquity (Esther 3:1-15)—Ahasuerus was persuaded by Haman, his newly appointed prime minister, to sign a law calling for the destruction of all Jews in the kingdom.

IV. Scene Four: A Throne Room (Esther 4:1–5:14)—Upon hearing of this plot from Mordecai, Esther risked her life by walking unannounced into the king's throne room. At her request, the king agreed to attend a banquet she would prepare for him and Haman alone.

V. Scene Five: A Bed Chamber (Esther 6:1-14)
   A. The sleepless potentate
      1. The king ordered the "Persian Congressional Record" to be read to him one night, hoping this would put him to sleep.
      2. Instead, he learned from the report that Mordecai had once saved his life, and he determined to reward him.

B. The heartless prime minister
1. At that moment Haman arrived at the palace, hoping to obtain permission to hang Mordecai.
2. By an ironic twist, Haman was forced to officiate over an honor parade for Mordecai.
VI. Scene Six: A Banquet Hall (Esther 7:1–10:3)
A. The reason for the banquet
1. Esther revealed to Ahasuerus the plot of Haman to kill both her and her countrymen.
2. Haman, not knowing that Esther was Jewish, begged for his life.
3. The king, however, assumed he did know and ordered him hanged on the very gallows prepared for Mordecai.
B. The results following the banquet
1. Ahasuerus gave Esther Haman's estate, and the signet ring he had once awarded to Haman was now presented to Mordecai.
2. Esther then begged the king to save her people from the coming holocaust.
3. Although unable to rescind his original decree, Ahasuerus issued another, whereby the Jews were permitted to defend themselves.
4. The Jews were later victorious over their enemies.
5. At Esther's request, Haman's 10 sons were hanged.
6. Ahasuerus promoted Mordecai to the office of prime minister.

STATISTICS

Father: Darius
Spouses: Vashti and Esther (Esther 1:9; 2:15-18)
First mention: Esther 1:1 (Xerxes in NIV)
Final mention: Esther 10:3
Meaning of his name: "Mighty, eye of man"
Frequency of his name: Referred to 28 times
Biblical books mentioning him: One book (Esther)
Occupation: King of the Medo-Persian empire (Esther 1:1-3)

Circumstances of death: He was eventually assassinated.
Important fact about his life: He married Esther (Esther 2:15-18).

Ahaz

CHRONOLOGICAL SUMMARY

I. Ahaz, the man
A. He began ruling at age 20 (2 Kings 16:2).
B. He was the 12th ruler of Judah.
C. He ruled for 16 years (2 Kings 16:2).
D. He was an evil king.
1. He offered sacrifices and burned incense to idols on hilltops, under every spreading tree, and on every street corner in Jerusalem (2 Kings 16:4; 2 Chron. 28:24).
2. He even sacrificed his own son in the fire (2 Kings 16:3).
II. Ahaz and Isaiah (Isa. 7:1-14)
A. The grievous rejection
1. Ahaz was attacked by Syria and Northern Israel.
2. The terrified king was reassured by God through Isaiah that Jerusalem would not be destroyed at that time.
3. In fact, Ahaz was offered any sign he wanted to demonstrate the fact of God's intention to save Jerusalem.
4. The faithless and foolish king, however, refused to put God to the test.
B. The glorious revelation—God then gave (in Ahaz's presence, but not for his benefit) a prophetical sign to the whole house of Israel that would prove the divine purpose to someday permanently deliver Jerusalem from all her enemies. "Behold, a virgin shall conceive, and bear a son, and shall call his name Immanuel" (Isa. 7:14).
III. Ahaz and his enemies
A. The Syrian army—This army took

many prisoners from Jerusalem to
Damascus (2 Chron. 28:5).
B. The Northern Israelite army
   1. Pekah, king of Northern Israel,
      attacked Ahaz and killed 120,000
      Judean soldiers, including Maase-
      iah, his son (2 Chron. 28:6-7).
   2. Pekah took captive 200,000
      women and children plus a great
      deal of plunder, carrying all this
      to Samaria (2 Chron. 28:8).
   3. However, Oded, a prophet from
      God, convinced Pekah to return
      to Judah all the captives and
      wealth his army had taken
      (2 Chron. 28:9-15).
IV. Ahaz and Tiglath-pileser
  A. Ahaz asked Tiglath-pileser the Assyr-
    ian king to help him against the
    Edomites and Philistines (2 Chron.
    28:16-20).
  B. He also turned to this pagan monarch
    for aid against Syria and Northern
    Israel, bribing him with gold and sil-
    ver taken from the temple (2 Kings
    16:7-8).
  C. After Tiglath-pileser had defeated the
    Syrians, Ahaz met him in Damascus.
    While there he saw a pagan altar
    which pleased him (2 Kings 16:9-
    10).
  D. He had a copy made and set it in the
    Jerusalem temple, replacing the regu-
    lar bronze altar (2 Kings 16:11-16).
  E. He also rearranged the other temple
    furniture in deference to the Assyrian
    king (2 Kings 16:17-18).
  F. He finally removed the temple furni-
    ture altogether, and shut the temple's
    doors (2 Chron. 28:24; 29:19).
  G. Sometime during this period he also
    constructed a special sundial (Isa.
    38:8).
 V. Ahaz and God—"In the time of his dis-
   tress did he trespass yet more against
   the LORD. . . . For he sacrificed unto the
   gods of Damascus, which smote him:
   and he said, Because the gods of the
   kings of Syria help them, therefore will
   I sacrifice to them, that they may help

me. But they were the ruin of him, and
of all Israel" (2 Chron. 28:22-23).

STATISTICS
Father: Jotham (2 Kings 15:38; 2 Chron.
  27:9)
Son: Hezekiah (2 Kings 16:20)
First mention: 2 Kings 15:38
Final mention: Matthew 1:9
Meaning of his name: "He holds"
Frequency of his name: Referred to 41 times
Biblical books mentioning him: Seven books
  (2 Kings, 1 Chronicles, 2 Chronicles, Isa-
  iah, Hosea, Micah, Matthew)
Occupation: King of Judah (2 Kings 16:1)
Important fact about his life: He was the first
  person to hear about the virgin birth
  prophecy (Isa. 7:11-14).

Ahaziah (1)

CHRONOLOGICAL SUMMARY
 I. His apostasy (1 Kings 22:10, 51-53)
  A. Ahaziah was the eight ruler of North-
    ern Israel.
  B. He ruled for two years.
  C. He was the son of Ahab and Jezebel.
  D. He turned his back on the true God.
    "And he did evil in the sight of the
    LORD, and walked in the way of his
    father, and in the way of his mother,
    and in the way of Jeroboam the son
    of Nebat, who made Israel to sin: for
    he served Baal, and worshipped him,
    and provoked to anger the LORD God
    of Israel, according to all that his fa-
    ther had done" (1 Kings 22:52-53).
 II. His accident: "And Ahaziah fell down
   through a lattice in his upper chamber
   that was in Samaria, and was sick: and
   he sent messengers, and said unto
   them, God, enquire of Baal-zebub the
   god of Ekron whether I shall recover of
   this disease" (2 Kings 1:2).
III. His angel (2 Kings 1:3-17).
  A. The object of his anger. Ahaziah is
    furious at Elijah the prophet, who

rebuked the king for looking to Baal instead of God to heal him.

B. The outburst of his anger
1. The king sent out 150 soldiers in three separate groups of 50 to arrest Elijah.
2. Elijah promptly called down fire from heaven, which destroyed his first two groups.
3. The captain of the third group cried out for and received mercy from Elijah.

C. The outcome of his anger: "And the angel of the LORD said unto Elijah, Go down with him: be not afraid of him. And he arose, and went down with him unto the king. And he said unto him, Thus saith the LORD, Forasmuch as thou hast sent messengers to enquire of Baal-zebub the God of Ekron, is it not because there is no God in Israel to enquire of his word? therefore thou shalt not come down off that bed on which thou art gone up, but shalt surely die. So he died according to the word of the LORD which Elijah had spoken" (2 Kings 1:15-17).

from Athaliah's bloody purge (2 Kings 11:2-3).

II. Ahaziah and Jehu—He was killed by Jehu while visiting the king of Israel in the city of Jezreel (2 Kings 8:28-29; 9:27-29).

STATISTICS

Father: Joram (2 Kings 8:24) (Jehoram in NIV)
Mother: Athaliah (2 Kings 8:26; 11:1; 2 Chron. 22:3)
Spouse: Zibiah (2 Chron. 24:1)
Sister: Jehosheba (2 Kings 11:2)
Son: Joash (2 Chron. 22:11)
First mention: 2 Kings 8:24
Final mention: 2 Chronicles 22:11
Meaning of his name: "Jehovah possesses"
Frequency of his name: Referred to 26 times
Biblical books mentioning him: Three books (2 Kings, 1 Chronicles, 2 Chronicles)
Occupation: Sixth king of Judah (2 Kings 8:24)
Place of death: Megiddo (2 Kings 9:27)
Circumstances of death: He was killed at Jehu's command (2 Kings 9:27).
Important fact about his life: He followed the ways of his wicked mother Athaliah (2 Chron. 22:3).

✍*Ahaziah (2)*

CHRONOLOGICAL SUMMARY

I. Ahaziah and Athaliah
A. His mother was Athaliah, the daughter of Ahab and Jezebel (2 Kings 8:26; 11:1; 2 Chron. 22:1, 3).
B. He was also called Jehoahaz and Azariah (2 Chron. 21:17).
C. He was 22 when he began ruling (2 Kings 8:26).
D. He was made king after the Arabs had killed all his older brothers (2 Chron. 22:1).
E. He ruled only one year (2 Kings 8:26).
F. He was an evil king (2 Chron. 22:4).
G. Ahaziah's sister, Jehosheba, later hid the king's little son, named Joash,

✍*Ahijah*

CHRONOLOGICAL SUMMARY

I. Predicting the division of a kingdom
A. He was a prophet from Shiloh (1 Kings 11:29).
B. He tore his new coat in 12 pieces and gave 10 of them to Jeroboam I, explaining this signified God's plan to give him rule over 10 of Israel's 12 tribes (1 Kings 11:29-36).
C. Ahijah then promised Jeroboam that God would establish his dynasty if the future king would but obey— which he did not (1 Kings 11:37-39).

II. Predicting the death of a son—Ahijah later told Jeroboam's wife that their ailing son would die because of the king's wickedness (1 Kings 14:1-18).

III. Predicting the destruction of a dynasty—He predicted that Jeroboam's family and descendants would later be cut off (1 Kings 14:10-11; 15:29-30).

STATISTICS
First mention: 1 Kings 11:29
Final mention: 2 Chronicles 10:15
Meaning of his name: "God is Brother"
Frequency of his name: Referred to 12 times
Biblical books mentioning him: Two books (1 Kings, 2 Chronicles)
Occupation: Prophet (1 Kings 11:29)
Important fact about his life: He predicted the division of the 12 tribes of Israel (1 Kings 11:29-32).

Ahimelech in mind (introduction to Ps. 52).

STATISTICS
Significant ancestor: Ithamar, Aaron's youngest son (Exod. 6:23; 1 Chron. 24:3)
First mention: 1 Samuel 21:1
Final mention: Psalm 52 (in the introduction)
Meaning of his name: "Brother of the king"
Frequency of his name: Referred to 16 times
Biblical books mentioning him: Four books (1 Samuel, 2 Samuel, 1 Chronicles, Psalms)
Occupation: High priest
Circumstances of death: He was executed by order of King Saul at the hands of Doeg the Edomite (1 Sam. 22:16-19).
Important fact about his life: He aided David in time of need (1 Sam. 21:6-9).

✑Ahimelech

CHRONOLOGICAL SUMMARY
I. He was deceived by David.
  A. Ahimelech was Israel's high priest living at Nob during the time Saul was attempting to kill David (1 Sam. 21:1).
  B. David lied to him during his flight from Saul, telling the high priest he was really on a secret mission for the king (1 Sam. 21:2).
  C. Ahimelech thereupon provided David with food and a sword (1 Sam.21:2-9).
II. He was destroyed by Saul.
  A. Ahimelech's kindness to David was seen and reported by Doeg, the vicious chief herdsman for King Saul (1 Sam. 21:7; 22:9-10).
  B. Saul ordered the high priest to be executed for befriending David (1 Sam. 22:11-19).
  C. Only Abiathar, Ahimelech's son, escaped the bloody purge among the 85 priests living at Nob (1 Sam. 22:20-23).
  D. David probably wrote Psalm 52 with

✑Ahithophel

CHRONOLOGICAL SUMMARY
I. The betrayal by Ahithophel
  A. He was a native of Giloh in the highlands of Judah (2 Sam. 15:12).
  B. He may have been Bath-sheba's grandfather (2 Sam. 11:3; 23:34).
  C. One of David's top 30 men was Eliam, son of Ahithophel (2 Sam. 23:34).
  D. He served for awhile as David's counselor (2 Sam. 15:12; 1 Chron. 27:33).
  E. He betrayed David, however, by siding in with Absalom during the rebellion (2 Sam. 15:12, 31).
II. The bitter end of Ahithophel
  A. David asked God to make Ahithophel offer foolish counsel to Absalom (2 Sam. 15:31).
  B. Ahithophel, however, gave wise advice to Absalom, but the foolish young rebel refused to listen (2 Sam. 17:1-4, 14).
  C. Upon realizing his counsel had been

rejected, Ahithophel went home and hung himself (2 Sam. 17:23).

STATISTICS
Son: Eliam (2 Sam. 23:34)
Significant descendant: Bath-sheba (2 Sam. 11:3; 23:34)
First mention: 2 Samuel 15:12
Final mention: 1 Chronicles 27:34
Meaning of his name: "Foolish brother"
Frequency of his name: Referred to 20 times
Biblical books mentioning him: Two books (2 Samuel, 1 Chronicles)
Occupation: Counselor (2 Sam. 16:23)
Place of death: In the city of Giloh (2 Sam. 15:12; 17:23)
Circumstances of death: He hanged himself (2 Sam. 17:23).
Important fact about his life: He betrayed David and gave support to Absalom (2 Sam. 15:12).

✐Aholiab

CHRONOLOGICAL SUMMARY
I. His appointment—He was appointed by God himself to serve as Bezaleel's chief assistant in the construction of the tabernacle (Exod. 31:2, 6).
II. His abilities
 A. He was a gifted teacher, instructing others in working with materials used to build the tabernacle (Exod. 35:34-35; 36:1-2).
 B. His special skill was in the area of engraving, weaving, and embroidering costly and colorful threads into fine linen cloth (Exod. 38:23).

STATISTICS
Father: Ahisamach (Exod. 31:6)
First mention: Exodus 31:6
Final mention: Exodus 38:23
Meaning of his name: "Father is my tent"
Frequency of his name: Referred to five times

Biblical books mentioning him: One book (Exodus)
Occupation: Craftsman and teacher (Exod. 38:23)
Important fact about his life: He served as the chief assistant to Bezaleel, who oversaw the construction of the tabernacle and everything in it, including the Ark of the Covenant (Exod. 31:1-6).

✐Amasa

CHRONOLOGICAL SUMMARY
I. His appointment by Absalom—He was David's nephew who was appointed commander-in-chief by Absalom during the rebellion against David (1 Chron. 2:16-17; 2 Samuel 17:25).
II. His agreement with David—After Absalom's death, Amasa agreed to help David regain his throne (2 Sam. 19:11-15; 20:4).
III. His assassination by Joab
 A. He was later murdered by Joab, David's commander-in-chief, for being a potential rival (2 Sam. 20:9-10).
 B. David regarded this as an act of cold-blooded murder until the day of his death (1 Kings 2:5).

STATISTICS
Father: Jether (1 Kings 2:5)
Mother: Abigail (1 Chron. 2:17)
First mention: 2 Samuel 17:25
Final mention: 1 Chronicles 2:17
Meaning of his name: "Burden bearer"
Frequency of his name: Referred to 15 times
Biblical books mentioning him: Three books (2 Samuel, 1 Kings, 1 Chronicles)
Occupation: Military leader (2 Sam. 17:25)
Place of death: By the great stone in Gibeon (2 Sam. 20:8-10)
Circumstances of death: He was killed by Joab (2 Sam. 20:8-10).
Important fact about his life: He was Absalom's military leader (2 Sam. 17:25).

✍Amaziah

CHRONOLOGICAL SUMMARY
I. His works
   A. He began reigning at age 25 (2 Kings 14:2; 2 Chron. 25:1). He was the ninth ruler of Judah.
   B. He reigned 29 years (2 Kings 14:2; 2 Chron. 25:1).
   C. He began by doing what was right (2 Kings 14:3; 15:3).
   D. Upon being established in power, he executed those officials who had killed his father, Joash (2 Kings 14:5).
   E. He did not, however, kill the children of the assassins because of the Mosaic Law that said: "The fathers shall not be put to death for the children, nor the children be put to death for the fathers; but every man shall be put to death for his own sin" (2 Kings 14:6).
   F. He rearranged the population and enlarged the army to 300,000 men (2 Chron. 25:5).
II. His warfare
   A. Against Edom—He defeated 20,000 Edomites in the Valley of Salt (2 Kings 14:7; 2 Chron. 25:11-12).
   B. Against Northern Israel
      1. The derision
         a. He challenged Jehoash, the Northern Israelite king, to do battle with him (2 Kings 14:8).
         b. Jehoash ridiculed Amaziah, referring to him as a thistle in Lebanon (2 Kings 14:9).
      2. The defeat—Amaziah continued his threat and war broke out. He was defeated, a portion of the Jerusalem wall was broken down, and all the gold, silver, and articles from the temple were taken by Jehoash (2 Kings 14:11-14).
III. His wickedness
   A. Amaziah on one occasion hired 100,000 soldiers from Northern Israel (2 Chron. 25:6).
   B. He was rebuked for this by a prophet of God (2 Chron. 25:7-9).
   C. He reluctantly dismissed the 100,000 hired troops (2 Chron. 25:10).
   D. He later learned that these soldiers had killed and plundered various Judean cities on their way home (2 Chron. 25:13).
   E. On another occasion (fearing he had offended the Edomite gods), Amaziah brought their idols to Jerusalem and worshiped them (2 Chron. 25:14).
   F. Again, he was severely rebuked for this by a prophet (2 Chron. 25:15-16).
   G. Amaziah was finally killed by his own officials in the city of Lachish (2 Chron. 25:27).

STATISTICS
Father: Joash (2 Kings 12:20-21)
Mother: Jehoaddin (2 Kings 14:1-2)
Son: Azariah (2 Kings 15:1)
First mention: 2 Kings 12:21
Final mention: 2 Chronicles 26:4
Meaning of his name: "God has strength"
Frequency of his name: Referred to 35 times
Biblical books mentioning him: Three books (2 Kings, 1 Chronicles, 2 Chronicles)
Occupation: King of Judah (2 Kings 14:1)
Place of death: In the city of Lachish (2 Chron. 25:27)
Circumstances of death: He was killed by his own officials (2 Chron. 25:27)
Important fact about his life: He was ridiculed as a thistle king (2 Kings 14:9).

✍Amnon

CHRONOLOGICAL SUMMARY
I. The rape of his half sister
   A. Amnon was David's eldest son (2 Sam. 3:2).
   B. He lusted after Tamar, his half sister and the full sister of Absalom (2 Sam. 13:1).
   C. Amnon tricked Tamar into caring for

him during a faked illness, at which time he raped her (2 Sam. 13:2-14).

D. His lust quickly turned to hate, causing him to completely disgrace Tamar by refusing to marry her (2 Sam. 13:15-19).

E. She then lived with Absalom, a broken and desolate woman (2 Sam. 13:20).

F. David was furious, but did nothing about it (2 Sam. 13:21).

II. The retaliation by his half brother—After two years of plotting revenge, Absalom had Amnon killed (2 Sam. 13:22-29).

STATISTICS

Father: David (2 Sam. 3:2)
Mother: Ahinoam (2 Sam. 3:2)
Brothers: His 18 half brothers are named (1 Chron. 3:1-8). The three most important were Absalom, Amnon, and Solomon (2 Sam. 3:2-4; 12:24).
Sister: Half sister named Tamar (2 Sam. 13:1)
First mention: 2 Samuel 3:2
Final mention: 1 Chronicles 3:1
Meaning of his name: "Tutelage, upbringing"
Frequency of his name: Referred to 27 times
Biblical books mentioning him: Two books (2 Samuel, 1 Chronicles)
Place of birth: Hebron (2 Sam. 3:2)
Place of death: At a banquet given by Absalom (2 Sam. 13:22-29)
Circumstances of death: He was killed by Absalom's servants (2 Sam. 13:29).
Important fact about his life: He raped his half sister Tamar (2 Sam. 13:10-14).

✐*Amon*

CHRONOLOGICAL SUMMARY

I. His apostasy
A. He was the 15th ruler of Judah.
B. He ruled for two years (2 Kings 21:19).
C. He was 22 when he became king (2 Kings 21:19).

D. He was an evil king (2 Kings 21:20).

E. He worshiped idols and forsook God (2 Kings 21:21).

F. Like his father Manasseh, Amon sacrificed to all the idols; but unlike his father, he did not repent of his sin (2 Chron. 33:22-23).

II. His assassination—His officials conspired against him and assassinated the king in his own palace (2 Kings 21:23).

STATISTICS

Father: Manasseh (2 Kings 21:18)
Mother: Meshullemeth (2 Kings 21:19)
Spouse: Jedidah (2 Kings 22:1)
Son: Josiah (2 Kings 21:24)
First mention: 2 Kings 21:18
Final mention: Matthew 1:10
Meaning of his name: "Workman"
Frequency of his name: Referred to 16 times
Biblical books mentioning him: Six books (2 Kings, 1 Chronicles, 2 Chronicles, Jeremiah, Zephaniah, Matthew)
Occupation: King of Judah (2 Kings 21:19)
Place of death: In the palace at Jerusalem (2 Kings 21:23)
Circumstances of death: He was assassinated by his own officials (2 Kings 21:23).
Important fact about his life: He repeated his father, Manasseh's, sins (2 Kings 21:21).

✐*Amos*

CHRONOLOGICAL SUMMARY

I. The grievous news—The majority of the book of Amos is a forceful portrayal of God's judgment of sin (Amos 1:1–9:10).
A. The denouncing of eight kingdoms (chapters 1–6)
1. The heathen kingdoms (1:1–2:3)
a. Their identities
(1) Syria—capital city, Damascus (1:3)
(2) Philistia—capital city, Gaza (1:6)
(3) Phoenica—capital city, Tyre (1:9)

(4) Edom—capital cities, Teman and Bozrah (1:12)

(5) Ammon—capital city, Rabbah (1:14)

(6) Moab—capital city, Kerioth (2:2)

b. Among their iniquities:

(1) Barbaric cruelty (1:13)

(2) Slave running (1:6)

(3) Treachery (1:9)

(4) Bloodshed (1:11)

(5) Desecration of the dead (2:1)

2. The Hebrew kingdoms—Judah and Northern Israel (2:4–6:14)

a. Among their perversions against God:

(1) Rejection of his law (2:4)

(2) Idolatry (2:8)

(3) Utter contempt for the poor (2:6)

(4) Gross materialism (2:6)

(5) Shameless immorality (2:7)

(6) Forcing Nazarites to break their vows (2:12)

(7) Forbidding the prophets and prophecy (2:12)

(8) Total hypocrisy in their formal and empty religion (2:4)

(9) Bribery and corruption of justice (2:6)

(10) Drunkenness (2:8)

b. Their punishment from God

(1) Their chief cities (Jerusalem, Beth-el, Samaria, Gilgal) would be burned with fire.

(2) Their armies would be totally defeated, suffering a 90 percent casualty rate.

(3) Their land would be occupied by enemy soldiers.

(4) Their people would be led into foreign captivity.

B. The announcing of five visions (chapters 7–9)

1. The locust plague vision—God showed Amos the horrible insect invasion which would fall upon sinful Israel. At the prophet's prayer for mercy, however, the plague did not occur (7:1-3).

2. The great fire vision—As was the case with the locusts, God heeded Amos' prayer and canceled this judgment also (7:4-6).

3. The plumbline vision—Amos saw the Lord standing by a wall (probably the Law of Moses) that had been built true to plumb, measuring Israel with a plumbline in his hand (7:7-9).

4. The basket of ripe fruit vision—Amos was shown a basket of summer fruit and was told by God it represented Israel, ripe for judgment (8:1-14).

5. The Lord at the altar vision—The prophet saw God standing at the altar as a Judge, passing sentence upon Israel (9:1-10).

II. The glorious news—A new day would dawn, replacing blight with blessing, sin with righteousness, and man's grief with God's glory (9:11-15).

A. The reaper will be overtaken by the plowman and the planter by the one treading grapes.

B. New wine will drip down from the mountains.

C. Israel will return to the land, nevermore to leave.

THEOLOGICAL SUMMARY

I. Amos' identity

A. Amos was not a prophet by calling, nor the son of a prophet (Amos 7:14).

B. He was, rather, a herdsman and gatherer of sycamore fruit (Amos 1:1; 7:14-15).

C. He ministered during the reigns of Uzziah, king of Judah, and Jeroboam II, king of Northern Israel.

D. He began his ministry two years before a mighty earthquake struck Israel (Amos 1:1-2). This earthquake was so severe that Zechariah referred to it some 250 years later (Zech. 14:5).

II. Amos' influence
　A. At the time of Amos' ministry, Israel, under powerful king Jeroboam II, was at its zenith of success (2 Kings 14:25). But along with the nation's prosperity had come religious perversion.
　B. James quoted from Amos to support the Jerusalem Council's decision not to require saved Gentiles to be circumcised (Amos 9:11-12; Acts 15:15-17): "To this agree the words of the prophets; as it is written, After this I will return, and will build again the tabernacle of David, which is fallen down; and I will build again the ruins thereof, and I will set it up: that the residue of men might seek after the Lord, and all the Gentiles, upon whom my name is called, saith the Lord, who doeth all these things" (Acts 15:15-17).
　C. Amos confronted and condemned Amaziah, the priest at Beth-el (Amos 7:10-17).
　　1. The twofold reason for this judgment
　　　a. Amaziah had slandered Amos before King Jeroboam II, calling him a traitor.
　　　b. Amaziah had personally threatened Amos, demanding that he leave the land.
　　2. The fourfold result of this judgment—Amos predicted four terrible things would befall the wicked priest.
　　　a. His wife would become a prostitute in the city.
　　　b. His sons and daughters would be killed.
　　　c. His land would be divided up.
　　　d. He himself would die in a heathen land.

STATISTICS
First mention: Amos 1:1
Final mention: Amos 8:2
Meaning of his name: "Burden bearer"

Frequency of his name: Referred to seven times
Biblical books mentioning him: One book (Amos)
Occupation: Herdsman, gatherer of sycamore fruit, prophet (Amos 7:14-15)
Place of birth: The town of Tekoa (Amos 1:1)
Important fact about his life: He was the "Billy Sunday" of the Old Testament prophets.

✐*Artaxerxes*

CHRONOLOGICAL SUMMARY
　I. Artaxerxes was the Persian king in the days of Ezra and Nehemiah who befriended both. His father was the Ahasuerus of the book of Esther.
　II. Artaxerxes and Ezra the scribe
　　A. He used his authority to help Ezra (Ezra 7:12-26).
　　　1. The king offered official aid in assisting Ezra to prepare for his long trip from Persia to Jerusalem.
　　　2. He instructed the scribe to take a copy of God's Word and send back a report concerning the religious progress being made there.
　　　3. He authorized Ezra:
　　　　a. To collect temple offerings from the Jews in Judah (7:16)
　　　　b. To requisition any additional money from the royal treasury (7:20)
　　　　c. To select and appoint his own judges and officials (7:25)
　　　　d. To teach God's Word to both Jews and pagans (7:25)
　　　4. Finally, he promised Ezra that anyone breaking either God's Law or the king's law would be put to death (7:26).
　　B. He used his assets to help Ezra (Ezra 7:12-26).
　　　1. The king personally presented Ezra with a large gift of silver and gold (7:15).
　　　2. He then instructed his Persian

officials west of the Euphrates River as follows:

a. They were to give Ezra anything he needed, up to $300,000 in silver, 1,225 bushels of wheat, 990 gallons of wine, and any amount of salt (7:22).

b. They were forbidden to tax any Jewish personnel working in the temple area (7:24).

III. Artaxerxes and Nehemiah the wall builder

A. Nehemiah's employment with the king—He served as Artaxerxes' royal cupbearer (Neh. 1:11).

B. Nehemiah's encouragement from the king—Artaxerxes granted Nehemiah's requests (Neh. 2:1-9)

1. That he be allowed to go to Judah and rebuild the walls around Jerusalem (2:5).

2. That the king write letters to his Persian officials west of the Euphrates River to assure Nehemiah safe passage (2:7).

3. That the manager of the king's forest be instructed to provide Nehemiah with building materials for his project (2:8).

STATISTICS

Father: Xerxes I (also called Ahasuerus)

First mention: Ezra 7:1

Final mention: Nehemiah 13:6

Meaning of his name: "Brave warrior"

Frequency of his name: Referred to nine times

Biblical books mentioning him: Two books (Ezra, Nehemiah)

Occupation: King of Persia (Ezra 7:1)

Important fact about his life: He supported Ezra and Nehemiah as they returned to Jerusalem (Ezra 7:13-28; Neh. 2:1-8).

## Asa

CHRONOLOGICAL SUMMARY

I. The first years—Asa the godly

A. The military leader

1. Asa reigned 41 years (1 Kings 15:9-10). He was the third ruler of Judah.

2. He built up fortified cities in Judah (2 Chron. 14:6-7).

3. He had an army of 300,000 men from Judah, equipped with large shields and spears (2 Chron. 14:8).

4. He also enlisted 280,000 men from Benjamin with small shields and bows (2 Chron. 14:8).

B. The spiritual leader

1. His concern for the Lord

a. He expelled the male shrine prostitutes from the land (1 Kings 15:11).

b. He got rid of the idols his fathers had made (1 Kings 15:12).

c. He even deposed his grandmother Maachah as queen because of her idolatry (1 Kings 15:13).

d. He repaired the altar of the Lord (2 Chron. 15:8).

2. His cry to the Lord

a. He was on one occasion threatened by a vast Ethiopian army led by Zerah who commanded 300 chariots (2 Chron. 14:9).

b. In utter despair he cried out to God: "LORD, it is nothing with thee to help, whether with many, or with them that have no power: help us, O LORD our God; for we rest on thee, and in thy name we go against this multitude. O LORD, thou art our God; let not man prevail against thee" (2 Chron. 14:11).

c. God answered Asa's prayer and struck down the Ethiopians, providing great spoils of war for the Judean army (2 Chron. 14:12-15).

d. Asa was both encouraged and warned by the prophet Azariah to continue serving God (2 Chron. 15:1-8).

e. He assembled his people at Jerusalem to offer praise and sacrifices to God. At that time, the people entered into a covenant to serve the LORD (2 Chron. 15:9-15).

II. The final years—Asa the godless
   A. He disobeyed God's precepts; He fought against Baasha, king of Northern Israel, and then made a treaty with Syria, seeking their help against Baasha. Both these actions were forbidden by God's Word (1 Kings 15:16-22; 2 Chron. 14:1).
   B. He disregarded God's prophet.
      1. Asa was rebuked for this by the prophet Hanani (2 Chron. 16:7-9).
      2. The angry king thereupon imprisoned Hanani and began to brutally oppress his own people (2 Chron. 16:10).
   C. He denied God's power—Asa suffered much from a foot disease during the final two years of his life, but refused God's help (2 Chron. 16:12-14).

STATISTICS
Father: Abijam (1 Kings 15:8; 1 Chron. 3:10)
Son: Jehoshaphat (1 Chron. 3:10)
First mention: 1 Kings 15:8
Final mention: Matthew 1:8
Meaning of his name: "Physician"
Frequency of his name: Referred to 58 times
Biblical books mentioning him: Five books (1 Kings, 1 Chronicles, 2 Chronicles, Jeremiah, Matthew)
Occupation: King of Judah (1 Kings 15:9)
Circumstances of death: He died of a foot disease (2 Chron. 16:12-13).
Important fact about his life: He was Judah's first saved king (1 Kings 15:11-14).

✐Asaph

CHRONOLOGICAL SUMMARY
I. His appointment
   A. By David
      1. He was chief of the Levite musi-
cians appointed by David to oversee the song services in the tabernacle (1 Chron. 6:39; 16:4-5; Neh. 12:46).
      2. He was one of the musicians the Levites picked at David's command to participate in the Ark's arrival at Jerusalem (1 Chron. 15:16-17).
   B. By Solomon—Solomon appointed him with several others to oversee the song service in the temple (2 Chron. 5:12).
II. His associates—He worked closely with Heman, Ethan, and Jeduthun (1 Chron. 15:19; 16:5; 2 Chron. 5:12).
III. His activities
   A. He sounded the bronze cymbals (1 Chron. 15:19).
   B. He ministered before the Ark, praying and giving thanks to God (1 Chron. 16:4-5).
   C. He led a choir consisting of 288 musicians (1 Chron. 25:7).
   D. He helped conduct a special musical service during the dedication of Solomon's temple, with 120 priests sounding trumpets (2 Chron. 5:12-14).
IV. His achievements
   A. He was the forefather of the prophet Jahaziel, who reassured King Jehoshaphat (2 Chron. 20:14).
   B. He had the gift of prophecy (1 Chron. 25:1-2; 2 Chron. 29:30).
   C. He may have composed the music for Psalm 105, one of David's great psalms of praise (1 Chron. 16:7-36).
   D. He personally wrote 12 psalms: Psalms 50, 73-83 (2 Chron. 29:30).

STATISTICS
Significant descendant: Jahaziel, who prophesied victory for King Jehoshaphat (2 Chron. 20:14)
First mention: 1 Chronicles 6:39
Final mention: Psalm 83 (in the introduction)
Meaning of his name: "Collector, gatherer"
Frequency of his name: Referred to 38 times

Biblical books mentioning him: Five books
  (1 Chronicles, 2 Chronicles, Ezra, Nehemiah, Psalms)
Occupation: Musician (1 Chron. 16:5)
Important fact about his life: He wrote 12 of
  the Psalms (Pss. 50, 73–83).

Athaliah

CHRONOLOGICAL SUMMARY
  I. Her godless reign
    A. She was a blasphemous queen—She
      allowed her pagan sons to loot the
      temple of God and offer up its sacred
      objects to Baal (2 Chron. 24:7).
    B. She was a bloody queen
      1. Athaliah became queen in Judah
        following the death of her son,
        Ahaziah (2 Kings 11:1).
      2. She immediately initiated a blood
        purge against the royal line of Da-
        vid, which succeeded in killing all
        male descendants except a small
        baby named Joash (2 Kings 11:1-2;
        2 Chron. 22:10-11).
    C. She was the seventh ruler of Judah.
  II. Her removal
    A. After a reign of six years she was
      killed by the Judean palace guard and
      Joash became king (2 Kings 11:3-16).
    B. The plot was led by the high priest
      Jehoiada and his wife Jehosheba, the
      couple who had previously hidden
      the lad Joash (2 Kings 11:2, 4;
      2 Chron. 22:11).

STATISTICS
Father: Ahab (2 Chron. 21:6)
Mother: Jezebel
Spouse: Jehoram (2 Chron. 21:6; 22:2)
Son: Ahaziah (2 Kings 8:26)
First mention: 2 Kings 8:26
Final mention: 2 Chronicles 24:7
Meaning of her name: "God is strong"
Frequency of her name: Referred to 15 times
Biblical books mentioning her: Two books
  (2 Kings, 2 Chronicles)
Occupation: Queen of Judah (2 Kings 11:1-3)

Place of death: Outside the Jerusalem palace
  (2 Kings 11:3-16)
Circumstances of death: She was killed by the
  sword at the command of Judah's high
  priest (2 Kings 11:15).
Important fact about her life: She attempted to
  purge all the royal seed of David (2 Kings
  11:1-3).

Baasha

CHRONOLOGICAL SUMMARY
  I. The perversions of Baasha
    A. He ruled for 24 years and was an evil
      king (1 Kings 15:33-34). He was the
      third ruler of Northern Israel.
    B. He built a "Berlin Wall" against Asa
      to prevent anyone from leaving or
      entering the territory of Judah
      (1 Kings 15:16-17).
    C. He was finally stopped by an alliance
      between Asa and Syria (1 Kings
      15:18-21).
    D. He murdered Nadab, Northern Isra-
      el's second king, and then killed all
      of the royal family (1 Kings 15:27,
      29).
  II. The prophecies against Baasha
    A. He was rebuked by the prophet Jehu,
      who warned Baasha that his house
      would suffer the same destruction he
      had wrought upon Nadab's family
      (1 Kings 16:1-5).
    B. This was fulfilled in the days of Zimri
      (1 Kings 16:11-13)

STATISTICS
Father: Ahijah (1 Kings 15:27)
Son: Elah (1 Kings 16:6)
First mention: 1 Kings 15:16
Final mention: Jeremiah 41:9
Meaning of his name: "Boldness"
Frequency of his name: Referred to 28 times
Biblical books mentioning him: Four books
  (1 Kings, 2 Kings, 2 Chronicles, Jeremiah)
Occupation: King of Northern Israel (1 Kings
  15:33)
Important fact about his life: He tried to build

a "Berlin Wall" against King Asa (1 Kings 15:17-21).

✎Balaam

CHRONOLOGICAL SUMMARY
I. The foolish prophet
   A. God's warning
      1. Balaam was a Midianite prophet.
      2. He resided at Pethor, a city of Mesopotamia (Num. 22:5).
      3. He was offered a bribe by Balak, king of Moab, to curse Israel (Num. 22:4-8).
      4. He refused the first bribe after being warned by God not to receive Balak's money (Num. 22:9-13).
      5. However, after the second attempted bribe, he was allowed by the Lord to accompany Balak's messengers to Moab (Num. 22:14-20).
   B. God's wrath
      1. An unseen angel
         a. En route he incurred the wrath of God and was nearly killed by the angel of the Lord who stood in the pathway with a drawn sword (Num. 22:21-28).
         b. At first, only his donkey saw the angel and was beaten by Balaam when the frightened animal bolted from the path (Num. 22:22-27).
      2. An unusual animal
         a. The Lord opened the donkey's mouth, and it protested the brutal treatment handed out by Balaam (Num. 22:28-30).
         b. Finally, Balaam saw the angel and was severely rebuked by him (Num. 22:31-33).
         c. Balaam acknowledged his sinfulness, but was commanded by God to continue the trip to Moab (Num. 22:34-35).

II. The frustrated prophet
   A. The occasions—Upon meeting Balak, the false prophet from Pethor attempted to pronounce a divine curse upon Israel on six separate occasions (Num. 22:39–24:25; Deut. 23:4-5; Mic. 6:5). Each time, however, when he opened his mouth to utter bad things against Israel, God filled it with blessings instead (Num. 22:39—24:25; Josh. 24:9-10; Neh. 13:2).
      1. First blessing—Numbers 23:7-10
      2. Second blessing—23:18-24
      3. Third blessing—24:3-9
      4. Fourth blessing—24:15-19
      5. Fifth blessing—24:20
      6. Sixth blessing—24:21-24
   B. The overview—At least six key prophecies were uttered by Balaam during these futile attempts to curse Israel.
      1. The aloofness of Israel (Num. 23:9)
      2. The population increase of Israel (Num. 23:10)
      3. The faithfulness and power of God enjoyed by Israel (Num. 23:19-24)
      4. The victories of Israel (Num. 24:8-9)
      5. The coming Messiah of Israel (Num. 24:17-19)
      6. The defeat of the enemies of Israel (Num. 24:20-24)
III. The filthy prophet—Unable to curse them, Balaam attempted with some success to corrupt them by encouraging sexual relations between Israelite men and Moabite women (Num. 25:1-3; 31:16).
IV. The fallen prophet—Balaam was eventually killed by the advancing Israelite armies (Num. 31:8).

THEOLOGICAL SUMMARY
I. Balaam's spiritual condition—Joshua said Balaam had practiced divination, i.e., the occult (Josh. 13:22).
II. Balaam's spiritual example—Three New Testament authors referred to Balaam.

A. Peter spoke of the way of Balaam (2 Pet. 2:15). He sold his gift to the highest bidder.

B. Jude spoke of the error of Balaam (Jude 11). Balaam falsely concluded God could be forced into condemning Israel because of the sins of that nation.

C. John spoke of the doctrine of Balaam (Rev. 2:14). In essence, this says if you can't condemn your enemy, then corrupt him.

STATISTICS

Father: Beor (Num. 22:5)

First mention: Numbers 22:5

Final mention: Revelation 2:14

Meaning of his name: "Pilgrim" or "lord of the people"

Frequency of his name: Referred to 61 times

Biblical books mentioning him: Eight books (Numbers, Deuteronomy, Joshua, Nehemiah, Micah, 2 Peter, Jude, Revelation)

Occupation: Prophet turned soothsayer (Num. 22-24; Josh. 13:22)

Place of birth: Pethor (Num. 22:5)

Circumstances of death: He was killed with the sword by the Israelites (Josh. 13:22).

Important fact about his life: He attempted to curse Israel (Num. 23–24).

✎Balak

CHRONOLOGICAL SUMMARY

I. His bribe—Balak, the king of Moab sent messengers on two occasions to bribe Balaam the prophet to put a curse on Israel during the Exodus march (Num. 22:1-21).

A. His first attempt was unsuccessful: "The elders of Moab and the elders of Midian departed with the rewards of divination in their hand; and they came unto Balaam, and spake unto him the words of Balak. . . . And Balaam rose up in the morning, and said unto the princes of Balak, Get

you into your land: for the LORD refuseth to give me leave to go with you" (Num. 22:7, 13).

B. His second attempt was successful: "Balak sent yet again princes, more, and more honourable than they. . . . And Balaam rose up in the morning, and saddled his ass, and went with the princes of Moab" (Num. 22:15, 21).

II. His bitterness—With growing frustration, Balak watched as Balaam attempted in vain to curse Israel. Each time the false prophet opened his mouth to blast Israel, God supernaturally caused him to bless instead.

A. The first attempt

1. Balaam's announcement—"How shall I curse, whom God hath not cursed? Or how shall I defy, whom the LORD hath not defied?" (Num. 23:8).

2. Balak's anger—"Balak said unto Balaam, What hast thou done unto me? I took thee to curse mine enemies, and, behold, thou hast blessed them altogether" (Num. 23:11).

B. The second attempt

1. Balaam's announcement—"Behold, the people shall rise up as a great lion, and lift up himself as a young lion: he shall not lie down until he eat of the prey, and drink the blood of the slain" (Num. 23:24).

2. Balak's anger—"Balak said unto Balaam, Neither curse them at all, nor bless them at all" (Num. 23:25).

C. The third attempt

1. Balaam's announcement—"How goodly are thy tents, O Jacob, and thy tabernacles, O Israel!" (Num. 24:5).

2. Balak's anger—"Balak's anger was kindled against Balaam, and he smote his hands together: and Balak said unto Balaam, I called thee to curse mine enemies, and,

behold, thou hast altogether blessed them these three times" (Num. 24:10).

THEOLOGICAL SUMMARY

I. Joshua mentioned Balak during his farewell address to Israel (Josh. 24:9).

II. Jephthah warned an enemy Ammonite king against attacking Israel, reminding him what God did to Balak (Judg. 11:25).

III. Micah reminded sinful Israel of God's past faithfulness in dealing with Balak (Mic. 6:3).

STATISTICS

Father: Zippor (Num. 22:2)
First mention: Numbers 22:2
Final mention: Micah 6:5
Meaning of his name: "Empty, void, waster"
Frequency of his name: Referred to 42 times
Biblical books mentioning him: Four books (Numbers, Joshua, Judges, Micah)
Occupation: King of Moab (Num. 22:4)
Important fact about his life: He hired Balaam to curse the nation of Israel (Num. 22:5-6).

Barak

CHRONOLOGICAL SUMMARY

I. The command to Barak

A. Barak was from the tribe of Naphtali, living in the city of Kedesh (Judg. 4:6).

B. He was commanded by Deborah, an Israelite prophetess, to gather an army of 10,000 soldiers from the tribes of Naphtali and Zebulun and defeat the Canaanites, who had oppressed Israel for 20 years (Judg. 4:3, 6).

II. The concern of Barak

A. He agreed, but only under the condition that Deborah accompany him (Judg. 4:8).

B. She concurred, but warned him that the credit for the victory would not be his, but rather would go to a woman (Judg. 4:9).

III. The charge of Barak

A. He gathered his 10,000 troops on Mt. Tabor (Judg. 4:12).

B. Sisera, the Canaanite military leader, assembled his army along with the 900 iron chariots he commanded (Judg. 4:13).

C. At Deborah's order, Barak's troops ran down the mountain and totally routed the enemy (Judg. 4:14-15).

D. The enemy was swept away by the river Kishon (Judg. 5:21).

E. It was later indicated that angels helped give Barak the victory (Judg. 5:20).

F. The fleeing Sisera was later killed by a woman named Jael, who thus received credit for the victory, as Deborah had predicted (Judg. 4:16-22; 5:24-27).

IV. The celebration of Barak

A. Barak and Deborah then composed and sang a victory song (Judg. 5:1).

B. This victory brought peace to the land for the next 40 years (Judg. 5:31).

C. Barak is mentioned in the New Testament "Hall of Faith" chapter (Heb. 11:32).

STATISTICS

Father: Abinoam (Judg. 4:6)
First mention: Judges 4:6
Final mention: Hebrews 11:32
Meaning of his name: "Lightning"
Frequency of his name: Referred to 14 times
Biblical books mentioning him: Two books (Judges, Hebrews)
Occupation: Military leader (Judg. 4:1-16)
Important fact about his life: He defeated the Canaanites at the base of Mt. Tabor (Judg. 4:14-16).

Baruch

CHRONOLOGICAL SUMMARY

I. The transaction

A. He was Jeremiah's scribe (Jer. 32:12-13, 16; 36:4).

B. He prepared the deed of purchase for a portion of land the imprisoned Jeremiah bought from his cousin Hanameel (Jer. 32:8-16).

C. He was then ordered to put the deed in a clay jar (Jer. 32:14).

II. The transmission—At Jeremiah's command, Baruch wrote Jeremiah's original prophetical scroll on a parchment and publicly read it in the temple (Jer. 36:5-8).

III. The tribulation

A. This original scroll was later burned by wicked King Jehoiakim (Jer. 36:22-23, 27).

B. Baruch became very discouraged, but was comforted by the Lord (Jer. 45:1-5).

C. He was falsely accused of treason by some godless Jews (Jer. 43:3).

D. Along with Jeremiah, he was forced by his own countrymen to leave Judah and live in Egypt (Jer. 43:4-7).

STATISTICS

Father: Neriah (Jer. 32:12)

First mention: Jeremiah 32:12

Final mention: Jeremiah 45:2

Meaning of his name: "Blessed"

Frequency of his name: Referred to 23 times

Biblical books mentioning him: One book (Jeremiah)

Occupation: Scribe (Jer. 36:4, 32)

Important fact about his life: He wrote down Jeremiah's prophecies (Jer. 36:4, 32).

Barzillai

CHRONOLOGICAL SUMMARY

I. The kindness he remitted to David

A. This man from Gilead brought bedding, bowls, articles of pottery, wheat, barley, flour, roasted grain, beans, lentils, honey, curds, sheep, and cheese to David during Absalom's revolt (2 Sam. 17:27-29).

B. At this time, he was advanced in age, around 80, and very wealthy (2 Sam. 19:32).

II. The kindness he received from David

A. He declined David's gracious invitation to join the king in Jerusalem after the revolt, pleading old age as his reason (2 Sam. 19:31-37).

B. As they parted, David expressed great appreciation to Barzillai (2 Sam. 19:38-39).

C. David, on his deathbed, instructed Solomon to show great kindness to the sons of Barzillai (1 Kings 2:7).

D. A female descendant of Barzillai and her husband (who himself bore the name Barzillai) are listed among those who returned to Jerusalem after the Decree of Cyrus (Ezra 2:61).

STATISTICS

First mention: 2 Samuel 17:27

Final mention: Nehemiah 7:63

Meaning of his name: "Strong, iron"

Frequency of his name: Referred to nine times

Biblical books mentioning him: Four books (2 Samuel, 1 Kings, Ezra, Nehemiah)

Important fact about his life: He brought David supplies during Absalom's rebellion (2 Sam. 17:27-29).

Bath-Sheba

CHRONOLOGICAL SUMMARY

I. Bath-sheba and David

A. Her misconduct with David

1. She was a very beautiful woman (2 Sam. 11:2).

2. She slept with David and became pregnant by him (2 Sam. 11:4-5).

B. Her marriage to David—After the battlefield death of Uriah her husband, whom David had killed, she became David's wife (2 Sam. 11:27).

II. Bath-sheba and Solomon

A. Seeking support for Solomon—She informed the dying David of an attempt by his oldest son Adonijah to steal the kingdom from Solomon (1 Kings 1:11-21).

B. Seeking support from Solomon—She was later tricked by Adonijah into asking Solomon if he (Adonijah) could marry Abishag, David's final concubine (1 Kings 2:13-21).

C. Jewish tradition says she composed and recited Proverbs 31 as an admonition to her son Solomon. Bathsheba is one of four women referred to in the New Testament genealogy leading to Christ (Matt. 1:6).

STATISTICS

Father: Eliam (2 Sam. 11:3)

Spouses: Uriah and David (2 Sam. 11:3, 27)

Sons: Five sons. one unnamed (2 Sam. 11:27; 12:18). Four are named: Solomon, Nathan, Shammua, and Shobab (2 Sam. 12:24; 1 Chron. 3:5).

Significant ancestor: Her grandfather was Ahithophel (2 Sam. 11:3; 23:34).

First mention: 2 Samuel 11:3

Final mention: Matthew 1:6 ("wife of Urias")

Meaning of her name: "Daughter of an oath"

Frequency of her name: Referred to 12 times

Biblical books mentioning her: Four books (2 Samuel, 1 Kings, Psalms, Matthew)

Important fact about her life: She was Solomon's mother (2 Sam. 12:24).

✍Belshazzar

CHRONOLOGICAL SUMMARY

I. The ball hosted by Belshazzar
   A. The who of the matter
      1. Belshazzar was probably the grandson of Nebuchadnezzar.
      2. He was the last king of the Neo-Babylonian empire.
   B. The what of the matter—The king had staged a huge state dinner and drinking party for 1,000 of his top officials (Dan. 5:1).
   C. The why of the matter—At this exact time Babylon was surrounded by its enemy, Persia. Thus the banquet was probably given for two reasons:
      1. To boost his officials' courage
      2. To show contempt for his enemies

II. The gall shown by Belshezzar—He ordered the gold and silver cups taken by his grandfather Nebuchadnezzar from the Jerusalem temple to be brought to this feast, that the king might drink wine from them and praise the Babylonian gods (Dan. 5:2-4).

III. The wall above Belshazzar—Suddenly he saw the fingers of a man's hand writing a mysterious message on the wall above his table (Dan. 5:5-6).

IV. The call by Belshazzar
   A. Belshazzar and the wise men—A terrified king quickly turned to his astrologers and soothsayers for help, but they could not interpret the writing (Dan. 5:7-9).
   B. Belshazzar and the queen—At the suggestion of the queen (probably his mother) he called for the prophet Daniel (Dan. 5:10-12).
   C. Belshazzar and Daniel (Dan. 5:13-29)—The king offered to make Daniel third ruler in the kingdom if he could but interpret the writing. Daniel quickly delivered a twofold message:
      1. Concerning Belshazzar's sin
         a. His sin of pride—"O thou king, the most high God gave Nebuchadnezzar thy father a kingdom, and majesty, and glory, and honour. . . . But when his heart was lifted up, and his mind hardened in pride, he was deposed from his kingly throne, and they took his glory from him. . . . And thou his son, O Belshazzar, hast not humbled thine heart, though thou knewest all this" (Dan. 5:18, 20, 22).
         b. His sin of perversion—"But hast lifted up thyself against the Lord of heaven; and they have brought the vessels of his house before thee, and thou, and thy lords, thy wives, and thy concubines, have drunk wine in them; and thou hast praised the gods of silver, and gold, of brass, iron, wood, and

stone, which see not, nor hear, nor know: and the God in whose hand thy breath is, and whose are all thy ways, hast thou not glorified" (Dan. 5:23).

2. Concerning Belshazzar's sentence—Refusing his offer to become third ruler in the kingdom, Daniel interpreted the writing for Belshazzar. It was a message from God to the king (Dan. 5:24-28).

   a. *Mene:* "God hath numbered thy kingdom, and finished it" (5:26).

   b. *Tekel:* "Thou art weighed in the balances, and art found wanting" (5:27).

   c. *Peres:* "Thy kingdom is divided, and given to the Medes and Persians" (5:28).

V. The fall of Belshazzar—That same night the Medes and Persians took the city and killed Belshazzar. Darius, the Mede, at age 62, became the new ruler (Dan. 5:30-31).

STATISTICS

First mention: Daniel 5:1
Final mention: Daniel 8:1
Meaning of his name: "The lord's leader"
Frequency of his name: Referred to eight times
Biblical books mentioning him: One book (Daniel)
Place of death: In the palace at Babylon
Circumstances of death: He was killed by order of Darius.
Important fact about his life: He received a written message from God on a wall during a banquet (Dan. 5:5, 22-28).

B. He struck down a huge Egyptian with only a club when his enemy was holding a spear. The Egyptian was seven and a half feet tall (2 Sam. 23:21; 1 Chron. 11:23).

C. He also defeated two of Moab's best soldiers (2 Sam. 23:20).

D. On one occasion he went down into a pit on a snowy day and killed a lion (2 Sam. 23:20).

I. Solomon's loyal supporter

   A. Protecting Solomon from his enemies

      1. He sided with Solomon during the attempted revolt headed up by Adonijah (1 Kings 1:8).

      2. He helped Nathan the prophet and Zadok the high priest formally crown Solomon as king over Israel (1 Kings 1:32-40).

   B. Purging Solomon of his enemies— Benaiah executed three of Solomon's enemies.

      1. Adonijah (1 Kings 2:24-25)

      2. Joab (1 Kings 2:33-34)

      3. Shimei (1 Kings 2:44-46)

STATISTICS

Father: Jehoiada (2 Sam. 8:18)
Son: Ammizabad (1 Chron. 27:6)
First mention: 2 Samuel 8:18
Final mention: 1 Chronicles 27:6
Meaning of his name: "God is intelligent"
Frequency of his name: Referred to 24 times
Biblical books mentioning him: Three books (2 Samuel, 1 Kings, 1 Chronicles)
Occupation: Military leader (2 Sam. 8:18)
Important fact about his life: He was a brave commander in the armies of both David and Solomon (2 Sam. 8:18; 1 Kings 2:35; 4:4).

✍Benaiah

CHRONOLOGICAL SUMMARY

I. David's loyal supporter

   A. He was considered one of the four best warriors in David's army (2 Sam. 23:22-23).

✍Benjamin

CHRONOLOGICAL SUMMARY

I. Growing up in Canaan

   A. He was Jacob's youngest son, and the only one born in Canaan (Gen. 46:19).

B. His mother, Rachel, died giving birth to him near the city of Bethlehem (Gen. 35:16-18).
   1. She named him "Benoni," meaning "son of my sorrow" (Gen. 35:18).
   2. Jacob, however, renamed him "Benjamin," meaning "son of my right hand" (Gen. 35:18).
C. Benjamin's only full brother was Joseph (Gen. 30:22-24; 46:19).
D. He had 10 half brothers (Gen. 35:23-26).
II. Going down to Egypt
A. His arrival in Egypt
   1. He did not accompany his 10 half brothers during their first trip to Egypt to buy food (Gen. 42:3-4).
   2. However, Joseph, who had become prime minister in Egypt (but was unrecognized by the 10 brothers) demanded that Benjamin be brought to him on the next trip (Gen. 42:18-20).
   3. A reluctant Jacob finally permitted Benjamin to go (Gen. 43:11-14).
   4. Joseph greeted his brothers, prepared a banquet for them, and gave Benjamin five times the food portion that he gave the rest (Gen. 43:15-34).
B. His arrest in Egypt
   1. After leaving for Canaan loaded down with food, the brothers were stopped en route and charged with stealing Joseph's special silver cup. Unknown to them, Joseph had secretly hidden it in Benjamin's sack (Gen. 44:1-12).
   2. After they were brought back to Egypt, Judah pleaded with Joseph, offering to become his slave if only Benjamin could be set free (Gen. 44:13-34).
C. His assurance in Egypt
   1. Unable to contain himself any longer, Joseph revealed his identity and sent them back to Canaan to get their father (Gen. 45:1-21).

2. Benjamin received more silver and clothing gifts from Joseph than did his brothers (Gen. 45:22).

STATISTICS
Father: Jacob (Gen. 46:19)
Mother: Rachel (Gen. 35:16-19; 46:19)
Sons: Belah, Beker, Ashbel, Gera, Naaman, Ehi, Rosh, Muppim, Huppim, and Ard (Gen. 46:21)
Brothers: Full brother: Joseph (Gen. 35:24). Half brothers: Reuben, Simeon, Levi, Judah, Issachar, Zebulun, Gad, Asher, Dan, and Naphtali (Gen. 35:23, 25, 26).
Sister: Half sister: Dinah (Gen. 30:21)
Significant descendants: The Old Testament and New Testament Sauls (1 Sam. 9:1-2; Phil. 3:5)
First mention: Genesis 35:18
Final mention: 1 Chronicles 7:6
Meaning of his name: "Son of my right hand"
Frequency of his name: Referred to 21 times
Biblical books mentioning him: Four books (Genesis, Exodus, Deuteronomy, 1 Chronicles)
Place of birth: Near Bethlehem (Gen. 35:16-19)
Important fact about his life: He was the youngest of Jacob's 12 sons (Gen. 42:13).

✍*Bezaleel*

CHRONOLOGICAL SUMMARY
I. His anointing
A. He was from the tribe of Judah (Exod. 31:2).
B. He was filled with the Spirit of God (Exod. 31:3).
II. His abilities
A. God had given him skills and knowledge in all kinds of building craft (Exod. 31:3).
B. He was also a gifted teacher (Exod. 35:34).
III. His associate—Bezaleel's helper was Aholiab, from the tribe of Dan (Exod. 31:6).
IV. His accomplishments

A. He crafted the golden, silver, and bronze structures and cut the stone and wood, all of which were used in the tabernacle construction (Exod. 31:4-5; 35:30-33).
B. He personally constructed the Ark of the Covenant and the brazen altar (Exod. 37:1-9; 2 Chron. 1:5).

STATISTICS

Father: Uri (Exod. 31:2)
Significant ancestor: Caleb was his great grandfather (1 Chron. 2:18-20)
First mention: Exodus 31:2
Final mention: 2 Chronicles 1:5
Meaning of his name: "God is protection"
Frequency of his name: Referred to eight times
Biblical books mentioning him: Three books (Exodus, 1 Chronicles, 2 Chronicles)
Occupation: Skilled craftsman in building materials (Exod. 31:3-5)
Important fact about his life: Assisted by Aholiab, he oversaw the construction of the tabernacle and everything in it, including the Ark of the Covenant (Exod. 31:6).

 *Bildad*

CHRONOLOGICAL SUMMARY

I. His concern—"Now when Job's three friends heard of all this evil that was come upon him, they came every one from his own place; Eliphaz the Temanite, and Bildad the Shuhite, and Zophar the Naamathite: for they had made an appointment together to come to mourn with him and to comfort him. And when they lifted up their eyes afar off, and knew him not, they lifted up their voice, and wept; and they rent every one his mantle, and sprinkled dust upon their heads toward heaven. So they sat down with him upon the ground seven days and seven nights, and none spake a word unto him: for

they saw that his grief was very great" (Job 2:11-13).
II. His criticism (Job 8, 18, 25)—It wasn't long before Bildad's compassion, as he viewed Job's suffering, turned into hostile and unfair criticism. Bildad was in error on two counts.
A. His assumption was wrong—Like his two friends Eliphaz and Zophar, Bildad assumed Job was suffering because of some terrible unconfessed sin. "Behold, God will not cast away a perfect man, neither will he help the evil doers" (Job 8:20). NOTE: Bildad based his assumption on tradition. (See Job 8:8-10.)
B. His advice was wrong—Bildad's counsel was simple; "Repent of your secret sin!" "If thou wouldest seek unto God betimes, and make thy supplication to the Almighty; if thou wert pure and upright; surely now he would awake for thee, and make the habitation of thy righteousness prosperous" (Job 8:5-6).
III. His chastisement
A. Bildad was later rebuked by God for his unkind and untrue opinion of Job (Job 42:7).
B. He was then required along with his two friends to offer up seven bulls and seven rams as burnt sacrifices for his sin of slander (Job 42:8-9).

STATISTICS

Significant ancestor: He was a descendant of Abraham through Keturah (Gen. 25:2).
First mention: Job 2:11
Final mention: Job 42:9
Meaning of his name: "Son of contention"
Frequency of his name: Referred to five times
Biblical books mentioning him: One book (Job)
Important fact about his life: He was one of Job's three "friends" whose comfort turned out to be criticism (Job 2:11; 6:24-27).

Bilhah

CHRONOLOGICAL SUMMARY

I. Her marriage to Jacob
   A. She was the servant girl given by Laban to his daughter Rachel following Rachel's marriage to Jacob (Gen. 29:28-29).
   B. The barren Rachel then presented her to Jacob for childbearing purposes (Gen. 30:1-4).
   C. Bilhah gave birth to two sons, Dan and Naphtali (Gen. 30:5-8; 35:25).
   D. Later, Bilhah became the grandmother of five grandsons, one born to Dan, and four born to Naphtali (Gen. 46:23-24).
II. Her misconduct with Reuben—She had an illicit sex affair with Reuben, Jacob's firstborn son, whose mother was Leah (Gen. 35:22).

STATISTICS

Spouse: Jacob (Gen. 30:1-4)
Sons: Dan and Naphtali (Gen. 30:5-8; 35:25)
First mention: Genesis 29:29
Final mention: 1 Chronicles 7:13
Meaning of her name: "Tender"
Frequency of her name: Referred to 10 times
Biblical books mentioning her: Two books
   (Genesis, 1 Chronicles)
Important fact about her life: She bore Jacob two sons (Gen. 35:25).

Boaz

CHRONOLOGICAL SUMMARY

I. His meetings with Ruth
   A. First meeting: In a wheat field
      1. Boaz was a close relative of the widow Naomi on her husband Elimelech's side (Ruth 2:1).
      2. He was a wealthy bachelor from the tribe of Judah (Ruth 2:1).
      3. He met Ruth in a field owned by him near Bethlehem (Ruth 2:4-8).
      4. He commended her for the kindly treatment she showed toward her mother-in-law Naomi (Ruth 2:5-13).
      5. He instructed his harvesters to make it easier for her to glean the grain in his field (Ruth 2:15-16).
      6. He provided this service for Ruth during the entire harvest season (Ruth 2:23).
   B. Second meeting: By a threshing floor
      1. Acting upon Naomi's instructions, Ruth proposed marriage to Boaz (Ruth 3:1-11).
      2. Boaz was more than willing, but told Ruth that permission had to be secured from a relative who was even closer to Elimelech than he was (Ruth 3:12–4:6).
II. His marriage to Ruth
   A. After Boaz received this permission, the marriage contract was ratified by the exchanging of shoes (Ruth 4:7-12).
   B. Boaz fathered a boy through Ruth named Obed (Ruth 4:13-17).
   C. He thus became the great grandfather of King David (Ruth 4:18-22).

STATISTICS

Father: Salmon (Ruth 4:21)
Mother: Rahab (Matt. 1:5)
Spouse: Ruth (Ruth 4:13)
Son: Obed (Ruth 4:13, 17)
Significant ancestor: Abraham (Matt. 1:2, 5)
Significant descendants: David, Joseph, Mary, and Jesus (Ruth 4:22; Matt. 1:16)
First mention: Ruth 2:1
Final mention: Luke 3:32
Meaning of his name: "Fleetness, strength"
Frequency of his name: Referred to 23 times
Biblical books mentioning him: Four books
   (Ruth, 1 Chronicles, Matthew, Luke)
Occupation: Wealthy farmer (Ruth 2:1, 3)
Place of birth: Probably Bethlehem
Important fact about his life: He married Ruth and became an ancestor of Jesus through

David's line (Ruth 4:13, 21-22; Matt. 1:5-16).

Cain

CHRONOLOGICAL SUMMARY
I. The apostate
   A. He brought some of the fruits of the ground as an offering to God, which was not acceptable (Gen 4:3-5).
   B. In anger, he rejected God's gracious invitation to bring a blood offering, as his brother Abel had done, which would be accepted (Gen. 4:5-7).
II. The assassin
   A. The crime
      1. He murdered his brother Abel in the field (Gen. 4:8).
      2. He then lied to God about what he had done (Gen. 4:9).
   B. The curse
      1. God pronounced a special judgmental curse upon Cain (Gen. 4:10-12).
      2. He was, however, protected by God from mob violence by a special mark (probably until human government could be established) (Gen. 4:13-15).
III. The architect
   A. He left God's presence and resided in the land of Nob, meaning "wandering," east of Eden (Gen. 4:16).
   B. He married one of his sisters (implied in Gen. 5:4) and fathered a son named Enoch (Gen. 4:17).
   C. He built earth's first city and named it after his son Enoch (Gen. 4:17).

A THEOLOGICAL SUMMARY
I. Hebrews contrasts Cain's unbelief and disobedience with his brother Abel's faith and obedience (Heb. 11:4).
II. John gave us both the source and reason which prompted Cain to kill Abel (1 John 3:12).
   A. The source—Satan himself
   B. The reason—Envy

III. Jude referred to Cain, using him to illustrate the works of an apostate (Jude 11).

STATISTICS
Father: Adam (Gen. 4:1)
Mother: Eve (Gen. 4:1)
Spouse: Unnamed wife (Gen. 4:17)
Son: Enoch (Gen. 4:17)
Brothers: Abel and Seth named (Gen. 4:2, 25) (See Gen. 5:4.)
First mention: Genesis 4:1
Final mention: Jude 1:11
Meaning of his name: "Acquisition"
Frequency of his name: Referred to 19 times
Biblical books mentioning him: Four books (Genesis, Hebrews, 1 John, Jude)
Occupation: Farmer, city builder (Gen. 4:3, 17)
Place of birth: Outside the Garden of Eden (Gen. 3:23–4:1)
Important fact about his life: He was the first baby to be born on earth (Gen. 4:1).

Caleb

CHRONOLOGICAL SUMMARY
I. His faithfulness, as revealed at 40
   A. His trip
      1. Caleb was one of the 12 men sent by Moses to spy out the land of Canaan (Num. 13:1-2, 6).
      2. He was from the tribe of Judah (Num. 13:6; 34:19).
   B. His testimony
      1. Along with Joshua, he gave a good report upon returning, urging Israel to enter the land, as opposed to the evil report rendered by the 10 spies (Num. 13:30; 14:6-9).
      2. Scripture refers to this act of faith on six specific occasions (Num. 14:24, 30, 38; 26:65; 32:12; Deut. 1:36).
      3. Because of his testimony, both Caleb and his descendants were assured by the Lord of a special

inheritance in Canaan (Num. 14:24).

II. His faithfulness, as rewarded at 85
 A. At age 85, he gave one of Scripture's greatest testimonies concerning the keeping power of God (Josh. 14:6-12).
 B. He was given Hebron, the land of some huge warriors known as the Anakites, for his inheritance. The old warrior promptly drove them out and occupied the land (Josh. 14:12; 15:13-15).

STATISTICS

Father: Jephunneh (Num. 13:6)
Spouses: Ephah and Maachah (1 Chron. 2:46, 48) (NOTE: NIDB and Dake's both distinguish between the Caleb who married these concubines and the Caleb being studied here. They distinguish between the Caleb in 1 Chron. 2:18-19, 46, 48 and in 1 Chron. 4:15.)
Sons: Mesha, Iru, Elah, and Naam (1 Chron. 2:42; 4:15) (See note above)
Daughter: Achsah (Josh. 15:16)
Brother: Jerahmeel (1 Chron. 2:42) (See note)
Significant descendant: Nabal (1 Sam. 25:3)
First mention: Numbers 13:6
Final mention: 1 Chronicles 6:56
Meaning of his name: "Bold, impetuous," or "dog"
Frequency of his name: Referred to 32 times
Biblical books mentioning him: Six books (Numbers, Deuteronomy, Joshua, Judges, 1 Samuel, 1 Chronicles)
Occupation: Soldier (Josh. 14:6-14)
Important fact about his life: He was a faithful partner with Joshua standing against the evil report of the 10 spies (Num. 14:6-9).

Canaan

CHRONOLOGICAL SUMMARY

I. His sin against Noah—He was involved in a sin (of a somewhat unclear nature) along with his father Ham against his grandfather Noah, when the old man was drunk (Gen. 9:20-24).

II. His sentence by Noah
 A. The what of this curse—His descendants would become servants to the descendants of Shem and Japheth (Gen. 9:25-27).
 B. The who of this curse would include the following:
  1. The Hittites, Jebusites, and Amorites (Gen. 10:15-19; 1 Chron. 1:8, 13-16).
  2. The citizens of Sodom and Gomorrah (Gen. 10:19).

STATISTICS

Father: Ham (Gen. 9:18)
Sons: Sidon and Heth (Gen. 10:15). Unnamed descendants (10:16-19)
Brothers: Cush, Mizraim, and Put (Gen. 10:6; 1 Chron. 1:8)
First mention: Genesis 9:18
Final mention: 1 Chronicles 1:13
Meaning of his name: "Low, flat"
Frequency of his name: Referred to nine times
Biblical books mentioning him: Two books (Genesis, 1 Chronicles)
Important fact about his life: He was cursed by his grandfather Noah (Gen. 9:25-27).

Chedorlaomer

CHRONOLOGICAL SUMMARY

I. The victor
 A. His campaign
  1. He was the king of Elam, located in ancient Mesopotamia, who instigated the first recorded war in the Bible (Gen. 14:5).
  2. Five Canaanite kings he had previously subdued suddenly rebelled against him (Gen. 14:1-4).
 B. His captives
  1. With an alliance of three other Mesopotamian kings, Chedorlaomer defeated the rebels and carried away many people as slaves (Gen. 14:5-11).
  2. One of the captives was Lot, nephew of Abraham, who was

living in the city of Sodom at the time (Gen. 14:12).

II. The vanquished—Upon hearing of this, Abraham attacked Chedorlaomer with 318 trained household servants and defeated him just north of the Galilean Sea (Gen. 14:13-16).

STATISTICS

First mention: Genesis 14:1
Final mention: Genesis 14:17
Meaning of his name: "Sheaf band"
Frequency of his name: Referred to five times
Biblical books mentioning him: One book (Genesis)
Occupation: King of Elam (Gen. 14:1)
Important fact about his life: He captured Lot but was defeated by Abraham (Gen. 14:1-17).

Cozbi

CHRONOLOGICAL SUMMARY

I. Her perversion
  A. She was the daughter of Zur, a chief official in Midian (Num. 25:15)
  B. Cozbi was guilty of immorality with Zimri, an Israelite man (Num. 25:6, 14-15).
II. Her punishment
  A. Both she and Zimri were killed with a javelin by Phinehas, high priest of Israel (Num. 25:7).
  B. This act of judgment ended a terrible divine plague which had come upon Israel because of the sins of idolatry and immorality (Num. 25:8).

STATISTICS

Father: Zur (Num. 25:15)
First mention: Numbers 25:15
Final mention: Numbers 25:18
Meaning of her name: "Fruitful"
Frequency of her name: Referred to two times
Biblical books mentioning her: One book (Numbers)
Place of death: In the tent of her lover (Num. 26:6-8)

Circumstances of death: She was killed with a javelin (Num. 25:7-8).
Important fact about her life: She was guilty of immorality with an Israelite man and helped bring a plague on Israel (Num. 25:8, 18).

Cyrus

CHRONOLOGICAL SUMMARY

I. Cyrus and Isaiah: The foretelling
  A. Cyrus was the founder of the Persian Empire.
  B. In an amazing prophecy given some 200 years before Cyrus' birth, Isaiah the prophet wrote:
    1. That he would be called Cyrus (Isa. 44:28).
    2. That he would conquer many lands (Isa. 45:1).
    3. That he would open the gates of Babylon and take the city (Isa. 45:1).
    4. That he would issue a decree allowing the Jews to return and rebuild both Jerusalem and the temple (Isa. 45:1).
II. Cyrus, Daniel, and Ezra: The fulfilling
  A. Cyrus and the book of Daniel—Daniel, who lived during Cyrus' (also called Darius) reign, described for us that fateful night when Cyrus took the city of Babylon (Dan. 5:1-31; 6:28; 10:1).
  B. Cyrus and the book of Ezra—Ezra provided for us the very words found in Cyrus' decree (Ezra 1:1-4).
    1. The author of 2 Chronicles also gave us the same decree (2 Chron. 36:22-23).
    2. Cyrus allowed the returning remnant to carry back those sacred vessels Nebuchadnezzar had previously taken from the temple of Solomon in Jerusalem (Ezra 1:7-11; 5:13-15).
    3. He also commanded the people of Sidon and Tyre to help the Jews

in rebuilding the second temple (Ezra 3:7).

4. Finally, he appointed a political leader named Zerubbabel (also known as Sheshbazzar) to guide the returning remnant (Ezra 2:2; 3:8; 4:2; 5:2, 14).

STATISTICS

First mention: 2 Chronicles 36:22
Final mention: Daniel 10:1
Meaning of his name: "Sun, throne"
Frequency of his name: Referred to 22 times
Biblical books mentioning him: Four books (2 Chronicles, Ezra, Isaiah, Daniel)
Occupation: King of Persia (2 Chron. 36:22)
Important fact about his life: He issued the return decree allowing the Jews to go back and rebuild Jerusalem (2 Chron. 36:22-23).

✎Daniel

CHRONOLOGICAL SUMMARY

I. A divine diet
   A. Daniel's resolution (Dan. 1:1-8)—(All references here are to Daniel except where specified otherwise.)
      1. Daniel and his three friends, Shadrach, Meshach, and Abednego, along with other Hebrew youths, were selected by Nebuchadnezzar to prepare themselves for a life of political service.
      2. He determined not to defile himself with the king's food, probably because it was forbidden by Mosaic Law and it might have been sacrificed to idols.
   B. His recommendation (1:9-14)—He proposed a test, suggesting a 10-day diet of only vegetables and water. At the end of this short time his superintendent could compare Daniel and his friends with the others who ate the king's rich food. The terms of this test were granted.

C. His rewards (1:15-20)
   1. At the hand of God
      a. They were many times stronger at the end of the 10-day test.
      b. They were 10 times smarter at the end of the three-year training period.
   2. At the hand of Nebuchadnezzar— Daniel was appointed to a political career.

II. A statue and a stone
   A. The Babylonians' frustration (2:1-13)
      1. Nebuchadnezzar had a terrifying nightmare and called his entire cabinet to relate and interpret his dream.
      2. Unable to do this, they were all condemned to death.
   B. God's revelation (2:14-30)—God revealed Nebuchadnezzar's dream to Daniel (who apparently was not present at the original demand of the king).
   C. Daniel's interpretation
      1. A chronology of the dream—What did the king see? (2:31-35).
         a. He saw a huge and powerful statue of a man. It was made up of various materials.
            (1) Its head was gold.
            (2) Its breast and arms were silver.
            (3) Its belly and thighs were brass.
            (4) Its legs were iron, and its feet part iron and part clay.
         b. This statue was then utterly pulverized into small powder by a special rock, supernaturally cut from a mountainside, which fell upon it.
         c. The rock then grew until it filled the entire earth. (2:30-35).
      2. A theology of the dream—What did this all mean? (2:36-45).
         a. The statue represented four Gentile world powers:
            (1) The golden head was Babylon.
            (2) The silver chest and arms were Persia.

(3) The brass belly and thighs were Greece.

(4) The iron legs and iron and clay feet were Rome.

b. The final Gentile power (Rome) will be revived during the tribulation and will consist of 10 nations. This is implied, for the great prophecies concerning the fourth power were not fulfilled in the history of ancient Rome.

c. In the days of the final world power the God of heaven would shatter all earthly kingdoms through his rock (the Lord Jesus Christ) and set up an eternal kingdom (2:44-45).

D. Nebuchadnezzar's adoration (2:46-49)

1. The king bowed down to Daniel and commanded his people to offer sacrifices and burn sweet incense before him (2:46).

2. He acknowledged the God of Daniel as "God of gods" (2:47).

3. He elevated Daniel to the highest office in Babylon, as chief magistrate in the king's court (2:48).

4. Daniel then appointed Shadrach, Meshach, and Abednego to high offices (2:49).

III. A fiery furnace

A. The king's command (3:1-7)

1. Nebuchadnezzar constructed a golden statue 90 feet high and nine feet wide. This was set up in the plain of Dura near Babylon.

2. On dedication day at a given musical signal all his officials were to bow down and worship the image. Failure to do so would result in a fiery death. "Whoso falleth not down and worshippeth shall the same hour be cast into the midst of a burning fiery furnace" (3:6).

3. The officials complied with the king's demand.

B. The Hebrews' stand (3:8-23)

1. Jealous Babylonians informed Nebuchadnezzar that Shadrach, Meshach, and Abednego refused to bow.

2. Nebuchadnezzar offered them another chance.

3. Upon their second refusal they were bound and cast into a fiery furnace, heated seven times hotter than usual.

C. The Lord's own man (3:24-30)

1. Peering into the furnace, an amazed king saw a fourth figure.

2. The three friends then walked out of the furnace unharmed with not even the smell of smoke upon them.

3. Nebuchadnezzar issued a decree, ordering the death penalty to anyone who blasphemed the God of Israel.

IV. A tree in turmoil

A. The tree—Nebuchadnezzar corrupted through vanity (4:1-27)

1. Nebuchadnezzar related another dream he had to Daniel (4:8-18).

a. He saw a large and leafy tree increasing in size until it reached the heavens and was viewed by all. The wild animals and birds were shaded and sheltered by its leafy branches, and the entire world was fed from its generous fruit supply (4:10-12).

b. Suddenly a heavenly figure appeared and ordered the tree cut down and its fruit scattered. Only the stump was to be left, banded with a chain of iron and brass. This felled tree represented a man who would be given the mind of an animal and remain in this pitiful condition for seven years (4:13-16).

c. This all was to be done so the entire world might know that "the most High ruleth in the kingdom of men, and giveth it to whomsoever he will, and setteth up over it the basest of men" (4:17).

2. Daniel revealed the dream to Nebuchadnezzar (4:19-27).

  a. The interpretation was so frightful that Daniel observed an hour of shocked silence (4:19).

  b. He then revealed the details:

    (1) The tree indeed stood for a man, and that man was Nebuchadnezzar.

    (2) The king would suffer a seven-year period of insanity for his pride. During this time he would act and think like a wild animal.

    (3) This affliction would end only when he realized that the powers that be are ordained of God.

    (4) Daniel then begged the proud monarch to "break off thy sins," but all to no avail.

B. The tree—Nebuchadnezzar corrected through insanity (4:28-37)

  1. Nebuchadnezzar's pride (4:28-30)—Twelve months after the dream, while the king was strolling on the roof of the royal palace in Babylon, he made an arrogant boast. "Is not this great Babylon, that I have built for the house of the kingdom by the might of my power, and for the honour of my majesty?" (4:30)

  2. Nebuchadnezzar's punishment (4:31-33)

    a. Even while the king spoke his proud words, God's judgment fell from heaven and he was driven from the palace (4:31).

    b. The sad results of his vanity: "He was driven from men, and did eat grass as oxen, and his body was wet with the dew of heaven, till his hairs were grown like eagles' feathers, and

his nails like birds' claws" (4:33).

  3. Nebuchadnezzar's praise (4:34-37)—Upon restoration his pride turned to praise.

V. A heavenly hand

  A. The ball (5:1)—Belshazzar the king staged a huge dinner and drinking party and invited his top 1,000 officers to attend.

  B. The gall (5:2-4)—He ordered the gold and silver cups taken by his grandfather Nebuchadnezzar from the Jerusalem temple to be brought to this feast that he might drink wine from them and praise the Babylonian gods.

  C. The wall (5:5-6)—Suddenly he saw the fingers of a man's hand writing a mysterious message on the wall next to his table.

  D. The call (5:7-29)

    1. A terrified king turned to his astrologers for help and interpretation, but they could not assist him.

    2. At the suggestion of the queen, he called for Daniel, offering to make the great prophet third ruler in the kingdom if he could interpret the message.

    3. Daniel refused the offer but interpreted the message anyway.

      a. *Mene:* "God hath numbered thy kingdom, and finished it" (5:26).

      b. *Tekel:* "Thou art weighed in the balances, and art found wanting" (5:27).

      c. *Peres:* "Thy kingdom is divided, and given to the Medes and Persians" (5:28).

  E. The fall (5:30-31)—Belshazzar was slain that very night, and the city was ruled by a 62-year-old Mede named Darius.

VI. The lions and the lion-hearted

  A. An evil plan (6:1-9)

    1. The organization—Darius, the Mede, immediately set about to

reorganize and consolidate this fantastic new kingdom called Babylon that he now ruled. He divided the kingdom into 129 provinces, each under a prince. These princes were accountable to three presidents, with Daniel being one of the three. Daniel, now over 80, was still blessed with so much skill and ability that Darius was considering elevating him over the other two presidents (6:1-3).

2. The orchestration
   a. This so infuriated both the presidents and the princes that they plotted against Daniel's life (6:4).
   b. Being unable to see the slightest flaw in his secular life, they determined to trap him in his religious life (6:5).
   c. Darius was tricked into signing a 30-day decree which said that all prayers during that time were to be directed to the king himself (6:6-9).

B. A kneeling man (6:10-20)
   1. The fearless prophet—Daniel learned of this and doubtless immediately saw through its clumsy effort to trap him. But the old warrior continued worshiping God as before (6:10).
      a. He kept his windows opened.
      b. He continued praying three times a day.
      c. He knelt down.
      d. He faced Jerusalem.
   2. The heartless plotters—Those vicious hunters who had set their trap now saw the prey inside and gleefully rushed to Darius to deliver the death blow. Darius realized he had been had and desperately sought to find a loophole in the immutable law of the Medes and the Persians, but all to no avail (6:11-15). Daniel was arrested and thrown into a den of hungry man-eating lions.

3. The sleepless potentate
   a. After sealing the mouth of the den with his own signet ring, Darius returned and spent a sleepless and miserable night in the royal palace (6:17-18).
   b. At daybreak the next morning he rushed to the den, ordered the capstone removed, and called out in anguish: "O Daniel, servant of the living God, is thy God, whom thou servest continually, able to deliver thee from the lions?" (6:20).

C. A heavenly ban
   1. Daniel's response—Out of the blackness of that den of doom there came a cheerful and clear voice: "O king, live for ever. My God hath sent his angel, and hath shut the lions' mouths, that they have not hurt me: forasmuch as before him innocency was found in me; and also before thee, O king, have I done no hurt" (6:21-22).
   2. Darius' reaction—The king's reaction to all this was twofold; he was both glad and mad.
      a. He rejoiced at Daniel's salvation and issued a decree ordering all the citizens of his kingdom to consider this almighty Judean God (6:23, 25-27).
      b. He took immediate vengeance upon those who had tricked him in the first place and ordered them along with all their families thrown into this same den. Their bodies were instantly torn apart by the lions (6:24).

VII. Godless kingdoms and the kingdom of God
   A. Nebuchadnezzar, the Babylonian lion (7:1-4)
      1. Daniel, in a vision, saw a great

storm on a mighty ocean with
four winds blowing from every
direction and four beasts emerg-
ing from the water.

2. The first beast symbolized Nebuchadnezzar and Babylon.
   a. It was like a lion.
   b. It had eagle's wings.
   c. Those wings were plucked.
   (See Dan. 4:33 and 5:31.)

B. Cyrus, the Persian bear (7:5)
1. This bear raised itself up on one
   side, probably referring to the
   stronger Persian part of the dual
   Medes and Persians alliance.
2. It had three ribs in its mouth, a
   reference to Babylon, Egypt, and
   Lydia, three nations Persia had
   just conquered.
3. It would devour much flesh. The
   Persian King Xerxes led a force
   of over one and a half million
   men and 300 ships into Greece
   alone.

C. Alexander, the Grecian leopard (7:6)
1. It was like a leopard but had four
   wings. Alexander traveled faster
   and conquered more land than
   any other man in recorded history.
2. It had four heads. After his untimely death at 32, his kingdom
   fell to four of his generals.

D. The Roman monster and the little
   horn (7:7-28)
1. This monster "retired" to its den
   in A.D. 476 for a while to hiber-
   nate.
2. It will be awakened in the form of
   10 nations during the tribulation
   by the little horn, who is none
   other than the Antichrist.
3. The Antichrist will defeat three of
   these 10 kingdoms (horns) in his
   rise to power (7:8).
4. He will have a universal rule during the final three and a half years
   of the tribulation (7:25).
5. He will shed blood upon this

earth in an unprecedented manner (7:7, 19).
6. He will wear out the saints of
   God (Israel) (7:25).
7. He will attempt to change seasons
   and laws (7:25).
8. He will blaspheme God (7:25).
9. He will be defeated at Christ's
   coming and his body given over
   to the flames of hell (7:11).

E. Jesus Christ, the King of kings (7:13-
14)
1. He will come in the clouds to
   claim his rightful earthly inheritance. "I saw in the night visions,
   and, behold, one like the Son of
   man came with the clouds of
   heaven, and came to the Ancient
   of days, and they brought him
   near before him" (7:13).
2. He will be given his universal and
   eternal throne by his Father, the
   Ancient of Days (7:9, 13-14). "I
   beheld till the thrones were cast
   down, and the Ancient of days
   did sit, whose garment was white
   as snow, and the hair of his head
   like the pure wool: his throne was
   like the fiery flame, and his
   wheels as burning fire. A fiery
   stream issued and came forth
   from before him: thousand thousands ministered unto him, and
   ten thousand times ten thousand
   stood before him: the judgment
   was set, and the books were
   opened" (7:9-10).

VIII. The horns of the heathen
A. A two-headed ram—Persia, as represented by the example of Darius III
   (8:1-4; see also 8:20)
1. In this vision Daniel saw himself
   in the fortress of Shushan (or
   Susa), a city some 230 miles east
   of Babylon and 120 miles north of
   the Persian Gulf (8:2).
2. He saw a victorious ram coming
   from the east and pushing its way
   westward, northward, and to the

south. This represented the Persian conquests (8:3-4).

B. A one-horned goat—Greece, as represented by Alexander the Great (8:5-8, 21)

   1. Daniel then saw a goat from the west that rushed the ram, smashed it to the ground, and stomped it to pieces.
   2. Daniel then saw this powerful horn suddenly broken and its might divided into four parts. Alexander died in Babylon during a drunken orgy at the age of 32, in 323 B.C. His kingdom was then divided among his four leading generals.

C. Two little-horned kings—Syria and the revived Roman Empire as represented by Antiochus Epiphanes and the Antichrist (8:9-27). The archangel Gabriel interpreted all this to Daniel. This is the first mention of him in the Bible (8:16).

   1. The historical little horn—Antiochus Epiphanes
      a. He was a Syrian.
      b. He came to the throne in 175 B.C. and ruled until 164 B.C.
      c. He was anti-Semitic to the core. He assaulted Jerusalem, murdering over 40,000 in three days, and selling an equal number into cruel slavery. It is thought that he began his evil actions on September 6, 171 B.C. and ended them on December 25, 165 B.C. This would account for the 2,300 days of 8:14.
      d. Daniel became physically ill upon seeing this terrible prophetical vision (8:27). "I Daniel fainted, and was sick certain days; afterward I rose up, and did the king's business; and I was astonished at the vision, but none understood it" (8:27).
   2. The prophetical little horn—the

Antichrist: The future enemy of Israel will do all his forerunner did and much more. The following comparisons can be seen between the two:

   a. Both would conquer much (Dan. 8:9; Rev. 13:4).
   b. Both would magnify themselves (Dan. 8:11; Rev. 13:15).
   c. Both would be masters of deceit (Dan. 8:25; 2 Thess. 2:10).
   d. Both would offer a false peace program (Dan. 8:25; 1 Thess. 5:2-3).
   e. Both would hate and persecute Israel (Dan. 8:25; Rev. 12:13).
   f. Both would profane the temple (Dan 8:11; Matt. 24:15).
   g. Both would be energized by Satan (Dan. 8:24; Rev. 13:2).
   h. Both would be active in the Middle East for about seven years (Dan. 8:14; 9:27).
   i. Both would speak against the Lord God (Dan. 8:25).
   j. Both would be utterly destroyed by God (Dan. 8:25; Rev. 19:19-20). "He shall also stand up against the Prince of princes; but he shall be broken without hand" (Dan. 8:25).

IX. The secret of the 70 seven's

A. Daniel—the prayer of a prophet (9:1-19)

   1. Reading God's message—This is one of the greatest chapters in all the Bible. It has a double theme, that of prayer and prophecy. At this time Daniel was about 85. He was reading from the book of Jeremiah (Daniel had probably become the official custodian of various Old Testament books after the destruction of the temple) and was reminded that God had determined Jerusalem must lie desolate for 70 years (see Jer. 25:11; 29:10).
   2. Pleading God's mercy—He then

began an intense and prolonged prayer to God, concerning both his personal sins and those national sins of Israel which had caused her captivity in the first place. His prayer was accompanied by fasting, sackcloth, and ashes (9:1-3).

a. He reminded God of his covenants (9:4).

b. He contrasted God's grace and goodness with Israel's immorality and idolatry (9:5-11).

   (1) Israel's immorality and idolatry—"We have . . . committed iniquity . . . and have rebelled" (9:5). "Yea, all Israel have transgressed thy law" (9:11).

   (2) God's grace and goodness—"O Lord, righteousness belongeth unto thee" (9:7). "To the Lord our God belong mercies and forgiveness" (9:9).

c. He mentioned Judah's kings (9:8). Two of them had been carried off into the Babylonian Captivity along with the Jewish people.

d. He fully agreed that Judah had gotten just what she deserved and that God meant just what he said when he warned them about disobedience and punishment (9:12-14). He ended his prayer by throwing both himself and his people completely upon the manifold grace of God (9:18).

B. Gabriel—the prophecy of an angel (9:20-27): Even while Daniel was praying, God sent Gabriel the archangel to both minister to him and explain the most important, the most amazing, and the most profound single prophecy in the entire Word of God! "Seventy weeks are determined upon thy people and upon thy holy city, to fin-ish the transgression, and to make an end of sins, and to make reconciliation for iniquity, and to bring in everlasting righteousness, and to seal up the vision and prophecy, and to anoint the most Holy. Know therefore and understand, that from the going forth of the commandment to restore and to build Jerusalem unto the Messiah the Prince shall be seven weeks, and threescore and two weeks: the street shall be built again, and the wall, even in troublous times. And after threescore and two weeks shall Messiah be cut off, but not for himself: and the people of the prince that shall come shall destroy the city and the sanctuary; and the end thereof shall be with a flood, and unto the end of the war desolations are determined. And he shall confirm the covenant with many for one week: and in the midst of the week he shall cause the sacrifice and the oblation to cease, and for the overspreading of abominations he shall make it desolate, even until the consummation, and that determined shall be poured upon the desolate" (9:24-27). We shall consider this prophecy by asking and attempting to answer six key questions:

1. To whom does this prophecy refer? It refers to Israel, "Thy people" (9:24).

2. What is meant by the term "seventy weeks"? The Hebrew word refers to 70 seven's of years, or a total of 490 years.

3. When was the 70-week period to begin? It was to begin with the command to rebuild Jerusalem's walls (9:25).

4. What are the distinct time periods mentioned within the 70-week prophecy and what was to happen during each period?

   a. First period—A period of seven weeks (49 years), from 445 B.C.

to 396 B.C. The key events during this time were the building
of the streets and walls of Jerusalem "even in troublous times"
(9:25).

b. Second period—A period of 62
weeks (434 years), from 396
B.C. to A.D. 30. (These don't
add up to 434 years, and the
same period mentioned below
gives different years that also
do not add up.) At the end of
this second period the Messiah
was to be crucified.

c. Third period—A period of one
week (seven years) from the
Rapture until the Millennium.

5. Do the 70 weeks run continuously? This is to say, is there a
gap somewhere between these
490 years, or do they run without
pause until they are completed?
Dispensational theology teaches
that these "weeks" do not run
continuously, but that there has
been a gap or parenthesis of
nearly 2,000 years between the
sixty-ninth and seventieth week.
This is known as the Age of the
Church.

6. Does the Bible offer any other examples of time gaps in divine programs? It does. At least three
instances come to mind in which
gaps of many centuries can be
found in a single short paragraph
(Isa. 9:6-7; 61:1-2; Zech. 9:9-10).
Here is a final brief review of the
70 weeks:

a. The six main accomplishments
of the 70 weeks:

(1) To bring to an end all human transgressions and sins,
especially those of the nation
Israel.

(2) To make reconciliation for
iniquity.

(3) To vindicate by fulfillment
all true prophets and their
prophecies.

(4) To prove the inability of the
devil to rightfully rule this
world.

(5) To destroy him and his chief
henchman, the Antichrist.

(6) To usher in the Millennium.

b. The three main time periods of
the 70 weeks (490 years)

(1) First period—49 years, or
seven weeks from 445 B.C.
to 396 B.C.

(2) Second period—434 years, or
62 weeks from 396 B.C. to
A.D. 32

(3) A time-out period—which
has already lasted almost 20
centuries

(4) Third period—seven years,
or one week from the Rap-
ture until the Millennium

c. The two main individuals of the
70 weeks:

(1) Messiah—the Lord Jesus
Christ

(2) "The prince that shall come"
(9:26)—the Antichrist

X. The conflict above the clouds

A. A man in mourning (10:1-4)—Daniel
had set aside a period of three weeks
to be alone with God. During that
time, he refrained from eating food,
drinking wine, and anointing himself.

B. An angel in attendance (10:5-21)

1. His description (10:5-9)—"I lifted
up mine eyes, and looked, and
behold a certain man clothed in
linen, whose loins were girded
with fine gold of Uphaz: his body
also was like the beryl, and his
face as the appearance of lightning, and his eyes as lamps of
fire, and his arms and his feet like
in colour to polished brass, and
the voice of his words like the
voice of a multitude" (10:5-6).

a. Daniel immediately grew pale
and weak with fright at such a
dazzling sight.

b. The men with Daniel were also

filled with terror, although they did not actually see the vision as did Daniel (10:7).

2. His declaration (10:10-19)

   a. He had been hindered by the prince of Persia (10:13). Who was this prince?

     (1) The prince was powerful— He singlehandedly blocked one of heaven's mightiest angels for 21 days.

     (2) The prince was perverted— He withstood God's divinely appointed messenger. Thus he must have been a high-ranking demon assigned by Satan to Persia to control the demonic activities in that kingdom.

   b. He had been helped by the archangel Michael (10:13). This is the other archangel mentioned in the Bible. This angel then proceeded to comfort, reassure, strengthen, and instruct Daniel concerning the end times.

3. His determination (10:20-21)—As he returned to God, the angel was aware that not only would he once again be confronted by the Persian demon, but also by the demon of Greece. Apparently Satan was throwing in new support by sending into battle his future appointee over the Grecian empire. But the angel was confident, knowing he could again count on the help of Michael.

XI. A chronology of Christless kings

  A. Alexander the Great (11:1-20) including his predecessors and successors

    1. Four Persian kings would rule after Cyrus (who was ruling when Daniel wrote this) and the fourth would be the richest of all. This happened (11:2).

    2. After this, a mighty king would rule (11:3). This was Alexander the Great (336-323 B.C.).

    3. This king would suddenly die in his prime. His kingdom would not be given to his posterity, but would be divided up by outsiders into four sections (11:4). This is what happened. Shortly after Alexander's death, Philip, his half brother; Alexander II, his legitimate son; and Hercules, his illegitimate son, were murdered. Alexander's four generals took over.

  B. Antiochus Epiphanes (11:21-35)

    1. He was the youngest son of Antiochus the Great and is immediately classified as a vile (or contemptible) person by the Word of God (11:21).

    2. He was nicknamed "Epimanes," meaning "madman," by those who knew him best.

    3. He practiced deceit and pretended to be a second-century B.C. Robin Hood (1 Macc. 3:29-31).

    4. Antiochus had hoped to capture Egypt but was stopped cold by the mighty Romans (11:30).

    5. He took out his insane rage on the city of Jerusalem (11:28-35).

  C. Antichrist (11:36-45)

    1. He shall do everything according to his own selfish will (11:36).

    2. He shall magnify himself and malign God (11:36). The word "marvelous things" here in this verse means literally "astonishing, unbelievable." The Antichrist will scream out unbelievable blasphemies against God—insults no one else could ever think of, or would dare say if they could.

    3. He will be allowed by God to prosper (given full rope) during the tribulation (the "indignation") (11:36).

    4. He will not regard "the God of his fathers" (11:37).

    5. He will not have the desire for (or of) women (11:37).

    6. His god will be the God of

fortresses (11:38). The Antichrist will spend all his resources on military programs.

7. In the latter days of the Tribulation, he shall be attacked by the king of the south (Egypt) and the king of the north (Russia) (11:40).

8. After the defeat of Russia, the Antichrist will occupy Palestine. Edom and Moab will not be occupied by him (11:41).

9. Upon establishing control in Palestine, the Antichrist will march into Egypt and control that land (11:42-43).

10. While he is in Egypt, he will hear alarming rumors from the east and the north (11:44). The exact nature of these rumors is uncertain.

11. He will quickly return and in great fury destroy many (11:44). Here again the identity of those who are destroyed cannot be dogmatically stated.

12. He will apparently successfully deal with the threat and establish his worldwide headquarters on Mt. Zion. Here he will remain until his total destruction by the King of kings at the end of the tribulation (11:45).

XII. Closing conditions

A. The ministry of Michael (12:1)

1. Michael is Israel's guardian angel.

2. He will help deliver Israel through the worst period of human history since the creation of the world.

B. The two resurrections—"Many of them that sleep in the dust of the earth shall awake, some to everlasting life, and some to shame and everlasting contempt. And they that be wise shall shine as the brightness of the firmament; and they that turn many to righteousness as the stars for ever and ever" (12:2-3).

1. The resurrection of those to eternal life—This will occur at the beginning of the Millennium and

will include all Old Testament and martyred tribulation saints. (See Job 19:25-26; Ps. 49:15; Isa. 25:8; 26:19; Hos. 13:14; Heb. 11:35; Rev. 20:4, 6.) The reward of all righteous soul winners is mentioned in Daniel 12:3.

2. The resurrection of those to shame and everlasting contempt—This will transpire after the Millennium, and will include all unsaved people who have ever lived (Rev. 20:5). Our Lord summarized these two resurrections in John 5:28-29.

C. The two last day prophecies (12:4)

1. An increase of knowledge

2. An increase of speed

D. The three time periods (12:5-13)

1. Daniel saw two other angels who had been listening to this private prophecy conference the mighty angel was conducting for the old statesman. One of the two suddenly asked how long this terrible tribulation period would last (12:6). Neither of these two angels had apparently overheard the details of the 70-week vision in 9:24-27. The mighty angel informed them that the duration of this final horrible half of the tribulation will last as long as it takes for the pride and power of the Jews to be broken, or three and a half years (12:7).

2. The 1,290 days (12:11)—This period refers to the same as mentioned above, but includes an additional 30 days. Although we cannot be dogmatic, it would seem reasonable to conclude that an additional month will be needed here to carry out the sheep and goat judgment mentioned in Matthew 25:31-46.

3. The 1,335 days (12:12)—Here again a period of time is added: 45 days. What will be the need of these 45 days? It may be the time

necessary for setting up the government machinery for carrying on the rule of Christ.

E. The four final conclusions

1. The mighty angel raised both hands to heaven as he attested to the veracity of all this (12:7).
2. Many shall be cleansed (saved) during the tribulation (12:1). This includes both Jews and Gentiles (Rev. 7:1-17).
3. The wicked, however, will continue their evil ways (Dan. 12:10; Rev. 9:20-21; 11:9-10)
4. Daniel was to carefully preserve his writings (12:4), but all their meaning would not be revealed to him until that glorious day when he stood alongside the righteous awaiting his inheritance lot (12:9, 13).

THEOLOGICAL SUMMARY

I. Daniel's example—He was referred to along with Noah and Job by Ezekiel to illustrate two godly virtues.
   A. The virtue of righteousness (Ezek. 14:14, 20)
   B. The virtue of wisdom (Ezek. 28:3)
II. Daniel's background
   A. Daniel was born in Israel from the tribe of Judah, of a royal family (Dan. 1:3).
   B. He was carried off by Nebuchadnezzar to Babylon during the first siege of Jerusalem in 606 B.C. (Dan. 1:1-2).
   C. He was described as being handsome, without physical defect, quick to understand, well-informed, and showing great learning potential (Dan. 1:4).
   D. He possessed the divine gift of prophecy and of dream interpretation (Dan. 2:29; 4:20).
III. When in captivity, without the slightest compromise, he faithfully served under the administration of three kings.
   A. Nebuchadnezzar (Dan. 1–4)
   B. Belshazzar (Dan. 5, 7–8)
   C. Darius (Dan. 6, 9–12)

IV. He himself was ministered to by both of heaven's archangels.
   A. Gabriel (Dan. 8:16-17; 9:21)
   B. Michael (Dan. 10:13; 12:1)
V. The preincarnate Christ appeared to Daniel on two occasions.
   A. In the lion's den (Dan. 6:22)
   B. By the Tigris River (Dan. 10:4-9, 16-17)
VI. The abomination of desolation—Jesus referred to the historical "abomination of desolation" as spoken of by Daniel, and tied it in with a prophetical event (Dan. 11:31; Matt. 24:15). "When ye therefore shall see the abomination of desolation, spoken of by Daniel the prophet, stand in the holy place, (whoso readeth, let him understand)" (Matt. 24:15).
   A. The historical abomination of desolation (Dan. 11:31)
      1. The actor involved—Antiochus Epiphanes, a Syrian king who hated Jews
      2. The action involved—He defiled the holy of holies in the second temple by slaughtering a pig.
   B. The prophetical abomination of desolation (2 Thess. 2:4; Rev. 13:6, 14-18)
      1. The actor involved—The Antichrist
      2. The action involved—He will pollute the holy of holies in the tribulational temple by placing there a statue of himself.
VII. The book of Daniel—The unusual feature of Daniel's book is that he wrote the central portion (2:4–7:28) in the Aramaic language.

STATISTICS

First mention: Ezekiel 14:14
Final mention: Mark 13:14
Meaning of his name: "God is Judge"
Frequency of his name: Referred to 87 times
Biblical books mentioning him: Four books (Ezekiel, Daniel, Matthew, Mark)
Occupation: Political leader and prophet (Dan. 2:48, 49; 5:10-12)
Place of birth: Judah (Dan. 1:1-6)

Place of death: Babylon
Important fact about his life: He served as
  prime minister in Babylon under Nebuchadnezzar and Darius (Dan. 2:48; 6:1-3).

✒Darius (1)

CHRONOLOGICAL SUMMARY

I. Darius and Belshazzar the king
  A. Darius was known as Darius the
     Mede (Dan. 5:31).
  B. He was the military general under
     Cyrus the Great who conquered Bab-
     ylon and killed Belshazzar (Dan.
     5:30).
  C. He is probably the man referred to as
     Gubaru in the Persian records.
  D. Darius was strengthened by an angel
     of God during the first year of his
     reign (Dan. 11:1).
II. Darius and Daniel the prophet
  A. An evil plan (Dan. 6:1-9)
     1. The organization—Darius, the
        Mede, immediately set about to
        reorganize and consolidate this
        fantastic new kingdom called Bab-
        ylon he now ruled. He divided
        the kingdom into 129 provinces,
        each under a prince. These
        princes were accountable to three
        presidents, with Daniel being one
        of the three. Daniel, now over 80,
        was still blessed with so much
        skill and ability that Darius was
        considering elevating him over
        the other two presidents (6:1-3).
     2. The orchestration
        a. This so infuriated both the
           presidents and the princes that
           they plotted against Daniel's
           life (6:4).
        b. Being unable to see the slight-
           est flaw in his secular life, they
           determined to trap him in his
           religious life (6:5).
        c. Darius was tricked into signing
           a 30-day decree which said that
           all prayers during that time

were to be directed to the king
himself (6:6-9).
  B. A kneeling man (6:10-20)
     1. The fearless prophet—Daniel
        learned of this and doubtless im-
        mediately saw through its clumsy
        effort to trap him. But the old
        warrior continued worshiping
        God as before (6:10).
        a. He kept his windows opened.
        b. He continued praying three
           times a day.
        c. He knelt down.
        d. He faced Jerusalem.
     2. The heartless plotters—Those vi-
        cious hunters who had set their
        trap now saw the prey inside and
        gleefully rushed to Darius to de-
        liver the death blow. Darius real-
        ized he had been had and
        desperately sought to find a loop-
        hole in the immutable law of the
        Medes and the Persians, but all to
        no avail (6:11-15). Daniel was ar-
        rested and thrown down into a
        den of hungry man-eating lions.
     3. The sleepless potentate
        a. After sealing the mouth of the
           den with his own signet ring,
           Darius returned and spent a
           sleepless and miserable night in
           the royal palace (6:17-18).
        b. At daybreak the next morning
           he rushed to the den, ordered
           the capstone removed, and
           called out in anguish: "O Dan-
           iel, servant of the living God, is
           thy God, whom thou servest
           continually, able to deliver thee
           from the lions?" (6:20).
  C. A heavenly ban
     1. Daniel's response—Out of the
        blackness of that den of doom
        there came a cheerful and clear
        voice: "O king, live for ever. My
        God hath sent his angel, and hath
        shut the lions' mouths, that they
        have not hurt me: forasmuch as
        before him innocency was found
        in me; and also before thee, O

king, have I done no hurt" (6:21-22).

2. Darius' reaction—The king's reaction to all this was twofold; he was both glad and mad.

a. He rejoiced at Daniel's salvation and issued a decree ordering all the citizens of his kingdom to consider this almighty Judean God (6:23, 25-27).

b. He took immediate vengeance upon those who had tricked him in the first place, and ordered them along with all their families thrown into this same den. Their bodies were instantly torn apart by the lions (6:24).

STATISTICS

First mention: Daniel 5:31
Final mention: Daniel 11:1
Meaning of his name: "He who upholds the good"
Frequency of his name: Referred to eight times
Biblical books mentioning him: One book (Daniel)
Occupation: King of the Medo-Persian empire (Dan. 6:12)
Important fact about his life: He was tricked into casting Daniel into the den of lions (Dan. 6:14-16).

✍Darius (2)

CHRONOLOGICAL SUMMARY

I. The request
   A. He was also known as Darius the Great.
   B. He took over the crumbling Persian empire after the suicide of King Cambyses.
   C. Darius received a letter from one of his officials named Tattenai concerning a situation in the city of Jerusalem (Ezra 5:3-17).
      1. The review given by Tattenai—He told the king he had approached the Jews in Jerusalem who were building a temple and demanded to know: "Who hath commanded you to build this house, and to make up this wall?" (5:3).
      2. The reply given to Tattenai—The Jews responded by saying they had received official permission to build their temple from Cyrus the Great himself (5:11-13).
      3. The request coming from Tattenai—In light of the situation, Tattenai suggested to Darius that he authorize a search in the royal archives to determine the validity of this claim.

II. The research—The king ordered such an investigation, and discovered the original decree issued by Cyrus (6:1-5).

III. The resolution—Darius thereupon drafted a letter to his officials in the Holy Land (Ezra 6:6-12).
   A. The wisdom of the king—Realizing God himself had prompted Cyrus's original decree, Darius instructed his officials not only to aid in the temple construction, but to pay for it through local taxes.
   B. The warning from the king—Anyone disobeying this command would lose both his house and his head. The temple was completed during the sixth year of his reign (Ezra 6:15).

STATISTICS

First mention: Ezra 4:5
Final mention: Zechariah 7:1
Meaning of his name: "He who upholds the good"
Frequency of his name: Referred to 16 times
Biblical books mentioning him: Three books (Ezra, Haggai, Zechariah)
Occupation: King of Persia (Ezra 4:5)
Important fact about his life: He ordered the work on the temple in Jerusalem, which had been halted, to resume (Ezra 6:1-12).

David

CHRONOLOGICAL SUMMARY

I. The former years

A. The shepherd

1. His provision for the sheep

a. "Samuel said unto Jesse, Are here all thy children? And he said, There remaineth yet the youngest, and, behold, he keepeth the sheep. And Samuel said unto Jesse, Send and fetch him: for we will not sit down till he come hither" (1 Sam. 16:11).

b. "David went and returned from Saul to feed his father's sheep at Beth-lehem" (1 Sam. 17:15).

c. "Now therefore so shalt thou say unto my servant David, Thus saith the LORD of hosts, I took thee from the sheepcote, from following the sheep, to be ruler over my people, over Israel" (2 Sam. 7:8).

d. "He chose David also his servant, and took him from the sheepfolds: from following the ewes great with young he brought him to feed Jacob his people, and Israel his inheritance" (Ps. 78:70-71).

2. His protection of the sheep— "David said unto Saul, Thy servant kept his father's sheep, and there came a lion, and a bear, and took a lamb out of the flock: and I went out after him, and smote him, and delivered it out of his mouth: and when he arose against me, I caught him by his beard, and smote him, and slew him. Thy servant slew both the lion and the bear: and this uncircumcised Philistine shall be as one of them, seeing he hath defied the armies of the living God" (1 Sam. 17:34-36).

B. The selected (1 Sam. 16:1-13)

1. The rejection of Jesse's older sons

a. The command—At God's order, Samuel the prophet visited the home of Jesse in Bethlehem to anoint one of his sons who would replace the rejected Saul as Israel's next king.

b. The confusion—Impressed by his appearance, Samuel mistakenly concluded that Eliab, Jesse's oldest son, would be God's choice. "It came to pass, when they were come, that he looked on Eliab, and said, Surely the LORD's anointed is before him" (1 Sam. 16:6).

c. The correction—"The LORD said unto Samuel, Look not on his countenance, or on the height of his stature; because I have refused him: for the LORD seeth not as man seeth; for man looketh on the outward appearance, but the LORD looketh on the heart" (1 Sam. 16:7).

2. The selection of Jesse's youngest son—"Again, Jesse made seven of his sons to pass before Samuel. And Samuel said unto Jesse, The LORD hath not chosen these. And Samuel said unto Jesse, Are here all thy children? And he said, There remaineth yet the youngest, and, behold, he keepeth the sheep. And Samuel said unto Jesse, Send and fetch him: for we will not sit down till he come hither. And he sent, and brought him in. Now he was ruddy, and withal of a beautiful countenance, and goodly to look to. And the LORD said, Arise, anoint him: for this is he. Then Samuel took the horn of oil, and anointed him in the midst of his brethren: and the Spirit of the LORD came upon David from that day forward. So Samuel rose up, and went to Ramah" (1 Sam. 16:10-13).

C. The singer (1 Sam. 16:14-23; 17:15)

1. The problem—"The Spirit of the LORD departed from Saul, and an evil spirit from the LORD troubled him" (1 Sam. 16:14).
2. The performance
   a. At the suggestion of his servants, Saul requested that David be invited to play his harp in the royal palace.
   b. When David played, the evil spirit left Saul.
   c. During this time David also served as Saul's armorbearer.
   d. He thus traveled to and fro from the palace to the pasture, serving as both singer and shepherd.
D. The soldier (1 Sam. 17:1-58)
   1. The criticism (David and Eliab)
      a. At his father Jesse's instruction, David carried some food supplies to his three older brothers, who were in Saul's army fighting the Philistines (17:13, 17).
      b. Upon arriving at the battle scene, David gazed upon a Philistine giant named Goliath (17:23).
      c. For 40 days this huge warrior (nearly 10 feet tall) had defied both Israel and God (17:16).
      d. During this time he had demanded that Saul send a soldier to fight him with the agreement that the entire army of the one defeated would surrender (17:8-10).
      e. The Israelite army, however, was terrified at such a proposal (17:11, 24).
      f. David wondered out loud why the defiance of this pagan giant was allowed to go unchallenged (17:26).
      g. Eliab, David's oldest brother, rebuked him for his bold statements.
         (1) The rebuke: "Why camest thou down hither? and with whom hast thou left those

few sheep in the wilderness? I know thy pride, and the naughtiness of thine heart; for thou art come down that thou mightest see the battle" (17:28).
         (2) The reply: "What have I now done? Is there not a cause?" (17:29).
   2. The concern (David and Saul)
      a. David met with Saul and volunteered to fight Goliath himself (17:32).
         (1) Saul's objection: "You're only a boy and Goliath is a seasoned and professional killing machine."
         (2) David's answer:
            (a) "In the past I have protected my father's sheep from a lion and a bear."
            (b) "When either animal turned on me, I killed it."
            (c) "The same God who delivered me from those animals will deliver me from this one."
      b. Saul then dressed David with the king's own coat of armor and brass helmet (17:38).
      c. David, however, decided against wearing this strange and untested equipment (17:39).
      d. Instead, choosing five smooth stones from the stream, he marched out to meet the giant with his sling (17:40).
   3. The contempt (David and Goliath)
      a. David was despised and cursed by Goliath, who vowed to give his flesh to the birds of the air and the beasts of the field (17:41-44).
      b. His answer to this hostile warrior was both concise and confident (17:45-47).
         (1) He would come against Goliath by the power of God.
         (2) He would slay the giant, cut

off his head, and feed his
flesh to the birds and beasts.

(3) By this, all men would know
that the battle was the
Lord's.

4. The conquest (David and God)

a. David killed Goliath by striking
the warrior in his forehead with
a stone hurled from his sling
(17:48-50).

b. He then cut off the Philistine's
head with the giant's own
sword (17:51).

c. With Goliath's head in his
hand, David stood before Saul
(17:57).

II. The frustrating years

A. The sought

1. The persecution by Saul

a. The background

(1) Following the battle, Saul
commanded David to live
with him in the king's court
(1 Sam. 18:2).

(2) Whatever he was sent to do,
David did it so successfully
that Saul soon gave him a
high rank in the army
(1 Sam. 18:5).

b. The basis—Saul soon turned
against David, prompted by
two factors (1 Sam. 18:6-10, 12).

(1) A victory song—The women
of Israel had composed a
song to celebrate the victory
of David and Israel over the
Philistines. The words ran:
"Saul has slain his thou-
sands, and David his tens of
thousands." Saul took a very
dim view of this song. "Saul
was very wroth, and the
saying displeased him; and
he said, They have ascribed
unto David ten thousands,
and to me they have as-
cribed but thousands: and
what can he have more but
the kingdom?" (1 Sam. 18:8).

(2) A vicious spirit—At this

time, the demon that David
had once driven from Saul
through his music (1 Sam.
16:14, 23) now returned to
plague him (1 Sam. 18:10).

c. The bungling—On numerous
occasions the wicked king attempted to kill David, but failed
every time.

(1) On at least three occasions,
Saul tried to kill David by
hurling a javelin at him
(1 Sam. 18:10, 11; 19:9-10).

(2) He offered his youngest
daughter, Michal, to David
in marriage. "Saul said,
Thus shall ye say to David,
The king desireth not any
dowry, but an hundred foreskins of the Philistines, to be
avenged of the king's enemies. But Saul thought to
make David fall by the hand
of the Philistines" (1 Sam.
18:25). To Saul's amazement
and anger, David presented
him with the foreskins of
200 Philistines and thus
qualified to become the
king's son-in-law (1 Sam.
18:27).

(3) Saul sent soldiers to kill David in his own home, but
Michal saved her husband
by lowering him down
through a bedroom window
(1 Sam. 19:11-17).

d. The blessing—Through all these
trying events, God's hand continued to rest upon David,
causing his fame to increase.

(1) On the home front—"David
behaved himself wisely in all
his ways; and the LORD was
with him. . . . All Israel and
Judah loved David, because
he went out and came in
before them" (1 Sam. 18:14,
16).

(2) On the battlefront—"There

was war again: and David
went out, and fought with
the Philistines, and slew
them with a great slaughter;
and they fled from him"
(1 Sam. 19:8).
e. The befriending
  (1) The great love and friend-
      ship between David and Jon-
      athan (Saul's son) had begun
      when David killed Goliath
      (1 Sam. 18:1, 3-4).
  (2) David was warned by Jona-
      than concerning his father's
      murderous intents (1 Sam.
      19:1-3).
  (3) After cautioning Saul against
      his hatred of David, Jona-
      than persuaded his father to
      declare a truce (1 Sam. 19:4-7).
  (4) David secretly met with Jon-
      athan (1 Sam. 20:1-23).
      (a) Jonathan had concluded
          (sincerely but incorrectly)
          that his father had finally
          given up plans to kill Da-
          vid.
      (b) Fearing the worst, David
          was reassured by Jona-
          than, who proposed a
          test to reveal Saul's true
          motives.
      (c) He would absent himself
          from the New Moon Fes-
          tival at the royal palace.
      (d) If Saul showed anger
          over his absence, this
          would mean he was still
          planning to kill him.
      (e) Following the banquet,
          Jonathan would let David
          know the true situation.
  (5) Upon learning of David's
      absence at the banquet table,
      Saul became furious (1 Sam.
      20:24-34).
      (a) He cursed his own son
          Jonathan for befriending
          David.
      (b) He actually attempted to

kill Jonathan with a
spear.
  (6) The following morning, as
      agreed upon, David was
      warned by Jonathan (1 Sam.
      20:35-41).
  (7) Both reaffirmed their loyalty
      to each other. "Jonathan said
      to David, Go in peace, foras-
      much as we have sworn
      both of us in the name of
      the LORD, saying, The LORD
      be between me and thee,
      and between my seed and
      thy seed for ever. And he
      arose and departed: and Jon-
      athan went into the city"
      (1 Sam. 20:42).
  (8) During this time, David had
      visited the city of Ramah
      and told Samuel the prophet
      all that Saul had done to
      him (1 Sam. 19:18).
2. The flight from Saul
  a. David at Nob (1 Sam. 21:1-9)—
     He fled to Nob, where the tab-
     ernacle was located, and lied to
     Ahimelech, the high priest.
     (1) The falsehood of David
         (a) That he was on a secret
             mission for King Saul
         (b) That it was therefore
             Ahimelech's duty to pro-
             vide him with food and
             weapons
     (2) The faithfulness of
         Ahimelech—The old priest
         gave David bread and Golia-
         th's sword, which was
         wrapped in a cloth behind
         the ephod.
  b. David at Gath (1 Sam. 21:10-15)
     (1) Leaving Nob, David went to
         Gath, a city in Philistia and
         the former home of Goliath.
     (2) David was immediately
         recognized by the servants
         of Achish, king of Gath.
     (3) David, however, successfully
         faked insanity before the

king and was allowed to leave the city.

c. David at Adullam

(1) Leaving Gath, David established temporary headquarters in a cave called Adullam, located near a Canaanite city halfway between Lachish and Jerusalem (1 Sam. 22:1).

(2) Here he was joined by his brothers, and his father's household, plus many in distress, in debt, or discontented. His followers now numbered about 400 (1 Sam. 22:1-2).

(3) These followers were men from the tribes of Benjamin and Judah who pledged their allegiance to David, realizing he was God's chosen one (1 Chron. 12:16-18).

d. David at Moab (1 Sam. 22:3-5)

(1) David asked and received permission from the king of Moab to move his father and mother there.

(2) He was then ordered by the Lord through the prophet Gad to return to Judah.

e. David in the forest of Hereth (1 Sam. 22:5-23)

(1) Here he learned from Abiathar (a son of the high priest Ahimelech) the horrible news concerning a massacre at the city of Nob.

(2) Saul had executed the high priest plus 85 other priests for befriending David.

(3) The murderous king had then put the entire city to the sword.

f. David at Keilah (1 Sam. 23:1-13)

(1) At God's command, David defeated the Philistines who had been robbing the threshing floors of the Israelite city Keilah.

(2) Upon learning of David's whereabouts, Saul sent an army to Keilah.

(3) God warned David to flee Keilah, for its fickle citizens were planning to hand him over to Saul.

g. David in the wilderness of Ziph (1 Sam. 23:14-18)

(1) At this time his army numbered some 600 men. These 600 men were highly skilled, being able to shoot arrows and sling stones both with their right or left hands (1 Chron. 12:1-7).

(2) He once again met briefly with Jonathan. "Jonathan Saul's son arose, and went to David into the wood, and strengthened his hand in God. And he said unto him, Fear not: for the hand of Saul my father shall not find thee; and thou shalt be king over Israel, and I shall be next unto thee; and that also Saul my father knoweth. And they two made a covenant before the LORD: and David abode in the wood, and Jonathan went to his house" (1 Sam. 23:16-18).

(3) This would be the final meeting of these close friends.

h. David at Carmel (1 Sam. 25:1-44)—Following the death of Samuel, David met and married Abigail, the widow of a wealthy but doltish sheepherder named Nabal.

(1) Nabal had both refused and ridiculed David's modest request for a small amount of food.

(2) An angry David had prepared to do battle against Nabal.

(3) Learning of this, Abigail

rode off to meet David with
a large food gift.

(4) David's wrath subsided and
he spared Nabal's life.

(5) Sometime later the drunken
Nabal was struck dead by
God.

(6) David then sent for Abigail
and she became his wife.

(7) Saul had given David's first
wife, Michal, to another
man.

3. The kindness to Saul—On two
separate occasions David spared
the life of his mortal enemy Saul.

a. The episode in a cave (1 Sam.
24:1-22)

(1) The restraint (24:1-7)

(a) David established his
headquarters in a cave
near the Dead Sea in the
wilderness of En-gedi.

(b) Upon learning that David
was in that area, Saul led
an army of 3,000 chosen
men to capture him.

(c) Totally unaware, Saul entered David's cave to re-
lieve himself.

(d) David refused to grant
his men's request to kill
Saul, but he secretly cut
off a corner of the king's
robe.

(e) Afterward, however, David's heart "smote him"
because he had shown
disrespect toward the
king.

(2) The reprimand (24:8-15)

(a) After Saul had left the
cave, David called out to
him.

(b) He pointed out how easily he could have slain
the king, showing Saul
the piece that had been
cut from his robe.

(c) He then demanded to
know why Saul was try-

ing to kill him, for he was
innocent of any wrong-
doing or rebellion.

(3) The remorse (1 Sam. 24:16-
22)—"It came to pass, when
David had made an end of
speaking these words unto
Saul, that Saul said, Is this
thy voice, my son David?
And Saul lifted up his voice,
and wept" (1 Sam. 24:16).

(a) Saul acknowledged Da-
vid's righteousness in not
killing him when he could
have done so.

(b) He said he knew David
would soon become king
over Israel.

(c) Saul asked for and received David's promise
that he would not cut off
his descendants or wipe
out his name when he did
become king.

b. The episode on a hill (1 Sam.
26:1-25)

(1) David and Abishai—the
courage involved (26:1-12)

(a) Saul once again led an
army of 3,000 chosen
troops against David,
hoping to capture him in
the southeast part of the
Judean desert.

(b) Spotting the king first,
David and Abishai se-
cretly entered his camp
one night and removed
from the sleeping mon-
arch his water jug and
spear.

(c) Again David refused to
kill Saul.

(d) God had caused the army
to sleep deeply.

(2) David and Abner—the contempt involved (26:13-16)

(a) From a nearby hill David
cried out and made his
presence known.

(b) He then heaped contempt upon Saul's general, Abner, who had slept through everything. "David said to Abner, Art not thou a valiant man? and who is like to thee in Israel? wherefore then hast thou not kept thy lord the king? for there came one of the people in to destroy the king thy lord. This thing is not good that thou hast done. As the LORD liveth, ye are worthy to die, because ye have not kept your master, the LORD's anointed. And now see where the king's spear is, and the cruse of water that was at his bolster" (1 Sam. 26:15-16).

(3) David and Saul—the confession involved (26:17-25)

(a) Saul tried to reestablish his friendship with David. "Saul knew David's voice, and said, Is this thy voice, my son David? And David said, It is my voice, my lord, O king. And he said, Wherefore doth my lord thus pursue after his servant? for what have I done? or what evil is in mine hand? . . . Then said Saul, I have sinned: return, my son David: for I will no more do thee harm, because my soul was precious in thine eyes this day: behold, I have played the fool, and have erred exceedingly" (1 Sam. 26:17-18, 21).

(b) David wisely decided to go his way with his men.

B. David, the sidetracked (1 Sam. 27:1-28:2; 29:1-30:31; 2 Sam. 1:1-27)

1. His backsliding—"David said in his heart, I shall now perish one day by the hand of Saul: there is nothing better for me than that I should speedily escape into the land of the Philistines; and Saul shall despair of me, to seek me any more in any coast of Israel: so shall I escape out of his hand" (1 Sam. 27:1).

a. Thus, in time of discouragement, David and his 600 men, for fear of Saul, left Judah and settled in the Philistine city of Ziklag, given to David by Achish the king. Here he would live for 16 months (1 Sam. 27:1-7).

b. During this time David went out and raided many Canaanite cities, but deceived Achish into believing they were Israelite settlements (1 Sam. 27:8-12).

c. After awhile, King Achish prepared to do battle with Israel and requested that David and his men assist in the attack (1 Sam. 28:1-2).

d. Just before the battle, however, the Philistine military commanders, over the objections of Achish, refused to allow David to join their attack, fearing he would betray them (1 Sam. 29:1-11).

2. His bravery (1 Sam. 30:1-31)

a. Upon returning to Ziklag, David learned the Amalekites had attacked and burned the city and carried away into slavery all the wives and families of both David and his men.

b. David's men, for some unrecorded reason, blamed him for their misfortune and threatened to stone him. "David was greatly distressed; for the people

spake of stoning him, because
the soul of all the people was
grieved, every man for his
sons and for his daughters: but
David encouraged himself in
the LORD his God" (1 Sam.
30:6).

c. God commanded David to pursue the Amalekites, assuring
his servant of total victory.

d. The Lord kept his promise, and
David utterly routed the enemy
(1 Sam. 30:9-20).

(1) A captured slave agreed to
lead David to the location of
the Amalekite camp.

(2) Finding them drinking and
reveling over the destruction
of Ziklag, David fell upon
them, killing all but some
young men who rode off on
camels and escaped.

(3) He then recovered all that
the enemy had taken, in-
cluding every single hostage.

e. For some reason 200 of David's
600 soldiers were too exhausted
to fight and were placed in
charge of the supplies as the
remaining 400 rode into battle
(30:21).

f. Following the victory, the 400
soldiers did not want to share
the spoils of war with the 200
men.

g. David, however, overruled this
objection: "Then said David, Ye
shall not do so, my brethren,
with that which the LORD hath
given us, who hath preserved
us, and delivered the company
that came against us into our
hand. For who will hearken
unto you in this matter? but as
his part is that goeth down to
the battle, so shall his part be
that tarrieth by the stuff: they
shall part alike. And it was so
from that day forward, that he

made it a statute and an ordinance for Israel unto this day"
(1 Sam. 30:23-25).

h. David later sent some of the
war plunder to his friends who
were elders in Judah (1 Sam.
30:26-31).

3. His bereavement (2 Sam. 1:1-27)

a. The reason for this bereavement—While in Ziklag, David
learned that both Saul and Jonathan had been killed in the
battle against the Philistines.

b. The reaction to this bereavement

(1) David ordered the execution
of an Amalekite man who
claimed he had personally
killed the mortally wounded
Saul.

(2) He then composed and cried
out a lament for Saul and
Jonathan.

(a) He ordered that the news
of their deaths not be
spread abroad, lest God's
enemies rejoice.

(b) He called for a divine
judgment of drought
and failing crops upon
Mt. Gilboa where Saul
fell.

c. He offered the highest praise
for Saul and Jonathan, saying:

(1) They were the glory of Israel.

(2) In life they were loved and
gracious.

(3) In death they were not
parted.

(4) They were swifter than eagles and stronger than lions.

d. He commanded all Israel to join
him in lamenting their deaths,
pointing out that:

(1) Saul would be remembered
as the one who had met Israel's physical needs.

(2) Jonathan would be remem-

bered as being David's dearest and closest friend.

III. The finest years

A. David the sovereign, at Hebron, his first capital

1. Anointed king over one tribe

a. At God's command, David left Ziklag at the death of Saul and moved to the city of Hebron (2 Sam. 2:1-3).

b. The men of Judah came to Hebron and anointed David as their king.

c. He would reign over this tribe for seven and a half years (2 Sam. 2:4, 11).

d. He commended the men of Jabesh-gilead for recovering Saul's body which the Philistines had fastened to a wall. The body was then given a decent burial (compare 1 Sam. 31:8-13 with 2 Sam. 2:4-7).

e. David entered into an agreement with Abner, former military commander under Saul (2 Sam. 3:12-21).

(1) Abner promised to bring the remaining 10 tribes of Israel under David's control.

(2) At David's request, Abner arranged to have Michal, the king's first wife, returned to him.

f. Later, David was furious upon learning that Abner had been murdered by Joab, the king's military commander, who had doubtless viewed Abner as a potential rival (2 Sam. 3:22-38).

g. Six of David's many sons were born during his reign in Hebron (2 Sam. 3:2-5); three of these would later cause him much grief.

(1) Amnon would rape his own half sister, Tamar.

(2) Absalom would murder Amnon for this and later lead a revolt against David.

(3) Adonijah would attempt to steal the throne from Solomon, even as David lay on his deathbed.

2. Anointed king over 12 tribes

a. David was presented with the head of Ish-bosheth (2 Sam. 4:1-12).

(1) Ish-bosheth was Saul's son whom Abner had made king over 11 of Israel's tribes following his father's death.

(2) David, however, ordered the deaths of the two military men who murdered him.

b. David was anointed at Hebron by all 12 tribes of Israel (2 Sam. 5:1-3; 1 Chron. 11:1-3; 12:8-15, 23-40).

(1) They acknowledged that even when Saul was king, it was really David who provided inspiration and led them to victory.

(2) A total of 336,100 soldiers from all 12 tribes celebrated this great event for three days.

(3) Troops from three tribes are especially noted by the sacred account:

(a) Gad, of whom it was said they were men of valor, trained for war with the strength of lions and the swiftness of roes (1 Chron. 12:8)

(b) Issachar, of whom it was said they had understanding of the times, to know what Israel ought to do (1 Chron. 12:32)

(c) Zebulun, of whom it was said they were men of single heart (1 Chron. 12:33)

c. David was 37 1/2 years old at this time (2 Sam. 5:4-5).

d. This marked David's third and final anointing.

B. David the sovereign, at Jerusalem, his final capital
   1. The city of God—David captured Jerusalem and made it his permanent headquarters (2 Sam. 5:6-12; 1 Chron. 11:4-9; 14:1-2).
      a. The Jebusites, pagan defenders of Jerusalem, had ridiculed David's plan to take the city.
      b. David promised that the first Israelite soldier to enter the city would become his military leader.
      c. Joab, David's nephew, accomplished this and assumed the position of army commander.
      d. Upon taking the city, David began to enlarge it.
      e. He then contracted with Hiram, King of Tyre, to build him a house.
   2. The Ark of God (2 Sam. 6:1-23; 1 Chron. 13:1-14; 15:1-29; 16:1-3)
      a. The journey of the Ark, part one:
         (1) The transportation
            (a) At the king's invitation, some 30,000 representatives from all over Israel accompanied him to the city of Kirjath-jearim (also called Baale of Judah) where the Ark of the Covenant was resting at the home of Abinadab (2 Sam. 6:1-4; 1 Chron. 13:1-7).
            (b) It was placed on a new cart, driven by Abinadab's two sons, Uzzah and Ahio (2 Sam. 6:3-4; 1 Chron. 13:7).
            (c) David and a multitude of worshipers ran before the cart, praising God with songs and musical instruments (2 Sam. 6:5; 1 Chron. 13:8).
         (2) The tragedy
            (a) Disaster struck when Uz-

zah's unwise handling of the Ark brought down the judgment of death from God (2 Sam. 6:6-7; 1 Chron. 13:9-10).
            (b) Fearful to continue his trip, David placed the Ark in the house of a man named Obed-edom where it would reside for three months (2 Sam. 6:8-12; 1 Chron. 13:11-14).
         (3) The transference—Realizing his problem resulted in the way the Ark was being transported, David discarded the cart and transferred the Ark to 762 Levitical priests, ordering them to carry it on their shoulders, as God had originally commanded Moses (1 Chron. 15:1-15).
      b. The journey of the Ark, part two:
         (1) The celebration
            (a) David began the final part of the trip by offering up animal sacrifices to God (2 Sam. 6:13).
            (b) Amid joyful shouting, singing, and the playing of musical instruments, David, the Levites, and the accompanying congregation entered the city of Jerusalem with the Ark (2 Sam. 6:15; 1 Chron. 15:16, 25-28).
            (c) David himself danced before the Ark with all his might (2 Sam. 6:14).
            (d) The Ark was then placed inside the tabernacle (2 Sam. 6:17; 1 Chron. 16:1).
            (e) David then assigned the priests a very important task. "He appointed certain of the Levites to minister before the ark of the

LORD, and to record, and
to thank and praise the
LORD God of Israel"
(1 Chron. 16:4).

(2) The criticism (2 Sam. 6:16,
20-23; 1 Chron. 15:29)

(a) Upon returning home to
bless his family, David
received a crushing blow.

(b) His wife Michal both ridiculed and rebuked him
for displaying such zeal
and praise to God.

(c) As a result of this, David
and Michal no longer
lived together as husband
and wife.

3. The covenant of God (2 Sam. 7:1-
17; 1 Chron. 17:1-15)

a. David's request—to build a
house for God

(1) After defeating all his enemies, David proposed to
build a temple to house the
Ark of the Covenant. "Now
it came to pass, as David sat
in his house, that David said
to Nathan the prophet, Lo, I
dwell in an house of cedars,
but the ark of the covenant
of the LORD remaineth under
curtains" (1 Chron. 17:1).

(2) Nathan the prophet encouraged David to do this
(2 Sam. 7:3; 1 Chron. 17:2).

(3) However, that very night
God revealed to Nathan in a
vision that it was not his will
for David to build the temple because of his much
bloodshedding in war
(2 Sam. 7:4-7; 1 Chron. 17:3-
6; 22:8-9).

b. God's response—to build a
house for David

(1) To the contrary, God would
construct a house (dynasty)
for David. "Also the LORD
telleth thee that he will

make thee an house"
(2 Sam. 7:11). "For thou, O
my God, hast told thy servant that thou wilt build him
an house" (1 Chron. 17:25).

(2) This "house covenant"
(known as the Davidic Covenant) had three key promises attached to it (2 Sam.
7:8-17; 1 Chron. 17:7-15).

(a) God would make David's
name great.

(b) His son Solomon would
succeed him and build
the temple.

(c) David's kingdom would
be established forever.

4. The worship of God—During this
time in his life, David worshiped
God by offering up three thanksgiving prayers.

a. Thanking and worshiping God
for his *presence*

(1) This had to do with the Ark
of the Covenant, over which
dwelt the glory of God
(1 Chron. 16:7-36). "On that
day David delivered first this
psalm to thank the LORD into
the hand of Asaph and his
brethren" (1 Chron. 16:7).

(2) The words in this hymn of
praise would later be in-
cluded in Psalms 96, 105,
and 106.

b. Thanking and worshiping God
for his *promise*—This had to do
with the features in the Davidic
Covenant (2 Sam. 7:18-29;
1 Chron. 17:16-27). "For thou,
O my God, hast told thy servant that thou wilt build him
an house: therefore thy servant
hath found in his heart to pray
before thee" (1 Chron. 17:25).

c. Thanking and worshiping God
for his *power*. This had to do
with the great military victories
God had given David (2 Sam.

22:1-51). "David spake unto the LORD the words of this song in the day that the LORD had delivered him out of the hand of all his enemies, and out of the hand of Saul" (2 Sam. 22:1). Much of this material is later repeated in Psalm 18.

5. The blessings of God—As has been previously noted, God empowered David to defeat his various enemies.

a. His military conquests

(1) Against the Philistines— David conducted six successful military campaigns against the Philistines.

(a) First campaign (2 Sam. 5:17-21; 23:13-17; 1 Chron. 11:15-19; 14:8-12)

i. On this occasion, David expressed his longing for a drink of water from the well in Bethlehem, which was occupied by the Philistines at the time.

ii. Risking their own lives, three of David's mighty men crept into the enemy area and secured a container of water for him.

iii. Unwilling to drink this water which was obtained under such selfless and dangerous conditions, David poured it out as an offering to God.

iv. He was then commanded by God to attack and defeat the Philistines, which he did.

(b) Second campaign (2 Sam. 5:22-25; 1 Chron. 14:13-17)

i. David was instructed by God to encircle the attacking Philistines, stationing his men in the midst of some mulberry trees.

ii. When he heard a sound like the marching of troops coming from the tops of the trees, he was to attack, for this would be God's signal for victory.

(c) Third campaign (2 Sam. 21:15-17)

i. During this battle a huge Philistine giant named Ishbi-benob attacked David with a ponderous sword, which apparently unnerved the king.

ii. But one of David's warriors, Abishai, stepped in and killed the Philistine.

iii. After the narrow escape, David's soldiers prevented him from exposing his life in battle, lest their beloved and irreplaceable king be taken from them.

(d) Fourth campaign (2 Sam. 21:18; 1 Chron. 20:4)— During this battle another Philistine giant known both as Saph and Sippai was killed.

(e) Fifth campaign (2 Sam. 21:19; 1 Chron. 20:5)— Lahmi, the brother of the Philistine giant Goliath, was killed by an Israelite soldier from Bethlehem named Elhanan.

(f) Sixth Campaign (2 Sam. 21:20-22; 1 Chron. 20:6-8)

i. This final battle was

fought in the Philistine city of Gath.

ii. A relative of David named Jonathan killed an especially fierce and blasphemous giant who had six fingers on each hand and six toes on each foot.

(2) Against the Moabites (2 Sam. 8:2; 1 Chron. 18:2)

(a) David devastated the land of Moab.

(b) He divided his victims by making them lie down side by side in rows.

(c) Two thirds of each row were then executed and the remaining one third became his servants.

(3) Against the Aramaeans (2 Sam. 8:3-4; 1 Chron. 18:3-4)

(a) He destroyed the forces of King Hadadezer in a battle at the Euphrates River.

(b) David captured 1,700 cavalry and 20,000 infantry.

(c) He then lamed all of the chariot horses except for 100 teams.

(4) Against the Edomites (2 Sam. 8:13-14; 1 Chron. 18:12-13)

(a) He destroyed 18,000 Edomites at the Valley of Salt.

(b) He then placed garrisons throughout Edom and forced the entire nation to pay tribute to Israel.

(5) Against the Ammonites

(a) First campaign (2 Sam. 10:1-14; 1 Chron. 19:1-15)

i. Upon learning of the death of his friend Nahash, the king of Ammon, David sent

ambassadors to comfort his son Hanun.

ii. Hanun, however, rejected and ridiculed these messengers, foolishly and falsely concluding they had been sent to spy out his land.

iii. The beards and clothes of the ambassadors were mutilated by Hanun.

iv. Later, realizing his stupid actions had aroused David's wrath, Hanun hired a Syrian army to help him attack Israel.

v. The alliance was, however, totally routed by Israel under the command of Joab, David's nephew.

(b) Second campaign (2 Sam. 12:26-31; 1 Chron. 20:1-3)

i. David captured Rabbah, the capital of Ammon.

ii. Tremendous amounts of loot were carried back to Jerusalem, and David took the king of Rabbah's crown—a $50,000 treasure made from solid gold set with gems—and placed it on his own head.

iii. He then made slaves of the people of the city.

(6) Against the Syrians

(a) First campaign (2 Sam. 8:5-8; 1 Chron. 18:5-8)

i. He killed 22,000 Syrians from Damascus.

ii. He then placed several army garrisons in Damascus and imposed tribute upon its people.

(b) Second campaign (2 Sam. 10:15-19; 1 Chron. 19:16-19)

b. His military champions—
Having considered David's military conquests, here is a list of his mighty men.

(1) Elhanan—He killed Lahmi, the giant brother of Goliath (2 Sam. 21:19; 1 Chron. 20:5).

(2) Jashobeam—He slew 300 enemy troops (1 Chron. 11:11).

(3) Adino—He killed 800 enemy troops (2 Sam. 23:8).

(4) Eleazar—He smote the enemy until his hand clave to his sword (2 Sam. 23:9-10; 1 Chron. 11:12).

(5) Shammah—He stood in a barley field and killed many Philistines (2 Sam. 23:11-12; 1 Chron. 11:13-14).

(6) Abishai—He killed 300 enemy troops and saved David's life by killing a huge Philistine warrior (2 Sam. 21:15-17; 23:18-19; 1 Chron. 11:20-21).

(7) Benaiah—He killed a lion in a pit in the snow. He also, armed only with a staff, slew a huge seven and a half-foot-high Egyptian warrior with his enemy's own enormous spear (2 Sam. 23:20-23; 1 Chron. 11:22-25).

6. The type of God (2 Sam. 9:1-13)

a. After securing his throne, David asked the following question: "Is there yet any that is left of the house of Saul, that I may shew him kindness for Jonathan's sake?" (2 Sam. 9:1).

b. He learned from Ziba, a former servant of Saul, that Jonathan had a crippled son living in Israel named Mephibosheth.

c. Upon finding him, David said: "Fear not: for I will surely show thee kindness for Jonathan thy father's sake, and will restore thee all the land of Saul . . . and thou shalt eat bread at my table continually" (2 Sam. 9:7).

d. David then commanded the 15 sons and 20 servants of Ziba to wait upon Mephibosheth.

e. Through all this David became a beautiful type of the Heavenly Father.

(1) The Heavenly Father seeks to show kindness to poor, lost, crippled sinners.

(2) He does this for Jesus' sake.

(3) Upon finding them, they are "accepted in the beloved" and invited to feast upon the riches of his grace (Eph. 1:6-7, 18).

IV. The frightful years

A. David, the sinner (2 Sam. 11:1-27)

1. His sin of adultery (2 Sam. 11:1-5)

a. Instead of leading his troops who were at that time fighting against the Ammonites, David was indulging himself in Jerusalem.

b. One night, unable to sleep, he went for a stroll on the roof of the palace.

c. Looking out over the city, he saw a beautiful woman taking her evening bath.

d. Upon learning her name was Bath-sheba, David sent for her, even though he also knew she was married to Uriah, one of his soldiers.

e. David lay with her and was soon told by her that she had become pregnant.

2. His sin of deceit (2 Sam. 11:6-13)

a. David brought Uriah home from the front lines, hoping he

would sleep with his wife and later assume the unborn child to be his.

b. But Uriah refused (probably realizing the truth) to cooperate with the king's deceitful plan.

c. When asked by David why he did not spend the night with Bath-sheba, Uriah replied in words that must have been a stinging slap to the king: "The ark, and Israel, and Judah, abide in tents; and my lord Joab, and the servants of my lord, are encamped in the open fields; shall I then go into mine house, to eat and to drink, and to lie with my wife? as thou livest, and as thy soul liveth, I will not do this thing" (2 Sam. 11:11).

3. His sin of murder (2 Sam. 11:14-27)

a. Realizing Uriah could not be compromised, David sent him back to the war with a sealed letter instructing Joab, Israel's military commander, to arrange for him to be killed in battle.

b. David soon received the message that Uriah had been slain in the fighting.

c. David eventually married Bathsheba, and their child, a boy, was born.

B. David, the sorrowful—"But the thing that David had done displeased the LORD" (2 Sam. 11:27).

1. The confrontation by the prophet—David was soundly rebuked by Nathan the prophet for his terrible sins of adultery, deceit, and murder (2 Sam. 12:1-9).

a. The illustration—Nathan related a story of how a rich farmer owning many flocks took from a poor farmer his only pet ewe lamb and served it up at a banquet.

b. The indignation—A furious David vowed the rich man would be forced to restore fourfold to the poor farmer and then forfeit his life.

c. The identification—"Nathan said to David, Thou art the man. Thus saith the LORD God of Israel, I anointed thee king over Israel, and I delivered thee out of the hand of Saul. . . . Wherefore hast thou despised the commandment of the LORD, to do evil in his sight? thou hast killed Uriah the Hittite with the sword, and hast taken his wife to be thy wife, and hast slain him with the sword of the children of Ammon" (2 Sam. 12:7, 9).

2. The chastisement from the LORD—"Now therefore the sword shall never depart from thine house; because thou hast despised me, and hast taken the wife of Uriah the Hittite to be thy wife. Thus saith the LORD, Behold, I will raise up evil against thee out of thine own house, and I will take thy wives before thine eyes, and give them unto thy neighbour, and he shall lie with thy wives in the sight of this sun. For thou didst it secretly: but I will do this thing before all Israel, and before the sun. . . . The child also that is born unto thee shall surely die" (2 Sam. 12:10-12, 14).

3. The confession of the king—"Have mercy upon me, O God, according to thy lovingkindness: according unto the multitude of thy tender mercies blot out my transgressions. Wash me thoroughly from mine iniquity, and cleanse me from my sin. For I acknowledge my transgressions: and my sin is ever before me. Against thee, thee only, have I sinned, and done this evil in thy sight: that thou mightest be justi-

fied when thou speakest, and be clear when thou judgest" (Ps. 51:1-4). "I acknowledged my sin unto thee, and mine iniquity have I not hid. I said, I will confess my transgressions unto the LORD; and thou forgavest the iniquity of my sin. Selah" (Ps. 32:5).

C. David, the submissive—David's first reaction to Nathan's parable was the demand that the guilty man first make a fourfold payment to the poor farmer and then be put to death. Apparently God imposed upon David the king's own sentence. While he would not die, David would nevertheless pay back fourfold for his sin against Uriah. The brokenhearted monarch now humbly submitted to the chastening hand of the Lord.

1. First sin payback—sickness and death (2 Sam. 12:15-25)
   a. The departure of Bath-sheba's first son
      (1) David's travail—"Nathan departed unto his house. And the LORD struck the child that Uriah's wife bare unto David, and it was very sick. David therefore besought God for the child; and David fasted, and went in, and lay all night upon the earth" (2 Sam. 12:15-16).
      (2) David's testimony—Upon hearing from his servant that his son had died, the king responded: "While the child was yet alive, I fasted and wept: for I said, Who can tell whether God will be gracious to me, that the child may live? But now he is dead, wherefore should I fast? can I bring him back again? I shall go to him, but he shall not return to me" (2 Sam. 12:22-23).
   b. The arrival of Bath-sheba's second son—"David comforted

Bath-sheba his wife, and went in unto her, and lay with her: and she bare a son, and he called his name Solomon: and the LORD loved him" (2 Sam. 12:24).

2. Second sin payback—incest (2 Sam. 13:1-21)
   a. Amnon deceived his half sister Tamar.
      (1) Amnon, son of David and half brother to Tamar, David's daughter, burned in his lust toward her.
      (2) Acting upon the advice of a crafty friend, Amnon feigned sickness and requested from David that Tamar be sent to nurse him.
   b. Amnon defiled his half sister Tamar.
      (1) When they were alone, Amnon raped Tamar.
      (2) He then compounded his vicious crime by refusing to marry her.
      (3) Instead, he literally had her thrown out of his bedroom.
      (4) David was furious upon hearing this, but did not punish Amnon for it.

3. Third sin payback—murder (2 Sam. 13:22-39)
   a. After planning for two full years, Absalom, David's son and Tamar's full brother, arranged to have his half brother Amnon murdered.
   b. Absalom then fled to the land of Geshur, where he remained for three years.
   c. Again, David seemed helpless, and could do nothing but mourn the loss of one son and the absence of another.

4. Fourth sin payment—rebellion (2 Sam. 14–20)
   a. The reconciliation (2 Sam. 14:1-33)
      (1) A mother, sent by Joab,

tricked David into bringing back Absalom from exile.

(2) She sought the king's favor, pretending she had two sons, one of which had killed the other.

(3) David reassured her that upon his return the rebellious son would not be punished.

(4) The woman then immediately applied the lesson parable to David.

(5) Absalom was allowed to return, but for two long years his father refused to see him.

(6) Finally, after Absalom burned Joab's barley field to get attention, David agreed to meet his son.

(7) The king and Absalom were reconciled.

b. The revolt (2 Sam. 15:1-12)

(1) The politics leading to the revolt—"It came to pass after this, that Absalom prepared him chariots and horses, and fifty men to run before him. And Absalom rose up early, and stood beside the way of the gate: and it was so, that when any man that had a controversy came to the king for judgment, then Absalom called unto him, and said, Of what city art thou? And he said, Thy servant is of one of the tribes of Israel. And Absalom said unto him, See, thy matters are good and right; but there is no man deputed of the king to hear thee. Absalom said moreover, Oh that I were made judge in the land, that every man which hath any suit or cause might come unto me, and I would do

him justice! And it was so, that when any man came nigh to him to do him obeisance, he put forth his hand, and took him, and kissed him. And on this manner did Absalom to all Israel that came to the king for judgment: so Absalom stole the hearts of the men of Israel" (2 Sam. 15:1-6).

(2) The place of this revolt— After a four-year period of preparation, Absalom went to the city of Hebron, blew a trumpet, and declared the revolt against his father.

c. The retreat (2 Sam. 15:13-17)— "There came a messenger to David, saying, The hearts of the men of Israel are after Absalom. . . . And the king went forth, and all his household after him. And the king left ten women, which were concubines, to keep the house" (2 Sam. 15:13, 16).

d. The resolve—At the edge of the city, David suddenly noticed that his foreign friend Ittai, who had been visiting Jerusalem from the Philistine city of Gath, was accompanying the king along with the 600 Gittite warriors who served under him (2 Sam. 15:18-22).

(1) David's advice—"What are you doing here? Go on back with your men . . . for you are a guest in Israel . . . Should I force you to wander with me . . . ? Go on back . . . and may the LORD be merciful to you."

(2) Ittai's answer—"As the LORD liveth, and as my lord the king liveth, surely in what place my lord the king shall be, whether in death or life,

even there also will thy servant be" (2 Sam. 15:21).

e. The remorse—"All the country wept with a loud voice, and all the people passed over: the king also himself passed over the brook Kidron, and all the people passed over, toward the way of the wilderness. . . . And David went up by the ascent of mount Olivet, and wept as he went up, and had his head covered, and he went barefoot: and all the people that was with him covered every man his head, and they went up, weeping as they went up" (2 Sam. 15:23, 30).

f. The reflection (2 Sam. 15:24-29)—"Lo Zadok also, and all the Levites were with him, bearing the ark of the covenant of God: and they set down the ark of God; and Abiathar went up, until all the people had done passing out of the city. And the king said unto Zadok, Carry back the ark of God into the city: if I shall find favour in the eyes of the LORD, he will bring me again, and shew me both it, and his habitation: But if he thus say, I have no delight in thee; behold, here am I, let him do to me as seemeth good unto him" (2 Sam. 15:24-26).

g. The ruse (2 Sam. 15:31-37; 16:15–17:23)

(1) Upon learning that his former advisor Ahithophel had joined Absalom's revolt, David ordered another loyal advisor, Hushai, to pretend to sell out to Absalom also, that he might frustrate and counter Ahithophel's counsel.

(2) This plan worked exactly as David hoped it would.

(a) The correct advice of Ahithophel—"Let me now choose out twelve thousand men, and I will arise and pursue after David this night: And I will come upon him while he is weary and weak handed, and will make him afraid: and all the people that are with him shall flee; and I will smite the king only" (2 Sam. 17:1-2).

(b) The crafty advice of Hushai—"The counsel that Ahithophel hath given is not good at this time. . . . Therefore I counsel that all Israel be generally gathered unto thee, from Dan even to Beer-sheba, as the sand that is by the sea for multitude; and that thou go to battle in thine own person" (2 Sam. 17:7, 11).

(3) The vain Absalom decided upon Hushai's counsel, thus unknowingly allowing David time to mobilize the royal troops.

(4) Upon having his advice refused, Ahithophel went home and hung himself.

(5) Hushai then sent messengers warning David to cross the Jordan River and prepare his men for battle.

h. The rendezvous—During the interval before the battle, David met with several individuals.

(1) His meeting with Ziba—Ziba, the chief steward of Mephibosheth (Jonathan's crippled son), approached David with both food and a falsehood (2 Sam. 16:1-4).

(a) The food—He brought

two donkeys, loaded
down with bread, raisins,
grapes, summer fruits
[figs?], and a barrel of
wine.

(b) The falsehood—Ziba slandered his master, saying
Mephibosheth was in Je-
rusalem hoping David
would be defeated so that
he could get back his
grandfather Saul's king-
dom. David (at first)
seemed to believe Ziba,
and gave him the estate
he had previously
awarded to Mephibo-
sheth. Later, however,
the king would refuse
this.

(2) His meeting with Shobi,
Machir, and Barzillai—These
three men, all non-Israelite
friends of David, met the
king and brought him mats
to sleep on, cooking pots,
serving bowls, wheat and
barley flour, parched grain,
beans, lentils, honey, butter,
and cheese (2 Sam. 17:27-
29).

i. The reviling (2 Sam. 16:5-13)

(1) The reviler—Shimei, a member of Saul's family, encoun-
tered David and hurled both
curses and rocks at the king.
"Come out, come out, thou
bloody man, and thou man
of Belial: The LORD hath returned upon thee all the
blood of the house of Saul,
in whose stead thou hast
reigned; and the LORD hath
delivered the kingdom into
the hand of Absalom thy
son: and, behold, thou art
taken in thy mischief, because thou art a bloody
man" (2 Sam. 16:7-8).

(2) The reviled—Abishai, one of

David's soldiers sought permission to kill Shimei for his
insults.

(a) The request—"Why
should this dead dog
curse my lord the king?
let me go over, I pray
thee, and take off his
head" (2 Sam. 16:9).

(b) The refusal—"David said
to Abishai, and to all his
servants, Behold, my son,
which came forth of my
bowels, seeketh my life:
how much more now
may this Benjamite do it?
let him alone, and let him
curse; for the LORD hath
bidden him. It may be
that the LORD will look on
mine affliction, and that
the LORD will requite me
good for his cursing this
day" (2 Sam. 16:11-12).

j. The rout (2 Sam. 18:1-8)—
David's seasoned troops met
Absalom's inexperienced sol-
diers at the Battle of Mount
Ephraim.

(1) The concern prior to the
battle

(a) The people's concern for
their king—"The king
said unto the people, I
will surely go forth with
you myself also. But the
people answered, Thou
shalt not go forth: for if
we flee away, they will
not care for us; neither if
half of us die, will they
care for us: but now thou
art worth ten thousand of
us: therefore now it is
better that thou succour
us out of the city" (2 Sam.
18:2-3).

(b) The king's concern for his
son—"The king com-
manded Joab and Abishai

and Ittai, saying, Deal gently for my sake with the young man, even with Absalom. And all the people heard when the king gave all the captains charge concerning Absalom" (2 Sam. 18:5).

(2) The casualties resulting from the battle
  (a) David's men killed 20,000 of Absalom's soldiers.
  (b) Even more than this number died of hunger, exposure, and exhaustion as a result of being scattered throughout the desolate and hostile countryside of Ephraim.

k. The reprisal (2 Sam. 18:9-18)— In spite of David's plan concerning his son, Joab found Absalom caught by his hair in the thick boughs of a great tree and killed him by thrusting three daggers into his heart.

l. The reprimands (2 Sam. 18:19– 19:7)
  (1) David's anguish—"The king was much moved, and went up to the chamber over the gate, and wept: and as he went, thus he said, O my son Absalom, my son, my son Absalom! would God I had died for thee, O Absalom, my son, my son!" (2 Sam. 18:33).
  (2) Joab's anger—"Joab came into the house to the king, and said, Thou hast shamed this day the faces of all thy servants, which this day have saved thy life, and the lives of thy sons and of thy daughters, and the lives of thy wives, and the lives of thy concubines; In that thou lovest thine enemies, and hatest thy friends. For thou

hast declared this day, that thou regardest neither princes nor servants: for this day I perceive, that if Absalom had lived, and all we had died this day, then it had pleased thee well. Now therefore arise, go forth, and speak comfortably unto thy servants: for I swear by the LORD, if thou go not forth, there will not tarry one with thee this night: and that will be worse unto thee than all the evil that befell thee from thy youth until now" (2 Sam. 19:5-7).

m. The return (2 Sam. 19:8–20:26)
  (1) The king on the east bank of the Jordan (2 Sam. 19:8-43)
    (a) David and Zadok—Both Zadok and Abiathar the priest were sent to the elders and Judah that they might create some interest for the king's return. It seemed all the other tribes except his very own wanted this to happen.
    (b) David and Amasa—David appointed his nephew Amasa to replace Joab as military commander-in-chief. Amasa thereupon convinced Judah's elders to urge David's return.
    (c) David and Shimei—David spared the life of Shimei, who now met him and begged for forgiveness.
    (d) David and Mephibosheth—Jonathan's lame son explained to David that Ziba had slandered him, falsely accusing him of treason. David, apparently not quite sure who to believe, divided Mephibosheth's estate

equally, giving half to the lame son and half to Ziba.

(e) David and Barzillai—David urged this 80-year-old Gileadite who had previously befriended him to come to Jerusalem and live in the king's palace. But the old friend respectfully declined, pleading old age.

(f) David and the men of Judah—The king was met by those from his own tribe who accompanied him across the Jordan River.

(2) The king at Jerusalem—At long last David had returned home. But two more bloody events would occur before peaceful conditions prevailed.

(a) Amasa's murder—Joab brutally and deceitfully murdered Amasa with a dagger, thus eliminating a future rival (2 Sam. 20:4-10).

(b) Sheba's malcontent—A Benjaminite named Sheba organized a brief revolt against David. At first, all the tribes but Judah followed him, deserting their king. But the revolt was short-lived, for Joab trapped Sheba in the city of Abel. He then demanded and received from its citizens the head of Sheba (2 Sam. 20:1-3, 14-22).

V. The final years

A. David, the statesman (2 Sam. 21:1-14)

1. He surveyed a problem.

a. There was a famine that lasted for three years and David spent much time in prayer about it.

b. Finally, God told him the famine was a divine judgment upon Israel because of past sins committed against the Gibeonites.

c. In Joshua 9, Israel had made a covenant with these pagan people that they would not be harmed, but Saul and his family had murdered many of them.

2. He solved the problem.

a. David negotiated with the Gibeonite leaders, and they determined that justice could be done only by allowing them to execute seven of Saul's sons, all of which probably participated in the former Gibeonite massacre.

b. This was done and the plague was stayed.

c. The life of Mephibosheth was, however, spared.

d. Later David ordered a decent burial to be given to two of these sons, upon learning that their mother had watched over their bodies during the entire harvest season, driving away the vultures and wild animals.

B. David, the statistician (2 Sam. 24; 1 Chron. 21)

1. The project—David commanded Joab, his military commander, to conduct a census throughout the land that he might know the population of Israel.

2. The protest

a. Joab objected to the project, but David insisted it be carried out.

b. At the end of nine months and 20 days Joab gave David the figures (2 Sam. 24:8).

3. The perception—Soon David realized this census was (for some

unrecorded reason) highly displeasing to God.

4. The plea—"David's heart smote him after that he had numbered the people. And David said unto the Lord, I have sinned greatly in that I have done: and now, I beseech thee, O Lord, take away the iniquity of thy servant; for I have done very foolishly" (2 Sam. 24:10).

5. The punishment—God allowed David to choose one of three possible punishments.
   a. A period of famine
   b. Ninety days of retreat before his enemies
   c. A three-day pestilence

6. The plague—David chose the third punishment. "David said unto Gad, I am in a great strait: let us fall now into the hand of the Lord; for his mercies are great: and let me not fall into the hand of man. So the Lord sent a pestilence upon Israel from the morning even to the time appointed: and there died of the people from Dan even to Beersheba seventy thousand men" (2 Sam. 24:14-15).

7. The pardon—"When the angel stretched out his hand upon Jerusalem to destroy it, the Lord repented him of the evil, and said to the angel that destroyed the people, It is enough: stay now thine hand. And the angel of the Lord was by the threshingplace of Araunah the Jebusite" (2 Sam. 24:16).

8. The purchase
   a. David was commanded to build an altar at the place where the plague stopped. David was able to see the angel.
   b. David built the altar, but not before buying the threshing

floor of Araunah (also called Ornan) the Jebusite.
   c. It was upon this spot that Abraham had once offered Isaac (Gen. 22:2), and on it the temple of Solomon would later be built (2 Chron. 3:1).
   d. God approved of David's offering by sending down fire from heaven to consume the sacrifice (1 Chron. 21:26).

C. David, the sponsor (1 Chron. 22–29)—"David said, Solomon my son is young and tender, and the house that is to be builded for the Lord must be exceeding magnifical, of fame and of glory throughout all countries: I will therefore now make preparation for it. So David prepared abundantly before his death" (1 Chron. 22:5).

1. The background involved—David was now nearly 70. When he was but 37, he had determined to build a temple for God but was forbidden to do so. "David said to Solomon, My son, as for me, it was in my mind to build an house unto the name of the Lord my God: But the word of the Lord came to me, saying, Thou hast shed blood abundantly, and hast made great wars: thou shalt not build an house unto my name, because thou hast shed much blood upon the earth in my sight. Behold, a son shall be born to thee, who shall be a man of rest; and I will give him rest from all his enemies round about: for his name shall be Solomon, and I will give peace and quietness unto Israel in his days. He shall build an house for my name; and he shall be my son, and I will be his father; and I will establish the throne of his kingdom over Israel for ever" (1 Chron. 22:7-10).

2. The purpose involved—It was to

provide a home for the Ark of
God (1 Chron. 22:19) and the
other vessels from a temporary
tabernacle, which was located at
Gibeon (1 Chron. 21:29). The original tabernacle of Moses had been
set up at Shiloh (Josh. 18:1; 19:51;
Judg. 18:31; 1 Sam. 1:9; 3:3) but
was destroyed along with the city
of Shiloh by the Philistines (see
Ps. 78:60; Jer. 7:12, 14; 26:6) in
1 Samuel 4.
3. The cost involved (1 Chron. 22:14,
16)
   a. It took 100,000 talents of gold
   and 1,000,000 talents of silver,
   plus untold tons of bronze,
   iron, and timber to build the
   temple. This would equal several billion dollars by today's
   standards.
   b. David himself contributed mil-
   lions to the project (1 Chron.
   29:3-5).
4. The workers involved—David appointed 38,000 Levites for the
temple construction (1 Chron.
23:3-5): 24,000 workers; 6,000 to
function as officers and judges;
4,000 temple guards.
5. The music involved
   a. There were 4,000 singers and
   musicians (1 Chron. 23:5).
   b. To this number David then appointed 288 special master musicians (1 Chron. 25:7-8).
6. The priests involved—At this time
David divided the priesthood into
24 divisions (1 Chron. 23:6; 24:1-3;
compare 1 Chron. 24:10 with Luke
1:5).
7. The army involved—David had an
army of 288,000 men, consisting
of 12 divisions of 24,000 warriors
(1 Chron. 27:1-15).
8. The blueprints involved—David
gave Solomon the temple building
plans which God had given him
(1 Chron. 28:11-12, 19).

9. The challenge involved (given by
David)
   a. The recipients of his challenge
      (1) Solomon (1 Chron. 22:11-13;
      28:9-10, 20)—"Wherefore Da-
      vid blessed the LORD before
      all the congregation: and Da-
      vid said, Blessed be thou,
      LORD God of Israel our fa-
      ther, for ever and ever"
      (1 Chron. 29:10). "Be strong
      and of good courage, and do
      it: fear not, nor be dismayed:
      for the LORD God, even my
      God, will be with thee; he
      will not fail thee, nor forsake
      thee, until thou hast finished
      all the work for the service
      of the house of the LORD"
      (1 Chron. 28:20).
      (2) The resident aliens in Israel
      (1 Chron. 22:2).
      (3) The religious, military, polit-
      ical, and financial leaders in
      Israel (1 Chron. 22:17-19;
      28:1-8)—"Is not the LORD
      your God with you? and
      hath he not given you rest
      on every side? for he hath
      given the inhabitants of the
      land into mine hand; and
      the land is subdued before
      the LORD, and before his
      people. Now set your heart
      and your soul to seek the
      LORD your God; arise there-
      fore, and build ye the sanc-
      tuary of the LORD God, to
      bring the ark of the covenant
      of the LORD, and the holy
      vessels of God, into the
      house that is to be built to
      the name of the LORD"
      (1 Chron. 22:18-19).
   b. The results of his challenge
      (1 Chron. 29:6-9, 20-21)
      (1) Concerning the princes of
      Israel—"Then the chief of the
      fathers and princes of the

tribes of Israel, and the captains of thousands and of hundreds, with the rulers of the king's work, offered willingly" (1 Chron. 29:6).

(2) Concerning the people of Israel—"Then the people rejoiced, for that they offered willingly, because with perfect heart they offered willingly to the LORD: and David the king also rejoiced with great joy" (1 Chron. 29:9).

10. The prayer involved (1 Chron. 29:10-19)

   (a) David's description of God—"Wherefore David blessed the LORD before all the congregation: and David said, Blessed be thou, LORD God of Israel our father, for ever and ever. Thine, O LORD, is the greatness, and the power, and the glory, and the victory, and the majesty: for all that is in the heaven and in the earth is thine; thine is the kingdom, O LORD, and thou art exalted as head above all. Both riches and honour come of thee, and thou reignest over all; and in thine hand is power and might; and in thine hand it is to make great, and to give strength unto all. Now therefore, our God, we thank thee, and praise thy glorious name. But who am I, and what is my people, that we should be able to offer so willingly after this sort? for all things come of thee, and of thine own have we given thee. For we are strangers before thee, and sojourners, as were all our fathers: our days on the earth are as a shadow, and there is none abiding. O LORD our God, all this store that we have prepared to build thee an house for thine holy name cometh of thine hand, and is all thine own (1 Chron. 29:10-16).

   (b) David's desire from God—"Give unto Solomon my son a perfect heart, to keep thy commandments, thy testimonies, and thy statutes, and to do all these things, and to build the palace, for the which I have made provision" (1 Chron. 29:19).

D. David, the sinking

   1. His final work

      a. The insurrection of Adonijah—On his deathbed David was visited by Bath-sheba and Nathan the prophet, who informed the king of the rebellion led by Adonijah (his oldest son) against Solomon (1 Kings 1:15-27).

      b. The instruction of David—The dying king quickly instructed Zadok the high priest and Nathan the prophet to do the following (1 Kings 1:32-40):

         (1) To place Solomon on the king's personal mule

         (2) To anoint Solomon (by Zadok)

         (3) To publicly crown Solomon amid the blowing of trumpets

         (4) To ride to the palace and sit upon David's throne

   2. His final words

a. To his Savior (2 Sam. 23:1-7)—
"Now these be the last words
of David. David the son of
Jesse said, and the man who
was raised up on high, the
anointed of the God of Jacob,
and the sweet psalmist of
Israel, said, The Spirit of the
LORD spake by me, and his
word was in my tongue. The
God of Israel said, the Rock of
Israel spake to me, He that
ruleth over men must be just,
ruling in the fear of God. And
he shall be as the light of the
morning, when the sun riseth,
even a morning without clouds;
as the tender grass springing
out of the earth by clear shining
after rain" (2 Sam. 23:1-4).
b. To his son (1 Kings 2:1-9)—
"Now the days of David drew
nigh that he should die; and he
charged Solomon his son, saying, I go the way of all the
earth: be thou strong therefore,
and shew thyself a man; and
keep the charge of the LORD thy
God, to walk in his ways, to
keep his statutes, and his commandments, and his judg-
ments, and his testimonies, as
it is written in the law of Moses, that thou mayest prosper
in all that thou doest, and
whithersoever thou turnest thyself" (1 Kings 2:1-3).
E. David, the scribe (the psalms that David wrote)
1. The number of his psalms—David
authored at least 75 of the 150
psalms.
a. Of these, 73 are ascribed to him
in the Old Testament. These
are: 3-9; 11-32; 34-41; 51-65; 68-
70; 86; 101; 103; 108-110; 122;
124; 131; 133; 138-145.
b. Two of the psalms are ascribed
to him in the New Testament.
These are:

(1) Psalm 2 (Acts 4:25)
(2) Psalm 95 (Heb. 4:7)
2. The nature of his psalms—The
historical background for some of
David's psalms is as follows:
a. Psalm 8—Written after his victory over Goliath (1 Sam. 17)
b. Psalm 11—Written while he
was still living in Saul's court
(1 Sam. 18)
c. Psalm 59—Written after his
wife Michal saved him from
Saul (1 Sam. 19)
d. Psalms 63, 143—Written when
fleeing from Saul (1 Sam. 19–31)
e. Psalms 34, 56—Written after
escaping from Achish, the Philistine king of Gath (1 Sam. 21)
f. Psalm 52—Written upon learning of the slaughter of the
priests at Nob by the cruel
Doeg (1 Sam. 22)
g. Psalms 57, 142—Written while
he was living in the cave of
Adullam (1 Sam. 22)
h. Psalm 54—Written after being
betrayed by the citizens of Ziph
(1 Sam. 23)
i. Psalm 18—Written after Saul
had given up trying to kill him
(1 Sam. 26:21)
j. Psalms 19, 101—Written to celebrate the capture of Jerusalem
(2 Sam. 5)
k. Psalms 15, 24, 68, 132—Written
when the Ark of the Covenant
was brought into Jerusalem
(2 Sam. 6)
l. Psalm 89—Written after receiving the Davidic Covenant
(2 Sam. 7)
m. Psalm 60—Written to celebrate
Joab's victory over the Edomites
(2 Sam. 8)
n. Psalm 21—Written after his
kingdom was established
(2 Sam. 8)
o. Psalms 32, 51—Written in regard to his sin of adultery and
murder

(1) Psalm 32 describes the terrible guilt he experienced before his confession (2 Sam. 11).

(2) Psalm 51 describes the prayer he offered during his confession (2 Sam. 12).

p. Psalms 3, 4, 35, 41—Written during his flight from Absalom's rebellion (2 Sam. 15–18)

q. Psalm 30—Written at the end of a divine plague caused by a census he took (2 Sam. 24)

r. Psalm 72—Written as a prayer for his son Solomon (1 Chron. 29).

THEOLOGICAL SUMMARY

I. David and God
   A. God's evaluation of David
      1. He was one who walked in God's image, obeying divine statutes and commands (1 Kings 3:14; 11:38).
      2. He was a man possessing integrity and uprightness (1 Kings 9:4; 14:8; 15:5).
      3. He was a man after God's own heart (1 Sam. 13:14; Acts 13:22).
   B. God's promises to David
      1. That he would be given an everlasting kingdom (2 Sam. 7:16)
      2. That Jerusalem would be the capital of the kingdom (1 Kings 11:36; 15:4)
      3. That the Messiah from the house of David would someday rule over the everlasting kingdom (Isa. 9:6-7; 16:5; Jer. 23:5; 33:15-17)
      4. That David would serve as vice regent under the Messiah during the Millennium (Jer. 30:9; Ezek. 34:24; 37:24-25; Hos. 3:5)

II. David and Israel—Israel and Judah were often saved from their enemies by God for David's sake. This happened during the reigns of:
   A. Solomon (1 Kings 11:12)
   B. Joram (2 Kings 8:19)
   C. Hezekiah (2 Kings 19:34; 20:6)

D. Jehoshaphat (2 Chron. 17:3)

III. David and Israel's kings—David became the standard and role model for Israel's kings. God used him to measure and evaluate the following monarchs:
   A. Solomon (1 Kings 3:14; 11:4, 6)
   B. Jeroboam (1 Kings 14:8)
   C. Abijah (1 Kings 15:3)
   D. Asa (1 Kings 15:11)
   E. Ahaz (2 Kings 16:2)
   F. Hezekiah (2 Kings 18:3)
   G. Josiah (2 Kings 22:2)

IV. David and Israel's cities—Two of the nation's most important cities were known as the city of David.
   A. Bethlehem (Luke 2:4, 11)
   B. Jerusalem (1 Kings 2:10; 2 Chron. 12:16; 14:1; 16:14; 21:1, 20; 24:16, 25; 27:9)

V. David and Gabriel—The angel of the Lord referred to David in his anouncement to Mary concerning the virgin birth of Christ (Luke 1:29-33).

VI. David and Zechariah—The old priest referred to David during his prophecy concerning his infant son, John the Baptist (Luke 1:69).

VII. David and Jesus
   A. Jesus referred to an event in David's life to defend his disciples, who were criticized for plucking grain on the Sabbath (Matt. 12:3-4; Mark 2:25-26).
   B. He mentioned David during his attempts to convince the wicked Pharisees of his own deity (Matt. 22:41-45).
   C. Christ was referred to as the son of David during his earthly ministry and after his death:
      1. By Matthew (Matt. 1:1)
      2. By two blind men (Matt. 9:27)
      3. By a crowd when he healed a blind and mute demoniac (Matt. 12:23)
      4. By a Canaanite mother (Matt. 15:22)
      5. By two blind men in Jericho (Matt. 20:30-31)
      6. By the crowd at his triumphal entry into Jerusalem (Matt. 21:9, 15)
      7. By the Pharisees (Matt. 22:41-42)

8. By Bartimaeus (Mark 10:46-48)
9. By Paul (Rom. 1:3; 2 Tim. 2:8)
10. By one of heaven's elders (Rev. 5:5)
11. By Jesus himself (Rev. 22:16)

VIII. David and Peter—Peter referred to those prophetical psalms of David that predicted at least four key events in the life of Christ.
  A. His betrayal—Psalms 41, 69, 109 (Acts 1:16-20)
  B. His resurrection—Psalm 16 (Acts 2:25-29)
  C. His ascension—Psalm 110 (Acts 2:34-35)
  D. His millennial reign—Psalm 2 (Acts 4:25-26)

IX. David and Paul
  A. Paul said Christ was from the seed of David (Acts 13:23; Rom. 1:3; 2 Tim. 2:8).
  B. He referred to the selection of David by God (Acts 13:22).
  C. He referred to David's Psalm 16, which predicted the resurrection of Christ (Acts 13:35-37).
  D. He used David to illustrate how God saves people by grace, apart from works (Rom. 4:6-8).
  E. He mentioned David to explain Israel's present-day spiritual blindness. According to David's prophecy (Ps. 69:22), this blindness was a divinely imposed judgment because of Israel's sin (Rom. 11:8-10).

X. David and Stephen—Stephen referred to David during his defense before the Sanhedrin (Acts 7:45).

XI. David and James—James referred to David during the Jerusalem Council (Acts 15:16).

XII. David and the book of Hebrews
  A. The author quoted from David's Psalm 95, using it as an example of warning about unbelief (Heb. 4:7-11).
    1. The historical example given by David—It was the sin of unbelief which once kept Moses' generation out of the promised land.
    2. The present-day warning—It is the sin of unbelief which will keep us out of the promised land, that is, the perfect will of God.
  B. The author referred to David as a role model for faith (Heb. 11:32).

STATISTICS

Father: Jesse (Ruth 4:17, 21)

Spouses: Michal, Ahinoam, Abigail, Maacah, Haggith, Abital, Eglah, and Bathsheba (1 Sam. 18:27; 2 Sam. 3:2-5; 11:27; 1 Chron. 3:1-8)

Sons: Amnon, Chileab (also called Daniel), Absalom, Adonijah, Shephatiah, Ithream, Shammua, Shobab, Nathan, Solomon, Ibhar, Elishua, Eliphelet, Nogah, Nepheg, Japhia, Elishama, Eliada, and Eliphelet (2 Sam. 3:2-5; 5:13-16; 1 Chron. 3:1-8; 14:3-5)

Brothers: Eliab, Abinadab, Shammah, Nethaneel, Raddai, and Ozem (1 Sam. 17:12-13; 1 Chron. 2:13-15); one unnamed

Sisters: Zeruiah, and Abigail (1 Chron. 2:16)

First mention: Ruth 4:17

Final mention: Revelation 22:16

Meaning of his name: "Beloved"

Frequency of his name: Referred to 1,118 times

Biblical books mentioning him: 28 books (Ruth, 1 Samuel, 2 Samuel, 1 Kings, 2 Kings, 1 Chronicles, 2 Chronicles, Ezra, Nehemiah, Psalms, Proverbs, Ecclesiastes, Song of Solomon, Isaiah, Jeremiah, Ezekiel, Hosea, Amos, Zechariah, Matthew, Mark, Luke, John, Acts, Romans, 2 Timothy, Hebrews, Revelation)

Occupation: Shepherd, soldier, king of Judah, king of all Israel (1 Sam. 16:11; 18:5; 2 Sam. 2:1-7; 5:1-5)

Place of birth: Bethlehem (Ruth; 1 Sam. 16:1)

Place of death: Jerusalem (1 Kings 2:10-11)

Age at death: 70 (2 Sam. 5:4-5)

Important fact about his life: He was Israel's greatest king and author of over half the Psalms.

✒Deborah

CHRONOLOGICAL SUMMARY
I. Her court
  A. She was a prophetess in the days of the judges (Judg. 4:4).
  B. She was a mother (Judg. 5:7).
  C. She was either from the tribe of Ephraim (Judg. 4:5) or of Issachar (Judg. 5:15).
  D. Deborah held court under the Palm of Deborah between the cities of Ramah and Beth-el in the hill country of Ephraim (Judg. 4:5).
II. Her command
  A. The revelation—She instructed a soldier named Barak that God wanted him to mobilize an army of 10,000 men from the tribes of Naphtali and Zebulun upon Mt. Tabor and defeat the Canaanite oppressors (Judg. 4:6-7).
  B. The reluctance
    1. Barak refused to do this unless Deborah accompanied him (Judg. 4:8).
    2. She agreed, but warned him that the credit for the victory would not go to him but to a woman (Judg. 4:9).
III. Her celebration
  A. At Deborah's order, Barak's army charged the Canaanites and totally routed them (Judg. 4:14-17).
  B. Following the battle, she and Barak composed and sang a victory song (Judg. 5:1-31).

STATISTICS
Spouse: Lapidoth (Judg. 4:4)
First mention: Judges 4:4
Final mention: Judges 5:15
Meaning of her name: "Bee, wasp"
Frequency of her name: Referred to nine times
Biblical books mentioning her: One book (Judges)
Occupation: Prophetess, judge (Judg. 4:4)
Important fact about her life: She aided Barak in defeating Israel's enemies (Judg. 4:8-9).

✒Delilah

CHRONOLOGICAL SUMMARY
I. Delilah and the Philistines—the bribe
  A. She was probably a Philistine harlot.
  B. She lived in the Sorek valley (Judg. 16:4).
  C. She was hired by the Philistines to discover the source of Samson's great strength (Judg. 16:5).
II. Delilah and Samson—The betrayal
  A. The testing
    1. Samson loved Delilah (Judg. 16:4).
    2. She was unsuccessful after her first three attempts to pry the answer from him (Judg. 16:6-14).
  B. The tears—She then demanded the right answer, accusing Samson of not loving her if he refused (Judg. 16:15).
  C. The treachery
    1. She learned that Samson's strength was in his hair, which had never been cut (Judg. 16:17).
    2. Having lulled him to sleep on her lap, she called a man to shave off the seven braids of his hair (Judg. 16:19).
    3. Delilah then awakened him and watched as the Philistines seized the helpless ex-strong man, gouged out his eyes, and carried him down to the city of Gaza (Judg. 16:20-21).

STATISTICS
First mention: Judges 16:4
Final mention: Judges 16:18
Meaning of her name: "Languishing"
Frequency of her name: Referred to six times
Biblical books mentioning her: One book (Judges)
Occupation: Probably prostitution
Important fact about her life: She betrayed Samson to the Philistines (Judg. 16:5, 18).

Dinah

CHRONOLOGICAL SUMMARY

I. The seduction
  A. Dinah was the only recorded daughter of Jacob. Her mother was Leah (Gen. 30:21).
  B. She was seduced by a pagan named Shechem, son of Hamor, a Hivite ruler (Gen. 34:2).
II. The slaughter
  A. Deceiving the Shechemites
    1. Realizing his son loved Dinah, Hamor proposed a marriage alliance to Jacob and his sons (Gen. 34:3-12).
    2. The deceitful sons of Jacob pretended to concur with the marriage and other possible future marriages between the two peoples, but only if the pagans agreed to circumcise themselves (Gen. 34:13-24).
  B. Destroying the Shechemites
    1. However, after three days, when the Shechemites were rendered helpless because of the pain and swelling, two of Dinah's brothers, Simeon and Levi, attacked the city and slaughtered every male (Gen. 34:25-29).
    2. Dinah was then taken back to the home of Jacob (Gen. 34:26).

STATISTICS

Father: Jacob (Gen. 30:19-21)
Mother: Leah (Gen. 30:19-21)
Brothers: Full brothers: Reuben, Simeon, Levi, Judah, Issachar, and Zebulun (Gen. 29:31-35; 30:17-20). Half brothers: Dan, Joseph, Benjamin, Naphtali, Gad, and Asher (1 Chron. 2:2).
First mention: Genesis 30:21
Final mention: Genesis 46:15
Meaning of her name: "Judged, avenged"
Frequency of her name: Referred to eight times
Biblical books mentioning her: One book (Genesis)

Important fact about her life: She was seduced by a pagan chief's son, precipitating the massacre of a town by two of her brothers (Gen. 34).

Doeg

CHRONOLOGICAL SUMMARY

I. Slandering the priest of God
  A. Doeg was an Edomite and head shepherd for King Saul (1 Sam. 21:7; 22:9).
  B. He betrayed Ahimelech the high priest to Saul, causing the jealous king to conclude that the man of God had sold out to David (1 Sam. 22:9-10).
II. Slaughtering the people of God—At Saul's command, the brutal and bloodthirsty Doeg slew with the sword:
  A. Ahimelech the high priest (1 Sam. 22:18)
  B. Eighty-five other priests (1 Sam. 22:18)
  C. The men, women, children, babies, and animals living in the city of Nob where Ahimelech resided (1 Sam. 22:19)
  D. David composed Psalm 52 upon learning of the horrible massacre.

STATISTICS

First mention: 1 Samuel 21:7
Final mention: Psalms 52 (in the introduction)
Meaning of his name: "Fearful"
Frequency of his name: Referred to six times
Biblical books mentioning him: Two books (1 Samuel, Psalms)
Occupation: Shepherd (1 Sam. 21:7)
Important fact about his life: He killed 85 priests by order of King Saul (1 Sam. 22:18).

✍️*Eglon*

CHRONOLOGICAL SUMMARY

I. His activities
 A. He was a Moabite king who oppressed Israel in the days of the
  judges (Judg. 3:12).
 B. God had allowed him to do this for
  some 18 years to punish Israel for
  their sin (Judg. 3:12-14).
 C. He was allied with the Ammonites
  and Amalekites (Judg. 3:13).
 D. He made Jericho his capital city
  (Judg. 3:13).
II. His assassination—He was killed by
 Ehud, a left-handed judge from the
 tribe of Benjamin, who used an 18-inch
 knife (Judg. 3:16-26).

STATISTICS

First mention: Judges 3:12
Final mention: Judges 3:17
Meaning of his name: "Circle"
Frequency of his name: Referred to four times
Biblical books mentioning him: One book
 (Judges)
Occupation: King of Moab (Judg. 3:12)
Place of death: In his Jericho summer parlor
 (Judg. 3:13, 20)
Circumstances of death: He was stabbed to
 death by Ehud (Judg. 3:21).
Important fact about his life: He was a Moabite
 king who oppressed Israel (Judg. 3:12-14).

✍️*Ehud*

CHRONOLOGICAL SUMMARY

I. His dagger of death
 A. Ehud was Israel's second judge
  (Judg. 3:15).
 B. He was from the tribe of Benjamin
  and a left-handed warrior (Judg.
  3:15).
 C. He executed Eglon, a Moabite king
  who had oppressed Israel for 18 years
  (Judg. 3:16-26).

 D. Ehud's weapon was an 18-inch dagger (Judg. 3:16).
II. His trumpet of victory
 A. He blew a trumpet, gathered an army
  of men, and defeated the Moabites,
  killing 10,000 of their troops (Judg.
  3:27-29).
 B. His victory led to an 80-year rest from
  war in that part of the promised land
  (Judg. 3:30).

STATISTICS

Father: Gera (Judg. 3:15)
First mention: Judges 3:15
Final mention: Judges 4:1
Meaning of his name: "Strong"
Frequency of his name: Referred to eight times
Biblical books mentioning him: One book
 (Judges)
Important fact about his life: He assassinated
 Eglon and brought rest to the land of Is-
 rael (Judg. 3:21-30).

✍️*Elah*

CHRONOLOGICAL SUMMARY

I. Elah, the apostate king
 A. He was the fourth king of Northern
  Israel.
 B. He ruled two years (1 Kings 16:8).
 C. He was a wicked king like his father
  Baasha (1 Kings 16:13).
II. Elah, the assassinated king
 A. He was plotted against by Zimri, one
  of his army officials who commanded
  half of his chariots (1 Kings 16:9).
 B. Zimri killed Elah as the king lay in a
  drunken stupor at the capital city of
  Tirzah (1 Kings 16:9-10).
 C. Zimri then killed off all of Elah's rela-
  tives (1 Kings 16:12).

STATISTICS

Father: Baasha (1 Kings 16:6)
First mention: 1 Kings 16:6
Final mention: 1 Kings 16:14
Meaning of his name: "Oak"
Frequency of his name: Referred to four times

Biblical books mentioning him: One book
(1 Kings)
Occupation: King of Northern Israel (1 Kings
6:8)
Place of death: In an official's home in Tirzah
(1 Kings 6:9)
Circumstances of death: He was killed by
Zimri, commander of half his chariots
(1 Kings 6:9-10).
Important fact about his life: He was Northern
Israel's fourth king.

Eldad

CHRONOLOGICAL SUMMARY

I. Eldad and Medad—These men, the only
two named, were among the 70 Israelite
elders upon whom the Spirit of God
rested, causing them to prophesy
(Num. 11:24-27).

II. Eldad and Moses

A. The request of Moses concerning
Eldad—"Joshua the son of Nun, the
servant of Moses, one of his young
men, answered and said, My lord
Moses, forbid them" (Num. 11:28).

B. The reply of Moses concerning
Eldad—"Enviest thou for my sake?
would God that all the LORD's people
were prophets, and that the LORD
would put his Spirit upon them!"
(Num. 11:29).

STATISTICS

First mention: Numbers 11:26
Final mention: Numbers 11:27
Meaning of his name: "God is a Friend"
Frequency of his name: Referred to two times
Biblical books mentioning him: One book
(Numbers)
Occupation: Elder in Israel (Num. 11:26)
Important fact about his life: He was one of
the 70 Israelite elders to whom were
given the ministry of the Holy Spirit
(Num. 11:25-26).

Eleazar

CHRONOLOGICAL SUMMARY

I. Eleazar and Moses

A. His association with Moses

1. He was the third son of Aaron
(Exod. 6:23; Num. 3:2).

2. He was Israel's second high priest
(Num. 20:25-28; Deut. 10:6).

3. He was the nephew of Moses
(Exod. 28:1).

4. Through a misunderstanding, he
once invoked Moses' anger, until
his father Aaron explained the
situation (Lev. 10:16-20).

B. His assignments by Moses

1. He served as the chief Levitical
leader who cared for the tabernacle (Num. 3:32; 4:16).

2. He was responsible with Moses
for conducting Israel's second census (Num. 26:1-3, 63).

3. He helped in the commissioning
of Joshua to succeed Moses
(Num. 27:18-23).

4. He aided Moses in the dividing
among the tribes of the immense
war spoils following the victory
over the Midianites (Num. 31).

II. Eleazar and Joshua

A. He helped Joshua assign the land
portions for each tribe after Israel had
entered Canaan (Num. 34:17; Josh.
14:1; 19:51).

B. He was buried in the city of Gibeah
(Josh. 24:33).

STATISTICS

Father: Aaron (Exod. 6:23; Num. 3:2)
Mother: Elisheba (Exod. 6:23)
Son: Phinehas (Exod. 6:25; Num. 25:7)
Brothers: Nadab, Abihu, and Ithamar (Exod.
6:23)
Significant descendant: Ezra (Ezra 7:1-5)
First mention: Exodus 6:23
Final mention: Ezra 7:5
Meaning of his name: "God is Helper"
Frequency of his name: Referred to 60 times
Biblical books mentioning him: Seven books

(Exodus, Leviticus, Deuteronomy, Joshua, Judges, 1 Chronicles, Ezra)

Occupation: High priest (Num. 20:22-29)

Place of death: The city of Gibeah (Josh. 24:33)

Important fact about his life: He was Israel's second high priest (Num. 20:22-29).

Eli

CHRONOLOGICAL SUMMARY

I. Eli and Hannah
A. His rebuke
  1. Eli ministered in the city of Shiloh, where the tabernacle was located (Josh. 18:1; 1 Sam. 1:3).
  2. On one occasion Eli rebuked Hannah in the temple as she stood praying silently with only her lips moving (1 Sam. 1:9-14).
B. His reassurance
  1. Upon realizing she was not drunk (as he had first concluded), Eli assured Hannah her prayers for a son would be answered (1 Sam. 1:15-18).
  2. In the course of time Hannah bore a son and named him Samuel (1 Sam. 1:19-20).
  3. After her son was weaned, Hannah brought him to Eli to be raised in the tabernacle (1 Sam. 1:21-28; 2:11).
  4. Eli prayed that God would give Hannah even more children. His request was granted, for she later bore three sons and two daughters (1 Sam. 2:20-21).

II. Eli and his sons—He had two wicked sons named Hophni and Phinehas (1 Sam. 1:3).
A. The nature of their wickedness
  1. They had no regard for God (1 Sam. 2:12).
  2. They took by force for themselves some of the sacrifices offered up by the people of Israel (1 Sam. 2:13-16).
  3. They actually committed adultery with some of the women who served at the entrance of the tabernacle (1 Sam. 2:22).
B. The cause leading to their wickedness
  1. To some extent, God held Eli responsible, for he did not properly discipline his sons (1 Sam. 3:13).
  2. What discipline he did offer was weak and totally ineffective (1 Sam. 2:22-25).
  3. In essence, Eli put his sons before the Lord (1 Sam. 2:29).
C. The consequences of their wickedness
  1. Because of his total failure as a father, Eli received some horrible news from a prophet of God (1 Sam. 2:27-36).
    a. All his descendants would die in the prime of life.
    b. Before their deaths, their sinful actions would grieve his heart and fill his eyes with tears.
    c. His two sons Hophni and Phinehas would die on the same day.
  2. Approximately 150 years after Eli's death, Solomon removed one of his descendants named Abiathar from the priesthood (1 Kings 2:27).

III. Eli and Samuel
A. As a boy growing up in the tabernacle, Samuel one night mistook the voice of God for the voice of Eli on three occasions (1 Sam. 3:1-8).
B. Realizing the source of the voice, Eli instructed Samuel just how he should respond to God's call, which Samuel did (1 Sam. 3:9-10).
C. The following morning Eli urged Samuel to relate God's message. Sadly, the old man learned it concerned his failure as a father (1 Sam. 3:11-18).

IV. Eli and the Ark of God
A. The anxiety—Eli sat on his chair by

the side of the road in Shiloh, awaiting news concerning the battle between Israel and the Philistines
(1 Sam. 4:13).
B. The agony (1 Sam. 4:12-18)
1. Soon a runner appeared and gave
the tragic report.
a. Israel had lost the battle.
b. Eli's two sons Hophni and
Phinehas were dead.
C. The Ark of the Covenant had been
captured by the Philistines.
2. Upon hearing all this Eli fell back-
ward off his chair, causing instant
death by a broken neck.
3. He was 98 and had led Israel for
40 years.

STATISTICS

Sons: Hophni and Phinehas (1 Sam. 1:3)
Significant ancestors: Aaron and Ithamar
First mention: 1 Samuel 1:3
Final mention: 1 Kings 2:27
Meaning of his name: "God is high"
Frequency of his name: Referred to 33 times
Biblical books mentioning him: Two books
(1 Samuel, 1 Kings)
Occupation: High priest (1 Sam. 1:9)
Place of death: Near the Shiloh main gate
(1 Sam. 4:12, 18)
Age at death: 98 (1 Sam. 4:15)
Circumstances of death: He died from a fall
which broke his neck (1 Sam. 4:18).
Important fact about his life: He was the high
priest when Samuel was born and when
the Ark of the Covenant was captured
(1 Sam. 1:17-20; 4:12-18).

✍️*Eliab*

CHRONOLOGICAL SUMMARY

I. Eliab and Samuel in Bethlehem
A. He was Jesse's eldest son (1 Sam.
17:13).
B. He was also called Elihu (1 Chron.
27:18).
C. He was handsome and tall (1 Sam.
16:6-7).

D. Samuel at first wrongly concluded
Eliab would become the successor of
King Saul (1 Sam. 16:6-7).
1. The prophet's confusion—"He
looked on Eliab, and said, Surely
the LORD's anointed is before him"
(1 Sam. 16:6).
2. The Lord's correction—"Look not
on his countenance, or on the
height of his stature; because I
have refused him: for the LORD
seeth not as man seeth; for man
looketh on the outward appearance, but the LORD looketh on the
heart" (1 Sam. 16:7).
II. Eliab and David in battle
A. Eliab joined the army of Saul in the
king's fight against the Philistines
(1 Sam. 17:13).
B. He became furious with David when
his younger brother wanted to know
why Goliath was allowed to slander
both God and Israel (1 Sam. 17:26-29).

STATISTICS

Father: Jesse (1 Sam. 17:13)
Daughter: Abihael (2 Chron. 11:18)
Brothers: Abinadab, Shammah, Nathan, Ne-
thaneel, Raddai, Ozem, and David
(1 Sam. 17:12-13; 1 Chron. 2:13-15)
Sisters: Zeruiah and Abigail (1 Chron. 2:13)
First mention: 1 Samuel 16:6
Final mention: 2 Chronicles 11:18
Meaning of his name: "God is Father"
Frequency of his name: Referred to six times
Biblical books mentioning him: Three books
(1 Samuel, 1 Chronicles, 2 Chronicles)
Important fact about his life: He criticized his
younger brother David (1 Sam. 17:28).

✍️*Eliakim*

CHRONOLOGICAL SUMMARY

I. His report to the king of Judah
A. He was the palace administrator under King Hezekiah of Judah (2 Kings
18:18).
B. He replaced the former dishonest pal-

ace administrator, Shebna (Isa. 22:15-20).

C. He headed up a delegation which attempted (unsuccessfully) to secure peace when Jerusalem was surrounded by the Assyrian army (2 Kings 18:26).

D. He then had to report to Hezekiah that the enemy had ridiculed their peace offer (2 Kings 18:37).

E. He was then sent by Hezekiah to inform the prophet Isaiah of the impending Assyrian invasion (2 Kings 19:1-2).

II. His reassurance from the King of kings

A. Reassurance for the present—"Thus saith the LORD, Be not afraid of the words which thou hast heard, with which the servants of the king of Assyria have blasphemed me. Behold, I will send a blast upon him, and he shall hear a rumour, and shall return to his own land; and I will cause him to fall by the sword in his own land" (2 Kings 19:6-7).

B. Reassurance for the future (Isa. 22:21-23)

1. That he would become a spiritual father to the people of Judah
2. That God would place on his shoulder the key to the house of David
3. That God would keep open what Eliakim opened and keep shut what he shut
4. That he would be driven and established like a peg into a firm place
5. That he would be honored

STATISTICS

Father: Hilkiah (2 Kings 18:18)
First mention: 2 Kings 18:18
Final mention: Isaiah 37:2
Meaning of his name: "God is setting up"
Frequency of his name: Referred to nine times
Biblical books mentioning him: Two books (2 Kings, Isaiah)
Occupation: Palace administrator (2 Kings 18:18)

Important fact about his life: He was Hezekiah's palace official when Jerusalem was saved by the death angel (Isa. 36–37).

Eliezer (1)

CHRONOLOGICAL SUMMARY

I. The seeking of a son

A. Eliezer was Abraham's chief servant (Gen. 15:2; 24:66).
B. He may have been born in Damascus (Gen. 15:2).
C. Abraham requested that he be allowed to adopt Eliezer and look upon him as the promised heir (Gen. 15:3).
D. God promised this would not be the case (Gen. 15:4).

II. The sending of a servant—Although unnamed, Eliezer is thought to be the servant sent by Abraham on a special mission in Genesis 24.

A. The reason for this mission—Unwilling to allow Isaac to marry a pagan Canaanite girl, Abraham sent Eliezer to the land of his fathers so that he might bring back a bride for his son (Gen. 24:1-4).

B. The results of this mission

1. Eliezer took 10 camels and departed for the city of Nahor in Mesopotamia (Gen. 24:10).
2. Outside the city, near a well, he prayed, asking God for a specific sign that he might recognize the girl who should become Isaac's wife (Gen. 24:11-14).
3. The requested sign was twofold (Gen. 24:14)
   a. That the girl would offer him water to drink
   b. That the girl would offer to water his camels
4. Even before he finished praying, Rebekah arrived at the well with a jar on her shoulder (Gen. 24:15).
5. Rebekah fulfilled both signs (Gen. 24:16-21).
6. Concluding she was indeed God's

choice, he gave her golden jewelry and explained the nature of his mission (Gen. 24:22-27).

7. The day after Eliezer's offer, Rebekah agreed to go with him and become Isaac's wife (Gen. 24:57-58).

8. They left immediately. Upon arrival in Canaan, Isaac and Rebekah were married (Gen. 24:61-67).

STATISTICS

First mention: Genesis 15:2
Final mention: Genesis 24:66 ("the servant")
Meaning of his name: "God is Help"
Frequency of his name: Referred to 13 times
Biblical books mentioning him: One book (Genesis)
Occupation: Abraham's chief steward (Gen. 15:2)
Important fact about his life: At Abraham's command, he brought Rebekah to Isaac (Gen. 24).

Eliezer (2)

CHRONOLOGICAL SUMMARY

I. He was the second son of Moses and Zipporah (Exod. 18:4).
II. Like his older brother Gershom, Eliezer was apparently born and raised in the Sinai desert (Exod. 18:3-4).
III. Eliezer later had many grandchildren through his only son Rehabiah (1 Chron. 23:17).

STATISTICS

Father: Moses (Exod. 18:2-4)
Mother: Zipporah (Exod. 18:2-4)
Son: Rehabiah (1 Chron. 23:17)
Brother: Gershom (Exod. 2:22)
First mention: Exodus 18:4
Final mention: 1 Chronicles 26:25
Meaning of his name: "God is help"
Frequency of his name: Referred to five times
Biblical books mentioning him: Two books (Exodus, 1 Chronicles)

Important fact about his life: He was Moses' second son (Exod. 18:2-4).

Elihu

CHRONOLOGICAL SUMMARY

I. The abstinence of Elihu
   A. He was the youngest of Job's four friends, the son of Barakel, of the family of Ram (Job 32:2).
   B. He was from the land of Buz (Job 32:2; Jer. 25:23).
   C. His lectures are found in Job 32–37.
   D. He waited a long while to speak because of his youth (Job 32:6).
   E. He finally felt he must speak out or burst from within (Job 32:18-20).
II. The anger of Elihu—He expressed anger toward Job as well as his three friends (Job 32:2-3).
   A. Toward Job, because he had attempted to justify himself rather than God
   B. Toward the three friends, because they had condemned Job without being able to refute him
III. The arrogance of Elihu
   A. He presumed to teach Job wisdom (Job 33:33).
   B. He assumed Job had little wisdom (Job 34:35; 35:16).
   C. In fact, he almost claimed his words were infallible (Job 36:4).
   D. He actually announced he was the one Job was wishing for, that person to stand between the suffering patriarch and God (Job 33:6).
IV. The assumption of Elihu—He, like the first three friends, assumed Job was being punished for his sins (Job 36:17, 21).
V. The analysis of Elihu—In spite of his youth and immaturity, Elihu does display a theological grasp of God's omnipotence (Job 37:1-24).

STATISTICS

Father: Barachel (Job 32:2)
First mention: Job 32:2

Final mention: Job 36:1
Meaning of his name: "God himself"
Frequency of his name: Referred to seven
  times
Biblical books mentioning him: One book (Job)
Important fact about his life: He was a young
  man who attempted to advise Job (Job
  32:6-10).

Elijah

CHRONOLOGICAL SUMMARY
I. Elijah and Ahab
  A. The prophet confronted the wicked
     king.
     1. Elijah was a prophet from the
        town of Tishbe in Gilead, that
        land east of the Jordan River
        (1 Kings 17:1).
     2. He warned Ahab of an impending
        drought from God as punishment
        for both the sins of the king and
        those of Northern Israel (1 Kings
        17:1; James 5:17-18).
  B. The prophet challenged the wicked
     king.
     1. After the drought had surpassed
        three years in duration, God sent
        Elijah back to Ahab with news
        that the rains would soon come
        (1 Kings 18:1).
     2. He then threw down a challenge
        to Ahab—"Send, and gather to
        me all Israel unto Mount Carmel,
        and the prophets of Baal four
        hundred and fifty, and the proph-
        ets of the groves four hundred,
        which eat at Jezebel's table"
        (1 Kings 18:19).
     3. The purpose of this gathering was
        to determine the true God.
  C. The prophet condemned the wicked
     king (1 Kings 21:17-24).
     1. The place involved—The meeting
        occurred in the vineyard of Na-

both, a godly Israelite whom the
wicked king had previously murdered to obtain his property.
     2. The punishment involved—The
        condemnation was threefold.
        a. The wild dogs of Jezreel would
           lick Ahab's blood outside the
           city just as they licked the
           blood of Naboth (see 1 Kings
           22:37-38 for fulfillment).
        b. The wild dogs of Jezreel would
           later eat the flesh of Jezebel,
           Ahab's notoriously wicked wife
           (see 2 Kings 9:35-36 for fulfill-
           ment).
        c. Ahab's entire family would
           eventually die terrible deaths
           (see 2 Kings 10:6-11 for fulfill-
           ment).
II. Elijah and the ravens—God supplied
    Elijah's needs with an unlikely source
    (1 Kings 17:2-7).
  A. After Elijah had first warned Ahab
     about the coming drought, he was
     commanded by God to hide himself
     by the Cherith brook at its eastern
     entrance into the Jordan River.
  B. He was fed by the ravens, who
     brought him bread and meat each
     morning and evening.
  C. After some time, however, the brook
     dried up.
III. Elijah and a widow
  A. Supernaturally feeding her family
     (1 Kings 17:8-16)
     1. Following the drying of the brook,
        Elijah was ordered to go and live
        in the village of Zarephath.
     2. There he met a desperately poor
        widow who was preparing a scant
        meal for her son with the last
        food she had left.
     3. Elijah greeted her with a request
        and a reassurance.
        a. The request—She was to give
           him her meager food.
        b. The reassurance—Neither the
           widow nor her son would be
           hungry again, for the prophet
           promised there would be a su-

pernatural supply of flour and oil left in her containers until the crops could grow again at the end of the drought.

    c. The results—She obeyed and found it to be exactly as Elijah had promised.

B. Supernaturally raising her son (1 Kings 17:17-24) Elijah raised to life the widow's son who had died of a sickness.

    1. The consternation—At first she felt Elijah might have been sent by God to punish her for some past sin.

    2. The confidence—Elijah restored the dead boy by stretching himself upon the corpse three times and calling out to God.

    3. The conclusion—The widow gratefully acknowledged he was indeed a prophet sent from God.

IV. Elijah and Obadiah

A. The command of Elijah (1 Kings 18:2-15)

    1. Near the end of the three and a half-year drought, Elijah met a secret believer named Obadiah.

    2. Obadiah was in charge of Ahab's household.

    3. Obadiah had previously hidden from Jezebel 100 prophets of God in two caves.

    4. Elijah commanded this timid official to arrange a meeting between the prophet and the king.

B. The concern of Obadiah (1 Kings 18:10-12, 15)

    1. Obadiah was terrified to do this, fearing God would remove Elijah to another place after the meeting had been set up.

    2. However, the prophet persuaded him to do this.

V. Elijah and the people of Israel—After he had challenged Ahab and the priests of Baal to a contest on Mt. Carmel, Elijah gathered the people of Israel and rebuked them. "How long halt ye between two opinions? if the LORD be

God, follow him: but if Baal, then follow him. And the people answered him not a word" (1 Kings 18:21).

VI. Elijah and the priests of Baal

A. The proposal (1 Kings 18:22-25)

    1. Elijah proposed to the pagan priests a test to determine the true God.

    2. Two bulls would be placed on two altars, one dedicated to Baal, the other to Jehovah God.

    3. The true God would then be asked to respond by sending down fire from heaven.

B. The problem (1 Kings 18:26-29)

    1. The priests of Baal soon ran into difficulty.

    2. Elijah allowed them to go first.

    3. From morning till noon they danced around the altar, crying out to Baal.

    4. Elijah ridiculed their futile attempts.

    5. From noon till evening they intensified their efforts, raving and cutting themselves with knives and swords, but all to no avail.

C. The preparation (1 Kings 18:30-35)

    1. When it was his turn, Elijah summoned the people around him.

    2. He first rebuilt the altar of God, using 12 stones, representing Israel's 12 tribes.

    3. He then dug a three-foot-wide trench around the altar and had it filled with 12 barrels of water.

D. The prayer (1 Kings 18:36-37)—He asked God to hear and hearken to his prayer, that "this people may know that thou art the LORD God, and that thou hast turned their heart back again" (1 Kings 18:37).

E. The purification—"Then the fire of the LORD fell, and consumed the burnt sacrifice, and the wood, and the stones, and the dust, and licked up the water that was in the trench" (1 Kings 18:38).

F. The praise—"When all the people saw it, they fell on their faces: and they said, The LORD, he is the God; the LORD, he is the God" (1 Kings 18:39).

G. The purge—"Elijah said unto them, take the prophets of Baal; let not one of them escape. And they took them: and Elijah brought them down to the brook Kishon, and slew them there" (1 Kings 18:40).

VII. Elijah and God

A. The prophet under a tree (1 Kings 19:1-7)

1. Upon learning of Jezebel's threat to kill him for destroying her priests, Elijah ran for his life.
2. After reaching Beer-sheba, he left his servant and started into the Sinai desert alone.
3. At the end of a day's journey, he sat down under a juniper tree and was ministered to by an angel who gave him food and water.

B. The prophet on a mount (1 Kings 19:8-12)

1. He heard God's words.
   a. Elijah was asked why he had come there.
   b. His feeble answer was three-fold.
      (1) That all Israel had forsaken God.
      (2) That he alone was true to the Lord.
      (3) That God's enemies were trying to kill him.
2. He saw God's works.
   a. Suddenly a mighty windstorm hit the mountain, but the Lord was not in the wind.
   b. Then there was a great earthquake, but the Lord was not in it.
   c. Finally there was a fierce fire, but again the Lord was not in it.
   d. However, after all these mighty wonders, there came to his heart "a still, small voice." God *was* in this.

C. The prophet in a cave (1 Kings 19:13-18)

1. God assigned Elijah—The prophet was to do three things.
   a. He was to anoint Hazael to be king over Syria.
   b. He was to anoint Jehu to be king over Northern Israel.
   c. He was to anoint Elisha to be his successor.
2. God assured Elijah.
   a. Once again Elijah complained to God that he was the only true believer left.
   b. God responded by assuring Elijah this was not true: "I have left me seven thousand in Israel, all the knees which have not bowed unto Baal, and every mouth which hath not kissed him" (1 Kings 19:18).

VIII. Elijah and Ahaziah—Elijah pronounced God's death penalty upon Ahaziah, eighth king of Northern Israel (2 Kings 1:1-17).

A. The circumstances leading to this judgment prophecy

1. Ahaziah had suffered from a fall and was desperately ill.
2. He turned to the pagan idol Baal-zebub for help instead of to God.
3. This action led to Elijah's death prediction.

B. The confirmation following this judgment prophecy

1. Upon hearing of this, Ahaziah sent out 150 soldiers in three separate companies of 50 to arrest the prophet.
2. Elijah called down fire from heaven which consumed the first two groups.
3. The captain of the third company, however, begged and received mercy from Elijah, who spared both him and his men.
4. Elijah then personally visited Ahaziah and reconfirmed the message of death.
5. Soon the wicked king died.

IX. Elijah and Joram—Prior to his translation, Elijah had sent a written message

to Joram (also called Jehoram)
(2 Chron. 21:12-19).

A. The contents of this message
1. Concerning Joram's family—
"Behold, with a great plague will
the LORD smite thy people, and
thy children, and thy wives, and
all thy goods" (2 Chron. 21:14).
2. Concerning Joram himself—"Thou
shalt have great sickness by disease of thy bowels, until thy bowels fall out by reason of the
sickness day by day" (2 Chron.
21:15).

B. The cause for the message—All this
would come upon Joram because the
wicked king had "made Judah and
the inhabitants of Jerusalem to go a
whoring, like to the whoredoms of
the house of Ahab, and also hast
slain thy brethren of thy father's
house, which were better than thyself" (2 Chron. 21:13).

X. Elijah and Elisha
A. Their first meeting (1 Kings 19:19-21)
1. Elisha ceased his work as a plowman.
a. While Elijah was in the cave on
Mt. Horeb, God had instructed
him to find and anoint Elisha as
his successor (1 Kings 19:16).
b. He found Elisha plowing in a
field with 12 yoke of oxen.
c. After some hesitation, Elisha
submitted to the call, killed and
sacrificed two of his oxen to
God, and followed Elijah.
2. Elisha commenced his work as a
prophet. "Then he arose, and
went after Elijah, and ministered
unto him" (1 Kings 19:21).
B. Their final meeting (2 Kings 2:1-11)
1. The realization—God revealed to
Elijah that he would soon take
him to heaven by a whirlwind.
2. The route
a. Elijah began his final earthly
journey, accompanied by Elisha.

b. Beginning at Gilgal, the two
men traveled through Beth-el
and Jericho en route to the Jordan River.
3. The Jordan River—"Elijah took his
mantle, and wrapped it together,
and smote the waters, and they
were divided hither and thither,
so that they two went over on dry
ground" (2 Kings 2:8).
4. The request (2 Kings 2:9)
a. Elijah's proposal—"Ask what I
shall do for thee, before I be
taken away from thee."
b. Elisha's answer—"I pray thee,
let a double portion of thy spirit
be upon me."
5. The requirement—"He said, Thou
hast asked a hard thing: nevertheless, if thou see me when I am
taken from thee, it shall be so
unto thee; but if not, it shall not
be so" (2 Kings 2:10).
6. The removal—"It came to pass, as
they still went on, and talked,
that, behold, there appeared a
chariot of fire, and horses of fire,
and parted them both asunder;
and Elijah went up by a whirlwind into heaven" (2 Kings 2:11).

THEOLOGICAL SUMMARY

I. Malachi and Elijah—Malachi predicted
Elijah would return and minister during
the days of the great tribulation (Mal.
4:5).
II. Gabriel and Elijah—The angel Gabriel
told Zacharias, father of John the Baptist, that his unborn son would someday minister in the spirit and power of
Elijah (Luke 1:17).
III. John the Baptist and Elijah—The Pharisees asked John if he was Elijah (John
1:21).
IV. Jesus and Elijah
A. Jesus compared John the Baptist to
Elijah on at least two occasions (Matt.
11:14; 17:11).
B. In the days of Christ's earthly minis-

try, some people mistakenly believed he was a reincarnation of Elijah (Matt. 16:14; Mark 6:15; 8:28; Luke 9:8).

C. Jesus referred to the historical account of Elijah and the widow of Zarephath to illustrate the unbelief he had found in Nazareth during his sermon in the synagogue there (Luke 4:26).

D. Both Elijah and Moses appeared to Christ on the Mount of Transfiguration to discuss his impending crucifixion in Jerusalem (Luke 9:30-31).

V. John the Apostle and Elijah—On one occasion, John the apostle and his brother James asked Jesus if they could call down fire from heaven and destroy God's enemies as Elijah had once done (Luke 9:54).

VI. The crowd at Calvary and Elijah—While Christ was on the cross, the wicked crowd that watched erroneously thought he was calling out for Elijah (Matt. 27:46-47).

VII. Paul and Elijah—The apostle referred to Elijah to illustrate the fact that God always has his chosen remnant on earth (Rom. 11:2-5).

VIII. The book of Hebrews and Elijah—Here the author may have referred to Elijah when he wrote: "Women received their dead raised to life again" (Heb. 11:35).

IX. James and Elijah—James mentioned Elijah to demonstrate the power of prayer (James 5:17-18).

A. Pointing out that he was a man, just like us

B. That he prayed earnestly that it would not rain

C. That it did not rain for 3 1/2 years

D. That he then prayed for rain, resulting in a downpour

STATISTICS

First mention: 1 Kings 17:1
Final mention: James 5:17
Meaning of his name: "God himself"
Frequency of his name: Referred to 95 times
Biblical books mentioning him: 10 books

(1 Kings, 2 Kings, 2 Chronicles, Malachi, Matthew, Mark, Luke, John, Romans, James)
Occupation: Prophet (1 Kings 19:14)
Place of birth: East side of the Jordan River
Place of death: Did not suffer death (2 Kings 2:11–12)
Important fact about his life: He defeated his enemies on Mt. Carmel and was later caught up into heaven without dying (1 Kings 18:16-45; 2 Kings 2:1-18).

Eliphaz (1)

CHRONOLOGICAL SUMMARY

I. The birth of his son—Of his seven sons, Amalek would later gain the most notoriety (Gen. 36:10-12, 15-16).

II. The bitterness wrought by his son

A. Amalek founded the Amalekites, an especially fierce and hostile people who constantly troubled Israel.

1. Moses and Joshua fought against them at the base of Mt. Sinai (Exod. 17:8-16; Deut. 25:17-18).

2. Ehud battled them in the time of the judges (Judg. 3:13-15, 26-30).

3. Saul's great sin was in sparing Agag, the king of the Amalekites, as well as the spoils of war (1 Sam. 15:3-23; 28:18-19).

B. The Amalekites are mentioned by the psalmist in his list of God's enemies (Ps. 83:1-7).

STATISTICS

Father: Esau (Gen. 36:4)
Mother: Adah (Gen. 36:4)
Spouse: Timna (Gen. 36:12) Also an unnamed spouse who had all the sons except Amalek
Sons: Amalek, Teman, Omar, Zephi, Gatam, Kenaz, and Timna (1 Chron. 1:36)
Brothers: Reuel, Jeush, Jaalam, and Korah (1 Chron. 1:35)
First mention: Genesis 36:4
Final mention: 1 Chronicles 1:36

Meaning of his name: "God is Dispenser"
Frequency of his name: Referred to nine times
Biblical books mentioning him: Two books (Genesis, 1 Chronicles)
Important fact about his life: He was the founder of the Amalekites.

Eliphaz (2)

CHRONOLOGICAL SUMMARY

I. The concern of Eliphaz—"When Job's three friends heard of all this evil that was come upon him, they came every one from his own place; Eliphaz the Temanite, and Bildad the Shuhite, and Zophar the Naamathite: for they had made an appointment together to come to mourn with him, and to comfort him. And when they lifted up their eyes afar off, and knew him not, they lifted up their voice, and wept; and they rent every one his mantle, and sprinkled dust upon their heads toward heaven. So they sat down with him upon the ground seven days and seven nights, and none spake a word unto him: for they saw that his grief was very great" (Job 2:11-13).

II. The criticism of Eliphaz—It wasn't long before the compassion of Eliphaz, as he viewed the suffering Job, turned into hostile and untrue criticism. Eliphaz was in error on two counts (Job 4–5, 15, 22).

A. His assumption was wrong. Like his two friends, Bildad and Zophar, Eliphaz assumed Job was suffering because of some terrible unconfessed sin. "Remember, I pray thee, who ever perished, being innocent? or where were the righteous cut off? Even as I have seen, they that plow iniquity, and sow wickedness, reap the same" (Job 4:7-8). "Thine own mouth condemneth thee, and not I: yea, thine own lips testify against thee" (Job 15:6). NOTE: Eliphaz

based his assumption on personal experience (see Job 4:8, 12-16; 5:3, 27; 15:17).

B. His advice was wrong. Eliphaz's counsel was simple—repent of your secret sin. "If thou return to the Almighty, thou shalt be built up, thou shalt put away iniquity far from thy tabernacles" (Job 22:23).

III. The chastisement of Eliphaz

A. Eliphaz was later rebuked by God for his unkind and untrue opinion of Job (Job 42:7).

B. He was then required along with his two friends to offer up seven bulls and seven rams as burnt offerings for his sin of slander (Job 42:8-9).

STATISTICS
First mention: Job 2:11
Final mention: Job 42:9
Meaning of his name: "God is Dispenser"
Frequency of his name: Referred to six times
Biblical books mentioning him: One book (Job)
Important fact about his life: He was one of Job's three "friends" whose "comfort" became criticism (Job 5:5-7).

Elisha

CHRONOLOGICAL SUMMARY

I. Faithful assistant to Elijah—a serving ministry

A. Their first meeting—In a field

1. The message—While Elijah was on Mt. Horab, God had spoken to him concerning Elisha. "Elisha . . . shalt thou anoint to be prophet in thy room" (1 Kings 19:16).

2. The mantle—"He departed thence, and found Elisha the son of Shaphat, who was plowing with twelve yoke of oxen before him, and he with the twelfth: and Elijah passed by him, and cast his mantle upon him. And he left the

oxen, and ran after Elijah, and said, Let me, I pray thee, kiss my father and my mother, and then I will follow thee. And he said unto him, Go back again: for what have I done to thee? And he returned back from him, and took a yoke of oxen, and slew them, and boiled their flesh with the instruments of the oxen, and gave unto the people, and they did eat. Then he arose, and went after Elijah, and ministered unto him" (1 Kings 19:19-21).

B. Their final meeting—By a riverside (2 Kings 2:1-11)
1. The realization—God revealed to Elijah that he would soon take him to heaven by a whirlwind.
2. The route
   a. Elijah began his final earthly journey, accompanied by Elisha.
   b. Beginning at Gilgal, the two men traveled through Beth-el and Jericho en route to the Jordan River.
3. The Jordan River—"Elijah took his mantle, and wrapped it together, and smote the waters, and they were divided hither and thither, so that they two went over on dry ground" (2 Kings 2:8).
4. The request (2 Kings 2:9)
   a. Elijah's proposal—"Ask what I shall do for thee, before I be taken away from thee."
   b. Elisha's answer—"I pray thee, let a double portion of thy spirit be upon me."
5. The requirement—"He said, Thou hast asked a hard thing: nevertheless, if thou see me when I am taken from thee, it shall be so unto thee; but if not, it shall not be so" (2 Kings 2:10).
6. The removal—"It came to pass, as they still went on, and talked, that, behold, there appeared a chariot of fire, and horses of fire,

and parted them both asunder; and Elijah went up by a whirlwind into heaven" (2 Kings 2:11).
II. The faithful ambassador for God—His supernatural ministry: Apart from Moses, Elisha probably performed more miracles than any other Old Testament individual, some 21 in number.
A. His personal miracles
1. Performed for himself
   a. Parting the Jordan River (2 Kings 2:13-18)
      (1) Following the removal of Elijah, Elisha put God to the test.
      (2) He struck the Jordan River with the cloak Elijah had left behind, and cried out: "Where is the LORD God of Elijah?" (2 Kings 2:14).
      (3) Immediately the waters parted and Elisha walked across on dry ground.
      (4) He then finally persuaded the young (and probably immature) prophets-in-training that Elijah had indeed been taken up into heaven.
   b. Punishing some troublemakers—He called down judgment from God upon some unruly youths from Beth-el who were insulting and threatening him (2 Kings 2:23-25).
      (1) The jeers—They ridiculed his bald head and dared him to "go up," a possible sarcastic reference to the previous removal of Elijah.
      (2) The judgment—Two female bears came out of the woods and mauled 42 of the youths.
2. Performed for his students
   a. Purifying some water—He purified some polluted water for those young prophets-in-training at Jericho by casting salt into the spring (2 Kings 2:19-22).

b. Creating oil for the poverty-stricken widow of a prophet (2 Kings 4:1-7)
   (1) Elisha learned that the creditors of this widow were coming to take her two sons as slaves.
   (2) He commanded her to borrow all the empty jars she could from her neighbors and pour what little oil she possessed into them.
   (3) This she did, and the oil continued pouring until the last jar was filled, thus allowing her to pay the creditors.
c. Purifying a stew (2 Kings 4:38-41)
   (1) A young man at Gilgal unknowingly added some poisonous wild gourds to a stew he was preparing for his fellow students.
   (2) After the men had tasted the stew, they realized it was poison.
   (3) Elisha then cast some meal into the kettle, which made the stew fit to eat.
d. Feeding 100 men—Elisha supernaturally increased 20 loaves of barley bread to provide sufficient food for 100 hungry men in the city of Gilgal (2 Kings 4:42-44).
e. Recovering an ax head (2 Kings 6:1-7)
   (1) Elisha approved some building expansion to enlarge his training program for the prophets of Jericho.
   (2) In chopping down trees for the project, one of his students accidentally cast a borrowed ax head into the Jordan River.
   (3) Elisha threw in a stick and made the iron float.

3. Performed for a supporter—He restored the dead son of a Shunammite woman (2 Kings 4:8-37).
   a. This woman and her husband had previously befriended Elisha by providing a spare room for him in their home.
   b. He returned the favor by predicting that God would touch her barren womb and give her a child the following year.
   c. Some years later the child became sick and died.
   d. The grief-stricken mother met Elisha and his servant Gehazi at the base of Mt. Carmel and told them the terrible news.
   e. When Elisha came he went into the boy's room, prayed, and stretched himself out upon the body.
   f. Soon the lad's body grew warm. After sneezing seven times he opened his eyes.
4. Performed for a servant—One morning Elisha and his servant (probably Gehazi) found themselves completely surrounded by enemy troops (2 Kings 6:14-17).
   a. The servant's terror—"When the servant of the man of God was risen early, and gone forth, behold, an host compassed the city both with horses and chariots. And his servant said unto him, Alas, my master! how shall we do?" (2 Kings 6:15).
   b. The prophet's testimony—"He answered, Fear not: for they that be with us are more than they that be with them. And Elisha prayed, and said, LORD, I pray thee, open his eyes, that he may see. And the LORD opened the eyes of the young man; and he saw: and, behold, the mountain was full of horses and chariots of fire round about Elisha" (2 Kings 6:16-17).

5. Performed for a soldier—Elisha healed Naaman, a Syrian military commander, of his leprosy (2 Kings 5:1-19).
   a. Naaman, the seeking soldier— He learned about the supernatural power of Elisha through a young Israelite maid who served in his household (2 Kings 5:2-3). Acting upon her testimony, he visited King Jehoram (the youngest son of Ahab) in Jerusalem, requesting that he be healed of his leprosy (2 Kings 5:4-6). This godless and powerless king could offer no help whatsoever, and was greatly relieved when Elisha agreed to meet with Naaman (5:7-8).
   b. Naaman, the sulking soldier— Upon his arrival at Elisha's home, Naaman was instructed by a servant of the prophet to wash himself seven times in the Jordan River for his healing (2 Kings 5:9-10).
      (1) The anger of Naaman—He expected Elisha to greet him personally and, in dramatic fashion, to heal him. He complained that if the washing process was indeed necessary, the rivers in Damascus were much cleaner than the Jordan (2 Kings 5:11-12).
      (2) The advice to Naaman—His servants gave their master some excellent advice: "My father, if the prophet had bid thee do some great thing, wouldest thou not have done it? how much rather then, when he saith to thee, Wash, and be clean?" (2 Kings 5:13).
   c. Naaman, the saved soldier
      (1) His physical salvation—

Naaman obeyed Elisha, washed himself seven times, and was instantly and totally healed (2 Kings 5:14).
      (2) His spiritual salvation—He stood before Elisha and acknowledged that the God of Israel was the only true God. He offered Elisha a gift, which the prophet refused. He vowed never again to offer sacrifices to any god except the true one. He even took two muleloads of Israelite earth with him back to Damascus (2 Kings 5:15-17).
B. His patriotic miracles
   1. Deceiving the enemy troops
      a. The desperation of the Israelite soldiers
         (1) Jehoshaphat, king of Judah, and Jehoram, king of Northern Israel, had joined in a military alliance against the Moabites (2 Kings 3:6-7).
         (2) After an ill-prepared roundabout march of seven days, the alliance found itself in the desert with no water (2 Kings 3:8-10).
         (3) Jehoshaphat sought God's counsel and discovered the great prophet Elisha had been traveling with the armies, unnoticed (2 Kings 3:11-12).
         (4) Elisha agreed to help the thirsty soldiers, but only for the sake of Jehoshaphat (2 Kings 3:13-14).
         (5) The prophet then provided, supernaturally, water for all to drink (2 Kings 3:15-20). Elisha had effected this miracle by ordering that ditches be dug, which were then filled with water by the Lord.

b. The deception of the Moabite soldiers—The following day God caused the eyes of the enemy to deceive them as they looked upon those ditches filled with water (2 Kings 3:21-27). "They rose up early in the morning, and the sun shone upon the water, and the Moabites saw the water on the other side as red as blood: And they said, This is blood: the kings are surely slain, and they have smitten one another: now therefore, Moab, to the spoil. And when they came to the camp of Israel, the Israelites rose up and smote the Moabites, so that they fled before them: but they went forward smiting the Moabites, even in their country" (2 Kings 3:22-24).

2. Revealing the war plans of the enemy troops—"The king of Syria warred against Israel, and took counsel with his servants, saying, In such and such a place shall be my camp. And the man of God sent unto the king of Israel, saying, Beware that thou pass not such a place; for thither the Syrians are come down. And the king of Israel sent to the place which the man of God told him and warned him of, and saved himself there, not once nor twice. Therefore the heart of the king of Syria was sore troubled for this thing; and he called his servants, and said unto them, Will ye not shew me which of us is for the king of Israel? And one of his servants said, None, my lord, O king: but Elisha, the prophet that is in Israel, telleth the king of Israel the words that thou speakest in thy bedchamber" (2 Kings 6:8-12).

3. Blinding the enemy troops (2 Kings 6:18-23)

a. The power involved—Elisha temporarily and supernaturally blinded some Syrian soldiers who had been dispatched to arrest him.

b. The pity involved—After leading them into Samaria, Elisha restored their sight and refused the request of the king of Northern Israel to kill them.

C. His predictive miracles—Elisha correctly predicted the following:

1. The leprosy judgment upon his servant Gehazi (2 Kings 5:20-27)

a. Gehazi the lustful—Gehazi was upset with Elisha for refusing the money offered by Naaman after his healing from leprosy. "Gehazi, the servant of Elisha the man of God, said, Behold, my master hath spared Naaman this Syrian, in not receiving at his hands that which he brought: but, as the LORD liveth, I will run after him, and take somewhat of him" (2 Kings 5:20).

b. Gehazi the liar—Gehazi told Naaman Elisha had changed his mind and now wanted some money for healing him.

c. Gehazi the leper—Upon his return Gehazi was severely rebuked by Elisha: "The leprosy therefore of Naaman shall cleave unto thee, and unto thy seed for ever. And he went out from his presence a leper as white as snow" (2 Kings 5:27).

2. The salvation of Samaria (2 Kings 6:24–7:20)

a. The agony of the city—Samaria was completely surrounded by the Syrians, causing great famine in the city (2 Kings 6:24-29).

(1) A donkey's head sold for about $50 and a pint of dove's dung brought about $3.

(2) Women were even boiling and eating their own children.

b. The anger of the king (2 Kings 6:30-31)

(1) Elisha was blamed by the king for Samaria's problem, for the prophet had previously refused to allow some blinded Syrian soldiers to be killed.

(2) The king thereupon threatened to kill Elisha.

c. The assurance of the prophet—Elisha predicted that within 24 hours, food in Samaria would be so plentiful that about two gallons of flour or about four gallons of barley grain could be purchased for less than a dollar (2 Kings 7:1).

3. The death of the king's chief assistant—Elisha predicted that this man, who had ridiculed the prophet's words, would surely see the food but would not eat of it (2 Kings 7:1-2, 18-20).

4. A seven-year famine—He advised the Shunammite woman, whose dead son he had raised, to move to another country, because God was sending a seven-year famine on Israel (2 Kings 8:1-2).

5. The death of Ben-hadad, king of Syria—Elisha predicted the future for both Ben-hadad, king of Syria, and his chief administrator, Hazael (2 Kings 8:7-15).

a. Prophecies concerning Ben-hadad

(1) That he would recover from a very serious sickness

(2) That he would, nevertheless, die—This strange prophecy was literally fulfilled, for the king did recover from his sickness, only to be murdered by Hazael.

b. Prophecies concerning Hazael

(1) That he would succeed Ben-hadad as king

(2) That he would then horribly mistreat the people of Israel

6. Israel's three victories over Syria—Elisha was visited on his deathbed by Jehoash, king of Israel (2 Kings 13:14-19).

a. At the prophet's command, the king was told to strike the floor with some arrows.

b. Jehoash did this three times and stopped.

c. Elisha was upset, telling the king he should have continued the action five or six times, for each strike assured him of a future victory over the enemy of Israel, Syria.

7. The avenging ministry of King Jehu—Elisha predicted the following concerning Jehu upon his anointing as Northern Israel's new king (2 Kings 9:6-10):

a. That he would destroy the family of Ahab

b. That he would avenge the murder of God's prophets who were killed by Jezebel

c. That dogs would eat Jezebel at the city of Jezreel and no one would bury her

D. His posthumous miracle—"Elisha died, and they buried him. And the bands of the Moabites invaded the land at the coming in of the year. And it came to pass, as they were burying a man, that, behold, they spied a band of men; and they cast the man into the sepulchre of Elisha: and when the man was let down, and touched the bones of Elisha, he revived, and stood up on his feet" (2 Kings 13:20-21).

STATISTICS

Father: Shaphat (1 Kings 19:16)
First mention: 1 Kings 19:16
Final mention: Luke 4:27

Meaning of his name: "God is Savior"
Frequency of his name: Referred to 58 times
Biblical books mentioning him: Three books (1 Kings, 2 Kings, Luke)
Occupation: Prophet (1 Kings 19:16)
Important fact about his life: He was Elijah's successor who parted the Jordan and healed Naaman of his leprosy (2 Kings 2:9-14; 5).

STATISTICS
Spouses: Hannah and Peninnah (1 Sam. 1:2)
Sons: Samuel (1 Sam. 1:19-20; 1 Chron. 6:25), plus three unnamed (1 Sam. 2:21)
Daughters: Two unnamed (1 Sam. 2:21)
Significant ancestor: Levi (1 Chron. 6:16, 26)
First mention: 1 Samuel 1:1
Final mention: 1 Chronicles 6:34
Meaning of his name: "God is possessing"
Frequency of his name: Referred to 10 times
Biblical books mentioning him: Two books (1 Samuel, 1 Chronicles)
Important fact about his life: He was Samuel's father (1 Sam. 1:19-20).

Elkanah

CHRONOLOGICAL SUMMARY
I. Elkanah and God
  A. He was a descendant of Levi through Kohath (1 Chron. 6:16, 21-27).
  B. He lived in Ramah, a city located in the hill country of Ephraim (1 Sam. 1:1; 2:11).
  C. He faithfully traveled each year with his entire family to the tabernacle at Shiloh in order to sacrifice and worship God (1 Sam. 1:3, 21).
II. Elkanah and Hannah
  A. He loved her more than his other wife, Peninnah (1 Sam. 1:5).
  B. He gave her presents (1 Sam. 1:5).
  C. He attempted to comfort her— Hannah was heartbroken over her inability to bear a child (1 Sam. 1:8).
  D. When God did bless Hannah's womb, Elkanah encouraged her to dedicate Samuel to the Lord (1 Sam. 1:23).
III. Elkanah and Eli
  A. Eli blessed Elkanah, praying that God would give him and Hannah other children to take the place of Samuel, who was being raised in the tabernacle (1 Sam. 2:20).
  B. God answered this prayer, for Elkanah eventually fathered three sons and two daughters through Hannah (1 Sam. 2:21).

Enoch

CHRONOLOGICAL SUMMARY
I. His relationship with God
  A. Enoch the pilgrim
    1. He possessed great faith (Heb. 11:5).
    2. He walked with God (Gen. 5:22).
    3. He pleased God (Heb. 11:5).
    4. He was included in the genealogy which led to Christ (Luke 3:37).
  B. Enoch the parent—His first son, Methuselah, lived 969 years, longer than any other recorded person in history (Gen. 5:21, 27).
  C. Enoch the preacher (Jude 14-15)
    1. He was the first recorded preacher in human history.
    2. He warned the godless teachers present even in his day about coming judgment (compare 2 Pet. 2:1-5).
    3. He predicted the eventual return of the Lord to this earth.
II. His removal by God—He was taken from earth without dying at the age of 365 (Gen. 5:23-24; Heb. 11:5).

STATISTICS
Father: Jared (Gen. 5:18)
Son: Methuselah (Gen. 5:21)

First mention: Genesis 5:18
Final mention: Jude 1:14
Meaning of his name: "Teacher"
Frequency of his name: Referred to nine times
Biblical books mentioning him: Five books (Genesis, 1 Chronicles, Luke, Hebrews, Jude)
Place of death: Did not suffer death (Gen. 5:24)
Age at death: 365 years old when God took him home without dying (Gen. 5:23-24)
Important fact about his life: He was the first of two people recorded in Scripture to leave earth without dying (Gen. 5:24; 2 Kings 2:11-12).

STATISTICS
Father: Joseph (Gen. 41:50, 52; 46:20)
Mother: Asenath (Gen. 41:50, 52)
Sons: Ezer, Elead, and Beriah (1 Chron. 7:22-23)
Daughter: Sherah (1 Chron. 7:24)
Brother: Manasseh (Gen. 41:51)
Significant descendants: Joshua (1 Chron. 7:27)
First mention: Genesis 41:52
Final mention: 1 Chronicles 7:22
Meaning of his name: "Doubly fruitful"
Frequency of his name: Referred to 14 times
Biblical books mentioning him: Three books (Genesis, Numbers, 1 Chronicles)
Important fact about his life: He was Joseph's second son (Gen. 41:52).

✏️*Ephraim*

CHRONOLOGICAL SUMMARY
I. His selection over his brother
   A. He and his older brother, Manasseh, were brought before their dying grandfather Jacob, in Egypt, to be blessed (Gen. 48:1).
   B. The old patriarch adopted them as his own sons (Gen. 48:5).
   C. To Joseph's surprise and displeasure, Jacob bestowed upon Ephraim, the younger brother, the greater blessing (Gen. 48:12-20).
   D. Jacob predicted that the tribe Ephraim later founded would be greater than the one founded by Manasseh (Gen. 48:19).
II. His sorrow over his sons
   A. Two of Ephraim's sons, Ezer and Elead, were murdered by the Philistines of Gath, in a dispute over cattle (1 Chron. 7:21).
   B. Ephraim mourned for them many days (1 Chron. 7:22)
   C. He then named a third son Beriah, meaning "misfortune" (1 Chron. 7:23).
   D. His daughter Sherah later built the city of Beth-horon (1 Chron. 7:24).

✏️*Er*

CHRONOLOGICAL SUMMARY
I. His wife
   A. Er's father, Judah, personally selected a woman named Tamar for his son to marry (Gen. 38:6).
   B. Tamar would eventually be included in the genealogy leading to Christ (Matt. 1:3).
II. His wickedness (Gen. 38:7)—Er was killed by God for some unrecorded act of wickedness.

STATISTICS
Father: Judah (Gen. 38:2-3)
Mother: Bathshua (Gen. 38:2-3) (Called "daughter of Shuah" in KJV and NIV)
Spouse: Tamar (Gen. 38:6)
Brothers: Onan and Shelah (Gen. 38:4-5)
First mention: Genesis 38:3
Final mention: 1 Chronicles 2:3
Meaning of his name: "Watcher"
Frequency of his name: Referred to eight times
Biblical books mentioning him: Three books (Genesis, Numbers, 1 Chronicles)

Circumstances of death: He was killed by God (Gen. 38:7).

Important fact about his life: He was a wicked son of Judah whose death helped bring about an illegitimate relationship between Judah and Tamar (Gen. 38:6-26).

Esau

CHRONOLOGICAL SUMMARY

I. The early years of his life
  A. Esau the hunter
    1. Despising the birthright
      a. He became a skillful hunter, a man of the open country (Gen. 25:27).
      b. He was the favorite of his father Isaac (Gen. 25:28).
      c. Upon returning from a hunting trip, the famished Esau sold his birthright to his brother Jacob for a pot of red stew (Gen. 25:20-34).
      d. He thus acquired the nickname of Edom, which means "red" (Gen. 25:30).
      e. He did this because he despised (looked upon with disdain) his birthright (Gen. 25:34; Heb. 12:16-17).
    2. Desiring the blessing
      a. Years later, Isaac (who incorrectly thought he was dying) told Esau to kill and prepare a meal of wild game. Following this, Isaac promised to impart to Esau the patriarchal blessing (Gen. 27:1-4).
      b. Rebekah overheard this conversation and tricked her nearly blind husband into giving Jacob, her favorite son, the blessing (Gen. 27:5-29).
      c. Upon learning of this deception, Esau cried out in bitter tears, demanding that Isaac give him the blessing regardless (Gen. 27:30-36, 38).
      d. Unable to do this, Isaac sadly predicted a hard and violent life for Esau (Gen. 27:39-40).
      e. Esau then vowed revenge, threatening to kill Jacob (Gen. 27:41).
  B. Esau the husband
      a. He married two Hittite girls, Judith and Bashemath, when he was 40 (Gen. 26:34).
      b. He later married some Canaanite wives (Gen. 36:2).
      c. These marriages were a source of grief to Isaac and Rebekah (Gen. 26:35; 27:46).
      d. Realizing his pagan wives saddened his parents, Esau married a descendant of Abraham named Mahalath, the daughter of Ishmael (Gen. 28:6-9).
II. The latter years of his life
  A. Finding his brother Jacob
    1. Jacob departed following his deception (Gen. 28:1-5).
    2. Then 20 years later they met again.
  B. Forgiving his brother Jacob
    1. Jacob was horrified to learn that Esau was riding to meet him with 400 men (Gen. 32:6; 33:1).
    2. The reunion, however, was a pleasant one (Gen. 33:4-11).
      a. Esau ran to meet Jacob, kissed him, and wept.
      b. Esau offered to return the generous gift of animals Jacob had sent before the meeting to appease his brother.
      c. Esau suggested he and Jacob travel together, but his offer was politely declined.
    3. The final meeting of the brothers occurred at the funeral of Isaac (Gen. 35:29).

THEOLOGICAL SUMMARY

I. One of Esau's five sons, Eliphaz, fathered Amalek through Timna (Gen. 36:12; 1 Chron. 1:35).
II. Amalek was founder of the Amalekites,

an especially fierce and hostile people who constantly troubled Israel.

A. Joshua fought them at Sinai (Exod. 17:8; Deut. 25:17).

B. Ehud fought them at Jericho (Judg. 3:13).

C. King Saul was rejected by God for refusing to kill Agag, ruler of the Amalekites (1 Sam. 15:3-20; 28:18-19).

III. Esau was also the founder of the Edomites (Gen. 36:43).

IV. Doeg, a vicious killer who later slew 85 priests at Saul's order, was an Edomite (1 Sam. 22:18).

V. King Herod the Great was part Edomite.

VI. God assigned to the Edomites the mountain region of Mt. Seir (Josh. 24:4).

VII. The entire book of Obadiah condemns the Edomites for their treachery against the Israelites, their own relatives.

VIII. God said he hated this kind of action (Mal. 1:3).

IX. Paul used the selection of Jacob over Esau as an example of God's sovereignty (Rom. 9:10-13).

X. The book of Hebrews related four things about Esau (Heb. 12:16-17).

A. That he was sexually immoral

B. That he was godless

C. That he looked down upon his birthright

D. That he unsuccessfully sought with tears to receive the patriarchal blessing

STATISTICS

Father: Isaac (Gen. 25:21-25)

Mother: Rebekah (Gen. 25:21-25)

Spouses: Judith and Bashemath (Gen. 26:34)

Sons: Eliphaz, Reuel, Jeush, Jalam, and Korah (Gen. 36:4-5; 1 Chron. 1:35)

Brother: Jacob (Gen. 25:26)

Significant descendant: Doeg (Gen. 36:43; 1 Sam. 22:18)

First mention: Genesis 25:25

Final mention: Hebrews 12:16

Meaning of his name: "Hairy"

Frequency of his name: Referred to 76 times

Biblical books mentioning him: Six books

(Genesis, Joshua, 1 Chronicles, Malachi, Romans, Hebrews)

Occupation: Sheepherder

Important fact about his life: He was Jacob's brother and the father of the Edomites (Gen. 25:26; 36:43).

 # Esther

CHRONOLOGICAL SUMMARY

I. The rise of Esther

A. The rejection of Vashti (1:2-21)

B. The selection of Esther (2:1-20)

C. The detection of Mordecai (2:19-23)

1. Mordecai, Esther's cousin, had become a palace official. He overheard a plot of two guards at the gate to assassinate Ahasuerus.

2. He reported this to Queen Esther, who, in turn, informed the king. Both guards were executed, and this was all duly recorded in the book of the history of King Ahasuerus' reign.

II. The lies of Haman

A. Infernal servitude

1. Soon after Esther had become queen, Ahasuerus appointed as his prime minister a vicious politician named Haman, an unwitting servant of Satan himself (3:1).

2. The arrogant Haman soon learned Mordecai was refusing to bow before him, as had been commanded (3:2-4).

3. Haman hatched a plot to exterminate not only Mordecai, but every other Jew living in the Persian Empire. He approached the king with the following "recommendations":

a. That there was a "certain people scattered abroad and dispersed among the people in all the provinces of thy kingdom; and their laws are diverse from all people; neither keep they the king's laws: therefore it is not for the king's profit to suffer them" (3:8). This, of course, was a brazen lie.

b. That he, Haman, would be happy to contribute the sum of $30 million into the royal treasury for the expense involved in this purge (3:9). He then planned to butcher the Jews like cattle.

c. The careless and heartless king agreed to this, without even checking the identity of this "certain people," to say nothing of their guilt. "The king took his ring from his hand, and gave it unto Haman the son of Hammedatha the Agagite, the Jews' enemy. And the king said unto Haman, The silver is given to thee, the people also, to do with them as it seemeth good to thee" (3:10-11).

d. Royal riders were sent forth to announce this edict of execution, which decreed that all Jews would be killed on February 28 of the following year, 473 B.C. (3:12-15).

B. Intestinal fortitude (4–5)

1. As seen in Mordecai (4:1-14)

a. Upon learning of the decree of death, Mordecai immediately identified with his people and went into deep mourning (4:1-3).

b. Unaware of the new law, Esther learned of her cousin's sorrow and inquired concerning the reason behind it (4:4-6).

c. Mordecai informed her and advised that she visit the king immediately (4:7-9).

d. Esther pointed out to him that she had not been summoned to Ahasuerus's inner court for 30 days, and to walk in uninvited would very possibly bring instant death.

e. Mordecai answered with what

is perhaps the key statement in the entire book. "Think not with thyself that thou shalt escape in the king's house, more than all the Jews. For if thou altogether holdest thy peace at this time, then shall there enlargement and deliverance arise to the Jews from another place; but thou and thy father's house shall be destroyed: and who knoweth whether thou art come to the kingdom for such a time as this?" (4:13-14).

2. As seen in Esther (4:15–5:14)

a. Esther immediately ordered a three-day fast among the Jews, and determined that she would "go in unto the king, which is not according to the law: and if I perish, I perish" (4:16).

b. Three days later Esther entered the king's inner court, uninvited. To her relief, she was warmly received and the king offered to grant her any request (5:1-3).

c. Esther asked only that the king and Haman attend a private banquet with her, to which the king readily agreed (5:4-5).

d. The queen did not reveal her request during her first banquet, but simply asked that both the king and Haman attend a second banquet she was preparing the next day. Ahasuerus quickly agreed (5:6-8).

e. After attending this first banquet, the vain Haman was puffed up with pride. But when he saw Mordecai standing at the palace gate, still refusing to bow, he was furious (5:9-10).

f. He related both his joy and frustration to Zeresh, his wife, and to friends at home (5:11-13).

g. They foolishly suggested

Haman build a gallows and have Mordecai hanged upon it the very next day (5:14).

III. The prize of faith
  A. The execution of a beast—Haman (6–8)
    1. Scene One—The king's bedroom (6)
      a. The sleepless king
        (1) Ahasuerus experienced a case of royal insomnia and ordered the reading of some historical records, hoping perhaps that this dull material would put him to sleep (6:1).
        (2) The reader, by "chance," began reading at the place which related how Mordecai had once saved the king's life by exposing an assassination plot (6:2).
        (3) "The king said, What honour and dignity hath been done to Mordecai for this? Then said the king's servants that ministered unto him, There is nothing done for him" (6:3).
        (4) At this exact moment, Haman had arrived at Ahasuerus's palace, seeking the king's permission to hang Mordecai. The king, still determined to reward Mordecai (neither Ahasuerus nor Haman, of course, knew what the other was thinking), used Haman as a sounding board and inquired: "What shall be done unto the man whom the king delighteth to honour?" (6:6).
      b. The shameless Haman—The arrogant and self-centered Haman immediately thought Ahasuerus had him in mind and brazenly suggested the following:

        (1) That the man to be honored be clothed in the king's own royal robes
        (2) That he be placed upon Ahasuerus's personal horse
        (3) That he be allowed to wear the king's crown
        (4) That the king's most noble prince lead this hero, seated upon the horse, through the streets of the city, shouting his praises for all to hear (6:7-9)
      c. The king quickly agreed to all this and then turned to Haman and ordered his wicked prime minister to perform all this for Mordecai (6:10). The totally dumbstruck Haman stumbled out to obey Xerxes' command and later hurried home utterly humiliated. Even there he received no comfort. "Haman told Zeresh, his wife, and all his friends every thing that had befallen him. Then said his wise men and Zeresh, his wife, unto him, If Mordecai be of the seed of the Jews, before whom thou hast begun to fall, thou shalt not prevail against him, but shalt surely fall before him" (6:13).
      d. While they yet spoke, he received the message to attend Esther's second banquet (6:14).
    2. Scene two—The king's banquet hall (7)
      a. The treachery learned (7:1-6)— "The king and Haman came to the banquet with Esther the queen. And the king said again unto Esther on the second day at the banquet of wine, What is thy petition, queen Esther? and it shall be granted thee: and what is thy request? and it shall be performed, even to the half of the kingdom" (7:1-2).

(1) Esther warned the king that a plot was underway to slaughter her and all her people. The king, filled with astonishment and then anger, asked: "Who is he, and where is he, that durst presume in his heart to do so?" (7:5)

(2) Esther pointed to Haman and replied: "The adversary and enemy is this wicked Haman" (7:6).

b. The tables turned (7:7–8:17)

(1) Ahasuerus, unable to speak because of fury, walked outside into his palace garden for a moment (7:7).

(2) Filled with fear, the cowardly Haman begged Esther to intercede to the king for him. In his terrible fright he accidentally fell upon the couch where Esther was reclining (7:8).

(3) At this point Ahasuerus walked back in and viewed what he interpreted to be a rape attempt on the part of Haman. Upon learning of the nearby gallows Haman had built for Mordecai, the king in his wrath ordered that Haman himself be hung that very night. The order was immediately carried out (7:9-10). "They hanged Haman on the gallows that he had prepared for Mordecai. Then was the king's wrath pacified" (7:10).

(4) After Haman's execution, Ahasuerus gave Esther Haman's estate and appointed Mordecai his new prime minister (8:1-2).

(5) Esther and Mordecai begged the king to reverse Haman's order, but the law of the Medes and the Persians, once made, was immutable. Not even Ahasuerus himself could change it. He then did the next best thing and ordered the Jews to defend themselves. Copies of this new decree were sent in the king's name to all the 127 provinces (8:3-14).

B. The institution of a feast—Purim (9–10)

1. The Jews prepared themselves and were able to slaughter their enemies (9:1-19).

2. Mordecai and Esther then instituted a new memorial feast called Purim to commemorate yearly their great salvation from Haman (9:20-32).

3. Mordecai became a great and godly statesman, respected by both Jews and Gentiles for his abilities and actions (10).

THEOLOGICAL SUMMARY

I. Esther, also called Hadassah, was from the tribe of Benjamin (Esther 2:5-7).

II. She was a very beautiful girl (Esther 2:7).

III. She was raised up in the city of Shushan in Persia by her cousin Mordecai (Esther 2:5-7).

IV. She won a Persian beauty contest and became the queen of King Ahasuerus (Esther 2:2-4, 8-17).

V. She did not, however, at that time reveal herself as a Jewish girl (Esther 2:10, 20).

VI. Esther was the second of two biblical books named after a woman. The other is Ruth.

A. Ruth is the story of a Moabite girl who married a Jewish husband.

B. Esther is the story of a Jewish girl who married a Gentile husband.

STATISTICS

Father: Abihail (Esther 2:15)
Spouse: Ahasuerus (Esther 2:17)
First mention: Esther 2:7

Final mention: Esther 9:32
Meaning of her name: "The planet Venus" (Star)
Frequency of her name: Referred to 55 times
Biblical books mentioning her: One book (Esther)
Occupation: Queen of the Medo-Persian empire (Esther 1:1-3; 2:17)
Place of birth: Shushan
Important fact about her life: She saved her people from an attempted holocaust (Esther 7:3-6; 8:3-8).

Eve

CHRONOLOGICAL SUMMARY

I. Her creation by God
  A. She was created (like Adam) in the image of God (Gen. 1:27).
  B. She was taken from the side of Adam (Gen. 2:22).
  C. She was married to Adam (Gen. 2:24-25).
  D. She was named by Adam (Gen. 3:20).

II. Her corruption by Satan
  A. The reason for her sin
    1. The falsehood—Satan urged Eve to disobey God and eat from the tree of knowledge of good and evil, promising her she would not die. "God doth know that in the day ye eat thereof, then your eyes shall be opened, and ye shall be as gods, knowing good and evil" (Gen. 3:5).
    2. The fascination—Eve saw that the tree was good for food, pleasant to the eyes, and a tree desired to make one wise (Gen. 3:6).
    3. The fall—"She took of the fruit thereof, and did eat, and gave also unto her husband with her; and he did eat" (Gen 3:6).
  B. The reaction to her sin
    1. She attempted to cover her nakedness (Gen. 3:7).
    2. She attempted to hide from God (Gen. 3:8).
    3. She attempted to blame the serpent (Gen. 3:13).
  C. The results of her sin
    1. She would suffer pain in childbirth (Gen. 3:16).
    2. She would be ruled over by her husband (Gen. 3:16).

III. Her conceptions by Adam
  A. First son—Cain (Gen. 4:1)—Eve's statement: "I have gotten a man from the LORD."
  B. Second son—Abel (Gen. 4:2)—Eve's statement: Not recorded
  C. Third son—Seth (Gen. 4:25)—Eve's statement: "God . . . hath appointed me another seed instead of Abel, whom Cain slew."

THEOLOGICAL SUMMARY

I. Jesus referred to Adam and Eve during his comments on the sanctity of marriage (Matt. 19:4).
II. Paul referred to Eve on two occasions.
  A. He warned the Corinthian believers that they were in danger of being deceived by the serpent's cunning devices, as was Eve (2 Cor. 11:3).
  B. He explained the divine rationale for placing the man over the woman. "Adam was first formed, then Eve. And Adam was not deceived, but the woman being deceived was in the transgression" (1 Tim. 2:13-14).

STATISTICS

Father: God/Adam (Gen. 2:22)
Mother: God/Adam (Gen. 2:22)
Spouse: Adam (Gen. 2:23-25)
Sons: Cain, Abel, Seth, and unnamed sons (Gen. 4:1-2, 25; 5:4)
Daughters: Several unnamed daughters (Gen. 5:4)
First mention: Genesis 3:20
Final mention: 1 Timothy 2:13
Meaning of her name: "Life, life-giving"
Frequency of her name: Referred to four times
Biblical books mentioning her: Three books (Genesis, 2 Corinthians, 1 Timothy)
Place of birth: Inside the Garden of Eden (Gen. 2:15, 21-22)

Important fact about her life: She was history's first woman and the first human to fall to temptation (Gen. 2:22; 1 Tim. 2:14).

✎ Ezekiel

CHRONOLOGICAL SUMMARY

I. The sanctification of the man of God—Ezekiel
   A. Ezekiel saw the vision of the living creatures (1:1-28). These creatures were identified later as the Cherubims (see 10:20).
      1. Each Cherubim had four faces.
         a. The face in front was as a man.
         b. The face on the right was as a lion.
         c. The face on the left was as an ox.
         d. The face in the back was as an eagle.
      2. Each had two pairs of wings.
         a. One pair spread out from the middle of the back.
         b. The other pair was used to cover the body.
      3. They had legs as of men, but cloven like calves' feet, which shone like burnished brass.
      4. They had four human hands, with one located under each wing.
      5. They apparently traveled in groups of four, and could move with the speed of light.
      6. A whirling wheel, sparkling like a precious stone and full of eyes on its rim, stood next to each creature.
   B. Ezekiel heard the voice of the living God (2-3, 33).
      1. He was to become a watchman for God (2:1-3; 3:17-21—also, see chapters 18, 24).
      2. He was to feed upon the Word of God (3:1-3).
      3. He was anointed by the Spirit of God (3:12, 14).
      4. He was allowed to see the glory of God (3:23).
      5. He was, however, for awhile unable to speak for God because God had struck him dumb (3:26; 24:27; 33:21-22).

II. The desolation of the city of God—Jerusalem
   A. There were three distinct phases in the Babylonian Captivity and the siege of Jerusalem.
      1. In 605 B.C.—At this time Daniel and other individuals of noble birth were carried away (Dan. 1:3-4; 2 Chron. 36:6-7).
      2. In 597 B.C.—During this phase both King Jehoiachin and Ezekiel, along with many others, were taken into Babylon (2 Kings 24:10-16).
      3. In 586 B.C.—At this final time Judah's last king, Zedekiah, was carried away, the walls of Jerusalem were destroyed, and both the temple and the city were burned (2 Kings 25:1-7). The events recorded in Ezekiel 4–24 took place between the second and third phase. Apparently there were false prophets, both in Jerusalem and Babylon, who brazenly assured the Jews that God would not dare destroy his own city, even though it had already suffered two bitter sieges. But Ezekiel knew otherwise, and he attempted through symbolic parables, dramatic acts, and messages to warn all that the Holy City would indeed suffer desolation and destruction.
   B. Ezekiel's 13 symbolic acts
      1. Drawing a map of Jerusalem with enemy camps around it—He drew a map of Jerusalem on a large flat tablet of soft clay, showing siege mounds being built against the city. He then added more details, portraying the enemy camps around it, and the placement of

the battering rams. He finally placed an iron plate between the map and himself. This was to indicate the impenetrable wall of the Babylonian army, and also to show the impossibility of escape (4:1-3).

2. Lying a few hours a day for 390 days on his left side—He lay on his left side a few hours each day for 390 days, to symbolize the iniquity of the Northern Kingdom. Each day was to represent a year (4:4-5).
3. Lying a few hours a day for 40 days on his right side—He then lay on his right side a few hours each day for 40 days, to depict the iniquity of Judah, the Southern Kingdom. Again, each day was to represent a year (4:6).
4. Preparing a scant meal with mixed grains and baked over cow dung—He prepared bread made with mixed grains and baked it over dried cow dung which had been set afire. This was to indicate the scarcity of food in Jerusalem (4:9-17).
5. Shaving his head and beard—He shaved his head and beard with a sharp knife and a razor, and then divided the hair into three equal parts (5:1-4).
   a. A third he burned.
   b. A third he cut up with the sword.
   c. A third he scattered to the wind.
   d. All this was to indicate what was in store for Judah and Jerusalem: one third of her citizens would die by fire in the Jerusalem siege; one third of the people would fall by the sword; and the remaining one third would be scattered to the wind.
6. Stamping his feet and clapping his hands—He was to stamp his feet and clap his hands to get the Jews' attention (6:11).
7. Digging an entrance through the city wall—He set some scant baggage outside his home. Then in the evening he dug an escape hole through the city wall. As he went through it carrying the baggage, he also covered his face. This was to vividly symbolize the following (12:1-16):
   a. The few articles of baggage represented the exiles hurriedly departing their homes.
   b. The hole in the wall symbolized their desperation to leave the doomed city of Jerusalem.
   c. The covered face depicted Zedekiah, Judah's last king, who was blinded by Nebuchadnezzar because of his rebellion, and led captive into Babylon (2 Kings 25:1-7).
8. Trembling as he ate his food (12:17-20)
9. Weeping in public (21:1-7)
10. Slashing a sword about (21:9-17)
11. Drawing a map of the Middle East with two routes on it—He drew a map of the Middle East and traced two routes for the king of Babylon to follow. One led to Jerusalem, and the other to Rabbath-Ammon. Both cities had rebelled against Nebuchadnezzar in 593 B.C. Ezekiel pictured the king here at the crossroads. Which city would be destroyed first? The sad answer is immediately forthcoming (21:18-22). "He made his arrows bright, he consulted with images, he looked in the liver. At his right hand was the divination for Jerusalem, to appoint captains, to open the mouth in the slaughter, to lift up the voice with shouting, to appoint battering rams against the gates, to cast a mount, and to build a fort" (21:21-22).

12. Boiling a pot of water until it baked itself dry—He filled a pot of boiling water with the choicest of meats and cooked it until the flesh fell off the bones. He then threw it all out and allowed the pot to bake itself dry to eliminate the scum and rust (24:1-14). Here, of course, the symbolism is clear. The judgment fire of God would utterly consume even the rich and noble of Jerusalem. All of its citizens would be cast out of the land, that his holy city might be cleansed of their moral scum and rust.

13. Remaining tearless at the funeral of his own wife—He was forbidden to express any outward sorrow over the sudden death of his beloved wife (24:15-18). "I spake unto the people in the morning: and at even my wife died; and I did in the morning as I was commanded" (24:18). God ordered him not to mourn over the death of his wife to emphasize that he, the Lord, would not mourn over Jerusalem's death. It is especially significant to observe that she died the very day that Nebuchadnezzar began his third and final assault upon Jerusalem (24:2).

C. Ezekiel's 12 judgment messages: 6:1-14; 7:1-27; 13:1-23; 14:1-12; 14:13-23; 18:1-32; 20:1-44; 20:45-49; 21:1-7; 22:1-16; 22:17-22; 22:23-31. A brief summary of Ezekiel's main points in these sermons:

   1. God had often held back his divine wrath in spite of Israel's brazen disobedience (20:7-10, 13, 21-22).
   2. God took no joy in judging his people even at this desperate stage, and again called for Judah's repentance (18:31-32).
   3. Judah would not listen, and her hour of doom was now at hand (7:6, 12; 12:26-28).
   4. Judah would then be destroyed, not because of the sins of their fathers, but because of their own vile wickedness (18:1-4, 20).
      a. Their prophets were wicked (13:1-16; 22:25, 28).
      b. Their princes were wicked (22:6, 27).
      c. Their priests were wicked (22:26).
      d. Their women were wicked (13:17-23).
   5. Even the presence of such godly men as Noah, Daniel, and Job could not spare the city of Jerusalem (14:14, 20).
   6. Her armies would be absolutely helpless in defending her (7:14).
   7. Her wealth could not purchase one additional minute of freedom (7:19).
   8. The Holy City of God had now become the harlot city of Satan.
   9. God would therefore bring into Jerusalem the worst of nations and people to occupy their lands and homes (7:24).
   10. Judah's cities would be burned, her idols smashed, and her temple destroyed (5:11; 6:4, 6; 7:24; 24:21).
   11. Four great punishments would fall upon her citizens: war, famine, ferocious beasts, and plagues (14:21).
   12. A remnant, however, would survive to testify of God's holiness and hatred for sin (6:8-10; 12:16; 14:22-23).

D. Ezekiel's six parables
   1. A fruitless vine tree (15:1-8)
   2. The adopted girl who became a harlot (16:1-63)
      a. God's concern for Israel
         (1) God had found in a field an abandoned, despised, and dying baby girl. Her name

was Israel (16:1-5). This is a
reference to Israel's bondage
to the Egyptians in the first
few chapters of Exodus (see
especially Exod. 1:13-14;
2:23; 3:7).

(2) God graciously adopted this
ragged little girl, and when
she came of age, he entered
into the sacred rite of marriage with her, and she le-
gally became his elected wife
(16:6-8).

(3) This, of course, all took
place at Mt. Sinai when God
ratified his covenant with
Israel (see Exod. 19:5; also
compare Ezek. 16:9 with
Exod. 19:14).

(4) After the marriage, God
dressed her in the most
beautiful clothes, adorned
her with the most costly
jewels, and provided the
finest food available for his
beloved (16:10-14).

(5) This occurred in Israel's history during the reigns of David and Solomon (see 2 Sam.
8:11; 1 Kings 3:13; 10:4-7).

b. Israel's contempt for God

(1) This little ex-orphan soon
spurned all his love and
faithfulness and became a
common harlot of the streets
(16:15-34).

(2) This intolerable action could
not continue unpunished,
for the beloved Husband
was also the righteous
Judge. He would, therefore,
turn her over to her own
murderous lovers to be
abused and punished (16:36-
41).

(3) Her wickedness by this time
had surpassed even that of
her older sister (Samaria, the
capital of the Northern Kingdom) and of her younger

sister (Sodom) (see Ezek.
16:46-51).

(4) After he had chastened her,
God would once again re-
store her to himself, because
of his love for her and his
promise to Abraham (16:53,
60, 63).

3. The two eagles—The events mentioned in this parable narrate the
international affairs of Judah, Babylon, and Egypt between 597 and
588 B.C. The figures involved are
Jehoiachin, Zedekiah, and Nebuchadnezzar (17:1-21). (For the recorded history of this period, see
2 Kings 24:8-20; 2 Chron. 36:9-13;
Jer. 37; 52:1-11.)

4. The tender twig (17:22-24)

a. The twig's growth—God himself stated he would someday
plant the finest and most tender twig of all upon Israel's
highest mountain (17:22). This
twig would grow into a noble
tree, blessing all who came near
it by its fruit and shade (17:23).

b. The twig's glory—Through all
this, the entire world would
know the plan and power of
God (17:24). These verses without question introduce a messi-
anic prophecy (see Isa. 2:2-4;
Mic. 4:1-4). The tender twig is
the Messiah (see Isa. 11:1; 53:2;
Jer. 23:5, 6; 33:15; Zech. 6:12;
Rev. 22:16) and the high mountain is Mount Zion (see Ps. 2:6).

5. The mother lioness and her cubs
(19:1-9)

a. A mother lioness had some
cubs. One of her whelps grew
up and learned to devour men.
For this he was trapped and
taken into Egypt (19:1-4).

b. Another of her cubs did the
same thing. He also was captured and carried away into
Babylon (19:5-9).

c. Some believe the mother

lioness here was Hamutal, the wife of Josiah, and mother of three Judean kings. The first cub was Jehoahaz (2 Kings 23:31-34), who was carried away into an Egyptian prison by Pharaoh Necho. The other cub was Zedekiah (Hamutal's youngest son). He was Judah's last king and was carried away by Nebuchadnezzar into Babylon (2 Kings 24:18–25:7).

6. The two harlot sisters (23:1-49)
   a. Their sin—two sisters began their sad history of prostitution by engaging in immorality with the Egyptians (23:1-3).
   b. Their symbolism—The names of these girls were Aholah and Aholibah, and they are identified as Samaria and Jerusalem (23:4).
      (1) The word Aholah means "her tent" and may be a reference to the fact that God never approved of the false religion of Samaria (capital of the Northern Kingdom) as instituted by its first king, Jeroboam (see 1 Kings 12:25-33). Thus, "her tent" meant she had her own religion which did not include God.
      (2) The word Aholibah means "my tent is in her," indicating perhaps that God's presence still dwelt in the Jerusalem temple in spite of Judah's sin. It is said here that both girls became harlots because of their Egyptian immorality. This may refer to the fact that both cities were impressed with the religious and political structures of Egypt. Aholah then began illicit relations with Assyria (23:5). This happened under Northern Israel's King Menahem, who

allied himself with Assyria (see 2 Kings 15:13-20). Aholibah did the same thing with Babylon (23:11). King Hezekiah treated the Babylonian representatives almost as if they were gods (see 2 Kings 20:12-19; 2 Chron. 32:31).
   c. Their sentence—God, therefore, determined to turn both sisters over to the full brutality of their respective lovers (23:9, 22, 24).

E. Ezekiel's extended temple vision (8–11).
   1. The departure of Judah from the glory of God
      a. Ezekiel was caught away in a vision from Babylon to Jerusalem (8:1-3).
      b. He saw 70 Israelite elders worshiping satanic images in the temple (8:4-12). "I went in and saw; and behold every form of creeping things, and abominable beasts, and all the idols of the house of Israel, pourtrayed upon the wall round about" (8:10).
      c. He saw some Jewish women weeping for the false Babylonian god Tammuz (8:13-14).
      d. He saw about 25 men with their backs to the temple, facing east and worshiping the sun (8:15-16).
      e. He saw six angels with weapons, one of whom had writing tools, go through Jerusalem at God's command killing all but those whom the one angel marked to be spared (9:1-11).
   2. The departure of the glory of God from Judah
      a. He viewed the glory cloud over the mercy seat (9:3).
      b. It then stood over the door of the temple (10:4).
      c. From there it moved to the east gate (10:18-19).

d. Finally it hovered over the Mt. of Olives and Ezekiel was returned to his home (11:23-24).
III. The condemnation of the enemies of God
A. Ammon—Their sin was the devilish glee they displayed over the destruction of the Jerusalem temple and the death of Judah's citizens (25:1-7).
B. Moab—They had degraded Jehovah, looking upon him as just another national and tribal god (25:8-11).
C. Edom—This nation had butchered helpless Jews during the Babylonian invasion (25:12-14; 35:1-15).
D. Philistia (25:15-17)—Revenge and vengeance
E. Tyre (26:1–28:19)
  1. The sin of Tyre
    a. Tyre had rejoiced over the fall of Judah (26:2).
    b. The city was totally corrupted with gross materialism (27:4-25).
  2. The ruler of Tyre—The ruler at the time Ezekiel wrote was Ithbaal II, who boasted he was as strong as a god and wiser than a Daniel (28:2-5).
  3. The punishment of Tyre—Perhaps here it should be noted that Tyre was actually two cities, one on the coastline some 60 miles northwest of Jerusalem, and the other on an island, a half mile out in the Mediterranean Sea. At the time of Ezekiel's prophecy, the Tyrians were in open revolt against Babylon.
    a. Various nations were to come up against Tyre like ocean waves (26:3).
    b. In spite of Tyre's strong watery protection, Ezekiel predicted her walls would be torn down and her very soil be scrapped, making her as bare as a rock; and both cities would become a place for the spreading of fishing nets (26:3-5).

c. The city would never again be inhabited (26:20-21). All this occurred later, during the days of Alexander the Great, exactly as Ezekiel had prophesied.
  4. The sinister force behind Tyre (28:11-19)
    a. The identity of this force—We have already noted that in 28:2-5 Ezekiel describes the pride of Ithbaal II, who was ruler of Tyre at that time. But the prophet now moves beyond the earthly scene and describes for us the creation and fall of a vile and vicious nonhuman angelic creature. This fearful being is Satan himself, the real force behind the wickedness of Tyre.
    b. The characteristics of this force—Satan, prior to his fall, was the sum total of wisdom and beauty.
      (1) He was the anointed cherub.
      (2) He had been in Eden.
      (3) He was covered with precious stones.
      (4) He was equipped with musical instruments.
      (5) He fell through pride.
F. Sidon (28:20-24)—Rebellion against God
G. Egypt (29:1–32:32)
  1. Her historical punishment (by Nebuchadnezzar)
    a. Egypt's sin, like that of so many other nations, was pride (29:3, 6).
    b. Ezekiel, therefore, pronounced doom upon Pharaoh, the people, and even the animals (29:8-12).
    c. In chapter 31, Egypt is described as a mighty cedar of Lebanon, towering above all other trees. The birds rested in its branches, and animals gave birth under its shade. But soon the tree was corrupted by pride and God ordered the

Babylonian wood choppers to hew it down.

d. Ezekiel informed us that Nebuchadnezzar conquered Egypt for its wealth in order to pay his soldiers after their long siege of Tyre (29:17-21).

e. Egypt was to be desolate for 40 years (29:9, 11).

f. After the 40-year punishment period, Egypt would be restored somewhat, but would forever remain a minor kingdom (29:13-15).

g. Israel would never again depend upon Egypt (29:16).

2. Her future punishment (by God) (30:1-19)—Although the name Nebuchadnezzar appears in this passage (v. 10), it is thought that the final fulfillment of the judgments mentioned here will transpire during the tribulation. According to Daniel (11:40-43), Egypt will be destroyed during the Tribulation.

IV. The presentation of the Shepherd of God—Jesus Christ

A. The many false shepherds (34:1-10)

1. They fed themselves instead of the flock (34:2-3).

2. They had not taken care of the weak, nor tended the sick, nor bound up the broken bones, nor sought the lost (34:4).

3. The sheep were then scattered, having no shepherd (34:5-6).

4. They had become prey to the wild animals (34:5).

5. Therefore, the shepherd would be punished (34:7-9).

a. Their positions as shepherds would be removed (34:10).

b. They would not themselves be fed by the Great Shepherd (34:9-10).

c. They would be judged and destroyed (34:16).

B. The one true Shepherd (34:11-31)

1. He would search out the lost sheep (34:11).

2. He would deliver them from their enemies (34:12).

3. He would gather them from all nations (34:13).

4. He would feed them upon the mountains of Israel (34:14).

5. He would give them rest in green pastures (34:15).

6. He would put splints and bandages upon their broken limbs (34:16).

7. He would heal their sick (34:16).

8. He would establish David as his trusted undershepherd (34:23). (See also Ezek. 37:24; Jer. 30:9; Hos. 3:5.)

9. He would make an eternal pact with them (34:25).

10. He would guarantee their safety and place them in a perfect paradise (34:25-28).

V. The restoration of the nation of God—Israel

A. The necessity of this restoration—Israel had been previously driven from Palestine because of their sin (36:17-19).

B. The reasons for this restoration

1. To shame those Gentile nations which had sneered at Israel's tragedy (36:1-7).

2. To exonerate the great name of God (36:20-23, 32). The rumor was being spread around that the God of Israel was unable (or unwilling) to protect and purify his own people.

C. The vision of this restoration (37:1-14)

1. Ezekiel was commanded to prophesy over a valley filled with old dry human bones, scattered everywhere (37:1-6).

2. Suddenly there was a rattling noise from all across the valley and the bones of each body came together and attached to each

other as they had once been
(37:7).

3. After this, the muscles and flesh
formed over the bones, and skin
covered them (37:8).

4. But the completed bodies had no
breath. Ezekiel was then commanded to prophesy over them to
give them breath. This he did
(37:9-13).

D. The symbol of this restoration (37:15-
22)

1. Ezekiel was to carve the following
words on two wooden sticks:

a. The first stick read: "For Judah,
and for the children of Israel
his companions" (37:16).

b. The second stick read: "For Joseph, the stick of Ephraim, and
for all the house of Israel his
companions" (37:16).

2. He was then to hold both sticks
together in one hand, indicating
the two kingdoms would someday be united again (37:17-22).

E. The results of this restoration

1. To once again become God's people (36:28; 37:27)—"Ye shall dwell
in the land that I gave to your fathers; and ye shall be my people,
and I will be your God" (36:28).
"My tabernacle also shall be with
them: yea, I will be their God,
and they shall be my people"
(37:27).

2. To be sprinkled by clear water
(36:25, 29, 33)—This, of course,
was an allusion to the Mosaic rite
of purification (see Num. 19:17-
19).

3. To possess the ministry of the in-
dwelling Holy Spirit (36:27; 37:14)

4. To be given new hearts and right
desires (36:26)

5. To enjoy the blessings of the new
temple (37:26-28)

6. To be ruled over by David (37:24-
25)

7. To be justified among the nations
(36:30)

8. To have abundant crops (36:29-30,
34-35)

9. To repopulate the cities of Israel,
especially Jerusalem (36:28)

10. To occupy the Holy Land forever
(37:25) (See also 11:16-17; 20:34;
28:25; 34:11-13)

VI. The demonstration of the wrath of
God—Russia

A. The identity of the invaders—In the
remarkable chapters of Ezekiel 38 and
39, the prophet described for us an
invasion into Palestine by a wicked
nation north of Israel in the latter
days. "Son of man, set thy face
against Gog, the land of Magog, the
chief prince of Meshech and Tubal,
and prophesy against him, And say,
Thus saith the Lord God: Behold, I
am against thee, O Gog, the chief
prince of Meshech and Tubal" (38:2-3).

B. The allies in the invasion—These will
be Persia, Ethiopia, Libya, Gomer,
and Togarmah (38:5-6).

C. The reason for the invasion—"I will
go . . . to take a spoil, and to take a
prey" (38:11-12).

D. The destruction of the invaders—The
nation will be totally defeated upon
the mountains of Israel. This smash-
ing defeat will be effected by the following events, caused by God
himself:

1. A mighty earthquake (38:19-20)

2. Mutiny among the troops (38:21)

3. A plague among the troops (38:22)

4. Floods, great hailstones, fire and
brimstone (38:22; 39:6)

E. The results of the invasion

1. That five-sixths (83 percent) of the
soldiers will be destroyed (39:2).

2. That the first grisly feast of God
will begin (39:4, 17-18, 19-20). A
similar feast would seem to take
place later, after the battle of Armageddon (Matt. 24:28; Rev.
19:17-18).

3. That the nation's threat will cease forever.
4. That seven months will be spent in burying the dead (39:11-15).
5. That seven years will be spent in burning the weapons of war (39:9-10).

VII. The manifestation of the glory of God—the temple
A. Its dimensions (40–42; 43:13-18)
B. Its purpose
   1. To provide a dwelling place for the cloud of glory (43:1-6)
   2. To provide a center for the King of Glory (43:7)
C. Its priesthood—The sons of Zadok will be the priests (see 40:46; 43:19; 44:15; 48:11). Zadok was the high priest in the days of King David.
D. Its prince—In his description of the temple, Ezekiel referred to a mysterious "prince" some 17 times (45:7-8, 17; 46:1-20). Whoever he is, he will occupy a very important role in the temple itself, apparently holding an intermediary place between the people and the priesthood. We are sure that he is not Christ, since he prepares a sin offering for himself (45:22), is married, and has sons (46:16). Some suggest that the prince is from the seed of King David, and that he will be to David what the false prophet was to the Antichrist.
E. Its unique features—Several articles and objects present in the temples of Moses, Solomon, and Herod will be absent from the millennial temple.
   1. There will be no veil.
   2. There will be no table of shewbread.
   3. There will be no lampstands.
   4. There will be no Ark of the Covenant.
   5. The east gate will be closed (44:2). This gate, it has been suggested, will remain closed for the following reasons:
      a. This will be the gate by which the Lord Jesus Christ enters the temple. As a mark of honor to an eastern king, no person could enter the gate by which he entered.
      b. It was from the eastern gate that the glory of God departed for the last time in the Old Testament (10:18-19). By sealing the gate, God will remind all those within that his glory will never again depart from his people.
F. Its sacrifices—As we have already seen, several pieces of furniture in the Old Testament temple will be missing in the millennial edifice. However, the brazen altar of sacrifice will again be present. There are at least four Old Testament prophecies which speak of animal sacrifices in the millennial temple (Isa. 46:6-7; 60:7; Jer. 33:18; Zech. 14:16-21). But why the need of these animal blood sacrifices during the golden age of the Millennium? They will function as:
   1. A reminder to all of the necessity of the new birth
   2. An object lesson of the costliness of salvation
   3. An example of the awfulness of sin
   4. An illustration of the holiness of God
G. Its river (47:1-12)
   1. The source of the river—It will proceed from beneath the temple (47:1).
   2. The course of the river—It will flow eastward and then south through the desert and Jordan River to the Dead Sea, where its sweet waters will purify that lifeless body of polluted water (47:1, 7, 9, 12).
   3. The force of the river—At first it reached Ezekiel's ankles, then his knees, after this his waist, and finally he swam into its unknown depths (47:3-5).
H. Its glory cloud (43:1-5)—"The glory of

the LORD came into the house by the way of the gate whose prospect is toward the east. So the spirit took me up, and brought me into the inner court; and, behold, the glory of the LORD filled the house" (43:4-5).

I. Its city
1. Jerusalem will become the worship center of the world and will occupy an elevated site (Zech. 14:10; see also Isa. 2:2-3).
2. The city will be six miles in circumference (Ezek. 48:35). In the time of Christ the city was about four miles. There will be 12 gates in the city wall. Each will be named for one of the 12 Israelite tribes.
3. The city will be named "Jehovah-Shammah," meaning "the LORD is there" (Ezek. 48:35).

THEOLOGICAL SUMMARY

I. Ezekiel recorded that God spoke to him personally on at least 90 occasions, more than any other biblical writer.
II. On each of these occasions, God referred to Ezekiel as "son of man."
III. Ezekiel knew of Daniel and mentioned him on two occasions.
   A. Referring to Daniel's righteousness (14:14, 20)
   B. Referring to Daniel's wisdom (28:3)
IV. Ezekiel had much to say about the glory cloud of God.
   A. He saw its removal (10:18).
   B. He saw its return (43:2).
V. Ezekiel can be compared to Hosea.
   A. Hosea depicted Israel as God's untrue and adulterous wife (Hos. 2:1–3:5).
   B. Ezekiel depicted Israel as God's ungrateful and immoral adopted orphan daughter (16).
VI. Ezekiel 34 can be compared to John 10. Both chapters speak of the characteristics of true and false shepherds.

STATISTICS

Father: Buzi (Ezek. 1:3)
Spouse: Unnamed wife (Ezek. 24:18)

First mention: Ezekiel 1:3
Final mention: Ezekiel 24:24
Meaning of his name: "God is strong"
Frequency of his name: Referred to 93 times
Biblical books mentioning him: One book (Ezekiel)
Occupation: Priest and prophet (Ezek. 1:3; 2:3-4)
Place of birth: Judah
Place of death: Babylon
Important fact about his life: He provided the most complete description of the Cherubim and millennial temple in the entire Bible (Ezek. 1:5-24; 41-44).

Ezra

CHRONOLOGICAL SUMMARY

I. First return trip
   A. Zerubbabel leading—This occurred before Ezra's time and is an historical account (1–6).
   B. The king proclaiming
      1. The decree—God placed a desire in Cyrus's heart to issue his return decree (1:2-3). "Thus saith Cyrus king of Persia, The LORD God of heaven hath given me all the kingdoms of the earth; and he hath charged me to build him an house at Jerusalem, which is in Judah. Who is there among you of all his people? his God be with him, and let him go up to Jerusalem, which is in Judah, and build the house of the LORD God of Israel, (he is the God,) which is in Jerusalem" (Ezra 1:2-3).
      2. The decision—A remnant of the Jews in captivity, some 42,360 (2:64), responded to this decree and began the trip to Jerusalem, carrying with them 5,400 golden and silver vessels Nebuchadnezzar had taken from the temple. They also took: the Urim and Thummim (2:63); 7,337 servants (2:65); 200 singers (2:65); 736

horses (2:66); 245 mules (2:66); 435 camels (2:67); 6,720 donkeys (2:67); 277,500 ounces of gold, worth approximately $100 million (2:69); 6250 pounds of silver, worth approximately $1.5 million (2:69); and 100 priestly garments (2:69).

3. The dedication
   a. Upon reaching Jerusalem, the altar was built and the Mosaic sacrificial system led by Jeshua (also called Joshua) was reinstituted. He was the grandson of Judah's last high priest before the Babylonian Captivity.
      (1) The altar was erected on the first day of the seventh month, which was the beginning of the Feast of Trumpets (3:6).
      (2) The Feast of Tabernacles (Booths) was then celebrated, from the fifteenth to the twenty-second of the seventh month (3:4; also Lev. 23:34-36).
   b. In June of 535 B.C. a most unusual temple groundbreaking ceremony was held (3:10-13).
      (1) Some of the people sang— These were of the younger generations, born in captivity, who now had a temple of their own for the first time.
      (2) Some of the people sorrowed—These were of the older generation, born in Jerusalem, who had seen the great temple of Solomon, and now compared it with the much smaller one being dedicated.

C. The devil, defaming—Satan tried his best to prevent the temple from going up.
   1. He tried accommodation (4:1-3).
      a. The request by the enemies of Judah—"Let us build with you:

for we seek your God, as ye do" (4:2).
      b. The rejection by the allies of Judah—Zerubbabel, Joshua, and the Jewish elders refused this request, knowing their enemies also worshiped idols.
   2. He tried intimidation—"Then the people of the land weakened the hands of the people of Judah, and troubled them in building" (4:4).
   3. He tried accusation (4:5-24).
      a. Their enemies hired counselors to frustrate them.
      b. They also wrote letters to slander them.

D. The Lord, sustaining—In spite of all this, God was at work.
   1. Both Haggai and Zechariah began their comforting ministries at this time (5:1-2).
   2. After Judah's enemies had stopped the work on the temple for awhile, it was continued and completed on March 12, 515 B.C. (6:15).
      a. The enemy officials wrote a letter to King Darius, requesting a search be made among the Persian records to validate the Jewish claim that King Cyrus had once issued the official permission to rebuild their temple (5:3-17).
      b. A search was made and the decree was discovered (6:1-5).
      c. Darius then sent orders not only for the temple work to continue, but for the local Persian officials to help finance it (6:6-12).
      d. The completed temple was then dedicated (6:16).
      e. The Passover was observed on April 14, 515 B.C. (6:19).

II. Second return trip
   A. The leadership from Ezra—This occurred during Ezra's time and is a biographical account (7–10). There is a period of some 60 years between

chapters 6 and 7 of Ezra. During this time Ezra was born. Thus, the first part of his book is historical (1–6), while the final part is biographical (7-10). "Ezra went up from Babylon; and he was a ready scribe in the law of Moses, which the LORD God of Israel had given: and the king granted him all his request, according to the hand of the LORD his God upon him. . . . For Ezra had prepared his heart to seek the law of the LORD, and to do it, and to teach in Israel statutes and judgments" (7:6, 10).

B. The cooperation from the king (Artaxerxes)—He greatly aided this second return by issuing an official letter addressed to three parties (7).

1. To all Jews in Babylon, encouraging them to return (7:11-20)

2. To all Persian officials west of the Euphrates River to help with the return (7:21-24)

   a. They were to contribute to the upkeep of the temple (7:21-23).

   b. They were forbidden to impose tax upon the temple (7:24).

3. To Ezra himself (7:25-28)—"I was strengthened as the hand of the LORD my God was upon me, and I gathered together out of Israel chief men to go up with me" (7:28).

C. The preparation for the trip (8)—Ezra left in March of 457 B.C. with approximately 5,000 people. They arrived in August of that year, carrying over $20 million with them (8:24-31).

1. A quick census taken en route several days after leaving for Jerusalem revealed that no Levites had joined the group (8:15).

2. A special delegation sent back by Ezra convinced 40 Levites to go (8:16-20).

3. Ezra proclaimed a fast by the Ahava River (8:21). "I was ashamed to require of the king a band of soldiers and horsemen to help us against the enemy in the

way: because we had spoken unto the king, saying, The hand of our God is upon all them for good that seek him; but his power and his wrath is against all them that forsake him. So we fasted and besought our God for this: and he was intreated of us" (8:22-23).

D. The supplication of the scribe (9)

1. Ezra soon learned that the Jews already in the Holy City had compromised their testimony by practicing heathen customs and even marrying pagan women (9:1-2).

2. The great Bible teacher immediately went into deep mourning and poured out his soul to God concerning this tragic situation (9:3-15).

   a. His pain—"When I heard this thing, I rent my garment and my mantle, and plucked off the hair of my head and of my beard, and sat down astonied" (9:3).

   b. His prayer

      (1) He acknowledged the former sins of Israel (9:6-7).

      (2) He acknowledged the present sins of Israel (9:10-15).

      (3) He acknowledged the continuous grace of God (9:8-9).

E. The purification of the people (10)

1. Soon conviction of sin settled down upon the hearts of the leaders. "When Ezra had prayed, and when he had confessed, weeping and casting himself down before the house of God, there assembled unto him out of Israel a very great congregation of men and women and children: for the people wept very sore" (10:1).

2. A proclamation went out throughout all Judah (10:3, 7, 9).

   a. The resolution—That the men of Israel make a covenant with God, agreeing to put away all their pagan wives

b. The response—"All the men of Judah and Benjamin gathered themselves together unto Jerusalem within three days. It was the ninth month, on the twentieth day of the month; and all the people sat in the street of the house of God, trembling because of this matter, and for the great rain" (10:9).

3. Upon hearing Ezra's sermon, the men agreed to dismiss their heathen wives (10:10-12).

THEOLOGICAL SUMMARY

I. Ezra's singular ministry
A. Ezra began his ministry in Persia under King Artaxerxes (7:1).
B. He was a priest (7:11; Neh. 12:26).
C. Ezra was also a gifted Bible teacher, well versed in the Law of Moses and given over totally to the proclamation of the Word of God (7:6, 10).
D. Ezra led the second of three Jewish returns from Persia to Judah.

II. Ezra's cooperative ministry
A. Several years later he was joined by Nehemiah the prophet (Neh. 2:11).
B. Standing on a high wooden platform in Jerusalem, Ezra read God's Word to the people assembled before the Water Gate from daybreak till noon (Neh. 8:1-4).
C. He then exhorted the people to rejoice upon hearing the Law of Moses and instructed them concerning how to celebrate the Feast of Tabernacles (Neh. 8:9, 12-17).
D. For a total of seven days Ezra continued his public reading from the Scriptures (Neh. 8:18).
E. Ezra then helped lead the musical celebration following the completion of the wall around Jerusalem (Neh. 12:27, 36).

STATISTICS

Father: Seraiah (Ezra 7:1)
Significant ancestors: Zadok and Aaron (Ezra 7:1-5)

First mention: Ezra 7:1
Final mention: Nehemiah 12:36
Meaning of his name: "Help"
Frequency of his name: Referred to 24 times
Biblical books mentioning him: Two books (Ezra, Nehemiah)
Occupation: Prophet, priest, scribe, teacher of the Law
Place of birth: Persia
Place of death: Jerusalem
Important fact about his life: He led the second (of three) Jewish returns from Persia to Jerusalem.

Gad

CHRONOLOGICAL SUMMARY

I. His revelation to David
A. Before David became king—He advised him to leave the cave of Adullam where David had been staying and return to the land of Judah (1 Sam. 22:5).
B. After David became king
1. He told David that God would allow him to choose one of three kinds of punishment after the king's sin of numbering the people (2 Sam. 24:11-14).
2. After the fulfillment of God's punishment, Gad informed David that the Lord wanted the king to build an altar on the threshing floor owned by Araunah (also called Ornan) the Jebusite (2 Sam. 24:16-19; 1 Chron. 21:18-19).

II. His record about David—Along with the prophets Samuel and Nathan, Gad later recorded the life and times of King David (1 Chron. 29:29, 30).

STATISTICS

First mention: 1 Samuel 22:5
Final mention: 2 Chronicles 29:25
Meaning of his name: "Seer, fortune"
Frequency of his name: Referred to 13 times
Biblical books mentioning him: Four books

(1 Samuel, 2 Samuel, 1 Chronicles, 2 Chronicles)

Occupation: Prophet (1 Sam. 22:5)

Important fact about his life: He ministered to David during the plague of the death angel (1 Chron. 21).

✐Gedaliah

CHRONOLOGICAL SUMMARY

I. His appointment by Nebuchadnezzar
   A. Gedaliah and Jeremiah
      1. Gedaliah was the grandson of Shaphan, who was King Josiah's secretary (2 Kings 25:22).
      2. He was appointed by Babylonian King Nebuchadnezzar to be governor over Judah after the fall of Jerusalem (2 Kings 25:23).
      3. He made his headquarters at the city of Mizpah (2 Kings 25:23; Jer. 40:10).
      4. Nebuchadnezzar released Jeremiah the prophet, who had been imprisoned for his fearless preaching on sin during Judah's final days, and entrusted him to Gedaliah for safekeeping (Jer. 39:11-14; 40:5-6).
   B. Gedaliah and Johanan
      1. Gedaliah was warned by Johanan, an Israelite army officer, that another soldier named Ishmael had been hired by the Ammonite king to assassinate him (Jer. 40:13-14).
      2. Gedaliah, however, refused to believe this report (Jer. 40:14-16).
II. His assassination by Ishmael
   A. Gedaliah was killed by Ishmael at a banquet in Mizpah (Jer. 41:1-2).
   B. His lifeless body was then thrown into a cistern once made by Judean King Asa (Jer. 41:9).

STATISTICS

Father: Ahikam (2 Kings 25:22)
First mention: 2 Kings 25:22
Final mention: Jeremiah 43:6

Meaning of his name: "God is great"
Frequency of his name: Referred to 27 times
Biblical books mentioning him: Two books (2 Kings, Jeremiah)
Occupation: Governor of Judah (2 Kings 25:22)
Place of death: At a banquet in Mizpah (Jer. 41:1-2)
Circumstances of death: He was killed by Ishmael and 10 men (Jer. 41:1-2).
Important fact about his life: He was appointed governor by Nebuchadnezzar after the destruction of Jerusalem (2 Kings 25:22).

✐Gehazi

CHRONOLOGICAL SUMMARY

I. Gehazi, the faithful servant
   A. Gehazi suggested that Elisha his master ask God to bless the barren womb of a woman living in Shunem who had shown great kindness to them. Elisha prayed, and the woman had a son (2 Kings 4:8-17).
   B. Upon the death of the boy much later, Elisha instructed Gehazi to take the prophet's staff and lay it on the corpse of the child (2 Kings 4:29-31).
   C. Soon Elisha arrived upon the scene, raised the boy to life and told Gehazi to bring the mother to a glad reunion (2 Kings 4:32-36).
   D. Gehazi later related this miracle of Elisha to the king of Israel. At that same time he was able to put in a good word to the king concerning the Shunammite woman. As a result of this, the land she had lost after moving to Philistia for seven years was then restored by the king (2 Kings 8:1-6).
II. Gehazi, the frightened servant
   A. The desperation—Gehazi's city of Dothan was surrounded by enemy troops sent by the king of Syria to arrest both him and Elisha (2 Kings 6:13-14).

B. The declaration
1. Gehazi—"Alas, my master! how shall we do?" (2 Kings 6:15)
2. Elisha—"Fear not: for they that be with us are more than they that be with them" (2 Kings 6:16).
C. The demonstration
1. The request—"Elisha prayed, and said, LORD, I pray thee, open his eyes, that he may see" (2 Kings 6:17).
2. The revelation—"The LORD opened the eyes of the young man; and he saw: and, behold, the mountain was full of horses and chariots of fire round about Elisha" (2 Kings 6:17).
III. Gehazi, the faithless servant
A. He became greedy and obtained money under false pretense from Naaman, a soldier Elisha had previously healed of leprosy (2 Kings 5:19-25).
B. For this he was punished by suffering the same kind of leprosy Naaman once had (2 Kings 5:26-27).

STATISTICS
First mention: 2 Kings 4:12
Final mention: 2 Kings 8:5
Meaning of his name: "Denier, diminisher"
Frequency of his name: Referred to 12 times
Biblical books mentioning him: One book (2 Kings)
Occupation: Chief servant to the prophet Elisha (2 Kings 4:12)
Circumstances of death: He died a leper (2 Kings 5:25-27).
Important fact about his life: He was Elisha's servant who attempted to deceive him by secretly accepting a gift from Naaman (2 Kings 5:21-25).

Geshem

CHRONOLOGICAL SUMMARY
I. The hostility of Geshem
A. He was an Arabian.
B. He was the third member of a trou-
blesome trio in the days of Nehemiah. The other two were Sanballat and Tobiah (Neh. 2:19).
II. The harassment of Geshem—He attempted (unsuccessfully) through various methods of harassment to prevent Nehemiah from rebuilding the wall around Jerusalem.
A. Ridicule (Neh. 2:19)
B. Murder (Neh. 6:1-2)
C. Slander (Neh. 6:6)

STATISTICS
First mention: Nehemiah 2:19
Final mention: Nehemiah 6:6
Meaning of his name: "Rain"
Frequency of his name: Referred to three times
Biblical books mentioning him: One book (Nehemiah)
Important fact about his life: He was one of three troublemakers who opposed Nehemiah (Neh. 2:19).

Gideon

CHRONOLOGICAL SUMMARY
I. The Angel of the Lord
A. Gideon was from the tribe of Manasseh.
B. An angel of God appeared to him under an oak tree in the city of Ophrah as he threshed wheat in a winepress to keep it from the Midianites (Judg. 6:11-12).
C. The angel commissioned him to raise up an army and defeat the Midianites (Judg. 6:13-16).
II. The altars
A. Building up an altar to God
1. Gideon offered up an animal sacrifice before the angel, who caused supernatural fire to consume it (Judg. 6:17-23).
2. He then built an altar and called it Jehovah-shalom, meaning "the Lord is Peace" (Judg. 6:24).
B. Tearing down an altar to Baal
1. That night God instructed him to

tear down his father's pagan altar
to Baal and replace it with an altar
to God, which he did (Judg. 6:25-
27).

2. Because of this, Gideon received
the nickname "Jerubbaal", meaning, "let Baal contend" (Judg. 6:32).

III. The anointing—The Spirit of God came
upon Gideon, and he blew a trumpet,
summoning an army from the tribes of
Manasseh, Asher, Zebulun, and Naphtali (Judg. 6:33-35).

IV. The assurance—Still needing God's reassurance, Gideon asked for and received two specific signs, both having to
do with a wool fleece he planned to
place on the threshing floor.

A. Wet fleece, dry ground—He asked
that the fleece be wet the next morning while the ground around it remain dry (Judg. 6:36-38).

B. Dry fleece, wet ground—He then
asked that on the following day the
fleece be dry and the ground around
it be wet (Judg. 6:39-40).

V. The army

A. Desiring that Gideon depend upon
God rather than human strength for
victory, God ordered him to reduce
his army (Judg. 7:1-2).

B. Almost immediately he saw his army
size drop (Judg. 7:3-6):
1. From 32,000 to 10,000
2. From 10,000 to 300

C. He was assured of victory with these
300 men, despite the fact that his enemy possessed 135,000 troops (Judg.
7:7; 8:10).

VI. The attack

A. Pre-battle events—Once again Gideon
was reassured on the eve of battle,
this time by secretly visiting the enemy camp and overhearing a conversation between two Midianite soldiers
concerning a divine dream, during
which his very name was mentioned
(Judg. 7:8-15).

B. Battle events
1. Gideon attacked the enemy with
his 300 men. At a given signal,

each man blew his trumpet,
smashed the jar he was carrying,
which revealed a burning torch,
and shouted out, "The sword of
the LORD, and of Gideon" (Judg.
7:16-20).

2. The Midianites fled in panic
(Judg. 7:22).

3. And 120,000 of the enemy were
slain by the sword (Judg. 8:10).

4. Four Midianite leaders were captured and killed during the course
of the battle (Judg. 7:25; 8:12, 21).

5. Gideon's victory resulted in a 40-
year period of peace for the land
(Judg. 8:28).

6. His great victory was referred to
in Hebrews 11:32.

C. Post-battle events—There were three
sad aspects to this glorious victory.

1. The hostility of the tribe of
Ephraim was aroused against Gideon, as they accused him of not
involving them in the battle (Judg.
8:1-3).

2. The punishment was imposed by
Gideon upon the Israelite city of
Succoth because of its refusal to
feed his famished troops (Judg.
8:4-8, 13-17).

3. Gideon's brothers were killed by
the Midianites (Judg. 8:18-20).

VII. The apostasy

A. Following the battle, Gideon refused
the invitation of the men of Israel to
reign over them, but did request that
he be given gold for an ephod (Judg.
8:22-27).

B. This request was quickly granted, but
with tragic results. "Gideon . . . put it
in his city . . . and all Israel went
thither a whoring after it: which thing
became a snare unto Gideon, and to
his house" (Judg. 8:27).

STATISTICS

Father: Joash (Judg. 6:11)
Sons: 71, two of which are named: Abime-
lech and Jotham (Judg. 9:1, 5)
First mention: Judges 6:11

Final mention: Hebrews 11:32
Meaning of his name: "Great warrior, hewer, feller"
Frequency of his name: Referred to 40 times
Biblical books mentioning him: Two books (Judges, Hebrews)
Occupation: Soldier, judge (Judg. 6:14; 8:28)
Place of birth: Ophrah (Judg. 6:11-12; 8:27)
Important fact about his life: He defeated a vastly superior army with 300 men (Judg. 7:22; 8:10-12).

✍Goliath

CHRONOLOGICAL SUMMARY

I. The background of Goliath
   A. He was a fierce Philistine warrior from the city of Gath (1 Sam. 17:5).
   B. He stood approximately 10 feet high (1 Sam. 17:4).
   C. He wore a bronze helmet on his head (1 Sam. 17:4).
   D. His coat of bronze scale armor weighed 125 pounds (1 Sam. 17:5).
   E. His spear shaft was like a weaver's rod and its iron point weighed 15 pounds (1 Sam. 17:7).
II. The boasting of Goliath
   A. He blasphemed God, challenging and terrifying the armies of Israel under Saul for 40 days (1 Sam. 17:11, 16, 24).
   B. He demanded Israel send out their champion to meet him in battle (1 Sam. 17:8-10).
   C. He was incensed when the lad David stepped out to meet him (1 Sam. 17:42).
   D. He cursed David by his gods and promised to give his flesh to the birds and beasts (1 Sam. 17:43-44).
III. The beheading of Goliath
   A. He was slain by David, who hurled a stone at him which struck the giant on the forehead (1 Sam. 17:49).

B. David then used Goliath's own sword to cut his head off (1 Sam. 17:50-51).

STATISTICS
Brother: Lahmi (1 Chron. 20:5)
First mention: 1 Samuel 17:4
Final mention: 1 Chronicles 20:5
Meaning of his name: "Exile, soothsayer"
Frequency of his name: Referred to six times
Biblical books mentioning him: Three books (1 Samuel, 2 Samuel, 1 Chronicles)
Occupation: Soldier (1 Sam. 17:4-10)
Place of death: On a battlefield (1 Sam. 17:1-2)
Circumstances of death: He was killed by a rock from David's sling (1 Sam. 17:49-51).
Important fact about his life: He was Scripture's tallest recorded person (1 Sam. 17:4).

✍Gomer

CHRONOLOGICAL SUMMARY

I. Gomer and the sin of harlotry
   A. She was the wife of Hosea the prophet (Hos. 1:2-3).
   B. Before her marriage, Gomer was a common prostitute (Hos. 1:2).
II. Gomer and the sin of adultery
   A. Gomer's lust
      1. After marriage, she soon returned to her previous immoral ways (Hos. 2:2; 3:3).
      2. She abandoned Hosea for worldly lovers (Hos. 2:5).
      3. She wound up in a slave market.
   B. Hosea's love
      1. In spite of her unfaithfulness, Gomer was still loved by Hosea, as Israel was loved by God (Hos. 3:1).
      2. He attempted to reason with her. Hosea even asked their children to plead with their mother (Hos. 2:1-2).
      3. He attempted to restrict her—"I will hedge up thy way with thorns, and make a wall, that she

shall not find her paths" (Hos. 2:6).

4. He redeemed her out of the slave market (Hos. 3:2).

STATISTICS

Father: Diblaim (Hos. 1:3)

Spouse: Hosea (Hos. 1:2)

Sons: Jezreel and Lo-ammi (Hos. 1:4-9)

Daughter: Lo-ruhamah (Hos. 1:4-9)

First mention: Hosea 1:3

Final mention: Hosea 3:2

Meaning of her name: "Completion, heat"

Frequency of her name: Referred to three times

Biblical books mentioning her: One book (Hosea)

Occupation: Harlot (Hos. 1:2-3)

Important fact about her life: She was the unfaithful wife of the prophet Hosea (Hos. 1:2-3; 3:1-2).

✍Habakkuk

CHRONOLOGICAL SUMMARY

I. Setting the scene—At the time of Habakkuk's writing, the Babylonians, new masters of the Middle East, had already threatened tiny Judah with extinction. But perhaps even worse, spiritual conditions at home were at an all-time low. This is the background which gives rise to the spiritual doubts and shouts in the book of Habakkuk.

II. The doubts

A. His question—"Will you punish our nation?" The prophet was grieved over Judah's wickedness.

1. The law was ignored (1:4).

2. Justice was perverted (1:4).

3. Righteousness was surrounded by wickedness (1:4).

B. God's answer—"I will, through Judah's foes." This would be done even during Habakkuk's lifetime (1:5). God was raising a new force on the world scene, the Chaldeans (1:6).

1. They were a law unto themselves (1:7).

2. Their horses were swifter than leopards and fiercer than wolves (1:8).

3. Their riders were like hungry eagles circling their prey (1:8).

4. They collected captives like sand (1:9).

5. They mocked at kings (1:10).

C. His question—"Will you punish these Chaldeans also?" Habakkuk could not comprehend why God would let this pagan nation punish his own people, even though they were admittedly guilty of gross sin (1:12-17). "Thou art of purer eyes than to behold evil, and canst not look on iniquity: wherefore lookest thou upon them that deal treacherously, and holdest thy tongue when the wicked devoureth the man that is more righteous than he?" (1:13). Habakkuk knew the Chaldeans would snare and treat their Hebrew captives like fish.

D. God's answer—"I will, through my woes!" Habakkuk climbed upon his watchtower to await God's answer. Soon it came (2:1-2).

1. God told him the Chaldeans would indeed be punished, but only at his appointed time (2:3).

2. Babylon was to be judged for their many sins (2:5-19).

   a. Slavery (2:5)

   b. Robbery (2:6, 8)

   c. Bloodshedding (2:8, 10, 12, 17)

   d. Drunkenness (2:5, 15)

   e. Idolatry (2:18-19)

3. Until then, Habakkuk was to live by faith (2:4).

   a. God was still in control over all the earth. "The LORD is in his holy temple: let all the earth keep silence before him" (2:20).

   b. God will someday rule over all the earth. "The earth shall be filled with the knowledge of the glory of the LORD, as the waters cover the sea" (2:14).

c. Habakkuk's final testimony reveals that he apparently learned to live by faith. "When I heard, my belly trembled; my lips quivered at the voice: rottenness entered into my bones, and I trembled in myself, that I might rest in the day of trouble: when he cometh up unto the people, he will invade them with his troops" (3:16).

III. The shouts

A. The soul of the prophet was revived. Deciding to follow his own advice ("the just shall live by his faith"), Habakkuk with childlike trust turned to God (3). "O LORD, I have heard thy speech, and was afraid: O LORD, revive thy work in the midst of the years, in the midst of the years make known; in wrath remember mercy" (3:2).

B. The eyes of the prophet were reassured. In 3:3-16 he saw an awesome manifestation of God's majestic glory. Some Hebrew scholars believe all the verbs found in 3:3-15 should be regarded as describing future events. If this is true, Habakkuk actually gave us the future coming of the returning Christ.

1. His schedule—"God came from Teman, and the Holy One from mount Paran. Selah. His glory covered the heavens, and the earth was full of his praise" (3:3).
   a. He will touch down upon the Mount of Olives (Zech. 14:4; Acts 1:10-12).
   b. He will then go to Teman (an ancient settlement in Edom), perhaps to rescue the Jews hiding out in Petra (Isa. 63:1; Rev. 12:13-17).

2. His appearance—"His brightness was as the light; he had horns coming out of his hand: and there was the hiding of his power" (3:4).

3. His actions—"Before him went the pestilence, and burning coals went forth at his feet. He stood, and measured the earth: he beheld, and drove asunder the nations; and the everlasting mountains were scattered, the perpetual hills did bow: his ways are everlasting. . . . Thou didst march through the land in indignation, thou didst thresh the heathen in anger" (3:5-6, 12).

4. His purpose—"Thou wentest forth for the salvation of thy people, even for salvation with thine anointed; thou woundedst the head out of the house of the wicked, by discovering the foundation unto the neck. Selah" (3:13).

C. The heart of the prophet was rejoiced. "Yet I will rejoice in the LORD, I will joy in the God of my salvation" (3:18).

D. The feet of the prophet were renewed. "The LORD God is my strength, and he will make my feet like hinds' feet, and he will make me to walk upon mine high places" (3:19).

THEOLOGICAL SUMMARY

I. Habakkuk's identity

A. He was apparently one of the Levitical choristers in the temple.

B. His closing statement, "to the chief singers on my stringed instruments," reveals the book is actually a song (Hab. 3:19).

C. Habakkuk has been called the Doubting Thomas of the Old Testament.

II. Habakkuk's insistence—His great theological declaration, "The just shall live by his faith" (2:4) is repeated three times in the New Testament.

A. Romans 1:17 emphasizes the first two words, "the just."

B. Galatians 3:11 emphasizes the second two words, "shall live."

C. Hebrews 10:38 emphasizes the final two words, "by faith."

III. Habakkuk's intentions—In essence, Habakkuk functioned more like a priest than a prophet. Instead of declaring God's message, and thus standing between God and the people, he pleaded God's mercy and thus stood between the people and God.

STATISTICS

First mention: Habakkuk 1:1
Final mention: Habakkuk 3:1
Meaning of his name: "Love's embrace"
Frequency of his name: Referred to two times
Biblical books mentioning him: One book (Habakkuk)
Occupation: Prophet and musician (Hab. 1:1; 3:1)
Important fact about his life: His phrase "the just shall live by . . . faith" is repeated three times in the New Testament (Hab. 2:4; Rom. 1:17; Gal. 3:11; Heb. 10:38).

 *Hagar*

CHRONOLOGICAL SUMMARY

I. Hagar and Sarah
  A. The marriage
    1. Hagar was the Egyptian maidservant to Sarah, Abraham's wife (Gen. 16:1).
    2. She was given to Abraham by the barren Sarah, that he might father the promised heir through her (Gen. 16:1-3).
  B. The malice—After becoming pregnant, Hagar's arrogant attitude invoked the wrath of Sarah, who drove her out into the desert (Gen. 16:4-6).
II. Hagar and Christ—She was met by the angel of the Lord, a title referring to Christ in the Old Testament (Gen. 16:7).
  A. He aided her.
  B. He advised her: "The angel of the LORD said unto her, Return to thy mistress, and submit thyself unto her hands" (Gen. 16:9).
  C. He assured her (Gen. 16:10-12).

    1. That he would greatly multiply her seed
    2. That the child she was carrying was a boy and he would be named Ishmael
    3. That Ishmael would be a wild one—free and untamed as a wild ass
    4. That he would be against everyone and everyone would feel the same toward him
III. Hagar and Abraham
  A. Hagar returned and gave birth to Ishmael (Gen. 16:15).
  B. Abraham was 86 when Ishmael was born (Gen. 16:16).
IV. Hagar and Ishmael
  A. Years later, Hagar was again dismissed to the desert, this time because her son mocked Isaac, the promised heir, on the very day of his weaning (Gen. 21:8-10).
  B. On this occasion God instructed Abraham to send both Hagar and Ishmael away, promising to take care of them (Gen. 21:11-14).
  C. When it came time for Ishmael to marry, Hagar brought a wife for him from Egypt (Gen. 21:20-21).

THEOLOGICAL SUMMARY

I. Paul used Hagar as an allegory of the Law of Moses in the book of Galatians
  A. She was a bondwoman (4:22).
  B. Her marriage to Abraham was flesh—directed (4:23).
  C. Her son Ishmael was naturally born (4:23).
  D. This son persecuted Abraham's second son, Isaac (4:29).
  E. Her child was not considered Abraham's rightful heir (4:30).
  F. Hagar represents the Mt. Sinai Covenant as she bore a slave child (Israel would also be slaves for awhile) (4:24).
  G. She corresponds to earthly Jerusalem (in Paul's day) due to her slavery (Jerusalem was occupied by the Romans at that time) (4:25).

II. Paul used Sarah as an allegory of grace.
  A. She was a freewoman (4:22).
  B. Her marriage to Abraham was Spirit-directed (4:23).
  C. Her son Isaac was supernaturally born (4:23).
  D. This son was persecuted by Ishmael (4:29).
  E. Her child was considered Abraham's rightful heir (4:30).
  F. Sarah represents the New Covenant, as she bore a free son (4:24-26).
  G. She corresponds to heavenly Jerusalem (4:23).

STATISTICS

Spouse: Abraham (Gen. 16:1-3)
Son: Ishmael (Gen. 16:15)
First mention: Genesis 16:1
Final mention: Galatians 4:25
Meaning of her name: "Wandering"
Frequency of her name: Referred to 14 times
Biblical books mentioning her: Two books (Genesis, Galatians)
Occupation: Handmaid to Sarah (Gen. 16:1)
Important fact about her life: She was Abraham's second wife and mother of Ishmael (Gen. 16:1-3, 15).

✍*Haggai*

CHRONOLOGICAL SUMMARY

  I. An August message, directed to the hands of the people—Perform! (Hag. 1:1-15).
  A. The people had about given up concerning the building of their temple. After 15 years it remained unfinished. Their lame excuse was, "The time is not come, the time that the LORD's house should be built" (1:2). Because of this carelessness, God could not and would not bless them with either spiritual or financial prosperity (1:4-6).
  B. God's advice to them—"Go up to the mountain, and bring wood, and build

the house; and I will take pleasure in it, and I will be glorified, saith the LORD" (1:8).
  C. The spirits of Zerubbabel (the governor) and Joshua (the high priest) were then stirred up by the Lord. This godly pair thus led the people to finish building the temple (1:14).
  II. An October message, directed to the hearts of the people—Patience! (2:1-9). In spite of the insignificant temple they had just built (see Ezra 3:8-13), there was weeping as well as joy at the dedication of the temple during Zerubbabel's time as some of the old men remembered the glories of Solomon's temple. The new temple was far inferior to that temple in size and cost. However, Haggai attempted to encourage even the old men as he spoke of the magnificent millennial temple that would someday be built (2:9).
  III. A December message, directed to the head of the people—Ponder! (2:10-23). There were four facts Haggai desired that the people ponder over.
  A. The fact of Judah's contamination (2:10-17)
    1. God asked Judah to answer two questions:
      a. If one of you is carrying a holy sacrifice in his robes, and happens to brush against some bread, or wine, or meat, will it too become holy (2:12)?
      b. The answer, of course, was, "No, holiness does not pass to other things that way."
      c. If someone touches a dead person, and so becomes ceremonially impure, and then brushes against something, does it become contaminated (2:13)?
      d. Here the answer was yes.
    2. The point God was making here is that whatever righteousness the nation of Israel might have once possessed was not automatically transferred upon them at this

time. But their own unrighteousness was affecting both them and their children.

B. The fact of God's determination—God promised them that because of their decision to finish the temple, he would bless them from that day on, even before the structure was completed (2:18-19).

C. The fact of the great tribulation—Someday God would destroy all those Gentile nations which had afflicted Israel throughout the years (2:20-22; see also Heb. 12:26; Rev. 16:18-20).

D. The fact of Zerubbabel's elevation—Some believe that Zerubbabel will be God's prime minister during the Millennium. "In that day, saith the LORD of hosts, will I take thee, O Zerubbabel, my servant . . . and will make thee as a signet: for I have chosen thee" (2:23).

THEOLOGICAL SUMMARY

I. Haggai was a contemporary with Zechariah the prophet (Ezra 5:1).

II. He joined the Jewish remnant (along with Zechariah, Zerubbabel the political leader, and Joshua the religious leader) during the return from Persia to Jerusalem in 536 B.C. to rebuild the temple (Ezra 5:1-2; 6:14).

III. His was the first prophetic voice to be heard after the Babylonian Captivity.

IV. His writings are the most precisely dated ones in the entire Bible. Here are the dates given to us at the times he delivered his messages:

A. First message—August 29, 520 B.C.

B. Second message—October 17, 520 B.C.

C. Third and fourth messages—December 18, 520 B.C.

V. His book is the second shortest in the Old Testament. Only Obadiah is shorter.

VI. In no other biblical book of its size is the fact of divine revelation so fre-

quently referred to. The phrase "thus saith the LORD" and its equivalent is found no less than 21 times.

VII. Haggai may have been one of the exiles who saw the temple of Solomon before it was destroyed in 586 B.C. If so, he would have been an elderly prophet (Hag. 2:3).

VIII. Haggai and Nehemiah can be favorably compared.

A. Both had a divine burden to build.

1. Haggai desired to rebuild the temple (Hag. 1:8).

2. Nehemiah desired to rebuild the wall around Jerusalem (Neh. 2:5, 17-18).

B. Both were men of action.

1. In just 23 days, after a delay of 14 years, Haggai led the people in the completion of the temple in Jerusalem (Hag. 1:1, 14-15).

2. In just 52 days, after a delay of 90 years, Nehemiah led the people in the completion of the walls around Jerusalem (Neh. 6:15).

IX. Haggai gave us a name for Christ not found anywhere else in the Bible, calling him "the desire of all nations" (Hag. 2:7).

X. In essence, Haggai's book is a tale of three temples.

A. The first temple, built by Solomon (Hag. 2:3)

B. The second temple, being built at Haggai's encouragement (1:7, 14)

C. The third temple, to be built by Christ himself (2:6-9)

STATISTICS

First mention: Ezra 5:1
Final mention: Haggai 2:20
Meaning of his name: "Festive"
Frequency of his name: Referred to 11 times
Biblical books mentioning him: Two books (Ezra, Haggai)
Occupation: Prophet (Ezra 5:1; Hag. 1:1)
Important fact about his life: He led the people in the completion of the second temple (Hag. 1:2-8).

*Ham*

CHRONOLOGICAL SUMMARY
I. His identity
  A. He was one of the three sons of Noah (Gen. 5:32).
  B. He was the father of Canaan (Gen. 9:18, 22).
II. His (possible) immorality—He may have been involved along with his son Canaan in the unnamed sin against Noah (Gen. 9:24).

STATISTICS
Father: Noah (Gen. 5:32)
Sons: Canaan, Cush, Mizraim, and Put (Gen. 9:18, 22; 10:6; 1 Chron. 1:8)
Brothers: Shem and Japheth (Gen. 5:32)
Significant descendant: Nimrod (Gen. 10:8-12)
First mention: Genesis 5:32
Final mention: 1 Chronicles 1:8
Meaning of his name: "Swarthy, dark, colored, warm"
Frequency of his name: Referred to 11 times
Biblical books mentioning him: Two books (Genesis, 1 Chronicles)
Important fact about his life: He was one of Noah's three sons and the father of Canaan (Gen. 5:32; 9:18). (See note on "Japheth.")

Haman

CHRONOLOGICAL SUMMARY
I. Haman, the haughty
  A. He was an Agagite, of Amalekite descent (Esther 3:1).
  B. He was elevated to the position of prime minister by the Persian King Ahasuerus, causing him to swell with pride (Esther 3:1).
II. Haman, the heartless
  A. He instigated the first attempted holocaust in history upon learning that a minor Jewish official named Mordecai was refusing to bow down and

honor him as he walked by (Esther 3:2-6).
  B. He began by lying about the Jews to the king, claiming they were disloyal, and urged that they be destroyed (Esther 3:7-8).
  C. He even offered to pay 10,000 talents of silver to cover the expense incurred in this proposed bloodbath. This would be approximately $30 million in today's currency (Esther 3:9).
  D. To Haman's surprise and delight, the king not only agreed to his proposal, but said Haman need not pay anything to finance the slaughter (Esther 3:10-11).
  E. After signing the death warrant, both men sat down and relaxed over a drink (Esther 3:15).
III. Haman, the honored
  A. He and the king attended a special banquet hosted by Queen Esther, and both were invited to attend a second one on the following day. Neither man at this point knew the purpose behind Esther's actions (Esther 5:1-8).
  B. In spite of having his pride fed by these honors, Haman was filled with rage upon seeing Mordecai continue in his refusal to kneel at his approach (Esther 5:9).
  C. At the advice of his wife, Zeresh, Haman had a 75-foot-high gallows built, upon which he planned to hang Mordecai, just before attending the queen's second banquet (Esther 5:10-14).
IV. Haman, the humbled
  A. The insomnia (Esther 6:1-3)
    1. At the same time Haman was constructing his gallows, the king was having difficulty falling to sleep.
    2. Hoping to solve his problem, Ahasuerus had the Persian daily "Congressional Record" read to him.
    3. Through a "chance" reading, however, he learned that

Mordecai had once saved his life. The king immediately decided to reward him.
  B. The irony (Esther 6:4-12)
    1. Just then, Haman arrived at the royal palace, seeking the king's permission to hang Mordecai.
    2. In one of history's most ironic twists, Haman not only failed to receive the desired permission, but actually wound up being forced to honor Mordecai in a celebration parade.
  V. Haman, the hanged
    A. Upon returning home following this humbling experience, the wretched Haman was warned by Zeresh that the plot against Mordecai and the Jews would surely lead to his total ruin (Esther 6:13).
    B. During the second banquet, Esther revealed her Jewish background to the king, and blamed Haman for the plot against her life (Esther 7:1-7).
    C. The furious king concluded (incorrectly) that Haman was aware of Esther's nationality and ordered his death (Esther 7:8-9).
    D. Haman was thus hanged upon the very gallows he had built for Mordecai (Esther 7:10).

STATISTICS

Father: Hammedatha (Esther 3:1)
Spouse: Zeresh (Esther 5:14)
Sons: 10 unnamed sons (Esther 9:10)
First mention: Esther 3:1
Final mention: Esther 9:24
Meaning of his name: "Celebrated"
Frequency of his name: Referred to 52 times
Biblical books mentioning him: One book (Esther)
Occupation: Chief associate under King Ahasuerus (Esther 3:1)
Place of death: On a gallows in the city of Shushan (Esther 7:10)
Important fact about his life: He was guilty of history's first attempted holocaust (Esther 3:8-9).

✍️*Hamor*

CHRONOLOGICAL SUMMARY

  I. The request by Hamor to Dinah's father
    A. Hamor was a Hivite chief who ruled over the city of Shechem in the days of Jacob (Gen. 34:1).
    B. Jacob had previously purchased from Hamor for 100 pieces of silver a field on which to spread his tent (Gen. 33:19).
    C. This event was mentioned later by both Joshua (Josh. 24:32) and Stephen (Acts 7:16).
    D. His son, also named Shechem, seduced Dinah, the daughter of Jacob, and requested Hamor to obtain the patriarch's permission to marry her (Gen. 34:2-6, 8-10).
  II. The retaliation against Hamor by Dinah's brothers
    A. He was deceived by them—Her brothers pretended to agree but insisted that all male Shechemites circumcise themselves first (Gen. 34:7, 13-17).
    B. He was destroyed by them (Gen. 34:18-29).
      1. Hamor and his people agreed, and all males were circumcised.
      2. Then, when they were rendered helpless because of the physical swelling, Simeon and Levi moved in and slaughtered them like helpless cattle.
      3. Hamor's city of Shechem was then totally plundered.

STATISTICS

Son: Shechem (Gen. 34:2-6)
First mention: Genesis 34:2
Final mention: Judges 9:28
Meaning of his name: "Large jackass"
Frequency of his name: Referred to 11 times
Biblical books mentioning him: Three books (Genesis, Joshua, Judges)
Occupation: Hivite chief (Gen. 34:2)
Place of death: In the city of Shechem

Circumstances of death: He was killed by Simeon and Levi (Gen. 34:25-26).

Important fact about his life: His son seduced Dinah, Jacob's daughter (Gen. 34:1-3).

✍Hananiah

CHRONOLOGICAL SUMMARY

I. The corrupt prophet
 A. His apostasy
  1. Hananiah was a false prophet in the reign of Zedekiah, the final king of Judah (Jer. 28:1).
  2. He falsely predicted that within two years, three events would occur (Jer. 28:2-4).
   a. All the articles Nebuchadnezzar had carried off from the Jerusalem temple to Babylon would be returned.
   b. Jehoiachin, a former Judean king also taken to Babylon, would come back along with the other exiles.
   c. The Babylonian empire would soon fall.
 B. His anger
  1. He was rebuked by Jeremiah, the true prophet in the temple, for speaking these false prophecies (Jer. 28:5-9).
  2. In a fit of anger Hananiah broke the yoke of straps and crossbars from around Jeremiah's neck, ordered placed there by God to symbolize the coming Babylonian Captivity (Jer. 27:2; 28:10).
II. The condemned prophet
 A. God warned Hananiah through Jeremiah that an iron yoke would be placed around his own neck (Jer. 28:12-13).
 B. Jeremiah then predicted that because of all his lies, this false prophet would die within that very year, which he did (Jer. 28:15-17).

STATISTICS

Father: Azur (Jer. 28:1)
First mention: Jeremiah 28:1
Final mention: Jeremiah 28:17
Meaning of his name: "God is gracious"
Frequency of his name: Referred to nine times
Biblical books mentioning him: One book (Jeremiah)
Occupation: False prophet (Jer. 28:15)
Place of death: Jerusalem
Circumstances of death: He died by the hand of God (Jer. 28:16).
Important fact about his life: He was a false prophet who opposed Jeremiah (Jer. 28:1-10).

✍Hannah

CHRONOLOGICAL SUMMARY

I. Her sorrow
 A. Hannah was one of Elkanah's two wives (1 Sam. 1:2).
 B. For many years she was barren and brokenhearted (1 Sam. 1:2, 7).
 C. She was especially loved by Elkanah (1 Sam. 1:5).
 D. However, she was ridiculed for her barrenness by Peninnah, the other wife who had children (1 Sam. 1:2, 6-7).
II. Her supplication
 A. The rebuke
  1. She visited the tabernacle in Shiloh and stood there praying silently, weeping and vowing she would raise any son God might give her as a Nazarite (1 Sam. 1:9-11).
  2. Eli, the high priest, watching her pray, thought at first that she was drunk and rebuked her (1 Sam. 1:12-14).
 B. The reassurance—Upon being aware of the actual situation, Eli sent

Hannah home, promising God would give her a son (1 Sam. 1:15-18).

III. Her son
  A. Hannah gave birth to Samuel (1 Sam. 1:19-20).
  B. She would later give birth to three more sons and two daughters (1 Sam. 2:21).

IV. Her sacrifice
  A. She offered up a lifeless sacrifice. "They slew a bullock" (1 Sam. 1:25).
  B. She offered up a living sacrifice. "For this child I prayed; and the LORD hath given me my petition which I asked of him. Therefore also I have lent him to the LORD; as long as he liveth he shall be lent to the LORD" (1 Sam. 1:27-28).

V. Her song—After the dedication, Hannah uttered a beautiful ode of praise which appears to be the basis of Mary's song found in Luke 1:46-55 (1 Sam. 2:1-10). In this remarkable prayer Hannah mentioned a number of God's divine attributes.
  A. His holiness—"There is none holy as the LORD" (2:2).
  B. His omniscience—"The LORD is a God of knowledge" (2:3).
  C. His omnipotence—"He bringeth low, and lifteth up" (2:7).
  D. His mercy—"He raiseth up the poor . . . and . . . beggar . . . to set them among princes" (2:8).
  E. His faithfulness—"He will keep the feet of his saints" (2:9).
  F. His justice—"The LORD shall judge the ends of the earth" (2:10).
  G. His Messiah—"He shall give strength unto his king, and exalt the horn of his anointed" (2:10).

STATISTICS

Spouse: Elkanah (1 Sam. 1:2)
Son: Samuel (1 Sam. 1:19-20)
First mention: 1 Samuel 1:2
Final mention: 1 Samuel 2:21
Meaning of her name: "Grace"

Frequency of her name: Referred to 13 times
Biblical books mentioning her: One book (1 Samuel)
Important fact about her life: She was the godly mother of Samuel (1 Sam. 1).

Hanun

CHRONOLOGICAL SUMMARY

I. His disrespect for David
  A. When Hanun became king over Ammon at the death of his father, Nahash (a close friend of David), David sent ambassadors to make a courtesy call (2 Sam. 10:2).
  B. Mistaking these men for spies, Hanun both mistreated and ridiculed them (2 Sam. 10:3-4).
    1. He shaved off half their beards.
    2. He cut their robes off at the buttocks and sent them home half naked.

II. His defeat by David
  A. Later, realizing his stupid blunder, Hanun hired a mercenary army consisting of 33,000 foot soldiers and 32,000 chariots to help him ward off an anticipated attack by David (2 Sam. 10:6; 1 Chron. 19:6-7).
  B. David attacked and soundly defeated both Hanun and his hired armies (2 Sam. 10:13-19).

STATISTICS

Father: Nahash (2 Sam. 10:1-2)
First mention: 2 Samuel 10:1
Final mention: 1 Chronicles 19:6
Meaning of his name: "Gracious"
Frequency of his name: Referred to nine times
Biblical books mentioning him: Two books (2 Samuel, 1 Chronicles)
Occupation: King of the Ammonites (2 Sam. 10:1)
Important fact about his life: He foolishly insulted some of David's ambassadors who came to him in peace (2 Sam. 10:3-4).

ᴥHazael

CHRONOLOGICAL SUMMARY

I. His wickedness
  A. He was originally a high official at Ben-hadad's court in Damascus (2 Kings 8:7-9).
  B. God instructed Elijah the prophet to anoint Hazael as Syria's next king (1 Kings 19:15).
  C. Even before he became king, however, Elisha (Elijah's successor) predicted with tears the bloody reign Hazael would have (2 Kings 8:7-12).
    1. He would murder his master Ben-hadad to secure the throne.
    2. He would then do grievous harm to the people of God.
      a. Setting fire to their fortified palaces
      b. Killing their young men with the sword
      c. Dashing their little children to the ground
      d. Ripping open their pregnant women
  D. Hazael denied he would do all these horrible things, but Elisha proved to be correct (2 Kings 8:13).
II. His warfare
  A. He later fought against an alliance of both Northern and Southern Israel at Ramoth-gilead and apparently defeated them (2 Kings 8:28).
  B. Joram, the king of Northern Israel, was wounded in this battle (2 Kings 8:29; 9:15).
  C. Because of his people's sin, God allowed Hazael to persecute Israel (2 Kings 10:32).
  D. On one occasion he surrounded Jerusalem, but was bought off with tribute money paid by Joash, the Judean king (2 Kings 12:17-18).
  E. In the midst of all this, however, Israel experienced the grace of God (2 Kings 13:22-24).
  F. Years later, Amos the prophet pronounced judgment upon the house of Hazael (Amos 1:4).

STATISTICS

First mention: 1 Kings 19:15
Final mention: Amos 1:4
Meaning of his name: "God sees"
Frequency of his name: Referred to 22 times
Biblical books mentioning him: Four books (1 Kings, 2 Kings, 2 Chronicles, Amos)
Occupation: King of Syria (1 Kings 19:15)
Important fact about his life: He was the bloody Syrian king anointed by Elisha (2 Kings 8:7-15).

ᴥHeman

CHRONOLOGICAL SUMMARY

I. Who he was
  A. He was Samuel's grandson and one of three key Levitical musicians in the time of David (1 Chron. 6:31, 33).
  B. His two associates were Asaph and Jeduthun (1 Chron. 6:39; 25:1).
II. What he did
  A. These three musicians, dressed in fine linen, played cymbals and were accompanied by 120 priests sounding trumpets at the dedication of Solomon's temple (2 Chron. 5:12).
  B. Heman also led his 14 sons and three daughters in the musical service of the tabernacle (1 Chron. 25:4-6).
  C. Heman later authored Psalm 88, which includes one of the most despondent prayers in all the Bible.

STATISTICS

Father: Joel (1 Chron. 6:33)
Significant ancestor His grandfather was Samuel (1 Chron. 6:33)
First mention: 1 Chronicles 6:33
Final mention: Psalm 88
Meaning of his name: "Faithful"
Frequency of his name: Referred to 13 times
Biblical books mentioning him: Three books (1 Chronicles, 2 Chronicles, Psalms)

Occupation: Levitical musician (1 Chron. 6:31)

Important fact about his life: He was a musician and author of Psalm 8.

✑Hezekiah

CHRONOLOGICAL SUMMARY

I. The heart of Hezekiah
  A. He was the thirteenth ruler of Judah.
  B. He ruled for 29 years (2 Kings 18:2).
  C. He was 25 when he began ruling (2 Kings 18:1-2).
  D. He was the finest king of Judah up to his time (2 Kings 18:3, 5).
  E. He was also the richest king since the time of Solomon (2 Chron. 32:27-29).

II. The hands of Hezekiah
  A. He repaired the palace (temple) of God—The very first month of his reign, Hezekiah opened the doors of the temple and repaired it (2 Chron. 29:3).
  B. He revived the people of God.
    1. The cleansing
      a. He removed the pagan high places, smashed the sacred stones, and cut down the Asherah poles (2 Kings 18:4).
      b. He broke into pieces the bronze snake Moses had made (see Num. 21) because his people had been worshiping it (2 Kings 18:4).
    2. The challenging
      a. He commanded the people to give of their substance (first fruits of their grain, new wine, oil, honey, herds and flocks, etc.) to the temple (2 Chron. 31:4).
      b. They responded in a tremendous way (2 Chron. 31:4-10).
  C. He reinstituted the Passover of God, and a special invitation was even sent out to the Northern Kingdom tribes (2 Chron. 30:1-27).

1. The request
   a. Turn to the God of Abraham.
   b. The God of Abraham will then turn to you.
2. The response
   a. Some ridiculed.
   b. Some returned.
3. The results
   a. Realizing some of the northern tribal people attending the Passover had not had the opportunity to purify themselves outwardly, Hezekiah prayed that God would accept their inward sincerity, which the Lord did, thus allowing them to eat the Passover meal.
   b. In fact, the king extended the regular seven-day feast for an additional seven days.
   c. The following number of animals were then offered:
      (1) A thousand bulls and 7,000 sheep given by Hezekiah for the assembly
      (2) A thousand bulls and 10,000 sheep given by the officials for the assembly
   d. This proved to be the greatest Passover since the days of David.
  D. He released the power of God.
    1. Relying upon the strength of God, he defeated the Philistines (2 Kings 18:8).
    2. He also rebelled against the king of Assyria and refused to serve him (2 Kings 18:7).
  E. He reorganized the priests of God.
    1. The speech—Hezekiah assembled the priests and Levites in the temple area and addressed them (2 Chron. 29:4-11).
      a. He challenged them to consecrate themselves to God.
      b. He reminded them of the northern tribes who were suffering from the Assyrian captivity because of their sin.

c. He announced his intentions to make a special covenant with God.

2. The singing—As the offerings began, he commissioned the Levites in the temple to sing, accompanied by the sound of cymbals, harps, and lyres (2 Chron. 29:25-28).

3. The sacrifices
   a. When the priests had consecrated themselves and the entire temple, Hezekiah ordered seven bulls, seven rams, seven male goats, and seven male lambs to be offered up as a sin offering for Judah (2 Chron. 29:18-24).
   b. He then instructed the entire assembly who had been present during the service to bring their sacrifices to the Lord (2 Chron. 29:31).
   c. The people then offered up the following animals (2 Chron. 29:32-33): 70 bulls; 100 rams; 200 male lambs; 600 oxen; and 3000 sheep and goats.
   d. Finally, the king assigned the priests and Levites by divisions to offer God both animal and praise sacrifices (2 Chron. 31:2).

III. The healing of Hezekiah
   A. His sickness
      1. Hezekiah became desperately ill and was told by Isaiah that he would die (2 Kings 20:1).
      2. This may have been a divine punishment because of his pride (2 Chron. 32:25).
      3. The king humbled himself and repented (2 Chron. 32:26).
   B. His supplication
      1. The king turned his face to the wall and prayed to God, reminding him of Hezekiah's past faithful service (2 Kings 20:2-3).
      2. God then commanded Isaiah to inform Hezekiah that his prayer

had been answered and he would not die. In fact, the Lord would add an additional 15 years to the king's life (2 Kings 20:4-6).

   C. His sign—In order to prove the validity of this prophecy, God offered Hezekiah through Isaiah one of two signs (2 Kings. 20:8-11).
      1. Did the king want the sun's shadow to go forward 10 steps on the stairway, or . . .
      2. Did he want it to go back 10 steps?
      3. Hezekiah chose the second, feeling this would be the greatest sign. As he watched in amazement, the miracle occurred.

IV. The hymns of Hezekiah
   A. In "the writing of Hezekiah king of Judah, when he had been sick, and was recovered of his sickness" (Isa. 38:9), the king reviewed two things:
      1. His despair upon hearing that he would die (Isa. 38:10-16)
      2. His dedication upon learning that he would not die (Isa. 38:17-20): "Behold, for peace I had great bitterness: but thou hast in love to my soul delivered it from the pit of corruption: for thou hast cast all my sins behind thy back" (Isa. 38:17). "The LORD was ready to save me: therefore we will sing my songs to the stringed instruments all the days of our life in the house of the LORD" (Isa. 38:20).
   B. It is believed by some scholars that these "songs" Hezekiah referred to were actually 15 psalms the king added to the Old Testament canon.
      1. Ten of these Psalms were written by Hezekiah himself, in memory of the 10 steps on the sundial. These were Psalms 120, 121, 123, 125, 126, 128, 129, 130, 132, and 134.
      2. He may then have added five more unpublished psalms of

David and Solomon to bring the total to 15, in honor of the 15 years God added to his life.

V. The hastiness of Hezekiah
  A. He received some ambassadors from the king of Babylon, who sent a gift, for he had heard of Hezekiah's sickness and recovery (2 Kings 20:12).
  B. Hezekiah foolishly showed these men all the gold, silver, spices, fine oil, etc., he kept in his storehouses (2 Kings 20:13).
  C. Upon learning of this, Isaiah soundly rebuked the king and predicted the following (2 Kings 20:14-18):
    1. Someday the Babylonians would return and carry off all the riches Hezekiah had shown them.
    2. Some of the king's own descendants would be taken away to Babylon.
  D. Hezekiah's response to all this was a very selfish one indeed: "Good is the word of the LORD which thou hast spoken. . . . Is it not good, if peace and truth be in my days?" (2 Kings 20:19). In other words, he was totally unconcerned as long as the terrible things did not happen during his reign.

VI. The helplessness of Hezekiah
  A. The problem
    1. During the fourth year of his reign, the Assyrians marched against Samaria. They took the city three years later, thus ending the Northern Kingdom (2 Kings 18:9-11).
    2. Seven years after the captivity of the 10 northern tribes, Assyrian King Sennacherib attacked Judah, capturing many of its cities (2 Kings 18:13).
    3. Being aware of Sennacherib's plan to destroy Jerusalem also, Hezekiah constructed a tunnel by which water was brought into the city (2 Kings 20:20; 2 Chron. 32:2-5).

4. Hezekiah then foolishly asked Sennacherib to forgive his past rebellion and agreed to pay the Assyrian king a huge tribute, stripping all the gold and silver from both the royal palace and temple (2 Kings 18:14-16).
    5. In spite of this, the Assyrian army surrounded Jerusalem (2 Kings 18:17).
    6. In fact, Sennacherib sent a personal threatening letter to Hezekiah (2 Kings 19:9-13).
  B. The prayer
    1. At first Hezekiah bravely attempted to encourage his people (2 Chron. 32:6-8).
    2. However, when he saw and heard the terrible threats of the enemy, he tore his clothes, put on sackcloth, and went into the temple to pray (2 Kings 19:1).
    3. In his prayer, the king both acknowledged and asked.
      a. He acknowledged:
        (1) The greatness and uniqueness of God (2 Kings 19:15)
        (2) The past victories of the Assyrians (2 Kings 19:17-18)
      b. He asked God to deliver Judah, that all the kingdoms might know who is the only true God (2 Kings 19:19).
    4. Hezekiah then sent word to Isaiah, urging him to seek God also (2 Kings 19:2-4).

VII. The help of Hezekiah
  A. The answer from the Lord—Hezekiah received from Isaiah a most reassuring message (2 Kings 19:20-34).
    1. God had heard the prayer of the king.
    2. God was angry over the pride of the Assyrians and over the insults they had heaped upon both him and Judah.
    3. Sennacherib would, therefore, not be permitted to enter Jerusalem.

4. No arrow from his soldiers would land inside.
5. The enemy would not build a siege ramp against the city.
6. Sennacherib would quickly leave the same way he came.
B. The angel of the Lord
   1. That very night the angel of the Lord went out and put to death 185,000 Assyrian soldiers (2 Kings 19:35).
   2. The Assyrian king quickly broke camp and withdrew (2 Kings 19:36).
   3. Shortly after reaching his capital city of Nineveh, Sennacherib was slain by two of his own sons while worshiping in the temple of his Assyrian god Nisroch (2 Kings 19:37).

STATISTICS
Father: Ahaz (2 Kings 16:20)
Mother: Abi (2 Kings 18:2)
Spouse: Hephzibah (2 Kings 21:1)
Son: Manasseh (2 Kings 21:1)
First mention: 2 Kings 16:20
Final mention: Matthew 1:10
Meaning of his name: "Strength of God"
Frequency of his name: Referred to 124 times
Biblical books mentioning him: Nine books
   (2 Kings, 1 Chronicles, 2 Chronicles, Proverbs, Isaiah, Jeremiah, Hosea, Micah, Matthew)
Occupation: King of Judah (2 Kings 18:1)
Place of birth: Jerusalem
Place of death: Jerusalem (2 Kings 20:21–21:1)
Important fact about his life: He was the king when God saved the city of Jerusalem from the Assyrians by the death angel (2 Kings 19).

✍️Hilkiah

CHRONOLOGICAL SUMMARY
I. His duties
   A. He was high priest in the time of Josiah, King of Judah (2 Kings 22:4).

B. He was trustee of a special fund given by the people to repair the temple (2 Kings 22:4; 2 Chron. 34:9).
II. His discovery
   A. He found a copy of the Law of Moses when repairing the temple (2 Kings 22:8; 2 Chron. 34:14).
   B. He gave it to Shaphan, secretary to Josiah, who then read it to the king (2 Kings 22:8-10).
   C. At the request of Josiah, he inquired of the prophetess Huldah what God was planning to do to Judah because of the people's sin (2 Kings 22:12-14).
III. His dedication
   A. The removal of paganism
      1. He was ordered by Josiah to remove all the idols from the temple (2 Kings 23:4).
      2. This he did, burning them outside Jerusalem in the Kidron valley, taking the ashes to Beth-el (2 Kings 23:4).
      3. He then did away with the pagan priests in the land (2 Kings 23:5-6).
      4. He also tore down the quarters of the male shrine prostitutes (2 Kings 23:7).
   B. The restoration of the Passover—He contributed greatly (along with two other priests) to Josiah's great Passover, giving 2,600 Passover offerings and 300 cattle (2 Chron. 35:8).

STATISTICS
Father: Shallum (1 Chron. 6:13)
Sons: Azariah and Gemariah (1 Chron. 6:13; Jer. 29:3)
Significant ancestor: His grandfather was Zadok (1 Chron. 6:12)
Significant descendant: Ezra (Ezra 7:1)
First mention: 2 Kings 22:4
Final mention: Jeremiah 29:3
Meaning of his name: "God is protection"
Frequency of his name: Referred to 20 times
Biblical books mentioning him: Five books
   (2 Kings, 1 Chronicles, 2 Chronicles, Ezra, Jeremiah)
Occupation: High priest (2 Kings 22:4)
Important fact about his life: He was the high

priest who found a copy of the Law in the temple during Josiah's reign (2 Kings 22:8).

✍ *Hiram (1)*

CHRONOLOGICAL SUMMARY

I. Hiram and David—He was the king of Tyre who helped David build his palace by furnishing cedar logs, carpenters, and stone masons (2 Sam. 5:11; 1 Chron 14:1).

II. Hiram and Solomon
   A. The construction
      1. Solomon's temple
         a. He was commissioned by Solomon to furnish some cedars of Lebanon to be used in constructing the temple (1 Kings 5:1-6).
         b. In addition, he sent trained stonedressers (1 Kings 5:18).
         c. Finally, he provided the required gold, some four and a half tons (1 Kings 9:11, 14).
         d. He then sent his chief architect (a man also called Hiram, Huram, and Huram-abi) to supervise the actual temple construction (1 Kings 7:13-14; 2 Chron. 2:13-14).
      2. Solomon's house—Hiram also helped build Solomon's home, which took 13 years to build, as contrasted with the temple, which was completed in seven years (1 Kings 7:1; 9:10).
   B. The compensation—For his work, Hiram received the following from Solomon:
      1. A yearly payment (for seven years) of 125,000 bushels of wheat and barley, and 115,000 gallons of pressed olive oil (1 Kings 5:10-12; 2 Chron. 2:10)
      2. Twenty towns in Galilee (1 Kings 9:11)
   C. The complaint—Hiram was disap-

pointed with these towns, calling them "Cabul," meaning, "good for nothing." He apparently gave them back (1 Kings 9:11-13; 2 Chron. 8:2).
   D. The commerce
      1. He sent his experienced sailors to serve in the fleet with Solomon's men on the Red Sea (1 Kings 9:26-27).
      2. Hiram's ships brought to Solomon from Ophir (a place in Saudia Arabia) precious and exotic objects and animals.
         a. The objects—gold, silver, ivory, cargoes of almug wood and various precious stones (1 Kings 10:11-12, 22)
         b. The animals—Apes and peacocks (1 Kings 10:22)

STATISTICS

First mention: 2 Samuel 5:11
Final mention: 2 Chronicles 9:21
Meaning of his name: "My brother is exalted"
Frequency of his name: Referred to 24 times
Biblical books mentioning him: Four books (2 Samuel, 1 Kings, 1 Chronicles, 2 Chronicles)
Occupation: King of Tyre (2 Sam. 5:11)
Important fact about his life: He was the king of Tyre who helped Solomon build the temple (1 Kings 5).

✍ *Hiram (2)*

CHRONOLOGICAL SUMMARY

I. His abilities
   A. He was also called Huram and Huram-abi (2 Chron. 2:13; 4:11).
   B. His mother was from either the tribe of Dan or Naphtali (1 Kings 7:14; 2 Chron. 2:14).
   C. His father was from Tyre and a craftsman in brass (1 Kings 7:14).
   D. Hiram was also highly skilled in bronze, gold, silver, iron, stone, wood, yarn, and fine linen, plus all

kinds of engraving (1 Kings 7:14;
2 Chron. 2:14).
II. His assignment—Hiram was sent by the
king of Tyre (also named Hiram) as
chief architect to superintend the building of the temple (2 Chron. 2:13; 4:11-
16).

STATISTICS
First mention: 1 Kings 7:13
Final mention: 2 Chronicles 4:16
Meaning of his name: "My brother is exalted"
Frequency of his name: Referred to seven
times
Biblical books mentioning him: Two books
(1 Kings, 2 Chronicles)
Occupation: Metal craftsman (1 Kings 7:14)
Important fact about his life: He served as the
chief architect for the temple built by Sol-
omon.

✏ *Hobab*

CHRONOLOGICAL SUMMARY
I. He was a Midianite scout and the
brother-in-law of Moses (Exod. 2:18; 3:1;
Num. 10:29).
II. He was urged by Moses to accompany
Israel to the promised land, but refused
to leave his home in the Sinai desert
(Num. 10:29-31).

STATISTICS
Sister: Zipporah (Exod. 2:21)
First mention: Numbers 10:29
Final mention: Numbers 10:29
Meaning of his name: "Beloved"
Frequency of his name: Referred to one time
Biblical books mentioning him: One book
(Numbers)
Occupation: Possibly a professional scout
(Num. 10:31)
Important fact about his life: He was Moses'
brother-in-law (Num. 10:29).

✏ *Hophni*

CHRONOLOGICAL SUMMARY
I. He was the corrupt priestly son of Eli.
A. The nature of this corruption
1. He and his brother Phinehas were
both dishonest and greedy in handling the tabernacle offerings, often threatening the people
(1 Sam. 2:12-17).
2. They actually committed adultery
with the women who came to the
tabernacle (1 Sam. 2:22).
B. The reason for this corruption—
Neither son had been properly disciplined by their father Eli (1 Sam. 2:23-
25; 3:13).
II. He was the condemned son of Eli.
A. The decision—Because of all this, God
determined to kill the brothers
(1 Sam. 2:25).
B. The declaration—A prophet warned
Eli both boys would die on the same
day (1 Sam. 2:34).
C. The defeat
1. In an attempt to rally the frightened Israelite troops, Hophni and
Phinehas carried the Ark of the
Covenant into a battle with the
Philistines (1 Sam. 4:4).
2. Israel lost the battle regardless,
and both sons were killed (1 Sam.
4:11).

STATISTICS
Father: Eli (1 Sam. 1:3)
Brother: Phinehas (1 Sam. 1:3)
First mention: 1 Samuel 1:3
Final mention: 1 Samuel 4:17
Meaning of his name: "Strong"
Frequency of his name: Referred to seven
times
Biblical books mentioning him: One book
(1 Samuel)
Occupation: Priest (1 Sam. 1:3)
Place of death: On a battlefield near Shiloh
(1 Sam. 4:10-12, 17)
Circumstances of death: He was killed by the
Philistines (1 Sam. 4:17).

Important fact about his death—He was Eli's wicked oldest son (1 Sam. 2:12-17, 22).

✎Hosea

CHRONOLOGICAL SUMMARY
I. The sin of adultery—Case study #1
  A. The individuals
    1. The injured spouse—Hosea
    2. The immoral spouse—Gomer
  B. The evaluation—God ordered Hosea the prophet to marry a harlot named Gomer so that this marriage would illustrate God's marriage to unfaithful Israel (1:1-3).
    1. The children from this marriage—The prophet fathered three children through Gomer. Each child was given a name (at God's command) which carried with it a prophetical meaning (1:4-11).
      a. The first child, a boy, was named Jezreel, meaning "to be scattered." This referred to two future events:
        (1) The setting aside of the dynasty of a Northern Israelite king named Jehu
        (2) The Assyrian invasion, at which time the entire Northern Kingdom would be scattered
      b. The second child, a girl, was named Lo-ruhamah, meaning "no more mercy," indicating that God's judgment was right around the corner.
      c. The third child, a boy, was named Lo-ammi, meaning "not my people."
    2. The concern for this marriage—Hosea attempted in vain to save his marriage. Gomer, a harlot before her marriage, soon became an adulteress following her marriage. In desperation, Hosea:
      a. Barred her from the markets of the world. In essence he tried to keep her home. But she found a way back to her old life and soon wound up as a sexual slave. Hosea then:
      b. Bought her from the markets of the world.
  C. The ending—We are not informed whether this marriage was eventually saved or not.
II. The sin of adultery—Case study #2
  A. The individuals
    1. The injured Spouse—God himself
    2. The immoral spouse—Ephraim (or Israel)
  B. The evaluation
    1. God's wife is described.
      a. Israel was as a backsliding heifer (4:16).
      b. She was aflame with lust like a baker's hot oven (7:4). God said the hearts of the people smoldered with evil plots during the night, and burst into flaming fire the next morning.
      c. They mingled with the heathen and had become as useless as a half-baked cake (7:8).
      d. They were as a silly dove, calling to Egypt and flying to Assyria for help (7:11).
      e. They were as a crooked bow, always missing the target, which was God's glory (7:16).
      f. They lay among the nations as a broken pot (8:8).
      g. They were as a wandering and lonely wild ass (8:9).
      h. They were as a dried-up root (9:16).
      i. They were as an empty vine (10:1).
    2. God's wife is denounced.
      a. Because of her ignorance (4:6)
      b. Because of her idolatry
        (1) Ephraim had prayed to idols (4:12).
        (2) She had sacrificed her sons to idols (4:13).
        (3) She had totally joined herself to idols (4:17).

3. God's wife was disciplined. "They have sown the wind, and they shall reap the whirlwind" (8:7; see also 10:13).
   a. God would therefore withhold his mercy from them (for awhile) (2:4).
   b. They would be many days without the following (3:4):
      (1) A king—In 721 B.C., Hoshea, Israel's last king, was dethroned, and in 587 B.C., Zedekiah, Judah's final king, was deposed. Some six centuries later Israel's only true king was rejected (John 19:15). Thus, this tragic situation will continue until he comes again (Rev. 19:11-16).
      (2) A prince—The next recorded prince in Israel's future will not minister until the Millennium (Ezek. 44:3).
      (3) A sacrifice—In A.D. 70 Titus destroyed the temple and all animal sacrifices ceased. During the tribulation they will once again be instituted, only to be stopped by the Antichrist (Dan. 9:27).
      (4) An image—This literally means "the pillars," and may refer to the temple. A temple will be rebuilt during the tribulation (Rev. 13; 2 Thess. 2), destroyed (Zech. 14:2), and another raised during the Millennium (Ezek. 40–48).
      (5) An ephod—A reference to Israel's high priesthood; the ephod was a garment he wore. Israel's last high priest personally planned the murder of the nation's own Messiah. (John 11:49-51; Matt. 26:57-68).
      (6) Terephim—These were normally figurines, or images in human form (Gen. 31:34). It is not known what Hosea had in mind here.
   c. They would go off as slaves into Assyria (10:6).
   d. They would be temporarily swallowed up among the nations (8:8; 9:17).
C. The ending
   1. The return of God's wife (3:5; 6:1-2)
   2. The restoration of God's wife (13:10, 14; 14:4-7)

THEOLOGICAL SUMMARY

I. Hosea may have ministered longer than any other Old or New Testament prophet.
II. He undoubtedly understood God's grieving heart over Israel's unfaithfulness because of his own tragic marriage.
III. He constantly referred to the Northern Kingdom of Israel as Ephraim, for this was the first of the 10 tribes to backslide.
IV. Paul quoted Hosea to support his position concerning the eventual restoration of Israel (Hos. 2:23; Rom. 9:25). "As he saith also in Osee, I will call them my people, which were not my people; and her beloved, which was not beloved" (Rom. 9:25).

STATISTICS

Father: Beeri (Hos. 1:1)
Spouse: Gomer (Hos. 1:2-3)
Sons: Jezreel and Lo-ammi (Hos. 1:4, 9)
Daughter: Lo-ruhamah (Hos. 1:6)
First mention: Hosea 1:1
Final mention: Romans 9:25
Meaning of his name: "Salvation"
Frequency of his name: Referred to four times
Biblical books mentioning him: Two books (Hosea, Romans)
Occupation: Priest (Prophet?)
Important fact about his life: He was commanded by God to marry a harlot (Hos. 1:2).

Hoshea

CHRONOLOGICAL SUMMARY
I. Hoshea and Pekah
  - A. Hoshea was the nineteenth and final king of Northern Israel.
  - B. He reigned nine years (2 Kings 17:1).
  - C. He murdered Pekah (the eighteenth ruler) to obtain his throne (2 Kings 15:30).
  - D. He was "evil in the sight of the LORD, but not as the kings of Israel that were before him" (2 Kings 17:2).
II. Hoshea and Shalmaneser
  - A. The rebellion against Shalmaneser
    1. At the beginning of his reign, Hoshea was threatened by the Assyrian monarch Shalmaneser.
    2. He at first attempted to appease him with tribute money (2 Kings 17:3).
  - B. The retaliation by Shalmaneser
    1. Later, however, Hoshea joined up with Egypt in plotting a rebellion against Shalmaneser (2 Kings 17:4).
    2. Upon discovering this, the Assyrian king cast Hoshea into prison (2 Kings 17:4).
    3. After a three-year siege, Shalmaneser conquered Hoshea's capital city of Samaria and carried the citizens off into captivity (2 Kings 17:5-6).

STATISTICS
Father: Elah (2 Kings 15:30)
First mention: 2 Kings 15:30
Final mention: 2 Kings 18:10
Meaning of his name: "God is help"
Frequency of his name: Referred to seven times
Biblical books mentioning him: One book (2 Kings)
Occupation: King of Northern Israel
Place of death: Probably Assyria (2 Kings 18:11)

Important fact about his life: He was the final king over Northern Israel (2 Kings 18:11).

Huldah

CHRONOLOGICAL SUMMARY
I. Her grievous prophecy
  - A. Huldah ministered in the days of godly King Josiah. She lived in the second district of Jerusalem (2 Kings 22:14).
  - B. Josiah sent Hilkiah the high priest to seek Huldah's counsel when workmen discovered a copy of the Law of Moses in the temple (2 Kings 22:8-13).
  - C. She warned Josiah that God was going to destroy Judah and Jerusalem because of their continuous and unrepentant sinning (2 Kings 22:15-17).
II. Her good prophecy—Huldah assured Josiah, however, that he would be spared this (2 Kings 22:18-20).

STATISTICS
Spouse: Shallum (2 Kings 22:14)
First mention: 2 Kings 22:14
Final mention: 2 Chronicles 34:22
Meaning of her name: "Weasel"
Frequency of her name: Referred to two times
Biblical books mentioning her: Two books (2 Kings, 2 Chronicles)
Occupation: Prophetess (2 Kings 22:14)
Important fact about her life: She was a prophetess in the days of King Josiah who warned of Judah's downfall (2 Kings 22:14-20).

Hur

CHRONOLOGICAL SUMMARY
I. His association with Moses—Hur was probably the husband of Miriam and thus brother-in-law of Moses, according to Jewish tradition.
II. His assistance to Moses—Along with

Aaron (Moses' older brother), Hur helped lift up the arms of Moses, thus assuring Israel victory during the battle against the Amalekites at the base of Mt. Sinai (Exod. 17:10-13).

III. His assignment from Moses—Moses placed Aaron and Hur in charge of the Israelite camp during the great lawgiver's 40-day session on Mt. Sinai (Exod. 24:14).

STATISTICS

Spouse: Thought to be Miriam, Moses' sister (Jewish tradition)

First mention: Exodus 17:10

Final mention: Exodus 24:14

Meaning of his name: "Free, noble"

Frequency of his name: Referred to three times

Biblical books mentioning him: One book (Exodus)

Important fact about his life: He helped uphold Moses' hands during a battle (Exod. 17:12).

Hushai

CHRONOLOGICAL SUMMARY

I. Hushai and David

A. A supporter of David

1. Hushai was an Arkite from a village west of Beth-el.

2. He was a friend and advisor of David who accompanied the king in his retreat from Jerusalem during the flight from Absalom (2 Sam. 15:32).

B. A spy for David—He was sent back to Jerusalem by David, who ordered him to pretend to side with Absalom so that the king might learn what the young rebel was planning (2 Sam. 15:33-37).

II. Hushai and Absalom

A. The subtlety

1. Absalom at first was suspicious of Hushai's offer to help, but soon accepted him as a valuable advisor (2 Sam. 16:15-20).

2. Realizing David's men needed time to organize a counterattack, Hushai advised Absalom to mobilize more men before attacking, and then suggested the young rebel himself lead the troops in battle (2 Sam. 17:6-13).

B. The success

1. The foolish and arrogant Absalom agreed, thus refusing the previous advice of Ahithophel, who had correctly counseled him to strike immediately (2 Sam. 17:1-4).

2. Hushai then told the high priest Zadok and his associate Abiathar of Absalom's plans, who in turn sent their two sons to warn David (2 Sam. 17:15-22).

III. Hushai and Solomon—Years later King Solomon (David's son) appointed Baanah, son of Hushai, as commissioner over one of the 12 tax districts in Israel (1 Kings 4:16).

STATISTICS

Son: Baanah (1 Kings 4:16)

First mention: 2 Samuel 15:32

Final mention: 1 Chronicles 27:33

Meaning of his name: "Quick"

Frequency of his name: Referred to 14 times

Biblical books mentioning him: Three books (2 Samuel, 1 Kings, 1 Chronicles)

Occupation: Advisor to David (2 Sam. 15:32-34)

Important fact about his life: He was a trusted advisor to both David and Solomon.

Isaac

CHRONOLOGICAL SUMMARY

I. Isaac and Abraham

A. The supernatural birth of Isaac

1. Isaac was promised to his parents and named by God himself even before he was born (Gen. 17:9, 21).

2. He was born from Sarah's barren

womb, which God had supernaturally touched (Gen. 18:10-11).

3. Abraham was 100 and Sarah was
90 at the birth of their son (Gen.
17:17; 21:5).

B. The submissive spirit of Isaac (Gen.
22:1-11)

1. Isaac accompanied Abraham upon
Mt. Moriah to become a sacrifice
as commanded by God.

2. At first he was unaware that he
himself would be the sacrifice.

3. He thus asked his father: "Behold
the fire and the wood: but where
is the lamb for a burnt offering?"
(Gen. 22:7).

4. Upon being told, he willingly allowed Abraham to bind him upon
the altar (Gen. 22:9).

C. The substitute lamb for Isaac (Gen.
22:12-14)

1. Abraham saw a ram nearby,
caught by his horns in a thicket.

2. At God's command, Abraham offered up the ram as a substitute
for Isaac.

II. Isaac and Ishmael

A. Isaac was ridiculed on the day of his
weaning by his older half brother Ishmael (Gen. 21:8-11).

B. Because of this, Abraham sent away
Ishmael and his mother Hagar (Gen.
21:12-14).

C. Isaac and Ishmael would be reunited
years later at the burial of their father
Abraham (Gen. 25:9).

III. Isaac and Rebekah

A. His marriage to Rebekah

1. Isaac married Rebekah, who was
selected and brought to him by
Abraham's servant from the Mesopotamian city of Nahor (Gen.
24:10, 62-67).

2. He was 40 years old at this time
(Gen. 25:20).

B. His prayer for Rebekah

1. God answered Isaac's prayer for
his barren wife Rebekah, resulting
in the birth of twins, Esau and
Jacob (Gen. 25:21-26).

2. Isaac was 60 at this time (Gen.
25:26).

C. His lie concerning Rebekah

1. In a time of famine, Isaac moved
to the Philistine city of Gerar
(Gen. 26:1).

2. Fearing the Philistines might kill
him in order to marry his wife,
Isaac lied about Rebekah, telling
the Philistine King Abimelech that
she was his sister (Gen. 26:7).

3. He was caught in this lie through
an embarrassing incident and rebuked by Abimelech (Gen. 26:8-
11).

IV. Isaac and the Philistines

A. In spite of his carnality, Isaac was
blessed by God, reaping a 100-fold
increase of his crops in one year
(Gen. 26:12-13).

B. This aroused the envy of the Philistines, who retaliated by filling up
Isaac's wells with debris (Gen. 26:14-
15).

C. Finally, at Abimelech's request, Isaac
moved away from Gerar and re-
opened those clogged wells (Gen.
26:16-22).

D. Realizing the blessings of God upon
Isaac, Abimelech visited him and requested they sign a peace treaty,
which they did (Gen. 26:26-33).

V. Isaac and God

A. The appearance at Gerar (Gen. 26:2-5)

1. He was warned not to go to
Egypt in time of famine as his father Abraham had once done.

2. God then reaffirmed the
Abrahamic Covenant to him,
which consisted of seed, soil, and
a Savior.

a. Seed—God would make his
seed "to multiply as the stars of
heaven" (26:4).

b. Soil—The land of Canaan
would be given to his descendants (26:3).

c. A Savior—Someday "in thy
seed shall all the nations of the
earth be blessed" (26:4).

B. The appearance at Beer-sheba (Gen. 26:23-25)
1. Once again the Abrahamic Covenant was confirmed to Isaac.
2. He built an altar there and worshiped God.

VI. Isaac and his sons
A. Esau, the favorite of Isaac
1. Both Isaac and Rebekah were grieved when Esau married two pagan Hittite women (Gen. 26:34-35).
2. In spite of this, however, Isaac looked upon Esau as his favorite son (Gen. 25:28).
3. One day, fearing his life might be ending, Isaac called for Esau (Gen. 27:1-4). Actually he would live many years longer, reaching the age of 180 (Gen. 35:28).
   a. He instructed his son to kill and prepare some wild game for him.
   b. He then promised to bestow upon Esau the patriarchal blessing.

B. Jacob, the favorite of Rebekah
1. Rebekah, upon overhearing the words of Isaac, quickly summoned Jacob, her favorite son (Gen. 25:28; 27:5-6).
2. Rapid plans were made for Jacob to deceive the dim-eyed Isaac (Gen. 27:7-17).
   a. He was to assume the identity of Esau so that he, Jacob, might receive the blessing.
   b. Rebekah quickly prepared the food Isaac had requested from Esau.
   c. She then dressed Jacob with Esau's clothes, covering his hands and the smooth part of his neck with goat skins.
3. Isaac was successfully deceived by Jacob and gave him the patriarchal blessing, predicting the following (Gen. 27:18-29):
   a. That Jacob would become a prosperous man

   b. That Esau's descendants would serve Jacob's descendants
   c. That other nations would serve Jacob's descendants
   d. That God would bless those who befriended Jacob and curse those who cursed him
4. A shocked Isaac later learned from Esau of Jacob's deception (Gen. 27:30-36).
5. At Esau's request, Isaac pronounced a modified blessing upon him, predicting the following (Gen. 27:37-40):
   a. That Esau's life would not be one of ease and luxury
   b. That he would live by the sword
   c. That for awhile he would serve his brother, but eventually he would shake loose from him
6. Realizing that Esau was planning to kill Jacob, Isaac did the following (Gen. 28:1-5):
   a. He called for Jacob and blessed him.
   b. He commanded him not to marry a Canaanite wife.
   c. He told him to find a wife among Rebekah's relatives in Nahor.
   d. Finally, he prayed that Jacob would eventually return and possess the land given him by the Abrahamic Covenant.

THEOLOGICAL SUMMARY
I. On at least 25 occasions in the Old Testament, God identified himself as the God of Abraham, Isaac, and Jacob.
II. These five individuals described the Lord as the God of Abraham, Isaac, and Jacob.
   A. Moses (Deut. 9:27)
   B. Elijah (1 Kings 18:36)
   C. David (1 Chron. 16:16; 29:18)
   D. The psalmist (Ps. 105:9-10)
   E. Hezekiah (2 Chron. 30:6)
III. Jesus and Isaac
   A. Jesus on two occasions referred to his

Father as the God of Abraham, Isaac, and Jacob (Matt. 22:32; Luke 20:37).
B. Jesus predicted that saved Gentiles would someday fellowship with Abraham, Isaac, and Jacob (Matt. 8:11).
IV. Peter and Isaac: Peter referred to God as the God of Abraham, Isaac, and Jacob (Acts 3:13).
V. Stephen and Isaac
A. Stephen referred to God as the God of Abraham, Isaac, and Jacob (Acts 7:32).
B. Stephen mentioned the birth and circumcision of Isaac (Acts 7:8).
VI. Paul and Isaac
A. Paul referred to Isaac and his two sons in illustrating the sovereignty of God (Rom. 9:7-15).
B. Paul referred to Isaac and Ishmael, using them to contrast law and grace (Gal. 4:28-31).
VII. James and Isaac—James referred to the offering up of Isaac on Mt. Moriah (James 2:21).
VIII. The book of Hebrews and Isaac
A. Hebrews mentions the offering up of Isaac on Mt. Moriah (Heb. 11:17).
B. It refers also to Isaac's faith in blessing Jacob and Esau (Heb. 11:20).

STATISTICS

Father: Abraham (Gen. 21:3)
Mother: Sarah (Gen. 21:3)
Spouse: Rebekah (Gen. 24:67)
Sons: Esau and Jacob (Gen. 25:24-26)
Brothers: Half brothers: Ishmael, Zimran, Jokshan, Medan, Midian, Ishbak, and Shuah (Gen. 16:16; 25:1-2)
First mention: Genesis 17:19
Final mention: James 2:21
Meaning of his name: "Laughter"
Frequency of his name: Referred to 128 times
Biblical books mentioning him: 21 books (Genesis, Exodus, Leviticus, Numbers, Deuteronomy, Joshua, 1 Kings, 2 Kings, 1 Chronicles, 2 Chronicles, Psalms, Jeremiah, Amos, Matthew, Mark, Luke, Acts, Romans, Galatians, Hebrews, James)
Place of death: At Mamre, near Hebron (Gen. 35:27-29)

Age at death—180 (Gen. 35:28)
Important fact about his life: He was Abraham's promised son and father of Jacob (Gen. 17:19; 25:21-26).

Isaiah

CHRONOLOGICAL SUMMARY

I. Israel, God's faithless servant (1–35)
A. Isaiah discussed the failures of Israel.
B. Isaiah discussed the future of Israel.
II. Hezekiah, God's frightened servant (36–39)
A. Jerusalem was surrounded by her foes.
B. Jerusalem was saved from her foes.
III. Christ, God's faithful servant (40–66)

TOPICAL SUMMARY

I. Isaiah and King Ahaz
A. Isaiah's first prophecy
1. Divinely sent reassurance—Isaiah and his son Shear-jashub were sent by God to reassure the frightened Judean King Ahaz (7:1-12).
2. The need for this reassurance—The city of Jerusalem had been surrounded by two of its enemies.
3. The contents of this reassurance
a. Ahaz was to keep calm and not be afraid.
b. God himself would soon put down the two invaders.
4. The reaction to this reassurance
a. God's invitation—God invited Ahaz to test him by asking for a sign, either in the deepest depths or in the highest heights.
b. Ahaz's unbelief—He refused to even put God to the test.
B. Isaiah's second prophecy—God then delivered through Isaiah a special divine sign of his own (7:13-14).
1. Its message—Someday a virgin would give birth to a son, whose name would be Immanuel.
2. Its meaning—This sign would

serve as proof of God's intention to someday deliver Jerusalem from all its enemies.

II. Isaiah and King Hezekiah

A. The siege—Isaiah delivered three messages during the time when Sennacherib, the Assyrian king, and his armies had surrounded the city of Jerusalem.

1. Isaiah's message to the frightened Judean King Hezekiah (2 Kings 19:5-7; Isa. 37:5-7)

a. The Assyrian king would receive bad news from home and would quickly return there.

b. When he arrived, he would be killed.

2. Isaiah's message to the people of Jerusalem (2 Kings 19:32-34)

a. The Assyrian king would not enter the city.

b. He would not build a ramp against its wall or even shoot an arrow into the city.

c. He would return by the road he came on.

d. God would personally save Jerusalem for his name's sake and that of David.

3. Isaiah's message to Sennacherib, the Assyrian king (2 Kings 19:20-28; Isa. 37:22-29)

a. The only reason Sennacherib was able to defeat the various nations was because God allowed him to.

b. God knew his plans and the evil things Sennacherib said about him.

c. Because of Sennacherib's arrogance against God, God would do the following:

(1) Put a hook in his nose

(2) Place a bridle in his mouth

(3) Turn him back on the road by which he came

B. The salvation—Isaiah and Hezekiah then called out to God, who sent an angel who destroyed 185,000 Assyrian troops (2 Kings 19:35; 2 Chron. 32:20-21).

C. The sickness—Isaiah delivered some terrible and then tremendous news to the ailing Hezekiah.

1. The terrible news

a. The nature of this news—Hezekiah was to put his house in order, for God said he would not recover but die (Isa. 38:1).

b. The reason for the news—Hezekiah had invoked God's judgment for allowing his heart to become proud and ungrateful (2 Chron. 32:25).

2. The tremendous news

a. The nature of this news (2 Kings 20:4-6)

(1) God had heard the king's prayer and had seen his tears.

(2) God would raise him up and add 15 years to his life.

b. The sign proof of this news—Isaiah offered Hezekiah one of two signs to prove the validity of the prophecy (2 Kings 20:8-11).

(1) Did the king want the sun's shadow to go forward 10 steps on the stairway of Ahaz?

(2) Or did he want it to go back 10 steps?

(3) Hezekiah chose the second, feeling this would be the greater sign. As the king watched, the miracle occurred.

c. The method employed to effect this news—Isaiah instructed Hezekiah to boil some dried figs, make a paste of them, and apply it to his body (2 Kings 20:7; Isa. 38:21).

D. The stupidity—Isaiah severely rebuked Hezekiah (2 Kings 20:12-18; Isa. 39:1-7).

1. The foolishness of the king's action—Hezekiah showed a

visiting envoy from Babylon all his vast riches, his treasure house of silver, gold, jewels, spices, and fine oils.

2. The fallout from the king's action—Isaiah predicted the following:

   a. Someday Babylonian soldiers would come to Jerusalem and carry off all the riches Hezekiah had made known.

   b. His own sons would become their slaves.

III. Isaiah and the Seraphims—Isaiah was called into full-time service the year that King Uzziah died (6:1-13).

A. Isaiah and the heaven of God

  1. His vision

   a. He saw the Lord seated on a throne, with his glory filling the temple.

   b. He saw the mighty six-winged angels known as the Seraphs.

   c. He heard them calling to one another, "Holy, holy, holy is the LORD of hosts: the whole earth is full of his glory" (6:3).

  2. His vexation—The prophet was made to realize he was an unclean man living among an unclean people.

  3. His visitation—One of the Seraphs touched Isaiah's mouth with a live coal taken from the heavenly altar, assuring him his guilt was removed and his sin atoned for.

B. Isaiah and the God of heaven

  1. Hearing God's voice—The prophet heard God say: "Whom shall I send, and who will go for us?" (6:8)

  2. Heeding God's voice—Isaiah responded, "Here am I; send me" (6:8).

IV. Isaiah and the fall of Lucifer (14:12-15)—The prophet records the five deadly "I wills" which caused Lucifer to become the devil. This arrogant angel coveted the following:

A. God's place—"I will ascend into heaven."

B. God's preeminence—"I will exalt my throne above the stars of God."

C. God's program—"I will sit also upon the mount of the congregation, in the sides of the north."

D. God's position—"I will ascend above the heights of the clouds."

E. God's power—"I will be like the most High."

V. Isaiah and the Gentile nations

A. Babylon (13–14, 21)

B. Assyria (14:24-27)

C. Philistia (14:28-32)

D. Moab (15–16)

E. Syria (17)

F. Ethiopia (18)

G. Egypt (19–20)—Isaiah was commanded by God to remove his outer clothing and walk barefoot for three years to predict how Assyria would strip Egypt and Ethiopia of their riches and possessions (Isa. 20:1-6).

H. Edom (21:11-12)

I. Arabia (21:13-17)

J. Tyre (23)

K. The whole world (24–25)

VI. Isaiah and the nation of Israel

A. He described Israel's sin.

  1. Willful ignorance (1:3; 5:13)

  2. Hypocrisy (1:14-15)

  3. Corrupt leadership (1:23; 9:16)

  4. Idolatry (2:8)

  5. Gross materialism (2:7)

  6. Godless women (3:16-26)

  7. Fruitlessness (5:1-7)

  8. Drunkenness (5:11; 28:7)

  9. Amorality (5:20)

  10. Humanism (5:21)

  11. Unscriptural alliances (31:1)

  12. Rebellion (30:9; 65:2)

  13. Infant sacrificing (57:5)

  14. Overall condition (1:6; 59:1-3, 7-8; 64:6)

B. He described Israel's punishment.

  1. Defeat (30:17)

2. Dullness of eyes (29:10-12)
3. Destruction (3:8; 10:6)
C. He described Israel's repentance.
   1. They will turn from their misdoings (31:7).
   2. They will turn to their Messiah (64:8-9).
D. He described Israel's rebirth.
   1. The travail involved (66:7-9)
   2. The time involved (66:8)
   3. The transformation involved (26:19)
E. He described Israel's restoration.
   1. The gathering by the Lord (27:12; 43:5-6)
   2. The glorifying of the Lord (27:13)

VII. Isaiah and the greatness of God
A. He wrote of God's intrinsic attributes.
   1. His glory (42:8; 59:19)
   2. His holiness (6:1-3; 57:15)
   3. His omniscience (40:13-14)
   4. His omnipotence (40:12, 15-17)
   5. His eternalness (57:15)
   6. His trinity (48:16)
   7. His uniqueness (45:5-6; 46:9)
B. He writes of God's imparted attributes.
   1. His righteousness (59:17)
   2. His grace (30:19)
   3. His mercy (14:1)
   4. His compassion (63:7-9)
   5. His wrath (30:27)
   6. His longsuffering (1:18)
   7. His faithfulness (25:1)
   8. His love (49:14-16)
   9. His salvation (12:2-5; 25:8-9; 45:22)
   10. His Word (40:6-8; 55:10-11)

VIII. Isaiah and the Son of God
A. He described the Lamb.
   1. His incarnation (7:14-15; 9:6)
   2. His lowliness and youth (7:15; 11:1-2; 53:2)
   3. His relationship to the Father (42:1; 50:4-5)
   4. His specific ministry to the Gentiles (9:1-2)
   5. His gracious ministry to all (42:2-3)
   6. His miracles (35:5-6)
   7. His message (61:1-2)

8. His suffering and death (50:6; 52:14; 53:1-10)
B. He described the Lion.
   1. His resurrection (53:10-12)
   2. His millennial reign (9:7; 32:1; 33:22)

IX. Isaiah and the great tribulation
A. He described the final woes.
   1. Divine plagues upon the soil (2:21; 13:13; 24:1, 6, 20)
   2. Divine plagues upon the sky (13:10; 34:4)
   3. Divine plagues upon sinners (2:19; 13:7-8; 34:1-2; 63:3)
B. He described the final war.
   1. The vengeance of the Lord (26:20, 21; 34:1-4; 66:15-16, 24)
   2. The victory of the Lord (63:1-6)

X. Isaiah and the glorious Millennium
A. The nations in the Millennium
   1. The Jews
     a. Their citizens will be purified (4:4).
     b. Their capital will be magnified (26:1-2; 52:1).
   2. The Gentiles
     a. Wars will cease (2:4).
     b. Worship will commence (2:2-3; 66:23).
B. The needy in the Millennium
   1. The blind will see (29:18; 35:5).
   2. The deaf will hear (29:18; 35:5).
   3. The lame will walk (35:6).
C. Nature itself in the Millennium
   1. The countryside
     a. Valleys will rise (40:4).
     b. Mountains will sink (40:4).
     c. Deserts will bloom (35:1, 6).
   2. The creatures
     a. Perfect harmony between the lion and the lamb (11:6-7; 65:25)
     b. Perfect harmony between the child and the cockatrice (11:8)

THEOLOGICAL SUMMARY

I. Isaiah and the Gospel writers
A. Matthew and Luke identified John the Baptist as the New Testament messenger predicted by Isaiah in the

Old Testament (compare Matt. 3:1-3; Luke 3:2-6 with Isa. 40:3-5).

1. The foretelling as described by Isaiah—"The voice of him that crieth in the wilderness, Prepare ye the way of the LORD, make straight in the desert a highway for our God. Every valley shall be exalted, and every mountain and hill shall be made low: and the crooked shall be made straight, and the rough places plain: And the glory of the LORD shall be revealed, and all flesh shall see it together: for the mouth of the LORD hath spoken it" (Isa. 40:3-5).

2. The fulfillment as described by Matthew—"In those days came John the Baptist, preaching in the wilderness of Judaea, And saying, Repent ye: for the kingdom of heaven is at hand. For this is he that was spoken of by the prophet Esaias, saying, The voice of one crying in the wilderness, Prepare ye the way of the Lord, make his paths straight" (Matt. 3:1-3).

B. Matthew identified Christ as the New Testament chosen servant foretold by Isaiah in the Old Testament.

1. The foretelling as described by Isaiah—"Behold my servant, whom I uphold; mine elect, in whom my soul delighteth; I have put my spirit upon him: he shall bring forth judgment to the Gentiles. He shall not cry, nor lift up, nor cause his voice to be heard in the street. A bruised reed shall he not break, and the smoking flax shall he not quench: he shall bring forth judgment unto truth. He shall not fail nor be discouraged, till he have set judgment in the earth: and the isles shall wait for his law" (Isa. 42:1-4).

2. The fulfillment as described by Matthew—"Behold my servant, whom I have chosen; my beloved, in whom my soul is well pleased: I will put my spirit upon him, and he shall shew judgment to the Gentiles. He shall not strive, nor cry; neither shall any man hear his voice in the streets. A bruised reed shall he not break, and smoking flax shall he not quench, till he send forth judgment unto victory. And in his name shall the Gentiles trust" (Matt. 12:18-21).

C. John wrote the following:

1. That the Jewish leaders had fulfilled Isaiah's prophecies about the unbelief Christ would face (Isa. 53:1; John 12:37-38).

2. That Isaiah had seen the glory of Christ and spoken of him (John 12:41)

II. Isaiah and Jesus

A. Jesus read from Isaiah's scroll during his sermon in Nazareth and claimed he was the fulfillment of the prophet's words concerning the Messiah.

1. The foretelling—"The Spirit of the LORD God is upon me; because the LORD hath anointed me to preach good tidings unto the meek; he hath sent me to bind up the brokenhearted, to proclaim liberty to the captives, and the opening of the prison to them that are bound; To proclaim the acceptable year of the LORD, and the day of vengeance of our God; to comfort all that mourn" (Isa. 61:1-2).

2. The fulfillment (Luke 4:16-21)—"He began to say unto them, This day is this scripture fulfilled in your ears" (Luke 4:21).

B. Jesus moved to Capernaum, a Galilean city in the region of Zebulun and Naphtali so that he might fulfill a prophecy given by Isaiah.

1. The foretelling—"the land of Zebulun and the land of Naphtali . . . by the way of the sea, beyond Jordan, in Galilee of the nations.

The people that walked in darkness have seen a great light: they that dwell in the land of the shadow of death, upon them hath the light shined" (Isa. 9:1-2).

2. The fulfillment—"Leaving Nazareth, he came and dwelt in Capernaum, which is upon the sea coast, in the borders of Zabulon and Nephthalim: That it might be fulfilled which was spoken by Esaias the prophet, saying, The land of Zabulon, and the land of Nephthalim, by the way of the sea, beyond Jordan, Galilee of the Gentiles" (Matt. 4:13-15).

C. Jesus healed many people to fulfill Isaiah's prophecy concerning the Messiah (Isa. 53:4; Matt. 8:16-17).

D. Jesus denounced the Pharisees on two occasions, saying they had fulfilled Isaiah's prophecies concerning them.

1. The first occasion (Isa. 6:9-10; Matt. 13:14-15)
2. The second occasion (Isa. 29:13; Matt. 15:7-9: Mark 7:6-7)

III. Isaiah and Philip

A. The passage—The Ethiopian eunuch was reading from Isaiah 53 when Philip caught up with him in the desert (Isa. 53:7-8; Acts 8:26-35)."The place of the scripture which he read was this, He was led as a sheep to the slaughter; and like a lamb dumb before his shearer, so opened he not his mouth: In his humiliation his judgment was taken away: and who shall declare his generation? for his life is taken from the earth" (Acts 8:32-33).

B. The puzzle—"The eunuch answered Philip, and said, I pray thee, of whom speaketh the prophet this? of himself, or of some other man?" (Acts 8:34).

C. The proclaiming—"Philip opened his mouth, and began at the same scripture, and preached unto him Jesus" (Acts 8:35).

IV. Isaiah and Paul—Paul often quoted from Isaiah, pointing out:

A. That unbelieving Israel had fulfilled Isaiah's prophecy about them (Isa. 6:9-10; 44:18; Acts 28:25-27)

B. That God had extended a long and intense invitation to Israel (Isa. 65:2; Rom. 10:21). "I have spread out my hands all the day unto a rebellious people, which walketh in a way that was not good, after their own thoughts" (Isa. 65:2).

C. That Israel would stumble over Christ when he appeared (Isa. 8:14; 28:16; Rom. 9:33)

D. That God would, nevertheless, reserve for himself a remnant in Israel (Isa. 10:22-23; Rom. 9:27-28): "Esaias also crieth concerning Israel, Though the number of the children of Israel be as the sand of the sea, a remnant shall be saved" (Rom. 9:27).

E. That this remnant would be preserved due to the grace of God alone (Isa. 1:9; Rom. 9:29): "As Esaias said before, Except the Lord of Sabaoth had left us a seed, we had been as Sodoma, and been made like unto Gomorrha" (Rom. 9:29).

F. That the Gentiles would find Christ (Isa. 9:6-7; 11:1, 10; 52:15; 65:1; Rom. 10:20; 15:12, 21): "Esaias is very bold, and saith, I was found of them that sought me not; I was made manifest unto them that asked not after me" (Rom. 10:20). "Esaias saith, There shall be a root of Jesse, and he that shall rise to reign over the Gentiles; in him shall the Gentiles trust" (Rom. 15:12).

STATISTICS

Father: Amoz (Isa. 38:1)

Spouse: A prophetess (Isa. 8:3)

Sons: Shear-jashub and Maher-shalal-hash-baz (Isa. 7:3; 8:1, 3)

First mention: 2 Kings 19:2

Final mention: Romans 15:12
Meaning of his name: "God's salvation"
Frequency of his name: Referred to 53 times
Biblical books mentioning him: Nine books
  (2 Kings, 2 Chronicles, Isaiah, Matthew,
  Mark, Luke, John, Acts, Romans)
Occupation: Prophet (2 Kings 19:2)
Important fact about his life: He was the Old
  Testament's greatest prophet.

Ish-bosheth

CHRONOLOGICAL SUMMARY
I. Crowned by a soldier
  A. The anointing
    1. He was one of Saul's sons who
      was made king over the 10 tribes
      of Israel by Abner, Saul's general,
      after the death of Saul (2 Sam.
      2:8).
    2. He was 40 years old at the time
      and reigned only two years
      (2 Sam. 2:10).
  B. The accusation
    1. Ish-bosheth accused Abner of
      sleeping with Rizpah, a former
      concubine of his father Saul
      (2 Sam. 3:7).
    2. In a rage, Abner threatened to
      turn over Ish-bosheth's kingdom
      to David (2 Sam. 3:8-11).
  C. The appeasement—In an attempt to
    appease both Abner and David, Ish-
    bosheth sent Michal, Saul's youngest
    daughter and David's first wife, back
    to David. During David's difficult
    days as an outlaw she had married
    another man (2 Sam. 3:12-16).
II. Killed by two soldiers—At the end of a
  two-year reign, Ish-bosheth was murdered by two of his soldiers (2 Sam.
  4:5-6).

STATISTICS
Father: Saul (2 Sam. 2:8)
First mention: 2 Samuel 2:8
Final mention: 2 Samuel 4:12

Meaning of his name: "Man of shame"
Frequency of his name: Referred to 11 times
Biblical books mentioning him: One book
  (2 Samuel)
Occupation: King of all Israel except Judah
  (2 Sam. 2:4, 8-9)
Place of death: In his own bedroom (2 Sam.
  4:5-7)
Circumstances of death: He was murdered by
  two rebels (2 Sam. 4:5, 11).
Important fact about his life: He succeeded his
  father, Saul, as king (2 Sam. 2:8-9).

Ishmael (1)

CHRONOLOGICAL SUMMARY
I. The prophecies concerning Ishmael
  A. Before his birth
    1. Ishmael's name was given to his
      mother Hagar by the Lord himself
      before his birth (Gen. 16:11).
    2. God also predicted he would live
      a wild life, fighting with both
      friend and foe (Gen. 16:12).
  B. After his birth
    1. God promised Abraham that he
      would bless Ishmael, and make
      him the father of 12 rulers (Gen.
      17:20; 25:13-16).
    2. Ishmael was circumcised by Abra-
      ham when he was 13 years old
      (Gen. 17:24-26).
II. The provocation by Ishmael
  A. Later Ishmael incurred the wrath of
    Sarah when he mocked her son Isaac
    on the day set aside to celebrate his
    weaning (Gen. 21:9-10).
  B. At the command of God, Abraham
    sent both Hagar and Ishmael away
    from his camp (Gen. 21:11-13).
III. The provision
  A. God made provision for Ishmael as
    he grew up in the desert of Paran,
    where he became an archer (Gen.
    21:20-21).
  B. He later married an Egyptian wife
    (Gen. 21:21).

C. One of his daughters was named Mahalath. She later became the wife of Esau (Gen. 28:9; 36:3).

STATISTICS
Father: Abraham (Gen. 16:15)
Mother: Hagar (Gen. 16:15)
Daughter: Mahalath (Gen. 28:9; 36:3)
Brothers: Half brothers were: Isaac, Zimran, Jokshan, Medan, Midian, Ishbak, and Shuah (Gen. 21:3; 25:2)
First mention: Genesis 16:11
Final mention: 1 Chronicles 1:31
Meaning of his name: "God is hearing"
Frequency of his name: Referred to 20 times
Biblical books mentioning him: Two books (Genesis, 1 Chronicles)
Occupation: Hunter (Archer? Gen. 21:20)
Age at Death 137 (Gen. 25:17)
Important fact about his life: He was Abraham's first son (Gen. 16:15).

✎Ishmael (2)

CHRONOLOGICAL SUMMARY
I. His background
   A. He was of royal blood (2 Kings 25:25).
   B. He had been one of the Judean king's officers (Jer. 41:1).
II. His bloodletting
   A. He killed Gedaliah.
      1. He was hired by Baalis, the Ammonite king, to do this (Jer. 40:14).
      2. Along with 10 men, he assassinated Gedaliah, the man appointed by Nebuchadnezzar to be governor over Judah after the destruction of Jerusalem (2 Kings 25:23, 25).
      3. Ishmael assassinated Gedaliah during a banquet hosted by the governor in the city of Mizpah (Jer. 41:1-2).
   B. He killed Gedaliah's companions. This included the Jewish guests at the

banquet as well as the Babylonian soldiers who were there (Jer. 41:3).
   C. He killed 70 (out of 80) men who were en route to offer up a sacrifice of grain and incense amid the ruins of the temple. He then threw their bodies into a cistern (Jer. 41:4-8).
   D. He made many captives.
      1. Ishmael carried off the remaining people in Mizpah (Jer. 41:10).
      2. These captives, however, were later rescued by a Judean army officer named Johanan and his troops, who chased Ishmael to the land of Ammon (Jer. 41:10-15).

STATISTICS
Father: Nethaniah (2 Kings 25:23)
First mention: 2 Kings 25:23
Final mention: Jeremiah 41:18
Meaning of his name: "God is hearing"
Frequency of his name: Referred to 23 times
Biblical books mentioning him: Two books (2 Kings, Jeremiah)
Occupation: Rebel soldier (2 Kings 25:23-25)
Important fact about his life: He was a rebel who killed Governor Gedaliah (2 Kings 25:25).

✎Ithamar

CHRONOLOGICAL SUMMARY
I. Ithamar and the assignment by Moses
   A. The work involved
      1. He was appointed a priest by God (Exod. 28:1).
      2. He was placed in charge of the materials used for the tabernacle (Exod. 38:21).
      3. He was also responsible for the transporting of the tabernacle (Num. 4:24-33).
   B. The warning involved—He was warned by Moses against carelessness in observing God's holiness after the deaths of his two brothers, Nadab and Abihu (Lev. 10:6-7).
II. Ithamar and the anger of Moses

A. He incurred the anger of Moses concerning the way he handled a sin offering in the sanctuary, until Moses realized he was blameless in this matter (Lev. 10:16-20).
B. A descendant of Ithamar named Daniel is mentioned as one who joined up with Ezra during the return to Jerusalem (Ezra 8:2).

STATISTICS
Father: Aaron (Exod. 6:23)
Mother: Elisheba (Exod. 6:23)
Brothers: Nadab, Abihu, and Eleazar (Exod. 6:23)
First mention: Exodus 6:23
Final mention: Ezra 8:2
Meaning of his name: "Island of the palm tree"
Frequency of his name: Referred to 20 times
Biblical books mentioning him: Five books (Exodus, Leviticus, Numbers, 1 Chronicles, Ezra)
Occupation: Priest (Exod. 28:1)
Important fact about his life: He was Aaron's youngest son (Exod. 6:23).

✍️Jabin

CHRONOLOGICAL SUMMARY
I. His oppression of Israel
A. He was a Canaanite king who reigned in Hazor during the times of the judges (Judg. 4:2).
B. Sisera was the commander of his army, which boasted of 900 iron chariots (Judg. 4:3).
C. Jabin had oppressed Israel for 20 years (Judg. 4:3).
II. His overthrow by Israel
A. Jabin's army was totally routed by an Israelite army led by Barak (Judg. 4:15-16).
B. Eventually Jabin himself was destroyed (Judg. 4:24).

C. The psalmist Asaph later referred to this (Ps. 83:9).

STATISTICS
First mention: Judges 4:2
Final mention: Psalms 83:9
Meaning of his name: "Intelligent"
Frequency of his name: Referred to seven times
Biblical books mentioning him: Two books (Judges, Psalms)
Occupation: Canaanite king (Judg. 4:2)
Important fact about his life: He sent 900 chariots against Israel only to suffer total defeat (Judg. 4:13-16).

✍️Jacob

CHRONOLOGICAL SUMMARY
I. Jacob, the younger twin
A. His birth was God's answer to Isaac's and Rebekah's prayer concerning children (Gen. 25:21-23).
1. God told them two nations were in Rebekah's womb.
2. One nation would be stronger than the other.
3. The older twin would serve the younger twin.
B. Jacob was thus the second born of twins (Gen. 25:24-26).
C. He was born with his hand grasping Esau's heel (Gen. 25:26).
II. Jacob, the devising brother
A. In contrast to Esau, who was an outdoorsman and a hunter, Jacob grew up a quiet man, staying among the tents (Gen. 25:27).
B. Jacob persuaded his famished brother Esau, who was returning from a hunting trip, to sell him the firstborn birthright for some bread and lentil stew (Gen. 25:29-34).
III. Jacob, the deceitful son
A. He was persuaded by Rebekah to assume the identity of Esau so that he might deceive and obtain from his

dim-eyed father the patriarchal blessing (Gen. 27:5-13).

B. Rebekah dressed him in Esau's clothes, covering his hands and the smooth part of his neck with goat skins (Gen. 27:14-16).

C. Jacob successfully deceived Isaac and received the following patriarchal blessing (Gen 27:17-30):

1. He would become a prosperous man.
2. Esau's descendants would serve his descendants.
3. Other nations would serve him.
4. God would bless those who befriended him and curse those who did not.

IV. The dreaming traveler

A. The vision of Jacob

1. He saw the angels of the Lord.
   a. Upon realizing that Esau planned to kill Jacob, Isaac and Rebekah sent Jacob away (Gen. 27:41–28:5).
      (1) They warned him not to marry a Canaanite woman.
      (2) They advised him to find a wife in the city of Nahor, among Rebekah's relatives.
   b. God appeared to Jacob en route to Nahor.
   c. In a dream he saw a stairway resting on the earth, with its top reaching to heaven, and the angels of God ascending and descending on it (Gen. 28:10-12).
2. He saw the Lord of the angels (Gen. 28:13-15)—God at this time reaffirmed to Jacob (as he had previously done for Isaac) the threefold features of the Abrahamic Covenant.
   a. The first feature dealt with the soil; that is, God would give the land of Canaan to Jacob's descendants.
   b. The second feature dealt with

the seed; that is, God would make of Jacob a great nation.

   c. The third feature dealt with a Savior; that is, someday the Messiah would come and bless all nations.

B. The vow of Jacob (Gen. 28:16-22)

1. Upon awakening, Jacob took the stone he had used as a pillow, poured oil upon it, and set it up as a pillar to God.
2. He then named that place Beth-el, meaning "house of God."
3. He promised that if God would protect and bless him, he would serve God and give back a tenth of all he possessed.

V. Jacob, the love-struck groom

A. His love for Rachel

1. Jacob arrived in Nahor of Padan-aram (Gen. 29:1-4).
2. He met Rachel, daughter of Laban, the brother of his mother Rebekah (Gen. 29:5-13).
   a. She arrived at a well to water her father's sheep.
   b. Jacob rolled a huge stone away from the entrance of the well for her.
3. Jacob then asked Laban that he be allowed to marry Rachel, agreeing to work seven years for her (Gen. 29:15-21).

B. His labor for Rachel

1. The diligence of Jacob—"Jacob served seven years for Rachel; and they seemed unto him but a few days, for the love he had to her" (Gen. 29:20).
2. The deception by Laban
   a. Laban deceived Jacob on the wedding night, substituting Leah, Rachel's older sister, for Rachel (Gen. 29:22-23).
   b. An angry Jacob confronted Laban the following morning (Gen. 29:25).
   c. Laban "explained" it was not their custom to give the

younger daughter in marriage
before the older one (Gen. 29:26).
  d. He then proposed the following
     (Gen. 29:27):
     (1) That Jacob fulfill Leah's one-
         week-long bridal celebration
     (2) That Laban would then give
         Rachel to Jacob
     (3) That Jacob would, however,
         agree to work yet another
         seven years for Rachel
  e. Jacob agreed and continued yet
     another seven years (Gen.
     29:28-30).
VI. Jacob, the fruitful family man
  A. Jacob fathered his first four sons
     through Leah.
     1. Reuben (Gen. 29:32)
     2. Simeon (Gen. 29:33)
     3. Levi (Gen. 29:34)
     4. Judah (Gen. 29:35)
  B. The barren and desperate Rachel pre-
     sented her maidservant Bilhah to Ja-
     cob, hoping this girl could bear
     children for her. Bilhah gave birth to
     two sons, Jacob's fifth and sixth.
     1. Dan (Gen. 30:6)
     2. Naphtali (Gen. 30:8)
  C. Leah did the same thing, giving her
     maidservant Zilpah to Jacob. Through
     her he fathered his seventh and
     eighth sons.
     1. Gad (Gen. 30:11)
     2. Asher (Gen. 30:13)
  D. Leah then resumed childbearing and
     presented Jacob with sons number
     nine and 10, plus his only recorded
     daughter.
     1. Issachar (Gen. 30:18)
     2. Zebulun (Gen. 30:20)
     3. Dinah (Gen. 30:21)
  E. At long last, Rachel gave birth to a
     son, Joseph (Gen. 30:24).
VII. Jacob, the enterprising employee
  A. Jacob and Laban—the suggestion
     1. Jacob planned to leave for Ca-
        naan, but was persuaded by La-
        ban to continue working for him
        as a flock tender (Gen. 30:25-30).

  2. Laban agreed to give Jacob all the
     speckled and spotted lambs,
     sheep and goats for his personal
     possessions (Gen. 30:31-42).
  3. Jacob's herds multiplied quickly,
     making him a very rich man
     (Gen. 30:43).
B. Jacob and Laban—the separation
   (Gen. 31:1-42)
   1. The reasons for this separation—
      After working for Laban 20 years,
      three factors prompted Jacob to
      return to Canaan (Gen. 31:1-18):
      a. A growing hostility between
         himself, Laban, and Laban's
         sons
      b. A revelation from God, in-
         structing Jacob to return to Ca-
         naan
      c. The support of his wives, who
         encouraged him to return
   2. The reunion following this separa-
      tion (Gen. 31:19-42)
      a. The frustration of Laban
         (1) Three days after Jacob had
             left, Laban discovered Jacob
             was gone.
         (2) After a seven-day chase, he
             caught up with his son-in-
             law in Gilead, that land east
             of the Jordan River.
         (3) Laban was furious at Jacob
             for two reasons:
             (a) First, because his son-in-
                 law had left without tell-
                 ing him
             (b) Second, because he incor-
                 rectly assumed Jacob had
                 stolen his household
                 gods. (Actually, Rachel
                 had taken them without
                 Jacob's knowledge.)
      b. The revelation to Laban—God
         appeared to Laban in a dream,
         warning him not to harm
         Jacob.
      c. The confrontation by Laban
         (1) Jacob was rebuked for his
             abrupt departure and was

accused of stealing Laban's household gods.

(2) Jacob denied this and allowed Laban to search through the camp.

(3) Laban failed to find them, for Rachel had hidden them inside her camel's saddle and was sitting upon them.

d. The explanation to Laban— Jacob said one of the key reasons he left was the fact that Laban had changed his wages 10 times during the 20 years he was employed by Laban.

C. Jacob and Laban—the symbol (Gen. 31:43-55)

1. The nature of this covenant—At Laban's demand, he and Jacob entered into an agreement involving the following points:

a. That God would punish Jacob if he ever mistreated Laban's daughters

b. That neither man would cross over a designated boundary line to harm the other

2. The symbol of this covenant—It consisted of a heap of stones.

3. The place of the covenant—It was called Mizpah, meaning "watchtower."

VIII. Jacob, the determined wrestler (Gen. 32:1-32)

A. His communion with God

1. The preparation—After being visited by the angels of God, Jacob learned that his brother Esau was riding to meet him with 400 men. He immediately did two things.

a. He divided his camp—In great fear, Jacob divided his camp into two groups so that if Esau attacked one group, the other could escape.

b. He delivered his bribe—Jacob instructed his servants to ride out and present the following to Esau: 200 female goats; 20 male goats; 200 ewes; 20 rams;

30 female camels with their young; 40 cows; 10 bulls; 20 female donkeys; and 10 male donkeys.

2. The supplication

a. Jacob spoke to God and cried out for deliverance from Esau.

b. Jacob struggled with God.

(1) The place—It was near the brook Jabbok, later named Peniel by Jacob, meaning, "Seeing God face to face."

(2) The persistence—Jacob refused to let go of God until he was blessed.

(3) The pronouncement—God changed Jacob's name to Israel, meaning "he who struggles with God."

(4) The proof—God touched the socket of Jacob's hip, causing him to limp. He never walked the same again after this wrestling session with the Lord.

B. His reunion with Esau—To Jacob's great relief, the meeting between him and Esau proved to be a very friendly one (Gen. 33:1-16).

IX. Jacob, the obedient patriarch

A. The required rendezvous of Jacob— He was ordered back to Beth-el by God (Gen. 35:1-15).

B. The rededication of Jacob

1. He ordered his household to give up their foreign gods, to purify themselves, and to change their clothes.

2. He built an altar at Beth-el and called it El-beth-el, meaning "the God of God's house."

C. The revelation to Jacob—God once again confirmed the promises of the Abrahamic Covenant to Jacob.

X. Jacob, the brokenhearted

A. Over the failure of his sons and the defilement of his daughter

1. The defilement of Dinah—His daughter was sexually violated by

a Hivite pagan named Shechem (Gen. 34:1-2).

2. Murder on the part of Simeon and Levi (Gen. 34:3-31)

   a. These two brothers tricked the Hivites into circumcizing themselves as a condition for any future marriages between them and the Israelites.

   b. On the third day when the Hivites were swollen and helpless, Simeon and Levi slaughtered them like wild animals.

3. Adultery on the part of Reuben—Reuben slept with Bilhah, one of Jacob's wives (Gen. 35:22).

4. Deceit and treachery on the part of his 10 sons

   a. The 10 sons and Joseph (Gen. 37:1-36)

      (1) Jacob made a brightly colored coat for his favorite son, Joseph.

      (2) He later gently rebuked his favorite son, however, for relating the unlikely details of two of his dreams in which Jacob, Rachel, and his brothers would someday bow down to him.

      (3) Jacob sent Joseph to check on the welfare of his 10 half brothers who were out tending their father's sheep.

      (4) After finding his half brothers, Joseph was sold into slavery by them and taken to Egypt.

      (5) Jacob was then deceived by his 10 sons into believing Joseph had been killed and eaten by a wild animal.

      (6) He was grief-stricken and could not be comforted.

   b. The 10 sons and Benjamin (Gen. 42:1–43:15)

      (1) Jacob sent his 10 sons to Egypt during a famine to buy food.

      (2) He refused, however, to allow his youngest son, Benjamin, to go lest he suffer harm.

      (3) Upon their return, the 10 brothers told Jacob about the strange food administrator they had met in Egypt, not realizing this powerful man was Joseph.

      (4) They related how he at first had accused them of being spies, that he had taken Simeon as hostage, and then demanded Benjamin be brought with them during their next trip to buy food.

      (5) Jacob at first refused to listen, concluding everything had turned against him, as he had lost both Simeon and Joseph.

B. Over the funerals of his wife, his wife's nurse, and his father

   1. Rebekah his wife (Gen. 35:16-19)

      a. She had died giving birth to Benjamin.

      b. Jacob buried her in or near the little town of Bethlehem.

   2. Deborah, the nurse of his wife (Gen. 35:8)

   3. Isaac, his father (Gen. 35:27-29)

XI. Jacob, the overjoyed father (Gen. 45:25—47:10)

A. An amazed and overjoyed Jacob learned his beloved son Joseph was not only alive, but was second in command over all the land of Egypt.

B. En route to Egypt to meet Joseph, Jacob was visited by God, who appeared to him at Beer-sheba.

C. God promised to bless Jacob in Egypt and someday bring his descendants back to Canaan.

D. Jacob arrived in Egypt with his family clan of 70 and was joyfully and tearfully reunited with Joseph.

E. Jacob met and blessed the pharaoh. At this time the old patriarch was 130.

XII. Jacob, the dying prophet
  A. The prophet and his two grandsons (Gen. 48:1-20)
    1. After living in Egypt for 17 years, Jacob realized his life was drawing to a close and called for Joseph's two sons, Manasseh and Ephraim, to be brought to him that he might bless them.
    2. He then blessed them and predicted that Ephraim (the younger grandson) would become greater than Manasseh, the firstborn.
  B. The prophet and his 12 sons (Gen. 49:1-28)
    1. Jacob's revelation concerning them—The old patriarch historically reviewed and prophetically previewed their lives and the tribes they would found.
      a. Reuben (Gen. 49:3-4)—Reuben was rebuked for his unruliness and immorality and was demoted from the position of being Jacob's firstborn.
      b. Simeon and Levi (Gen. 49:5-7)—They were also rebuked for their uncontrolled anger and cruelty.
      c. Judah (Gen. 49:8-12)
        (1) His brothers would praise him.
        (2) He would destroy his enemies as a lion would.
        (3) From his tribe the Messiah (Shiloh) would someday come.
      d. Zebulun (Gen. 49:13)—His people would dwell on the shores of the sea and offer harbors for ships.
      e. Issachar (Gen. 49:14-15)—His people would lovingly and diligently till the ground.
      f. Dan (Gen. 49:16-18)—His tribe would be known for its treachery.
      g. Gad (Gen. 49:19)
        (1) He would be attacked by a band of raiders.

        (2) He would counterattack them at their heels.
      h. Asher (Gen. 49:20)—His people would produce rich food, fit for kings.
      i. Naphtali (Gen. 49:21)—His tribe would be as a deer let loose, producing lovely fawns.
      j. Joseph (Gen. 49:22-26)
        (1) He was like a fruitful tree beside a fountain, whose branches shade the wall, extending over it.
        (2) Although he had suffered persecution, the mighty Rock of Israel would protect and abundantly bless him.
      k. Benjamin (Gen. 49:27)—He was as a wild wolf that prowled, devouring his enemies in the morning and dividing the spoils in the evening.
    2. Jacob's death (Gen. 49:29–50:13)
      a. He desired that after death his body be carried back to Canaan and buried in the cave of Machpelah alongside Abraham, Isaac, Sarah, Rebekah, and Leah.
      b. At the age of 147 Jacob died (Gen. 47:28).
      c. His embalming process required 40 days.
      d. After this came a 70-day period of national mourning.
      e. He was then carried into Canaan by his 12 sons.

THEOLOGICAL SUMMARY

  I. Both Joshua and Samuel referred to Jacob during their final addresses to the elders of Israel.
    A. Joshua (Josh. 24:4)
    B. Samuel (1 Sam. 12:8)
  II. Malachi contrasted Jacob with Esau to illustrate God's love toward Israel (Mal. 1:2-3).
  III. Paul contrasted Jacob with Esau to prove God's sovereignty (Rom. 9:13).

IV. Matthew and Luke included his name in their genealogies.
   A. Matthew did this as he traced the line of Christ through Solomon, the son of David (Matt. 1:2).
   B. Luke did this as he traced the line of Christ through Nathan, another son of David (Luke 3:34).
V. Jesus referred to Jacob on several occasions.
   A. To emphasize the salvation of all believing Gentiles (Matt. 8:11)
   B. To emphasize the fact that all departed believers are now conscious and in God's presence (Matt. 22:29-32)
VI. The Samaritan woman asked Jesus if he was greater than Jacob (John 4:12).
VII. Stephen referred to Jacob six times during his defense before the Sanhedrin (Acts 7:8, 12, 14-15, 32, 46).
   A. The fact that he fathered 12 sons
   B. The fact that he sent those sons to Egypt for food
   C. The fact that he himself later moved to Egypt
VIII. The book of Hebrews speaks of Jacob's faith.
   A. In living a simple life in tents while awaiting his heavenly home (Heb. 11:9)
   B. In blessing Joseph's two sons and predicting their future (Heb. 11:21)

STATISTICS

Father: Isaac (Gen. 25:21-26)
Mother: Rebekah (Gen. 25:21-26)
Spouses: Leah, Rachel, Bilhah, and Zilpah (Gen. 29:23, 28; 30:4, 9)
Sons: From Leah: Reuben, Simeon, Levi, Judah, Issachar, and Zebulun (Gen. 29:32-35; 30:18-20). From Rachel: Joseph and Benjamin (Gen. 30:22-24; 35:16-18). From Bilhah: Dan and Naphtali (Gen. 30:5-8). From Zilpah: Gad and Asher (Gen. 30:10, 13).
Daughter: Dinah (Gen. 30:21)
Brother: Esau (Gen. 25:25)
First mention: Genesis 25:26
Final mention: Hebrews 11:21

Meaning of his name: "Following after, supplanter"
Frequency of his name: Referred to 252 times
Biblical books mentioning him: 16 books (Genesis, Exodus, Leviticus, Numbers, Deuteronomy, Joshua, 1 Samuel, 2 Kings, Malachi, Matthew, Mark, Luke, John, Acts, Romans, Hebrews)
Place of death: Egypt (Gen. 49:33–50:3)
Age at death: 147 (Gen. 47:28)
Important fact about his life: He fathered 12 sons, who later founded Israel's 12 tribes (1 Chron. 2-8).

Jael

CHRONOLOGICAL SUMMARY

I. Jael and Sisera
   A. She assisted him.
      1. Jael was the wife of Heber the Kenite. The Kenites were one of the 10 tribal peoples living in Palestine in the time of the judges (Judg. 4:17).
      2. She invited Sisera, the defeated Canaanite army commander, into her tent during his flight from Barak (Judg. 4:18).
      3. After receiving some milk from her, he fell asleep (Judg. 4:19-21).
   B. She assassinated him by driving a tent peg through his temple (Judg. 4:21).
II. Jael and Barak
   A. After this she invited the Jewish military commander Barak into her tent to view the dead Sisera (Judg. 4:22).
   B. Later both Deborah and Barak praised her for this act of bravery in their song of praise (Judg. 5:24).

STATISTICS

Spouse: Heber (Judg. 4:17)
First mention: Judges 4:17
Final mention: Judges 5:24
Meaning of her name: "Chamois"
Frequency of her name: Referred to six times

Biblical books mentioning her: One book
(Judges)
Occupation: Housewife
Important fact about her life: She killed Sisera,
the enemy of Israel (Judg. 4:21).

Japheth

CHRONOLOGICAL SUMMARY
I. Japheth and his father's ship—He was
one of eight human beings who entered
Noah's ark and survived the universal
flood (Gen. 7:13).
II. Japheth and his father's sin
A. He helped his brother Shem cover
their drunken father's nakedness
(Gen. 9:23).
B. Noah later predicted that God would
extend the territory of Japheth's
descendants and that he would live in
the tents of Shem (Gen. 9:27).

STATISTICS
Father: Noah (Gen. 5:32; 1 Chron. 1:4)
Brothers: Shem and Ham (Gen. 5:32;
1 Chron. 1:4)
First mention: Genesis 5:32
Final mention: 1 Chronicles 1:5
Meaning of his name: "Extender"
Frequency of his name: Referred to 11 times
Biblical books mentioning him: Two books
(Genesis, 1 Chronicles)
Important fact about his life: He was Noah's
youngest son (Gen. 5:32; 1 Chron. 1:4).

Jeduthun

CHRONOLOGICAL SUMMARY
I. His appointment—He was one of the
288 Levitical musicians (along with his
sons) appointed by King David
(1 Chron. 16:41-42; 25:7).
II. His assignment
A. He was, along with another musician
named Heman, responsible for
sounding the trumpets and cymbals

and for the playing of other instruments in the tabernacle at Gibeon
(1 Chron. 16:39, 42).
B. He helped lead the music in the celebration following the completion of
Solomon's temple (2 Chron. 5:12).
C. He had the gift of prophecy
(1 Chron. 25:1), as did six of his sons,
who also played the harp (1 Chron.
25:3).
D. He may have composed the music for
Psalms 39, 62, and 77.

STATISTICS
Son: Obed-edom (1 Chron. 16:38)
First mention: 1 Chronicles 9:16
Final mention: Psalm 77 (in the introduc-
tion)
Meaning of his name: "Choir of praises"
Frequency of his name: Referred to 15 times
Biblical books mentioning him: Four books
(1 Chronicles, 2 Chronicles, Nehemiah,
Psalms)
Occupation: Levitical musician (1 Chron.
16:41-42)
Important fact about his life: He may have
written the music for Psalms 39, 62,
and 77

Jehoahaz (1)

CHRONOLOGICAL SUMMARY
I. The character of the king of Israel
A. He was the eleventh king of North-
ern Israel.
B. He ruled for 17 years (2 Kings 13:1).
C. He was, for the most part, an evil
king (2 Kings 13:2).
II. The compassion of the King of kings
A. Jehoahaz did, on one occasion, turn
to God for help from the terrible op-
pression Israel was suffering at the
hands of the Syrians (2 Kings 13:4).
B. His army had been reduced to 50
horsemen, 10 chariots, and 10,000
foot soldiers (2 Kings 13:7).
C. God heard his cry and answered it—
"The LORD was gracious unto them,

and had compassion on them, and had respect unto them, because of his covenant with Abraham, Isaac, and Jacob, and would not destroy them, neither cast he them from his presence as yet" (2 Kings 13:23).

STATISTICS
Father: Jehu (2 Kings 10:35)
Son: Jehoash (2 Kings 13:10)
First mention: 2 Kings 10:35
Final mention: 2 Chronicles 25:25
Meaning of his name: "God upholds"
Frequency of his name: Referred to 15 times
Biblical books mentioning him: Two books
   (2 Kings, 2 Chronicles)
Occupation: King of Northern Israel (2 Kings 13:1)
Important fact about his life: He was Jehu's son who, because of his and his people's sin, saw God reduce Northern Israel's army to 50 horsemen, 10 chariots, and 10,000 foot soldiers (2 Kings 13:7).

☜Jehoahaz (2)

CHRONOLOGICAL SUMMARY
I. Jehoahaz, the evil king
   A. He was the seventeenth king of Judah.
   B. He ruled for three months (2 Kings 23:31).
   C. He was 23 when he began to reign.
   D. He was also called Shallum (1 Chron. 3:15; Jer. 22:11).
   E. He was a godless king (2 Kings 23:32).
II. Jehoahaz, the enslaved king
   A. He was put in chains and deposed to Egypt by Pharaoh Necho (KJV: "Pharaoh-nechoh") (2 Kings 23:33-34).
   B. Jeremiah rightly predicted Jehoahaz would never return to Judah, but die in Egypt (Jer. 22:11-12).
   C. Necho then made Jehoahaz's brother

Jehoiakim (also called Eliakim) king in his place (2 Kings 23:34).

STATISTICS
Father: Josiah (2 Kings 23:30)
Mother: Hamutal (2 Kings 23:31)
Brothers: Johanan, Jehoiakim, and Zedekiah
   (1 Chron. 3:15)
First mention: 2 Kings 23:30
Final mention: Jeremiah 22:11
Meaning of his name: "God upholds"
Frequency of his name: Referred to eight times
Biblical books mentioning him: Four books
   (2 Kings, 1 Chronicles, 2 Chronicles, Jeremiah)
Occupation: King of Judah (23:31)
Place of birth: Jerusalem
Place of death: Egypt (2 Kings 23:34)
Important fact about his life: He was Josiah's youngest son (1 Chron. 3:15).

☜Jehoash

CHRONOLOGICAL SUMMARY
I. Jehoash and Ben-hadad
   A. He was the twelfth king of Northern Israel.
   B. He ruled for 16 years (2 Kings 13:10).
   C. He was an evil king (2 Kings 13:11).
   D. He recaptured from Ben-hadad and the Syrians some towns taken in the days of his father, Jehoahaz (2 Kings 13:25).
II. Jehoash and Amaziah
   A. His warning to Amaziah
      1. Jehoash was challenged to battle by Amaziah, the king of Judah (2 Kings 14:8).
      2. Jehoash responded by relating the parable of a thistle in Lebanon (2 Kings 14:9-10).
         a. The content of the parable—An insignificant thistle dared suggest to a mighty cedar tree in Lebanon that its daughter be given in marriage to the thistle's son.

b. The conclusion of the parable—
The ultimate in folly was Amaziah (the thistle) challenging
Jehoash (the mighty cedar) to
battle.
B. His warfare against Amaziah (2 Kings
14:11-14)
1. Realizing his parable had gone
unheeded, Jehoash attacked and
utterly defeated Amaziah.
2. He captured Amaziah himself.
3. He broke down a 600-foot section
of the Jerusalem wall.
4. He confiscated the gold, silver,
and precious articles in the temple.
5. He removed the treasuries of the
royal palace.
6. He took hostages and returned to
Samaria.

STATISTICS
Father: Jehoahaz (2 Kings 13:10)
Son: Jeroboam II (2 Kings 13:13)
First mention: 2 Kings 13:10
Final mention: 2 Chronicles 25:17
Meaning of his name: "God supports"
Frequency of his name: Referred to nine times
Biblical books mentioning him: One book
(2 Kings)
Occupation: King of Northern Israel (2 Kings
13:10)
Important fact about his life: He ridiculed Judean King Amaziah, calling him a thistle
king, and soundly defeated him in battle
(2 Chron. 25:17-24).

✐*Jehoiachin*

CHRONOLOGICAL SUMMARY
I. Jehoiachin and God
A. He was the nineteenth ruler of Judah.
B. He ruled for three months (2 Kings
24:8).
C. He began to rule when he was 18
(2 Kings 24:8).
D. He was an evil king (2 Kings 24:9).

E. He was also called Jeconiah and
Coniah (1 Chron. 3:16; Jer. 22:24;
Matt. 1:11).
F. God said the following about this
wicked king (Jer. 22:24-30):
1. Even if he were a signet ring on
God's right hand, the Lord would
still remove him.
2. He would be handed over to
those he feared the most, the Babylonians.
3. He would be carried away along
with his mother to Babylon, never
to return.
4. None of his offspring would prosper or sit on the throne of David.
II. Jehoiachin and Nebuchadnezzar
A. He was taken prisoner to Babylon by
King Nebuchadnezzar (2 Kings
24:15).
B. His mother and wives were also
taken (2 Kings 24:15).
C. Mordecai and Esther were carried
away with him at this time (Esther
2:5-6).
III. Jehoiachin and Evil-merodach
A. After spending 37 years in a Babylonian prison, Jehoiachin was released
by a new king named Evil-merodach
(2 Kings 25:27-30).
B. He spoke kindly to Jehoiachin and
gave him a seat of honor.
C. He allowed him to eat at the king's
table.
D. He gave him a regular allowance.
IV. Jehoiachin and Ezekiel—It was during
the fifth year of Jehoiachin's exile that
God gave Ezekiel his prophecies (Ezek.
1:2-3).

STATISTICS
Father: Jehoiakim (2 Kings 24:6)
Mother: Nehushta (2 Kings 24:8)
Sons: Assir, Salathiel, Malchiram, Pedaiah,
Shenazar, Jecamiah, Hoshama, and Nedabiah (1 Chron. 3:17-18)
First mention: 2 Kings 24:6
Final mention: Matthew 1:12
Meaning of his name: "God establishes"
Frequency of his name: Referred to 23 times

Biblical books mentioning him: Seven books
(2 Kings, 1 Chronicles, 2 Chronicles, Esther, Jeremiah, Ezekiel, Matthew)
Occupation: King of Judah (2 Kings 24:8)
Place of birth: Jerusalem
Place of death: Babylon (2 Kings 25:27-
30)
Important fact about his life: He was warned
by God that none of his offspring would
sit upon the throne of David (Jer. 22:24-
30).

✍*Jehoiada*

CHRONOLOGICAL SUMMARY
I. Jehoiada and Joash
  A. The protecting of Joash
    1. Jehoiada was the high priest dur-
      ing the bloody reign of Queen
      Athaliah (2 Chron. 22:11).
    2. He and his wife hid the baby Jo-
      ash, the only male to survive
      Athaliah's purge of the royal fam-
      ily (2 Chron. 22:10-12).
    3. Six years later, Jehoiada success-
      fully planned the overthrow and
      death of the queen (2 Kings 11:4-
      15).
  B. The perfecting of Joash—Jehoiada was
    able to keep King Joash on the right
    road as long as he (Jehoiada) lived
    (2 Kings 12:2).
II. Jehoiada and Judah
  A. Reviving the people
    1. He led Judah in a national revival
      (2 Kings 11:17-20).
    2. The place of Baal was torn down.
    3. The prophet of Baal was struck
      down.
  B. Repairing the temple
    1. He prepared a special chest with a
      hole bored in its lid to gather of-
      ferings for the repair of the tem-
      ple (2 Kings 12:9-12).
    2. Because of his godly service, Je-
      hoiada was buried with the kings
      in Jerusalem (2 Chron. 24:16).

STATISTICS
Spouse: Jehosheba (2 Kings 11:2; 2 Chron.
22:11)
Son: Zechariah (2 Chron. 24:20)
First mention: 2 Kings 11:4
Final mention: 2 Chronicles 24:25
Meaning of his name: "God knows"
Frequency of his name: Referred to 28 times
Biblical books mentioning him: Two books
(2 Kings, 2 Chronicles)
Occupation: High priest (2 Kings 11)
Place of death: Jerusalem (2 Chron. 24:15-
16)
Important fact about his life: He hid the baby
Joash from wicked Queen Athaliah
(2 Kings 11).

✍*Jehoiakim*

CHRONOLOGICAL SUMMARY
I. The charge of Jehoiakim
  A. He was the eighteenth king of Judah.
  B. He ruled for 11 years (2 Kings 23:36).
  C. He was also called Eliakim (2 Kings
    23:34; 2 Chron. 36:4).
  D. He was given charge over the affairs
    of Judah by Pharaoh Necho in place
    of his brother Jehoahaz, whom the
    Egyptian monarch had deposed
    (2 Kings 23:34).
II. The conspiracy of Jehoiakim
  A. After the Babylonian King Nebuchad-
    nezzar had defeated the Egyptians,
    he invaded Judah. Jehoiakim became
    his vassal for three years (2 Kings
    24:1).
  B. Jehoiakim then rebelled against Nebu-
    chadnezzar, but was quickly subdued
    and bound with bronze shackles. At
    first the Babylonian king planned to
    carry him off into captivity, but for
    some unknown reason did not do so
    (2 Chron. 36:6).
III. The cruelty of Jehoiakim
  A. He dragged the prophet Urijah back
    from Egypt (where he had fled in

fear of the wicked king) and had him
murdered by the sword for denouncing Jehoiakim's sin (Jer. 26:20-23).

B. He shed innocent blood, and oppressed and cheated his people
(2 Kings 24:4).

IV. The contempt of Jehoiakim
A. His contempt for God's sheep
1. He was totally materialistic (Jer.
22:13-14).
a. He built a huge palace for himself with spacious upper rooms
and large windows.
b. He paneled it with cedar and
decorated it in red.
c. He set his heart and eyes only
upon dishonest gain (Jer.
22:17).
B. His contempt for God's Scriptures—
Jehoiakim burned the scroll of Jeremiah the prophet (Jer. 36:21-32).
1. Jehudi, a palace official, read Jeremiah's scroll to the king.
2. It was winter and Jehoiakim was
sitting near a fireplace.
3. After Jehudi had read three or
four columns of the scroll, Jehoiakim cut them off with a knife and
threw them into the fire.
4. He did this in spite of the palace
official's request that he not do it.
5. He then ordered the arrest of Jeremiah and Baruch (Jeremiah's
scribe), but God hid them.
6. God commanded Jeremiah to rewrite the scroll and add to it, predicting Jehoiakim's unlamented
funeral and that he would have
no one to sit on his throne.
V. The condemnation of Jehoiakim
A. Jeremiah severely rebuked Jehoiakim
(Jer. 22:15-16).
1. The prophet reminded him that
riches did not make a king.
2. He also told the wicked king he
was a far cry from his godly father, Josiah.
a. Josiah had defended the poor.
b. Jehoiakim, however, had de-
frauded them.

B. Jeremiah then predicted that when
Jehoiakim died, he would not be
mourned, but rather would receive
the burial of a donkey, to be dragged
away and thrown outside the gates of
Jerusalem (Jer. 22:18-19).

STATISTICS

Father: Josiah (1 Chron. 3:15)
Mother: Zebudah (2 Kings 23:36)
Son: Jehoiachin (2 Chron. 36:8)
Brothers: Johanan, Zedekiah, and Jehoahaz
(1 Chron. 3:15)
First mention: 2 Kings 23:34
Final mention: Daniel 1:2
Meaning of his name: "God sets up"
Frequency of his name: Referred to 41 times
Biblical books mentioning him: Five books
(2 Kings, 1 Chronicles, 2 Chronicles, Jere-
miah, Daniel)
Occupation: King of Judah (2 Kings 23:36)
Place of birth: Jerusalem
Place of death: Jerusalem (Jer. 22:18-19)
Important fact about his life: He burned the
scroll Jeremiah had dictated to Baruch
(Jer. 36:23, 32).

✑Jehoram

CHRONOLOGICAL SUMMARY

I. Jehoram and Elisha
A. Providing
1. Elisha provided water for the
thirsty king and his people
(2 Kings 3:1-20).
a. Jehoram was the ninth king of
Northern Israel.
b. He reigned for 12 years.
c. He was an evil king, but not as
bad as was his father Ahab.
d. He destroyed the sacred image
stone of Baal which Ahab had
made.
e. He did, however, continue
worshiping other idols as Jeroboam, Northern Israel's first
king, had done.
f. On one occasion he mobilized

an army against Moab, who had rebelled against him, persuading both Jehoshaphat, king of Judah, and the king of Edom to join him in the attack.

g. Because of some careless marching, his army soon became stranded in the burning desert without water.

h. The prophet Elisha, who had been traveling unnoticed with the army, agreed to supernaturally provide water for all, but only for the sake of godly King Jehoshaphat.

2. Elisha provided food for the starving king and his people (2 Kings 6:24–7:20).

a. The Syrians had surrounded the capital city of Samaria, causing a terrible famine inside.

b. Conditions soon became desperate (2 Kings 6:25, 28-29).
  (1) A donkey's head sold for 50 dollars.
  (2) A pint of dove's dung brought three dollars.
  (3) Some mothers were even eating their own children.

c. Jehoram wrongly blamed Elisha for all this and vowed to kill him that very day.

d. Ignoring the king's threats, Elisha calmly predicted that within 24 hours there would be an abundance of food in the city.

e. In fact, he said two gallons of flour or four gallons of barley grain would bring only one dollar in the markets of Samaria.

f. All this happened just as the prophet had promised.

B. Protecting (2 Kings 6:8-23)

1. The revelation by Elisha—On several occasions during a war between Syria and Israel, Elisha revealed (supernaturally) to Jeho-

ram the battle plans of his enemy, thus saving him from defeat.

2. The refusal by Elisha

a. Upon learning the source of their problems, the Syrians attempted to arrest Elisha, but were temporarily blinded by God.

b. Elisha then led those sightless soldiers into Samaria, but refused Jehoram's request to kill them.

II. Jehoram and Naaman (2 Kings 5:1-8)

A. The visit by the captain—A Syrian military commander named Naaman visited Jehoram, desiring to be healed of his leprosy, for he had been told there was someone in Israel who could help him.

B. The vexation of the king—Upon reading a letter written to him by the king of Syria requesting healing, Jehoram tore his clothes and cried out: "Am I God, to kill and to make alive, that this man doth send unto me to recover a man of his leprosy? wherefore consider, I pray you, and see how he seeketh a quarrel against me" (2 Kings 5:7).

C. The verification from the prophet— "When Elisha the man of God had heard that the king of Israel had rent his clothes . . . he sent to the king, saying, Wherefore hast thou rent thy clothes? let him come now to me, and he shall know that there is a prophet in Israel" (2 Kings 5:8).

III. Jehoram and Jehu (2 Kings 9:14-15, 24-26)

A. Jehoram was wounded in a battle against the Syrians and had returned to Jezreel to recover from his wounds.

B. It was there that he was killed by an army officer named Jehu.

C. Jehoram's lifeless body was then dumped on the field that had once belonged to Naboth, a godly farmer who had previously been murdered by Ahab and Jezebel (Jehoram's fa-

ther and mother) to secure his vineyard.

STATISTICS
Father: Ahab (2 Kings 3:1)
Mother: Jezebel (2 Kings 9:22)
Brother: Ahaziah (1 Kings 22:51; 2 Kings 1:2, 17)
First mention: 2 Kings 1:17
Final mention: 2 Chronicles 22:7
Meaning of his name: "God is high"
Frequency of his name: Referred to seven times
Biblical books mentioning him: Two books (2 Kings, 2 Chronicles)
Occupation: King of Northern Israel (2 Kings 3:1)
Place of death: At the city of Jezreel (2 Kings 9:14, 24)
Circumstances of death: He was killed by Jehu (2 Kings 9:24).
Important fact about his life: He was king when Naaman came to Samaria to be healed of his leprosy (2 Kings 5:6-7).

✍️*Jehoshaphat*

CHRONOLOGICAL SUMMARY
I. The glorious aspect of his reign
  A. Jehoshaphat and the Word of God
    1. The king proclaimed it.
      a. Jehoshaphat was the fourth ruler of Judah.
      b. He ruled for 25 years (1 Kings 22:42).
      c. He was, for all purposes, a good king (1 Kings 22:43).
      d. He instituted a nationwide program to instruct the people in the Word of God, sending out teachers to all the towns of Judah (2 Chron. 17:7-9).
    2. The king proved it.
      a. He was surrounded by a vast allied enemy army, consisting of Moabites, Ammonites, and Edomites (2 Chron. 20:1-2).

      b. The terrified king proclaimed a national fast and, standing in the temple courtyard, offered up one of Scripture's great prayers for deliverance (2 Chron. 20:3-12).
        (1) He referred to the eternal sovereignty of God.
        (2) He reviewed the past faithfulness of God.
        (3) He related the present need for and dependence upon God, concluding with these words: "O our God, wilt thou not judge them? for we have no might against this great company that cometh against us; neither know we what to do: but our eyes are upon thee" (2 Chron. 20:12).
      c. God's Spirit suddenly fell upon Jahaziel, a Levite, with some reassuring words indeed (2 Chron. 20:14-17): "Thus saith the LORD unto you, Be not afraid nor dismayed by reason of this great multitude; for the battle is not yours, but God's" (20:15).
      d. Greatly encouraged, Jehoshaphat prepared for battle by appointing the temple Levitical choir to lead the troops into battle, singing a song of praise to the Lord (2 Chron. 20:18-21).
      e. God himself, as he had promised, intervened, and the enemy soldiers were totally routed (2 Chron. 20:22-24).
      f. A grateful Jehoshaphat then ordered a special praise service to the Lord in a valley he named Berachah, which means "praise" (2 Chron. 20:25-26).
  B. Jehoshaphat and his works for God
    1. What the king did for God
      a. His religious activities
        (1) He rid the land of the male shrine prostitutes (1 Kings 22:46).

(2) He did not consult Baal
(2 Chron. 17:3).

(3) He removed the high places
and the Asherah poles from
Judah (2 Chron. 17:6).

b. His legal activities

(1) He appointed judges in the
land, admonishing them to
judge carefully and to depend upon God for their
verdict (2 Chron. 19:5-
10).

(2) He recognized the separation of church and state
(2 Chron. 19:11).

(a) By appointing Amariah,
the chief priest, to preside
over religious matters

(b) By appointing Zebadiah
to preside over political
and legal matters

c. His military activities

(1) He obeyed God's previous
command which forbade
Northern Israel and Judah
from fighting with each
other (1 Kings 22:44).

(2) He built forts and store cities
in Judah (2 Chron. 17:12).

(3) He maintained a fighting
army of 1,160,000 men
(2 Chron. 17:14-19).

2. What God did for the king

a. God established his kingdom
(2 Chron 17:3-5).

(1) All Judah brought gifts to
him.

(2) He enjoyed great wealth and
honor.

b. Even his enemies brought him
presents (2 Chron. 17:10-11).

(1) The Philistines gave him
silver.

(2) The Arabs gave him flocks—
7,700 rams and 7,700 goats.

II. The grievous aspects of his reign

A. His compromise with Ahab

1. The military compromise

a. Jehoshaphat joined up with
Ahab, the wicked Northern Is-

raelite king, in an alliance
against Syria (1 Kings 22:1-
33).

b. Prior to the battle, however,
Jehoshaphat suggested the two
kings seek counsel from the
Lord.

c. The 400 false prophets on
Ahab's payroll quickly "predicted" victory against Syria.

d. Still not convinced, Jehoshaphat
persuaded Ahab to allow a special prophet named Micaiah,
whom the wicked king had
kept in prison, to speak.

e. This true prophet predicted
both the defeat of the alliance
and the death of Ahab.

f. In spite of this, Jehoshaphat
foolishly joined Ahab in the
attack.

g. Jehoshaphat was almost killed
in battle when the Syrian archers for a moment mistook
him for Ahab.

h. Only the intervention of God
saved him (2 Chron. 18:31).

i. He was later soundly rebuked
by the prophet Jehu for all this
(2 Chron. 19:1-3).

2. The matrimonial compromise—
Jehoshaphat allowed one of his
sons, Joram, to marry Athaliah,
the wicked daughter of Ahab and
Jezebel (2 Kings 8:18).

B. His compromise with Ahaziah

1. Jehoshaphat and Ahaziah, a son
of Ahab, built a fleet of trading
ships to go to Ophir for gold.
They were wrecked at Ezion-geber
before they could set sail (1 Kings
22:48).

2. The prophet Eliezer had predicted
God would destroy their ships
(2 Chron. 20:35-37).

C. His compromise with Jehoram

1. Jehoshaphat joined up with Jehoram, another son of Ahab, in an
alliance against the Moabites
(2 Kings 3:6-7).

2. After an ill-prepared roundabout march of seven days, the alliance found itself in the desert with no water (2 Kings 3:8-10).
3. Jehoshaphat sought out God's counsel and discovered the great prophet Elisha had been traveling with the armies, unnoticed (2 Kings 3:11-12).
4. Elisha agreed to help the thirsty soldiers, but only for the sake of Jehoshaphat (2 Kings 3:13-14).
5. The prophet then provided, supernaturally, water for all to drink (2 Kings 3:15-20).

STATISTICS

Father: Asa (1 Kings 15:24)
Mother: Azubah (1 Kings 22:42)
Sons: Jehoram, Azariah, Jehiel, Zechariah, Azariah, Michael, and Shephatiah (1 Kings 22:50; 2 Chron. 21:2)
First mention: 1 Kings 15:24
Final mention: Matthew 1:8
Meaning of his name: "God is Judge"
Frequency of his name: Referred to 77 times
Biblical books mentioning him: Five books (1 Kings, 2 Kings, 1 Chronicles, 2 Chronicles, Matthew)
Occupation: King of Judah (1 Kings 22:41)
Place of birth: Jerusalem
Important fact about his life: He instituted a nationwide Bible teaching program (2 Chron. 17:7-9).

Jehu (1)

CHRONOLOGICAL SUMMARY

I. Rebuking
  A. Jehu rebuked Baasha
    1. The foretelling—He rebuked Baasha, third king of Northern Israel, for his sin, and predicted his seed dying in the city would be eaten by the dogs, and those dying in the countryside by the birds of the air (1 Kings 16:2-4).
    2. The fulfilling—Following Baasha's

death, his son Elah became king. After a reign of only two years, Zimri, one of his chariot commanders, killed the king and all his seed, thus fulfilling Jehu's prophecy (1 Kings 16:7-13).
  B. Jehu rebuked Jehoshaphat—Jehoshaphat was rebuked for his unwise military alliance with wicked Ahab, king of Northern Israel (2 Chron. 19:1-2).
II. Recording—Jehu later wrote a book on the kings of Israel (2 Chron. 20:34).

STATISTICS

Father: Hanani (1 Kings 16:1)
First mention: 1 Kings 16:1
Final mention: 2 Chronicles 20:34
Meaning of his name: "God is He"
Frequency of his name: Referred to five times
Biblical books mentioning him: Two books (1 Kings, 2 Chronicles)
Occupation: Prophet (1 Kings 16:7)
Important fact about his life: He pronounced judgment upon Baasha and rebuked Jehoshaphat (1 Kings 16:1-7; 2 Chron. 19:1-3).

Jehu (2)

CHRONOLOGICAL SUMMARY

I. Jehu—His anointing
  A. The person involved
    1. Jehu was the tenth king of Northern Israel.
    2. He ruled 28 years (2 Kings 10:36).
    3. He was a notorious chariot driver (2 Kings 9:20).
    4. His chariot officer was Bidkar (2 Kings 9:25).
    5. God had ordered Elijah to anoint Jehu as king (1 Kings 19:16).
    6. For some reason, however, Elijah did not do this, leaving the task to his successor Elisha (2 Kings 9:1-3).
  B. The prophecy involved—The servant of Elisha, at his master's command, carried out the actual anointing and,

by divine revelation, predicted the following (2 Kings 9:4-10):

1. That Ahab's house would be destroyed by Jehu
2. That the wild dogs of Jezreel would eat the dead body of Jezebel

II. Jehu—His assassinations
  A. Jehoram, the king of Northern Israel, by an arrow (2 Kings 9:21-24)
  B. Ahaziah, the king of Judah, by an arrow (2 Kings 9:27-29)
  C. Jezebel, wife of Ahab, by ordering her to be thrown from an upper window (2 Kings 9:30-37)
  D. The 70 sons of Ahab, by ordering the citizens in their hometown of Samaria to behead them (2 Kings 10:1-7)
  E. The close relatives of Ahab, by the sword (2 Kings 10:17)
  F. The 42 relatives of Ahaziah, king of Judah, by the sword (2 Kings 10:12-14)
  G. The priests of Baal, by the sword (2 Kings 10:18-28)
    1. Jehu lured these priests into a building under the pretext of conducting a worship service for Baal.
    2. At Jehu's command, 80 of his soldiers ran in and slaughtered all these pagan ministers.

III. Jehu—His assurance
  A. For his faithfulness in ridding the land of Baalism, God promised Jehu his descendants would sit on Northern Israel's throne to the fourth generation (2 Kings 10:30).
  B. This was fulfilled by Zachariah, Jehu's great grandson, and Northern Israel's fourteenth king, who represented the fourth generation (2 Kings 15:12).

IV. Jehu—His apostasy—He did not turn away from the sins of Jeroboam I, namely, the worship of the golden calves at Beth-el and Dan (2 Kings 10:29, 31).

STATISTICS

Father: Nimshi (1 Kings 19:16)
Son: Jehoahaz (2 Kings 10:35)

First mention: 1 Kings 19:16
Final mention: Hosea 1:4
Meaning of his name: "God is here"
Frequency of his name: Referred to 48 times
Biblical books mentioning him: Four books (1 Kings, 2 Kings, 2 Chronicles, Hosea)
Occupation: King of Northern Israel (2 Kings 10:36)
Important fact about his life: He had Jezebel and all the priests of Baal killed (2 Kings 9:30-37; 10:18-28).

Jephthah

CHRONOLOGICAL SUMMARY

I. His vocation
  A. The scorned
    1. He was raised up in Gilead, the land east of the Jordan River (Judg. 11:1).
    2. His mother was a prostitute (Judg. 11:1).
    3. He was driven from his home by his own half brothers because of his harlot mother (Judg. 11:2).
  B. The soldier
    1. He settled in the land of Tob (located in northeast Syria), where he gathered a group of mercenary troops (Judg. 11:3).
    2. The elders of Gilead later looked to Jephthah for help when their land was threatened by the Ammonites (Judg. 11:4-5).
    3. Jephthah was at first reluctant, remembering past injustices, but then, upon being promised to become head of the Gileadites, agreed to fight the Ammonites (Judg. 11:6-10).
    4. His treaty with the elders was ratified during a ceremony in Mizpeh (Judg. 11:11).
    5. On assuming command, Jephthah attempted to come to terms with the enemy by peaceful means (Judg. 11:12).

6. The Ammonites responded by claiming Joshua had stolen the land in question during his march to Canaan (Judg. 11:13).
7. Jephthah attempted to show them that historically this was not the case. To the contrary, Israel had peacefully occupied the land for the past 300 years and their settlements had never been disputed (Judg. 11:14-27).
8. However, the Ammonites refused to listen and Jephthah prepared to attack (Judg. 11:28-29).

II. His vow
A. The Holy Spirit now came upon Jephthah (Judg. 11:29).
B. On the eve of battle, he made a rash vow promising that if God gave him the victory, upon his return to Mizpeh he would offer up the first thing that came out of his door as a burnt sacrifice (Judg. 11:30-31).

III. His victory—Jephthah defeated the enemy, devastating 20 of their towns (Judg. 11:32-33).

IV. His vexation
A. The agony
1. Upon his return, the first person to greet him was his only daughter (Judg. 11:34).
2. The heartbroken Jephthah determined to keep his vow regardless (Judg. 11:35).
B. The agreement
1. The daughter agreed, but requested two months to lament her virginity (Judg. 11:36-38).
2. After this period she returned and Jephthah fulfilled his vow (Judg. 11:39).
C. The annual event—This event instigated a special yearly four-day commemoration by the young women of Israel to the memory of Jephthah's daughter (Judg. 11:39-40).

V. His vengeance
A. Following all this, Jephthah was rebuked and threatened by the jealous men of Ephraim for not allowing them to share the glory of victory over the Ammonites (Judg. 12:1).
B. Jephthah reminded them he had asked for their help but was refused (Judg. 12:2-3).
C. He then attacked them and killed some 42,000 of their troops at the fords of the Jordan (Judg. 12:4-6).
D. After leading Israel for six years, he died (Judg. 12:7).

THEOLOGICAL SUMMARY
I. Samuel used Jephthah as an example of God's power to deliver (1 Sam. 12:11).
II. Hebrews refers to his faith (Heb. 11:32).

STATISTICS
Mother: Unnamed prostitute (Judg. 11:1)
Daughter: Unnamed virgin daughter (Judg. 11:34, 37)
First mention: Judges 11:1
Final mention: Hebrews 11:32
Meaning of his name: "Opposer"
Frequency of his name: Referred to 28 times
Biblical books mentioning him: Three books (Judges, 1 Samuel, Hebrews)
Occupation: Professional soldier (Judg. 11:3-11)
Important fact about his life: He made a rash vow which he later bitterly regretted (Judg. 11:30-40).

✐*Jeremiah*

CHRONOLOGICAL SUMMARY
I. The personal history of Jeremiah
A. Jeremiah, the man
1. The selection
a. He was called into full-time service during the reign of Josiah (1:1-10).
b. He was to remain unmarried (16:2).
(1) Jeremiah was the son of Hilkiah, a priest living in Anathoth, some three miles

northeast of Jerusalem in the land of Benjamin (1:1).

(2) He received his call to full-time service during the thirteenth year of godly King Josiah (1:2).

c. Jeremiah at first protested this call (as Moses once did—see Exodus 3–4), pleading his youth as an excuse (1:4-6).

d. He was quickly, however, reassured by God (1:7-10).

(1) God's witness would be beside him.

(2) God's words would be within him.

2. The symbols—As he began his ministry, God showed him three things which underlined the nature and importance of his call.

a. He was shown an almond tree rod (1:11). Because it flowers earlier than the other trees, the almond signified the near fulfillment of God's proposed judgment.

b. He saw a pot of boiling water, tipping southward from the north. This symbolized the Babylonian invasion (1:13).

c. He then saw two baskets of figs in the temple. One basket had fresh, well-ripened figs, but the other contained rotten ones (24:1-3). God explained that the fresh figs represented the Jewish exiles in Babylon (men such as Daniel and Ezekiel), while the rotten fruit depicted Zedekiah and his corrupt officials (24:4-8).

3. The sign

a. Jeremiah was ordered to make a yoke and fasten it upon his neck with leather thongs (27:1-2).

b. He was then to send messages to the kings of Edom, Moab, Ammon, Tyre, and Sidon through their ambassadors in Jerusalem, warning them that God had given their nations over to Babylon. Those who submitted and wore the yoke of punishment with true repentance would be spared, but those who refused would be destroyed (27:3-11).

c. After God had used Nebuchadnezzar to punish Judah and his neighbor nations, he would chastise Babylon itself (27:7). Judah was reassured that after the Babylonian Captivity she would be gathered back to Jerusalem (27:22).

4. The search

a. He was given a command reminiscent of the Greek philosopher Diogenes, who repeatedly roamed the streets of Athens with a lantern trying to find an honest man. God had once made a similar arrangement with Abraham concerning Sodom (Gen. 18:23-33). "Run ye to and fro through the streets of Jerusalem, and see now, and know, and seek in the broad places thereof, if ye can find a man, if there be any that executeth judgment, that seeketh the truth, and I will pardon it" (5:1).

b. Jeremiah admitted this dreadful condition existed among the poor and ignorant, but felt he could find honest men within the ranks of Judah's educated and rich rulers. But they too had utterly rejected God (5:4-5).

c. After a fruitful 31-year reign, Josiah died. A weeping prophet attended his funeral (2 Chron. 34:1; 35:25). Judah's last good king had gone, and it would be downhill spiritually from that point on.

5. The settlement—Jeremiah visited

the settlement where the Rechabite families lived.

a. These individuals belonged to a religious order founded by Jonadab, son of Rechab, during the reign of Jehu (841–814 B.C.). They assisted in the eradication of Baalism from Israel. Avoiding city life, they lived as shepherds, drinking no wine.

b. Jeremiah was commanded to test them by offering them wine. They immediately refused (35:1-6).

c. Jeremiah then related this sterling example to Judah, and contrasted the obedience of the Rechabites to the disobedience of Jerusalem (35:12-19).

6. The sale

a. Jeremiah, while in prison, was ordered by God to buy a field from his cousin Hanameel. This was to illustrate that in spite of the advancing Babylonian armies, "houses and fields and vineyards shall be possessed again in this land" (32:15).

b. The background of all this: God told Jeremiah that his cousin, Hanameel, was soon to visit him and attempt to sell the prophet a farm he owned in Anathoth. Jeremiah was to buy it for 17 shekels of silver (32:6-12). Baruch was then to place the sealed deed in a pottery jar and bury it. All this was to demonstrate that someday people would once again own property in Judah, and buy and sell (32:14-15).

c. Jeremiah was comforted at this time in prison by God's gracious promise. "Call unto me, and I will answer thee, and shew thee great and mighty things, which thou knowest not" (33:3).

d. These tremendous and thrilling

"things" are listed in chapters 30–31 and 33. They include the following:

(1) In spite of the impending Babylonian Captivity, the time was coming when God would heal Jerusalem's hurt and give her prosperity and peace (33:4-6).

(2) He still loved Israel with an everlasting love (31:3).

(3) Israel would be gathered into Palestine from the earth's farthest ends (30:3, 10-11; 31:8-9, 12).

7. The sufferings

a. The sources of Jeremiah's sufferings

(1) His family

(2) His hometown

(3) The religious world

(4) The political world

b. The nature of his sufferings

(1) His own brothers and family turned against him, plotting to kill him (12:6).

(2) The men of Anathoth attempted to kill him (11:21-23).

(3) Pashur, the chief temple priest, had him whipped and put in stocks (20:1-3).

(4) He was almost murdered by a wild mob of priests and prophets after one of his messages (26:7-9).

(a) He preached a sermon at the temple gate and was nearly killed by an angry mob for predicting the temple would be destroyed (26:6-9).

(b) He was defended by some of Judah's wise old men, who reminded the angry mob that Jeremiah's message was like that of the prophet Micah (Jer. 26:17-19; Mic. 3:12).

(5) He was ridiculed by a false

prophet named Hananiah
(28).

(a) Jeremiah was accused of
lying by a false prophet
named Hananiah who
had predicted the Babylo-
nian Captivity would last
only for two years and
that those already in exile
(such as King Jehoiachin,
Daniel, Ezekiel, etc.)
would be returned, along
with all the temple trea-
sury which had been
taken (28:1-4).

(b) To dramatize his accusation, Hananiah broke the
yoke worn by Jeremiah
(28:10-11).

(6) He was threatened by King
Jehoiakim (36:26).

(7) He was arrested, flogged,
and accused of treason
(37:11-16).

(a) Jeremiah attempted to
visit the land of Benjamin
on one occasion to inspect
some property he had
bought (37:11-12).

(b) However, a guard named
Irijah arrested him at the
city gate and accused him
of defecting to the Bab-
ylonians (37:13).

(c) Jeremiah denied this, but
was flogged and thrown
into prison (37:14-16).

(d) He was secretly sent for
by Zedekiah, the king
(37:17). Zedekiah placed
him in the palace prison
instead of returning him
to the dungeon he was
formerly in (37:21).

(8) He was cast down into an
empty but filthy prison
(38:1-13).

(a) In the palace, pressure
from the religious officials
who despised Jeremiah

eventually forced Zede-
kiah to return the prophet
to a more crude confine-
ment.

(b) This time he was lowered
by ropes into an empty
cistern in the prison yard,
where he soon sank
down into a thick layer of
mire at the bottom (38:1-6).

(c) Eventually an Ethiopian
friend, Ebed-melech, per-
suaded Zedekiah to re-
move him from this filthy
place. It took 30 men to
haul him from the cistern.
He was returned to the
prison palace (38:7-13).

(d) Jeremiah again predicted
the fall of Jerusalem
(38:14-17; see also 32:1-5).
He would remain in
prison until the city was
taken (38:28).

(9) He had his original manu-
script burned by wicked
King Jehoiakim (36:21-23).

(a) God ordered Jeremiah to
have his scribe Baruch
write down all those oral
messages he had been
given for the past 23
years (36:1-2).

(b) Baruch did this and read
them to the people in the
temple (36:8). He then
was invited to read them
to the religious officials.
When he finished, they
were badly frightened
and decided King Jehoia-
kim should also hear
them (36:14-16).

(c) An official named Jehudi
thereupon read them to
Jehoiakim as the sullen
king sat in front of his
fireplace. As Jehudi fin-
ished reading three or
four columns, Jehoiakim

would take his knife, slit off the section of the roll, and throw it into the fire. Finally, the entire scroll was destroyed (36:21-23).

(d) Jeremiah was then commanded to rewrite the burned sections plus a good deal of additional material, including some fearful words about Jehoiakim: "Thus saith the LORD of Jehoiakim king of Judah; He shall have none to sit upon the throne of David: and his dead body shall be cast out in the day to the heat, and in the night to the frost. And I will punish him and his seed and his servants for their iniquity; and I will bring upon them, and upon the inhabitants of Jerusalem, and upon the men of Judah, all the evil that I have pronounced against them; but they hearkened not. Then took Jeremiah another roll, and gave it to Baruch the scribe, the son of Neriah; who wrote therein from the mouth of Jeremiah all the words of the book which Jehoiakim king of Judah had burned in the fire: and there were added besides unto them many like words" (36:30-32).

(e) After Jehoiakim had burned the scroll, Baruch became despondent. It had probably taken him a year to write the material. God then both warned and encouraged him through Jeremiah (45:1-5).

(10) He experienced frustration and depression (20:7-9, 14-18).

(a) Jeremiah had become so frustrated over his inability to call Judah back to God that he wrote the following: "Then I said, I will not make mention of him, nor speak any more in his name. But his word was in mine heart as a burning fire shut up in my bones, and I was weary with forbearing, and I could not stay" (20:9; see also 1 Kings 19:3-4; Jon. 1:1-3; 1 Cor. 9:16).

(b) At this time, he uttered one of the most despondent prayers in all the Bible: "Cursed be the day wherein I was born: let not the day wherein my mother bare me be blessed. Cursed be the man who brought tidings to my father, saying, A man child is born unto thee; making him very glad. And let that man be as the cities which the LORD overthrew, and repented not: and let him hear the cry in the morning, and the shouting at noontide; Because he slew me not from the womb; or that my mother might have been my grave, and her womb to be always great with me. Wherefore came I forth out of the womb to see labour and sorrow, that my days should be consumed with shame?" (20:14-18).

B. Jeremiah, the minister
    1. Rulers he ministered under

a. Josiah—Jeremiah was called by God during the reign of Josiah, Judah's last good king.
b. Jehoiakim—This wicked king burned Jeremiah's original written prophecy scroll.
c. Jehoiachin—This 90-day wonder was soundly condemned by Jeremiah (22:24-30).
d. Zedekiah—The prophet suffered much under the reign of Zedekiah, Judah's final king.
   (1) Zedekiah sent word to Jeremiah asking for his prayers after Nebuchadnezzar had declared war on Judah (21:1-2).
   (2) Jeremiah sent word back to the wicked king stating that prayers were useless on this subject, for God would use the Babylonians to punish Jerusalem, and Zedekiah himself was to be given over to Nebuchadnezzar (21:3-7).
   (3) Jeremiah told Zedekiah that Jerusalem would be burned and he was to be captured and carried into Babylon (34:1-5).
   (4) Zedekiah had proclaimed freedom for all the slaves in the city, but the owners had gone back on their word. Jeremiah rebuked those rich Jewish homeowners who had violated the Mosaic Law, which demanded all Hebrew servants to be set free after serving six years (34:8-16).
   (5) Pharaoh Hophra's Egyptian armies had arrived to aid Judah in fighting Nebuchadnezzar. Jeremiah warned Zedekiah that their political alliance would fail, for Nebuchadnezzar would defeat the Egyptians (37:5-10). Zed-

ekiah, however, refused to take the counsel of Jeremiah (2 Chron. 36:12).
e. Nebuchadnezzar—Jeremiah was treated with respect by the great Babylonian conqueror.
   (1) Zedekiah attempted to escape the doomed city but was captured near Jericho and brought back to Jerusalem. Here he was forced to witness the execution of his own sons, and then submit to the agony of having his eyes gouged out (39:4-7; 52:6-11).
   (2) Nebuchadnezzar instructed his chief-of-staff, Nebuzaradan, to treat Jeremiah with kindness (39:11-12).
   (3) Jeremiah was released from prison and taken by Nebuzar-adan to Ramah. Here he was offered his choice of going on to Babylon or returning to Jerusalem. Jeremiah chose to return and was placed under the protection of the new Jewish governor of Jerusalem, a man named Gedaliah (39:14; 40:1-6).
f. Gedaliah—He was appointed by Nebuchadnezzar to govern the fallen city of Jerusalem.
   (1) Gedaliah attempted to institute a moderate post-war administration over the devastated city of Jerusalem (40:7-12).
   (2) This soon aroused the fury of a Jewish rebel leader named Ishmael, who plotted to assassinate Gedaliah. The governor was warned of this plot by a man named Johanan but refused to take it seriously (40:13-16).
   (3) Gedaliah was murdered by Ishmael along with many

other Jewish officials, pilgrims, and some Babylonian soldiers. Some of their bodies were hurled down into an empty cistern (41:1-9).

(4) Johanan arrived upon the scene of the massacre and soon restored order (41:11-16).

g. Johanan—He took over after the tragic assassination of Gedaliah and later forced Jeremiah to accompany a Jewish remnant to Egypt.

(1) Johanan asked Jeremiah to determine God's will for the tiny Jewish remnant still in Jerusalem (42:1-6).

(2) After a 10-day prayer session with God, Jeremiah was told the Lord desired the remnant to remain in Jerusalem and not go to Egypt, as some were already planning to do (46:7-22).

(3) Upon hearing this unwelcome report, Johanan and other leaders accused Jeremiah of lying. They then disobeyed the clearly revealed word of God by going to Egypt. Jeremiah was forced to accompany them (43:1-7).

(4) Upon reaching Egypt, many of the Jews resorted to their old habits of idolatry. They began burning incense to the queen of heaven. This was another name for the pagan goddess Ishtar, the Mesopotamian goddess of love and war (44:8-10, 15-19).

(5) Jeremiah pronounced the divine death penalty upon all who refused to repent and return to Jerusalem (44:7-14, 28).

(6) To dramatize this bitter truth, he buried some large rocks between the pavement stones at the entrance of Pharaoh's palace. This signified that Nebuchadnezzar would occupy Egypt and set his throne upon those stones. Jeremiah predicted he would then kill many of the Jewish remnant who refused to return. The others would die of various plagues or be enslaved (43:9-13).

2. Groups he ministered to

a. Jeremiah cautioned the majority—He warned the majority still in Judah about the coming Babylonian Captivity.

(1) He pleaded with Judah to return to God (3:12-14; 26:1-7).

(a) God would repeatedly invite Israel back to him (2:9).

(b) He would receive Israel even after her immorality with other lovers (3:1).

(2) Jeremiah pleaded with them to plow up the hardness of their hearts, lest all be choked up by thorns and suffer the fire of God's wrath (4:3-4).

(a) They could still escape judgment by cleansing their hearts and purifying their thoughts (4:14).

(b) To repent meant they could remain in the land (7:3). To refuse meant to be covered by thick darkness (13:16).

(3) He fearlessly pronounced coming judgment at the hands of the Babylonians. He then outlined Judah's sins, often using metaphors and similes.

(a) Judah had forsaken the

fountain of divine water (2:13).

(b) They had built broken cisterns which could not hold water (2:13).

(c) The nation had become a race of evil men, symbolized by good seed producing a degenerate plant (2:21).

(d) No amount of soap or lye could make them clean (2:22).

(e) The rulers had stained their clothes with the blood of the innocent and poor (2:34).

(f) They were as an unashamed prostitute (3:3).

(g) They worshiped false gods upon every hill and under every shade tree (3:6).

(h) They had killed their prophets as a lion would slaughter his prey (2:30).

(i) They were as insolent as brass, and hard and cruel as iron (6:28).

(j) They had set up idols right in the temple and worshiped the pagan queen of heaven (7:18; 44:17). "The children gather wood, and the fathers kindle the fire, and the women knead their dough, to make cakes to the queen of heaven, and to pour out drink offerings unto other gods, that they may provoke me to anger" (7:18).

(k) They had actually sacrificed their little children as burnt offerings to devil gods (7:31; 19:5).

(4) He warned them concerning the terrible results of their disobedience.

(a) Great armies would march upon Jerusalem (1:14-15).

(b) Neither Assyria nor Egypt would be able to help Judah against Babylon (2:18, 36).

(c) People would flee from Judah's cities as one runs from a hungry lion (4:5-7).

(d) Jerusalem would be surrounded, as hunters would move in on a wild and wounded animal (4:17; 6:3-5).

(e) They would cry out as a woman in delivery (4:31; 6:24; 13:21).

(f) Jerusalem's own trees would be cut down and used against her walls as battering rams (6:6).

(g) The temple would be destroyed (7:14).

(h) Enemy troops would then move among the people like poisonous snakes (8:17).

(i) Many would die by the following methods: sword (15:3); disease (21:9); starvation (21:9).

(j) Some would be scattered as chaff by the fierce desert winds (13:24). Unburied corpses would litter the valleys outside Jerusalem, and become food for wild animals and birds (7:32; 9:22; 12:8-9; 15:3).

(k) Judah's enemies would break open the sacred graves of her kings, priests, and prophets, and spread out their bones on the ground before the sun, moon, and stars (8:1-2).

(l) Thousands would be carried away into Babylon for a period of 70 years (7:15; 25:11; 29:10).

(m) The severity of Judah's punishment would astonish the onlooking pagan Gentile nations (19:8; 22:8; 25:11).

(5) When the people ridiculed and rejected his message, the warning prophet became the weeping prophet (4:19; 8:21; 9:1-2, 10; 13:17; 14:17). "Oh that my head were waters, and mine eyes a fountain of tears, that I might weep day and night for the slain of the daughter of my people!" (9:1).

b. Jeremiah comforted the minority—Jeremiah wrote a letter of encouragement to the Jewish exiles in Babylon (29:1-32).

(1) They were to settle down for a long 70-year stay.

(2) They were to pray for the peace and prosperity of Babylon, that their own lives might be peaceful.

(3) They were to ignore the lies of those false prophets and mediums there in Babylon, lest they be punished along with them.

(a) Jeremiah pronounced God's death sentence upon two of these prophets named Ahab and Zedekiah for their lying messages and their sin of adultery (29:20-23).

(b) He also warned the exiles concerning a man named Shemaiah, who was sending poison pen letters from Babylon to the influential leaders in Jerusalem against Jeremiah (29:24-32).

(4) God still loved them and would someday bring them back to Jerusalem. "I know the thoughts that I think toward you, saith the LORD, thoughts of peace, and not of evil, to give you an expected end. Then shall ye call upon me, and ye shall go and pray unto me, and I will hearken unto you. And ye shall seek me, and find me, when ye shall search for me with all your heart. And I will be found of you, saith the LORD: and I will turn away your captivity, and I will gather you from all the nations, and from all the places whither I have driven you, saith the LORD; and I will bring you again into the place whence I caused you to be carried away captive" (29:11-14).

c. Jeremiah condemned the multitudes—He pronounced judgment upon nine Gentile nations (46–51).

(1) Egypt (46:1-26)
(2) Philistia (47:1-6)
(3) Moab (48:1-47)
(4) Ammon (49:1-6)
(5) Edom (49:7-22)
(6) Damascus (49:23-27)
(7) Kedar and Hazor (49:28-33)
(8) Elam (49:34-39)
(9) Babylon (50–51)—Two Babylons seem to be referred to in these verses.

(a) One is the historical Babylon, captured by Darius the Persian in October of 539 B.C. (Dan. 5).

(b) The other is future Babylon which will be destroyed by God himself (Rev. 17–18).

(c) After the destruction of both Babylons, Israel would seek their God. This happened historically (Ezra 1); and it will occur in the future (Zech. 13:9).

(d) After the final destruction of Babylon (Rev. 18) the city will never be inhabited again (Jer. 51:26).

(e) The ungodly nations would weep over the destruction of both Babylons (Jer. 50:46; Rev. 18).

(f) The Israelites were to flee from both Babylons (Jer. 51:6; Rev. 18:4).

(g) Both cities are depicted as golden cups filled with iniquities from which the nations have drunk and become mad (Jer. 51:7; Rev. 17:1-6).

(h) All heaven would rejoice over the destruction of both Babylons (Jer. 51:10; 48; Rev. 18:20).

II. The public prophecies of Jeremiah
  A. The group prophecies
    1. Concerning Judah's people
      a. The fall of Jerusalem (1:14-16; 4:5-9; 5:15-17; 6:1-6; 32:2-3; 38:17-18)
      b. The destruction of the temple (7:11-15; 26:6-9)
      c. The 70-year captivity of Judah into Babylon (25:11; 29:10)
      NOTE: In 31:15-16, Jeremiah predicted that the loud wails and bitter weeping of Rachel for her children in Ramah would disappear. Ramah is an ancient reference to the area in and around Bethlehem. It was here that Nebuchadnezzar killed many sick and feeble exile captives who would not be able to endure the long trip to Babylon. Rachel, the historical wife of Jacob, is of course symbolic of all weeping Israelite mothers. In Matthew 2:18 this sad verse is linked to that occasion when Herod murdered the babies of Bethlehem in an attempt to kill Christ.

      d. The kindly treatment of the exiles in Babylon (24:1-7)
      e. The restoration after the 70 years to Jerusalem (27:19-22; 30:3, 10-11, 18-21; 31:9, 12, 38-39; 33:3-9)
        (1) Israel would be gathered back from all over the world (3:14; 31:8-10; 32:37-43).
        (2) God would appoint for them leaders after his own heart (3:15).
        (3) Palestine would once again be filled with the glory of God, and the people of God (3:16-18). This would be a far greater and grander event than that of the original Exodus, when he brought them out of Egypt (16:14-15; 23:7).
        (4) A Righteous Branch (the Savior) will occupy King David's throne, ruling with wisdom and justice (23:5-6; 30:21; 33:17).
        (5) Jerusalem will be rebuilt and filled with joy and great thanksgiving (31:4, 7-9, 12-14, 23-25; 33:10-12).
        (6) During the Millennium, Israel will understand the necessity for and the purpose of all their sufferings (31:18-19).
        (7) The cities of Israel will be rebuilt and Jerusalem will become the praise and power center of all the earth (30:18-21; 31:38-39; 33:7-9).

2. Concerning Judah's potentates
  a. The death of the deposed Judean King Jehoahaz in Egypt (22:10-12)
  b. The ignoble and unlamented death of King Jehoiakim (36:29-30)
    (1) He soundly condemned Jehoiakim for his wicked reign (22:13-19).
      (a) He was constructing an extravagant palace with forced labor.
      (b) He had murdered the innocent and oppressed the poor.
      (c) He was filled with selfish greed and dishonesty.
    (2) About this time one of Jeremiah's fellow prophets, Urijah, was murdered by Jehoiakim for his fearless preaching (26:20-23). Therefore, Jeremiah predicted the following:
      (a) The king would die unlamented.
      (b) He would be buried like a dead donkey.
      (c) He would be dragged out of Jerusalem.
      (d) He would be thrown on the garbage dump beyond the gate.
  c. The cutting off from the royal line of King Jehoiachin (22:24-30)
    (1) This young son of Jehoiakim ruled only three months, but so aroused the divine wrath of heaven that, Jeremiah was told, had he been the signet ring of God's right hand, he would still have been cast off and given to the Babylonians (22:24-25)
    (2) Jeremiah predicted that this 90-day wonder would:
      (a) Be given over to Nebuchadnezzar

      (b) Be cast out of the land along with his mother
      (c) Die in a foreign land
      (d) Be regarded as a discarded and broken dish
      (e) Be considered childless (even though he had offspring) as far as the throne of David was concerned (22:25-29)
  d. The capture of Zedekiah (21:3-7; 34:1-5; 37:17; see 39:4-7; 52:6-11 for fulfillment)
3. Concerning Judah's prophets
  a. The death of two false prophets (Zedekiah and Ahab) and the punishment of another (Shemaiah) who were ministering among the first Jewish captive exiles in Babylon (29:20-32)
  b. The death of a false Jerusalem prophet named Hananiah (28:13-17)—Jeremiah predicted Hananiah's death in the near future by God's hand for his lying ministry. Within two years he was dead.
4. Concerning Judah's persecutors
  a. The failure of the Egyptian-Judean military alliance against Babylon (37:5-10)
  b. The defeat of Egypt by Babylon (46:1-26)—Jeremiah described in vivid detail the world-famous battle at Carchemish at the very moment when it was being fought. Egypt suffered a resounding defeat at the hands of Nebuchadnezzar (46:1-12).
  c. The eventual occupation of Egypt by Babylon (43:9-13)
  d. The defeat of Babylon after the 70 years (25:12; 27:7) NOTE: The punishment Babylon would receive from God as found in Jeremiah 50 and 51 evidently referred not only to the historical judgment (Dan. 5), but also that future judgment (Rev. 18). Jeremiah warned a man named

Seraiah that he would be taken captive by Nebuchadnezzar at a later date. This literally happened some six years later (51:59). Seraiah was then given a scroll containing Jeremiah's prophecies against Babylon. The prophet commanded him to publicly read it when he arrived there and then to tie a rock to the scroll and throw it into the Euphrates River. This symbolized that Babylon would sink, never to rise again (51:60-64).

B. The great prophecy—The New Covenant (31:31-34)
  1. The nature of the New Covenant (31:31-34)
    a. It would embrace the entire house of Israel.
    b. It would be totally unlike the old Mosaic Covenant.
    c. God would inscribe his laws upon their hearts. Israel had always suffered with self-inflicted spiritual heart trouble.
      (1) The divine diagnosis—"The sin of Judah is written with a pen of iron, and with the point of a diamond: it is graven upon the table of their heart" (17:1).
      (2) The divine prognosis—Under the New Covenant the heavenly Physician would offer them perfect and guaranteed successful heart transplants. This nation with the new hearts would then once again become God's people, and he their God.
  2. The time of the New Covenant
    a. It will go into effect "after those days" (31:33).
    b. It will follow the "time of Jacob's trouble" (30:7).
    c. Both these terms refer to the coming great tribulation. Thus,

the New Covenant will begin to function after the time of Jacob's trouble, at the start of the glorious Millennium.
  3. The superiority of the New Covenant
    a. It will be eternal as opposed to the Mosaic Covenant (Exod. 19:5-8; Jer. 31:32). God himself assured Israel of the duration of this New Covenant when he declared: "If heaven above can be measured, and the foundations of the earth searched out beneath, I will also cast off all the seed of Israel" (31:37; see also 33:20-26).
    b. It will be unconditional (31:34).
    c. It will be immutable (31:36-37).
  4. The Mediator of the New Covenant—The Son of David himself (30:9; 33:15-18)

THEOLOGICAL SUMMARY

I. Jeremiah's great prophecy concerning the 70-year Babylonian Captivity (Jer. 29:10) is referred to by three Old Testament authors.
  A. The author of 2 Chronicles mentioned it (2 Chron. 36:21).
  B. Ezra mentioned it (Ezra 1:1).
  C. Daniel referred to it (Dan. 9:2).
II. Matthew recorded the tragic fulfillment of two of Jeremiah's prophecies.
  A. Concerning the slaughter of the infants at Bethlehem (compare Jer. 31:15 with Matt. 2:17-18)
  B. Concerning the purchase of a potter's field where Judas was buried (compare Jer. 32:6-9 with Matt. 27:9-10)
III. Some of the Jews in the time of Christ believed the Savior was really a return of Jeremiah (Matt. 16:14).
IV. Jeremiah was the most persecuted prophet in the Old Testament, and in many ways his sufferings foreshadowed the sufferings of Christ.
  A. Both were mistreated by their own families (Jer. 12:6; John 7:5).

B. Both were plotted against by the citizens of their own hometowns (Jer. 11:21; Luke 4:28-30).

C. Both were hated by the religious world (Jer. 26:7-9; John 11:47-53).

D. Both were denounced by the two leading synagogue leaders of their day (Jer. 20:1; 28:1; John 18:13, 24).

E. Both were temporarily aided by a ruler (Jer. 38:16; Luke 23:4).

F. Both were described in similar fashion (Jer. 11:19; Isa. 53:7).

G. Both wept often over the city of Jerusalem (Jer. 9:1; Matt. 23:37; Luke 19:41).

H. Both predicted the destruction of the temple in their day (Jer. 7:11-15; Matt. 24:1-2).

V. Jeremiah, like Job, on occasion suffered from extreme depression (Job 3; Jer. 20:14-18).

VI. Like Elijah, Jeremiah once decided to resign (1 Kings 19:4; Jer. 20:9).

VII. However, he persevered, and his book became a great source of inspiration to the prophet Daniel years later (Dan. 9:2).

VIII. The book of Jeremiah gives the final of three great immutable Old Testament covenants.

A. The Abrahamic Covenant (Gen. 12:1-3) —This has to do with a land (Canaan), a people (Israel), and a Savior.

B. The Davidic Covenant (2 Sam. 7:4-16; 1 Chron. 17:3-15)—This had to do with a king to rule in that land over that people.

C. The New Covenant (Jer. 31:31-34)— This has to do with changed hearts so that the people in the land will allow that king to rule over them.

IX. Jeremiah may have been the only biblical writer to have died in Egypt.

STATISTICS

Father: Hilkiah (Jer. 1:1)
First mention: 2 Chronicles 35:25
Final mention: Matthew 27:9
Meaning of his name: "Jehovah is high"
Frequency of his name: Referred to 134 times

Biblical books mentioning him: Five books (2 Chronicles, Ezra, Jeremiah, Daniel, Matthew)
Occupation: Prophet (Matt. 27:9)
Place of birth: Anathoth, in Israel (Jer. 1:1)
Place of death: Egypt
Important fact about his life: He was known as the weeping prophet and authored the longest book in the Bible (apart from the Psalms).

Jeroboam I

CHRONOLOGICAL SUMMARY

I. Jeroboam, the supervisor

A. He was the first king of Northern Israel.

B. He ruled for 22 years (1 Kings 14:20).

C. He was from the tribe of Ephraim and lived in the city of Zeredah (1 Kings 11:26).

D. He had great natural organizational ability (1 Kings 11:28).

E. Realizing this, King Solomon made him supervisor over the labor force of the tribes of Ephraim and Manasseh (1 Kings 11:28).

II. Jeroboam, the sovereign

A. His rule foretold

1. The seer involved—Ahijah the prophet informed Jeroboam that he would soon become king over 10 of Israel's 12 tribes (1 Kings 11:29-39).

2. The sin involved—Both Solomon and Israel had forsaken God and were worshiping idols. God therefore would punish his people by dividing their kingdom.

3. The sign involved

a. Ahijah took off his new cloak, tore it into 12 pieces, and gave Jeroboam 10 pieces.

b. God then assured Jeroboam he would be blessed if he would but obey as did David.

B. His rule fulfilled

1. The refuge

a. Solomon learned of all this and attempted to kill Jeroboam (1 Kings 11:40).

b. Jeroboam fled to Egypt and took refuge there until Solomon's death (1 Kings 11:40).

2. The revolt

a. Upon his return, Jeroboam became the spokesman for the disgruntled 10 tribes that demanded tax relief from Israel's new king, Rehoboam, the son of Solomon (1 Kings 12:1-4).

C. When Rehoboam foolishly threatened to be even more harsh with Israel than his father had been, Jeroboam led a revolt and became the first ruler over the 10-tribe kingdom (1 Kings 12:6-16, 20).

III. Jeroboam, the sinner

A. His apostasy

1. He constructed two golden calves and set up false worship centers with a calf in each center in the cities of Bethel and Dan, lest his people return to sacrifice in the Jerusalem temple (1 Kings 12:25-29).

2. This caused Northern Israel to sin greatly (1 Kings 12:30).

3. He built shrines on high places (1 Kings 12:31).

4. He appointed worthless men who were not Levites to function as priests (1 Kings 12:31).

5. This resulted in the return to Jerusalem of those genuine Levites whom Jeroboam had rejected (1 Kings 11:14).

6. He replaced the regular feast days in Jerusalem with his own in Bethel and Dan (1 Kings 12:32).

7. He even created a new feast day on the fifteenth day of the eighth month (1 Kings 12:33).

8. Jeroboam's sin and evil ways are mentioned some 22 times, more than the sins of any other person in the entire Bible.

B. His altar—Jeroboam was rebuked by a prophet of God as he stood by his false altar in Bethel to offer up a sacrifice (1 Kings 13:1-9).

1. The prophecy against Jeroboam

a. A future godly Judean king named Josiah would someday burn the bones of Jeroboam's false prophets on that altar.

b. As a sign that God had indeed spoken through the prophet, Jeroboam was told the altar he stood by would be split apart and its ashes poured out. This happened immediately.

2. The punishment of Jeroboam— His hand was suddenly shriveled up as he reached out to seize the prophet.

3. The plea by Jeroboam

a. He begged the prophet to pray that his hand be restored. This plea was granted.

b. He invited the prophet to join him at his palace for dinner. This plea was refused.

c. In spite of all this, Jeroboam continued in his evil ways (1 Kings 13:33-34).

IV. Jeroboam, the soldier

A. There was constant war between Jeroboam and Rehoboam (1 Kings 14:30).

B. He also fought against Abijam, the son of Rehoboam (1 Kings 15:7; 2 Chron. 13:1-20).

1. The soldiers involved

a. Jeroboam had 800,000 troops.

b. Abijam had 400,000 troops.

2. The speech involved

a. While Abijam was delivering a long speech before the battle, attempting to persuade the 10 tribes back into the Judean fold, Jeroboam secretly surrounded him.

b. However, God routed Jeroboam's army and caused him to suffer 500,000 casualties.

c. He never really recovered from this terrible defeat.

V. Jeroboam, the seeker
  A. Jeroboam's son, Abijah, became ill (1 Kings 14:1).
  B. At the king's command, his wife disguised herself and went to Shiloh to ask Ahijah the prophet whether their son would recover (1 Kings 14:1-4).
  C. In spite of his near blindness and her disguise, the old prophet saw through everything and told Jeroboam's wife by divine revelation what the future held (1 Kings 14:4-16).
      1. Concerning her son, Abijah
         a. He would die upon her return home.
         b. He would, however, because of his goodness, be saved spiritually.
      2. Concerning her husband, Jeroboam
         a. His kingdom would not last.
         b. His male descendants and relatives would die unnatural and unlamented deaths. This was fulfilled by King Baasha (1 Kings 15:28-29).
      3. Concerning her nation, Israel— The people of Northern Israel would later be uprooted and scattered beyond the Euphrates River (1 Kings 14:15).
VI. Jeroboam, the slain—God struck Jeroboam down, and the evil king died (2 Chron. 13:20).

STATISTICS

Father: Nebat (1 Kings 11:26)
Mother: Zeruah (1 Kings 11:26)
Sons: Abijah and Nadab (1 Kings 14:1; 15:25)
First mention: 1 Kings 11:26
Final mention: 2 Chronicles 13:20
Meaning of his name: "Enlarger"
Frequency of his name: Referred to 84 times
Biblical books mentioning him: Three books (1 Kings, 2 Kings, 2 Chronicles)
Occupation: King of Northern Israel (1 Kings 12:19, 20)
Place of birth: Zeredah (1 Kings 11:26)

Circumstances of death: He died of a plague from God.
Important fact about his life: He was the first king of the 10-tribe confederation of Northern Israel (1 Kings 12:19-20).

Jeroboam II

CHRONOLOGICAL SUMMARY

I. Jeroboam and the true prophets of his day
  A. He was the thirteenth king of Northern Israel.
  B. He ruled for 41 years (2 Kings 14:23).
  C. He was an evil king (2 Kings 14:24).
  D. He was, however, allowed by God to restore the boundaries of his kingdom which had been previously occupied by Israel's enemies (2 Kings 14:25).
  E. All this was foretold by Jonah the prophet (2 Kings 14:25).
  F. The reason was due to God's grace. "The LORD saw the affliction of Israel, that it was very bitter: for there was not any . . . helper for Israel. And the LORD . . . saved them by the hand of Jeroboam" (2 Kings 14:26-27).
  G. Hosea and Amos also prophesied during the reign of Jeroboam (Hos. 1:1; Amos 1:1).
II. Jeroboam and a false prophet of his day
  A. Amaziah, false prophet of Beth-el, had complained to Jeroboam concerning the prophecies of Amos (Amos 7:10-11).
  B. He claimed that Amos had predicted the death of Jeroboam by the sword (this was a lie).
  C. He claimed Amos predicted Israel would later be led into captivity (this was the truth).

STATISTICS

Father: Jehoash (2 Kings 13:13; 14:16)
Son: Zechariah (2 Kings 14:29)
First mention: 2 Kings 13:13
Final mention: Amos 7:11

Meaning of his name: "Enlarger"
Frequency of his name: Referred to 14 times
Biblical books mentioning him: Four books
(2 Kings, 1 Chronicles, Hosea, Amos)
Occupation: King of Israel (2 Kings 14:16)
Important fact about his life: He was the king
who strengthened Israel during the pro-
phetical ministries of Jonah, Hosea, and
Amos.

✍︎Jesse

CHRONOLOGICAL SUMMARY

I. Jesse and Saul
   A. Jesse was a sheep raiser who lived in
   Bethlehem (1 Sam. 16:1).
   B. He allowed his youngest son, David,
   to visit Saul and play the harp for the
   troubled king (1 Sam. 16:19-23).
II. Jesse and Samuel
   A. The rejection of Jesse's older sons
   (1 Sam. 16:5-10)
      1. Samuel visited Jesse and informed
      him he was there to select the fu-
      ture king of Israel.
      2. Jesse presented his seven oldest
      sons, but all were rejected by
      Samuel.
   B. The selection of Jesse's youngest son
   (1 Sam. 16:11-13)
      1. At Samuel's command, Jesse sent
      for David who was caring for the
      sheep.
      2. David was chosen by God and
      anointed by Samuel.
III. Jesse and David—Jesse sent David with
   a food package to visit his brothers who
   were in Saul's army (1 Sam. 17:17-19).

STATISTICS

Father: Obed (Ruth 4:22)
Sons: Eliab, Abinadab, Shammah, Nethan-
eel, Raddai, Ozem, and David (1 Sam.
17:12-13; 1 Chron 2:13-15) Daughters—
Zeruiah and Abigail (1 Chron. 2:16)
Significant ancestors: Boaz and Ruth were his
grandparents (Ruth 4:13, 21)
First mention: Ruth 4:17
Final mention: Romans 15:12

Meaning of his name: "God exists"
Frequency of his name: Referred to 46 times
Biblical books mentioning him: 12 books (Ruth,
1 Samuel, 2 Samuel, 1 Kings, 1 Chronicles, 2 Chronicles, Psalms, Isaiah, Matthew, Luke, Acts, Romans)
Occupation: Sheepherder
Important fact about his life: He was David's
father (Ruth 4:17).

✍︎Jethro

CHRONOLOGICAL SUMMARY

I. The father-in-law of Moses
   A. Jethro is also called Reuel (Exod.
   2:18).
   B. He was a priest of Midian, and a
   sheep raiser (Exod. 3:1).
   C. Moses married Zipporah, one of
   Jethro's seven daughters (Exod. 2:16,
   21).
   D. Jethro was a descendant of Abraham
   through Keturah (Gen. 25:1-2).
II. The friend to Moses
   A. The journey to Egypt—Jethro encour-
   aged Moses to return to Egypt (Exod.
   4:18).
   B. The judging at Sinai
      1. Jethro and Moses were reunited at
      Sinai following the Red Sea cross-
      ing, during the Exodus march
      (Exod. 18:1-12).
      2. He advised Moses to appoint ca-
      pable men to help ease the load of
      the burdened lawgiver in matters
      of judging the people of Israel
      (Exod. 18:13-26).
      3. Jethro elected not to accompany
      Moses en route to the promised
      land (Exod. 18:27).

STATISTICS

Son: Hobab (Num. 10:29) Daughters—
seven, one of whom was Zipporah (Exod.
2:16, 21)
First mention: Exodus 3:1
Final mention: Exodus 18:12
Meaning of his name: "Preeminence"
Frequency of his name: Referred to 11 times

Biblical books mentioning him: One book (Exodus)
Occupation: Priest of Midian (Exod. 3:1)
Important fact about his life: He was Moses' father-in-law (Exod. 3:1).

Jezebel

CHRONOLOGICAL SUMMARY

I. The perversions of Jezebel
   A. Her blasphemy
      1. She worshiped Baal (1 Kings 16:31).
      2. She fed and cared for 850 false prophets of Baal and Asherah (1 Kings 18:19).
      3. She urged Ahab her husband to do evil in the sight of God (1 Kings 21:25).
   B. Her bloodletting
      1. She murdered many of God's prophets (1 Kings 18:4).
      2. She plotted the murder of godly Naboth so that Ahab could possess his vineyard (1 Kings 21:4-15).
      3. She vowed to kill Elijah after he executed her false prophets on Mt. Carmel (1 Kings 19:1-2).
II. The prophecies against Jezebel
   A. The facts—Elijah and Elisha both predicted dogs would eat Jezebel by the wall of Jezreel as her punishment for the murder of Naboth (1 Kings 21:23; 2 Kings 9:1-10).
   B. The fulfillment
      1. Years later, Jehu, a king of Northern Israel, ordered that Jezebel be thrown out of a window in the city of Jezreel (2 Kings 9:30-33).
      2. The dogs of the city then ate her smashed corpse (2 Kings 9:35-37).

STATISTICS

Father: Ethbaal (1 Kings 16:31)
Spouse: Ahab (1 Kings 16:30-31)
Son: Jehoram (2 Kings 9:22)
Daughter: Athaliah

First mention: 1 Kings 16:31
Final mention: 2 Kings 9:37
Meaning of her name: "Without cohabitation"
Frequency of her name: Referred to 20 times
Biblical books mentioning her: Two books (1 Kings, 2 Kings)
Occupation: Queen of Israel (1 Kings 16:29, 31)
Place of death: Jezreel (2 Kings 9:30-37)
Circumstances of death: She was thrown from a window (2 Kings 9:33).
Important fact about her life: She promoted Baal worship and tried to have Elijah killed (1 Kings 19:1-2).

Joab

CHRONOLOGICAL SUMMARY

I. Joab, under the reign of David
   A. His conquests
      1. He was the son of Zeruiah, David's sister, and thus the nephew of David (1 Chron. 2:16).
      2. He was commander-in-chief of David's army (2 Sam 8:16; 20:23).
      3. His armor bearer was Nahari (2 Sam. 23:37).
      4. He was victorious over the following:
         a. The Ammonites—He attacked and defeated them after they had spurned David's act of kindness (2 Sam. 10).
         b. The Edomites (1 Kings 11:15-16)
         c. The city of Rabbah (2 Sam. 12:26)
         d. The city of Jerusalem—He took the city from the Jebusites (1 Chron. 11:4-6).
   B. His conniving
      1. He arranged (at David's command) to have Uriah killed in battle so that the king might marry Bath-sheba, the soldier's wife (2 Sam. 11).
      2. He arranged by deception to have Absalom brought back to Jerusa-

lem after the young rebel had been banished by his father David for murdering Amnon (2 Sam. 14).

C. His cruelty
  1. He killed Abner.
     a. Joab was involved in a skirmish that almost led to an all-out war with Abner, Saul's general, who continued to be commander even after the king's death (2 Sam. 2:12-32).
     b. During this incident, Abner, acting in self-defense, killed Joab's younger brother, Asahel (2 Sam. 2:22-23).
     c. Soon after this, Joab murdered Abner to avenge his dead brother (2 Sam. 3:24-28).
     d. David was furious upon learning about this act of treachery (2 Sam. 3:28-39).
  2. He killed Absalom.
     a. In defiance of David's specific command, Joab killed the helpless Absalom after defeating him in battle (2 Sam. 18:5, 14).
     b. Joab then rebuked David for mourning over the death of his rebellious son (2 Sam. 19:1-7).
  3. He killed Amasa—Amasa was the son of David's sister Abigail and commander of Absalom's troops. Joab murdered him so he would not be replaced by him (2 Sam. 20:9-10).
  4. He killed Sheba—Joab arranged to have Sheba killed by his own townspeople of Abel for leading a rebellion against David (2 Sam. 20:15-22).
  5. On his deathbed, David requested that Solomon eventually punish Joab for all his crimes and bloodshedding (1 Kings 2:5).
D. His census—Against his better judgment, Joab, at David's command, conducted a census to determine the number of Israelite fighting men (2 Sam. 24:2-9; 1 Chron. 21:2-6).

II. Joab, under the reign of Solomon
  A. His plot against Solomon—Joab joined the unsuccessful conspiracy against Solomon led by Adonijah, the oldest half brother of the king (1 Kings 1:7).
  B. His punishment by Solomon—Realizing the plot had failed, Joab took refuge in the tabernacle but was killed by Solomon's order (1 Kings 2:28-34).

STATISTICS

Mother: Zeruiah (2 Sam. 2:13)
Brothers: Abishai and Asahel (2 Sam. 2:18)
First mention: 1 Samuel 26:6
Final mention: 1 Chronicles 27:34
Meaning of his name: "God is Father"
Frequency of his name: Referred to 138 times
Biblical books mentioning him: Four books (1 Samuel, 2 Samuel, 1 Kings, 1 Chronicles)
Occupation: General of David's army (1 Chron. 27:34)
Place of death: At the brazen altar in the temple at Jerusalem (1 Kings 2:28-34)
Circumstances of death: He was executed on Solomon's order (1 Kings 2:29).
Important fact about his life: He murdered Abner, Absalom, and Amasa (2 Sam. 3:27; 18:14; 20:10).

✥Joash (1)

CHRONOLOGICAL SUMMARY

I. His wrongdoing
  A. Joash was the father of Gideon, from the tribe of Manasseh, who lived in the city of Ophrah (Judg. 6:11; 8:32).
  B. He was a worshiper of Baal and Asherah (Judg. 6:25).

II. His wisdom—He defended Gideon from an angry mob who planned to kill his son for tearing down an altar of Baal. Joash successfully reasoned with the mob that if Baal did indeed exist, he could defend and avenge himself (Judg. 6:28-32).

STATISTICS

Son: Gideon (Judg. 6:11)
First mention: Judges 6:11
Final mention: Judges 8:32
Meaning of his name: "God supports"
Frequency of his name: Referred to nine times
Biblical books mentioning him: One book
   (Judges)
Important fact about his life: He was Gideon's
   father (Judg. 6:11).

Joash (2)

CHRONOLOGICAL SUMMARY

I. Joash—the better years
   A. His safekeeping by God
      1. He was the eighth ruler of Judah.
      2. He ruled for 40 years (2 Kings 12:1).
      3. He was also called Jehoash.
      4. He began to reign when he was only seven (2 Kings 11:21).
      5. Joash alone survived a bloody purge instigated by his own grandmother, Queen Athaliah, who was determined to eliminate all the seed of David (2 Kings 11:1).
      6. He was hidden, however, by his aunt Jehosheba and her high priest husband, Jehoiada, for the first six years of his life (2 Kings 11:2-3).
      7. When he was seven, Athaliah was executed and Joash became king (2 Kings 11:16, 21).
      8. Jehoiada chose two wives for Joash (2 Chron. 24:3).
   B. His service for God
      1. He was basically a good king (2 Kings 12:2).
      2. He collected a sizable amount of money for his people to repair the Jerusalem temple (2 Kings 12:4-8).

II. Joash—the bitter years
   A. His sins against God
      1. He did not remove the pagan high places (2 Kings 12:3).
      2. After the death of Jehoiada the high priest, Joash abandoned God (2 Chron. 24:17-19).
      3. Instead of looking to God for deliverance, he paid tribute to the Syrians who had attacked Jerusalem, giving them gold from the temple and royal palace (2 Kings 12:17-18).
      4. When godly Zechariah, son of Jehoiada, cried out against the king's sins, Joash ordered him stoned to death in the temple courtyard (2 Chron. 24:20-22).
   B. His sufferings from God
      1. God allowed the Syrians to invade both Judah and Jerusalem, killing all the leaders of the people (2 Chron. 24:23-24).
      2. Joash himself was severely wounded (2 Chron. 24:25).
      3. Later, his palace officials killed him in his own bed for ordering the death of Zechariah the high priest (2 Chron. 24:25).
      4. Two men were involved in his execution (2 Chron. 24:26).
         a. Zabad, an Ammonite
         b. Jehozabad, a Moabite

STATISTICS

Father: Ahaziah (2 Kings 11:2)
Mother: Zibiah (2 Kings 12:1)
Spouse: Jehoaddan (2 Kings 14:1-2)
Son: Amaziah (2 Kings 12:21)
First mention: 2 Kings 11:2
Final mention: 2 Chronicles 25:25
Meaning of his name: "God supports"
Frequency of his name: Referred to 25 times
Biblical books mentioning him: Three books
   (2 Kings, 1 Chronicles, 2 Chronicles)
Occupation: King of Judah (2 Kings 12:1)
Place of birth: Jerusalem
Place of death: On his own bed in Jerusalem
   (2 Chron. 24:25)

Circumstances of death: He was killed by his own officials (2 Chron. 24:25).

Important fact about his life: He alone survived Queen Athaliah's family massacre (2 Kings 11:1-2).

Job

CHRONOLOGICAL SUMMARY

I. His terrible trials
A. The nature of these trials
1. First trial—His oxen and donkeys were stolen and his farm hands were killed by a Sabean raid (1:14-15).
2. Second trial—His sheep and herdsmen were burned up by fire (1:16).
3. Third trial—His camels were stolen and his servants killed by a Chaldean raid (1:17).
4. Fourth trial—His sons and daughters perished in a mighty wind (1:18).
5. Fifth trial—Job himself was struck with a terrible case of boils (2:7).
B. The reason for these trials—A conversation took place in the heavenlies between God and Satan concerning Job. The devil sneeringly charged that Job only worshiped God because of two selfish benefits.
1. Because God had given his servant much wealth—"Hast not thou made an hedge about him, and about his house, and about all that he hath on every side? thou hast blessed the work of his hands, and his substance is increased in the land" (1:10).
2. Because God had given his servant good health—Satan argued that if he could but remove these two elements, Job would curse God to his face. Thus, to shut the devil's mouth, God gave him permission to remove both Job's wealth and health. Notice that

Satan cannot tempt a believer apart from God's specific permission.
C. The faith shown through these trials—"Job arose, and rent his mantle, and shaved his head, and fell down upon the ground, and worshipped, And said, Naked came I out of my mother's womb, and naked shall I return thither: the LORD gave, and the LORD hath taken away; blessed be the name of the LORD. In all this Job sinned not, nor charged God foolishly" (1:20-22).

II. His whimpering wife—"Then said his wife unto him, Dost thou still retain thine integrity? curse God, and die. But he said unto her, Thou speakest as one of the foolish women speaketh. What? shall we receive good at the hand of God, and shall we not receive evil? In all this did not Job sin with his lips" (2:9-10).

III. His fickle friends
A. Four friends (including Elihu mentioned later) of Job came to comfort Job when they heard of the calamity that had befallen him. Their initial reaction was one of sympathy (2:11-13).
B. Their true feelings, however, emerged in a series of speeches (Job 3–37).
1. The speeches of Eliphaz (chapters 4–5, 15, 22; see Gen. 36:10)
a. He claimed Job was suffering for his sins (4:7-8).
b. He based his conclusions on personal experience (4:8, 12-16).
c. He urged Job to repent and turn back to God (22:23).
2. The speeches of Bildad (chapters 8, 18, 25)
a. He claimed Job was suffering for his sins (8:20).
b. He based his conclusions on tradition (8:8).
c. He urged Job to repent and turn back to God (8:5-6).
3. The speeches of Zophar (chapters 11, 20)

a. He claimed Job was suffering for his sins (20:4-5).

b. He based his conclusions on sheer dogmatism (11:6; 20:4).

c. He urged Job to repent and turn back to God (11:13-15).

4. The speeches of Elihu (chapters 32–37)

IV. His defenses and dialogues

A. The suffering patriarch responded to his accusers in nine separate speeches.

1. Job 3
2. Job 6–7
3. Job 9–10
4. Job 12–14
5. Job 16–17
6. Job 19
7. Job 21
8. Job 23–24
9. Job 26–31

B. During these nine speeches, Job discussed 14 topics.

1. I am righteous, and therefore not suffering for my sin (27:6; 31:1-40)—"My righteousness I hold fast, and will not let it go: my heart shall not reproach me so long as I live" (27:6).

2. "In the past I have performed many good works" (29:12-17; 30:25).

a. He had helped the poor and fatherless (29:12).

b. He had aided the blind and lame (29:15).

c. He had wept with the sorrowing (30:25).

3. "Oh, for those good old days when I enjoyed health, wealth, and respect" (29:1-11, 20-25).

4. "But now I am being unfairly punished by God" (9:16-17, 30-33; 10:2, 7-8; 13:26-27; 19:6-11; 30:20-21).

5. "My three so-called friends are miserable comforters" (12:2; 13:4; 16:2; 19:3).

6. "If they were in my place, I would help them and not unjustly accuse them" (16:4-5).

7. "Even my neighbors, associates, and servants have turned against me" (19:13-22; 30:1, 9-10).

8. "I wish I could find the answers for all this" (28:12-28).

9. "I wish I could find God" (23:8-9).

10. "My flesh is clothed with worms" (7:5, 13-14; 30:17-18, 30).

11. "I wish I had never been born" (3:3-11, 16; 10:18).

12. "I wish I were dead" (6:8-9; 7:15-16).

13. "I have no hope" (10:20-22).

14. "In spite of all, I'll trust God" (13:15; 16:19; 23:10). "Though he slay me, yet will I trust in him: but I will maintain mine own ways before him" (13:15). "My witness is in heaven, and my record is on high" (16:19). "He knoweth the way that I take: when he hath tried me, I shall come forth as gold" (23:10).

V. His glorious God—Suddenly from out of a whirlwind came the mighty voice of God. The sullen Job was then subjected to a 60-question quiz (Job 38–41). Here are some of the questions:

A. God's first series of questions (Job 38–39)

1. Job 38:4—"Where wast thou when I laid the foundations of the earth? declare, if thou hast understanding."

2. Job 38:18—"Hast thou perceived the breadth of the earth? declare if thou knowest it all."

3. Job 38:19—"Where is the way where light dwelleth? and as for darkness, where is the place thereof."

4. Job 38:24—"By what way is the light parted, which scattereth the east wind upon the earth?"

5. Job 38:28—"Hath the rain a father? or who hath begotten the drops of dew?"

6. Job 40:2—"Shall he that contendeth with the Almighty instruct him? he that reproveth God, let him answer it."

B. Job's reply—"Behold, I am vile; what shall I answer thee? I will lay mine hand upon my mouth. Once have I spoken; but I will not answer: yea, twice; but I will proceed no further" (40:4-5).

C. God's second series of questions (Job 40:6–41:33)

  1. Job 40:15—"Behold now behemoth, which I made with thee; he eateth grass as an ox."

  2. Job 41:1—"Canst thou draw out leviathan with an hook? or his tongue with a cord which thou lettest down?" NOTE: These two creatures may very well refer to a land dinosaur and a sea dinosaur.

D. Job's reply—"I know that thou canst do every thing, and that no thought can be withholden from thee. Who is he that hideth counsel without knowledge? therefore have I uttered that I understood not; things too wonderful for me, which I knew not. Hear, I beseech thee, and I will speak: I will demand of thee, and declare thou unto me. I have heard of thee by the hearing of the ear: but now mine eye seeth thee. Wherefore I abhor myself, and repent in dust and ashes" (42:2-6).

VI. His bountiful blessings—Job had been subjected to five fiery trials and had participated in five painful debates, but now he received at the hand of God a 10-fold blessing (Job 42:7-17).

A. He was allowed to see the glory of God.

B. He saw himself as God saw him. (This is always a blessing.)

C. He was vindicated by God before the eyes of his three critical friends.

D. He discovered the joy of praying for these three friends.

E. His former health was fully restored.

F. He was comforted by his brothers and sisters.

G. He was given money, showered with gifts, and ended up with double his former wealth.

H. He was given seven more sons and three more daughters.

I. He lived to enjoy his grandchildren and great grandchildren.

J. He was given an additional 140 years—twice the number normally accorded a man (see Ps. 90:10).

THEOLOGICAL SUMMARY

I. Job lived in the land of Uz (thought to be the land of Edom) in the days of Abraham, Isaac, and Jacob, or perhaps even before their time (1:1).

II. We are told four facts about Job.

A. He was a godly man—He feared the Lord and avoided evil (Job 1:1).

B. He was a family man—Job had (at the beginning of the account) seven sons and three daughters (Job 1:2).

C. He was a wealthy man (Job 1:3).

  1. He owned 7,000 sheep, 3,000 camels, 500 teams of oxen, and 500 female donkeys.

  2. He employed many servants.

D. He was (apparently) a healthy man.

III. God allowed Satan to tempt Job in the following areas of his life:

A. His fortune (Job 1:14-17)

  1. His animals were stolen.

  2. His servants were slaughtered.

B. His family (Job 1:18-19; 2:9)

  1. The destruction of his children— In one day Satan killed all 10.

  2. The derision of his wife. "Then said his wife unto him, Dost thou still retain thine integrity? curse God, and die" (Job 2:9).

C. His flesh—"So went Satan forth from the presence of the LORD, and smote Job with sore boils from the sole of his foot unto his crown" (Job 2:7).

D. His friends (Job 2–37)

  1. Their assumptions were wrong— They assumed he was being

divinely punished for some terrible secret sin.
2. Their advice was wrong—They attempted to force him to confess for wrongdoings he had not done.

IV. After Job had suffered, God blessed the four areas of his life that Satan had afflicted.
   A. His fortune—The number of his herds previously owned was doubled (42:12).
   B. His family—God gave him 10 additional children, seven sons and three daughters (42:13-15).
   C. His flesh—Job's former health returned, allowing him to live an additional 140 years (Job 42:16).
   D. His friends—They admitted the error of their ways and asked his forgiveness (Job 42:7-9).

V. The book of Job may be the oldest in the Bible. This is indicated by the following:
   A. The many ancient historical allusions, such as the pyramids (3:14), the cities of the plains (15:28), and the great flood (22:16)
   B. The omission of Israel's history—There is no reference to the Law, the Exodus of Israel, the Red Sea crossing, or any of the kings of Israel.
   C. The usage of the ancient patriarchal name for God, El Shaddai—It is used 31 times in Job (see 5:17; 6:4).

VI. The theme of his book is not Job's suffering (although this is certainly involved), but rather God's sovereignty. This is one of the two Old Testament books giving a brief glimpse of the confrontation activities going on in heaven.
   A. Job 1–2
   B. Zechariah 3

VII. The book deals with a great misconception, namely, that suffering is always caused by personal sin.

VIII. Actually, Job was allowed to suffer to accomplish several things:
   A. That Satan might be silenced (1:9-11; 2:4-5)

B. That Job might see God (42:5)
C. That Job might see himself (40:4; 42:6)
D. That Job might learn to pray for, rather than to lash out against his critics (42:10)
E. To show that God remains in full control at all times (38:4)

IX. Job was later mentioned by both Ezekiel and James.
   A. Ezekiel referred to his righteousness (Ezek. 14:14, 20).
   B. James referred to his patience (James 5:11).

X. His disease may have been leprosy complicated by elephantiasis, one of the most loathsome and painful diseases known in the world of his time.

XI. In the midst of terrible suffering, Job uttered one of the truly great testimonies found in the entire Old Testament: "For I know that my redeemer liveth, and that he shall stand at the latter day upon the earth: And though after my skin worms destroy this body, yet in my flesh shall I see God" (Job 19:25-26).

XII. Job also revealed a very precious truth, namely, that Satan cannot tempt or afflict a believer without the express permission of God himself (Job 1:12; 2:6). Furthermore, in the New Testament we are told God knows just how much we can bear, and will not let Satan go beyond that point (1 Cor. 10:13).

XIII. Finally, Job may be considered as a commentary on Jesus' words in Luke 22:31-32: "Simon, Simon, behold, Satan hath desired to have you, that he may sift you as wheat: But I have prayed for thee, that thy faith fail not: and when thou art converted, strengthen thy brethren" (Luke 22:31-32).

STATISTICS

Spouse: Unnamed and unhelpful wife (Job 2:9)
Sons: 14 sons (Job 1:2; 42:13)
Daughters: Six daughters, three are named:

Jemima, Kezia, and Keren-happuch (Job 1:2; 42:13-14)
First mention: Job 1:1
Final mention: James 5:11
Meaning of his name: "Where is the Father?"
Frequency of his name: Referred to 56 times
Biblical books mentioning him: Three books (Job, Ezekiel, James)
Occupation: Wealthy rancher (Job 1:3)
Place of birth: Land of Uz (probably Edom) (Job 1:1)
Important fact about his life: He was accused by Satan before God and allowed to suffer, but was eventually totally restored (Job 1:9-12; 2:2-6; 42:10).

Jochebed

CHRONOLOGICAL SUMMARY

I. The sowing of her faith
  A. Jochebed's problem—After a three-month period, Jochebed realized she could no longer hide her infant son Moses from the pharaoh, who had ordered the death of all male Hebrew babies (Exod. 2:1-2).
  B. Jochebed's plan—She placed Moses in a papyrus basket coated with tar and pitch, and set it afloat on the Nile River (Exod. 2:3).
II. The reaping of her faith
  A. As seen in the rescue of the baby—In the providence of God the infant Moses was rescued from drowning by the daughter of the same pharaoh who had originally imposed the death penalty (Exod. 2:5-6).
  B. As seen in the raising of the baby
    1. God arranged for Jochebed to be paid by the pharaoh's daughter for nursing her own son (Exod. 2:7-9).
    2. Both the faith and courage of Jochebed are referred to in the New Testament (Heb. 11:23).

STATISTICS

Spouse: Amram (Exod. 6:20)
Sons: Aaron and Moses (Exod. 6:20; Num. 26:59)
Daughter: Miriam (Num. 26:59)
First mention: Exodus 6:20
Final mention: Hebrews 11:23 (by inference)
Meaning of her name: "God is honor"
Frequency of her name: Referred to three times
Biblical books mentioning her: Three books (Exodus, Numbers, Hebrews)
Important fact about her life—She was Moses' mother (Exod. 6:20; Num. 26:59).

Joel (1)

CHRONOLOGICAL SUMMARY

I. His appointment
  A. This firstborn son of Samuel was also known as Vashni (1 Chron. 6:28).
  B. He was appointed by Samuel, along with his brother Abijah, to serve as a judge at Beer-sheba (1 Sam. 8:2).
  C. His son Heman was a musician who later served in the tabernacle during the reign of King David (1 Chron. 6:33; 15:17).
II. His apostasy
  A. Joel turned aside after dishonest gain, accepted bribes, and perverted justice (1 Sam. 8:3).
  B. Both his and his brother's evil ways contributed to Israel's untimely and unwise demand for a king (1 Sam. 8:4-5).

STATISTICS

Father: Samuel (1 Sam. 8:2)
Son: Heman (1 Chron. 6:33; 15:17)
Brother: Abiah (1 Sam. 8:2)
First mention: 1 Samuel 8:2
Final mention: 1 Chronicles 15:17
Meaning of his name: "God is God"

Frequency of his name: Referred to three times
Biblical books mentioning him: Two books
  (1 Samuel, 1 Chronicles)
Occupation: Judge (1 Sam. 8:2)
Important fact about his life: He was the oldest
  of Samuel's two wicked sons (1 Sam. 8:2).

✍🏼Joel *(2)*

CHRONOLOGICAL SUMMARY

I. Joel reviewed present conditions in Israel. At the time of his writing, the people were suffering grievously (Joel 1).
 A. The nature of their sufferings—A terrible locust plague, unprecedented in
   history, had fallen upon the land.
 B. The reason for their sufferings—The
   plague had been sent to punish them
   for their sin against God.
 C. The answer to their sufferings
   1. A fast was to be announced.
   2. A solemn meeting was to be
     called.
   3. Both priests and people were to
     dress in sackcloth, weep, repent,
     and cry out to God for forgive-
     ness.

II. Joel previewed future conditions in Israel. Using the locust plague as an illustration and object lesson, Joel described
in some detail three future events which
would occur in the land (Joel 2–3).
 A. The Day of Pentecost
   1. Foretold by Joel in 2:28-32
     a. God's Spirit would be poured
       out upon all flesh.
     b. Israel's sons and daughters
       would prophesy.
     c. Israel's old men would dream
       dreams.
     d. Israel's young men would see
       visions.
   2. Fulfilled (in part) at Pentecost
     (Acts 2:16-21)
 B. The Day of the Lord—The seven-year
   great tribulation
   1. The deluge of the soldiers—

Enemy troops from all nations
will invade Israel like the locusts
in Joel's day (2:1-10).
   2. The deliverance of the saints—At
     that crucial hour, Israel as a na-
     tion will repent and return with
     their whole heart to God (2:12).
   3. The darkening of the skies—The
     sun and moon will be darkened
     and the stars will withdraw their
     light as the LORD prepares to do
     battle (2:10-11).
   4. The destruction of the sinners—
     God will utterly consume his ene-
     mies who attempted to destroy
     him, his holy city, and his people
     (2:18-20).
 C. The day of Christ—The Millennium
   (3:18)
   1. Sweet wine will drip from the
     mountains.
   2. The hills shall flow with milk.
   3. Water will fill the dry stream
     beds.
   4. A fountain will burst forth from
     the temple.

THEOLOGICAL SUMMARY

I. A unique prophet
 A. Joel was the first biblical prophet to
   use the phrase, "the day of the
   LORD," a title used to describe the
   great tribulation (Joel 1:15).
 B. He is the only prophet to pinpoint
   the crucial action during the battle of
   Armageddon at the end of the tribulation in a place called the Valley of Jehoshaphat, believed to be an Old
   Testament name for the Kidron Valley
   (Joel 3:2, 12).
II. A unique point of view—In describing
this battle, Joel reversed the order of
peace and war as described by Isaiah
and Micah.
 A. The action according to Isaiah and
   Micah (Isa. 2:4; Mic. 4:3)
   1. Nations will melt their swords
     into plowshares and beat their
     spears into pruninghooks.

2. Nations will gather for worship.
B. The action according to Joel (Joel 3:9-11)
   1. Nations will melt their plowshares into swords and beat their pruninghooks into spears.
   2. Nations will gather for war.

STATISTICS

Father: Pethuel (Joel 1:1)
First mention: Joel 1:1
Final mention: Acts 2:16
Meaning of his name: "Jehovah is God"
Frequency of his name: Referred to two times
Biblical books mentioning him: Two books (Joel, Acts)
Occupation: Prophet (Acts 2:16)
Important fact about his life: He used a locust plague in his day to illustrate the coming great tribulation (Joel 2:1-11).

✍*Johanan*

CHRONOLOGICAL SUMMARY

I. His warning
   A. He was a Jewish army captain living in Judah after the destruction of Jerusalem by Nebuchadnezzar (Jer. 40:7).
   B. He warned Gedaliah (the Jewish governor over Judah appointed by Nebuchadnezzar) concerning a plot to assassinate him by a Jewish rebel named Ishmael (Jer. 40:13-14).
   C. He volunteered to kill Ishmael, but the governor refused this offer (Jer. 40:15-16).
II. His warfare
   A. Ishmael did carry out his plot and assassinated Gedaliah (Jer. 41:1-2).
   B. Johanan attacked Ishmael, rescued some hostages the rebel had taken captive, and drove him out of the land (Jer. 41:11-15).
III. His wrongdoing
   A. Requesting Jeremiah's advice—He asked Jeremiah to seek direction from God concerning where the Jewish

remnant should live following the destruction of the temple, promising to obey whatever advice was given (Jer. 42:1-6).
   B. Rejecting Jeremiah's advice—When Jeremiah reported back saying God desired the remnant to remain in Jerusalem, Johanan accused him of lying and forced the prophet to accompany him to Egypt (Jer. 42:7-43:7).

STATISTICS

Father: Kareah (2 Kings 25:23)
First mention: 2 Kings 25:23
Final mention: Jeremiah 43:5
Meaning of his name: "God is gracious"
Frequency of his name: Referred to 13 times
Biblical books mentioning him: Two books (2 Kings, Jeremiah)
Occupation: Jewish army captain (Jer. 43:4-5)
Important fact about his life: He forced Jeremiah to accompany him and a Jewish group to Egypt (Jer. 43:5-6).

✍*Jonadab*

CHRONOLOGICAL SUMMARY

I. Jonadab and Jehu the king—He accompanied the Northern Israelite King Jehu when the ruler killed Ahab's family in Samaria, as well as the priests of Baal (2 Kings 10:15-27).
II. Jonadab and Jeremiah the prophet
   A. Jonadab's righteousness—Years after Jonadab's death, the prophet Jeremiah referred to his testimony and legacy, as demonstrated in the life of his descendants (Jer. 35:1-17).
      1. His stand against drinking wine
      2. His simple, nonmaterialistic lifestyle
      3. The fact that he remained in Jerusalem
   B. Jonadab's reward—As a result of Jonadab's faithfulness, God had

promised to use his descendants in his service forever (Jer. 35:18-19).

STATISTICS

Father: Rechab (2 Kings 10:15)
First mention: 2 Kings 10:15
Final mention: Jeremiah 35:19
Meaning of his name: "God is liberal"
Frequency of his name: Referred to 10 times
Biblical books mentioning him: Two books (2 Kings, Jeremiah)
Important fact about his life: Jeremiah pointed to his life as an example of true godliness (Jer. 35:13-14).

✍️*Jonah*

CHRONOLOGICAL SUMMARY

I. The refusal: Jonah's protest—A demonstration of God's patience (chapter 1)
   A. The prophet's order—God commanded him to go to Nineveh and warn that wicked city that divine judgment would fall unless it repented.
   B. The prophet's objection—Jonah disobeyed and set sail at Joppa for Tarshish.
   C. The prophet's ordeal
      1. God created a great storm, which threatened to sink the ship Jonah was in.
      2. After praying to their gods and throwing the cargo overboard, the terrified sailors awakened Jonah and asked him what they should do.
      3. He instructed them to cast him into the sea, explaining that his act of disobedience had brought about the storm in the first place.
      4. He was thrown overboard, causing the raging sea to become calm immediately.
      5. Jonah was swallowed by a great fish, prepared by God, whose

huge stomach would house the prophet for three days and three nights.

II. The resolution: Jonah's prayer—A demonstration of God's power (chapter 2)
   A. The prophet's despair—Inside the fish, he acknowledged his disobedience and cried out for help.
   B. The prophet's dedication—Jonah promised to make good his former vows to God.
   C. The prophet's deliverance—At God's command, Jonah was vomited up by the fish onto dry ground.

III. The revival: Jonah's proclamation—A demonstration of God's pardon (chapter 3)
   A. The warning—He told the people of Nineveh their city would be destroyed by God at the end of 40 days unless they repented.
   B. The mourning—One of the greatest revivals in all human history then took place as a result of Jonah's preaching.
      1. A citywide fast was declared which included both people and animals.
      2. The king of Nineveh led the way, taking off his royal robes, covering himself with sackcloth, and sitting down in the dust.
      3. The entire city turned from its wicked ways.
   C. The transforming—Viewing all this from heaven, the compassionate God saved the people both physically and spiritually.

IV. The resentment: Jonah's pout—A demonstration of God's pity (chapter 4)
   A. The twofold complaint of Jonah—In great bitterness he prayed for death.
      1. First occasion—Concerning the sparing of the city. This carnal prophet apparently preferred death to life if it meant seeing God's salvation extended to the pagan Ninevites.
      2. Second occasion—Concerning the glaring sun

a. God had allowed a vine to grow quickly and spread its broad leaves over Jonah's head to shade him.

b. The Lord then prepared a worm that ate through the plant's stem, causing it to die.

c. Finally, God ordered a scorching east wind to blow on Jonah, which only intensified the power of the fierce sun already beating down upon his head.

B. The manifold compassion of God— God contrasted his great heart with the grubby one displayed by the prophet.

1. The selfish heart—Jonah felt pity only for himself and the vine which the worm destroyed.

2. The sovereign heart—God's compassion embraced:

a. The adults of Nineveh

b. Their 120,000 children (This may be a reference to 120,000 people in Nineveh who were spiritually ignorant.)

c. The cattle of Nineveh

THEOLOGICAL SUMMARY

I. Jonah was probably the only Old Testament prophet who enjoyed some degree of popularity, for he predicted a "bull market" time of prosperity for Northern Israel during the reign of Jeroboam II (2 Kings 14:25).

II. He became the most famous "foreign missionary" in the Old Testament.

III. He was from the city of Gath-hepher in Zebulun of Galilee, which in fact contradicted the claim of the Pharisees (2 Kings 14:25): "Nicodemus saith unto them, (he that came to Jesus by night, being one of them,) Doth our law judge any man, before it hear him, and know what he doeth? They answered and said unto him, Art thou also of Galilee? Search, and look: for out of Galilee ariseth no prophet" (John 7:50-52).

IV. Some believe Jonah actually died in the fish's belly and was raised again (compare Jon. 2:2, 6 with Matt. 12:40).

V. Jonah may be compared to John Mark and Simon Peter in the New Testament.

A. Jonah and John Mark

1. Jonah failed God the first time but was given a second chance and succeeded (compare Jon. 1:2-3 with 3:1-3).

2. John Mark failed God the first time but was given a second chance and succeeded (compare Acts 13:13; 15:36-40 with 2 Tim. 4:11).

B. Jonah and Simon Peter

1. In Joppa, God called Jonah, a Hebrew prophet, to minister to some Gentiles (Jon. 1).

2. In Joppa, God called Peter, a Hebrew apostle, to minister to some Gentiles (Acts 10).

VI. According to Jewish tradition, Jonah was the son of the widow of Zarephath, whom Elijah raised from the dead (1 Kings 17:8-24).

VII. Jesus referred to the life of Jonah on two occasions when he was confronted by the Pharisees.

A. Concerning their demands (Matt. 12:38-40; 16:1-4; Luke 11:29-30)— "Then certain of the scribes and of the Pharisees answered, saying, Master, we would see a sign from thee. But he answered and said unto them, An evil and adulterous generation seeketh after a sign; and there shall no sign be given to it, but the sign of the prophet Jonas: For as Jonas was three days and three nights in the whale's belly; so shall the Son of man be three days and three nights in the heart of the earth" (Matt. 12:38-40).

B. Concerning their disbelief (Matt. 12:40; Luke 11:32)—"The men of Nineve shall rise up in the judgment with this generation, and shall condemn it: for they repented at the preaching of Jonas; and, behold, a greater than Jonas is here" (Luke 11:32).

STATISTICS
Father: Amittai (2 Kings 14:25)
First mention: 2 Kings 14:25
Final mention: Luke 11:32
Meaning of his name: "Dove"
Frequency of his name: Referred to 27 times
Biblical books mentioning him: Four books
   (2 Kings, Jonah, Matthew, Luke)
Occupation: Prophet (2 Kings 14:25)
Place of birth: Gath-hepher (2 Kings 14:25)
Important fact about his life: He survived being swallowed by a fish, and he preached a great revival in Nineveh (Jon. 2:10–3:5).

✒Jonathan (1)

CHRONOLOGICAL SUMMARY
I. Jonathan and his foes—the Philistines
   A. He bravely attacked a Philistine outpost at Geba, thus triggering an all-out Israelite and Philistine war (1 Sam. 13:3-5).
   B. He attacked another Philistine outpost and, aided only by his armor bearer, killed 20 enemy troops. God then sent a panic among the Philistines which routed their entire army (1 Sam. 14:1-15).
II. Jonathan and his father—Saul
   A. In pursuing the enemy, Saul issued a stupid order forbidding his troops to eat any food until final victory had been won. Unaware of this command, Jonathan ate some honey (1 Sam. 14:24-27).
   B. Upon discovery of this, Saul ordered the death of Jonathan. However, the Israelite soldiers stepped in and refused to allow this national hero to die (1 Sam. 14:43-45).
III. Jonathan and his friend—David
   A. He honored his friend.
      1. Jonathan loved David (1 Sam. 18:1-4; 20:16-17).
      2. He warned and defended David

   a. He told David about the threat of Saul to kill him (1 Sam. 19:1-3).
   b. He attempted to change his father's mind concerning David and succeeded, but only for a brief time (1 Sam. 19:4-9).
   c. In spite of the evidence at hand, Jonathan still found it difficult to believe Saul would actually murder David (1 Sam. 20:1-2).
   d. Finally, upon being convinced of Saul's evil intentions, Jonathan warned David by a previously agreed upon signal (1 Sam. 20:10-40).
   e. At this time, the beloved friends said good-bye (1 Sam. 20:41-42).
   f. Saul cursed Jonathan for befriending David and actually attempted to kill his own son (1 Sam. 20:30-33).
      3. He encouraged David—Jonathan and David met for a final time at Horesh, during which time he encouraged David in the Lord and reassured him that he (David) would someday indeed rule over all of Israel (1 Sam. 23:16-18).
   B. He was honored by his friend.
      1. The death of Jonathan
         a. Jonathan, along with his two brothers and father, was killed in a battle with the Philistines (1 Sam. 31:2-6).
         b. Upon hearing of this, a brokenhearted David lamented the death of his dear friend, especially referring to his courage, saying he was swifter than an eagle and stronger than a lion (2 Sam. 1:17, 22-26).
         c. David later secured the bones of Jonathan and buried them near Jerusalem (2 Sam. 21:11-14).
      2. The descendant of Jonathan
         a. Jonathan had a son named Mephibosheth who was crippled

as the result of an accident when he was only five years old (2 Sam. 4:4).

b. David tracked down Mephibosheth and showed great kindness to him for Jonathan's sake (2 Sam. 9:1-13).

c. David later protected Mephibosheth from the Gibeonites, who demanded the blood of all Saul's descendants for past injustices on the part of the wicked king. Remembering his covenant with Jonathan, David refused to allow Mephibosheth to be harmed (2 Sam. 21:7).

STATISTICS

Father: Saul (1 Sam. 14:1)
Mother: Ahinoam (1 Sam. 14:49-50)
Son: Mephibosheth (2 Sam. 4:4)
Brothers: Ishui, Melchi-shua, and Abinadab (1 Sam. 14:49; 1 Chron. 8:33)
Sisters: Merab and Michal (1 Sam. 14:49)
First mention: 1 Samuel 13:2
Final mention: 1 Chronicles 10:2
Meaning of his name: "God has given"
Frequency of his name: Referred to 91 times
Biblical books mentioning him: Three books (1 Samuel, 2 Samuel, 1 Chronicles)
Place of death: On a battlefield at Mt. Gilboa (1 Sam. 31:1-2)
Circumstances of death: He was killed by Philistine soldiers (1 Sam. 31:2).
Important fact about his life: He was Saul's son and David's closest friend (1 Sam. 14:1; 18:1-4).

Jonathan (2)

CHRONOLOGICAL SUMMARY

I. His support for King David

A. He was the son of Abiathar, one of Israel's two chief priests in the days of David (2 Sam. 15:27).

B. He undertook a dangerous mission to warn David concerning the plans of

the king's wicked son Absalom during the revolt (2 Sam. 17:17-21).

II. His sin against King Solomon

A. Jonathan later joined in with Adonijah, eldest half brother of Solomon, in an attempt to steal the throne of Israel.

B. It fell to Jonathan to tell the plotters their scheme had failed (1 Kings 1:42-49).

STATISTICS

Father: Abiathar (2 Sam. 15:27)
First mention: 2 Samuel 15:27
Final mention: 1 Kings 1:43
Meaning of his name: "God has given"
Frequency of his name: Referred to six times
Biblical books mentioning him: Two books (2 Samuel, 1 Kings)
Important fact about his life: He undertook a dangerous mission to warn David (2 Sam. 17:17-21).

Joram

CHRONOLOGICAL SUMMARY

I. Joram's debauchery

A. The king's wicked wife

1. Joram (also called Jehoram) was the fifth king of Judah.
2. He ruled for eight years (2 Kings 8:17).
3. He was 32 when he became king (2 Kings 8:17).
4. He was a godless king (2 Kings 8:18).
5. He married an equally evil wife named Athaliah, who was the daughter of Ahab and Jezebel (2 Kings 8:18).

B. The king's wicked ways

1. He killed his brothers at the beginning of his reign (2 Chron. 21:4).
2. He built high places on the hills of Judah to worship pagan gods (2 Chron. 21:11).

II. Joram's defeat
  A. Joram attacked Edom, who had re-
     belled against him, hoping to regain
     control of that land (2 Kings 8:20-21).
  B. However, he did not succeed, and
     finding himself surrounded, barely
     broke through by night and fled back
     home (2 Kings 8:21).
III. Joram's destruction
  A. The message from God—He received
     a letter from Elijah the prophet
     (2 Chron. 21:12-16).
     1. Concerning what Joram had done
        against God
        a. He had caused Judah and Jeru-
           salem to prostitute themselves.
        b. He had murdered his own
           brothers, men better than he.
     2. Concerning what God would do
        against Joram
        a. He would punish the people.
        b. He would punish the king.
  B. The misery from God
     1. Joram suffered from an invasion—
        God himself aroused the hostility
        of the Philistines and Arabs
        against Joram, causing them to
        invade Judah (2 Chron. 21:16-17).
        a. They carried off all the goods in
           the royal palace.
        b. They took Joram's sons and
           wives; only the youngest son,
           Ahaziah (also called Jehoahaz),
           was left.
     2. Joram suffered from an infirmity.
        a. As Elijah had predicted, God
           afflicted Joram with an incur-
           able disease of the bowels
           (2 Chron. 21:15, 18).
        b. After two years of suffering
           great pain, Joram died and was
           unlamented by the people of
           Judah (2 Chron. 21:19-20).

STATISTICS

Father: Jehoshaphat (1 Kings 22:50)
Spouse: Athaliah (2 Kings 8:18)
Son: Ahaziah (2 Kings 8:24)
Daughter: Jehosheba (2 Kings 11:2)
First mention: 1 Kings 22:50

Final mention: Matthew 1:8
Meaning of his name: "God is high"
Frequency of his name: Referred to 21 times
Biblical books mentioning him: Five books
  (1 Kings, 2 Kings, 1 Chronicles, 2 Chroni-
  cles, Matthew)
Occupation: King of Judah (2 Kings 22:50)
Place of birth: Jerusalem
Place of death: Jerusalem (2 Chron. 21:20)
Age at death: 40 (2 Chron. 21:20)
Circumstances of death: He was plagued by
  God with an incurable bowel disease
  (2 Chron. 21:15).
Important fact about his life: He married Je-
  zebel's daughter Athaliah and killed all
  his brothers (2 Chron. 21:1-6).

✍ Joseph

CHRONOLOGICAL SUMMARY

I. Joseph, the favored son
  A. Loved by his father (Gen. 37:3)
     1. The reasons involved
        a. Because he had been born to
           Jacob in his old age
        b. Because he was the firstborn
           son of Rachel, Jacob's beloved
           wife
     2. The reward involved—Jacob gave
        him a brightly colored coat.
  B. Loathed by his brothers (Gen. 37:2-11)
     1. The reasons involved
        a. Because he reported to his fa-
           ther some of their bad actions
        b. Because of his two dreams,
           both in which he saw his 10
           brothers bowing down before
           him
     2. The results involved (Gen. 37:2,
        12-35)
        a. The trip—Jacob sent Joseph to
           check up on his brothers. He
           finally located them near the
           town of Dothan. He was 17 at
           this time, and was a shepherd.
        b. The treachery

(1) The brothers at first planned to kill him.

(2) They stripped him of his brightly colored robe.

(3) They then decided to throw him into a dry cistern and leave him to starve to death.

c. The transaction—Finally, seeing some Ishmaelite and Midianite merchants passing by en route to Egypt, they sold Joseph for 20 shekels of silver.

d. The trickery—The brothers then dipped Joseph's coat in the blood of a slaughtered goat, leading Jacob to believe his son had been killed and devoured by a wild animal.

II. Joseph, the faithful steward

A. His service

1. Upon reaching Egypt, Joseph was sold by the merchants as a slave to Potiphar, one of Pharaoh's military officials (Gen. 37:36).

2. Joseph was soon entrusted to run the entire household of Potiphar (Gen. 39:1-6).

B. His self-control

1. The request—Joseph was repeatedly urged by Potiphar's wife to sleep with her (Gen. 39:7).

2. The refusal—Joseph refused her sexual advances for two reasons (Gen. 39:8-9):

a. He would not sin against his master.

b. He would not sin against his God.

3. The revenge—The rejected wife falsely accused Joseph of attempted rape (Gen. 39:10-19).

C. His sufferings—Potiphar believed his wife and had Joseph thrown into prison (Gen. 39:20).

III. Joseph, the forgotten slave

A. Joseph, the prison keeper—"The LORD was with Joseph, and shewed him mercy, and gave him favour in the sight of the keeper of the prison. And the keeper of the prison committed to Joseph's hand all the prisoners that were in the prison; and whatsoever they did there, he was the doer of it" (Gen. 39:21-22).

B. Joseph and the prisoners (Gen. 40:1-23)

1. Who they were

a. Among the inmates there were two political prisoners.

b. One was the royal chief cupbearer and the other was the chief baker, both of whom had angered Pharaoh for some reason.

2. What they dreamed—Both these men experienced strange dreams and told them to Joseph, hoping he could explain their meaning (Gen. 40:5-23).

a. The information in the dreams

(1) The chief cupbearer's dream

(a) He saw a vine with three branches loaded down with grapes.

(b) He saw himself squeezing the grapes into Pharaoh's cup and handing it to him.

(2) The chief baker's dream

(a) He saw himself carrying three baskets of bread on his head for Pharaoh.

(b) The birds, however, ate the bread.

b. The interpretation of the dreams

(1) The chief cupbearer's dream—Joseph predicted that within three days the cupbearer would be restored by Pharaoh to his original office.

(2) The chief baker's dream—Joseph predicted within three days the baker would be hanged by Pharaoh and the birds would eat his flesh. Within three days both prophecies were fulfilled.

IV. Joseph, the famed statesman
 A. The dreams of Pharaoh—The king of
    Egypt, like the two prisoners, also
    experienced two dreams which both-
    ered him. Suddenly the cupbearer
    remembered Joseph's ability to ex-
    plain dreams. At Pharaoh's com-
    mand, Joseph was brought before
    him and interpreted the dreams
    (Gen. 41:1-32).
   1. The information in the dreams
    a. Pharaoh's first dream
     (1) He saw 14 cows coming up
        out of the Nile River—seven
        were fat, and seven were
        skinny.
     (2) The seven skinny cows ate
        up the seven fat ones.
    b. Pharaoh's second dream
     (1) He saw 14 heads of grain—
        There were seven healthy
        ones on a single stalk, and
        seven thin and scorched
        ones on another stalk.
     (2) The seven thin heads of
        grain swallowed up the
        seven healthy ones.
   2. The interpretation of the dreams
    a. The 14 cows and the 14 stalks
       represented 14 years.
    b. The first seven years would be
       a time of great crop growth.
    c. The second seven years would
       be a time of terrible famine.
 B. The decree of Pharaoh
   1. Joseph's proposal—Joseph pre-
      sented a plan of action in light of
      Pharaoh's dreams (Gen. 41:33-
      36).
    a. The king should appoint a food
       administrator.
    b. The king should collect and
       store 20 percent of all food pro-
       duced during the first seven
       abundant years to prepare for
       the following seven years of
       famine.
   2. Joseph's promotion—Pharaoh ap-
      pointed Joseph on the spot to this
      office (Gen. 41:37-44).

    a. He placed on Joseph's finger
       the king's own signet ring.
    b. He dressed him in robes of fine
       linen and put a gold chain
       around his neck.
 C. He gave him the chariot of his
    second-in-command.
   3. Joseph's program
    a. Joseph was now 30 years old.
       He married an Egyptian girl
       and fathered two sons through
       her (Gen. 41:45-46, 50-52).
    b. He stored up enormous quanti-
       ties of food during the seven
       abundant years (Gen. 41:47-49).
    c. As he had predicted, the seven
       fruitful years gave way to seven
       years of famine (Gen. 41:53-
       57).
     (1) The Egyptians immediately
        came to Joseph for food.
     (2) The nations eventually came
        to Joseph for food.
V. Joseph, the forgiving saint
 A. Joseph and his brothers
   1. The forgotten brother
    a. The first trip of the brothers to
       Egypt (Gen. 42:6-26)
     (1) Joseph's brothers traveled to
        Egypt to buy food. He im-
        mediately recognized them,
        but they did not know him.
     (2) They bowed at his feet, thus
        fulfilling the two dreams he
        once had experienced.
     (3) To test them, he accused
        them of being spies and
        placed them in custody for
        three days.
     (4) He finally agreed to sell
        them the needed food and
        allow them to return under
        two conditions:
      (a) One of the brothers, Sim-
         eon, had to stay behind
         as a hostage.
      (b) The remaining nine
         brothers had to promise
         to bring Benjamin (Jo-
         seph's youngest brother)

back with them during
their next trip for food.

(5) Joseph gave orders to fill
their bags with grain and to
return each man's silver
back to his sack.

(6) The nine then returned
home.

b. The second trip of the brothers
to Egypt (Gen. 43:15–44:34)

(1) Upon their arrival in Egypt,
this time with Benjamin,
Joseph invited his brothers
to a meal.

(2) He reassured the guilt-
stricken brothers (who still
did not recognize him) that
he meant them no harm.

(3) At the noon meal, the
brothers once again bowed
down to Joseph.

(4) After their meeting and
speaking to Benjamin, Jo-
seph was so moved he was
forced to leave the room for
a moment to weep.

(5) Joseph sent his brothers
back to Canaan, but not
before secretly hiding his
silver cup in the sack belonging to Benjamin.

(6) Shortly after they left, his
steward (at Joseph's com-
mand) caught up with the
brothers and accused them
of stealing his master's silver cup.

(7) They denied the charge,
agreeing that if one had
stolen it, he would become
the steward's Joseph's
slave.

(8) A systematic search revealed the cup in Ben-
jamin's sack.

(9) The shocked and grief-
stricken brothers followed
the steward back to Jo-
seph's house.

(10) Joseph confronted his

brothers for a final time before revealing himself to
them.

(11) The brothers continued to
maintain their innocence,
but requested that they all
might stay with Benjamin
as slaves.

(12) Joseph, however, refused,
saying that only Benjamin
would be allowed to stay.

(13) A distraught brother, Judah, begged Joseph to keep
him in place of Benjamin,
or else their aged father
Jacob would die with grief.

2. The forgiving brother (Gen. 45:1-15)

a. The revelation by Joseph

(1) Unable to control himself
any longer, Joseph ordered
all his attendants out.

(2) He then told his astonished
and terrified brothers who
he was.

b. The reassurance by Joseph

(1) He told them not to be distressed or angry with themselves, for it was God who
had allowed them to sell
him that he might save
many lives.

(2) He requested that they return home and bring Jacob
to Egypt, for the famine
would continue for another
five years.

(3) He promised to provide for
all of them in Egypt.

B. Joseph and his father

1. Pharaoh promised Joseph he
would personally see to it that his
father and brothers enjoyed the
best Egypt could offer (Gen.
45:16-20).

2. Joseph and his father were reunited at Goshen for the first time
in 15 years (Gen. 46:29).

3. Joseph formally presented his father and brothers to Pharaoh
(Gen. 47:1-10).

4. He then settled and provided for them in the district of Goshen (Gen. 47:11-12).
5. Joseph governed wisely over Egypt during the final five years of drought, as the famine increased.
   a. When the Egyptians ran out of money to buy food, he agreed to take their livestock as payment.
   b. When the livestock was gone, he accepted their land.
   c. When the land was given up, he provided opportunities for the people to serve for their food.
   d. Even though Joseph easily could have enslaved the people, he did not, but to the contrary decreed that each farmer could keep 80 percent of what he raised, requiring only 20 percent to be given back to Pharaoh.
C. Joseph and his sons
   1. Joseph brought his two sons, Manasseh and Ephraim, to Jacob for a final blessing (Gen. 48:1).
   2. Over the initial objection of Joseph, Jacob pronounced a greater blessing upon Ephraim, the second son, than he gave Manasseh, the firstborn (Gen. 48:8-20).
VI. Joseph, the fruitful shade tree
A. Joseph received his father's blessings (Gen. 49:22-26).
   1. Even though Joseph was the eleventh son, Jacob gave him the rights of the firstborn son (Gen. 48:21-22; 1 Chron. 5:1-2).
   2. Jacob predicted Joseph would continue to be as a fruitful vine near a spring, with extended branches, helping others.
   3. In spite of persecution, God himself would continue to both protect and prosper him.

B. Joseph removed his father's body.
   1. The return
      a. At the age of 147 Jacob died (Gen. 47:28; 49:33).
      b. Joseph and his brothers carried their father's body back to Canaan for burial (Gen. 50:1-14).
   2. The reassurance—He once again reassured his concerned brothers he meant them no harm. "Fear not . . . ye thought evil against me; but God meant it unto good, to bring to pass, as it is this day, to save many people alive. . . . I will nourish you, and your little ones. And he comforted them, and spake kindly unto them" (Gen. 50:20-21).
   3. The request—Just prior to his death at age 110, Joseph desired a favor and described the future (Gen. 50:22-26).
      a. The future described—He predicted that God would someday lead the people of Israel out of Egypt back to Canaan.
      b. The favor desired
         (1) He requested that, at that time, his bones be carried back to Canaan.
         (2) Moses later took these bones with him when he left Egypt (Exod. 13:19).
         (3) When Joshua entered the promised land he buried them at Shechem (Josh. 24:32).
VII. Joseph, the foreshadow of the Savior— Joseph was the most pronounced foreshadow and type of Christ in the entire Old Testament. Notice the amazing similarities between the two:
A. Both were beloved by their fathers (Gen. 37:3; Matt. 3:17).
B. Both regarded themselves as shepherds (Gen. 37:2; John 10:11-16).
C. Both were sent by their fathers to their brethren (Gen. 37:13-14; Luke 20:13; Heb. 2:12).
D. Both were unjustly hated by their

brethren (Gen. 37:4-5, 8; John 1:11; 7:5; 15:25).

E. Both were plotted against by their brethren (Gen. 37:20; John 11:53).

F. Both were severely tempted (Gen. 39:7; Matt. 4:1).

G. Both were taken to Egypt (Gen. 37:36; Matt. 2:14-15).

H. Both were stripped of their robes (Gen. 37:23; John 19:23-24).

I. Both were sold for the price of a slave (Gen. 37:28; Matt. 26:15).

J. Both were bound (Gen. 39:20; Matt. 27:2).

K. Both remained silent and offered no defense (Gen. 39:20; Isa. 53:7).

L. Both were falsely accused (Gen. 39:16-18; Matt. 26:59-60).

M. Both experienced God's presence through everything (Gen. 39:2, 21, 23; John 16:32).

N. Both were respected by their jailors (Gen 39:21; Luke 23:47).

O. Both were placed with two prisoners, one of which was later lost, the other saved (Gen. 40:2-3; Luke 23:32).

P. Both were 30 at the beginning of their ministry (Gen. 41:46; Luke 3:23).

Q. Both were highly exalted after their sufferings (Gen. 41:41; Phil. 2:9-11).

R. Both took non-Jewish brides (Gen. 41:45; Eph. 3:1-12).

S. Both were lost to their brethren for awhile (Gen. 42:7-8; Rom. 10:1-3, 11:7-8).

T. Both forgave and restored their repentant brothers (Gen. 45:1-15; Zech. 12:10-12).

U. Both visited and were honored by all earthly nations (Gen. 41:57; Isa. 2:2-3; 49:6).

THEOLOGICAL SUMMARY

I. The psalmist referred to five events in Joseph's life (Ps. 105:17-22).

A. Being sold as a slave

B. Having his feet bruised with shackles

C. Being placed in irons

D. Interpreting Pharaoh's dreams

E. Ruling over all of Egypt under Pharaoh

II. John mentioned the fact that Jesus met the Samaritan woman near the plot of ground Jacob once gave to Joseph (John 4:5).

III. Stephen referred to Joseph during his defense before the Sanhedrin, pointing out the following (Acts 7:9-14):

A. That he was sold by his envious brothers into Egyptian slavery

B. That God was nevertheless with him, both delivering him and giving him wisdom

C. That he became ruler over all Egypt

D. That he later forgave his brothers in Egypt

IV. The book of Hebrews refers to his faith (Heb. 11:22).

A. As demonstrated through his predictions concerning the Exodus

B. As demonstrated by his request to have his bones carried back to Canaan

STATISTICS

Father: Jacob (Gen. 35:22-26)

Mother: Rachel (Gen. 30:22-24)

Spouse: Asenath (Gen. 41:45)

Sons: Manasseh and Ephraim (Gen. 41:51-52)

Brothers: Full brother: Benjamin (Gen. 35:24). Half brothers: Reuben, Simeon, Levi, Judah, Issachar, Zebulun, Dan, Naphtali, Gad, and Asher (Gen. 35:23-26).

Sister: Half sister: Dinah (Gen. 30:21)

First mention: Genesis 30:24

Final mention: Hebrews 11:22

Meaning of his name: "Increaser"

Frequency of his name: Referred to 214 times

Biblical books mentioning him: 16 books (Genesis, Exodus, Numbers, Deuteronomy, Joshua, Judges, 2 Samuel, 1 Kings, 1 Chronicles, Psalms, Ezekiel, Amos, Obadiah, John, Acts, Hebrews)

Occupation: Chief associate to Pharaoh (Gen. 41:37-40)

Place of birth: Haran (Gen. 27:43; 30:25)

Place of death: Egypt (Gen. 50:26)

Age at death: 110 (Gen. 50:22)

Important fact about his life: He was Jacob's

favorite son who used his position in Egypt to rescue his family from famine (Gen. 37:3; 45:7-11).

Joshua (1)

CHRONOLOGICAL SUMMARY

I. Joshua, the trip to Canaan
  A. From Egypt to Sinai
   1. Functioning as a soldier (Exod. 17:8-16)—"Then came Amalek, and fought with Israel in Rephidim. And Moses said unto Joshua, Choose us out men, and go out, fight with Amalek: tomorrow I will stand on the top of the hill with the rod of God in mine hand. So Joshua did as Moses had said to him, and fought with Amalek: and Moses, Aaron, and Hur went up to the top of the hill. . . . And Joshua discomfited Amalek and his people with the edge of the sword" (Exod. 17:8-10, 13).
   2. Functioning as a servant
    a. During the entire Exodus march, Joshua served as a faithful servant to Moses (Exod. 24:13; Num. 11:28).
    b. In fact, his original name, Oshea, meaning "salvation," was changed by Moses to that of Joshua, meaning "Jehovah is salvation" (Num. 13:16).
    c. He was a man filled with God's Spirit (Num. 27:18; Deut. 34:9).
  B. At Sinai—He accompanied Moses partway up Mt. Sinai, where the great lawgiver received the Ten Commandments (Exod. 24:13; 32:17).
  C. From Sinai to Kadesh-barnea—He had his request denied by Moses that two prophets named Eldad and Medad be forbidden to prophesy in the camp (Num. 11:26-29).
  D. At Kadesh-barnea
   1. His trip to the promised land—Joshua, representing the tribe of

Ephraim, was one of the 12 men sent by Moses to search out the land of Canaan (Num. 13:1-3, 8, 16).
   2. His testimony concerning the promised land—Upon the return of the 12 men, only two, Joshua and Caleb, gave a positive report about Canaan (Num. 14:6-9).
    a. They said God had indeed provided a land flowing with milk and honey.
    b. They said God indeed would protect them in that land. "Only rebel not ye against the LORD, neither fear ye the people of the land; for they are bread for us: their defence is departed from them, and the LORD is with us: fear them not" (Num. 14:9).
  E. From Kadesh-barnea to the eastern bank of the Jordan River (Num. 27:15-23)
   1. The concern of the lawgiver—"Moses spake unto the LORD, saying, Let the LORD, the God of the spirits of all flesh, set a man over the congregation, Which may go out before them, and which may go in before them, and which may lead them out, and which may bring them in; that the congregation of the LORD be not as sheep which have no shepherd" (Num. 27:15-17).
   2. The command of the Lord—"Take thee Joshua the son of Nun, a man in whom is the spirit, and lay thine hand upon him; And set him before Eleazar the priest, and before all the congregation; and give him a charge in their sight. And thou shalt put some of thine honour upon him, that all the congregation of the children of Israel may be obedient" (Num. 27:18-20).
  F. On the eastern bank of the Jordan River

1. Joshua and Moses (Deut. 31:7-8, 23)—"Moses called unto Joshua, and said unto him in the sight of all Israel, Be strong and of a good courage: for thou must go with this people unto the land which the LORD hath sworn unto their fathers to give them; and thou shalt cause them to inherit it. And the LORD, he it is that doth go before thee; he will be with thee, he will not fail thee, neither forsake thee: fear not, neither be dismayed" (Deut. 31:7-8).

2. Joshua and God—
   a. God assured Joshua of victory before the death of Moses. "The LORD said unto Moses, Behold, thy days approach that thou must die: call Joshua, and present yourselves in the tabernacle of the congregation, that I may give him a charge. And Moses and Joshua went and presented themselves in the tabernacle of the congregation. And the LORD appeared in the tabernacle in a pillar of a cloud: and the pillar of the cloud stood over the door of the tabernacle" (Deut. 31:14-15).
   b. God reassured Joshua following the death of Moses (Josh. 1:1-9).
      (1) What Joshua should do— "Moses my servant is dead; now therefore arise, go over this Jordan, thou, and all this people, unto the land which I do give to them, even to the children of Israel. . . . Be strong and of a good courage: for unto this people shalt thou divide for an inheritance the land, which I sware unto their fathers to give them. . . . This book of the law shall not depart out of thy mouth; but thou shalt meditate therein day and night, that thou

mayest observe to do according to all that is written therein: for then thou shalt make thy way prosperous, and then thou shalt have good success" (Josh. 1:2, 6, 8).
      (2) What God would do— "Every place that the sole of your foot shall tread upon, that have I given unto you, as I said unto Moses. . . . There shall not any man be able to stand before thee all the days of thy life: as I was with Moses, so I will be with thee: I will not fail thee, nor forsake thee. . . . The LORD said unto Joshua, This day will I begin to magnify thee in the sight of all Israel, that they may know that, as I was with Moses, so I will be with thee" (Josh. 1:3, 5; 3:7).

3. Joshua and the people—"Joshua commanded the officers of the people, saying, Pass through the host, and command the people, saying, Prepare you victuals; for within three days ye shall pass over this Jordan, to go in to possess the land, which the LORD your God giveth you to possess it. . . . Joshua said unto the people, Sanctify yourselves: for to morrow the LORD will do wonders among you" (Josh. 1:10-11; 3:5).

4. Joshua and the priests—"Joshua spake unto the priests, saying, Take up the ark of the covenant, and pass over before the people. And they took up the ark of the covenant, and went before the people. . . . It shall come to pass, as soon as the soles of the feet of the priests that bear the ark of the LORD, the LORD of all the earth, shall rest in the waters of Jordan, that the waters of Jordan shall be cut off from the waters that come down from above; and they shall

stand upon an heap" (Josh 3:6, 13).

5. Joshua and the two and a half tribes (Josh. 1:12-18)—The tribes of Reuben, Gad, and the half tribe of Mannasseh met with Joshua concerning a previous agreement they had had with Moses.

   a. The request involved—That these two and a half tribes be allowed to settle on the eastern side of the Jordan River.

   b. The requirement involved— This request would only be granted if they agreed to cross over the Jordan and help the remaining nine and a half tribes defeat the Canaanites.

6. Joshua and the two spies (Josh. 2:1-23)

   a. Their trip—"Joshua the son of Nun sent out of Shittim two men to spy secretly, saying, Go view the land, even Jericho. And they went, and came into an harlot's house, named Rahab, and lodged there" (Josh. 2:1).

   b. Their testimony—"The two men returned, and descended from the mountain, and passed over, and came to Joshua the son of Nun, and told him all things that befell them: And they said unto Joshua, Truly the LORD hath delivered into our hands all the land; for even all the inhabitants of the country do faint because of us" (Josh. 2:23-24).

II. Joshua, the taking of Canaan

A. The crossing involved

   1. The path in the river (Josh. 3:15-17; 4:17-18)

     a. The priests advanced to the river, carrying the Ark of the Covenant.

     b. When their feet touched the waters, the Jordan was rolled back.

     c. After all Israel had crossed over on dry ground, the priests stepped out, causing the waters to return.

   2. The pyramid of stones—On the west bank (before the waters returned) Joshua chose 12 men, one from each tribe, for a special task (Josh. 4:1-9, 20-24).

     a. What they were to do—Each man was to carry a rock from the middle of the Jordan to be used in constructing a pile of boulders on the west bank.

     b. Why they were to do this— These rocks would serve as a memorial for the following generations, reminding them of God's faithfulness in parting the river.

     c. Joshua himself built a pile of stones in the middle of the Jordan itself for a similar purpose.

   3. The panic of the heathen—"When all the kings of the Amorites, which were on the side of Jordan westward, and all the kings of the Canaanites, which were by the sea, heard that the LORD had dried up the waters of Jordan from before the children of Israel, until we were passed over, that their heart melted, neither was there spirit in them any more, because of the children of Israel" (Josh. 5:1).

   4. The purification of the people (Josh. 5:2-9)—"The LORD said unto Joshua, Make thee sharp knives, and circumcise again the children of Israel the second time" (Josh. 5:2).

     a. The need involved—No male in that entire generation, with the exception of Joshua and Caleb, had been circumcised as proscribed by Abraham.

     b. The name involved—The location where the ceremony took

place was called Gilgal, meaning "to roll away," in this case, the reproach of Egypt.

5. The Passover of the lamb—"The children of Israel encamped in Gilgal, and kept the Passover on the fourteenth day of the month at even in the plains of Jericho" (Josh. 5:10).

6. The provision of the land—"They did eat of the old corn of the land on the morrow after the passover, unleavened cakes, and parched corn in the selfsame day. And the manna ceased on the morrow after they had eaten of the old corn of the land; neither had the children of Israel manna any more; but they did eat of the fruit of the land of Canaan that year" (Josh. 5:11-12).

7. The presence of the Lord
   a. The warfare by Christ—"It came to pass, when Joshua was by Jericho, that he lifted up his eyes and looked, and, behold, there stood a man over against him with his sword drawn in his hand: and Joshua went unto him, and said unto him, Art thou for us, or for our adversaries?" (Josh. 5:13).
   b. The worship of Christ—"He said, Nay; but as captain of the host of the LORD am I now come. And Joshua fell on his face to the earth, and did worship, and said unto him, What saith my lord unto his servant? And the captain of the LORD's host said unto Joshua, Loose thy shoe from off thy foot; for the place whereon thou standest is holy. And Joshua did so" (Josh. 5:14-15).

B. The campaigns involved
   1. The central campaign—Here the main action took place in two cities and upon two mountains.
      a. The two cities

(1) Jericho—Joshua received instructions from God concerning the battle against Jericho (Josh. 6:1-25).
   (a) What Israel should do
      i. The army was to march around the city once daily for six straight days.
      ii. On the seventh day, the army was to march seven times around Jericho.
      iii. During the seventh trip, the priests were to follow, blowing their trumpets.
      iv. The people were then to give a loud shout.
      v. No soldier was to take any of the spoils of war for himself.
      vi. Only Rahab the harlot, her immediate family, and anyone found in her house were to be spared.
   (b) What God would do
      i. He promised to cause the walls of Jericho to fall flat.
      ii. God kept his word and Jericho was taken.
   (c) What Joshua then did— He pronounced a prophetic oath over the devastated city. "Cursed be the man before the LORD, that riseth up and buildeth this city Jericho: he shall lay the foundation thereof in his firstborn, and in his youngest son shall he set up the gates of it" (Josh. 6:26). NOTE: See 1 Kings 16:34 for the amazing fulfillment of this prophecy.

(2) Ai—Joshua sent 3,000 soldiers to defeat the enemy at

Ai, only to have his troops themselves utterly defeated (Josh. 7:1-26).

(a) The concern over this defeat

  i. Joshua tore his clothes, sprinkled dust on his head, and fell on his face before the Ark of God.

  ii. He then complained to the Lord for allowing this defeat, suggesting it would have been better had Israel remained on the eastern bank of the Jordan.

(b) The causes leading to the defeat

  i. God's rebuke—He told Joshua to stop complaining and stand on his feet.

  ii. God's revelation—Joshua was told Israel had lost the battle because of sin. Someone had disobeyed by stealing and lying.

(c) The course of action in light of this defeat—God told Joshua that on the following morning he would single out the particular tribe involved, then the clan within the tribe, and finally the guilty family within the clan.

(d) The culprit punished for this defeat—The divine finger pointed to the tribe of Judah, the clan of the Zarhites, and the family of Zabdi, the immediate family of Achan.

  i. What he did—Achan confessed to stealing a beautiful Babylonian robe, 200 shekels of silver, and a wedge of gold.

  ii. How he died—Achan and his family (who doubtless had played a part in his crime) were stoned to death and their bodies were burned.

(e) The conquest following this defeat—Joshua was now reassured that Israel would be able to defeat Ai, and quickly devised a battle plan (Josh. 8:1-28).

  i. He chose 30,000 of his best fighting men, who were ordered to lie in ambush behind the city of Ai.

  ii. Joshua then attacked Ai with another army and pretended to retreat, that the enemy might be drawn out from the city to counterattack.

  iii. When this happened, the 30,000 men entered Ai and destroyed it.

b. The two mountains (Josh. 8:30-35)

  (1) Joshua built an altar on Mt. Ebal as Moses had previously commanded.

  (2) He made it of uncut stones on which no iron tool had been used.

  (3) As the people watched, he carved upon the stones the Ten Commandments.

  (4) He then sacrificed burnt and peace offerings upon the altar.

  (5) Finally, he ordered the priests to read out loud the entire Law of Moses to the people.

  (a) The blessings for obeying the Law were read from the top of Mt. Gerizim.

(b) The curses for disobeying the Law were read from the top of Mt. Ebal.

2. The southern campaign

a. The deception of Joshua—Joshua was deceived by a pagan group in Canaan known as the Gibeonites (Josh. 9:1-27).

(1) The contents of this deception

(a) How they deceived Joshua—A delegation met with Joshua, pretending they had come from a far country. They carried worn-out sacks and old wine skins. They wore patched sandals and ragged clothes. Their food supply was dry and moldy (Josh. 9:3-13).

(b) Why they deceived Joshua—They feared the military power of Israel and realized Joshua would not sign a peace treaty with the local Canaanites, which they were. But he might do so with a delegation from a far-off country.

(2) The cause of the deception—Why did Israel and Joshua fall for this trick? The reason is given in nine short words. We are told that Israel "asked not counsel at the mouth of the LORD" (Josh. 9:14).

(3) The consequences following this deception

(a) Only after signing the treaty did Joshua learn the truth. Israel had given its word. The enemy could not be harmed.

(b) Joshua did, however, make them wood cutters and water carriers (Josh. 9:27).

b. The destruction by Joshua—Joshua waged war against Adoni-zedek, king of Jerusalem, and his allies (Josh. 10:1-27).

(1) The reason for the battle

(a) Adoni-zedek attacked the Gibeonites for signing a peace treaty with Joshua.

(b) The city of Gibeon appealed to Joshua for help.

(2) The reassurance before the battle—"The LORD said unto Joshua, Fear them not: for I have delivered them into thine hand; there shall not a man of them stand before thee" (Josh. 10:8).

(3) The results of the battle

(a) God hurled down large hailstones from the sky upon the enemy.

(b) Joshua then worked one of the great miracles found in the Old Testament. "He said in the sight of Israel, Sun, stand thou still upon Gibeon; and thou, Moon, in the Valley of Aijalon. And the sun stood still, and the moon stayed, until the people had avenged themselves upon their enemies. . . . So the sun stood still in the midst of heaven, and hasted not to go down about a whole day. And there was no day like that before it or after it. . . for the LORD fought for Israel" (Josh. 10:12-14).

(4) The reprisal following the battle

(a) Following his great victory, Joshua captured and executed the five enemy kings who had declared war on him (Josh. 10:26).

(b) He then conquered the eight key southern Canaanite cities (Josh. 10:28-43).

3. The northern campaign—Joshua defeated the allied northern Canaanite forces near the waters of Merom, just north of the Galilean Sea (Josh. 11:1-22).

  a. He burned Hazor, the key city of the confederacy.

  b. He hamstrung the enemy's horses and burned their chariots. "Joshua took the whole land, according to all that the LORD said unto Moses; and Joshua gave it for an inheritance unto Israel according to their divisions by their tribes. And the land rested from war" (Josh. 11:23).

III. Joshua, the time in Canaan

A. The casting of lots—He divided the land among the 12 tribes.

  1. The parties involved—He was aided in this by Eleazar the high priest and the leaders of Israel (Josh. 19:51).

  2. The place involved—This was done at Shiloh, the location of the tabernacle (Josh. 18:1, 10).

  3. The procedure involved—The land allotment was determined by the casting of lots (Josh. 18:10; 19:51).

  4. The partitions involved

    a. Land east of the Jordan, as assigned to the two and a half tribes (Josh. 13:15-32)

    b. Land west of the Jordan, as assigned to the nine and a half tribes (Josh. 15–19)

B. The champion of God—Caleb (Josh. 14:6-14)

  1. His review of the past—"Forty years old was I when Moses the servant of the LORD sent me from Kadesh-barnea to espy out the land; and I brought him word again as it was in mine heart. Nevertheless my brethren that went up with me made the heart of the people melt: but I wholly followed the LORD my God. And Moses sware on that day, saying, Surely the land whereon thy feet have trodden shall be thine inheritance, and thy children's for ever, because thou hast wholly followed the LORD my God. And now, behold, the LORD hath kept me alive, as he said, these forty and five years, even since the LORD spake this word unto Moses, while the children of Israel wandered in the wilderness: and now, lo, I am this day fourscore and five years old. As yet I am as strong this day as I was in the day that Moses sent me: as my strength was then, even so is my strength now, for war, both to go out, and to come in" (Josh. 14:7-11).

  2. His request for the future—"Now therefore give me this mountain, whereof the LORD spake in that day" (Josh. 14:12).

C. The cities of refuge—Joshua designated the six cities of refuge (Josh. 20:1-9).

  1. Cities west of the Jordan River

    a. Kadesh, in the tribe of Naphtali

    b. Shechem, in the tribe of Ephraim

    c. Hebron, in the tribe of Judah

  2. Cities east of the Jordan River

    a. Bezer, in the tribe of Reuben

    b. Ramoth, in the tribe of Gad

    c. Golan, in the tribe of Manasseh

  3. Joshua then assigned 48 cities to the Levites (Josh. 21:1-8).

D. The challenge of faith

  1. Given by Joshua to the two and a half tribes (Josh. 22:1-34)

    a. The contents of the message

      (1) He commended them for their obedience to God on the west side of the river.

"Ye have kept all that Moses the servant of the Lord commanded you, and have obeyed my voice in all that I commanded you: Ye have not left your brethren these many days unto this day, but have kept the charge of the commandment of the Lord your God" (Josh. 22:2-3).

(2) He cautioned them to continue their obedience on the east side of the river. "Behold, I have divided unto you by lot these nations that remain, to be an inheritance for your tribes, from Jordan, with all the nations that I have cut off, even unto the great sea westward. And the Lord your God, he shall expel them from before you, and drive them from out of your sight; and ye shall possess their land, as the Lord your God hath promised unto you" (Josh. 23:4-5).

b. The confusion following the message

(1) What the two and a half tribes actually did—En route home, they built an altar on the western bank of the Jordan before crossing over to serve as a reminder of their common heritage with the remaining nine and a half tribes.

(2) What the nine and a half tribes assumed they did—They at first misinterpreted this, viewing it as an altar of rebellion. The matter was quickly clarified, however, averting a possible civil war.

2. Given by Joshua to the nine and a half tribes (Josh. 23:1-16)—He reviewed what God had done for them in former days. "Ye have seen all that the Lord your God hath done unto all these nations because of you; for the Lord your God is he that hath fought for you. . . . For the Lord hath driven out from before you great nations and strong: but as for you, no man hath been able to stand before you unto this day. . . . And, behold, this day I am going the way of all the earth: and ye know in all your hearts and in all your souls, that not one thing hath failed of all the good things which the Lord your God spake concerning you; all are come to pass unto you, and not one thing hath failed thereof" (Josh. 23:3, 9, 14).

3. Given by Joshua to the entire nation (Josh. 24:1-28)

a. God's covenant with Israel was reviewed—Joshua summarized the faithfulness of God in the past (Josh. 24:1-13).

(1) He brought Abraham from a pagan land to Canaan.

(2) He gave him many descendants through Isaac and Jacob.

(3) He called Moses and Aaron to lead Israel out of Egypt.

(4) He fought Israel's battles in the wilderness.

(5) He brought their generation into the promised land.

b. God's covenant with Israel was renewed.

(1) The consecration of the people—They promised to fear, obey, and serve the Lord.

(2) The contract of the prophet—Joshua drew up for them the terms of their agreement, recording it in the book of the Law of God. He then took a large stone and set it under an oak tree

near the tabernacle to serve as a reminder of this renewed covenant. Joshua died at the age of 110 and was buried in the hill country of Ephraim (Josh. 24:29-30).

THEOLOGICAL SUMMARY

I. Joshua is referred to on only two occasions in the New Testament, and both are found in the book of Hebrews. His frailty is mentioned—The author showed that Joshua was inferior to Jesus, for he was unable to provide that perfect rest that only Christ can offer (Heb. 4:8-9).

II. His faith is mentioned—"By faith the walls of Jericho fell down, after they were compassed about seven days" (Heb. 11:30).

STATISTICS

Father: Nun (Exod. 33:11)
First mention: Exodus 17:9
Final mention: Hebrews 4:8
Meaning of his name: "Jehovah saves"
Frequency of his name: Referred to 201 times
Biblical books mentioning him: Eight books (Exodus, Numbers, Deuteronomy, Joshua, Judges, 1 Kings, 1 Chronicles, Hebrews)
Occupation: Soldier and national leader (Exod. 17:9; Deut. 34:9)
Place of birth: Egypt
Place of death: Hill country of Ephraim (Josh. 24:29-30)
Age at death: 110 (Josh. 24:29)
Important fact about his life: He was Moses' successor who led Israel into the promised land (Josh. 1:1-3).

⟨⟨Joshua (2)

CHRONOLOGICAL SUMMARY

I. Joshua, the cleansed
   A. He is also called Jeshua (Ezra 2:2).
   B. Joshua was the first high priest of Ju-

dah after the return from the Babylonian Captivity (Hag. 1:1; 2:2).
   C. He led the returning remnant in the building of the altar and temple (Ezra 3:2, 8; 5:2).
   D. He was a contemporary of the political leader Zerubbabel (Ezra 2:2).
   E. The prophet Zechariah saw a vision of Joshua, who stood in heaven being accused by Satan but defended and cleansed by the angel of the Lord (Zech. 3:1-5).

II. Joshua, the challenged—The Lord then spoke to Joshua (Zech. 3:6-10)
   A. Urging him to live a godly life
   B. Promising him a special place of service if he obeyed
   C. Predicting that Christ (referred to as the Branch of God) would someday remove Israel's sin and restore his chosen people to their land

III. Joshua, the crowned—Joshua had a golden crown placed on his head by Zechariah to demonstrate the future work of Christ, who would accomplish two things (Zech. 6:9-15):
   A. He would build the millennial temple.
   B. He would combine the two great Old Testament offices of priest and king.

STATISTICS

Father: Jozadak (Ezra 3:2)
Son: Joiakim (Neh. 12:10)
Brothers: Maaseiah, Eliezer, Jarib, and Gedaliah (Ezra 10:18)
First mention: Ezra 2:2
Final mention: Zechariah 6:11
Meaning of his name: "God saves"
Frequency of his name: Referred to 23 times
Biblical books mentioning him: Four books (Ezra, Nehemiah, Haggai, Zechariah)
Occupation: High priest (Zech. 6:11)
Important fact about his life: He was Israel's first high priest after the return to rebuild Jerusalem (Zech. 6:9-15).

✍️*Josiah*

CHRONOLOGICAL SUMMARY

I. Doing the work of God

A. The prophecy involved

1. He was the sixteenth ruler of Judah.
2. He ruled for 31 years (2 Kings 22:1).
3. He was eight years old when he became king (2 Kings 22:1).
4. He really began seeking God when he was only 16 (2 Chron. 34:3).
5. He was the greatest king since David (2 Kings 23:25).
6. His birth, name, and ministry were predicted nearly three centuries in advance by a prophet of God in the city of Beth-el (1 Kings 13:1-2).

B. The purge involved—When he was 20, Josiah began his great work of reform (2 Kings 23:4-20; 2 Chron. 34:3-7).

1. He purged Judah and Jerusalem of the pagan high places.
2. He destroyed the Asherah poles, carved idols, and cast images.
3. He cut down the idols of Baal.
4. He then broke them to pieces and scattered them over the graves of those who had sacrificed to them, burning the bones of the priests on their altars.
5. He thus fulfilled the three-century-old prophecy concerning him (see 1 Kings 13:1-2).
6. He did away with the pagan priests appointed by previous evil kings of Judah.
7. He tore down the quarters of the male shrine prostitutes and executed them.
8. He desecrated Topheth, a place in the valley of Hinnom, so no one could use it to sacrifice his sons or daughters in the fire of Molech, the devil god.
9. He removed the sacred horses from the entrance of the temple which had been dedicated by previous evil Judean kings to the sun god.
10. He burned the sacred chariots which were also dedicated to the sun god.
11. He smashed to pieces the pagan high places Solomon himself had once built.
12. He carried out similar reforms outside of Judah in Beth-el and Samaria.

C. The Passover involved—Josiah organized and presided over a special Passover service when he was 26 (2 Chron. 35:1-19).

1. He began by ordering the Ark of the Covenant to be put back in the holy of holies. For some undisclosed reason it had apparently been removed. This marked the last known whereabouts of the Ark.
2. He then provided the following animals to be sacrificed for his people: 30,000 sheep and goats; 3000 cattle.
3. His officials also contributed animals for this purpose: 7600 lambs; 800 cattle.
4. This was said to be the greatest Passover since the days of the prophet Samuel.

II. Discovering the Word of God

A. When he was 26, Josiah gave orders to repair the temple of God (2 Chron. 34:8).

B. During a cleaning of the temple, a copy of the Law of Moses (perhaps the only one in existence) was found. Upon hearing it read, the king went into mourning, then assembled the priests, Levites, and common people into the temple area, where he personally read them the Law and urged all to follow it (2 Chron. 34:19, 29-32).

C. He then received a special message from God through the prophetess Huldah (2 Chron. 34:22-28).

1. God would soon bring down upon the people of Judah all the curses of the Law because of their sin.
2. Josiah, however, would be spared all this because of his godly behavior.

III. Disregarding the warning of God
   A. The foolish war—Josiah refused to honor the request of Necho, king of Egypt (who had acted at God's command) to peacefully march through the land of Judah to Carchemish to do battle with the Babylonians (2 Chron. 35:20-21).
   B. The fatal wound
   1. Josiah attacked Necho and was mortally wounded by the Egyptian archers at Megiddo (2 Chron. 35:22-24; 2 Kings 23:29).
   2. Jeremiah the prophet composed a funeral dirge in memory of Josiah (2 Chron. 35:25).

STATISTICS

Father: Amon (2 Kings 21:24)
Mother: Jedidah (2 Kings 22:1)
Spouses: Hamutal and Zebidah (2 Kings 23:30-36)
Sons: Johanan, Jehoiakim, Zedekiah, and Jehoahaz (also called Shallum) (1 Chron. 3:15)
First mention: 1 Kings 13:2
Final mention: Matthew 1:11
Meaning of his name: "God supports"
Frequency of his name: Referred to 51 times
Biblical books mentioning him: Seven books (1 Kings, 2 Kings, 1 Chronicles, 2 Chronicles, Jeremiah, Zephaniah, Matthew)
Occupation: King of Judah
Place of birth: Jerusalem
Place of death: On a battlefield at Megiddo (2 Chron. 35:22)
Circumstances of death: He was killed in battle by the Egyptians (2 Chron. 35:20-24).
Important fact about his life: He was both the finest and final saved king of Judah (2 Chron. 34:1, 26-28).

✍🏻 Jotham

CHRONOLOGICAL SUMMARY

I. The king constructing
   A. He was the 11th ruler of Judah.
   B. He ruled for 16 years (2 Chron. 27:1).
   C. He had charge of the palace and governed the people even before his leprous father Uzziah died (2 Kings 15:5; 2 Chron. 26:21).
   D. He was 25 when he began to rule as king (2 Kings 15:33).
   E. Jotham, for the most part, was a good king (2 Kings 15:34-35).
   F. Isaiah, Hosea, and Micah prophesied during his reign (Isa. 1:1; Hos. 1:1; Mic. 1:1).
   G. He rebuilt the upper gate of the temple and did extensive work on the wall at the hill of Ophel (2 Chron. 27:3).
   H. He built cities in the Judean hills, and forts and towers in the wooded areas (2 Chron. 27:4).

II. The king conquering—He attacked and conquered the Ammonites, imposing a huge yearly tribute from them (2 Chron. 27:5).

STATISTICS

Father: Uzziah (2 Chron. 27:1-2)
Mother: Jerushah (2 Chron. 27:1)
Spouse: Abi (2 Kings 18:2)
Son: Ahaz (2 Kings 15:38)
First mention: 2 Kings 15:5
Final mention: Matthew 1:9
Meaning of his name: "God is perfect"
Frequency of his name: Referred to 20 times
Biblical books mentioning him: Seven books (2 Kings, 1 Chronicles, 2 Chronicles, Isaiah, Hosea, Micah, Matthew)
Occupation: King of Judah (2 Kings 15:32)
Place of birth: Jerusalem
Place of death: Jerusalem (2 Kings 15:38)
Important fact about his life: He rebuilt the upper gate of the temple (2 Chron. 27:3).

✏️*Judah*

CHRONOLOGICAL SUMMARY

I. Judah and Joseph
   A. Pleading mercy for Joseph
      1. Judah was the fourth son of Jacob by Leah (Gen. 29:35; 35:23).
      2. He urged his nine brothers to sell Joseph into slavery instead of killing him (Gen. 37:26-27).
   B. Pleading mercy from Joseph
      1. Just prior to the second trip of Jacob's sons to buy food in Egypt, Judah promised his father he would assume personal responsibility for the life of Benjamin, whose appearance was demanded by the chief officer before he would sell the brothers more food. The officer was of course Joseph, at that time unrecognized by the brothers (Gen. 43:3-10).
      2. When Joseph's silver cup (secretly placed there by Joseph) was found in Benjamin's sack, a brokenhearted Judah begged that he be punished in place of Benjamin (Gen. 44:1-34).

II. Judah and Tamar
   A. His choice
      1. He selected a wife by the name of Tamar for Er his son (Gen. 38:6).
      2. When Er was killed by God for his wickedness, Tamar married Onan, his brother. Soon Onan was also slain for his evil ways (Gen. 38:7-10).
      3. Judah promised Tamar she could marry Shelah, his youngest son, when he was of age, but went back on his word (Gen. 38:11, 14).
   B. His carnality
      1. Tamar disguised herself as a roadside harlot and enticed Judah to lie with her, asking only for his seal, bracelets, and staff as a pledge for later payment (Gen. 38:13-19).
      2. Later, upon learning that Tamar was pregnant, the outraged Judah ordered her to be burned to death (Gen. 38:24).
   C. His confession
      1. Judah's rage, however, was quickly changed to shame when Tamar, by displaying the seal, bracelets, and staff, identified him as the father (Gen. 38:25-26).
      2. Tamar gave birth to twins named Pharez and Zarah (Gen. 38:27-30).

III. Judah and Jacob
   A. On his deathbed Jacob predicted the following about Judah and his descendants (Gen. 49:8-12):
      1. His 11 brothers would honor and praise him.
      2. He would defeat his enemies.
      3. The Messiah would eventually come from the tribe of Judah.
   B. Judah's tribe later proved to be the strongest of the 12 (1 Chron. 5:2).

STATISTICS

Father: Jacob (Gen. 29:35; 35:23)
Mother: Leah (Gen. 29:35; 35:23)
Spouses: Shuah (and Tamar?) (Gen. 38:3-5, 27-30)
Sons: Er, Onan, Shelah, Pharez, and Zarah (Gen. 38:3-5, 27-30)
Brothers: Full brothers: Reuben, Simeon, Levi, Issachar, and Zebulun (Gen. 35:23). Half brothers: Dan, Joseph, Benjamin, Naphtali, Gad, and Asher (Gen. 35:24-26).
Sister: Dinah (Gen. 30:21)
Significant descendant: Christ (Gen. 49:10; Heb. 7:14)
First mention: Genesis 29:35
Final mention: Luke 3:33
Meaning of his name: "Praise"
Frequency of his name: Referred to 43 times
Biblical books mentioning him: Eight books (Genesis, Exodus, Numbers, Ruth, 1 Chronicles, Nehemiah, Matthew, Luke)
Place of birth: Haran (Gen. 29:4, 35)
Important fact about his life: He was Jacob's

fourth son, from whose line Christ would eventually come (Gen. 49:10; Heb. 7:14).

✍Keturah

CHRONOLOGICAL SUMMARY
I. Keturah, the wife—She was the third and final wife of Abraham (Gen. 25:1).
II. Keturah, the mother
  A. She bore six sons to Abraham (Gen. 25:2; 1 Chron. 1:32).
  B. She became an ancestress of Zipporah, wife of Moses (Exod. 2:15-21).

STATISTICS
Spouse: Abraham (Gen. 25:1)
Sons: Zimran, Jokshan, Medan, Midian, Ishbak, and Shuah (Gen. 25:2)
Significant descendants: Zipporah (Exod. 2:15-21)
First mention: Genesis 25:1
Final mention: 1 Chronicles 1:33
Meaning of her name: "Fragrance"
Frequency of her name: Referred to four times
Biblical books mentioning her: Two books (Genesis, 1 Chronicles)
Important fact about her life—She was Abraham's third and final wife (Gen. 16:1-3; 25:1-8).

✍Kohath

CHRONOLOGICAL SUMMARY
I. His background
  A. He was the second son of Levi (Gen. 46:11).
  B. He went to Egypt with his father, Levi, and his two brothers (Gen. 46:8-11).
  C. His four sons were probably born in Egypt (Exod. 6:18).
  D. His grandson was the troublemaker Korah (Num. 16:1).
II. His brothers—The descendants of Kohath and his two brothers, Gershon and

Merari, were later entrusted solely with the care for the tabernacle.
  A. The descendants of Gershon—They were entrusted with the tents and curtains (Num. 3:25-26).
  B. The descendants of Kohath—They were responsible for the sanctuary furniture (brazen laver, altar, lampstand, etc.). These pieces they were to personally carry on their shoulders (Num. 3:28-31; 4:4-20; 7:9).
  C. The descendants of Merari—They took care of the tent frames, posts, ropes, pegs, and crossbars (Num. 3:36-37).

STATISTICS
Father: Levi (Gen. 46:11)
Sons: Amram, Izhar, Hebron, and Uzziel (Exod. 6:18)
Brothers: Gershon and Merari (Gen. 46:11)
Significant descendants: Moses and Aaron (Num. 26:58-59)
First mention: Genesis 46:11
Final mention: 1 Chronicles 23:12
Meaning of his name: "Assembly"
Frequency of his name: Referred to 31 times
Biblical books mentioning him: Five books (Genesis, Exodus, Numbers, Joshua, 1 Chronicles)
Age at death: 133 (Exod. 6:18)
Important fact about his life: He was Levi's second son (Gen. 46:11).

✍Korah

CHRONOLOGICAL SUMMARY
I. The wickedness of Korah—This great grandson of Levi and first cousin of Moses led a revolt against the great lawgiver during the Exodus journey (Exod. 6:16, 18, 20; Num. 16).
  A. The reason for this rebellion—Korah and 250 influential Israelite leaders challenged both Moses and Aaron concerning the political and religious authority God had entrusted to them (Num. 16:1-3).

B. The results of this rebellion
   1. He and his followers were judged when the very ground they stood upon supernaturally opened and swallowed them into the heart of the earth (Num. 16:31-34).
   2. Korah's revolt would eventually cause the deaths of 14,700 people who continued making trouble even after the earth had consumed him (Num. 16:41-50).
II. The writings of Korah's descendants (Num. 26:11)
   A. Korah's line did not die out during this time.
   B. Some of his descendants would later write Psalms 42, 44, 45, 46, 47, 48, 49, 87, and 88.

STATISTICS

Father: Izhar (Exod. 6:21)
Sons: Assir, Elkanah, and Abiasaph (Exod. 6:24)
Brothers: Nepheg and Zichri (Exod. 6:21)
Significant ancestors: His great grandfather was Levi (Exod. 6:16-21).
First mention: Exodus 6:21
Final mention: 1 Chronicles 9:19
Meaning of his name: "Boldness"
Frequency of his name: Referred to 19 times
Biblical books mentioning him: Three books (Exodus, Numbers, 1 Chronicles)
Place of death: Near Kadesh-barnea
Circumstances of death: He was crushed by the earth, which opened up and swallowed him (Num. 16:32-33).
Important fact about his life: He led the revolt against Moses in the wilderness (Num. 16:1-3).

✍Laban

CHRONOLOGICAL SUMMARY

I. Laban and the servant of Abraham—Eliezer
   A. He extended hospitality to Eliezer upon learning of his mission, namely, that the servant had been sent by Abraham to find a bride for Isaac (Gen. 24:29-33).
   B. He encouraged his sister Rebekah (whom Eliezer had selected) to accompany the servant back to Canaan and marry Isaac (Gen. 24:50-61).
II. Laban and the grandson of Abraham—Jacob
   A. The trickery
      1. Years later, when Jacob (Rebekah's son) visited the land of his mother, Laban agreed to give him his daughter Rachel in marriage if he would serve him seven years (Gen. 29:18-20).
      2. Jacob agreed, but seven years later, Laban secretly replaced Rachel with Leah (his older and less attractive daughter) on the wedding night (Gen. 29:23).
      3. He then required Jacob to work yet another seven years for Rachel (Gen. 29:26-28).
      4. He provided each of his daughters with a maidservant, Zilpah for Leah, and Bilhah for Rachel (Gen. 29:24, 29).
      5. He urged Jacob to continue working for him, realizing the hand of God was upon him (Gen. 30:25-28).
   B. The trouble
      1. Friction later developed between them (Gen. 31:1-2).
      2. In great anger he caught up with Jacob in the hill country of Gilead after his son-in-law had left without telling him (Gen. 31:22-23).
      3. He was warned, however, by God en route not to harm Jacob (Gen. 31:24).
      4. He complained to Jacob concerning two matters (Gen. 31:26-30).
         a. That Jacob had left without even allowing Laban to say good-bye to his daughters and grandchildren
         b. That Jacob had stolen his household gods
   C. The truce—He suggested an uneasy

truce be arranged between them, ratified by a pile of stones (Gen. 31:43-53).

STATISTICS

Father: Bethuel (Gen. 24:50; 28:5)
Daughters: Rachel and Leah (Gen. 29:16)
Sister: Rebekah (Gen. 24:29)
First mention: Genesis 24:29
Final mention: Genesis 46:25
Meaning of his name: "White, glorious"
Frequency of his name: Referred to 50 times
Biblical books mentioning him: One book
  (Genesis)
Occupation: Livestock raiser (Gen. 30:25-34)
Important fact about his life: He was Jacob's
  father-in-law (Gen. 29:21-30).

✒ *Lamech* (1)

CHRONOLOGICAL SUMMARY
  I. His polygamy—Lamech was the first
     recorded polygamist.
     A. His two wives—He married Adah
        and Zillah (Gen. 4:19).
     B. His three sons (Gen. 4:20-22)
        1. Jabal was the father of those who
           would live in tents and raise live-
           stock.
        2. Jubal was the father of all who
           played the harp and flute.
        3. Tubal-cain was the father of those
           who forged tools out of brass and
           iron.
 II. His pride—He bragged to his wives that
     he had killed a man who injured him,
     claiming he was seven times more im-
     portant than was Cain, his famous an-
     cestor (Gen. 4:23-24).

STATISTICS
Father: Methusael (Gen. 4:18)
Spouses: Adah and Zillah (Gen. 4:19)
Sons: Jabal, Jubal, and Tubal-cain (Gen.
  4:20-22)
Daughter: Naamah (Gen. 4:22)
Significant ancestors: Cain (Gen. 4:17-18)
First mention: Genesis 4:18

Final mention: Genesis 4:24
Meaning of his name: "Overthrower, wild"
Frequency of his name: Referred to four times
Biblical books mentioning him: One book
  (Genesis)
Important fact about his life: He was the first
  recorded polygamist (Gen. 4:19).

✒ *Lamech* (2)

CHRONOLOGICAL SUMMARY
  I. Lamech the parent—He was the father
     of Noah (Gen. 5:28-29).
 II. Lamech the prophet—He predicted his
     son would comfort the family in the la-
     bor and painful toil of their hands
     caused by the ground God had cursed
     (Gen. 5:29).

STATISTICS
Father: Methuselah (Gen. 5:25)
Son: Noah (Gen. 5:28-29)
First mention: Genesis 5:25
Final mention: Luke 3:36
Meaning of his name: "Overthrower"
Frequency of his name: Referred to four times
Biblical books mentioning him: Three books
  (Genesis, 1 Chronicles, Luke)
Age at death: 777 (Gen. 5:31)
Important fact about his life: He was Noah's
  father (Gen. 5:28-29).

✒ *Leah*

CHRONOLOGICAL SUMMARY
  I. Leah and her spouse
     A. The unexpected bride
        1. She was Laban's eldest daughter,
           plagued with weak eyes (Gen.
           29:16-17).
        2. She was secretly substituted by
           Laban for Rachel on the night of
           Jacob's wedding (Gen. 29:23).
     B. The unloved wife
        1. She was unloved by Jacob (Gen.
           29:31).

2. In spite of this, God loved and blessed her (Gen. 29:31-35).
II. Leah and her sons—She bore Jacob six of his 12 sons and his only recorded daughter.
III. Leah and her servant
   A. Laban gave Zilpah to Leah to help her (Gen. 29:24).
   B. Leah gave Zilpah to Jacob for purposes of childbearing (Gen. 30:9).
IV. Leah and her sister
   A. The malice—Leah accused Rachel of stealing Jacob's love from her (Gen. 30:15).
   B. The mandrakes
      1. Her son Reuben presented his mother with some mandrakes he had found (Gen. 30:14).
      2. Mandrakes were a leafy plant eaten by peasant women who supposed this would aid them in becoming pregnant.
      3. After eating them, Leah slept with Jacob and Issachar was born (Gen. 30:16-18).
V. Leah and her sepulcher—Leah was later buried by Jacob along with Abraham and Sarah in the cave of Machpelah (Gen. 49:31).

STATISTICS

Father: Laban (Gen. 29:16)
Spouse: Jacob (Gen. 29:23)
Sons: Reuben, Simeon, Levi, Judah, Issachar, and Zebulun (Gen. 35:23)
Daughter: Dinah (Gen. 30:21)
Sister: Rachel (Gen. 29:16)
First mention: Genesis 29:16
Final mention: Ruth 4:11
Meaning of her name: "Weary"
Frequency of her name: Referred to 34 times
Biblical books mentioning her: Two books (Genesis, Ruth)
Place of birth: Haran (Gen. 29:4, 16)
Place of death: Hebron (Gen. 49:30-31)
Important fact about her life: She bore Jacob six sons and one daughter (Gen. 30:21; 35:23).

Levi

CHRONOLOGICAL SUMMARY

I. The reprisal by Levi
   A. Levi was the third son of Jacob by Leah (Gen. 29:34).
   B. He was guilty along with his brother Simeon in the treacherous murder of some helpless pagans (Gen. 34:25-29).
      1. Why he did this—This was done because the son of the pagan chief had seduced Levi's sister Dinah and wanted to marry her (Gen. 34:1-12).
      2. How he did this—He and his brothers pretended to agree, but insisted the pagans circumcize themselves first (Gen. 34:15).
II. The reprimand of Levi—On two separate occasions Levi's father Jacob rebuked him for this.
   A. First occasion—Right after it happened (Gen. 34:30)
   B. Second occasion—When Jacob was on his deathbed in Egypt (Gen. 49:5-7)

STATISTICS

Father: Jacob (Gen. 35:22-23)
Mother: Leah (Gen. 35:22-23)
Sons: Gershon, Kohath, and Merari (Gen. 46:11)
Brothers: Full brothers: Reuben, Simeon, Judah, Issachar, and Zebulun (Gen. 35:23). Half brothers: Joseph, Benjamin, Dan, Naphtali, Gad, and Asher (Gen. 35:24-26).
Sister: Dinah (Gen. 30;21)
Significant descendants: Moses, Aaron, and Korah (Exod. 6:16-21; Num. 16:1)
First mention: Genesis 29:34
Final mention: Ezra 8:18
Meaning of his name: "Joined"
Frequency of his name: Referred to 18 times
Biblical books mentioning him: Four books (Genesis, Exodus, Numbers, 1 Chronicles)
Place of birth: (Gen. 28:43; 29:30)
Age at death: 137 (Exod. 6:16)
Important fact about his life: He was Jacob's

third son, from whom the priestly line would come (Num. 18:1-6).

✑*Lot*

CHRONOLOGICAL SUMMARY

I. Lot and Abraham
A. His uncle raised him.
1. Lot was the son of Haran, brother of Abraham (Gen. 11:27).
2. He was adopted and raised by Abraham after the death of Haran (Gen. 11:28; 12:4).
3. He was taken by Abraham to the land of Canaan (Gen. 12:5).
4. He later accompanied Abraham during his uncle's trip to Egypt (Gen. 13:1).
B. His uncle respected him.
1. Upon their return from Egypt to Canaan, a quarrel broke out between Abraham's herdsmen and Lot's herdsmen concerning grazing rights (Gen. 13:5-7).
2. Abraham offered Lot his choice of the land, not desiring to argue (Gen. 13:8-9).
3. Lot foolishly chose that section of land located near the wicked city of Sodom (Gen. 13:10-13).
C. His uncle rescued him.
1. Soon after this, Lot moved into Sodom, but was among those taken captive when a Mesopotamian king named Chedorlaomer defeated the city during a war (Gen. 14:1-12).
2. Upon learning of this, Abraham defeated Chedorlaomer in a surprise attack with his 318 trained men and rescued Lot (Gen. 14:13-16).
3. After this, Lot unwisely moved right back into Sodom and actually became a city leader (Gen. 19:1).
II. Lot and two angels
A. The purpose of the angels' visit— They warned Lot to leave Sodom, for

God was planning to destroy that wicked city (Gen. 19:12-13).
B. The perversion during their visit
1. The blasphemy of the Sodomites (Gen. 19:1-10)
a. The homosexual men of Sodom demanded that Lot turn his visitors over to them for sexual perversion.
b. At this time, Lot was so backslidden that he actually offered his two virgin daughters to the perverts in the place of the two angels.
2. The blinding of the Sodomites (Gen. 19:9-11)
a. Spurning Lot's offer, the perverted men attempted to break down the door to get at the angels.
b. The angels supernaturally blinded these vile men.
III. Lot and his family (Gen. 19:12-38)
A. His married daughters
1. Lot was instructed to gather all his family members and flee the doomed city.
2. They ridiculed his warning, however, leaving only his two unmarried daughters and wife.
3. These four were forced by the angels out of Sodom.
4. Unwilling to take refuge on a mountain as the angel first commanded, Lot asked and received permission to seek shelter in a small town near Sodom called Zoar.
B. His wife—His wife disobeyed God's command not to look upon the burning city. As she turned to view her former home, she perished (Gen. 19:17, 26).
C. His unmarried daughters
1. Lot and his two daughters left Zoar and climbed the mountain as originally commanded.
2. Fearing they would remain childless, the daughters caused Lot to be drunk, lay with him, and even-

tually bore two sons, Moab and Benammi (Gen. 19:31-38).

THEOLOGICAL SUMMARY

I. Centuries later, Joshua was forbidden to initiate a war against the Moabites, for they were the descendants of Lot through the son born by his oldest daughter (Gen. 19:37; Deut. 2:9).
II. Jesus referred to Lot on two occasions.
   A. He predicted similar conditions which prevailed in Lot's time to occur just before Sodom's destruction would be repeated, just prior to the final destruction of the earth (Luke 17:28-30).
   B. He used Lot's wife as an example, warning against disobedience (Luke 17:32).
III. Peter also mentioned Lot.
   A. He called him a righteous man, but concluded he "vexed his righteous soul" by staying in Sodom (2 Pet. 2:7-8).
   B. He referred to his deliverance from Sodom as an example of how God can deliver us from our trials today (2 Pet. 2:9).

STATISTICS

Father: Haran (Gen. 11:27)
Sons: Moab and Ben-ammi (Gen. 19:31-38)
Daughters: He fathered his sons through two unnamed daughters (Gen. 19:31-38).
First mention: Genesis 11:27
Final mention: 2 Peter 2:7
Meaning of his name: "Concealed, dark, colored"
Frequency of his name: Referred to 34 times
Biblical books mentioning him: Five books (Genesis, Deuteronomy, Psalms, Luke, 2 Peter)
Important fact about his life: He was Abraham's nephew (Gen. 12:4-5).

✐Maher-Shalal-Hash-Baz

CHRONOLOGICAL SUMMARY

I. This younger son of Isaiah the prophet had the longest name of anyone in the Bible (Isa. 8:3).
II. His name was to serve as a divine prediction concerning the imminent destruction of Damascus and Samaria by Assyria (Isa. 8:3-4).

STATISTICS

Father: Isaiah (Isa. 8:3)
Brother: Shear-jashub (Isa. 7:3)
First mention: Isaiah 8:1
Final mention: Isaiah 8:3
Meaning of his name: "Quick to the plunder"
Frequency of his name: Referred to two times
Biblical books mentioning him: One book (Isaiah)
Important fact about his life: He was Isaiah's son.

✐Mahlah

CHRONOLOGICAL SUMMARY

I. Her request
   A. Mahlah was the eldest daughter of Zelophehad, a man from the tribe of Manasseh who died during the Exodus march, leaving no son (Num. 26:33).
   B. Mahlah and her four sisters petitioned both Moses and Joshua, requesting that they receive the property inheritance which normally would have been passed on to the son.
      1. Her petition to Moses (Num. 27:1-4)
      2. Her petition to Joshua (Josh. 17:3-4)
II. Her reward—God honored her bold stand and the request was granted (Num. 27:5-11; Josh. 17:4-6).

STATISTICS

Father: Zelophehad (Num. 26:33)
Sisters: Noah, Hoglah, Milcah, and Tirzah (Num. 26:33)
First mention: Numbers 26:33
Final mention: Joshua 17:3
Meaning of her name: "Mildness"
Frequency of her name: Referred to four times
Biblical books mentioning her: Two books (Numbers, Joshua)
Important fact about her life: She and her sisters requested and received from Moses the land rights of their father (Num. 27:1-11).

Malachi

CHRONOLOGICAL SUMMARY

I. The love of God stated—In verse 2 of his book, Malachi listed the first of six rather flippant questions the carnal Israelites had asked of God. Each question challenged a previous clear statement from God.

A. In what way have you loved us? (1:2) Answer: I have demonstrated this love by choosing as my special servants Jacob and his descendants, rather than Esau and his descendants.

B. In what way have we despised your name? (1:6) Answer: You have despised my name by refusing to give me the honor a son would give to his father or a servant to his master.

C. In what way have we polluted you? (1:7) Answer: You offer me defiled food and blemished animals.

D. In what way have we wearied you? (2:17) Answer: You have wearied me not only by trying to make evil good, but by implying that I delight in evil because I do not dispense immediate justice.

E. How have we robbed you? (3:8) Answer: You have robbed me in unpaid tithes.

F. What have we spoken so much

against you? (3:13) Answer: You have spoken against me in saying it is vain to serve me unless I bless you with immediate prosperity.

II. The love of God scorned

A. By the prophets

1. They cheated the Lord through their shabby offerings (1:6–2:9).

a. They had offered lame and sick animals to God. These cheap sacrifices were refused by the Lord, who challenged them with an ironic comparison. "Offer it now unto thy governor; will he be pleased with thee, or accept thy person?" (1:8).

b. They had not offered that proper honor and respect to God that

(1) A child should give to his father (1:6)

(2) A servant should render to his master (1:6)

(3) A citizen should pay to his king (1:14)

2. They cheated the people through their shabby example (2:7-9).

B. By the people

1. Through their inequalities—"Have we not all one father? hath not one God created us? why do we deal treacherously every man against his brother, by profaning the covenant of our fathers?" (2:10).

2. Through their intermarriages (2:11)

3. Through their immorality (2:14)

4. Through their insincerity (2:17)

5. Through their indebtedness—"Will a man rob God? Yet ye have robbed me. But ye say, Wherein have we robbed thee? In tithes and offerings. Ye are cursed with a curse: for ye have robbed me, even this whole nation. Bring ye all the tithes into the storehouse, that there may be meat in mine house, and prove me now herewith, saith the LORD of hosts, if I

will not open you the windows of heaven, and pour you out a blessing, that there shall not be room enough to receive it" (3:8-10).

6. Through their incriminations (3:13-15)—"Ye have said, It is vain to serve God: and what profit is it that we have kept his ordinance, and that we have walked mournfully before the LORD of hosts?" (Mal. 3:14).

III. The love of God shown

A. By remembering his own saints— "Then they that feared the LORD spake often one to another: and the LORD hearkened, and heard it, and a book of remembrance was written before him for them that feared the LORD, and that thought upon his name. And they shall be mine, saith the LORD of hosts, in that day when I make up my jewels; and I will spare them, as a man spareth his own son that serveth him" (3:16-17).

B. By sending his own Son

1. His first coming would be introduced by John the Baptist (Mal. 3:1; Mark 1:2).

2. His second coming will be introduced by Elijah the prophet (Mal. 4:5-6; see also Rev. 11:3-14). Elijah thus will be awarded the privilege of preparing this cruel, corrupt, and cursed old world for its greatest, grandest, and most glorious moment—the visible appearance of the King of kings and Lord of lords.

a. He shall come to punish the Gentiles (4:1).

b. He shall come to purify Israel (3:2-4).

c. He shall come to publish his great name (1:11).

THEOLOGICAL SUMMARY

I. The prophet Malachi may be compared with the Apostle John.

A. Malachi wrote the last book in the Old Testament—Malachi.

B. John wrote the last book in the New Testament—Revelation.

C. Malachi referred to Christ as the "Sun of righteousness" (Mal. 4:2).

D. John referred to Christ as the "bright and morning star" (Rev. 22:16).

E. Malachi ended his book with a warning (Mal. 4:6).

F. John ended his book with a warning (Rev. 22:18-19).

II. Like Isaiah, Malachi predicted the New Testament ministry of John the Baptist (compare Isa. 40:3-5 with Mal.3:1).

III. Malachi presented his book in a question-and-answer format. There are no fewer than 25 examples of this.

IV. He also offered a sevenfold overview concerning God's will for Israel. The chosen nation was to:

A. Respond to God's love (1:2-5)

B. Honor God (1:6—2:9)

C. Be faithful to God (2:10-16)

D. Hope in God (2:17—3:6)

E. Obey God (3:7-12)

F. Fear God (3:13—4:3)

G. Remember God's Word (4:4-6)

V. In essence, Malachi recorded the following:

A. The most famous Old Testament passage on giving (3:8-10)

B. The most wonderful diary of all time (3:16)

C. The only biblical passage in which believers are called jewels (3:17)

D. The only Old Testament book predicting the return of Elijah to minister during the coming great tribulation (4:5)

STATISTICS

First mention: Malachi 1:1
Final mention: Malachi 1:1
Meaning of his name: "Messenger of God"
Frequency of his name: Referred to one time
Biblical books mentioning him: One book (Malachi)
Occupation: Prophet (Mal. 1:1)
Important fact about his life: He wrote the final Old Testament book (Mal. 1:1).

Manasseh (1)

CHRONOLOGICAL SUMMARY

I. Manasseh, the firstborn
   A. He was the eldest son of Joseph (Gen. 41:51).
   B. Both he and his brother Ephraim were born in Egypt (Gen. 41:51-52).

II. Manasseh, the second blessed
   A. He and Ephraim were brought by Joseph to Jacob, their dying grandfather, to receive his blessing (Gen. 48:1).
   B. The old patriarch adopted them as his own sons (Gen. 48:5).
   C. To Joseph's surprise and displeasure, Jacob bestowed the greater blessing upon Ephraim the younger brother, rather than upon Manasseh, the eldest (Gen. 48:12-20).

STATISTICS

Father: Joseph (Gen. 41:51)
Mother: Asenath (Gen. 41:50)
Sons: Machir and Asriel (Num. 26:29-31; 1 Chron. 7:14)
Brother: Ephraim (Gen. 41:52)
First mention: Genesis 41:51
Final mention: 1 Chronicles 7:17
Meaning of his name: "Causing forgetfulness"
Frequency of his name: Referred to 28 times
Biblical books mentioning him: Six books (Genesis, Numbers, Deuteronomy, Joshua, 1 Kings, 1 Chronicles)
Important fact about his life: He was Joseph's oldest son (Gen. 41:51).

Manasseh (2)

CHRONOLOGICAL SUMMARY

I. Manasseh, the unique king
   A. He was the fourteenth king of Judah.
   B. He ruled for 55 years, longer than any other king in the Bible (2 Kings 21:1).
   C. He was 12 years old when he began to reign (2 Kings 21:1).

II. Manasseh, the ungodly king (2 Kings 21:2-16; 2 Chron. 33:2-10).
   A. He rebuilt the pagan high places his father Hezekiah had destroyed.
   B. He erected altars to Baal and made an Asherah pole.
   C. He bowed down to the starry hosts and worshiped them.
   D. He built pagan altars in the temple of God.
   E. He sacrificed his own sons in the fire in the Valley of Hinnom, outside Jerusalem.
   F. He practiced sorcery, divination, and witchcraft.
   G. He consulted mediums and spiritists.
   H. He did more evil than the original Canaanites in the land had done.
   I. He filled Jerusalem from end to end with the blood of innocent people who were slaughtered at his command.
   J. Tradition says he ordered Isaiah to be sawn asunder (Heb. 11:37).
   K. He continued to do all these things in spite of repeated warnings from God.
   L. Jeremiah the prophet later referred to Manasseh as a symbol of evil (Jer. 15:4).

III. Manasseh, the upright king
   A. The record of his conversion
      1. The prison—God punished Manasseh for all this by allowing the Assyrians to take him prisoner, put a hook in his nose, bind him with bronze shackles, and take him to Babylon (2 Chron. 33:11).
      2. The prayer
         a. In his distress, Manasseh turned to God and begged for forgiveness (2 Chron. 33:12).
         b. God heard his prayer, saved him, and brought him back to Jerusalem (2 Chron. 33:13, 18-19).

B. The results of his conversion
1. Military accomplishments—Manasseh rebuilt the outer wall of the city of David, making it much higher, and stationed military commanders in all the fortified cities of Judah (2 Chron. 33:14).
2. Moral accomplishments
a. He got rid of the foreign gods and altars, removing them from the temple (2 Chron. 33:15).
b. He urged all Judah to serve God (2 Chron. 33:16).

STATISTICS

Father: Hezekiah (2 Kings 20:21)
Mother: Hephzibah (2 Kings 21:1)
Spouse: Meshullemeth (2 Kings 21:19)
Son: Amon (2 Kings 21:18)
First mention: 2 Kings 20:21
Final mention: Matthew 1:10
Meaning of his name: "Causing forgetfulness"
Frequency of his name: Referred to 26 times
Biblical books mentioning him: Five books (2 Kings, 1 Chronicles, 2 Chronicles, Jeremiah, Matthew)
Occupation: King of Judah (2 Kings 21:17)
Place of birth: Jerusalem
Place of death: Jerusalem
Important fact about his life: He was Judah's most wicked king, but he turned to God and was saved (2 Chron. 33:12-17).

✐Manoah

CHRONOLOGICAL SUMMARY

I. The prophecy to Manoah and his wife (concerning the birth of their son)
A. The revelation—The angel of the Lord appeared to Manoah's wife, revealing three things (Judg. 13:3-5):
1. That Manoah's barren wife would give birth to a son
2. That the son would become a Nazarite
3. That he would deliver Israel from the bondage of the Philistines

B. The response—Manoah asked God to send the messenger again, which God did (Judg. 13:6-23).
1. Manoah asked for wisdom in raising the child.
2. He inquired concerning the name of the angel.
3. He offered up a burnt offering and a meal offering to the Lord.
4. He saw the angel ascend in the flames coming from the altar.
C. The realization—As the angel had promised, Manoah's wife bore him a child (Judg. 13:24-25).
1. He was named Samson.
2. He was empowered by the Holy Spirit.
II. The preparation by Manoah and his wife (concerning a bride for their son)
A. Samson's command—The carnal Samson instructed his father to seek a Philistine bride for him (Judg. 14:1-2).
B. Manoah's concern (Judg. 14:3-4, 10)
1. He asked his son to consider marrying an Israelite girl rather than a pagan one.
2. Samson was persistent, so Manoah made the necessary arrangements.

STATISTICS

Son: Samson (Judg. 13:19-25)
First mention: Judges 13:2
Final mention: Judges 16:31
Meaning of his name: "Rest"
Frequency of his name: Referred to 16 times
Biblical books mentioning him: One book (Judges)
Important fact about his life: He was Samson's father (Judg. 13:19-25).

✐Medad

CHRONOLOGICAL SUMMARY
I. Medad and Eldad—These men, the only 2 named, were part of 70 Israelite elders upon which the Spirit of God rested, causing them to prophesy (Num. 11:25-26).
II. Medad and Moses (Num. 11:27-29)
  A. The request to Moses concerning Medad—"Joshua the son of Nun, the servant of Moses, one of his young men, answered and said, My lord Moses, forbid them" (Num. 11:28).
  B. The reaction of Moses concerning Medad—"Enviest thou for my sake? would God that all the LORD's people were prophets, and that the LORD would put his spirit upon them!" (Num. 11:29).

STATISTICS
First mention: Numbers 11:26
Final mention: Numbers 11:27
Meaning of his name: "Love"
Frequency of his name: Referred to two times
Biblical books mentioning him: One book (Numbers)
Occupation: Prophet (Elder?)
Important fact about his life: He was one of the 70 Israelite elders to whom was given the ministry of the Holy Spirit (Num. 11:25-26).

✐Melchizedek

CHRONOLOGICAL SUMMARY
I. The blessing he remitted to Abraham
  A. Who he was—He was the mysterious king and priest of the city known as Salem (Gen. 14:18).
  B. What he did
    1. He met Abraham when the patriarch was returning from a war (Gen. 14:17).
    2. He brought out bread and wine (Gen. 14:18).

    3. He blessed Abraham in the name of "the most high God, possessor of heaven and earth" (Gen. 14:19).
II. The bounty he received from Abraham—Abraham gave to Melchizedek a tithe of all he possessed (Gen. 14:20).

THEOLOGICAL SUMMARY
I. David predicted that the Messiah would be a priest forever after the order of Melchizedek (Ps. 110:4).
II. The book of Hebrews refers to this truth on six occasions (Heb. 5:6, 10; 6:20; 7:11, 15, 17).
  A. Hebrews states Melchizedek was without father or mother, without genealogy, and without beginning of days or end of life (Heb. 7:3).
  B. Hebrews demonstrates the high priesthood of Melchizedek is superior to the high priesthood of Aaron (Heb. 7:11-19).

STATISTICS
First mention: Genesis 14:18
Final mention: Hebrews 7:21
Meaning of his name: "My king is righteous"
Frequency of his name: Referred to 11 times
Biblical books mentioning him: Three books (Genesis, Psalms, Hebrews)
Occupation: King and priest (Gen. 14:18)
Important fact about his life: He was the mysterious king/priest of Jerusalem to whom Abraham paid tithes (Gen. 14:18-20).

✐Menahem

CHRONOLOGICAL SUMMARY
I. His butchery
  A. He was the sixteenth king of Northern Israel.
  B. He ruled 10 years (2 Kings 15:17).
  C. He murdered Shallum to obtain his throne (2 Kings 15:14).
  D. Menahem was an unusually brutal king, slaughtering even the women

of his enemies and ripping open those with child (2 Kings 15:16).

II. His bribe
  A. He bribed an Assyrian king with 1,000 talents of silver that he might be allowed to continue as the puppet king over Israel (2 Kings 15:19).
  B. He raised this money by imposing a huge tax upon the rich Israelites living in his kingdom (2 Kings 15:20).

STATISTICS

Father: Gadi (2 Kings 15:17)
Son: Pekahiah (2 Kings 15:22)
First mention: 2 Kings 15:14
Final mention: 2 Kings 15:22
Meaning of his name: "Comforter"
Frequency of his name: Referred to seven times
Biblical books mentioning him: One book (2 Kings)
Occupation: King of Northern Israel (2 Kings 15:17)
Important fact about his life: He was an especially brutal king who bribed the Assyrian monarch to allow him to continue ruling over Israel (2 Kings 15:14, 19-20).

☙Mephibosheth

CHRONOLOGICAL SUMMARY

I. Befriended by David
  A. He was the son of Jonathan and grandson of Saul (2 Sam. 4:4).
  B. He was accidentally dropped by his nurse at age five, making him a cripple in both feet (2 Sam. 4:4; 9:13).
  C. After Jonathan's death he was sought out by David, who invited him to live at the palace to honor the memory of the king's dear friend (2 Sam. 9:1-13).
II. Betrayed by Ziba
  A. He was betrayed by Ziba (the servant David gave him), who slandered his master before the king during the time of Absalom's rebellion (2 Sam. 16:1-4).
  B. Mephibosheth was eventually able to

defend himself before the king (2 Sam. 19:24-30).
  C. David later spared Mephibosheth from the wrath of the Gibeonites, who were allowed to kill seven of Saul's descendants (2 Sam. 21:1-7, 14).

STATISTICS

Father: Jonathan (2 Sam. 4:4)
Son: Micha (2 Sam. 9:12)
Significant ancestor: His grandfather was King Saul (2 Sam. 4:4)
First mention: 2 Samuel 4:4
Final mention: 2 Samuel 21:7
Meaning of his name: "Utterance of Baal"
Frequency of his name: Referred to 14 times
Biblical books mentioning him: One book (2 Samuel)
Important fact about his life: He was the crippled son of Jonathan befriended by David (2 Sam. 4:4; 9; 21:7).

☙Mesha

CHRONOLOGICAL SUMMARY

I. The rebellious act of Mesha
  A. Mesha was a Moabite king who rebelled in the days of Elisha, refusing to pay tribute to Israel (2 Kings 3:4-5).
  B. This led to a war between Israel and Moab (2 Kings 3:5-8).
  C. Through a miracle from God, wrought by Elisha, Israel's thirsty army received water in the desert and defeated Moab (2 Kings 3:15-26).
II. The ruthless act of Mesha—In a desperate but futile attempt to appease his gods and still win the battle, Mesha offered up his firstborn son as a sacrifice on a Moabite city wall (2 Kings 3:26-27).

STATISTICS

Son: He sacrificed his unnamed son (2 Kings 3:26-27)
First mention: 2 Kings 3:4
Final mention: 2 Kings 3:4
Meaning of his name: "Freedom"
Frequency of his name: Referred to one time

Biblical books mentioning him: One book
  (2 Kings)
Occupation: Moabite king (2 Kings 3:4)
Important fact about his life: He sacrificed his
  own son to a pagan Moabite god (2 Kings
  3:26-27).

✒︎*Meshach*

CHRONOLOGICAL SUMMARY
I. Meshach and the king's food (Dan. 1:1-
   20)
   A. His resolve
      1. He was one of the four Jewish
         youths among the thousands
         taken from Judah to Babylon by
         King Nebuchadnezzar in 606 B.C.
         (Dan. 1:1-7).
      2. He was also called Mishael. The
         names of his three friends were:
         a. Daniel (also called Belteshazzar)
         b. Azariah (also called Abednego)
         c. Hananiah (also called Shadrach)
      3. Meshach determined (along with
         his three friends) not to defile his
         body with the king's food and
         wine, but instead requested a spe-
         cial, simple diet (Dan. 1:8-14).
   B. His reward
      1. God honored Meshach's decision,
         and gave him great ability to mas-
         ter all the literature and science he
         was taught in Nebuchadnezzar's
         school (Dan. 1:17).
      2. Upon completion of his three-year
         training program, Meshach was
         found by the king to possess 10
         times the knowledge and wisdom
         of those who had remained on
         the royal diet (Dan. 1:18-20).
II. Meshach and the king's frustration
    (Dan. 2:1-19)
    A. Nebuchadnezzar dreamed a dream
       which he could not understand.
    B. Meshach joined Daniel and his
       friends in asking God to reveal the
       content and meaning of Nebuchad-
       nezzar's dream.

C. God answered their request that very
   night.
III. Meshach and the king's furnace (Dan.
     3:1-30)
     A. His resolve
        1. Meshach, along with Abednego
           and Shadrach, refused to bow
           down and worship a golden pa-
           gan statue Nebuchadnezzar had
           built.
        2. After rejecting the king's final of-
           fer (after having been given a sec-
           ond chance), the three Hebrew
           youths were bound and cast into
           a fiery furnace.
     B. His reward
        1. Christ himself joined his three
           faithful servants in the fire, pro-
           tecting them from all harm.
        2. The three men stepped from the
           fire without even the smell of
           smoke upon them.
        3. Meshach received a promotion
           from Nebuchadnezzar and pros-
           pered greatly.

STATISTICS
First mention: Daniel 1:7 (His Jewish name
  was Mishael)
Final mention: Daniel 3:30
Meaning of his name: "Who is like Aku, the
  moon god?"
Frequency of his name: Referred to 20 times
Biblical books mentioning him: One book
  (Daniel)
Occupation: Political leader (Dan. 3:30)
Place of birth: Judah (Dan. 1:1-6)
Place of death: Babylon
Important fact about his life: He was preserved
  in the fiery furnace by Christ himself
  (Dan. 3:23-25).

✒︎*Methuselah*

CHRONOLOGICAL SUMMARY
I. Methuselah, the son—He was Enoch's
   first son, born when his father was 65
   (Gen. 5:21).

II. Methuselah, the senior citizen—He became the oldest person ever recorded, reaching the age of 969 (Gen. 5:27).

STATISTICS

Father: Enoch (Gen. 5:21)
Son: Lamech (Gen. 5:25)
First mention: Genesis 5:21
Final mention: Genesis 5:27
Meaning of his name: "Man of the javelin"
Frequency of his name: Referred to five times
Biblical books mentioning him: One book (Genesis)
Age at death: 969 (Gen. 5:27)
Important fact about his life: His age was the oldest recorded.

✍*Micah* (1)

CHRONOLOGICAL SUMMARY
I. The dishonesty of Micah (Judg. 17:1-4)
   A. He was a man from the tribe of Ephraim who stole some money from his mother.
   B. After getting it back, she foolishly used it to make a carved pagan idol.
II. The idolatry of Micah (Judg. 17:5-13; 18:14-27)
   A. Micah added this idol to his household shrine and installed one of his sons as priest.
   B. He employed a traveling Levite from Bethlehem to serve as his full-time priest.
   C. Later, over the bitter but unsuccessful protests of Micah, the Levite priest left to become priest for the tribe of Dan.

STATISTICS
First mention: Judges 17:1
Final mention: Judges 18:31
Meaning of his name: "Who is like God?"
Frequency of his name: Referred to 21 times
Biblical books mentioning him: One book (Judges)

Important fact about his life: He made an idol and hired a priest to serve him (Judg. 17:7-11).

✍*Micah* (2)

CHRONOLOGICAL SUMMARY
I. The outward look: Micah's public sermons
   A. Proclaiming the retribution upon Israel in three sermons (1–3)
      1. First sermon (chapter 1)
         a. God himself would soon respond in judgment because of the sins found in Samaria and Jerusalem (1:1-5).
         b. Samaria would be utterly destroyed.
            (1) The sin of the city was terminal (1:9).
            (2) The very foundation of its buildings would be exposed (1:6).
            (3) The idols of Samaria would be thrown into the surrounding valley (1:7).
         c. The enemy would come up to the very gates of Jerusalem (1:9).
      2. Second sermon (chapter 2)
         a. God condemned those who lay awake at night, plotting wickedness, and rose at dawn to perform it (2:1).
         b. Their punishment would only end when the Messiah (the breaker and king of 2:13) led them out of exile through the gates of their cities of captivity, back to their own land. God would then regather Israel (2:12).
      3. Third sermon (chapter 3)
         a. Israel's leaders were especially rebuked by God. They were supposed to know right from wrong, but were themselves the vilest sinners of all (3:1-7).

(1) The shepherds had become the butchers of God's flock (3:3).

(2) The prophets had become treacherous liars (3:5).

(3) The Lord therefore would hide his face from both leaders and people (3:4, 6-7).

b. Micah alone of the prophets at that time was described as "full of power by the spirit of the LORD, and of judgment, and of might, to declare unto Jacob his transgression, and to Israel his sin" (3:8).

c. Because of those false money-loving prophets, Jerusalem would later be plowed as a field and become a heap of rubble. The very spot on Mt. Moriah where the temple stood would be overgrown with brush (3:12).

B. Prophesying the restoration of Israel (4–5)—In spite of her terrible sins, God would someday, after Israel's punishment had been consummated, restore her to Palestine.

1. The chronology leading to this restoration

a. Judah would first suffer the 70-year Babylonian Captivity. "Thou shalt go even to Babylon: there shalt thou be delivered; there the LORD shall redeem thee from the land of thine enemies" (4:10). This was a remarkable passage indeed, for at the time Micah wrote, Babylon was anything but a world power. Assyria was the strong nation then.

b. Judah's Messiah would be born in Bethlehem. "But thou, Bethlehem Ephratah, though thou be little among the thousands of Judah, yet out of thee shall he come forth unto me that is to be ruler in Israel; whose go-

ings forth have been from of old, from everlasting" (5:2).

c. God will set them aside awhile as a nation until their spiritual rebirth during the tribulation (5:3).

d. The nations will gather together against Israel at Armageddon (4:11).

e. These nations will be utterly destroyed (5:15).

2. The final results of this restoration (4:1-6)

a. All nations will learn the Word of God.

b. All nations will forget the ways of war.

C. Pleading for the repentance of Israel (6)

1. What God had done for Israel

a. He brought them up out of Egypt (6:4).

b. He showed them the right way (6:8). "He hath shewed thee, O man, what is good; and what doth the LORD require of thee, but to do justly, and to love mercy, and to walk humbly with thy God?" (6:8).

2. What Israel was doing against God—They were walking in the evil ways of Ahab (6:16).

3. What God would do to Israel

a. "Thou shalt eat, but not be satisfied" (6:14).

b. "Thou shalt sow, but thou shalt not reap" (6:15).

II. The inward look: Micah's personal sentiments

A. The collapse of Micah's hope—"Woe is me! for I am as when they have gathered the summer fruits, as the grapegleanings of the vintage: there is no cluster to eat: my soul desired the firstripe fruit" (7:1).

B. The collapse of the judicial system (7:2-4)

C. The collapse of friendship—"Trust ye not in a friend, put ye not confidence in a guide" (7:5).

D. The collapse of the family unit
1. "Keep the doors of thy mouth from her that lieth in thy bosom" (7:5).
2. "For the son dishonoureth the father, the daughter riseth up against her mother, the daughter-in-law against her mother-in-law; a man's enemies are the men of his own house" (7:6).

III. The upward look: Micah's prayerful supplications
A. His decision for God
1. He would wait for the future salvation of the Lord (7:7-8, 10-17).
2. He would endure the present indignation from the Lord (7:9).
B. His description of God (7:18-20)
1. Micah wrote of his forgiveness.
a. How God deals with his saints—He pardons them, loves them, has compassion upon them, and is merciful to them.
b. How God deals with their sins—He treads their sins beneath his feet and throws them into the depths of the ocean.
2. Micah wrote of his faithfulness. He will keep the promises he made to Abraham concerning the nation of Israel.

THEOLOGICAL SUMMARY
I. Micah prophesied during the reigns of Judean kings Jotham, Ahaz, and Hezekiah (1:1).
II. A quotation from the book of Micah probably saved the life of Jeremiah the prophet years later.
A. The decision to slay Jeremiah—His fearless preaching of coming judgment upon Judah, Jerusalem, and the temple because of sin had incensed the Jewish leaders. "Then spake the priests and the prophets unto the princes and to all the people, saying, This man is worthy to die; for he hath prophesied against this city, as ye have heard with your ears" (Jer. 26:11).
B. The defense that saved Jeremiah— "Then rose up certain of the elders of the land, and spake to all the assembly of the people, saying, Micah the Morasthite prophesied in the days of Hezekiah king of Judah, and spake to all the people of Judah, saying, Thus saith the LORD of hosts; Zion shall be plowed like a field, and Jerusalem shall become heaps, and the mountain of the house as the high places of a forest. Did Hezekiah king of Judah and all Judah put him at all to death? did he not fear the LORD, and besought the LORD, and the LORD repented him of the evil which he had pronounced against them? Thus might we procure great evil against our souls" (Jer. 26:17-19).
III. Another quotation from his book directed the wise men to Bethlehem after their arrival in Jerusalem (Mic. 5:2; Matt. 2:5-6).
A. The request—"When Jesus was born in Beth-lehem of Judaea in the days of Herod the king, behold, there came wise men from the east to Jerusalem, Saying, Where is he that is born King of the Jews? for we have seen his star in the east, and are come to worship him" (Matt. 2:1-2).
B. The reply—"In Beth-lehem of Judea: for thus it is written by the prophet, And thou Beth-lehem, in the land of Judah, art not least among the princes of Judah: for out of thee shall come a Governor, that shall rule my people Israel" (Matt. 2:5-6).

STATISTICS
First mention: Jeremiah 26:18
Final mention: Micah 1:1
Meaning of his name: "Who is like God?"
Frequency of his name: Referred to two times
Biblical books mentioning him: Two books (Jeremiah, Micah)
Occupation: Prophet (Jer. 26:18)

Place of birth: Moresheth (Mic. 1:1)
Important fact about his life: He predicted the birthplace of the Messiah would be Bethlehem (Mic. 5:2; Matt. 2:6).

✍*Micaiah*

CHRONOLOGICAL SUMMARY

I. The fearlessness of Micaiah
A. He was a godly and faithful prophet imprisoned by wicked Ahab, king of Northern Israel (1 Kings 22:8).
B. At the request of godly Jehoshaphat, visiting king of Judah, Micaiah appeared before both rulers who were planning to attack Syria (1 Kings 22:15).
C. En route to the throne room, he was warned to issue a favorable prediction concerning the outcome of the battle, but refused to compromise his message (1 Kings 22:14).
D. Micaiah at first apparently ridiculed Ahab (1 Kings 22:15).

II. The foretelling of Micaiah
A. He then correctly predicted both the defeat of Israel and the death of Ahab in battle (1 Kings 22:17).
B. Through a divine vision he announced Ahab was actually being drawn into the battle by demons at the command of God. (1 Kings 22:19-23).
C. At the conclusion of his prophecy, Micaiah was slapped in the face by Zedekiah, Ahab's chief false prophet (1 Kings 22:24).
D. Micaiah was sent back to prison by Ahab on a diet of bread and water (1 Kings 22:27).
E. His prophecy came true, for Ahab was killed in the battle (1 Kings 22:37-38).

STATISTICS

Father: Imlah (1 Kings 22:8)
First mention: 1 Kings 22:8
Final mention: 2 Chronicles 18:27

Meaning of his name: "Who is like God?"
Frequency of his name: Referred to 18 times
Biblical books mentioning him: Two books (1 Kings, 2 Chronicles)
Important fact about his life: He was a godly and imprisoned prophet who told Ahab the king that he would die in battle (1 Kings 22:19-27).

✍*Michal*

CHRONOLOGICAL SUMMARY

I. Defending her husband David
A. She was Saul's younger daughter (1 Sam. 14:49).
B. She loved David deeply (1 Sam. 18:20, 28).
C. She was given to David by Saul in an unsuccessful attempt to have him killed on the battlefield by the Philistines (1 Sam. 18:20-27).
D. She became David's first wife (1 Sam. 18:27).
E. She saved David's life by letting him down through a window of their house when Saul sent men to kill him (1 Sam. 19:11-12).
F. She was given to another man by Saul during those years David was being hunted by the wicked king (1 Sam. 25:44).

II. Denouncing her husband David
A. After Saul's death, David demanded Michal be brought back to him (2 Sam. 3:13-15).
B. She would, however, later ridicule David for the great zeal he demonstrated upon the return of the Ark of the Covenant to Jerusalem (2 Sam. 6:16, 20).
C. Because of this, David rebuked her sharply, and they no longer lived together as husband and wife (2 Sam. 6:21-23).

STATISTICS

Father: Saul (1 Sam. 14:49)
Mother: Ahinoam (1 Sam. 14:49-50)

Spouses: David and Phaltiel (1 Sam. 18:27; 2 Sam. 3:15)
Brothers: Ishui, Melchi-shua, Abinadab, and Jonathan (1 Sam. 14:49; 1 Chron. 8:33)
Sister: Merab (1 Sam. 14:49)
First mention: 1 Samuel 14:49
Final mention: 1 Chronicles 15:29
Meaning of her name: "Who is like God?"
Frequency of her name: Referred to 18 times
Biblical books mentioning her: Two books (1 Samuel, 1 Chronicles)
Important fact about her life: She was Saul's youngest daughter and David's first wife (1 Sam. 14:49; 18:27).

✐Midian

CHRONOLOGICAL SUMMARY
I. Midian was the fourth of six sons of Abraham through Keturah.
II. The descendants of Midian settled in that area near Mt. Sinai.
III. Some five centuries later, Moses, a descendant of Abraham through Sarah, would meet and marry Zipporah, a descendant of Abraham through Keturah (Exod. 2:21; 3:1).

STATISTICS
Father: Abraham (Gen. 25:1-2)
Mother: Keturah (Gen. 25:1-2)
Sons: Ephah, Epher, Hanoch, Abidah, and Eldaah (Gen. 25:4)
Brothers: Full brothers: Zimran, Jokshan, Medan, Ishbak, and Shuah (Gen. 25:2). Half brothers: Ishmael and Isaac (Gen. 16:16; 21:2-3).
Significant descendant: Zipporah (Exod. 2:15-21)
First mention: Genesis 25:2
Final mention: 1 Chronicles 1:33
Meaning of his name: "Contention"
Frequency of his name: Referred to four times
Biblical books mentioning him: Two books (Genesis, 1 Chronicles)
Important fact about his life: He was Abraham's son through Keturah who founded the Midianite people (Gen. 25:1-4).

✐Miriam

CHRONOLOGICAL SUMMARY
I. Her care for her brother Moses
   A. Miriam was the elder sister of Aaron and Moses (Exod. 15:20; 1 Chron. 6:3).
   B. She may have been married to a man named Hur (Exod. 17:10-12; 24:14).
   C. She cleverly arranged for her baby brother Moses to be raised by his own mother when he was rescued from the Nile River by Pharaoh's daughter (Exod. 2:1-9).
II. Her celebration with her brother Moses
   A. Miriam was Scripture's first recorded prophetess (Exod. 15:20).
   B. She led the Israelite women in a victory song and celebration following the destruction of Pharaoh's army at the Red Sea (Exod. 15:20-22).
III. Her criticism of her brother Moses
   A. The reason for her criticism—Both she and Aaron criticized Moses for two reasons:
      1. Because he had married a Cushite wife (Num. 12:1)
      2. Because he assumed he was God's only spokesman—which of course he was (Num. 12:2)
   B. The results of her criticism
      1. Both Miriam and Aaron were rebuked by God, and she was punished with leprosy (Num. 12:4-10).
      2. At Aaron's tearful plea, Moses prayed to God and she was healed of her leprosy. She thus became the only Israelite to be healed of leprosy in the Old Testament (Num. 12:11-15).
      3. Miriam died and was buried at Kadesh in the wilderness during the Exodus march (Num. 20:1).

STATISTICS
Father: Amram (Num. 26:59)
Mother: Jochebed (Num. 26:59)
Spouse: Thought to be Hur (Exod. 17:12)

Brothers: Moses and Aaron (Exod. 15:20;
  1 Chron. 6:3)
First mention: Exodus 15:20
Final mention: Micah 6:4
Meaning of her name: "Fat, thick, strong"
Frequency of her name: Referred to 14 times
Biblical books mentioning her: Five books (Exo-
  dus, Numbers, Deuteronomy, 1 Chroni-
  cles, Micah)
Occupation: Prophetess (Exod. 15:20)
Place of death: In the Kadesh wilderness
  (Num. 20:1)
Important fact about her life: She was Moses'
  only sister (1 Chron. 6:3).

✎Mordecai

CHRONOLOGICAL SUMMARY

I. The dedication of Mordecai
  A. He was a Benjamite who had been
    carried into exile from Jerusalem by
    Nebuchadnezzar (Esther 2:5-6).
  B. He had raised up his cousin (or niece)
    named Esther (also called Hadassah)
    at the death of her parents (2:7).
  C. When Esther became queen, he
    advised her not to reveal her nation-
    ality or background (2:10).

II. The detection of Mordecai
  A. He discovered and reported to Esther
    concerning a plot on the part of two
    royal gatekeepers to assassinate King
    Ahasuerus (2:21-22).
  B. The rebels were quickly arrested and
    executed (2:23).

III. The defiance of Mordecai—He refused
    to bow and pay honor to Haman, Per-
    sia's wicked and arrogant prime minis-
    ter appointed by the king (3:2; 5:9).

IV. The distress of Mordecai
  A. Haman noted this refusal and plotted
    to kill not only Mordecai, but all the
    Jews in the entire kingdom (3:3-15).
  B. Learning of this, Mordecai went into
    deep mourning (4:1).

V. The direction of Mordecai—Mordecai
  informed Esther concerning Haman's

death decree, and gave her the follow-
ing advice (4:13-14):
  A. Don't think you will escape the fate
    of your people simply because you
    live in the palace.
  B. If you refuse to keep quiet, God will
    deliver the Jews from some other
    source, but you will die.
  C. You have probably been brought
    to the kingdom for such a time as
    this.

VI. The delight of Mordecai
  A. At Esther's request, he gathered the
    Jewish leaders in Susa for a three-day
    fast as the queen prepared to ap-
    proach (uninvited) her husband the
    king (4:15-17).
  B. Shortly after this, in the marvelous
    providence of God, two totally unex-
    pected events occurred.
    1. The king suddenly learned that
      Mordecai had once saved his life
      and determined to reward him
      (6:1-3).
    2. Haman was forced by the king to
      arrange an honor parade for the
      detested Mordecai (6:10-11).

VII. The decree of Mordecai
  A. Haman was eventually hanged upon
    the very gallows he had previously
    built for Mordecai (5:14; 7:9-10).
  B. Following Haman's death, Mordecai
    was appointed by Esther over the
    wicked prime minister's estate
    (8:1-2).
  C. At Ahasuerus' command, Mordecai
    wrote out a new royal edict, permit-
    ting the Jews to defend themselves
    against their enemies (8:7-14).
  D. Mordecai then became very powerful
    in the kingdom (9:3-4).
  E. Following the victory over their ene-
    mies, the Jewish leaders received a
    letter from Mordecai commanding
    them to celebrate the newly estab-
    lished Feast of Purim (9:20-32).
  F. Mordecai was eventually placed in
    authority directly under the king him-
    self (10:1-3).

STATISTICS

Father: Jair (2:5)
First mention: Esther 2:5
Final mention: Esther 10:3
Meaning of his name: "Dedicated to Mars"
Frequency of his name: Referred to 56 times
Biblical books mentioning him: One book (Esther)
Occupation: Prime minister (10:3)
Important fact about his life: He was Esther's cousin and prime minister of Persia (2:7; 10:3).

ᴁ*Moses*

CHRONOLOGICAL SUMMARY—THE PRINCE OF EGYPT

I. The baby in the boat
 A. Moses and his parents (Exod. 2:1-3)
  1. Moses was born in Egypt of parents who were from the tribe of Levi.
  2. He was an especially beautiful baby.
  3. To escape the wrath of Pharaoh (who had ordered the death of all male Hebrew babies), Moses' parents placed him in a little boat on the Nile River when he was three months old.
 B. Moses and the princess (2:4-10)
  1. He was found and rescued by Pharaoh's daughter.
  2. Miriam, Moses' sister, who was watching, suggested to the princess that she hire "a nurse of the Hebrew women" to feed the child.
  3. The princess agreed, and Miriam quickly hired Moses' own mother to nurse him.
  4. The princess adopted him as her son and called him Moses, meaning "to draw out."
II. The man in the middle
 A. The helpless slave (2:11-13)
  1. Upon reaching manhood, Moses

killed an Egyptian who was cruelly mistreating a Hebrew slave.
  2. The following day Moses saw two Hebrew slaves fighting.
 B. The hostile slave (2:14-15)
  1. Upon Moses' attempting to separate them, one slave sarcastically asked Moses if he intended to kill him as he did the Egyptian.
  2. Realizing his act was now well known and that Pharaoh was seeking to kill him, Moses fled to the land of Midian in the Sinai desert.

CHRONOLOGICAL SUMMARY—THE SHEPHERD OF MIDIAN

I. The marriage of Moses
 A. He assisted a Midianite girl at a well. "The priest of Midian had seven daughters: and they came and drew water, and filled the troughs to water their father's flock. And the shepherds came and drove them away: but Moses stood up and helped them, and watered their flock" (2:16-17).
 B. He accepted a Midianite girl as his wife (2:18-22). "Moses was content to dwell with the man: and he gave Moses Zipporah his daughter" (2:21).
II. The mission of Moses (2:23—3:10)
 A. The matters preceding the burning bush (2:23-25)—"God looked upon the children of Israel, and God had respect unto them" (2:25).
 B. The miracle of the burning bush (3:1-3)
  1. As he was tending the flock for his father-in-law, Moses saw a bush on fire, but the fire was not consuming it.
  2. He approached the bush for a closer look.
 C. The message from the burning bush (3:4-10)
  1. "Take your shoes off."
   a. God himself spoke, telling Moses he was standing on holy ground.

b. God then informed Moses he had heard the cries of his enslaved people in Egypt and would deliver them. "I am come down to deliver them out of the hand of the Egyptians, and to bring them up out of that land unto a good land and a large . . . flowing with milk and honey; unto the place of the Canaanites" (3:8).

2. "Put your shoes back on." "Come now therefore, and I will send thee unto Pharaoh, that thou mayest bring forth my people the children of Israel out of Egypt" (3:10).

III. The misgivings of Moses

A. Moses' three protests—Simply stated, Moses did not want to obey God, offering three excuses why he could not go. God quickly answered each excuse.

1. Excuse: "Israel will not know who is sending me" (3:13). Answer: "Tell them the great I AM THAT I AM, the God of their ancestors Abraham, Isaac, and Jacob has sent you" (3:14-15).

2. Excuse: "Israel will not believe that you have sent me" (4:1). Answer: "I'll give you a twofold demonstration of my power" (4:2-9).

   a. The shepherd's rod of Moses became a snake and then turned back into a rod again.

   b. Moses' hand became leprous, and then returned to normal.

3. Excuse: "I'm not a good speaker. In fact, I have a speech impediment" (4:10). Answer: "I promise you the following" (4:11-17):

   a. "To help you speak"

   b. "To tell you what to say"

   c. "To allow your brother Aaron to accompany you"

B. God's five prophecies (3:12, 18-22)

1. That Israel's elders would accept his message

2. That Pharaoh at first would refuse his message

3. That Pharaoh would, however, be persuaded through divine miracles of judgment

4. That Israel would leave Egypt with much riches, given to them by their masters

5. That following the Exodus, Israel would worship God on the very mountain Moses stood upon at that moment

IV. The mistake of Moses (4:24-26)

A. The anger of God—For some reason Moses had carelessly neglected, or perhaps refused, to circumcise his firstborn son, Gershom. "It came to pass by the way in the inn, that the LORD met him, and sought to kill him" (4:24).

B. The arbitration by Zipporah—Realizing the terrible danger her husband was in, Zipporah quickly circumcised Gershom.

CHRONOLOGICAL SUMMARY—
THE LAWGIVER OF ISRAEL

I. Liberating the people of God

A. The problems—"Afterward Moses and Aaron went in, and told Pharaoh, Thus saith the LORD God of Israel, Let my people go, that they may hold a feast unto me in the wilderness" (5:1).

1. Coming from Pharaoh (5:2, 4-9)

   a. He insulted the God of Israel. "Pharaoh said, Who is the LORD, that I should obey his voice to let Israel go? I know not the LORD, neither will I let Israel go" (5:2).

   b. He increased the burden of Israel. "Pharaoh commanded the same day the taskmasters of the people, and their officers, saying, Ye shall no more give the people straw to make brick, as heretofore: let them go and gather straw for themselves" (5:6-7).

2. Coming from the people
   a. At first Israel's elders believed Moses concerning his mission and rejoiced (4:29-31).
   b. But then, blaming Moses for their increased work burden, they heaped abuses upon him (5:10-21).
   c. Moses complained to God about this, but was again reassured that eventually his mission would be accomplished (5:22–6:13).
B. The preview—Prior to the terrible 10 plagues, Moses performed some miracles for the king (7:8-12).
   1. The purpose involved—Both Pharaoh and Moses (for different reasons) needed to see the only true God in action.
   2. The power involved
      a. Under Moses' direction, Aaron turned his rod into a serpent.
      b. When Pharaoh's magicians did a similar thing, Aaron's serpent swallowed their serpents.
C. The plagues
   1. The plague upon the Nile River and all other water which God turned into blood (7:15-25)
   2. The plague of frogs (8:1-15)
   3. The plague of lice (8:16-19)
   4. The plague of flies (8:20-32)
   5. The plague upon the cattle (9:1-7)
   6. The plague of boils upon man and beast (9:8-12)
   7. The plague of hail and lightning which devastated the land (9:13-35).
   8. The plague of locusts (10:1-20)
   9. The plague of the three-day darkness (10:21-29)
   10. The plague of death upon the firstborn (11:1–12:36)
D. The promises—During four of the plagues, Pharaoh vowed to free Israel if Moses would stop the judgment, but lied about his real intentions each time.
   1. During the frog plague (8:8, 15)

2. During the fly plague (8:28, 32)
3. During the hail and lightning plague (9:27-28, 34).
4. During the locust plague (10:16-17, 27)
E. The plot—During the plagues Pharaoh suggested four compromises, attempting to weaken Moses' mission, but all were rejected.
   1. Worship your God here in Egypt (8:25-26).
   2. Go, but don't go too far (8:28-29).
   3. Go, but leave your children behind (10:10-11).
   4. Go, but leave your flocks and herds behind (10:24).
F. The provision—Just prior to the final plague God told Moses to both warn and instruct.
   1. The pharaoh of Egypt was warned—He was told by Moses that God himself planned to slay the eldest son in every Egyptian home, plus the firstborn of all the animals (11:1-10).
   2. The people of Israel were instructed (12:1-27).
      a. The details of a new annual feast given by God to Israel were described.
      b. The name of the feast was the Passover.
      c. On the eve of God's death visit, each family was to sacrifice a lamb and, by means of hyssop branches, spread its blood upon the doors of their homes.
      d. The Lord would then pass over all such blood-sprinkled homes.
G. The proclamation
   1. By Pharaoh—Immediately following the terrible Passover plague, Moses was summoned by Pharaoh (who had lost his firstborn) and told to assemble the Israelites and leave Egypt immediately (12:28-36).
   2. By the Lord
      a. The selection of the firstborn (13:1-2, 12-16)

(1) God told Moses to dedicate
to him all of Israel's firstborn
sons, plus every firstborn
male animal.

(2) Moses gathered the bones of
the patriarch Joseph as he
prepared to leave Egypt
(13:19).

H. The possessions (12:33-36)

1. The fact of the matter—"The children of Israel did according to the
word of Moses; and they borrowed of the Egyptians jewels of
silver, and jewels of gold, and
raiment: And the LORD gave the
people favour in the sight of the
Egyptians, so that they lent unto
them such things as they required. And they spoiled the
Egyptians" (12:35-36).

2. The foretelling of the matter—God
had previously told both Abraham
(Gen. 15:14) and Moses (3:21-22)
that this very thing would happen.

II. Leading the people of God

CHRONOLOGICAL SUMMARY— FROM EGYPT TO SINAI

A. Phase 1—Israel at the Red Sea

1. The decision of Pharaoh—To follow up (14:5-9)—"It was told the
king of Egypt that the people fled:
and the heart of Pharaoh and of
his servants was turned against
the people, and they said, Why
have we done this, that we have
let Israel go from serving us? And
he made ready his chariot, and
took his people with him: And he
took six hundred chosen chariots,
and all the chariots of Egypt, and
captains over every one of them"
(14:5-7).

2. The despair of the people—To
give up (14:10-12).

a. Upon seeing the advancing
Egyptian army, God's people
were filled with fear.

b. They immediately turned upon
Moses. "They said unto Moses,
Because there were no graves
in Egypt, hast thou taken us
away to die in the wilderness?
wherefore hast thou dealt thus
with us, to carry us forth out of
Egypt?" (14:11).

3. The declaration of the prophet—
To look up (14:13-14)—"Moses
said unto the people, Fear ye not,
stand still, and see the salvation
of the LORD, which he will shew
to you today: for the Egyptians
whom ye have seen to day, ye
shall see them again no more for
ever. The LORD shall fight for you,
and ye shall hold your peace"
(14:13-14).

B. Phase 2—Israel crossing the Red Sea

1. The cloudy pillar—Protecting—
"The angel of God, which went
before the camp of Israel, removed and went behind them;
and the pillar of the cloud went
from before their face, and stood
behind them: And it came between the camp of the Egyptians
and the camp of Israel; and it was
a cloud and darkness to them, but
it gave light by night to these: so
that the one came not near the
other all the night" (14:19-20).

2. The Red Sea—Parting—"Moses
stretched out his hand over the
sea; and the LORD caused the sea
to go back by a strong east wind
all that night, and made the sea
dry land, and the waters were
divided. And the children of Israel went into the midst of the sea
upon the dry ground: and the waters were a wall unto them on
their right hand, and on their left"
(14:21-22).

3. The Egyptian army—Perishing
(14:23-28)—"The Egyptians pursued, and went in after them to

the midst of the sea, even all Pharaoh's horses, his chariots, and his horsemen" (14:23).

   a. At God's command, Moses stretched out his hand over the sea.

   b. The waters then fell upon the Egyptians, drowning every one of them.

4. The Lord's people—Praising (14:30—15:21)—"Thus the LORD saved Israel that day out of the hand of the Egyptians; and Israel saw the Egyptians dead upon the sea shore. And Israel saw that great work which the LORD did upon the Egyptians: and the people feared the LORD, and believed the LORD, and his servant Moses" (14:30-31). "Then sang Moses and the children of Israel this song unto the LORD, and spake, saying, I will sing unto the LORD, for he hath triumphed gloriously: the horse and his rider hath he thrown into the sea" (15:1).

C. Phase 3—Israel at Marah (15:22-26)

1. The galling water—The problem— "When they came to Marah, they could not drink of the waters of Marah, for they were bitter: therefore the name of it was called Marah" (15:23).

2. The goodly tree—the purification—"The LORD shewed [Moses] a tree, which when he had cast into the waters, the waters were made sweet" (15:25).

3. The Great Physician—The promise—God made the following promise to both Moses and Israel: "If thou wilt diligently hearken to the voice of the LORD thy God, and wilt do that which is right in his sight, and wilt give ear to his commandments, and keep all his statutes, I will put none of these diseases upon thee, which I have brought upon the Egyptians: for I

am the LORD that healeth thee" (15:26).

D. Phase 4—Israel at Elim—"They came to Elim, where were twelve wells of water, and threescore and ten palm trees: and they encamped there by the waters" (15:27).

E. Phase 5—Israel in the wilderness of Sin (16:1-36)

1. A special diet—The manna (16:1-22, 31-36). After Israel had complained about the lack of food, God spoke to Moses, promising him and the people their physical needs would be supernaturally met. "Then said the LORD unto Moses, Behold, I will rain bread from heaven for you; and the people shall go out and gather a certain rate every day, that I may prove them, whether they will walk in my law, or no" (16:4). "When the dew that lay was gone up, behold, upon the face of the wilderness there lay a small round thing, as small as the hoar frost on the ground. And when the children of Israel saw it, they said one to another, It is manna: for they wist not what it was. And Moses said unto them, This is the bread which the LORD hath given you to eat" (16:14-15). "The children of Israel did eat manna forty years, until they came to a land inhabited; they did eat manna, until they came unto the borders of the land of Canaan" (16:35).

2. A special day—The Sabbath (16:23-30)—"He said unto them, This is that which the LORD hath said, Tomorrow is the rest of the holy sabbath unto the LORD: bake that which ye will bake today, and seethe that ye will seethe; and that which remaineth over lay up for you to be kept unto the morning" (16:23). "See, for that

the LORD hath given you the sabbath, therefore he giveth you on the sixth day the bread of two days; abide ye every man in his place, let no man go out of his place on the seventh day. So the people rested on the seventh day" (16:29-30).

F. Phase 6—Israel at Rephidim (17:1-16)
  1. The rock struck open by Moses—Moses struck a rock with his rod, producing from it a supernatural stream of water for the thirsty crowd (17:1-7).
  2. The enemy struck down by Moses (17:8-16)
    a. The foe involved—Israel was suddenly attacked by a fierce desert people called the Amalekites.
    b. The faith involved—"Moses said unto Joshua, Choose us out men, and go out, fight with Amalek: tomorrow I will stand on the top of the hill with the rod of God in mine hand. So Joshua did as Moses had said to him, and fought with Amalek: and Moses, Aaron, and Hur went up to the top of the hill. And it came to pass, when Moses held up his hand, that Israel prevailed: and when he let down his hand, Amalek prevailed. But Moses' hands were heavy; and they took a stone, and put it under him, and he sat thereon; and Aaron and Hur stayed up his hands, the one on the one side, and the other on the other side; and his hands were steady until the going down of the sun" (17:9-12).
    c. The firsts involved—This biblical passage records three "firsts."
      (1) The first recorded military victory of Israel
      (2) The first mention of Joshua

(3) Possibly the first part of the Bible to have been written—"The LORD said unto Moses, Write this for a memorial in a book, and rehearse it in the ears of Joshua: for I will utterly put out the remembrance of Amalek from under heaven" (17:14).

CHRONOLOGICAL SUMMARY— AT MOUNT SINAI (Exod. 18–40; Lev. 1–27; Num. 1:1–10:10)

A. Phase 1—The constitution of Israel (Moses and the Law of God)
  1. The circumstances leading to this constitution (Exod. 18:1–19:19)
    a. The welcome (18:1-12)
      (1) Arriving at the base of Mt. Sinai, Moses was greeted by Jethro, his father-in-law, and Zipporah, his wife.
      (2) They rejoiced when Moses told them how God had delivered Israel out of Egypt.
    b. The wisdom (18:13-25)—"It came to pass on the morrow, that Moses sat to judge the people: and the people stood by Moses from the morning unto the evening. And when Moses' father-in-law saw all that he did to the people, he said, What is this thing that thou doest to the people? why sittest thou thyself alone, and all the people stand by thee from morning unto even?" (18:13-14).
      (1) At Jethro's advice, Moses selected capable Israelite men to help him judge over the people.
      (2) Each judge was appointed over 1,000 individuals with others assisting him over groups of 100, 50, and 10.
    c. The wonder (19:1-19)
      (1) Moses explained to Israel God's desire to adopt them

as his special flock. "Moses went up unto God, and the LORD called unto him out of the mountain, saying, Thus shalt thou say to the house of Jacob, and tell the children of Israel; Ye have seen what I did unto the Egyptians, and how I bare you on eagles' wings, and brought you unto myself. Now therefore, if ye will obey my voice indeed, and keep my covenant, then ye shall be a peculiar treasure unto me above all people: for all the earth is mine: And ye shall be unto me a kingdom of priests, and an holy nation. These are the words which thou shalt speak unto the children of Israel" (19:3-6).

(2) He then helped the people to sanctify themselves in preparation for a promised visit within two days by God himself.

(3) On the morning of the third day, Moses and all Israel stood in awe, gazing upon the glory of God being manifested on Mt. Sinai.

(4) Thunder, lightning, and a huge cloud came down upon the mountain.

(5) A long, loud blast, as from a ram's horn, was heard.

(6) Then, almighty God himself descended in the form of a fire, causing smoke to billow into the sky as from a great furnace.

(7) The entire mountain shook with a violent earthquake.

2. The contents in the constitution— Moses was called to the top of Mt. Sinai and received the Law from God (19:20). The Law consisted of three codes.

a. The moral code (the Ten Commandments—20:1-17)— Vertical laws

(1) "Thou shalt have no other gods before me" (20:3).

(2) "Thou shalt not make unto thee any graven image" (20:4).

(3) "Thou shalt not take the name of the LORD thy God in vain" (20:7).

(4) "Remember the sabbath day, to keep it holy" (20:8).

b. The moral code—Horizontal laws

(1) "Honour thy father and thy mother" (20:12).

(2) "Thou shalt not kill" (20:13).

(3) "Thou shalt not commit adultery" (20:14).

(4) "Thou shalt not steal" (20:15).

(5) "Thou shalt not bear false witness" (20:16).

(6) "Thou shalt not covet" (20:17).

c. The social code (community laws—Exod. 21–23; Lev. 11–15, 18–20, 25–27)—These laws governed:

(1) Property rights

(2) Purity of individuals

(3) Peace and war

(4) Personal injuries, etc.

d. The spiritual code (laws dealing with Israel's worship life— Exod. 24–31, 34–40; Lev. 1–10, 16–17, 21–24)—The confirmation of this constitution

(1) Moses descended Mt. Sinai, read these laws to Israel, and confirmed God's covenant with his people by building an altar with 12 pillars and sacrificing upon it (Exod. 24:3-8).

(2) Moses, Aaron, Nadab, and Abihu (Aaron's two sons), and 70 Israelite elders were allowed to see the glory of God (24:9-11). "They saw the

God of Israel: and there was under his feet as it were a paved work of a sapphire stone, and as it were the body of heaven in his clearness" (24:10).

(3) Moses spent 40 days on Mt. Sinai. He received the Ten Commandments from God in permanent written form (24:12; 31:18).

B. Phase 2—The prostitution of Israel: Moses and the golden calf

1. The perversion by Israel—Moses was ordered to go down the mountain immediately to deal with a terrible crisis which had developed in the camp below (32:1-8).

   a. The why of the crisis— Concluding that Moses would not return, the people had taken matters into their own hands.

   b. The what of the crisis

      (1) Idolatry—A golden calf had been constructed that it might be worshipped. Through this action Israel had violated the vertical laws of the Ten Commandments

      (2) Immorality—Following the pagan worship service, the people involved themselves in sexual perversions. Through this action Israel had violated the horizontal laws of the Ten Commandments

   c. The who of this crisis—Aaron, Moses' own brother and Israel's first high priest, had been persuaded to organize this crisis of corruption.

2. The punishment of Israel (32:15-29)

   a. Moses entered the camp, carrying the Ten Commandments

which had been written upon two stone tablets.

   b. Upon seeing Israel's idolatry and immorality, Moses did the following five things:

      (1) He broke the two stone tablets.

      (2) He melted down the golden calf and ground it to powder.

      (3) He mixed it with water and made the people drink it.

      (4) He severely rebuked Aaron for his part in this terrible transgression.

      (5) He commanded the men of Levi, who apparently were not involved in the sin, to execute 3,000 of the key troublemakers who had instigated the entire matter.

3. The prayers for Israel—During this entire tragedy, Moses offered up two sessions of prayer for sinful Israel.

   a. His first prayer (32:9-14)

      (1) Moses begged that Israel be forgiven because of God's eternal character, that is, his reputation among the nations. "Wherefore should the Egyptians speak, and say, For mischief did he bring them out, to slay them in the mountains, and to consume them from the face of the earth? Turn from thy fierce wrath, and repent of this evil against thy people" (32:12).

      (2) Moses begged that Israel be forgiven because of God's earlier commitment, that is, his promises to Abraham, Isaac, and Jacob. "Remember Abraham, Isaac, and Israel, thy servants, to whom thou swarest by thine own self, and saidst unto them, I will multiply your seed as the

stars of heaven, and all this land that I have spoken of will I give unto your seed, and they shall inherit it for ever" (32:13).

b. His second prayer (32:30–34:28)

(1) The grief of the prophet— "Moses returned unto the LORD, and said, Oh, this people have sinned a great sin, and have made them gods of gold. Yet now, if thou wilt forgive their sin—; and if not, blot me, I pray thee, out of thy book which thou hast written" (32:31-32).

(2) The glory of the Lord

(a) As revealed to Moses (33:11, 17-23; 34:5-7)— "The LORD spake unto Moses face to face, as a man speaketh unto his friend" (33:11). "The LORD said unto Moses . . . thou hast found grace in my sight, and I know thee by name. And he said, I beseech thee, shew me thy glory. And he said, I will make all my goodness pass before thee, and I will proclaim the name of the LORD before thee; and will be gracious to whom I will be gracious, and will shew mercy on whom I will shew mercy. And he said, Thou canst not see my face: for there shall no man see me, and live. And the LORD said, Behold, there is a place by me, and thou shalt stand upon a rock: And it shall come to pass, while my glory passeth by, that I will put thee in a clift of the rock, and will cover thee with my hand while I pass by: And I will take

away mine hand, and thou shalt see my back parts: but my face shall not be seen" (33:17-23). "The LORD descended in the cloud, and stood with him there, and proclaimed the name of the LORD. And the LORD passed by before him, and proclaimed, The LORD, the LORD God, merciful and gracious, long suffering, and abundant in goodness and truth, Keeping mercy for thousands, forgiving iniquity and transgression and sin, and that will by no means clear the guilty; visiting the iniquity of the fathers upon the children, and upon the children's children, unto the third and to the fourth generation" (34:5-7).

(b) As reflected by Moses (34:29-35)—"It came to pass, when Moses came down from mount Sinai with the two tables of testimony in Moses' hand, when he came down from the mount, that Moses wist not that the skin of his face shone while he talked with him. And when Aaron and all the children of Israel saw Moses, behold, the skin of his face shone; and they were afraid to come nigh him" (34:29-30). "Afterward all the children of Israel came nigh: and he gave them in commandment all that the LORD had spoken with him in mount Sinai. And till Moses had done speaking with them, he put a vail on his face" (34:32-33).

C. Phase 3—The restitution of Israel: Moses and the tabernacle
1. The background
   a. On top of Mt. Sinai Moses received the plans for building the tabernacle. "Let them make me a sanctuary; that I may dwell among them. According to all that I shew thee, after the pattern of the tabernacle, and the pattern of all the instruments thereof, even so shall ye make it" (25:8-9).
   b. At the base of Mt. Sinai Moses issued the order to build the tabernacle. "Moses spake unto all the congregation of the children of Israel, saying, This is the thing which the LORD commanded, saying, Take ye from among you an offering unto the LORD: whosoever is of a willing heart, let him bring it, an offering of the LORD; gold, and silver, and brass" (35:4-5). "Every wise hearted among you shall come, and make all that the LORD hath commanded; The tabernacle, his tent, and his covering, his taches, and his boards, his bars, his pillars, and his sockets" (35:10-11).
2. The builders—At God's command, he appointed Bezaleel, grandson of Hur, from the tribe of Judah to serve as general contractor (35:30-31).
3. The building—The summary of facts about the tabernacle proper
   a. The framework—It consisted of three sections.
      (1) The outer court—150 feet long, 75 feet wide, seven and a half feet high
      (2) The inner court
      (3) The holy of holies
   b. The furniture

(1) In the outer court—A bronze altar and bronze laver
(2) In the inner court—The table of shewbread, the lampstand and the altar of incense
(3) In the holy of holies—The Ark of the Covenant
   a. The sacrifices—Those offered to maintain fellowship
      (1) The burnt offering (Lev. 1)
      (2) The meal offering (Lev. 2)
      (3) The peace offering (Lev. 3)
   b. The sacrifices—Those offered to restore fellowship
      (1) The sin offering (Lev. 4)
      (2) The trespass offering (Lev. 5)
   c. The suppers—Those feasts depicting God's work of creation
      (1) The weekly Sabbath (20:8-11; Lev. 23:1-3)
      (2) The seven-year Sabbath (23:10-11; Lev. 25:2-7)
      (3) The 50-year Sabbath (Lev. 25:8-16)
   d. The suppers—Those feasts depicting God's work of redemption:
      (1) The Passover feast—Speaking of the death of Christ (Lev. 23:4-8; 1 Cor. 5:7)
      (2) The feast of firstfruits—Speaking of Christ's resurrection (Lev. 23:9-14; 1 Cor. 15:23)
      (3) The feast of Pentecost—Speaking of the coming of the Holy Spirit (Lev. 23:15-25; Acts 2)
      (4) The feast of trumpets—Speaking of Christ's return (Lev. 23:23-25; 1 Thess. 4:13-18; Rev. 11:15)
      (5) The Day of Atonement feast—Speaking of the great tribulation (Lev. 23:26-32; Rev. 6–18)
      (6) The feast of trumpets—Speaking of the Millennium (Lev. 23:33-44; Rev. 20:1-6)

e. The stewards—Facts about the Levitical priesthood:
  (1) Their garments (Exod. 28-39)
  (2) Their separation (Lev. 8–9, 22; Num. 8)
  (3) Their duties (Num. 3–4)
f. The separated
  (1) The setting apart of the tribe of Levi (Exod. 28)—"Take thou unto thee Aaron thy brother, and his sons with him, from among the children of Israel, that he may minister unto me in the priest's office, even Aaron, Nadab and Abihu, Eleazar and Ithamar, Aaron's sons" (Exod. 28:1).
  (2) The setting apart of the Nazarites (Num. 6)
g. The survey (census)—Moses ordered the construction of two trumpets of beaten silver (Num. 10:1-9).
4. The brothers (Lev. 10)—this chapter Moses became involved with Aaron's four sons.
  a. The malicious act of Nadab and Abihu (Lev. 10:1-11)
    (1) These two brothers were killed by God for offering pagan fire before the LORD, perhaps while drunk.
    (2) Moses warned Aaron not to display sorrow over the deaths of these young blasphemers.
  b. The misunderstood act of Eleazar and Ithamar (Lev. 10:12-20)—Moses became angry with these brothers concerning the manner in which they offered up a sacrifice, until Aaron pointed out it had been done properly.
5. The blessing—Moses blessed the people for their faithfulness in finishing the tabernacle. "According to all that the LORD commanded Moses, so the children of

Israel made all the work. And Moses did look upon all the work, and, behold, they had done it as the LORD had commanded, even so had they done it: and Moses blessed them" (Exod. 39:42-43). "Moses and Aaron went into the tabernacle of the congregation, and came out, and blessed the people: and the glory of the LORD appeared unto all the people. And there came a fire out from before the LORD, and consumed upon the altar the burnt offering and the fat: which when all the people saw, they shouted, and fell on their faces" (Lev. 9:23-24).
6. The brightness—"Then a cloud covered the tent of the congregation, and the glory of the LORD filled the tabernacle. And Moses was not able to enter into the tent of the congregation, because the cloud abode thereon, and the glory of the LORD filled the tabernacle" (Exod. 40:34-35). "For the cloud of the LORD was upon the tabernacle by day, and fire was on it by night, in the sight of all the house of Israel, throughout all their journeys" (40:38).
7. The benediction—"The LORD spake unto Moses, saying, Speak unto Aaron and unto his sons, saying, On this wise ye shall bless the children of Israel, saying unto them, The LORD bless thee, and keep thee: The LORD make his face shine upon thee, and be gracious unto thee: The LORD lift up his countenance upon thee, and give thee peace" (Num. 6:22-26).

CHRONOLOGICAL SUMMARY— FROM MOUNT SINAI TO KADESH-BARNEA

A. Phase 1—The signal involved (God's glory cloud): "When the cloud was taken up from over the tabernacle, the children of Israel went onward in all their journeys: But if the cloud were not taken up, then they journeyed not till the day that it was taken up" (Exod. 40:36-37). "The cloud of the LORD was upon them by day, when they went out of the camp. And it came to pass, when the ark set forward, that Moses said, Rise up, LORD, and let thine enemies be scattered; and let them that hate thee flee before thee. And when it rested, he said, Return, O LORD, unto the many thousands of Israel" (Num. 10:34-36).

B. Phase 2—The steps involved
  1. Defiance (Num. 11:1-3)—"When the people complained, it displeased the LORD: and the LORD heard it; and his anger was kindled; and the fire of the LORD burnt among them, and consumed them that were in the uttermost parts of the camp. And the people cried unto Moses; and when Moses prayed unto the LORD, the fire was quenched" (Num. 11:1-2).
  2. Despair (Num. 11:10-30)
     a. Moses complained to God, stating that his burden in leading such a rebellious group was too heavy for him to bear.
     b. God appointed 70 Israelite leaders to aid Moses.
     c. Two of the 70, Eldad and Medad, were praised by Moses for their faithful service.
  3. Destruction (Num. 11:4-6, 31-34)
     a. The provocation by Israel— "The mixed multitude that was among them fell a lusting: and the children of Israel also wept again, and said, Who shall give us flesh to eat? We remember the fish, which we did eat in Egypt freely; the cucumbers, and the melons, and the leeks, and the onions, and the garlick: But now our soul is dried away: there is nothing at all, beside this manna, before our eyes" (Num. 11:4-6).
     b. The punishment by God— "There went forth a wind from the LORD, and brought quails from the sea, and let them fall by the camp, as it were a day's journey on this side, and as it were a day's journey on the other side, round about the camp, and as it were two cubits high upon the face of the earth" (Num. 11:31). "While the flesh was yet between their teeth, ere it was chewed, the wrath of the LORD was kindled against the people, and the LORD smote the people with a very great plague" (Num. 11:33).
  4. Disrespect (Num. 12:1-16)
     a. Moses was criticized by both Miriam and Aaron on two counts.
        (1) A domestic one— "Miriam and Aaron spake against Moses because of the Ethiopian woman whom he had married: for he had married an Ethiopian woman" (Num. 12:1).
        (2) A political and religious one—"They said, Hath the LORD indeed spoken only by Moses? hath he not spoken also by us? And the LORD heard it" (Num. 12:2).
     b. Miriam was struck with leprosy for her criticism.
     c. At Aaron's request, Moses prayed for his sister, who was then healed by the Lord but had to remain outside of the camp for seven days.

CHRONOLOGICAL SUMMARY— AT KADESH-BARNEA

A. Phase 1—The penetration by the spies: Moses sent 12 Israelite men (one from each of the 12 tribes) on a twofold mission (Num. 13:1-20).

1. They were to check out the foes in Canaan.
2. They were to carry back the fruit of Canaan.

B. Phase 2—The lamentation by the people

1. The report of the 12
    a. The 10-man majority report— "They brought up an evil report of the land which they had searched unto the children of Israel, saying, The land, through which we have gone to search it, is a land that eateth up the inhabitants thereof; and all the people that we saw in it are men of a great stature. And there we saw the giants, the sons of Anak, which come of the giants: and we were in our own sight as grasshoppers, and so we were in their sight" (Num. 13:32-33).
    b. The two-man minority report— "Caleb stilled the people before Moses, and said, Let us go up at once, and possess it; for we are well able to overcome it" (Num. 13:30). "If the LORD delight in us, then he will bring us into this land, and give it us; a land which floweth with milk and honey. Only rebel not ye against the LORD, neither fear ye the people of the land; for they are bread for us: their defence is departed from them, and the LORD is with us: fear them not" (Num. 14:8-9).
2. The reaction of the crowd
    a. To reject the land of Canaan— "All the children of Israel murmured against Moses and against Aaron: and the whole congregation said unto them, Would God that we had died in the land of Egypt! or would

God we had died in this wilderness!" (Num. 14:2).
    b. To return to the land of Egypt—"They said one to another, Let us make a captain, and let us return into Egypt" (Num. 14:4).

C. Phase 3—The supplication by the prophet—Realizing the awesome anger of God, Moses once again interceded for Israel, praying that they be spared for two reasons:

1. That God's power might be confirmed among the heathen nations—"Now if thou shalt kill all this people as one man, then the nations which have heard the fame of thee will speak, saying, Because the LORD was not able to bring this people into the land which he sware unto them, therefore he hath slain them in the wilderness" (Num. 14:15-16).
2. That God's pity might be confirmed among his chosen nation— "Pardon, I beseech thee, the iniquity of this people according unto the greatness of thy mercy, and as thou hast forgiven this people, from Egypt even until now" (Num. 14:19).

D. Phase 4—The condemnation by the Lord (Num. 14:20-39)

1. All those under 20 years of age would dwell in the wilderness until . . .
2. All those over 20 years of age would die in the wilderness. The only exceptions would be Joshua and Caleb.

CHRONOLOGICAL SUMMARY— FROM KADESH-BARNEA TO THE JORDAN RIVER

A. Phase 1—The troublemakers

1. A Sabbath breaker—Moses ordered the death of a man who had defied the Law of God by working on the Sabbath (Num. 15:32-36).

2. Korah—This great-grandson of
Levi and first cousin of Moses led
a revolt against the great lawgiver
(Num. 16:1-35).
   a. The reason for this revolt—He
   and 250 influential Israelite
   leaders challenged both Moses
   and Aaron concerning their political and religious leadership,
   entrusted to them by God.
   b. The results of the rebellion
   (1) He and his followers were
       judged when the very
       ground they stood upon su-
       pernaturally opened and
       swallowed them into the
       heart of the earth.
   (2) Korah's revolt would even-
       tually cause the deaths of
       14,700 people who contin-
       ued their rebellion even after
       the earth had consumed
       their leaders (Num. 16:36-
       50).
3. Some Edomites (Num. 20:14-22)
   a. Israel was refused passage
   through the land of Edom by
   its king in spite of a personal
   twofold appeal by Moses.
   (1) He reminded the king of the
       common bloodline. Both
       Edom and Israel were
       descendants of Isaac through
       Esau and Jacob.
   (2) He reassured the king they
       would stay on the main
       route and not as much as
       drink a cup of water from
       his wells.
   b. The king's refusal forced the
   people to turn back and travel a
   longer and more difficult route.
4. Balaam and the Moabites—Moses
   ordered the execution of those
   Israelite leaders who had been
   seduced to worship Baal by Balaam the false prophet and some
   Moabite women (Num. 25:1-5).
B. Phase 2—The tragedy—Moses committed his great sin at a place named

Meribah, meaning "rebel waters"
(Num. 20:2-13).
   1. The disbelief of Israel—"There
   was no water for the congregation: and they gathered themselves together against Moses and
   against Aaron. And the people
   chode with Moses, and spake saying, Would God that we had died
   when our brethren died before
   the LORD!" (Num. 20:2-3).
   2. The directive of God—"The LORD
   spake unto Moses, saying, Take
   the rod, and gather thou the assembly together, thou, and Aaron
   thy brother, and speak ye unto
   the rock before their eyes; and it
   shall give forth his water, and
   thou shalt bring forth to them water out of the rock: so thou shalt
   give the congregation and their
   beasts drink" (Num. 20:7-8).
   3. The disobedience of Moses—
   "Moses and Aaron gathered the
   congregation together before the
   rock, and he said unto them,
   Hear now, ye rebels; must we
   fetch you water out of this rock?
   And Moses lifted up his hand,
   and with his rod he smote the
   rock twice: and the water came
   out abundantly, and the congregation drank, and their beasts
   also. And the LORD spake unto
   Moses and Aaron, Because ye believed me not, to sanctify me in
   the eyes of the children of Israel,
   therefore ye shall not bring this
   congregation into the land which I
   have given them" (Num. 20:10-
   12).
C. Phase 3—The transitions
   1. Two deaths
   a. The death of Miriam, Moses'
   sister—Moses buried her in the
   desert near Kadesh (Num.
   20:1).
   b. The death of Aaron, Moses'
   brother (Num. 20:23-29)
   (1) The preparation for his

death—God told both Moses and Aaron that the time for Israel's first high priest to die had come.

(2) The place of his death—He died and was buried on top of Mt. Hor. Israel then mourned him for 30 days.

2. Two replacements
   a. Eleazar succeeded Aaron. "Take Aaron and Eleazar his son, and bring them up unto mount Hor: And strip Aaron of his garments, and put them upon Eleazar his son: and Aaron shall be gathered unto his people, and shall die there. And Moses stripped Aaron of his garments, and put them upon Eleazar his son; and Aaron died there in the top of the mount: and Moses and Eleazar came down from the mount" (Num. 20:25-26, 28).
   b. Joshua succeeded Moses (Num. 27:12-23).
      (1) God informed Moses that the time would soon come for him to die.
      (2) He would not be allowed to enter Canaan because of his sin in striking the rock.
      (3) After praying that God would appoint a capable leader to succeed him, Moses was commanded to transfer his authority to Joshua. "Moses did as the LORD commanded him: and he took Joshua, and set him before Eleazar the priest, and before all the congregation: And he laid his hands upon him, and gave him a charge, as the LORD commanded by the hand of Moses" (Num. 27:22-23).

D. Phase 4—The tabulation—Moses was commanded to take a census of the new generation. "Take the sum of all the congregation of the children of Israel, from twenty years old and upward, throughout their fathers' house, all that are able to go to war in Israel" (Num. 26:2). "These were the numbered of the children of Israel, six hundred thousand and a thousand seven hundred and thirty" (Num. 26:51).

E. Phase 5—The triumphs
   1. Victory over King Og—When attacked by the giant warrior king of Bashan, Moses was reassured that God himself would fight the battle for them (Num. 21:31-35).
   2. Victory over the Midianites—Moses issued his final military orders, commanding Israel to attack the Midianites (Num. 31:1-53).
      a. The reasons for this battle—Midian had previously led Israel into the twin sins of immorality and idolatry (Num. 25:16-18; 31:1).
      b. The results of this battle—Total victory was effected by 12,000 chosen soldiers, 1,000 from each of the 12 tribes.
      c. The reprimand following this battle
         (1) The soldiers invoked Moses' anger by sparing some of the very Midianite women who had previously led Israel into sin.
         (2) At his order, these women were killed.
         (3) Moses then issued instructions for dividing the spoils of war.

F. Phase 6—The types—"Moreover, brethren, I would not that ye should be ignorant, how that all our fathers were under the cloud, and all passed through the sea; and were all baptized unto Moses in the cloud and in the sea; and did all eat the same spiritual meat; and did all drink the same spiritual drink: for they drank of that spiritual Rock that followed them: and that Rock was Christ" (1 Cor. 10:1-4). Here Paul stated that some of the events occurring during the wilderness march may be looked upon as spiritual types of New Testament truths. Among these are the following:

1. Types of Christ
   a. The red heifer and the serpent of brass—Types of Christ's death
      (1) The red heifer (Num. 19:1-22)
      (2) The serpent of brass (Num. 21:5-9)—"The LORD sent fiery serpents among the people, and they bit the people; and much people of Israel died. Therefore the people came to Moses, and said, We have sinned, for we have spoken against the LORD, and against thee; pray unto the LORD, that he take away the serpents from us. And Moses prayed for the people. And the LORD said unto Moses, Make thee a fiery serpent, and set it upon a pole: and it shall come to pass, that every one that is bitten, when he looketh upon it, shall live. And Moses made a serpent of brass, and put it upon a pole, and it came to pass, that if a serpent had bitten any man, when he beheld the serpent of brass, he lived" (Num. 21:6-9).
   b. Aaron's rod that budded—A type of Christ's resurrection (Num. 17:1-10)—To prevent the constant complaining by Israel against Moses and Aaron, God ordered his servant to do the following:
      (1) Each tribal leader was to bring a wooden rod with his name on it.
      (2) Aaron's name was to be printed on the rod representing the tribe of Judah.
      (3) All 12 rods were then placed overnight in the tabernacle.
      (4) The next morning it was discovered that Aaron's rod had budded, was blossoming, and had ripe almonds hanging from it.
      (5) Moses then permanently placed Aaron's rod inside the sacred Ark of the Covenant (Num. 17:10; Heb. 9:4).
   c. The six cities of refuge—A type of the security in Christ (Num. 35:6-34)
2. A type of the worldly believer—Moses granted, perhaps sadly, the request of two and a half tribes, Reuben, Gad, and the half tribe of Manasseh (Num. 32:1-42).
   a. Their request—That they be allowed to settle on the eastern side of the Jordan River
   b. His reply—This would be permitted only if the two and a half tribes agreed to join the other nine and a half tribes during the invasion of Canaan and do their part in conquering the land.
3. A type of the overcoming life (Num. 34:1-29)
   a. God gave Moses specific instructions concerning the land of Canaan.
   b. In the book of Hebrews, Canaan is depicted as a type of the victorious life (Heb. 3:7-13; 4:1, 9-11).

CHRONOLOGICAL SUMMARY— THE STATESMAN OF GOD—The book of Deuteronomy is the eighth longest book in the Bible. In a nutshell, it records the final words, wisdom, and works of Moses, the man of God.

I. The sermons—The bulk of Deuteronomy (chapters 1–30) is given over to recording those messages delivered by Moses as he stood on the eastern bank of the Jordan River. Those sermons will be considered both chronologically and theologically.

A. A chronological consideration—First sermon (chapters 1–4)

1. Moses spoke about the sin at Kadesh.

   a. The sin of the people—Moses reminded Israel that a trip which should have taken only 11 days (from Mt. Sinai to Canaan) actually took nearly 40 years (see also Num. 14:23-34). "(There are eleven days' journey from Horeb by the way of mount Seir unto Kadesh-barnea) . . . . Notwithstanding ye would not go up, but rebelled against the commandment of the LORD your God" (Deut. 1:2, 26).

   b. The sin of the prophet—He spoke of his own sin which would keep him out of the promised land (Deut. 1:37; 3:23-27; 4:21-22). "The LORD was wroth with me for your sakes, and would not hear me: and the LORD said unto me, Let it suffice thee; speak no more unto me of this matter. Get thee up into the top of Pisgah, and lift up thine eyes westward, and northward, and southward, and eastward, and behold it with thine eyes: for thou shalt not go over this Jordan" (Deut. 3:26-27).

2. Moses spoke about the splendor at Sinai. "For what nation is there so great, who hath God so nigh unto them, as the LORD our God is in all things that we call upon him for? . . . Specially the day that thou stoodest before the LORD thy God in Horeb, when the LORD said unto me, Gather me the people together, and I will make them hear my words, that they may learn to fear me all the days that they shall live upon the earth, and that they may teach their children. . . . And the LORD spake unto you out of the midst of the fire: ye heard the voice of the words, but saw no similitude; only ye heard a voice. . . . Did ever people hear the voice of God speaking out of the midst of the fire, as thou hast heard, and live? . . . Out of heaven he made thee to hear his voice, that he might instruct thee: and upon earth he shewed thee his great fire; and thou heardest his words out of the midst of the fire" (Deut. 4:7, 10, 12, 33, 36).

B. Second sermon (chapters 5–26)

1. Repetition—The Ten Commandments were repeated (Deut. 5:7-21).

2. Reflection—He recalled his meeting with God on Mt. Sinai (Deut. 9:9-21). "When I was gone up into the mount to receive the tables of stone, even the tables of the covenant which the LORD made with you, then I abode in the mount forty days and forty nights, I neither did eat bread nor drink water" (Deut. 9:9).

   a. How his prayer had saved the people of Israel—"I fell down before the LORD, as at the first, forty days and forty nights: I did neither eat bread, nor drink water, because of all your sins which ye sinned, in doing wickedly in the sight of the LORD, to provoke him to anger. For I was afraid of the anger and hot displeasure, wherewith the LORD was wroth against you to destroy you. But the LORD hearkened unto me at that time" (Deut. 9:18-19).

   b. How his prayer had saved the

priest of Israel—"The LORD was very angry with Aaron to have destroyed him: and I prayed for Aaron also the same time" (Deut. 9:20).

3. Reminder—He reminded them concerning their stewardship obligations (Deuteronomy 26). "It shall be, when thou art come in unto the land which the LORD thy God giveth thee for an inheritance, and possessest it, and dwellest therein; That thou shalt take of the first of all the fruit of the earth, which thou shalt bring of thy land that the LORD thy God giveth thee, and shalt put it in a basket, and shalt go unto the place which the LORD thy God shall choose to place his name there" (Deut. 26:1-2).

4. Restraint—The prophet warned Israel against the following:

   a. Intermarriage—He forbade Israel to intermarry with the pagans in Canaan. "Neither shalt thou make marriages with them; thy daughter thou shalt not give unto his son, nor his daughter shalt thou take unto thy son. For they will turn away thy son from following me, that they may serve other gods: so will the anger of the LORD be kindled against you, and destroy thee suddenly" (Deut. 7:3-4).

   b. Imposters—"If there arise among you a prophet, or a dreamer of dreams, and giveth thee a sign or a wonder, and the sign or the wonder come to pass, whereof he spake unto thee, saying, Let us go after other gods, which thou hast not known, and let us serve them; Thou shalt not hearken unto the words of that prophet, or that dreamer of dreams: for the LORD your God proveth

you, to know whether ye love the LORD your God with all your heart and with all your soul" (Deut. 13:1-3). "The prophet, which shall presume to speak a word in my name, which I have not commanded him to speak, or that shall speak in the name of other gods, even that prophet shall die. And if thou say in thine heart, How shall we know the word which the LORD hath not spoken? When a prophet speaketh in the name of the LORD, if the thing follow not, nor come to pass, that is the thing which the LORD hath not spoken, but the prophet hath spoken it presumptuously: thou shalt not be afraid of him" (Deut. 18:20-22).

   c. Idolatry—"When thou art come into the land which the LORD thy God giveth thee, thou shalt not learn to do after the abominations of those nations" (Deut. 18:9).

   d. Injustice (Deut. 24:6-22)—"Thou shalt not remove thy neighbour's landmark, which they of old time have set in thine inheritance, which thou shalt inherit in the land that the LORD thy God giveth thee to possess it. One witness shall not rise up against a man for any iniquity, or for any sin, in any sin that he sinneth: at the mouth of two witnesses, or at the mouth of three witnesses, shall the matter be established" (Deut. 19:14-15).

   e. Indulgence—"If a man have a stubborn and rebellious son, which will not obey the voice of his father, or the voice of his mother, and that, when they have chastened him, will not hearken unto them: Then shall

his father and his mother lay
hold on him, and bring him out
unto the elders of his city, and
unto the gate of his place; . . .
And all the men of his city shall
stone him with stones, that he
die: so shalt thou put evil away
from among you; and all Israel
shall hear, and fear" (Deut.
21:18-19, 21).
f. Immorality (Deut. 22:13-30;
23:17)
g. Indifference—"When thou shalt
vow a vow unto the LORD thy
God, thou shalt not slack to
pay it: for the LORD thy God
will surely require it of thee;
and it would be sin in thee"
(Deut. 23:21).
h. Inhumanity—"If there be a controversy between men, and
they come unto judgment, that
the judges may judge them;
then they shall justify the righteous, and condemn the
wicked. And it shall be, if the
wicked man be worthy to be
beaten, that the judge shall
cause him to lie down, and to
be beaten before his face, according to his fault, by a certain
number. Forty stripes he may
give him, and not exceed: lest,
if he should exceed, and beat
him above these with many
stripes, then thy brother should
seem vile unto thee" (Deut.
25:1-3).
5. Reassurance—Moses reassured
Israel by giving a glowing description of the land of Canaan (Deut.
6:10-11; 8:7-9; 11:8-12). "For the
LORD thy God bringeth thee into a
good land, a land of brooks of
water, of fountains and depths
that spring out of valleys and
hills; a land of wheat, and barley,
and vines, and fig trees, and
pomegranates; a land of oil olive,
and honey; a land wherein thou

shalt eat bread without scarce-
ness, thou shalt not lack any
thing in it; a land whose stones
are iron, and out of whose hills
thou mayest dig brass" (Deut. 8:7-9).
"A land which the LORD thy God
careth for: the eyes of the LORD
thy God are always upon it, from
the beginning of the year even
unto the end of the year" (Deut.
11:12).
6. Regulations—He gave them rules
concerning the following:
a. The central sanctuary (Deut.
12:5, 18)
b. Diet (Deut. 14:3-21; 17:1)
c. The sabbatic year (Deut. 15:1-
15)
d. Religious feasts (Deut. 16:1-17)
e. Cities of refuge (Deut. 19:1-13)
f. Retribution (Deut. 19:15-21)
g. Warfare (Deut. 20:1-20)
h. Domestic situations (Deut.
21:10-17; 22:1-8)
i. Personal hygiene (Deut. 23:9-
14)
j. Divorce (Deut. 24:1-4)
7. Review—In one simple statement
Moses summarized God's overall
dealings with Israel in the Old
Testament: "He brought us out
from thence, that he might bring
us in, to give us the land which
he sware unto our fathers" (Deut.
6:23).
C. Third sermon (chapters 27–30)
1. A command
a. To build an altar to God—Israel
was to take out boulders from
the river bottom of the Jordan
and build an altar upon Mt.
Ebal (Deut. 27:1-7).
b. To broadcast the Law of God
(1) The curses of the Law (resulting from disobedience)
were to be read to the people by the priests upon Mt.
Ebal (Deut. 27:13-26; 28:15-
68).
(2) The blessings of the Law

(resulting from obedience) were to be read to the people by the priests upon Mt. Gerizim (Deut. 27:12; 28:1-14).

2. A covenant—Deuteronomy 28–30 records the features of the Palestinian Covenant, given by God to Israel. It is in seven parts.

a. Israel will be dispersed for disobedience (28:36, 49–53, 63–68; 30:1). This takes in the Assyrian, Babylonian, and Roman captivities, in addition to Israel's trials during the past 20 centuries. It would almost seem that Moses had Hitler's armies in mind when he wrote Deuteronomy 28:64-67. "The LORD shall scatter thee among all people, from the one end of the earth even unto the other; and there thou shalt serve other gods, which neither thou nor thy fathers have known, even wood and stone. And among these nations shalt thou find no ease, neither shall the sole of thy foot have rest: but the LORD shall give thee there a trembling heart, and failing of eyes, and sorrow of mind: and thy life shall hang in doubt before thee; and thou shalt fear day and night, and shalt have none assurance of thy life: In the morning thou shalt say, Would God it were even! and at even thou shalt say, Would God it were morning! for the fear of thine heart wherewith thou shalt fear, and for the sight of thine eyes which thou shalt see." During this time Israel would become a byword (28:37), and be the tail instead of the head (compare 28:13 with 28:44).

b. Israel will repent while in dispersion (30:2).

c. The return of Christ will occur—"The LORD thy God will turn thy captivity, and have compassion upon thee, and will return and gather thee from all the nations, whither the LORD thy God hath scattered thee" (30:3).

d. Israel will be restored to the land—"The LORD thy God will bring thee into the land which thy fathers possessed, and thou shalt possess it; and he will do thee good, and multiply thee above thy fathers" (30:5).

e. The nation will receive a new heart (30:6).

f. Israel's oppressors will be judged (30:7).

g. The nation will experience prosperity (30:9).

D. A theological consideration—During these three sermons Moses expounded upon the following great theological themes:

1. The faithfulness of God (2:7; 4:33-38; 7:6-8; 8:3-4; 9:4-6; 29:5-6; 32:9-14)

a. They had lacked nothing for 40 years (2:7).

b. Both food and clothing had been provided (8:3-4; 29:5-6).

c. He cared for Israel as an eagle cares for its own (32:9-14).

d. He did all this in spite of their constant sin (9:4-6).

2. The Word of God (4:1-2, 7-9; 11:18-21; 30:11-14)

a. Don't add to it or take away from it (4:1-2).

b. Teach it to your sons and daughters (4:7-9; 11:19-20)—"Ye shall teach them your children, speaking of them when thou sittest in thine house, and when thou walkest by the way, when thou liest down, and when thou risest up. And thou shalt write them upon the door posts of thine house, and upon thy gates" (Deut. 11:19-20).

c. Meditate upon it personally—"Therefore shall ye lay up these my words in your heart and in your soul, and bind them for a sign upon your hand, that they may be as frontlets between your eyes" (Deut. 11:18).

3. The person of God (6:4-5; 7:9; 32:39-42)—"Hear, O Israel: The LORD our God is one LORD: And thou shalt love the LORD thy God will all thine heart, and with all thy soul, and with all thy might" (6:4-5). "See now that I, even I, am he, and there is no god with me: I kill, and I make alive; I wound, and I heal: neither is there any that can deliver out of my hand. For I lift up my hand to heaven, and say, I live for ever" (Deut. 32:39-40).

4. The love of God (7:6-8, 13)—"For thou art an holy people unto the LORD thy God: the LORD thy God hath chosen thee to be a special people unto himself, above all people that are upon the face of the earth. The LORD did not set his love upon you, nor choose you, because ye were more in number than any people; for ye were the fewest of all people: But because the LORD loved you, and because he would keep the oath which he had sworn unto your fathers, hath the LORD brought you out with a mighty hand, and redeemed you out of the house of bondmen, from the hand of Pharaoh king of Egypt" (Deut. 7:6-8).

5. The glory of God (4:39; 10:17-18)

6. The grace of God (7:6-9; 9:4-6)—"Speak not thou in thine heart, after that the LORD thy God hath cast them out from before thee, saying, For my righteousness the LORD hath brought me in to possess this land: but for the wicked-ness of these nations the LORD doth drive them out from before thee . . . and that he may perform the word which the LORD sware unto thy fathers, Abraham, Isaac, and Jacob. Understand therefore, that the LORD thy God giveth thee not this good land to possess it for thy righteousness; for thou art a stiffnecked people" (Deut. 9:4-6).

7. The coming great prophet of God—"The LORD thy God will raise up unto thee a Prophet from the midst of thee, of thy brethren, like unto me; unto him ye shall hearken . . . . And it shall come to pass, that whosoever will not hearken unto my words which he shall speak in my name, I will require it of him" (Deut. 18:15, 19).

8. The will of God (10:12-16)—"Now, Israel, what doth the LORD thy God require of thee, but to fear the LORD thy God, to walk in all his ways, and to love him, and to serve the LORD thy God with all thy heart and with all thy soul, To keep the commandments of the LORD, and his statutes, which I command thee this day for thy good?" (Deut. 10:12-13).

9. The kings of God (17:14-20)
   a. They were not to multiply to themselves wives, gold, or horses (17:15-17).
   b. They were to be diligent students of God's Word (17:18-20).

10. The Israel of God (4:25-31; 11:16-17)
   a. To be scattered for unbelief—"The LORD shall scatter you among the nations, and ye shall be left few in number among the heathen, whither the LORD shall lead you" (Deut. 4:27).
   b. To be kept nevertheless through tribulation
   c. To repent and be gathered back into the land—"When thou art in tribulation, and all these

things are come upon thee, even in the latter days, if thou turn to the LORD thy God, and shalt be obedient unto his voice; (For the LORD thy God is a merciful God;) he will not forsake thee, neither destroy thee, nor forget the covenant of thy fathers which he sware unto them" (Deut. 4:30-31).

II. The setting apart

A. Of the 12 tribes

1. Moses briefed them—"Moses went and spake these words unto all Israel. And he said unto them, I am an hundred and twenty years old this day; I can no more go out and come in: also the LORD hath said unto me, Thou shalt not go over this Jordan. The LORD thy God, he will go over before thee, and he will destroy these nations from before thee, and thou shalt possess them: and Joshua, he shall go over before thee, as the LORD hath said" (Deut. 31:1-3). "He brought us out from thence, that he might bring us in, to give us the land which he sware unto our fathers" (Deut. 6:23).

2. Moses blessed them.

a. His legacy of the written word—"Moses wrote this law, and delivered it unto the priests the sons of Levi, which bare the ark of the covenant of the LORD, and unto all the elders of Israel. . . . And it came to pass, when Moses had made an end of writing the words of this law in a book, until they were finished, that Moses commanded the Levites, which bare the ark of the covenant of the LORD, saying, Take this book of the law, and put it in the side of the ark of the covenant of the LORD your God, that it may be there for a witness against thee" (Deut. 31:9, 24-26).

b. His legacy of the spoken word (Deut. 33)—"This is the blessing, wherewith Moses the man of God blessed the children of Israel before his death. And he said, The LORD came from Sinai, and rose up from Seir unto them; he shined forth from mount Paran, and he came with ten thousands of saints: from his right hand went a fiery law for them. Yea, he loved the people; all his saints are in thy hand: and they sat down at thy feet; every one shall receive of thy words" (Deut. 33:1-3).

(1) His blessing upon Reuben (Deut. 33:6)—"Let Reuben live forever and may his tribe increase!"

(2) His blessing upon Judah (Deut. 33:7)—"Hear his cry, O LORD, unite him, and fight for him against his enemies!"

(3) His blessing upon Levi (Deut. 33:8, 11)—"Give to him your Urim and Thummim. . . . Bless him as he teaches your Law and works in your temple."

(4) His blessing upon Benjamin (Deut. 33:12)—"Surround him with your loving care and protect him."

(5) His blessings upon Ephraim and Manasseh (Deut. 33:13-17)—"Bless their land and increase their crops."

(6) His blessing upon Zebulun (Deut. 33:18)—"Cause him to rejoice in the outdoor life."

(7) His blessing upon Issachar (Deut. 33:18-19)—"Give him the riches of the sea."

(8) His blessing upon Gad (Deut. 33:20-21)—"Let him be a ruler and judge for God."

(9) His blessing upon Dan (Deut. 33:22)—"May he increase in strength like a lion's cub."

(10) His blessing upon Naphtali (Deut. 33:23)—"Give him the Mediterranean coast and the Negeb as his homeland."

(11) His blessing upon Asher (Deut. 33:24-25)—"Bathe his feet in oil and give him strength the length of his days."

(12) His blessing upon all Israel—"The eternal God is thy refuge, and underneath are the everlasting arms: and he shall thrust out the enemy from before thee; and shall say, Destroy them. Israel then shall dwell in safety alone: the fountain of Jacob shall be upon a land of corn and wine; also his heavens shall drop down dew. Happy art thou, O Israel: who is like unto thee, O people saved by the LORD, the shield of thy help, and who is the sword of thy excellency! and thine enemies shall be found liars unto thee; and thou shalt tread upon their high places" (Deut. 33:27-29).

B. Of the man Joshua (Deut. 1:38; 3:21-22, 28; 31:7-8, 23)—"Joshua the son of Nun, which standeth before thee, he shall go in thither: encourage him: for he shall cause Israel to inherit it" (Deut. 1:38). "Moses called unto Joshua, and said unto him in the sight of all Israel, Be strong and of a good courage: for thou must go with this people unto the land which the LORD hath sworn unto their fathers to give them; and thou shalt cause them to inherit it. And the LORD, he it is that doth go before thee; he will be with thee, he will not fail thee, neither forsake thee: fear not, neither be dismayed" (Deut. 31:7-8).

III. The song

A. The command to write the song— "Now therefore write ye this song for you, and teach it the children of Israel: put it in their mouths, that this song may be a witness for me against the children of Israel. . . . And Moses spake in the ears of all the congregation of Israel the words of this song, until they were ended" (Deut. 31:19-30).

B. The contents of the song (Deut. 32:1-43)—"Give ear, O ye heavens, and I will speak; and hear, O earth, the words of my mouth" (Deut. 32:1).

1. He wrote about the greatness of God. "Because I will publish the name of the LORD: ascribe ye greatness unto our God. He is the Rock, his work is perfect: for all his ways are judgment: a God of truth and without iniquity, just and right is he" (Deut. 32:3-4).

2. He wrote about the grace of God. "For the LORD's portion is his people; Jacob is the lot of his inheritance. He found him in a desert land, and in the waste howling wilderness; he led him about, he instructed him, he kept him as the apple of his eye. As an eagle stirreth up her nest, fluttereth over her young, spreadeth abroad her wings, taketh them, beareth them on her wings" (Deut. 32:9-11).

3. He wrote about the grief of God. "O that they were wise, that they understood this, that they would consider their latter end! How

should one chase a thousand, and two put ten thousand to flight, except their Rock had sold them, and the LORD had shut them up?" (Deut. 32:29-30).

   a. His grief because of what Israel had done—"They provoked him to jealousy with strange gods, with abominations provoked they him to anger. They sacrificed unto devils, not to God; to gods whom they knew not, to new gods that came newly up, whom your fathers feared not. Of the Rock that begat thee thou art unmindful, and hast forgotten God that formed thee. . . . For they are a nation void of counsel, neither is there any understanding in them" (Deut. 32:16-18, 28).

   b. His grief concerning what he must do—"I will hide my face from them" (32:20). "To me belongeth vengeance, and recompence; their foot shall slide in due time" (32:35). "For the LORD shall judge his people" (32:36).

  4. He wrote about the guarantee of God. In spite of Israel's sin and chastisement, the story will have a happy ending. "Rejoice, O ye nations, with his people: for he will avenge the blood of his servants, and will render vengeance to his adversaries, and will be merciful unto his land, and to his people" (Deut. 32:43).

IV. The summons

  A. The proclaiming of Moses' death— "The LORD said unto Moses, Behold, thy days approach that thou must die: call Joshua, and present yourselves in the tabernacle of the congregation, that I may give him a charge. And Moses and Joshua went, and presented themselves in the taberna-

cle of the congregation. And the LORD appeared in the tabernacle in a pillar of a cloud: and the pillar of the cloud stood over the door of the tabernacle" (Deut. 31:14-15).

  B. The place of Moses' death—He would die on Mt. Nebo in the land of Moab, on the eastern bank of Jordan (Deut. 32:48-50; 34:5-6).

  C. The panoramic view before Moses' death—"Moses went up from the plains of Moab unto the mountain of Nebo, to the top of Pisgah, that is over against Jericho. And the LORD shewed him all the land of Gilead, unto Dan, and all Naphtali, and the land of Ephraim, and Manasseh, and all the land of Judah, unto the utmost sea, and the south, and the plain of the valley of Jericho, the city of palm trees, unto Zoar. And the LORD said unto him, This is the land which I sware unto Abraham, unto Isaac, and unto Jacob, saying, I will give it unto thy seed: I have caused thee to see it with thine eyes, but thou shalt not go over thither" (Deut. 34:1-4).

V. The sorrow—"The children of Israel wept for Moses in the plains of Moab thirty days: so the days of weeping and mourning for Moses were ended" (Deut. 34:8).

VI. The successor—"Joshua the son of Nun was full of the spirit of wisdom; for Moses had laid his hands upon him: and the children of Israel hearkened unto him, and did as the LORD commanded Moses" (Deut. 34:9).

VII. The summary—"Moses was an hundred and twenty years old when he died: his eye was not dim, nor his natural force abated. . . . And there arose not a prophet since in Israel like unto Moses, whom the LORD knew face to face, in all the signs and the wonders, which the LORD sent him to do in the land of Egypt to Pharaoh, and to all his servants, and to all his land, and in all that mighty hand, and in all the great terror which Moses shewed in the sight of all Israel" (Deut. 34:7, 10-12).

THEOLOGICAL SUMMARY

I. Caleb reminded Joshua of a promise Moses had once made to him. "Moses sware on that day, saying, Surely the land whereon thy feet have trodden shall be thine inheritance, and thy children's for ever, because thou hast wholly followed the Lord my God" (Josh. 14:9).

II. Joshua, Samuel, and David referred to Moses during their final speeches.
   A. Joshua (Josh. 24:5)
   B. Samuel—"When Jacob was come into Egypt, and your fathers cried unto the Lord, then the Lord sent Moses and Aaron, which brought forth your fathers out of Egypt, and made them dwell in this place" (1 Sam. 12:8).
   C. David (as he spoke to Solomon)— "Keep the charge of the Lord thy God, to walk in his ways, to keep his statutes, and his commandments, and his judgments, and his testimonies, as it is written in the law of Moses, that thou mayest prosper in all that thou doest, and whithersoever thou turnest thyself" (1 Kings 2:3).

III. Solomon mentioned Moses during his dedicatory prayer for the temple (1 Kings 8:53, 56). "Blessed be the Lord, that hath given rest unto his people Israel, according to all that he promised: there hath not failed one word of all his good promise, which he promised by the hand of Moses his servant" (1 Kings 8:56).

IV. The author of 1 and 2 Chronicles referred to Moses (1 Chron. 23:14; 2 Chron. 30:16).

V. Ezra referred to him (Ezra 3:2).

VI. Nehemiah mentioned Moses during a prayer (Neh. 1:7-8).

VII. The Levites mentioned him during a praise and confession service (Neh. 9:14).

VIII. Moses was the author of Psalm 90.
   A. He wrote concerning the eternality of God. "Before the mountains were brought forth, or ever thou hadst formed the earth and the world, even from everlasting to everlasting, thou art God. For a thousand years in thy sight are but as yesterday when it is past, and as a watch in the night" (Ps. 90:2, 4).
   B. He wrote concerning the mortality of man. "Thou carriest them away as with a flood; they are as a sleep: in the morning they are like grass which groweth up. In the morning it flourisheth, and groweth up; in the evening it is cut down, and withereth . . . . The days of our years are threescore years and ten; and if by reason of strength they be fourscore years, yet is their strength labour and sorrow; for it is soon cut off, and we fly away" (Ps. 90:5-6, 10).

IX. Moses was referred to often in the Psalms.
   A. How God used him (Ps. 77:20; 103:7; 105:26-27)—"Behold, he smote the rock, that the waters gushed out, and the streams overflowed" (Ps. 78:20). "He sent Moses his servant; and Aaron whom he had chosen. They shewed his signs among them, and wonders in the land of Ham" (Ps. 105:26-27).
   B. How God heard and answered him— "Moses and Aaron among his priests, and Samuel among them that call upon his name; they called upon the Lord, and he answered them. He spake unto them in the cloudy pillar: they kept his testimonies, and the ordinance that he gave them" (Ps. 99:6-7). "Therefore he said that he would destroy them, had not Moses his chosen stood before him in the breach, to turn away his wrath, lest he should destroy them" (Ps. 106:23).

X. Isaiah referred to him during his praise to God for past faithfulness to Israel (Isa. 63:11-12).

XI. Jeremiah was told by God that Judah had become so wicked that even the prayers of both Moses and Samuel could not save that nation from divine punishment (Jer. 15:1).

XII. Daniel referred to Moses during his great prayer of confession for the people of Israel (Dan. 9:11, 13).

XIII. Micah referred to Moses when rebuking Israel, reminding them of God's faithfulness once shown in the days of Moses (Mic. 6:4).

XIV. The final two individuals referred to in the Old Testament are Moses and Elijah (Mal. 4:4-5)—"Remember ye the law of Moses my servant, which I commanded unto him in Horeb for all Israel, with the statutes and judgments" (Mal. 4:4).

XV. Jesus referred to Moses on various occasions.

A. When he healed a leper—"See thou tell no man; but go thy way, shew thyself to the priest, and offer the gift that Moses commanded, for a testimony unto them" (Matt. 8:4).

B. In explaining the plan of salvation to Nicodemus—"As Moses lifted up the serpent in the wilderness, even so must the Son of man be lifted up" (John 3:14).

C. In comparing the Old Testament manna with himself—"Moses gave you not that bread from heaven; but my Father giveth you the true bread from heaven. For the bread of God is he which cometh down from heaven, and giveth life unto the world" (John 6:32-33).

D. In refuting the cynicism of the Sadducees concerning the resurrection from the dead—"As touching the dead, that they rise: have ye not read in the book of Moses, how in the bush God spake unto him, saying, I am the God of Abraham, and the God of Isaac, and the God of Jacob? He is not the God of the dead, but the God of the living: ye therefore do greatly err" (Mark 12:26-27).

E. In dealing with the Pharisees

1. He defended the healing of a cripple on the Sabbath by referring to Moses (John 5:1-16)—"Moses therefore gave unto you circumcision; (not because it is of Moses, but of the fathers;) and ye on the sabbath day circumcise a man. If a man on the sabbath day receive circumcision, that the law of Moses should not be broken; are ye angry at me, because I have made a man every whit whole on the sabbath day?" (John 7:22-23).

2. He rebuked the Pharisees for their low view of marriage by referring to Moses: "Moses because of the hardness of your hearts suffered you to put away your wives: but from the beginning it was not so" (Matt. 19:8).

3. He warned the Pharisees Moses himself would someday judge them—"Do not think that I will accuse you to the Father: there is one that accuseth you, even Moses in whom ye trust. For had ye believed Moses, ye would have believed me: for he wrote of me. But if ye believe not his writings, how shall ye believe my words?" (John 5:45-47).

4. He condemned the Pharisees.
   a. For substituting the laws of God with their own laws (Mark 7:8-13)
   b. For attempting to kill him— "Did not Moses give you the law, and yet none of you keepeth the law? Why go ye about to kill me?" (John 7:19).

F. In ministering to his disciples on the first Easter Sunday

1. To the two disciples on the Emmaus road—"O fools, and slow of heart to believe all that the prophets have spoken: Ought not Christ to have suffered these things, and

to enter into his glory? And beginning at Moses and all the prophets, he expounded unto them in all the scriptures the things concerning himself" (Luke 24:25-27).

    2. To the 10 disciples in the Upper Room—"These are the words which I spake unto you, while I was yet with you, that all things must be fulfilled, which were written in the law of Moses, and in the prophets, and in the psalms, concerning me" (Luke 24:44).

XVI. Moses and Elijah appeared with Christ during his transfiguration (Matt. 17:3; Mark 9:4; Luke 9:30-31)—"There talked with him two men, which were Moses and Elias: Who appeared in glory, and spake of his decease which he should accomplish at Jerusalem" (Luke 9:30-31).

XVII. Abraham referred to Moses while talking to the lost rich man in hell (Luke 16:19-31).

  A. The request of the rich man—He wanted Abraham to send a person back to earth from the dead. "For I have five brethren; that he may testify unto them, lest they also come into this place of torment" (Luke 16:28).

  B. The refusal of Abraham—"If they hear not Moses and the prophets, neither will they be persuaded, though one rose from the dead" (Luke 16:31).

XVIII. Both Peter and Stephen quoted from Moses, showing the Jewish leaders how Israel's great lawgiver had predicted the ministry of Christ.

  A. Peter's statement—"Moses truly said unto the fathers, A prophet shall the LORD your God raise up unto you of your brethren, like unto me; him shall ye hear in all things whatsoever he shall say unto you. . . . Unto you first God, having raised up his Son Jesus, sent him to bless you, in turn-

ing away every one of you from his iniquities" (Acts 3:22, 26).

  B. Stephen's statement—"This is that Moses, which said unto the children of Israel, A prophet shall the LORD your God raise up unto you of your brethren, like unto me; him shall ye hear" (Acts 7:37).

XIX. Both Stephen and Paul were falsely accused by their enemies of speaking against Moses.

  A. They lied about Stephen—"Then they suborned men, which said, We have heard him speak blasphemous words against Moses, and against God. . . . For we have heard him say, that this Jesus of Nazareth shall destroy this place, and shall change the customs which Moses delivered us" (Acts 6:11, 14).

  B. They lied about Paul—"Thou teachest all the Jews which are among the Gentiles to forsake Moses, saying that they ought not to circumcise their children, neither to walk after the customs" (Acts 21:21).

XX. During his defense before the Sanhedrin, Stephen referred to no less than 13 events in the life of Moses.

  A. The first three months of his life in Egypt

  B. His rescue from the Nile River by Pharaoh's daughter—"In which time Moses was born, and was exceeding fair, and nourished up in his father's house three months" (Acts 7:20).

  C. His education and formal training in Egypt—"Moses was learned in all the wisdom of the Egyptians, and was mighty in words and in deeds" (Acts 7:22).

  D. His act in defending a Hebrew slave by killing the Egyptian taskmaster who was beating him (Acts 7:23-24)

  E. His being maligned by that same slave the very next day (Acts 7:25-28)

  F. His flight into Midian to escape the wrath of Pharaoh for killing the taskmaster (Acts 7:29)

G. The fact that he fathered two sons (Acts 7:29)

H. His burning bush mission call from God (Acts 7:30-34)

I. How he delivered Israel from Egypt (Acts 7:35-36)

J. His prophecy concerning Christ— "This is that Moses, which said unto the children of Israel, A prophet shall the LORD your God raise up unto you of your brethren, like unto me; him shall ye hear" (Acts 7:37).

K. How he gave Israel the Law of God (Acts 7:38)

L. How Israel rejected both Moses and God (Acts 7:39-42)

M. How he constructed the tabernacle (Acts 7:44)

XXI. Paul referred to Moses on three occasions in the book of Acts.

A. Showing the Jews at Pisidian Antioch that Moses could not justify them as Christ did (Acts 13:39)

B. Proving to King Agrippa that Jesus was indeed the Christ (Acts 26:22)

C. Attempting to convince the Jews in Rome that Jesus was the Christ (Acts 28:23)

XXII. Paul referred to Moses often in his own epistles.

A. Contrasting:

1. The Law of Moses with the gift of Christ (Rom. 5:14; 10:5; see also Heb. 3:3)

2. The glory of the Law with the glory of the gospel (2 Cor. 3:7)

B. Proving the sovereignty of God in choosing Israel—"For he saith to Moses, I will have mercy on whom I will have mercy, and I will have compassion on whom I will have compassion" (Rom. 9:15).

C. Predicting God's plan to use Gentile people—"But I say, Did not Israel know? First Moses saith, I will provoke you to jealousy by them that are no people, and by a foolish nation I will anger you" (Rom. 10:19).

D. Illustrating:

1. That those who preach the gospel should be supported by the gospel—"For it is written in the law of Moses, Thou shalt not muzzle the mouth of the ox that treadeth out the corn. Doth God take care for oxen?" (1 Cor. 9:9).

2. That saving faith is a personal matter—Many Israelites during the Exodus died in unbelief in spite of witnessing the mighty miracles God performed through Moses (1 Cor. 10:1-12).

3. How godless men corrupt the truth and oppose godly men— "Now as Jannes and Jambres withstood Moses, so do these also resist the truth: men of corrupt minds, reprobate concerning the faith" (2 Tim. 3:8).

E. Explaining why Moses put a veil on his face after coming down from Mt. Sinai, namely, that Israel might not see the fading glory of the Law (2 Cor. 3:13).

F. Lamenting the fact that Israel had allowed the Law of Moses to blind them to the light of Christ (2 Cor. 3:15).

XXIII. The author of Hebrews mentioned Moses on various occasions:

A. Comparing the faithfulness of Moses with the faithfulness of Christ (Heb. 3:1-2, 5)

B. Referring to:

1. The unbelief at Kadesh-barnea during the days of Moses (Heb. 3:16)

2. The building of the tabernacle by Moses (Heb. 8:5)

3. The ratification of the Law at Mt. Sinai and the awesome fear he felt (Heb. 9:19; 12:21)—"So terrible was the sight, that Moses said, I exceedingly fear and quake" (Heb. 12:21).

4. The consequences of rejecting Moses' law during the Exodus march—"He that despised Moses' Law died without mercy under

two or three witnesses" (Heb.
10:28).

C. Illustrating:

1. The faith displayed by his parents
   who hid him from the Egyptian
   authorities until he was three
   months old—"By faith Moses,
   when he was born, was hid three
   months of his parents, because
   they saw he was a proper child;
   and they were not afraid of the
   king's commandment" (Heb.
   11:23).
2. The faith he displayed:
   a. When he forsook the riches of
      Egypt for the righteousness of
      Christ—"By faith Moses, when
      he was come to years, refused
      to be called the son of Pha-
      raoh's daughter; choosing
      rather to suffer affliction with
      the people of God, than to en-
      joy the pleasures of sin for a
      season; esteeming the reproach
      of Christ greater riches than the
      treasures in Egypt: for he had
      respect unto the recompence of
      the reward" (Heb. 11:24-26).
   b. When he kept the Passover—
      "Through faith he kept the
      passover, and the sprinkling of
      blood, lest he that destroyed
      the firstborn should touch
      them" (Heb. 11:28).
   c. When he led Israel across the
      Red Sea—"By faith they passed
      through the Red sea as by dry
      land: which the Egyptians as-
      saying to do were drowned"
      (Heb. 11:29).

XXIV. Jude informed us that Michael the Archangel and Satan were once involved in a
dispute over the dead body of Moses
(Jude 9).

XXV. John the apostle wrote that Jewish believers will someday sing the song of
Moses during the great tribulation—
"They sing the song of Moses the servant of God, and the song of the Lamb,
saying, Great and marvellous are thy

works, LORD God Almighty; just and
true are thy ways, thou King of saints.
Who shall not fear thee, O LORD, and
glorify thy name? for thou only art holy:
for all nations shall come and worship
before thee; for thy judgments are made
manifest" (Rev. 15:3-4).

STATISTICS

Father: Amram (Exod. 6:20)
Mother: Jochebed (Exod. 6:20)
Spouse: Zipporah (Exod. 2:21)
Sons: Gershom and Eliezer (Exod. 18:2-4)
Brother: Aaron (Exod. 6:20)
Sister: Miriam (Num. 26:59)
First mention: Exodus 2:10
Final mention: Revelation 15:3
Meaning of his name: "The one drawn out"
Frequency of his name: Referred to 804 times
Biblical books mentioning him: 31 books (Exo-
dus, Leviticus, Numbers, Deuteronomy,
Joshua, Judges, 1 Samuel, 1 Kings,
2 Kings, 1 Chronicles, 2 Chronicles, Ezra,
Nehemiah, Psalms, Isaiah, Jeremiah,
Daniel, Micah, Malachi, Matthew, Mark,
Luke, John, Acts, Romans, 1 Corinthians,
2 Corinthians, 2 Timothy, Hebrews, Jude,
Revelation)
Occupation: Lawgiver, prophet, and leader
of Israel (Deut. 34:10-12)
Place of birth: Egypt (Exod. 1:15–2:2)
Place of death: Mt. Nebo (Deut. 34:1-5)
Age at death: 120 (Deut. 34:7)
Important fact about his life: He was Israel's
great lawgiver and author of the
Pentateuch (Exod. 17:14; 24:5-7; Num.
33:2; Deut. 31:9; Josh. 23:6; Luke 24:27,
44; John 1:17; 5:46).

✍Naaman

CHRONOLOGICAL SUMMARY

I. Naaman, the successful soldier
  A. He was commander of the Syrian
     army in the days of Elisha the
     prophet (2 Kings 5:1).

B. He was a good and brave man, used by God to give victory to the Syrian people (2 Kings 5:1).

II. Naaman, the suffering soldier—He was a leper (2 Kings 5:1).

III. Naaman, the seeking soldier

A. He learned about the supernatural power of Elisha through a young Israelite maid who served in his household (2 Kings 5:2-3).

B. Acting upon her testimony, he visited King Jehoram in Jerusalem (the youngest son of Ahab), requesting that he be healed of his leprosy (2 Kings 5:4-6).

C. This godless and powerless king could offer no help whatsoever, and was greatly relieved when Elisha agreed to meet with Naaman (2 Kings 5:8).

IV. Naaman, the sulking soldier—Upon his arrival at Elisha's home, Naaman was instructed by a servant of the prophet to wash himself seven times in the Jordan River for his healing (2 Kings 5:9-10).

A. The anger of Naaman (2 Kings 5:11-12)

1. He expected Elisha to personally greet him and, in dramatic fashion, to heal him.

2. He complained that if indeed the washing process was necessary, the rivers in Damascus were much cleaner than the Jordan.

B. The advice to Naaman—His servants gave him some excellent advice (2 Kings 5:13): "My father, if the prophet had bid thee do some great thing, wouldest thou not have done it? how much rather then, when he saith to thee, Wash, and be clean?"

V. Naaman, the saved soldier

A. His physical salvation—Naaman obeyed Elisha, washed himself seven times, and was instantly and totally healed (2 Kings 5:14).

B. His spiritual salvation (2 Kings 5:15-17)

1. He stood before Elisha and acknowledged that the God of Israel was the only true God.

2. He offered Elisha a gift, which the prophet refused.

3. He vowed never again to offer burnt sacrifices to any god except the true one.

4. He even took two muleloads of Israelite earth with him back to Damascus in order to make an altar to the Lord at his home.

VI. Naaman, the seduced soldier (2 Kings 5:20-27)

A. En route back to Syria, Naaman was approached by Gehazi, Elisha's servant, who for personal greed lied to him, claiming the prophet had changed his mind and needed Naaman's gift to help some other prophets.

B. Naaman gave him two money bags and two expensive robes.

C. Upon arriving back home, however, Gehazi was punished for this by having Naaman's leprosy supernaturally placed upon him.

THEOLOGICAL SUMMARY

I. Jesus used the story of Naaman's healing during a sermon preached in his hometown synagogue of Nazareth to illustrate the faith of the Gentiles and the faithlessness of Israel. He said: "And many lepers were in Isarel in the time of Elisha, the prophet; and none of them was cleansed, but only Naaman, the Syrian" (Luke 4:27).

II. Naaman thus became the only male in the entire Old Testament to be healed of leprosy.

STATISTICS

First mention: 2 Kings 5:1
Final mention: Luke 4:27
Meaning of his name: "Pleasant"
Frequency of his name: Referred to 11 times
Biblical books mentioning him: Two books (2 Kings, Luke)
Occupation: Military commander (2 Kings 5:1)

Important fact about his life: He was cured of leprosy.

Nabal

CHRONOLOGICAL SUMMARY

I. The character of Nabal
 A. He was a wealthy shepherd living in Maon, a city in Judah seven miles southeast of Hebron (1 Sam. 25:2).
 B. He was a descendant of Caleb (1 Sam. 25:3).
 C. He was married to an intelligent and beautiful woman named Abigail (1 Sam. 25:3).
 D. He, however, was surly and mean in his dealings (1 Sam. 25:3).
II. The conduct of Nabal
 A. He refused to honor the modest request of David and his men concerning some needed bread and water (1 Sam. 25:4-11).
 B. An angered David then rode out to punish him (1 Sam. 25:12-13).
 C. Disaster was averted, however, by the wise and prompt actions of Abigail, who provided David with the requested food supplies and apologized for her stupid husband (1 Sam. 25:14-31).
III. The condemnation of Nabal
 A. Ten days later, Nabal was killed by God for his wickedness (1 Sam. 25:36-38).
 B. Soon after this David took Abigail as his third wife (1 Sam. 25:39-43).

STATISTICS

Spouse: Abigail (1 Sam. 25:3)
First mention: 1 Samuel 25:3
Final mention: 2 Samuel 2:2
Meaning of his name: "Fool"
Frequency of his name: Referred to 19 times
Biblical books mentioning him: Two books (1 Samuel, 2 Samuel)
Occupation: Sheep raiser (1 Sam. 25:5-8)
Place of death: Maon (a city near Hebron) (1 Sam. 25:2, 36)

Circumstances of death: He was killed by God (1 Sam. 25:37-38).
Important fact about his life: He was Abigail's brutish first husband who refused to return David's kindness (1 Sam. 25:5-12).

Naboth

CHRONOLOGICAL SUMMARY

I. His bravery—Naboth and Ahab (1 Kings 21:1-2)
 A. Ahab's request
 1. Naboth was a Jezreelite of the tribe of Issachar (Josh. 19:17-18; 1 Kings 21:1).
 2. He owned a vineyard close to the palace of King Ahab (1 Kings 21:1).
 3. He was pressured to sell this vineyard to Ahab, who wanted it for a vegetable garden.
 B. Naboth's refusal—"The LORD forbid it me, that I should give the inheritance of my fathers unto thee" (1 Kings 21:3).
II. His betrayal—Naboth and Jezebel
 A. Slandering him
 1. Ahab returned home sullen, angry, and refusing to eat (1 Kings 21:4).
 2. Upon learning of Ahab's problem, Jezebel his wicked wife instigated a murderous plot against Naboth (1 Kings 21:5-10).
 a. She wrote letters in Ahab's name to the elders living in Naboth's city.
 b. She commanded them to proclaim a day of fasting and hire two lying scoundrels to testify against Naboth, accusing him of cursing both God and king.
 c. She instructed the elders to stone him to death.
 B. Slaughtering him
 1. The sowing
 a. The cowardly elders did all that

Jezebel commanded (1 Kings 21:11-14).

b. Upon hearing of Naboth's death, Ahab hurried down to take possession of the vineyard (1 Kings 21:15-16).

c. Here he was confronted by Elijah, who pronounced a threefold judgment upon the house of Ahab for the murder of Naboth.

(1) Upon Ahab himself—The dogs would someday lick the blood of the wicked king in the same spot where they had licked Naboth's blood (1 Kings 21:19).

(2) Upon Jezebel—The dogs would eat her flesh by the wall of Jezreel (1 Kings 21:23).

(3) Upon their posterity—Their sons would be cut down (1 Kings 21:21, 24).

2. The reaping

a. Ahab's blood was licked up by the dogs (1 Kings 22:38).

b. Jezebel was eaten by the dogs (2 Kings 9:35).

c. Jehoram, their son, was killed on the very plot of ground once owned by Naboth (2 Kings 9:21-26).

STATISTICS

First mention: 1 Kings 21:1

Final mention: 2 Kings 9:26

Meaning of his name: "Prominence"

Frequency of his name: Referred to 20 times

Biblical books mentioning him: Two books (1 Kings, 2 Kings)

Place of death: Outside the city of Jezreel (1 Kings 21:13)

Circumstances of death: He was stoned to death (1 Kings 21:13).

Important fact about his life: He refused to sell his vineyard to wicked King Ahab (1 Kings 21:3).

Nadab (1)

CHRONOLOGICAL SUMMARY

I. He saw the glory of God

A. He was appointed by God himself to be a priest (Exod. 28:1).

B. He accompanied Moses, Aaron (his father), Abihu (his brother), and 70 Israelite elders part way up Mt. Sinai (Exod. 24:1).

C. He was given a view of God's majesty—"They saw the God of Israel: and there was under his feet as it were a paved work of a sapphire stone, and as it were the body of heaven in his clearness" (Exod. 24:10).

II. He scorned the God of glory—Nadab and his brother Abihu were both killed by the Lord (Lev. 10:1-11).

A. The method of his death—Fire fell from heaven and consumed him.

B. The reasons for his death—The context suggests (Lev. 10:9) that he may actually have been drunk when he offered his "strange fire before the LORD" (Lev. 10:1).

C. The lesson from his death—It served to illustrate the holiness of God.

D. The remembrance of his death—It is mentioned on two later occasions (Num. 3:4; 26:61).

STATISTICS

Father: Aaron (Exod. 6:23)

Mother: Elisheba (Exod. 6:23)

Brothers: Abihu, Eleazar, and Ithamar (Exod. 6:23)

First mention: Exodus 6:23

Final mention: 1 Chronicles 24:2

Meaning of his name: "Liberal, willing"

Frequency of his name: Referred to 12 times

Biblical books mentioning him: Four books (Exodus, Leviticus, Numbers, 1 Chronicles)

Occupation: Priest (Exod. 28:1)

Place of death: In the tabernacle at Kadesh-barnea

Circumstances of death: He was killed by God (Lev. 10:2).

Important fact about his life: He offered pagan fire to God in the tabernacle (Lev. 10:1).

☞*Nadab* (2)

CHRONOLOGICAL SUMMARY
I. The apostate king
  A. He was the second king of Northern Israel.
  B. He ruled for two years (1 Kings 15:25).
  C. He was evil like his father, Jeroboam I (1 Kings 15:26).
II. The assassinated king
  A. One of his soldiers from the tribe of Issachar plotted against him and killed Nadab as the king was attempting to capture a Philistine town (1 Kings 15:27-28).
  B. Baasha then killed all of Nadab's family and relatives (1 Kings 15:29).

STATISTICS
Father: Jeroboam I (1 Kings 14:20)
Brother: Abijah (1 Kings 14:1)
First mention: 1 Kings 14:20
Final mention: 1 Kings 15:31
Meaning of his name: "Liberal, willing"
Frequency of his name: Referred to four times
Biblical books mentioning him: One book (1 Kings)
Occupation: King of Northern Israel (1 Kings 15:25)
Place of death: Near the Philistine city of Gibbethon (1 Kings 15:27)
Circumstances of death: He was killed by Baasha (1 Kings 15:27).
Important fact about his life: He was the son of Jeroboam I, and Northern Israel's second king (1 Kings 15:25).

☞*Nahash*

CHRONOLOGICAL SUMMARY
I. His terrible demand
  A. He was a cruel Ammonite king who besieged the Israelite city of Jabesh-gilead shortly after Saul had been anointed ruler over Israel (1 Sam. 11:1).
  B. When the helpless city asked for peace terms, his condition was that each citizen submit to having his or her right eye gouged out (1 Sam. 11:1-2).
II. His total destruction—Upon learning of this, a furious Saul raised an army of 330,000 men and, falling upon Nahash, totally destroyed his army (1 Sam. 11:4-11).

STATISTICS
First mention: 1 Samuel 11:1
Final mention: 1 Samuel 12:12
Meaning of his name: Oracle
Frequency of his name: Referred to four times
Biblical books mentioning him: One book (1 Samuel)
Occupation: King of the Ammonites (1 Sam. 12:12)
Place of death: Probably outside the city of Jabesh-gilead (1 Sam. 11:1, 11)
Important fact about his life: He threatened to gouge out the right eye of those Israelites living in Jabesh-gilead (1 Sam. 11:2).

☞*Nahum*

CHRONOLOGICAL SUMMARY
I. The why concerning Nineveh's destruction
  A. To protect Judah—Nahum said God is jealous over those he loves and takes vengeance on those who would hurt them (1:2).
  B. To punish Nineveh
    1. Because of her haughty heart (3:4)
      a. Nineveh had sold herself to the enemies of God.
      b. She had enticed the nations with her beauty.
      c. She had bewitched them, teaching people to worship idols.
    2. Because of her bloody hands (2:12; 3:19)

a. She had crushed her enemies to feed her citizens.

b. She had filled her city and home with captured goods and slaves.

c. Her wound of sin was far too deep to cure.

d. All nations had suffered from her cruelty.

II. The how concerning Nineveh's destruction

  A. By the overflowing of the Tigris's waters (1:8; 2:6)

  B. By the onslaught of the Babylonian warriors (2:3-4)

    1. Their shields would flash red in the sunlight.

    2. Their chariots would rush through the streets, pulled by prancing steeds.

III. The who concerning Nineveh's destruction—God himself

  A. His patience was over—Nahum said God is slow in getting angry, but when aroused, his power is incredible (1:3).

  B. His punishment would begin.

    1. Nineveh's soldiers would desert the city (2:8).

    2. The vast wealth of the city would be taken (2:9).

    3. The hearts of the people would melt and their knees would quake in terror (2:10).

    4. Their finest youth would lie dead in the streets (2:13).

    5. The city would stagger like a drunkard and be put to the torch (3:11, 13).

    6. The people would be scattered to the wind (3:18).

THEOLOGICAL SUMMARY

I. Nahum has but one theme; the destruction of Nineveh, the second most notorious pagan city in the Old Testament.

II. Nahum may be compared to Jonah:

  A. Jonah had, a century and a half ago, proclaimed deliverance to the city. A repentant Nineveh was then delivered.

  B. Nahum proclaimed destruction upon the city. An unrepentant Nineveh would be destroyed.

    1. The time span between the ministry of Jonah and Nahum is a classic example of Genesis 15:16, "for the iniquity of the Amorites is not yet full."

    2. The New Testament city of Capernaum, meaning "village of Nahum," may have been named in honor of this Old Testament prophet.

STATISTICS

First mention: Nahum 1:1

Final mention: Nahum 1:1

Meaning of his name: "Comforter"

Frequency of his name: Referred to one time

Biblical books mentioning him: One book (Nahum)

Occupation: Prophet

Place of birth: Capernaum?

Important fact about his life: He predicted the total destruction of Nineveh (Nah. 2:8-10).

Naomi

CHRONOLOGICAL SUMMARY

I. Naomi, the grief-stricken

  A. She lost her spouse.

    1. She left Bethlehem with her family during a famine and moved to the land of Moab (Ruth 1:2).

    2. She became a widow in Moab (Ruth 1:3).

  B. She lost her sons

    1. Naomi witnessed the marriage of her two sons to Orpah and Ruth, two Moabite women (Ruth 1:4).

    2. Ten years later she lost both sons in death (Ruth 1:5).

II. Naomi, the guardian

  A. Naomi and Ruth in Moab

    1. Naomi's despair

a. Naomi decided to return to Bethlehem.
b. Both her daughters-in-law offered to accompany her, but Naomi discouraged this, telling them to remain in Moab, for "the hand of the LORD is gone out against me" (Ruth 1:13).
c. Orpah took her advice and left (Ruth 1:14).
2. Ruth's decision—Unlike Orpah, Ruth would not be put off (Ruth 1:15-16). "Entreat me not to leave thee; or to return from following after thee: for whither thou goest, I will go; and where thou lodgest, I will lodge: thy people shall be my people, and thy God my God" (Ruth 1:16).
B. Naomi and Ruth in Bethlehem
1. Ruth helped Naomi secure food.
a. Upon reaching Bethlehem, Naomi demanded that her own neighbors and friends no longer call her by that name, but refer to her as "Mara," which means "bitter." At this time she was indeed a bitter woman (Ruth 1:13, 20-21).
b. Naomi let Ruth glean in the fields for food (Ruth 2:2).
2. Naomi helped Ruth secure a family.
a. Upon learning that Ruth had met Boaz, a close relative of her dead husband, and a very eligible bachelor, Naomi began planning for a wedding (Ruth 2:19–3:2).
b. She instructed Ruth to approach Boaz and request that he fulfill his office of the kinsman redeemer, referring to his duty in caring for and even, if he himself was unmarried, to marry the widowed relative (Ruth 2:1; 3:2-9).
c. Boaz agreed, but informed Ruth there was a legal problem concerning an even closer kinsman redeemer (Ruth 3:10-15).

d. Upon her return, Naomi reassured Ruth, knowing the love and determination of Boaz (Ruth 3:16-18).
III. Naomi, the grandmother
A. Boaz resolved the legal problem and married Ruth, who later gave birth to a boy named Obed (Ruth 4:13, 17).
B. The overjoyed Naomi was allowed to help care for her grandson (Ruth 4:16).
C. In the providence of God, Naomi would eventually become the great-great-grandmother of King David (Ruth 4:18-21).

STATISTICS
Spouse: Elimelech (Ruth 1:2)
Sons: Mahlon and Chilion (Ruth 1:2)
First mention: Ruth 1:2
Final mention: Ruth 4:17
Meaning of her name: "Pleasant"
Frequency of her name: Referred to 21 times
Biblical books mentioning her: One book (Ruth)
Important fact about her life: She was Ruth's mother-in-law (Ruth 1:3-6).

✐*Nathan* (1)

CHRONOLOGICAL SUMMARY
I. Nathan under David
A. His reaction concerning the king's temple
1. He was a prophet to King David (2 Sam. 7:2).
2. He, along with another prophet named Gad, helped organize the musical ministry of the priests and Levites (2 Chron. 29:25-26).
3. On one occasion he mistakenly gave David some wrong advice.
a. David's desire—The king desired to build a temple for God (2 Sam. 7:2).
b. Nathan's disservice—He unintentionally gave the wrong

advice. "Go, do all that is in thine heart; for the LORD is with thee" (2 Sam. 7:3).

c. God's disapproval—The Lord told Nathan to inform David he would not be allowed to build the temple, but that his son Solomon would do this (1 Chron. 17:3, 11-12).

B. His rebuke concerning the king's transgression

1. The parable (2 Sam. 12:1-6)

a. He began by relating a parable of a rich farmer who stole and butchered a little ewe lamb from a poor farmer, serving it at a special dinner for a visiting friend.

b. A furious David decreed that the wretched rich farmer would be forced to pay back fourfold and then be executed.

2. The punchline—"Nathan said to David, Thou art the man" (2 Sam. 12:7).

a. Nathan reviewed David's sin—The king, who had many wives, had stolen Bath-sheba from Uriah and then ordered him killed (2 Sam. 12:7-9).

b. Nathan revealed David's sentence (2 Sam. 12:10-14).

(1) God would not kill David.

(2) However, the sword of rebellion and death would never depart from his house.

(3) David's child born to him by Bath-sheba would die. David later wrote Psalm 51 which records his prayer of repentance following the rebuke and prophecy of Nathan.

c. Nathan renamed David's son—Following the birth of David's second son through Bath-sheba, whom the king named Solomon, God informed Nathan to also call him Jedidiah, meaning,

"loved by the LORD" (2 Sam. 12:24-25).

II. Nathan under Solomon

A. Nathan remained true to Solomon during an attempted coup led by Adonijah, Solomon's eldest half brother (1 Kings 1:8, 22-27).

B. The dying David instructed Nathan to help anoint Solomon as Israel's next king (1 Kings 1:32-40).

C. Years later Nathan coauthored a book concerning the life and times of both David and Solomon (1 Chron. 29:29-30; 2 Chron. 9:29).

STATISTICS

First mention: 2 Samuel 7:2
Final mention: Psalm 51 (in the introduction)
Meaning of his name: "Giver"
Frequency of his name: Referred to 28 times
Biblical books mentioning him: Five books (2 Samuel, 2 Kings, 1 Chronicles, 2 Chronicles, Psalms)
Occupation: Prophet (2 Sam. 7:2)
Important fact about his life: He condemned David for the twin sins of adultery and murder (2 Sam. 12:1-12).

✐Nathan (2)

CHRONOLOGICAL SUMMARY

I. He was one of David's five sons he bore with Bath-sheba (2 Sam. 5:14; 1 Chron. 3:5).

II. He was the ancestor of Mary (Luke 3:31).

STATISTICS

Father: David (1 Chron. 3:1, 5)
Mother: Bath-sheba (1 Chron. 3:5)
Son: Mattatha (Luke 3:31)
Brothers: Solomon, Shammua, and Shobab (1 Chron. 3:5)
Significant descendants: Mary (Luke 3:31)
First mention: 2 Samuel 5:14
Final mention: Luke 3:31

Meaning of his name: "Giver"
Frequency of his name: Referred to four times
Biblical books mentioning him: Three books
 (2 Samuel, 1 Chronicles, Luke)
Important fact about his life: He was one of
 David's sons by Bath-sheba from whose
 line Mary was born (1 Chron. 3:4; Luke
 3:31).

Nebuchadnezzar

CHRONOLOGICAL SUMMARY

I. Nebuchadnezzar and the city of God
 A. The background—Nebuchadnezzar
  defeated the Egyptians at the battle
  of Carchemish beside the Euphrates
  River in 605 B.C., thus making Babylon the master of the Middle East
  (Jer. 46:2).
 B. The blockades—Nebuchadnezzar then
  headed west and surrounded the city
  of Jerusalem on three occasions.
  1. The first siege (605 B.C.)—He
   punished Judean King Jehoiakim,
   put the city to tribute, and carried
   off thousands of Jewish hostages,
   including Daniel and his three
   friends (2 Kings 24:1; 2 Chron.
   36:6-7; Dan. 1:3-4).
  2. The second siege (597 B.C.)—He
   enslaved Judean King Jehoiachin,
   took more tribute money, and carried off additional hostages, including Ezekiel and his wife
   (2 Kings 24:8-16; Jer. 24:1; Ezek.
   1:2.
  3. The third siege (586 B.C.)
   a. He blinded and enslaved Ju-
    dean King Zedekiah, burned
    the city, and destroyed the tem-
    ple (2 Kings 25:1-21; Jer. 39:1-
    10; 52:4-16).
   b. He appointed a Jewish leader
    named Gedaliah to govern over
    the people left in Judah
    (2 Kings 25:22).
   c. He ordered that Jeremiah the

prophet be treated with kindness (Jer. 39:11-12).
   d. He then removed many of the
    golden and silver objects from
    the Jerusalem temple and
    placed them in his pagan tem-
    ple in Babylon (2 Chron. 36:6,
    10; Dan. 5:2; Ezra 1:7; 5:14; 6:5).
II. Nebuchadnezzar and the champions of
 God
 A. The king and Daniel—The relationship between Nebuchadnezzar and
  Daniel centered around two dreams
  experienced by the king.
  1. The first dream (Dan. 2)
   a. A chronology of the dream—
    What did the king see? (2:31-35)
    (1) He saw a huge and powerful
     statue of a man made up of
     various materials.
     (a) Its head was gold.
     (b) Its breast and arms were
      silver.
     (c) Its belly and thighs were
      brass.
     (d) Its legs were iron and its
      feet part iron and part
      clay.
    (2) This statue was then utterly
     pulverized into small pow-
     der by a special rock, super-
     naturally cut from a
     mountainside, which fell
     upon it.
    (3) The rock then grew until it
     filled the entire earth.
   b. A theology of the dream—What
    did this all mean? (2:36-45)
    (1) The statue represented four
     Gentile world powers.
     (a) The golden head was
      Babylon.
     (b) The silver chest and arms
      were Persia.
     (c) The brass belly and thighs
      were Greece.
     (d) The iron legs and iron
      and clay feet were Rome.
    (2) In the days of the final
     world power, the God of

heaven would shatter all earthly kingdoms through his Rock, the Lord Jesus Christ, and set up an eternal kingdom (2:44-45).

(3) The final Gentile power (Rome) would be revived during the tribulation and would consist of 10 nations. This was implied, for the great prophecies concerning the fourth power were not fulfilled in the history of ancient Rome.

c. An acknowledgment of the dream

(1) The king bowed down to Daniel and commanded his people to offer sacrifices and burn sweet incense before him (2:46).

(2) He acknowledged the God of Daniel as being "God of gods" (2:47).

(3) He elevated Daniel to the highest office in Babylon, as chief magistrate in the king's court (2:48).

2. The second dream (Dan. 4)

a. It told how a tree had been corrupted through vanity (4:1-22).

(1) Nebuchadnezzar related his dream to Daniel (4:8-18).

(a) He saw a large and leafy tree increasing in size until it reached the heavens and was viewed by all. The wild animals and birds were shaded and sheltered by its leafy branches, and the entire world was fed from its generous fruit supply (4:10-12).

(b) Suddenly a heavenly figure appeared and ordered the tree cut down and its fruit scattered. Only the stump was to be left, banded with a chain of iron and brass. This felled tree represented a man who would be given the mind of an animal and remain in this pitiful condition for seven years (4:13-16).

(c) This all was to be done so the entire world might know that . . . "The most High ruleth in the kingdom of men, and giveth it to whomsoever he will, and setteth up over it the basest of men" (4:17).

(2) Daniel revealed the dream to Nebuchadnezzar (4:19-27).

(a) The interpretation was so frightful that Daniel observed an hour of shocked silence (4:19).

(b) He then revealed the details:

i. The tree indeed stood for a man, and that man was Nebuchadnezzar.

ii. The king would suffer a seven-year period of insanity for his pride. During this time he would act and think like a wild animal.

iii. This affliction would end only when he realized that the powers that be are ordained of God.

(c) Daniel then begged the proud monarch to "break off thy sins," but all to no avail.

b. It told how this tree would be corrected through insanity (4:28-37).

(1) The pride of Nebuchadnezzar—Once, 12 months after the dream, the king was strolling on the roof of the royal palace in

Babylon. He gave an arrogant boast (4:28-30): "Is not this great Babylon, that I have built for the house of the kingdom by the might of my power, and for the honour of my majesty?" (4:30).

(2) The punishment of Nebuchadnezzar (4:31-33)

(a) Even while the king spoke his proud words, the judgment of God fell from heaven and he was driven from the palace (4:31).

(b) The sad results of his vanity—"He was driven from men, and did eat grass as oxen, and his body was wet with the dew of heaven, till his hairs were grown like eagles' feathers, and his nails like birds' claws" (4:33).

(3) The praise of Nebuchadnezzar—Upon restoration his pride turned to praise.

B. The king and three Hebrew young men (Dan. 3)

1. The king's command (3:1-7)

a. Nebuchadnezzar constructed a golden statue 90 feet high and nine feet wide.

b. This was set up in the plain of Dura near Babylon.

c. On dedication day, at a given musical signal, all his officials were to bow down and worship the image. Failure to do so would result in a fiery death. "Whoso falleth not down and worshippeth shall the same hour be cast into the midst of a burning fiery furnace" (3:6).

2. The Hebrews' stand (3:8-23)

a. Shadrach, Meshach, and Abed-nego refused to bow.

b. This was brought to the attention of the king by some jealous Babylonians. Nebuchadnezzar offered the Hebrews another chance. Upon their second refusal the three were bound and cast into a fiery furnace, heated seven times hotter than usual.

3. The Lord's own Man (3:24-30)

a. Peering into the furnace, an amazed king saw a fourth figure.

b. The three friends then walked out of the furnace unharmed, with not even the smell of smoke upon them.

c. Nebuchadnezzar issued a decree, making it a crime punishable by the death penalty to blaspheme the God of Israel.

STATISTICS

Father: Nabopolassar
First mention: 2 Kings 24:1
Final mention: Daniel 5:18
Meaning of his name: "Nabu protects"
Frequency of his name: Referred to 91 times
Biblical books mentioning him: Nine books (2 Kings, 1 Chronicles, 2 Chronicles, Ezra, Nehemiah, Esther, Jeremiah, Ezekiel, David)
Occupation: King of Babylon (2 Kings 24:1)
Important fact about his life: He was the founder of the Neo-Babylonian Empire and the one who cast three Hebrew men into a furnace of fire (Dan. 4:30; 3).

✒ *Nebuzar-Adan*

CHRONOLOGICAL SUMMARY

I. He burned the temple of Judah.

A. Nebuzar-adan was the Babylonian general who served as Nebuchadnezzar's royal bodyguard and chief of staff (2 Kings 25:8).

B. He supervised the burning of the temple and the tearing down of Jerusalem's walls (2 Kings 25:9-10).

II. He executed the high priest of Judah—Nebuzar-adan brought Seraiah the high priest to Nebuchadnezzar and, at the king's command, had him executed (2 Kings 25:18-21).

III. He separated the people of Judah, placing them in one of two groups (2 Kings 25:18-22; Jer. 52:30; 39:10).

A. Some were sent away into the Babylonian Captivity. Five years later, he returned and carried off more Jews into Babylon.

B. Others were left to care for the crops and vineyards.

IV. He released the prophet of Judah—Nebuzar-adan freed Jeremiah from prison where Judean King Zedekiah had placed him, and returned the prophet to his own house (Jer. 39:11-14).

V. He appointed the post-war governor of Judah—Nebuzar-adan placed a Jew by the name of Gedaliah as governor over Judah after the temple was destroyed (Jer. 41:10).

STATISTICS

First mention: 2 Kings 25:8
Final mention: Jeremiah 52:26
Meaning of his name: "Nabu has given offspring"
Frequency of his name: Referred to 14 times
Biblical books mentioning him: Two books (2 Kings, Jeremiah)
Occupation: Military commander (2 Kings 25:8)
Important fact about his life: He was the military commander-in-chief under Nebuchadnezzar (2 Kings 25:8).

✏Nehemiah

CHRONOLOGICAL SUMMARY

I. The news concerning the wall (chapter 1)

A. Learning—The information: In December of 446 B.C., Nehemiah learned of the pitiful state of Jerusalem from a returning Jew named Hanani, his own brother (1:2; 7:2). The report broke his heart (1:3-4).

B. Lamenting—The intercession: Upon hearing this, Nehemiah began a time of confession and intercession (1:4-11).

1. He addressed the God of heaven, a special title for God during the captivity (1:5).

2. He identified with his people Israel and their sin (1:6).

3. He acknowledged the righteousness of God in punishing his people (1:7).

4. He reminded God of his promise to regather his people (1:8-10).

5. He asked God to soften the heart of the king (1:11; see also Ezra 4:21).

II. The request to build the wall (2:1-8)

A. In April of 445 B.C., after a prayer period of four months, Nehemiah asked the king to . . . "Send me unto Judah, unto the city of my fathers' sepulchres, that I may build it" (2:5).

B. Artaxerxes agreed to give Nehemiah the necessary assistance.

III. The necessity for the wall (2:9-20)—Soon after reaching Jerusalem, Nehemiah made a secret midnight ride around the city itself. The next morning he assembled Judah's leaders and shared with them the burden of his heart (2:17-18).

A. His evaluation—"The wall and the gates are burned with fire."

B. His exhortation—"Let us rise up and build!"

C. It may be concluded that there were at least two compelling reasons for building the wall:

1. It was necessary for protection, to keep the outsiders out. This would protect against sneak attacks (7:1-3).

2. It was necessary for separation, that is, to keep the insiders in. This would cut down on the growing worldliness of the Jews who had been associating freely with the surrounding pagan people.

IV. The gates in the wall (3)—The various gates mentioned here are in themselves a beautiful picture summary of the Christian life:
   A. The sheep gate—This speaks of the cross (Neh. 3:1; John 10:11).
   B. The fish gate—This speaks of soul winning (Neh. 3:3; Matt. 4:19).
   C. The old gate—This speaks of our old nature (Neh. 3:6; Rom. 6:1-23).
   D. The valley gate—This speaks of sufferings and testing (Neh. 3:13; 2 Cor. 1:3-5).
   E. The dung gate—This speaks of the works of the flesh (Neh. 3:14; Gal. 5:16-21).
   F. The fountain gate—This speaks of the Holy Spirit (Neh. 3:15; John 7:27-30).
   G. The water gate—This speaks of the Word of God (Neh. 3:26; John 4:10-14).
   H. The horse gate—This speaks of the believer's warfare (Neh. 3:28; Eph. 6:10-17).
   I. The east gate—This speaks of the return of Christ (Neh. 3:29; Ezek. 43:1-2).
   J. The Miphkad gate—This was thought to be the judgment gate and therefore speaks of the judgment seat of Christ (Neh. 3:31; 1 Cor. 3:9-15; 2 Cor. 5:10).
V. The opposition to the wall—"When Sanballat the Horonite, and Tobiah the servant, the Ammonite, heard of it, it grieved them exceedingly that there was come a man to seek the welfare of the children of Israel" (Neh. 2:10). A work for God will always be met by both human and Satanic opposition. These combined forces did their perverted best to halt the wall building. Many methods were employed to accomplish this.
   A. Ridicule (4:1-3)
      1. "They laughed us to scorn."
      2. "Sanballat . . . mocked the Jews" (4:1).
      3. "Tobiah . . . said, Even that which they build, if a fox go up, he shall even break down their stone wall" (4:3).
   B. Discouragement—"Judah said, The strength of the bearers of burdens is decayed, and there is much rubbish; so that we are not able to build the wall" (4:10).
   C. Conspiracy (4:7-8, 11)—"They were very wroth, and conspired all of them together to come and to fight against Jerusalem, and to hinder it" (4:7-8). "Our adversaries said, They shall not know, neither see, till we come in the midst among them, and slay them, and cause the work to cease" (4:11).
   D. Laziness—"Next unto them the Tekoites repaired; but their nobles put not their necks to the work of their Lord" (3:5).
   E. Internal strife—Some of the more well-to-do Jews were guilty of extortion toward their less fortunate countrymen (5:1-5).
   F. Compromise (6:1-4)
      1. Nehemiah's enemies' proposal—"Come, let us meet together. . . . But they thought to do me mischief" (6:2).
      2. Nehemiah's answer—"I am doing a great work, so that I cannot come down" (6:3).
   G. Slander—Sanballat spread vicious rumors that Nehemiah was actually plotting to become king and revolt against Persia (6:5-9).
   H. Treachery (6:10-14)—"Shemaiah claimed to have a special revelation about a plot against Nehemiah's life and suggested that the Holy Place in the Temple would be the only safe place for Nehemiah. But the suggestion unmasked Shemaiah's treachery, since only the priests could enter the Holy Place (Num. 18:7). If Nehemiah had done so, his testimony would have been ruined" (*The Ryrie Study Bible*, p. 718).
   I. Outright fear (6:9, 14)—"They all made us afraid, saying, Their hands shall be weakened from the work, that it be not done. Now therefore, O God, strengthen my hands" (Neh. 6:9).

VI. The builder of the wall—Nehemiah
   A. He set an unselfish example for all
      the people (5:14-18).
      1. During his entire 12-year ministry
         as governor, Nehemiah took no
         salary (5:14).
      2. In fact, he paid for the food con-
         sumed by 150 of his helpers (5:17-
         18).
      3. He worked hard on the wall him-
         self (5:16).
      4. He loaned money to needy Jews
         without interest (5:10).
   B. He displayed total confidence in God
      both during and following the build-
      ing of the wall (4:14; 8:9-10).
      1. Before—"I looked, and rose up,
         and said unto the nobles, and to
         the rulers, and to the rest of the
         people, Be not ye afraid of them:
         remember the LORD, which is
         great and terrible, and fight for
         your brethren, your sons, and
         your daughters, your wives, and
         your houses" (4:14).
      2. After—"Then he said unto them,
         Go your way, eat the fat, and
         drink the sweet, and send por-
         tions unto them for whom noth-
         ing is prepared: for this day is
         holy unto our LORD: neither be ye
         sorry; for the joy of the LORD is
         your strength" (8:10).
   C. He refused to compromise (2:20).
   D. He prayed constantly (4:4-5, 9; 6:9).
   E. He contended for the faith (4:16-23).
      1. Nehemiah assigned half the men
         to work, carrying building tools,
         and the other half to stand guard,
         carrying weapons.
      2. A trumpeter stood by Nehemiah's
         side ready to sound the alarm at a
         moment's notice.
      3. All the workers toiled from sun-
         rise to sunset, not even taking
         time to wash their clothes.
VII. Blessings of the completed wall—In
     spite of all the persecution and hard-
     ships, Nehemiah had the wall up and
     completed in early September, just 52

days after they had begun (6:15-16). "It
came to pass, that when all our enemies
heard thereof, and all the heathen that
were about us saw these things, they
were much cast down in their own
eyes: for they perceived that this work
was wrought of our God" (6:16). It resulted in many blessings indeed, including:
   A. The reading of the Word of God (8:1-8;
      9:3)
      1. Ezra stood and read it for six
         hours (8:3).
      2. He stood on a specially built
         wooden podium (8:4).
      3. Various Bible teachers helped the
         crowd to understand what was
         being read (8:8). "They read in the
         book in the law of God distinctly,
         and gave the sense, and caused
         them to understand the reading"
         (8:8).
   B. The restoration of the feast of taber-
      nacles (8:13-18)
   C. The prayer recitation of Israel's his-
      tory (9:6-38)—In this remarkable pub-
      lic prayer, the Levites summarized:
      1. The creation of the world (9:6)
      2. The history of Israel
         a. From Abraham to Moses (9:7-8)
         b. From Moses to Joshua (9:9-23)
         c. From Joshua to the Judges
            (9:24-25)
         d. From the Judges to the Captiv-
            ity (9:26-30)
         e. From the Captivity to Nehemi-
            ah's time (9:31-37)
      3. The God of Israel
         a. Creator (9:6)
         b. Communicator (9:13)
         c. Leader (9:12)
         d. Sustainer (9:15, 21)
         e. Forgiver of sins (9:16-17)
         f. Instructor (9:20, 30)
   D. The ratification of a special covenant
      (9:38; 10:1-29)—"Because of all this
      we make a sure covenant, and write
      it; and our princes, Levites, and
      priests, seal unto it" (9:38).
      1. They would not marry heathens.

2. They would keep the Sabbath and holy days free from commercial activity.
3. They would observe the sabbatical year.
4. They would support the temple.

E. The repopulating of the city of David—Lots were cast to bring one tenth of the country's population into Jerusalem (11:1-2).

F. The renunciation of sins
   1. Of ungodly alliances (9:1-3; 13:3)
   2. Of untithed money (10:32-39; 12:44-47; 13:10-12)
   3. Of unlawful Sabbath work (10:31; 13:15-22)
   4. Of unequal marriages (10:30; 13:23, 25)
   5. Of unauthorized usage of the temple (13:1-10)
      a. Nehemiah's fantastic zeal and fearless actions helped bring into being all this repentance over sin.
      b. Nehemiah had gone back to Persia for awhile (13:6), but upon returning he discovered several very disquieting things:
         (1) Eliashib, the temple high priest, had actually converted a storage room into a beautiful guest room for (of all people) Israel's enemy, Tobiah.
         (2) Eliashib was the grandson of Joshua the high priest.
         (3) Nehemiah ordered Tobiah to leave, and threw out all his belongings from the room (13:9).
         (4) He then had to regather the temple choir, which had dissolved during his absence (13:10).
      c. His last recorded act was to chase off Joiada (the very son of Eliashib, the high priest) because of his unlawful marriage to Sanballat's daughter. (13:28).

G. The rejoicing of all the remnant— When God's work is done in God's way, joy will follow. Note the various references to this.
   1. The thanksgiving from within
      a. The people sent presents to each other and ate festive meals. "All the people went their way to eat, and to drink, and to send portions, and to make great mirth, because they had understood the words that were declared unto them" (8:12).
      b. The Levitical choir sang and played with cymbals, psalteries, and harps (9:4; 12:27-28).
      c. Nehemiah divided the people into two groups. Each walked in opposite directions upon the completed wall singing their songs of praise to God (12:31-39).
      d. Ezra led a special corps of trumpet playing priests (12:35-37).
   2. The testimony from without—The result of all this was that the joy of Jerusalem was heard from afar off (12:43).

THEOLOGICAL SUMMARY

I. Nehemiah was the younger contemporary of Ezra.
   A. Ezra was a priest and Bible teacher. His main job concerned the purification of the people of Israel.
   B. Nehemiah was a politician and builder. His main job concerned the protection of the people of Israel.
II. His is the only completely autobiographical book in the Bible.
III. His book marks the end of historical chronology in the Old Testament.
IV. Nehemiah was the royal cupbearer for Artaxerxes, the king of Persia (Neh. 2:1)
V. He led the final (of three) Jewish returns from Persia back to Judah.
   A. Zerubbabel led the first (Ezra 3:8).

B. Ezra led the second (Ezra 7:1).

C. Nehemiah led the third (Neh. 2:9).

VI. Nehemiah participated in the final of eight Israelite Old Testament revivals. These were:

A. During the days of Samuel (1 Sam. 7:3-6)

B. During the days of Rehoboam (2 Chron. 12:5-7)

C. During the days of Asa (2 Chron. 14:1-6)

D. During the days of Joash and Jehoiada (2 Chron. 23:16-21)

E. During the days of Hezekiah (2 Chron. 29:3-14)

F. During the days of Josiah (2 Chron. 34:3-33)

G. During the days of Ezra (Ezra 10:1-19)

H. During the days of Nehemiah (Neh. 8:1–9:3)

VII. He and Ezra made up the final of six famous Old Testament teams for God. These are:

A. Moses and Aaron

B. Joshua and Caleb

C. Elijah and Elisha

D. Zerubbabel and Joshua (Ezra 3:2)

E. Haggai and Zechariah (Ezra 5:1)

F. Ezra and Nehemiah (Neh. 8:9)

VIII. Nehemiah pinpointed the starting point of Daniel's prophecy concerning the 70 weeks.

A. The prophecy—"From the going forth of the commandment to restore and to build Jerusalem" (Dan. 9:25).

B. The beginning—"Let . . . me . . . come into Judah . . . to make beams for the gates . . . and for the wall of the city. . . . And the king granted me" (Neh. 2:7-8).

IX. The book of Nehemiah also includes the last of three great prayers of confession by a man of God concerning the sins of Israel.

A. Daniel's prayer (Dan. 9:3-19).

B. Ezra's prayer (Ezra 9:5-15)

C. Nehemiah's prayer (Neh. 1:4-11)

X. He provided for us the only listing of the names of the Jerusalem gates in the Bible (Neh. 3).

STATISTICS

Father: Hachaliah (Neh. 1:1)

Brother: Hanani (Neh. 1:2)

First mention: Nehemiah 1:1

Final mention: Nehemiah 12:47

Meaning of his name: "Jehovah is great"

Frequency of his name: Referred to five times

Biblical books mentioning him: One book (Nehemiah)

Occupation: Political leader, wall builder (Neh. 2)

Place of birth: Persia

Place of death: Jerusalem

Important fact about his life: He led the final Jewish return from Persia to Jerusalem and rebuilt the wall around the city (Neh. 7:1).

✎Nimrod

CHRONOLOGICAL SUMMARY

I. The accomplishments of Nimrod

A. Nimrod was a mighty warrior and hunter (Gen. 10:8, 9; 1 Chron. 1:10).

B. The heart of his empire included Babel in the land of Shinar (Gen. 10:10).

C. From there he extended his reign to Assyria, building the city of Nineveh and other settlements (Gen. 10:11-12).

D. Centuries later the prophet Micah referred to this entire area as the land of Nimrod (Mic. 5:6).

II. The apostasy of Nimrod

A. He may have been the organizer of the tower of Babel (Gen. 11:1-4).

B. Secular history and tradition tell us Nimrod married a woman named Semrimus, who claimed that their son, Tammuz, was the fulfillment of the promised seed referred to in Genesis 3:15.

STATISTICS

Father: Cush (Gen. 10:8; 1 Chron. 1:10)

Significant ancestors: His grandfather was Ham and great-grandfather was Noah (Gen. 10).

First mention: Genesis 10:8
Final mention: 1 Chronicles 1:10
Meaning of his name: "Valiant, strong"
Frequency of his name: Referred to three times
Biblical books mentioning him: Two books (Genesis, 1 Chronicles)
Occupation: Warrior and hunter (Gen. 10:8-14)
Important fact about his life: He may have been the instigator of the tower of Babel (Gen. 10:10).

Noah

CHRONOLOGICAL SUMMARY

I. His spirituality
  A. Noah was born some 600 years before the great flood (Gen. 7:11).
  B. At birth he was named Noah by his father, who said: "This same shall comfort us concerning our work and toil of our hands, because of the ground which the LORD hath cursed" (Gen. 5:29).
  C. He was a righteous man, blameless among the people of his time, walking with God (Gen. 6:9).

II. His ship
  A. The order—God warned him 120 years in advance of a coming universal flood and ordered him to construct a ship (Gen. 6:3, 13-16).
    1. It was to be a floating rectangular box, made of cypress wood.
    2. It was to be 450 feet long, 75 feet wide, and 45 feet high.
  B. The occupants
    1. From the human community—Noah was to enter the ark, along with his wife, their three sons and their three wives (Gen. 6:18).
    2. From the animal community
      a. A male and female representing each species of unclean animal, bird, and reptile (Gen. 6:20)
      b. Seven males and seven females, representing each species of

clean animal and bird (Gen. 7:2-3)

III. His safety—For the next year Noah would remain in the ark, protected from the terrible water judgment outside (Gen. 7:11; 8:13-14).

IV. His sacrifice
  A. After the ark had settled on Mt. Ararat, Noah sent out a raven and a dove to determine the level of the water (Gen. 8:6-12).
  B. He was commanded to leave the ark (Gen. 8:15-19).
  C. He built an altar outside and offered up a clean animal for a burnt sacrifice (Gen. 8:20).
  D. He and his sons were commanded by God to be fruitful and increase in number (Gen. 9:1, 7).

V. His sign—God designated the rainbow as a sign to Noah, indicating two things (Gen. 8:21-22; 9:9-17):
  A. As long as the earth remained, there would be springtime and harvest, cold and heat, winter and summer, day and night.
  B. The earth would never again be destroyed through a great flood.

VI. His shame
  A. The failure
    1. Noah planted a vineyard and became drunk from its wine (Gen. 9:20-21).
    2. Ham (and his son Canaan) saw Noah's nakedness (Gen. 9:22).
    3. Shem and Japheth quickly covered their father's nakedness (Gen. 9:23).
  B. The foretelling
    1. Upon sobering up, Noah pronounced judgment upon Canaan for some undisclosed reason (Gen. 9:24-25).
    2. Noah then issued a threefold prediction.
      a. That the descendants of Canaan would serve the descendants of Shem and Japheth (Gen. 9:25)
      b. That the line of Shem would

become the blessed of the LORD (Gen. 9:26)

c. That God would extend the territory of Japheth and his descendants (Gen. 9:27)

3. Noah lived 350 years after the flood and died at age 950 (Gen. 9:28-29).

THEOLOGICAL SUMMARY

I. God referred to Noah in a prophecy given to Israel through Isaiah (Isa. 54:9).
   A. He said he once promised Noah he would never again destroy the world through a flood.
   B. He said he promised never to pour out his anger upon Israel again.
II. Noah's righteousness was favorably compared with that of Job and Daniel by the prophet Ezekiel (Ezek. 14:14, 20).
III. Jesus referred to Noah on two occasions.
   A. He warned that the great tribulation judgment would come as suddenly and unexpectedly upon its generation as did the great flood judgment upon Noah's generation (Matt. 24:39-40).
   B. He predicted the same godless conditions which once prevailed prior to the great flood in Noah's day would again prevail, just before the second coming of Christ (Matt. 24:37-38; Luke 17:26-27).
IV. Both Noah's fear of God and his faith are praised in the book of Hebrews (Heb. 11:7).
   A. His fear prompted him to build the ark.
   B. His faith saved his family and condemned the world.
V. Peter referred to Noah in each of his two epistles.
   A. He mentioned the universal disobedience of men and the marvelous patience of God in the days before the great flood (1 Pet. 3:20).
   B. He used Noah as an example, showing how God is able to do two things (2 Pet. 2:5, 9):

1. He is able to protect the righteous from judgment.
2. He is able to punish the unrighteous by judgment.

STATISTICS

Father: Lamech (Gen. 5:28)
Sons: Shem, Ham, and Japheth (Gen. 5:32)
Significant ancestors: His grandfather was Methuselah and his great-grandfather was Enoch (Gen. 5:21, 25).
First mention: Genesis 5:29
Final mention: 2 Peter 2:5
Meaning of his name: Referred to 50 times
Biblical books mentioning him: Nine books (Genesis, 1 Chronicles, Isaiah, Ezekiel, Matthew, Luke, Hebrews, 1 Peter, 2 Peter)
Occupation: Ship captain and vineyard owner (Gen. 7:1; 9:20)
Age at death: 950 (Gen. 9:28-29)
Important fact about his life: He built a ship and survived the flood (Gen. 6:9–8:19).

✒️Obadiah (1)

CHRONOLOGICAL SUMMARY

I. His ministry
   A. He was the Jewish superintendent of the palace during the reign of wicked King Ahab (1 Kings 18:3).
   B. He was a secret (and somewhat timid) believer who had hidden and fed 100 prophets of God in two caves during the bloody purge of Jezebel (1 Kings 18:3-4).
II. His mission—He was sent on a mission by Ahab to find water during a terrible drought (1 Kings 18:5-6).
III. His meeting (1 Kings 18:7-16)
   A. En route, Obadiah met Elijah the prophet.
   B. After some fearful objections, he granted Elijah's request and arranged a meeting between the prophet and Ahab.

STATISTICS

First mention: 1 Kings 18:3
Final mention: 1 Kings 18:16
Meaning of his name: "Servant of Jehovah"
Frequency of his name: Referred to seven times
Biblical books mentioning him: One book (1 Kings)
Occupation: Chief assistant to King Ahab (1 Kings 18:3)
Important fact about his life: He was Ahab's steward who once hid 100 prophets from Jezebel and met Elijah (1 Kings 18:7-13).

Obadiah (2)

CHRONOLOGICAL SUMMARY

I. The house of Edom, to be reduced by God (Obad. 1-16)
  A. Edom's contempt for God
    1. Their thankless heart (1-10)
    2. Their treacherous hand (10-14)
  B. Edom's condemnation by God (15-16)
II. The house of Jacob, to be restored by God (17-21)
  A. They would occupy the land of God.
  B. They would obey the Lamb of God.

THEOLOGICAL SUMMARY

I. Obadiah wrote the shortest Old Testament book.
II. He may have been the first of the minor prophets.
III. He was one of three prophets who wrote exclusively to a non-Jewish nation.
  A. Habakkuk wrote to Babylon.
  B. Nahum wrote to Assyria.
  C. Obadiah wrote to Edom.

STATISTICS

First mention: Obadiah 1:1
Final mention: Obadiah 1:1
Meaning of his name: "Servant of God"
Frequency of his name: Referred to one time

Biblical books mentioning him: One book (Obadiah)
Important fact about his life: He predicted the divine destruction of Edom (Obad. 1-14).

Obed-Edom

CHRONOLOGICAL SUMMARY

I. Obed-edom and the Ark—The background
  A. He was a Gittite (a native of Gath), and possibly Philistine (2 Sam. 6:10).
  B. David entrusted the Ark of the Covenant to Obed-edom for a 90-day period of time while it was en route to the city of Jerusalem following the tragic divine judgment upon Uzzah (2 Sam. 6:1-11).
II. Obed-edom and the Ark—The blessing
  A. During these three months God blessed Obed-edom and his entire household (2 Sam. 6:11).
  B. The Ark was taken from his house by David to Jerusalem (2 Sam. 6:12-15).

STATISTICS

First mention: 2 Samuel 6:10
Final mention: 1 Chronicles 15:25
Meaning of his name: "Servant of Edom"
Frequency of his name: Referred to eight times
Biblical books mentioning him: Two books (2 Samuel, 1 Chronicles)
Important fact about his life: He kept the Ark of the Covenant for a 90-day period in the time of David (2 Sam. 6:11; 1 Chron. 13:14).

Og

CHRONOLOGICAL SUMMARY

I. The size of Og
  A. He was the giant king of Bashan occupying that land east of the Sea of Galilee (Num. 21:33).

B. His bed was made of iron. It exceeded 13 feet in length and was six feet wide (Deut. 3:11).

II. The demise of Og

A. He was defeated by Joshua when he challenged Israel near Edrei, one of the royal cities in Bashan (Num. 21:33-35; Josh. 13:31).

B. Israel then captured and destroyed every one of the 60 cities controlled by Og (Deut. 3:4).

C. The Israelites killed Og with all his descendants Num. 21:35.

D. One-half of the tribe of Manasseh then took over the land of Og (Deut. 3:13).

E. The defeat of Og was used by Moses to encourage Israel just prior to their Jordan River crossing (Deut. 31:1-6).

F. News of Og's defeat struck fear in the hearts of those living in Jericho (Josh. 2:8-11).

G. This same fear later prompted the Gibeonites to deceive Joshua into signing a peace treaty with them (Josh. 9:1-13).

H. Years later, following the rebuilding of the wall around Jerusalem, the Levites mentioned Og's defeat in their prayer of praise to God (Neh. 9:22).

I. The psalmist referred to this event on two occasions (Pss. 135:11; 136:20).

STATISTICS

First mention: Numbers 21:33
Final mention: Psalm 136:20
Meaning of his name: "Long-necked giant"
Frequency of his name: Referred to 22 times
Biblical books mentioning him: Six books (Numbers, Deuteronomy, Joshua, 1 Kings, Nehemiah, Psalms)
Occupation: King of Bashan (Num. 21:33)
Important fact about his life: He was the giant king of Bashan defeated by the Israelites (Num. 21:33-35).

Oholiab

(See Aholiab)

CHRONOLOGICAL SUMMARY

I. The appointment of Oholiab—He was appointed by God himself to serve as Bazaleel's chief assistant in the construction of the tabernacle (Exod. 31:2, 6)

II. The abilities of Oholiab

A. He was a gifted teacher, instructing others in working with those materials that went into the building of the Tabernacle (Exod. 35:34-35; 36:1-2).

B. His special skill was in the area of engraving, weaving, and embroidering costly and colorful threads into fine linen cloth (Exod. 38:23).

Omri

CHRONOLOGICAL SUMMARY

I. His command

A. He was the sixth king of Northern Israel.

B. He reigned 12 years (1 Kings 16:23).

C. He was the father-in-law of Jezebel and father of Ahab (1 Kings 16:28, 30-31).

D. He was commander of Israel's army before defeating King Zimri and occupying his throne (1 Kings 16:16-17).

II. His capital—He built the city of Samaria and made it the capital of Northern Israel (1 Kings 16:24).

III. His corruption

A. He sinned even more than did the previous five Northern kings (1 Kings 16:25).

B. Years later the prophet Micah condemned Northern Israel for observing the evil ways of both Omri and Ahab (Mic. 6:16).

STATISTICS

Son: Ahab (1 Kings 16:28)
First mention: 1 Kings 16:16
Final mention: Micah 6:16

Meaning of his name: "Apportions"
Frequency of his name: Referred to 15 times
Biblical books mentioning him: Four books
  (1 Kings, 2 Kings, 2 Chronicles, Micah)
Occupation: Military leader, then king of
  Northern Israel (1 Kings 16:16)
Important fact about his life: He built the city
  of Samaria and made it the capital of
  Northern Israel (1 Kings 16:24, 28-29).

Onan

CHRONOLOGICAL SUMMARY

  I. Onan's disobedience
    A. He was the brother of Er, whom God
      had killed for wickedness (Gen. 38:7).
    B. Onan was commanded by his father
      Judah to marry Tamar, Er's widow,
      and raise up a child as the law re-
      quired (Gen. 38:8).
    C. Onan married Tamar but refused to
      father a child, spilling his seed before
      sexual contact (Gen. 38:9).
  II. Onan's death—He was executed by God
    for doing this (Gen. 38:10).

STATISTICS

Father: Judah (Gen. 38:3-4)
Brothers: Full brothers: Er and Shelah (Gen.
  38:3, 5). Half brothers: Pharez and Zerah
  (Gen. 38:29-30).
First mention: Genesis 38:4
Final mention: 1 Chronicles 2:3
Meaning of his name: "Strength"
Frequency of his name: Referred to six times
Biblical books mentioning him: Three books
  (Genesis, Numbers, 1 Chronicles)
Circumstances of death: He was killed by God
  (Gen. 38:8-10).
Important fact about his life: He was Judah's
  second son who refused to raise children
  for his older brother (Gen. 38:3-4, 8-10).

Othniel

CHRONOLOGICAL SUMMARY

  I. Othniel's wife—His wife, Achsah, (also
    his first cousin), was given to him by
    Caleb, her father, after Othniel defeated
    the Canaanite city of Kirjath-sepher
    (Josh. 15:16-17; Judg. 1:12-13).
  II. Othniel's warfare
    A. The accomplishments
      1. He was the first judge (military
        leader) mentioned in the book of
        Judges (Judg. 3:9).
      2. He delivered Israel from the cap-
        tivity of the enemy for 40 years
        (Judg. 3:11).
    B. The anointing (Judg. 3:10)—He did
      this through the power of the Holy
      Spirit.

STATISTICS

Father: Kenaz (Josh. 15:17)
Spouse: Achsah (Josh. 15:17)
Sons: Hathath and Meonothai (1 Chron.
  4:13-14)
Brother: Seraiah (1 Chron. 4:13)
First mention: Joshua 15:17
Final mention: 1 Chronicles 27:15
Meaning of his name: "God is Force"
Frequency of his name: Referred to seven
  times
Biblical books mentioning him: Three books
  (Joshua, Judges, 1 Chronicles)
Occupation: Soldier and judge (Josh. 15:16-
  17; Judg. 3:7-11)
Important fact about his life: He was Caleb's
  nephew and a judge who brought 40
  years of peace to Israel (Josh. 15:17; Judg.
  3:7-11).

Pashur

CHRONOLOGICAL SUMMARY

  I. The prejudice of Pashur
    A. He was the chief officer in the temple
      during Jeremiah's time (Jer. 20:1).

B. He had Jeremiah beaten and put in prison stocks (Jer. 20:2).
II. The prophecy against Pashur
A. Upon his release, Jeremiah renamed this wicked official, calling him Magor-missabib, meaning "terror on every side" (Jer. 20:3).
B. Jeremiah then issued a threefold prophecy against Pashur (Jer. 20:4-6).
1. He would become a terror both to himself and to all his friends.
2. He would witness their deaths by the Babylonians.
3. He himself, along with his family, would go into Babylonian exile, never to return to Jerusalem.

STATISTICS

Father: Immer (Jer. 20:1)
Son: Gedaliah (Jer. 38:1)
First mention: Jeremiah 20:1
Final mention: Jeremiah 38:1
Meaning of his name: "Free"
Frequency of his name: Referred to six times
Biblical books mentioning him: One book (Jeremiah)
Occupation: Chief officer in the temple (Jer. 20:1)
Place of birth: Jerusalem
Place of death: Babylon (Jer. 20:6)
Important fact about his life: He was the chief temple officer who had Jeremiah beaten and imprisoned (Jer. 20:2).

✍Pekah

CHRONOLOGICAL SUMMARY
I. Pekah and Pekahiah
A. Pekah was the eighteenth ruler of Northern Israel.
B. He ruled for 20 years (2 Kings 15:27).
C. He was an officer in Pekahiah's army (2 Kings 15:25).
D. He then murdered Pekahiah to obtain his throne (2 Kings 15:25).
E. Pekah was an evil king (2 Kings 15:28).

II. Pekah and Tiglath-pileser—During his reign, the Assyrian King Tiglath-pileser invaded the land and carried off many Israelites into captivity (2 Kings 15:29).
III. Pekah and Ahaz
A. Pekah joined military forces with Rezin, the king of Syria, in an effort to destroy Jerusalem when Ahaz was king of Judah.
B. God told Isaiah the prophet to reassure Ahaz that this alliance would fail (Isa. 7:1, 7).
C. Pekah did, however, succeed in killing 120,000 men of Judah in a single day. God allowed this because of Judah's sin (2 Chron. 28:6).
IV. Pekah and Hoshea—Hoshea conspired against and murdered Pekah to obtain his throne (2 Kings 15:30).

STATISTICS

Father: Remaliah (2 Chron. 28:6)
First mention: 2 Kings 15:25
Final mention: Isaiah 7:1
Meaning of his name: "Watchfulness"
Frequency of his name: Referred to 11 times
Biblical books mentioning him: Three books (2 Kings, 2 Chronicles, Isaiah)
Occupation: King of Northern Israel (2 Kings 15:23-25)
Circumstances of death: He was killed by Hoshea (2 Kings 15:30).
Important fact about his life: He attacked Judah, killing 120,000 of their soldiers in one day (2 Chron. 28:6).

✍Pekahiah

CHRONOLOGICAL SUMMARY
I. The apostate king
A. He was the seventeenth ruler of Northern Israel.
B. He ruled for two years (2 Kings 15:23).
C. He was an evil king (2 Kings 15:24).
II. The assassinated king—One of his army commanders named Pekah conspired

against him and killed him in his own palace (2 Kings 15:25).

STATISTICS

Father: Menahem (2 Kings 15:22)
First mention: 2 Kings 15:22
Final mention: 2 Kings 15:26
Meaning of his name: "God watches"
Frequency of his name: Referred to three times
Biblical books mentioning him: One book (2 Kings)
Occupation: King of Northern Israel (2 Kings 15:23)
Place of death: In his palace at Samaria (2 Kings 15:25)
Circumstances of death: He was killed by Pekah (2 Kings 15:25).
Important fact about his life: He was the son of Menahem and the seventeenth king of Northern Israel (2 Kings 15:22).

✍*Peninnah*

CHRONOLOGICAL SUMMARY

I. Peninnah and Elkanah
  A. She was one of his two wives (1 Sam. 1:2).
  B. She had children by him (1 Sam. 1:2).
II. Peninnah and Hannah
  A. Hannah was the other wife of Elkanah.
  B. She was barren (1 Sam. 1:2).
  C. Peninnah constantly taunted Hannah for her barrenness, laughing and scoffing at her, causing her great affliction of soul (1 Sam. 1:6-7).

STATISTICS

Spouse: Elkanah (1 Sam. 1:1, 2)
First mention: 1 Samuel 1:2
Final mention: 1 Samuel 1:4
Meaning of her name: "Pearl"
Frequency of her name: Referred to two times
Biblical books mentioning her: One book (1 Samuel)
Important fact about her life: She ridiculed Hannah for her barrenness (1 Sam. 1:6).

✍*Phinehas* (1)

CHRONOLOGICAL SUMMARY

I. Phinehas and the transgressors
  A. He succeeded his father Eleazar and became Israel's third high priest (Num. 25:10-13).
  B. He was greatly blessed by God (1 Chron. 9:20).
  C. He slew a defiant Israelite man named Zimri along with his Midianite mistress, Cozbi, during the rebellion in the days of Balaam, and thus stopped a divine plague in the camp (Num. 25:1-9).
  D. For this action God promised that both he and his descendants would have a lasting priesthood (Num. 25:10-13).
  E. This event is referred to in the Psalms (Ps. 106:30-31).
II. Phinehas and the tribes
  A. He prevented an intertribal war in the days of Joshua—Phinehas headed up a fact-finding peace committee which narrowly prevented a civil war between the 12 tribes due to a misunderstanding in the latter days of Joshua's rule (Josh. 22:13, 30-33).
  B. He proclaimed an intertribal war in the days of the judges—He sent the 11 Israelite tribes to war against the tribe of Benjamin (Judg. 20:26-28).

STATISTICS

Father: Eleazar (Exod. 6:25)
Son: Abishua (1 Chron. 6:4)
Significant descendants: Ezra and Zadok (1 Chron. 6:8; Ezra 7:1-5)
First mention: Exodus 6:25
Final mention: Psalm 106:30
Meaning of his name: "Oracle"
Frequency of his name: Referred to 14 times
Biblical books mentioning him: Seven books (Exodus, Numbers, Joshua, Judges, 1 Chronicles, Ezra, Psalms)
Occupation: High priest (Josh. 22:30-32)
Important fact about his life: He was Israel's

third high priest (Exod. 28:1; Num. 20:25, 26; Josh. 22:30-32).

✐Phinehas (2)

CHRONOLOGICAL SUMMARY

I. Phinehas, the corrupt priestly son of Eli
   A. The nature of this corruption
      1. Both Phinehas and his brother Hophni were wicked priests (1 Sam. 2:12).
      2. They were dishonest and greedy in handling the tabernacle offerings, and they threatened the people (1 Sam. 2:12-16).
      3. They actually committed adultery with the women who came to the tabernacle (1 Sam. 2:22).
   B. The reason for this corruption— Neither son had been properly disciplined by Eli (1 Sam. 2:23-25; 3:13).
II. Phinehas, the condemned priestly son of Eli
   A. His destruction foretold
      1. God determined to destroy both wicked sons (1 Sam. 2:25).
      2. A prophet warned Eli they would die on the same day (1 Sam. 2:34).
   B. His destruction fulfilled
      1. In an attempt to rally the frightened Israelite troops, Hophni and Phinehas carried the Ark of the Covenant into a battle with the Philistines (1 Sam. 4:4).
      2. Israel lost the battle, the Ark of the Covenant was captured, and both Phinehas and Hophni were killed (1 Sam. 4:10-11).
      3. Upon learning of her husband's death, and of the fate of the Ark, Phinehas' wife, who was herself dying in childbirth, named her infant son Ichabod, meaning "the glory of the LORD has departed" (1 Sam. 4:19-22).

STATISTICS

Father: Eli (1 Sam. 1:3)
Son: Ichabod (1 Sam. 4:19-22)
Brother: Hophni (1 Sam. 1:3)
First mention: 1 Samuel 1:3
Final mention: 1 Samuel 14:3
Meaning of his name: "Oracle"
Frequency of his name: Referred to six times
Biblical books mentioning him: One book (1 Samuel)
Occupation: Priest (1 Sam. 1:3)
Place of death: On a battlefield near Shiloh (1 Sam. 4:10-12, 17)
Circumstances of death: He was killed by the Philistines (1 Sam. 4:17).
Important fact about his life: He was the godless son of Eli, whose dying wife gave birth to Ichabod (1 Sam. 2:12-17, 22; 4:19-22).

✐Potiphar

CHRONOLOGICAL SUMMARY

I. Potiphar and his faithful servant
   A. He was an Egyptian captain of Pharaoh's guard to whom Joseph was sold as a slave (Gen. 37:36; 39:1).
   B. He placed the loyal and capable Joseph in charge of his entire household estate (Gen. 39:5).
II. Potiphar and his faithless spouse—He later believed the lying accusations of his wife (Gen. 39:7-20).
   A. What she said—After Joseph refused her sexual advances, Potiphar's wife accused him of attempted rape.
   B. What he did—The foolish Potiphar believed his wife's lie and had the innocent Joseph thrown into prison.

STATISTICS

First mention: Genesis 37:36
Final mention: Genesis 39:1
Meaning of his name: "Belonging to the sun-god Ra"
Frequency of his name: Referred to four times
Biblical books mentioning him: One book (Genesis)

Occupation: Captain of Pharaoh's guard (Gen. 39:1)

Important fact about his life: He purchased Joseph as a slave and later had him imprisoned (Gen. 39:1, 19-20).

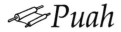

Puah

CHRONOLOGICAL SUMMARY

I. Puah and Shiphrah (Exod. 1:15-16)—These two courageous women were the chief midwives who were ordered by the Egyptian pharaoh to kill all Hebrew baby boys at birth.

II. Puah and God (Exod. 1:17-21)

A. Her resolve—She feared God and refused to carry out Pharaoh's command.

B. Her reward—God blessed her greatly, giving her children of her own.

STATISTICS

First mention: Exodus 1:15
Final mention: Exodus 1:15
Meaning of her name: "Mouth"
Frequency of her name: Referred to one time
Biblical books mentioning her: One book (Exodus)
Occupation: Midwife
Important fact about her life: She feared God and refused to kill the Hebrew male babies in Egypt (Exod. 1:17).

Rab-Shakeh

CHRONOLOGICAL SUMMARY

I. Rab-shakeh, the loudmouth

A. He was a chief officer of the Assyrian army under King Sennacherib, whose soldiers had surrounded the city of Jerusalem in the days of Judean King Hezekiah (2 Kings 18:13, 17).

B. He loudly and arrogantly demanded the surrender of the city (2 Kings 18:19-25).

1. He refuted the hope that Egypt would help the Jews.

2. He ridiculed the hope that God would help the Jews.

C. He added insult to injury by spouting all his demands in the Hebrew language so that those on the wall of Jerusalem could understand (2 Kings 18:26-28).

II. Rab-shakeh, the liar

A. He even claimed that the Lord himself had instructed him to destroy Jerusalem (2 Kings 18:25).

B. He called Hezekiah a liar for promising the people divine deliverance (2 Kings 18:29-35).

C. He promised the Jews a good life in a new land if they would surrender (Isa. 36:16-18).

D. He warned them, however, if they refused, they would be reduced to eating their own filth and drinking their own urine (2 Kings 18:27).

STATISTICS

First mention: 2 Kings 18:17
Final mention: Isaiah 37:8
Meaning of his name: "Head of cupbearers"
Frequency of his name: Referred to 16 times
Biblical books mentioning him: Two books (2 Kings, Isaiah)
Occupation: A chief officer of the Assyrian army (2 Kings 18:13, 17)
Important fact about his life: He was one of Sennacherib's chief officers when the Assyrians surrounded Jerusalem (2 Kings 18:17).

Rachel

CHRONOLOGICAL SUMMARY

I. Her husband

A. She was the youngest daughter of Laban, brother of Rebekah (Gen. 29:5-6, 16).

B. She worked as a shepherdess and was a beautiful girl (Gen. 29:9, 17).

C. Jacob worked a total of 14 years for her hand in marriage (Gen. 29:18-20, 26-30).

II. Her handmaid
  A. Laban presented her with Bilhah to serve as her handmaid (Gen. 29:29).
  B. Rachel was barren for a number of years (Gen. 29:31).
  C. Rachel then presented Bilhah to Jacob, hoping that she could bear children to Jacob through her handmaid (Gen. 30:1-3).

III. Her sister
  A. She became jealous of her sister's fruitful womb and demanded that Jacob give her children, lest she die (Gen. 30:1).
  B. She even ate some mandrake plants in hope that this would help her bear children (Gen. 30:14-16).
  C. She, along with her sister Leah, encouraged Jacob to leave his father-in-law (and their father) Laban and return to Canaan (Gen. 31:14-16).

IV. Her father
  A. Rachel stole her father's household gods before they left for Canaan (Gen. 31:19).
  B. She hid them inside her camel's saddle, and lied about taking them, thus preventing Laban from finding them when he caught up with Jacob in the wilderness (Gen. 31:34-35).

V. Her sons
  A. She gave birth to Joseph in Haran (Gen. 30:23-24).
  B. She gave birth to Benjamin near Bethlehem (Gen. 35:16-20).
    1. Realizing she was dying in childbirth, Rachel named him Ben-oni, meaning "son of my trouble."
    2. However, Jacob called him Benjamin, meaning "son of my right hand."
    3. A special pillar was made by Jacob and placed over her grave (Gen. 35:20).

THEOLOGICAL SUMMARY
I. Years later a doubtful Saul was told by Samuel he would meet two men by Rachel's tomb with a reassuring message concerning his role as Israel's first king (1 Sam. 10:2).

II. Because of Rachel's hard life, she would become a symbol for future Israelite mothers who wept over their children. Two historical events illustrated this.
  A. When Jewish mothers wept at Ramah over the deaths of their babies killed by Nebuchadnezzar (Jer. 31:15)
  B. When Jewish mothers wept at Bethlehem over the deaths of their babies killed by Herod (Matt. 2:18)

STATISTICS
Father: Laban (Gen. 29:16)
Spouse: Jacob (Gen. 29:18, 30)
Sons: Joseph and Benjamin (Gen. 30:23-24; 35:16-20)
Sister: Leah (Gen. 29:16)
First mention: Genesis 29:6
Final mention: Matthew 2:18
Meaning of her name: "Lamb"
Frequency of her name: Referred to 47 times
Biblical books mentioning her: Five books (Genesis, Ruth, 1 Samuel, Jeremiah, Matthew)
Place of death: Bethlehem (Gen. 35:16-20)
Circumstances of death: She died in childbirth (Gen. 35:16-20).
Important fact about her life: She was the beloved wife of Jacob and mother of both Joseph and Benjamin (Gen. 29:18; 30:23-24; 35:16-20).

✍*Rahab*

CHRONOLOGICAL SUMMARY
I. Her assistance to Israel's spies—She was a converted harlot living in Jericho who protected the two Israelite spies from being killed by the king of Jericho (Josh. 2:1-7).
II. Her assurance from the Israelite spies
  A. She asked and received assurance from the two men that she and her entire family would be spared when

the Israelite army defeated Jericho (Josh. 2:8-21).

B. Upon the defeat of the city, she and her loved ones were spared (Josh. 6:17, 23, 25).

C. She later married a man from the tribe of Judah named Salmon and bore him a son called Boaz (Matt. 1:5).

D. This made her the second mother-in-law to Ruth.

E. She would later become the great great grandmother of King David (Matt. 1:5-6).

F. Her name is mentioned in the genealogy leading to Christ himself (Matt. 1:1-16).

THEOLOGICAL SUMMARY

I. The New Testament refers to Rahab on two occasions, mentioning both the fact of her faith and the proof of her faith.

II. The fact of her faith is found in Hebrews 11:31.

III. The proof of her faith is found in James 2:25.

STATISTICS

Spouse: Salmon (Matt. 1:5)

Son: Boaz (Matt. 1:5)

Significant descendant: David (Matt. 1:5-6)

First mention: Joshua 2:1

Final mention: James 2:25

Meaning of her name: "Breadth"

Frequency of her name: Referred to eight times

Biblical books mentioning her: Four books (Joshua, Matthew, Hebrews, James)

Occupation: Former harlot (Josh. 2:1)

Place of birth: Jericho

Important fact about her life: She was Boaz's mother and the ex-harlot who saved the lives of the two Israelite spies in Jericho (Matt. 1:5; Josh. 2:6).

✐Rebekah

CHRONOLOGICAL SUMMARY

I. The diligence of Rebekah

A. She was the grand niece of Abraham (Gen. 24:15).

B. She grew up in Nahor, a town located in northwest Mesopotamia (Gen. 24:10).

C. She was a very beautiful girl (Gen. 24:16).

D. Abraham sent his servant Eliezer to Nahor that he might find a bride for Isaac (Gen. 24:1-4).

E. Outside the city, Eliezer prayed to be shown the girl he should select. God immediately answered, even before he had finished his prayer (Gen. 24:10-21).

1. Rebekah was the first girl to approach him beside a wall.

2. She volunteered to give him a drink and also to draw water for his camels, thus fulfilling the two signs Eliezer had asked God for.

II. The decision of Rebekah—She agreed to go with Eliezer and marry Isaac (Gen. 24:58-67)

III. The dilemma of Rebekah—After Rebekah remained barren for 20 years, God answered Isaac's prayer and she conceived (Gen. 25:21).

A. Her question: "The children struggled together within her; and she said, If it be so, why am I thus? And she went to enquire of the LORD" (Gen. 25:22).

B. Her answer—"The LORD said unto her, Two nations are in thy womb, and two manner of people shall be separated from thy bowels; and the one people shall be stronger than the other people; and the elder shall serve the younger" (Gen. 25:23).

IV. The deference of Rebekah

A. The twins were born and named— Esau, the firstborn, and Jacob (Gen. 25:24-26).

B. Rebekah unwisely preferred Jacob

over Esau as the boys were growing up (Gen. 25:28).

V. The distress of Rebekah

A. She was compromised by Isaac (Gen. 26:6-11).

1. In time of famine Isaac took Rebekah to the land of the Philistines and lied about her (as Abraham had once done to Sarah in Egypt), saying she was his sister.

2. Isaac was fearful he would be killed so that the Philistine ruler might marry Rebekah.

3. The lie was discovered, however, when the king saw them caressing each other.

B. She was concerned over Esau—His marriage to two pagan Hittite girls brought grief to Rebekah (Gen. 26:34-35).

VI. The deception of Rebekah

A. She overheard Isaac's plan to give Esau the blessing (Gen. 27:1-5).

B. She then instructed Jacob to pretend to be Esau and thus receive the blessing (Gen. 27:5-17).

C. Upon learning of Esau's plan to kill Jacob for cheating him, Rebekah sent her beloved son to her brother Laban in northwest Mesopotamia (Gen. 27:42-46).

VII. The death of Rebekah—She died and was buried along with Abraham and Sarah in the cave of Machpelah (Gen. 49:30-31).

THEOLOGICAL SUMMARY

In the New Testament, Paul referred to the birth of Rebekah's twin sons as an example of God's sovereign activities in human affairs (Rom. 9:10-13).

STATISTICS

Father: Bethuel (Gen. 22:23)
Spouse: Isaac (Gen. 24:67)
Sons: Esau and Jacob (Gen. 25:21-26)
Brother: Laban (Gen. 24:29)
First mention: Genesis 22:23
Final mention: Romans 9:10

Meaning of her name: "Flattering"
Frequency of her name: Referred to 29 times
Biblical books mentioning her: Two books (Genesis, Romans)
Place of birth: Nahor (Gen. 24:10)
Place of death: Hebron
Important fact about her life: She was Isaac's wife and Jacob's mother (Gen. 24:67; 25:26).

✍︎Rehoboam

CHRONOLOGICAL SUMMARY

I. The anointing of Rehoboam

A. He was the first king of Judah.

B. He ruled for 17 years (1 Kings 14:21).

C. He came to Shechem following the death of his father Solomon, to be anointed as Israel's fourth king (1 Kings 12:1).

D. He was 41 at the time (1 Kings 14:21).

II. The arrogance of Rehoboam

A. Receiving a sensible request

1. He was approached by some Israelite leaders representing the 10 northern tribes, requesting that he lighten the terrible tax load his father Solomon had imposed upon them (1 Kings 12:3-4).

2. Rehoboam asked for a three-day period in which to make his decision. He then sought counsel from two groups of individuals (1 Kings 12:5-11).

a. The elders who had once served Solomon—They advised him to grant Israel's request and make life easier for the people.

b. The young men who had grown up with Rehoboam— These immature and inexperienced individuals urged him to give the following answer: "My little finger shall be thicker than my father's loins. And now whereas my father did lade you with a heavy yoke, I will add to your yoke: my father hath chastised you with whips, but I will chastise you with scorpions" (1 Kings 12:10-11).

B. Returning a senseless reply

1. Rehoboam foolishly followed the advice of the young men and delivered the harsh and hateful decision to the elders (1 Kings 12:12-14).
2. This stupid action resulted in a civil war, for 10 of Israel's 12 tribes revolted against Rehoboam and proclaimed Jeroboam, a former official under Solomon, as their new king (1 Kings 12:16, 20).
3. To show their contempt for Rehoboam, the 10 tribes stoned to death Adoniram, the official in charge of forced labor (1 Kings 12:18).

III. The army of Rehoboam

A. Arriving back in Jerusalem, Rehoboam gathered an army of 180,000 men to crush the revolt, but was forbidden by God to fight against the 10 tribes (1 Kings 12:21-24).

B. In spite of God's command, there was continuous warfare between Rehoboam and Jeroboam (1 Kings 14:30).

C. To protect himself he fortified various towns in Judah, including Jerusalem, Bethlehem, and Hebron (2 Chron. 11:5-10).

IV. The apostasy of Rehoboam

A. The perversions involved—"When Rehoboam had established the kingdom, and had strengthened himself, he forsook the law of the LORD, and all Israel with him" (2 Chron. 12:1).

1. The people built pagan shrines under every green tree and upon every high hill (1 Kings 14:23).
2. There was an increase of sodomy and other vile sexual activities (1 Kings 14:24).
3. Rehoboam practiced polygamy, marrying 18 wives and 60 concubines (2 Chron. 11:21).
4. From these wives were born 28 sons and 60 daughters (2 Chron. 11:21).

B. The punishment involved

1. God allowed Shishak, the king of Egypt, to attack Jerusalem and carry off immense amounts of riches, including (1 Kings 14:22-28):
   a. The treasures of the temple
   b. The treasures of the royal palace
   c. The gold shields Solomon had made—To save face at this point, Rehoboam made bronze shields to replace them.
2. Rehoboam did (temporarily) humble himself, and thus God did not totally destroy Judah at this time (2 Chron. 12:12).

STATISTICS

Father: Solomon (1 Kings 11:43)
Mother: Naamah (1 Kings 14:21)
Spouses: Mahalath, Abihail, and Maachah are named among 18 wives and 36 concubines (2 Chron. 11:18-21).
Sons: Jeush, Shemariah, Zaham, Abijam, Attai, Ziza, and Shelomith are named among 28 sons and 36 daughters (2 Chron. 11:19-21; 1 Kings 14:31).
First mention: 1 Kings 11:43
Final mention: Matthew 1:7
Meaning of his name: "Freer of the people"
Frequency of his name: Referred to 50 times
Biblical books mentioning him: Four books (1 Kings, 1 Chronicles, 2 Chronicles, Matthew)
Occupation: King of Judah (1 Kings 14:21)
Place of birth: Jerusalem
Important fact about his life: He was Solomon's son and the first king over the southern kingdom of Judah (1 Kings 11:43–12:24).

✍*Reuben*

CHRONOLOGICAL SUMMARY

I. Reuben and Leah

A. He was the first son of Jacob through Leah (Gen. 29:32).

B. He brought some mandrake plants to his mother, hoping this would help her to bear more children (Gen. 30:14).

II. Reuben and Bilhah

A. He committed adultery with Bilhah, one of his father Jacob's wives (Gen. 35:22).

B. On his deathbed, Jacob reminded Reuben of and rebuked him for this immoral act (Gen. 49:3-4).

C. By this act Reuben forfeited his right as the firstborn son (1 Chron. 5:1).

III. Reuben and his brothers

A. The event at Dothan (Gen. 37:19-30)

1. He secretly attempted to prevent his nine brothers from killing Joseph, planning to bring the lad back to his father.

2. He succeeded in the first goal (Joseph was not killed), but failed to accomplish the second (Joseph was sold into slavery).

B. The event in Egypt—When he and the nine brothers ran into trouble years later at the hands of Joseph (whom they had not yet recognized), Reuben warned them it was due to their past sin against their younger half brother (Gen. 42:22).

IV. Reuben and Jacob—Reuben and Judah finally convinced a reluctant Jacob that Benjamin, youngest and most beloved remaining son of the old patriarch, be permitted to accompany the brothers on their second trip to Egypt for food, promising to assume full responsibility for his safety (Gen. 42:37; 43:8-10).

V. Reuben and Joseph—He later moved to Egypt along with Jacob and his brothers to live with Joseph (Gen. 46:5-7; Exod. 1:1-2).

STATISTICS

Father: Jacob (Gen. 29:21-32)
Mother: Leah (Gen. 29:32)
Sons: Hanoch, Phallu, Hezron, and Carmi (Gen. 46:9)
Brothers: Full brothers: Simeon, Levi, Judah, Issachar, and Zebulun (Gen. 35:23). Half

brothers: Dan, Joseph, Benjamin, Naphtali, Gad, and Asher (Gen. 35:24-26).
First mention: Genesis 29:32
Final mention: 1 Chronicles 5:3
Meaning of his name: "Behold, a son"
Frequency of his name: Referred to 26 times
Biblical books mentioning him: Six books (Genesis, Exodus, Numbers, Deuteronomy, Joshua, 1 Chronicles)
Important fact about his life: He was Jacob's first son (Gen. 35:23).

✑Rizpah

CHRONOLOGICAL SUMMARY

I. Rizpah, the mistress

A. She was the concubine of King Saul (2 Sam. 3:7).

B. After Saul's death his son Ishbosheth, who briefly succeeded him, accused Abner, commander of Saul's army, of sleeping with Rizpah (2 Sam. 3:7).

II. Rizpah, the mother

A. Later, her two sons were put to death by the Gibeonites and their bodies left exposed on a hill (2 Sam. 21:9).

B. The grieving Rizpah then took sackcloth and spread it out for herself on a rock (2 Sam. 21:10).

C. From the beginning of the harvest until the coming of the rains, she remained there, not letting the birds touch them by day or the wild animals by night (2 Sam. 21:10).

STATISTICS

Father: Aiah (2 Sam. 3:7)
Spouse: Saul (2 Sam. 3:7)
Sons: Armoni and Mephibosheth (2 Sam. 21:8)
First mention: 2 Samuel 3:7
Final mention: 2 Samuel 21:11
Meaning of her name: "Hot stone"
Frequency of her name: Referred to four times
Biblical books mentioning her: One book (2 Samuel)

Important fact about her life: She protected the dead bodies of her two sons (2 Sam. 21:10).

✍Ruth

CHRONOLOGICAL SUMMARY

I. Ruth in a pagan land—Moab
   A. Her travail
      1. Ruth was a Moabite girl who married Mahlon, eldest son of Elimelech and Naomi (Ruth 1:1-4; 4:10).
      2. After 10 years of marriage, Mahlon died (Ruth 1:5).
   B. Her testimony (Ruth 1:11-17)
      1. The decision of Ruth—Refusing to stay in Moab, as Naomi had strongly advised her to do, Ruth decided to accompany her mother-in-law back to Bethlehem and live there.
      2. The declaration of Ruth "Whither thou goest, I will go; and where thou lodgest, I will lodge: thy people shall be my people, and thy God my God" (Ruth 1:16).
II. Ruth in the Promised Land—Bethlehem
   A. Her missions for Naomi
      1. Reaping in a barley field
         a. Ruth met Boaz as she picked up the leftover grain in his field for Naomi and herself (Ruth 2:1-16).
            (1) Boaz praised her for the kindness she had shown to Naomi (who was a close relative) after the death of Elimelech.
            (2) He invited her to share his lunch.
            (3) He then privately instructed the harvesters to leave extra grain behind, thus making her work easier.
         b. Upon returning home Ruth told Naomi what had happened; Naomi immediately began planning for a wedding (Ruth 2:17-23).
      2. Requesting by a barley floor
         a. Ruth was instructed by Naomi to approach Boaz by night and request that he exercise his responsibility as a kinsman redeemer (Ruth 3:1-4).
         b. Ruth did this, but learned from Boaz that there was a closer kinsman than himself who first must agree concerning who would care for Naomi and Ruth (Ruth 3:5-16).
         c. Ruth was reassured by Naomi of Boaz's determination (Ruth 3:17-18).
   B. Her marriage to Boaz (Ruth 4:1-22)
      1. Boaz solved his legal problem and married Ruth.
      2. She gave birth to a boy named Obed.
      3. Ruth later became the great-grandmother of King David and occupied a place in the genealogy leading to Christ himself (Ruth 4:21-22; Matt. 1:5, 16).

STATISTICS
Spouses: Mahlon and Boaz (Ruth 4:10-13)
Son: Obed (Ruth 4:13, 17)
Significant descendant: David (Ruth 4:21-22)
First mention: Ruth 1:4
Final mention: Matthew 1:5
Meaning of her name: "Friendship"
Frequency of her name: Referred to 13 times
Biblical books mentioning her: Two books (Ruth, Matthew)
Important fact about her life: She was Boaz's wife and David's great grandmother (Ruth 4:13, 21-22).

✍Samson

CHRONOLOGICAL SUMMARY

I. His mission
   A. Samson's mother was visited by the angel of the Lord, who told her of his

future birth. "There was a certain man of Zorah, of the family of the Danites, whose name was Manoah; and his wife was barren, and bare not. And the angel of the LORD appeared unto the woman, and said unto her, Behold now, thou art barren, and bearest not: but thou shalt conceive, and bear a son" (Judg. 13:2-3).

B. This heavenly messenger instructed the parents that their child was to be raised a Nazarite (13:4, 5). According to Numbers 6:1-6, the Nazarite had three restrictions placed upon him.

    1. He was not to touch wine or any other product of the vine.

    2. His hair was to remain untouched by a razor.

    3. He must not touch a dead body. Note: Samson's mother was also commanded not to drink wine or eat any product of the vine (13:4, 14).

C. On this occasion Samson's parents prayed a prayer all expectant Christian parents should pray (13:8, 12). "Manoah intreated the LORD, and said, O my LORD, let the man of God which thou didst send come again unto us, and teach us what we shall do unto the child that shall be born. . . . And Manoah said, Now let thy words come to pass. How shall we order the child, and how shall we do unto him?" (13:8, 12)

D. Samson was born and empowered by the Holy Spirit even as he grew up (13:24-25).

II. His marriage

A. He determined to marry an unbelieving Philistine girl, to the dismay of his parents. Already Samson's carnal nature was coming to the surface. In spite of his sensuality, he was still used for God's glory (14:1-4).

B. En route to Philistia he killed a lion (14:5-6).

C. Later he discovered that a swarm of bees had chosen the carcass of the lion to make honey in it. At his wedding feast Samson used this experience as a basis for a riddle (Judg. 14:12-14). "Out of the eater came forth meat, and out of the strong came forth sweetness. And they could not in three days expound the riddle" (Judg. 14:14).

D. The guests eventually dishonestly solved this riddle, getting it from Samson's bride. He was furious at this and paid his debt to the wedding guests, but only at the expense of 30 Philistine victims (14:15-19).

E. He then went home in anger, leaving his wife with her father.

F. He returned the following harvest, only to find that the girl's father had given his bride to Samson's best man! In the act of revenge, the Hebrew strongman did the following: "Samson went and caught three hundred foxes, and took firebrands, and turned tail to tail, and put a firebrand in the midst between two tails. And when he had set the brands on fire, he let them go into the standing corn of the Philistines, and burnt up both the shocks, and also the standing corn, with the vineyards and olives" (15:4-5).

III. His miracles

A. He then killed many Philistines (15:8).

B. After this, the Philistines threatened to destroy the tribe of Judah unless they delivered Samson bound to them. Samson meekly allowed himself to be tied up, but as the enemy came in view he broke the ropes, grabbed the jawbone of an ass, and slaughtered 1,000 Philistines (15:9-17)!

C. He prayed one of his only two recorded prayers. Both were totally carnal and self-centered (Compare 15:18 with 16:28). "He was sore athirst, and called on the LORD, and said, Thou hast given this great deliverance into the hand of thy servant: and now shall I die for thirst, and fall into the hand of the uncircumcised? But God clave an hollow place that was in the jaw, and there came water thereout; and when he had drunk, his spirit came again, and he revived: wherefore he called the name thereof Enhakkore, which is in Lehi unto this day" (15:18, 19).

IV. His misconduct
   A. At Gaza (a Philistine city) Samson once again avoided capture, this time by tearing off the gate of the city (16:1-3). His purpose in going to Gaza was to visit a harlot!
   B. Samson was finally done in by a Philistine woman named Delilah, who discovered the source of his great strength (16:4-20). NOTE: At this point, Samson had probably violated all three Nazarite vows:
      1. He had touched the carcass of a lion (14:8, 9).
      2. He may have drunk wine at his wedding feast (14:10).
      3. He had allowed his hair to be cut (16:19).

V. His misery
   A. Samson now learned the high cost of low living. "The Philistines took him, and put out his eyes, and brought him down to Gaza, and bound him with fetters of brass; and he did grind in the prison house" (16:21).
   B. In prison he regained his strength as his hair grew out again.
   C. He was then allowed by God to destroy thousands of Philistines who had gathered in their heathen temple for a drunken orgy. In the following destruction Samson himself perished (16:22-31). "Samson called unto the LORD, and said, O Lord GOD, remember me, I pray thee, and strengthen me, I pray thee, only this once, O God, that I may be at once avenged of the Philistines for my two eyes. And Samson took hold of the two middle pillars upon which the house stood, and on which it was borne up, of the one with his right hand, and of

the other with his left. And Samson said, Let me die with the Philistines. And he bowed himself with all his might; and the house fell upon the lords, and upon all the people that were therein. So the dead which he slew at his death were more than they which he slew in his life" (16:28-30).

THEOLOGICAL SUMMARY
   I. Samson was the first of three famous biblical Nazarites.
      A. Samson (Judg. 13:4-5)
      B. Samuel (1 Sam. 1:11-28)
      C. John the Baptist (Luke 1:13-17)
   II. His faith is referred to in Heb. 11:32.

STATISTICS
Father: Manoah (Judg. 13:2)
Spouse: Unnamed wife (Judg. 14:10-18)
First mention: Judges 13:24
Final mention: Hebrews 11:32
Meaning of his name: "Distinguished, strong"
Frequency of his name: Referred to 36 times
Biblical books mentioning him: Two books (Judges, Hebrews)
Occupation: Judge (Judg. 15:20)
Place of death: At the arena at Gaza (Judg. 16:21-30)
Circumstances of death: He was crushed by a falling building (Judg. 16:30).
Important fact about his life: He was history's strongest man (Judg. 14:6, 19; 15:14).

✐Samuel

CHRONOLOGICAL SUMMARY
   I. The pre-ministry of Samuel—A boy in the tabernacle
      A. Hannah was his mother.
         1. Her prayer for her son
            a. Samuel was born as a result of God's answering Hannah's prayer and touching her barren womb (1 Sam. 1:2, 19, 20).
            b. He was promised to the Lord

even before his birth (1 Sam.
1:10-12).

c. He became the second of two
famous Old Testament
Nazarites. Samson was the first
(Judg. 13:7, 13-14; 1 Sam.
1:11).

2. Her presentation of her son—
After he was weaned, Hannah
dedicated him in the tabernacle
(1 Sam. 1:23-28).

B. Eli was his mentor

1. He then was raised for God's service by the old priest Eli in the
tabernacle (1 Sam. 2:11, 18, 21).

2. He was visited yearly by his
mother and presented with new
clothes (1 Sam. 2:19).

II. The ministry of Samuel—A prophet in
the land

A. Samuel, the anointed—Samuel and
God

1. His call

a. Samuel, like Jesus in the New
Testament, grew in stature and
in favor with God and men
(Compare 1 Sam. 2:26; 3:1 with
Luke 2:52).

b. God spoke to Samuel one night
as the lad lay on his cot in the
tabernacle (1 Sam. 3:1-14).

(1) He mistook the voice of God
for that of Eli on the first
two occasions.

(2) Realizing what was happen-
ing, Eli advised Samuel to
answer the mysterious voice
on the next occasion with
the words: "Speak, Lord; for
thy servant heareth" (1 Sam.
3:9).

(3) Samuel did this and heard a
fearful message from God
concerning the future di-
vinely caused deaths of Eli's
two wicked sons.

c. The next morning Samuel related all this to Eli (1 Sam. 3:15-
18).

d. Samuel now began a very fruitful ministry as a prophet
(1 Sam. 3:19-21).

(1) God let none of his words
fall to the ground.

(2) All of Israel recognized him
as a great prophet.

(3) God continued to reveal
himself to Samuel.

2. His covenant—Samuel led Israel
in a great revival (1 Sam. 7:1-13).

a. He ordered the people to assemble at Mizpeh.

b. The Philistines attacked this
assembled crowd but were destroyed by God.

c. Samuel then set aside a large
rock to commemorate all this,
naming it Ebenezer, meaning,
"hitherto hath the Lord helped
us."

3. His circuit—He established a
circuit-riding ministry, traveling
from Beth-el to Gilgal to Mizpeh,
judging Israel in all these places
(1 Sam. 7:15-16).

4. His city—Ramah became his
home and headquarters (1 Sam.
7:17).

B. Samuel, the anointer—Samuel and
Saul

1. Events leading to the crowning of
Saul

a. The request by Israel

(1) When he grew older, Samuel unwisely appointed his
ungodly sons, Joel and
Abiah, as judges over Israel
(1 Sam. 8:1-3).

(2) Because of this and other
reasons, the leaders of Israel
demanded that Samuel ap-
point a king to rule over
them (1 Sam. 8:4-5).

b. The revelation from God

(1) Samuel was displeased at
this request, but was told by
God Israel had rejected their
heavenly king and not their

earthly prophet (1 Sam. 8:6-7).

(2) God then instructed Samuel to grant their request, but to warn them of the consequences (1 Sam. 8:8-21).

  (a) The king would make soldiers of their sons.

  (b) Others would be forced into farming the ground.

  (c) Their daughters would become the king's cooks and bakers.

  (d) He would take the best of their fields, vineyards, and olive groves.

  (e) They would have a 10 percent tax enforced upon them.

(3) In spite of all these warnings, Israel still demanded a king!

(4) God told Samuel a man from the tribe of Benjamin would knock on his door the next day seeking information concerning some lost animals. The man's name was Saul and he would become Israel's first king (1 Sam. 9:1-18).

c. The reassurance to Saul

(1) When Saul arrived, Samuel told him all this and anointed him with oil (1 Sam. 9:19–10:1).

(2) Samuel then gave Saul four signs to confirm his divine selection (1 Sam. 10:2-7).

  (a) Two men would greet him at Rachel's tomb.

  (b) Three men would greet him by the plain of Tabor.

  (c) A procession of prophets would greet him at Gibeah.

  (d) Finally, Saul himself would be led by the Holy Spirit to prophesy with them.

d. The review by Samuel

(1) Samuel publicly anointed Saul at Mizpeh (1 Sam. 10:17-24).

(2) He then explained and reviewed for the people the regulations of the kingship and wrote them down (1 Sam. 10:25).

(3) After Saul had proven himself in battle (I Sam. 11:1-11), Samuel once again gathered the people, this time at Gilgal, to reaffirm the kingship (1 Sam. 11:14-15).

(4) At this time he delivered his final public speech (1 Sam. 12:1-25).

  (a) He reminded Israel of his faithful service to their nation.

  (b) He reminded them of God's faithfulness in the past and chided them for demanding a king.

  (c) He urged them to serve God from that day on.

  (d) He warned them of the consequences of disobedience.

  (e) He promised to pray for them.

  (f) He validated his message by praying down a thunder and rain storm.

2. Events following Saul's coronation

(1) The rejection of Israel's first king—Saul was set aside by God for two reasons.

  (a) For doing what he should not have done—Samuel severely rebuked Saul at Gilgal for intruding into the office of the priesthood by offering up a burnt sacrifice (1 Sam. 13:8-14).

i. Samuel told him his kingdom would not continue.

ii. God himself had sought out a man after his own heart.

(b) For not doing what he should have done—By order of the Lord, Samuel instructed Saul to attack the Amalekites and destroy everything, both people and livestock (1 Sam. 15:1-35).

  i. Saul disobeyed by sparing Agag, king of the Amalekites, and the best of the livestock (1 Sam. 15:7-9).

  ii. Samuel learned of all this from the Lord, who was grieved over Saul's disobedience. This caused the prophet to weep all that night (1 Sam. 15:10-11).

  iii. When Samuel confronted Saul about this on the following day, the disobedient king lied about it (1 Sam. 15:12-13).

  iv. He then attempted to shift the blame concerning why he had saved the best of the animals to the people, saying . . . "The people spared the best of the sheep and of the oxen, to sacrifice unto the LORD" (1 Sam. 15:15).

  v. Upon hearing this Samuel utterly condemned Saul, saying . . . "Behold, to obey is better than sacrifice,

and to hearken than the fat of rams. For rebellion is as the sin of witchcraft, and stubbornness is as iniquity and idolatry. Because thou hast rejected the word of the LORD, he hath also rejected thee from being king" (1 Sam. 15:22-23).

  vi. As Samuel turned to leave, Saul caught hold of his robe and tore it. Samuel told him God would likewise tear the kingdom from him and give it to one of the king's neighbors (1 Sam. 15:27-29).

  vii. Samuel then personally executed King Agag (1 Sam. 15:32-33).

  viii. This was the final meeting between Samuel and Saul before the death of the prophet (1 Sam. 15:34-35).

(2) The selection of Israel's finest king

  (a) Samuel was instructed to visit the home of Jesse in Bethlehem and anoint a new king (1 Sam. 16:1).

  (b) Following Samuel's instructions, Jesse paraded his seven sons before the prophet, but none were selected by God (1 Sam. 16:4-10).

  (c) Jesse's youngest son was finally brought in from the sheep pasture. At God's command, Samuel anointed this lad, David, as Israel's new king (1 Sam. 16:11-13).

  (d) Later David visited Samuel during that time

when Saul was attempting to kill him (1 Sam. 19:18).

III. The post-ministry of Samuel—A voice from the grave
A. The desperation of Saul
1. All Israel's leaders assembled at Ramah when Samuel died to mourn and honor their great prophet (1 Sam. 25:1; 28:3).
2. Sometime later a desperate Saul succeeded in contacting Samuel from the grave that he might ask the prophet concerning the outcome of a battle with the Philistines (1 Sam. 28:10-14).
B. The condemnation by Samuel— Samuel's stern answer was devastating to Saul (1 Sam. 28:15-20).
1. He reminded the king that God had rejected him because of disobedience.
2. He stated David would soon be Israel's new king.
3. He predicted Saul would not only be defeated in battle, but that both he and his sons would be killed!

THEOLOGICAL SUMMARY

I. Samuel probably wrote most of the material found in 1 Samuel and 1 Chronicles (1 Chron. 29:29-30).
II. The psalmist mentioned Samuel along with Moses and Aaron as three examples of God's faithfulness (Ps. 99:6).
III. Jeremiah refered to Samuel, along with Moses, to emphasize Israel's tragic sinful condition. "Then said the LORD unto me, Though Moses and Samuel stood before me, yet my mind could not be toward this people: cast them out of my sight, and let them go forth" (Jer. 15:1).
IV. Simon Peter used Samuel as a source of authority concerning the Messiah during his sermon by the temple gate called Beautiful (Acts 3:24).

V. Paul referred to Samuel during his message to the Jews in Pisidian Antioch (Acts 13:20).
VI. The author of Hebrews referred to the great faith of Samuel (Heb. 11:32).

STATISTICS

Father: Elkanah (1 Sam. 1:19-20)
Mother: Hannah (1 Sam. 1:19-20)
Sons: Joel and Abiah (1 Sam. 8:1-3)
Brothers: Three brothers (1 Sam. 2:21)
Sisters: Two sisters (1 Sam. 2:21)
First mention: 1 Samuel 1:20
Final mention: Hebrews 11:32
Meaning of his name: "Hand of God"
Frequency of his name: Referred to 134 times
Biblical books mentioning him: Seven books (1 Samuel, 1 Chronicles, 2 Chronicles, Psalms, Jeremiah, Acts, Hebrews)
Occupation: Prophet and priest (1 Sam. 3:1, 20)
Place of birth: Near Mt. Ephraim (1 Sam. 1:1, 19-20)
Place of death: Ramah (1 Sam. 25:1)
Important fact about his life: He anointed both Saul and David as king over Israel (1 Sam. 9:27–10:1; 16:13).

✍️*Sanballat*

CHRONOLOGICAL SUMMARY

I. The hostility of Sanballat
A. He was a Horonite who lived in Beth-horon, an area north of Jerusalem (Neh. 2:10).
B. He held a post in the Persian government during the days of Nehemiah (Neh. 2:10).
C. He co-conspired with Tobiah the Ammonite, and Geshem the Arab in attempting to prevent Nehemiah from rebuilding the wall around Jerusalem (Neh. 2:10, 19).
II. The harassment by Sanballat
A. He began by ridiculing the project (Neh. 2:19; 4:1-2).

B. He then became furious as the work progressed (Neh. 4:1-7).
C. He plotted to attack the workers (Neh. 4:8).
D. He attempted on five occasions to meet with Nehemiah, intending to harm or assassinate him (Neh. 6:1-9).
  1. On the fifth occasion, Sanballat threatened to accuse Nehemiah of treason against the king of Persia.
  2. On every instance however, Nehemiah refused to meet with Sanballat, saying he was far too busy with the work of the Lord to dialogue with an envoy of Satan.
E. Sanballat finally hired a friend of Nehemiah by the name of Shemaiah to betray him, but Nehemiah quickly saw through this plot (Neh. 6:10-13).
F. Sanballat did succeed in arranging for one of his daughters to marry a grandson of the Jewish high priest Eliashib (Neh. 13:28).

STATISTICS
First mention: Nehemiah 2:10
Final mention: Nehemiah 13:28
Meaning of his name: "Sin save the life"
Frequency of his name: Referred to 10 times
Biblical books mentioning him: One book (Nehemiah)
Occupation: An official in the Persian government (Neh. 2:9-10)
Important fact about his life: He was the chief troublemaker who opposed Nehemiah (Neh. 4:1-2).

✒Sarah

CHRONOLOGICAL SUMMARY
I. Sarai, her first name
  A. Sarai and her husband
    1. The trip to Canaan
      a. She was originally known as Sarai (Gen. 11:29).
      b. She was, along with her husband Abraham, probably born and raised in the city of Ur of the Chaldees.
      c. She was barren until God touched her womb (Gen. 11:30).
      d. She was probably converted to God about the same time Abraham became a believer.
      e. She followed her husband to Haran, and then to Canaan (Gen. 11:31; 12:5).
      f. She was 65 at this time (Gen. 12:4-5; 17:17).
    2. The trip to Egypt
      a. She was taken by Abraham to Egypt in time of a famine.
      b. Because of her great beauty, Abraham required that she pretend to be his sister, and not his wife, fearing Pharaoh might kill him in order to marry her.
      c. Believing this deception, Pharaoh did indeed consider marrying her, but was warned by God in a dream not to do this.
  B. Sarai and her handmaid
    1. In her frustration, the barren Sarai presented Hagar, her handmaid, to Abraham, planning to adopt the first son born by her (Gen. 16:1-3).
    2. Upon becoming pregnant however, Hagar's attitude angered Sarai, who mistreated Hagar until she fled into the desert (Gen. 16:4-6).
    3. At the command of God, Hagar returned to the camp and submitted herself to her mistress. Sarai was 76 at this time (Gen. 16:7-15).
II. Sarah, her final name
  A. Sarah and God
    1. Her name was changed by God from Sarai, meaning "contentious," to Sarah, meaning "princess." This occurred when she was 89 (Gen. 17:1, 15-17).
    2. God again told Abraham Sarah would bear him a child in his old age. Both the sex and name of the baby were predicted (Gen. 17:19).

a. It would be a boy.

b. He would be called Isaac.

3. Sarah and Abraham were visited by God and two angels. Sarah baked bread for them (Gen. 18:6).

4. As she sat in the tent, Sarah laughed in unbelief upon overhearing God tell Abraham that Isaac would be born the very next year (Gen. 18:9-15).

B. Sarah and Abimelech—She was once again forced to assume the role of sister to her fearful husband when the couple visited in Gerar, a Philistine city (Gen. 20:1-2).

C. Sarah and Isaac—At age 90, Sarah gave birth to Isaac (Gen. 21:1-7).

D. Sarah and Ishmael

1. On the day of Isaac's weaning, old hostilities between Sarah and Hagar once again surfaced. "Sarah saw the son of Hagar the Egyptian, which she had born unto Abraham, mocking" (Gen. 21:9).

2. Sarah's reaction was both swift and stern. "Wherefore she said unto Abraham, Cast out this bondwoman and her son: for the son of this bondwoman shall not be heir with my son, even with Isaac" (Gen. 21:10).

3. Sarah died at age 127 in the city of Hebron and was buried by Abraham in the cave of Machpelah (Gen. 23:1-2, 19).

THEOLOGICAL SUMMARY

I. Sarah was looked upon by God as being the mother of the nation of Israel (Isa. 51:1-2).

II. The New Testament writers referred to Sarah on several occasions.

A. To illustrate the power of God (Rom. 4:19)

B. To illustrate the sovereignty of God (Rom. 9:6-9)

C. To illustrate the faithfulness of God (Heb. 11:11)

D. Peter commended Sarah for her obe-

dience to Abraham and her inward beauty (1 Pet. 3:1-6).

STATISTICS

Father: Terah (Gen. 11:26; 20:12)

Spouse: Abraham (Gen. 11:29)

Son: Isaac (Gen. 21:1-7)

First mention: Genesis 11:29

Final mention: 1 Peter 3:6

Meaning of her name: "Princess"

Frequency of her name: Referred to 56 times

Biblical books mentioning her: Five books (Genesis, Isaiah, Romans, Hebrews, 1 Peter)

Place of death: Hebron (Gen. 23:1-2, 19)

Age at death: 127 (Gen. 23:1-2)

Important fact about her life: She was Abraham's wife and Isaac's mother (Gen. 11:29; 21:1-7).

Sargon II

CHRONOLOGICAL SUMMARY

I. Sargon and Shalmaneser V—Sargon seized the Assyrian throne when Shalmaneser died during the siege of Samaria.

II. Sargon and Isaiah (Isa. 20)

A. When Sargon captured the Philistine city of Ashdod, God told Isaiah the prophet to take off his clothes and walk around barefoot.

B. This action would illustrate what Sargon would later do to both Egypt and Ethiopia, literally stripping those nations of all their wealth.

C. Sargon was killed in 704 B.C. and succeeded by his son Sennacherib.

STATISTICS

Son: Sennacherib

First mention: Isaiah 20:1

Final mention: Isaiah 20:1

Meaning of his name: "Lawful king"

Frequency of his name: Referred to one time

Biblical books mentioning him: One book (Isaiah)

Occupation: King of Assyria (Isa. 20:1)

Important fact about his life: He completed the sacking of Samaria.

✍Saul

CHRONOLOGICAL SUMMARY

I. Saul, the seeker
  A. The servant and Saul
    1. Saul was from the tribe of Benjamin (1 Sam. 9:1-2).
    2. He was very tall and equally impressive (1 Sam. 9:2).
    3. He was sent by his father to look for some donkeys which had strayed away (1 Sam. 9:3).
    4. After a futile search, Saul determined to return home, lest his father begin to worry about him.
    5. Saul's servant, however, suggested they ask Samuel the seer (prophet) who lived in a nearby town if he could help them.
  B. The seer and Saul (1 Sam. 9:15–10:8).
    1. The announcements
      a. God's announcement to Samuel
        (1) On the previous day, God had told Samuel he would send a man to the prophet from the tribe of Benjamin within 24 hours.
        (2) Samuel was to anoint this man as Israel's first king.
      b. Samuel's announcement to Saul
        (1) At the meeting of the two men, God revealed to Samuel that Saul was the one.
        (2) Samuel greeted the astonished Saul with a twofold message. "Your father's donkeys have been found!" "You will become Israel's first king!"
    2. The anointing
      a. Saul agreed to have supper with Samuel and stay with him for the night.
      b. Before the men parted on the following day, Samuel anointed Saul with oil.
    3. The assurance—The prophet gave Saul a threefold sign to prove he would indeed become king.
      a. First sign—Samuel predicted Saul would meet two men near Rachel's tomb who would tell him his father's donkeys had been found.
      b. Second sign—Three men en route to Beth-el would meet him under the great tree at Tabor and offer him two loaves of bread.
      c. Third sign—Near the town of Gibeah, he would meet a procession of prophets, playing musical instruments and prophesying. Saul himself would then join in and prophesy with them in the power of God. All three signs were fulfilled.
    4. The acclamation—Saul was proclaimed king over all Israel by Samuel during a ceremony at Mizpeh (1 Sam. 10:17-27).
    5. The abasement—At the beginning of his reign, on three separate occasions, Saul demonstrated great humility and seemed actually reluctant to assume the throne.
      a. First occasion—When Samuel first told him he was God's choice to be king, Saul replied . . . "Am not I a Benjamite, of the smallest of the tribes of Israel? and my family the least of all the families of the tribe of Benjamin? wherefore then speakest thou so to me?" (1 Sam. 9:21).
      b. Second occasion—When it came time to be crowned, Saul disappeared and hid himself (1 Sam. 10:21-22).
      c. Third occasion—When he became established in power, Saul

displayed a merciful spirit, refusing the request to punish those who had previously ridiculed him. "The people said unto Samuel, Who is he that said, Shall Saul reign over us? Bring the men, that we may put them to death. And Saul said, There shall not a man be put to death this day: for to day the LORD hath wrought salvation in Israel" (1 Sam. 11:12-13).

II. Saul, the sovereign—Saul was confirmed in the kingship when he rescued the Israelite city of Jabesh-gilead (1 Sam. 11:1-11).

A. The terrible demand by Nahash
1. Nahash, an Ammonite king had surrounded Jabesh-gilead.
2. When the city attempted to make peace, he imposed the following conditions:
   a. What he demanded—He stated his intention to gouge out the right eye of all the citizens.
   b. Why he demanded this— Nahash knew this would bring disgrace upon all Israel.

B. The total destruction of Nahash
1. Upon hearing of this, an angry Saul quickly raised an army of 330,000 men.
2. He did this by cutting a pair of oxen into pieces and sending them throughout the land, threatening to do the same to the oxen of anyone not following him.
3. Saul separated his army into three divisions and utterly destroyed the Ammonite enemy.

III. Saul, the sinner—Israel's first king was guilty of at least five grievous sins.

A. He was guilty of disobedience.
1. First occasion—Before a battle (1 Sam. 13:1-15)—At this time the king was rebuked by Samuel the prophet.
   a. The background of this rebuke
      (1) Saul had attacked a small

Philistine outpost with 3,000 Israelite soldiers and had aroused the anger of his bitter enemy. It looks from the verses that Jonathan attacked the outpost and defeated it with 1000 men.
      (2) The Philistines thus assembled a vast army of foot soldiers along with 30,000 chariots and 6,000 horsemen, creating great fear among Saul's troops, causing many of them to flee in panic.
   b. The basis for this rebuke
      (1) Saul was instructed to wait for Samuel in Gilgal for seven days, at which time the prophet would appear, sacrifice an offering, and bless the troops.
      (2) At the end of the seven days the impatient king offered up the sacrifice himself, only to see Samuel appear!
      (3) Samuel told Saul two tragic things would result from his act of disobedience.
         (a) His kingdom would not endure.
         (b) God had sought out a man after his own heart.
2. Second occasion—After a battle— In spite of his first act of disobedience, Saul was allowed by God (for the sake of Israel) to defeat his various enemies, including the Moabites, Edomites, Ammonites, Amalekites, and Philistines (1 Sam. 14:47). However, once again disobedience entered his life. Are the Amalekites being equated with "the kings of Zobah" here? Should this be the case?
   a. The king of Israel set aside the God of Israel (1 Sam. 15:1-9).
      (1) Saul was commanded to

utterly destroy the Amalekites and their king because of past hostility against Israel.

(2) Not even their animals were to be spared.

(3) Saul disobeyed however, sparing Agag, the Amalekite king, plus the best of the sheep and cattle.

b. The God of Israel set aside the king of Israel (1 Sam. 15:10-35). Upon being asked by Samuel why he spared the animals, Saul weakly replied . . . "The people took of the spoil, sheep and oxen, the chief of the things which should have been utterly destroyed, to sacrifice unto the LORD thy God in Gilgal" (1 Sam. 15:21).

(1) The rebuff—"Samuel said, Hath the LORD as great delight in burnt offerings and sacrifices, as in obeying the voice of the LORD? Behold, to obey is better than sacrifice, and to hearken than the fat of rams" (1 Sam. 15:22).

(2) The remorse—"Saul said unto Samuel, I have sinned: for I have transgressed the commandment of the LORD, and thy words: because I feared the people, and obeyed their voice" (1 Sam. 15:24).

(3) The request—"Now therefore, I pray thee, pardon my sin, and turn again with me, that I may worship the LORD" (1 Sam. 15:25).

(4) The rejection—"Samuel said unto Saul, I will not return with thee: for thou hast rejected the word of the LORD, and the LORD hath rejected thee from being king over Israel. And as Samuel turned about to go away, he laid hold upon the skirt of his mantle, and it rent. And Samuel said unto him, The LORD hath rent the kingdom of Israel from thee this day, and hath given it to a neighbor of thine, that is better than thou" (1 Sam. 15:26-28).

B. He was guilty of self-will—Saul ordered the death of his own son Jonathan for disobeying his command (1 Sam. 14:24-46).

1. The stupidity of Saul's command

a. Saul forbade his soldiers as they went into battle against the Philistines to eat any food whatsoever until he had exacted full revenge upon his enemies.

b. The hero of this battle, Jonathan, unaware of the order, ate some honey.

2. The sin caused by Saul's command

a. Following the victorious battle, the famished Israelite troops quickly butchered some sheep and oxen and ate the raw, bloody meat, thus breaking the Mosaic Law which prohibited the eating of blood.

b. Upon learning what Jonathan had done, the self-willed Saul ordered his execution. The Israelite soldiers refused, however, to allow the death of Jonathan.

C. He was guilty of hatred—Saul turned against David, hating him with a passion.

1. The root of his hatred

a. The background—During their first two meetings, the two men got along quite well.

(1) First meeting—Saul and David the singer (1 Sam. 16:14-23)

(a) Saul was troubled by an evil spirit.

(b) A search was conducted for a skilled harpist

whose music would hopefully soothe the troubled king.

(c) David's fame reached Saul and he was brought to the royal court.

(d) At the playing by David the evil spirit left Saul.

(2) Second meeting—Saul and David the soldier (1 Sam. 17:1-58)

(a) Saul and Goliath—During a battle with the Philistines, Israel had been challenged for 40 days by mighty Goliath to send out a champion to fight him. Neither Saul nor any of his soldiers were willing to do this.

(b) Saul and David—David convinced a reluctant Saul that he be permitted to fight Goliath. The king offered David his own armor, but David refused to wear it. With but a sling in his hand, David slew Goliath.

b. The basis—What was it that turned Saul's affection for David to hatred? The answer is very clear. "It came to pass as they came, when David was returned from the slaughter of the Philistine, that the women came out of all cities of Israel, singing and dancing, to meet king Saul, with tabrets, with joy, and with instruments of musick. And the women answered one another as they played, and said, Saul hath slain his thousands, and David his ten thousands. And Saul was very wroth, and the saying displeased him; and he said, They have ascribed unto David ten thousands, and to me they have ascribed but thousands: and what can he have more but the kingdom? And Saul eyed David from that day and forward" (1 Sam. 18:6-9).

2. The fruit of his hatred—Saul displayed his loathing of David through both private and public attempts to kill him.

a. Private attempts to kill David

(1) He began by demoting David from a high-ranking army officer to that of a lower rank (1 Sam. 18:5, 13).

(2) He attempted on two occasions to kill David with a spear (1 Sam. 18:10-11; 19:9-10).

(3) He tried to arrange for David to be killed in battle (1 Sam. 18:20-30).

(a) Aware of David's love for Michal, Saul's daughter, the king offered her hand in marriage, but only if David could bring proof that he had killed 100 Philistines in battle, secretly hoping the young man himself would be killed in the attempt.

(b) David however, soon presented Saul with evidence that he had killed 200 enemy soldiers! (1 Sam. 18:25-27)

(4) He put pressure on his own son Jonathan to kill David (1 Sam. 19:1).

(5) He then pretended to have a change of heart (or was temporarily sorry) and assured Jonathan no harm would came to David (1 Sam. 19:6).

(6) Upon realizing, however, the depth of Jonathan's loyalty to David, Saul lost total control. He cursed his son and actually attempted to

kill him with a spear (1 Sam. 20:30-33).

b. Public attempts to kill David

(1) Saul and David—The malice

(a) He sent soldiers to arrest David in his own home, but Michal helped her husband to escape (1 Sam. 19:11-17).

(b) He dispatched three companies of soldiers to capture David in the home of Samuel. Each attempt was unsuccessful, however, for the troops wound up prophesying (1 Sam. 19:18-21).

(c) He himself then went to Samuel's house, only to end up also prophesying as the soldiers had done (1 Sam. 19:22-24).

(d) He attempted to trap David in the city of Keilah, but God revealed to his servant the king's wicked intentions (1 Sam. 23:7-13).

(e) On one occasion Saul was closing in on David, but was forced to break off pursuit upon learning the Philistines had invaded Israel (1 Sam. 23:26-28).

(f) Time and again, for some years Saul vainly and publicly sought out the life of David (1 Sam. 23:14).

(2) David and Saul—The mercy: Saul's life was spared by David on two occasions.

(a) First occasion—In a cave (1 Sam. 24:1-22). During one of his pursuits of David, Saul entered a cave down by the Dead Sea to go to the toilet. David and his men were in the cave and watched Saul who was utterly unaware of their presence. David refused to allow his men to kill Saul, but secretly cut off a corner of the king's robe. From a safe distance David later showed Saul this piece of cloth and demanded to know why the king was trying to kill him. Realizing his life had indeed been spared, Saul responded . . . "Is this thy voice, my son David? And Saul lifted up his voice, and wept. And he said to David, Thou art more righteous than I: for thou hast rewarded me good, whereas I have rewarded thee evil. . . . And now, behold, I know well that thou shalt surely be king, and that the kingdom of Israel shall be established in thine hand. Swear now therefore unto me by the LORD, that thou wilt not cut off my seed after me, and that thou wilt not destroy my name out of my father's house" (1 Sam. 24:16-17, 20-21).

(b) Second occasion—On a hillside (1 Sam. 26:1-25). Under cover of night, David and a soldier secretly visited Saul's camp and removed from the sleeping king his spear and water jug. Standing on a nearby hill David then called out and awakened Saul, showing him the spear and jug which had been taken. Once again David demanded to know why Saul was trying to kill him. Saul responded, "I have sinned: return,

my son David: for I will
no more do thee harm,
because my soul was pre-
cious in thine eyes this
day: behold, I have
played the fool, and have
erred exceedingly"
(1 Sam. 26:21).

D. He was guilty of murder—Saul instigated a terrible slaughter at the town
of Nob (1 Sam. 22:6-19).

1. Whom he had killed—At the
king's order, Ahimelech, Israel's
high priest, along with 84 other
priests, plus all the men, women,
children and livestock at Nob
were put to the sword in a bloody
massacre.

2. Why he had them killed—Saul
learned that Ahimelech had inno-
cently befriended David (who had
lied to the high priest, claiming he
was on a secret mission for Saul),
providing him with food and a
weapon.

E. He was guilty of apostasy—Saul visited the witch of Endor (1 Sam. 28:3-
25).

1. The reasons for the visit
a. He was faced with a vast and
imminent Philistine invasion.
b. The prophets could not offer
him advice or assurance.
c. The Lord would not offer him
advice or assurance.

2. The results of his visit
a. The king's trickery—Disguising
himself, Saul visited the witch
and requested that she put him
in contact with the dead Samuel.
b. The witch's terror—two events
quickly filled her with fear.
(1) She recognized Saul.
(2) She saw an old man wearing
a robe ascending up from
the earth. This was Samuel.
c. The prophet's testimony—
Samuel told Saul the what and
the why of the future.

(1) The what
(a) Saul would lose the battle
the next day.
(b) Both he and his sons
would be killed.
(c) The kingdom then would
go to David.
(2) The why—All this would
happen because of Saul's
disobedience.

d. Upon hearing this, the nearly
fainting Saul accepted some
food from the witch and left.

IV. Saul—The suicide (1 Sam. 31:1-13)

A. The place of his death—He died during the battle with the Philistines on
Mt. Gilboa.

B. The particulars of his death
1. The method
a. He was critically wounded by
the Philistine archers.
b. He fell upon his sword to escape being captured alive by
the enemy.
2. The mutilation involved
a. The Philistines cut off his head.
b. His body was then nailed on
the city wall of Beth-shan.
c. Saul's body was later recovered
by the men of Jabesh-gilead
and given a decent burial.

C. The pain over his death—Upon learning of Saul's death, David lamented
over him (2 Sam. 1:17-27). "The
beauty of Israel is slain upon thy high
places: how are the mighty fallen!
Saul and Jonathan were lovely and
pleasant in their lives, and in their
death they were not divided: they
were swifter than eagles, they were
stronger than lions" (2 Sam. 1:19, 23).

D. The perversion that caused his
death—"Saul died for his transgression which he committed against the
Lord, even against the word of the
Lord, which he kept not, and also for
asking counsel of one that had a fa-
miliar spirit, to enquire of it; And en-
quired not of the Lord: therefore he
slew him, and turned the kingdom

unto David the son of Jesse"
(1 Chron. 10:13-14).

THEOLOGICAL SUMMARY
I. Saul did not revere the ark of God (as did David) during his reign (1 Chron. 13:3).
II. He was mentioned in the titles of the following psalms:
  A. Psalm 18—A psalm written by David after God had delivered him from the hand of Saul. In some cases, his name is in the introduction only.
  B. Psalm 52—Written by David after Saul had killed the priests at Nob (See 1 Samuel 22)
  C. Psalm 54—Written when the Ziphites attempted to betray David into Saul's hand (See 1 Samuel 23)
  D. Psalm 57—Written when David hid in a cave from Saul (See 1 Sam. 22)
  E. Psalm 59—Written when Saul attempted to kill David in his own house (See 1 Sam. 19)
III. Saul was referred to by Paul the Apostle during his message in Pisidian Antioch (Acts 13:21).
IV. The Saul of the Old Testament can be both compared and contrasted with the Saul of the New Testament.
  A. The Old Testament Saul—
    1. Was tall and impressive (1 Sam. 9:2)
    2. Was from the tribe of Benjamin (1 Sam. 9:1-2)
    3. Began as God's friend (1 Sam. 9:16; 10:6-7)
    4. Ended as God's enemy (1 Sam. 28:6)
    5. Went to the witch in the hour of death (1 Sam. 28:7)
    6. Took his own life in great fear (1 Sam. 31:4)
    7. Was characterized by disobedience (1 Sam. 13:13; 15:22-23)
  B. The New Testament Saul—
    1. Was short and unimpressive (Gal. 4:13-14; 2 Cor. 10:10)
    2. Was from the tribe of Benjamin (Phil. 3:5)
    3. Began as God's enemy (Acts 9:1)
    4. Ended as God's friend (2 Tim. 4:18)
    5. Went to the Word in the hour of death (2 Tim. 4:13)
    6. Gave his own life with great expectation (2 Tim. 4:6-8)
    7. Was characterized by obedience (Acts 26:19)

STATISTICS
Father: Kish (1 Sam. 9:1-2)
Spouse: Ahinoam (1 Sam. 14:50)
Sons: Jonathan, Ishui, Melchi-shua, and Abinadab (1 Sam. 14:49; 1 Chron. 8:33)
Daughters: Merab and Michal (1 Sam. 14:49)
First mention: 1 Samuel 9:2
Final mention: Acts 13:21
Meaning of his name: "Asked for"
Frequency of his name: Referred to 388 times
Biblical books mentioning him: Six books (1 Samuel, 2 Samuel, 1 Chronicles, Psalms, Isaiah, Acts)
Occupation: King of Israel
Place of death: At the base of Mt. Gilboa (1 Sam. 31:1-2)
Circumstances of death: He was killed by the Philistines as a direct judgment by God (1 Sam. 28:16-19).
Important fact about his life: He was Israel's first king (1 Sam. 8–10).

✍Sennacherib

CHRONOLOGICAL SUMMARY
I. Sennacherib and Sargon II. He succeeded to the Assyrian throne in 704 B.C. when his father, Sargon II, was killed.
II. Sennacherib and Hezekiah
  A. The compromise of Hezekiah—When Sennacherib invaded Northern Israel, Judean King Hezekiah foolishly attempted to appease him with a huge bribe, hoping Jerusalem would be spared (2 Kings 18:13-16).
  B. The contempt of Sennacherib—

Ignoring this attempt for peace, the Assyrian king . . .

1. Surrounded the city of Jerusalem (2 Kings 18:17).
2. Sent a letter to Hezekiah demanding his surrender (2 Chron. 32:17; Isa. 37:9-13). It read:
   a. Don't be deceived by the empty promises of your God to deliver Jerusalem from me.
   b. I have already defeated the gods of other nations.
   c. Your God is no different!

III. Sennacherib and God (2 Kings 19:21-28, 35-37; Isa. 37:22-29, 33-38)
   A. The pride involved—God told both Isaiah the prophet and Hezekiah that he was angry over the pride of Sennacherib and his insults.
   B. The prophecy involved—A threefold prediction was now given against Sennacherib.
      1. He would not enter Jerusalem.
      2. His troops would not build a siege ramp against the city, nor would an enemy arrow fall inside.
      3. The Assyrian king would quickly leave the same way he came.
   C. The punishment involved—That very night the angel of the Lord put to death 185,000 Assyrian soldiers.
   D. The panic involved—Sennacherib immediately broke camp and quickly withdrew.

IV. Sennacherib and his sons (2 Kings 19:37; 2 Chron. 32:20, 21; Isa. 37:37-38)
   A. Upon his return to Nineveh, the king entered the temple of Nisroch to worship his pagon god.
   B. Here he was murdered with a sword by two of his sons, Adrammelech and Sharezer.
   C. He was succeeded by another son, Esarhaddon.

STATISTICS
Father: Sargon II
Sons: Adrammelech, Sharezer, and Esarhaddon (Isa. 37:37-38)
First mention: 2 Kings 18:13

Final mention: Isaiah 37:37
Meaning of his name: "The god Zin"
Frequency of his name: Referred to 13 times
Biblical books mentioning him: Three books (2 Kings, 2 Chronicles, Isaiah)
Occupation: King of Assyria (2 Kings 18:13)
Place of death: In a pagan temple at Nineveh (Isa. 37:37-38)
Circumstances of death: He was murdered with a sword by his two sons (Isa. 37:38).
Important fact about his life: His armies were destroyed at Jerusalem by the death angel (2 Kings 19:32-35).

✍*Seraiah* (1)

CHRONOLOGICAL SUMMARY
He was Israel's chief priest when Nebuchadnezzar destroyed Jerusalem (2 Kings 25:18). He was dragged before the Babylonian king and killed (2 Kings 25:18-21; Jer. 52:24-27).

STATISTICS
Father: Azariah (1 Chron. 6:14)
Son: Jehozadak (1 Chron. 6:14)
Significant descendant: Ezra (Ezra 7:1)
First mention: 2 Kings 25:18
Final mention: Jeremiah 52:24
Meaning of his name: "Warrior of God"
Frequency of his name: Referred to four times
Biblical books mentioning him: Four books (2 Kings, 1 Chronicles, Ezra, Jeremiah)
Occupation: High priest (2 Kings 25:18)
Place of birth: Jerusalem
Place of death: Riblah (2 Kings 25:20-21)
Circumstances of death: He was killed by order of Nebuchadnezzar (2 Kings 25:1, 21).
Important fact about his life: He was Israel's final high priest before the Babylonian Captivity (2 Kings 25:21).

✍*Seraiah* (2)

CHRONOLOGICAL SUMMARY
I. Seraiah and Zedekiah the king—He was the chief officer to Judean King

Zedekiah, and accompanied him into the Babylonian Captivity (Jer. 51:59).

II. Seraiah and Jeremiah the prophet (Jer. 51:59-64)

A. Seraiah was the brother of Baruch, Jeremiah's personal scribe (Jer. 32:12; 51:59).

B. Jeremiah gave him a scroll which contained God's scheduled punishments upon Babylon.

C. Upon reaching Babylon, Seraiah was to tie a rock to the scroll and cast it into the Euphrates River.

D. This action would symbolize that Babylon would eventually sink, never to rise.

STATISTICS

Father: Neriah (Jer. 51:59)
Brother: Baruch (Jer. 32:12; 51:59)
First mention: Jeremiah 51:59
Final mention: Jeremiah 51:61
Meaning of his name: "Warrior of God"
Frequency of his name: Referred to three times
Biblical books mentioning him: One book (Jeremiah)
Occupation: Officer to King Zedekiah (Jer. 51:59)
Place of birth: Jerusalem
Place of death: Babylon
Important fact about his life: He was the brother of Baruch, Jeremiah's scribe, and he carried a prophetic message for Jeremiah to Babylon (Jer. 32:12; 51:59-64).

✑Seth

CHRONOLOGICAL SUMMARY

I. Seth in the Old Testament (Gen. 4:25; 5:3)

A. He was the third son of Adam and Eve.

B. His line, eventually leading to the Messiah, replaced that of Abel, killed by Cain.

C. He was one of 10 major patriarchs listed in Genesis 5 as living before the great flood (Gen. 5:3).

D. He was born when his father Adam was 130 (Gen. 5:3).

II. Seth in the New Testament—He is included by Luke in the genealogy leading to Mary and the Messiah himself (Luke 3:23-38).

STATISTICS

Father: Adam (Gen. 4:25)
Mother: Eve (Gen. 4:25)
Son: Enos (Gen. 4:26)
Brothers: Cain and Abel (Gen. 4:1-2)
First mention: Genesis 4:25
Final mention: Luke 3:38
Meaning of his name: "Compensation, sprout"
Frequency of his name: Referred to nine times
Biblical books mentioning him: Three books (Genesis, 1 Chronicles, Luke)
Important fact about his life: He was Adam's third son, whose line led to Christ (Gen. 4:1-2, 25; Luke 3:38).

✑Shadrach

CHRONOLOGICAL SUMMARY

I. Shadrach and the king's food (Dan. 1:1-20)

A. His resolve

1. He was one of the four Jewish youths among the thousands who were taken from Judah to Babylon by King Nebuchadnezzar in 606 B.C. (Dan. 1:1-7).

2. He was also called Hananiah. The names of his three friends were:
a. Daniel (also called Belteshazzar)
b. Azariah (also called Abednego)
c. Mishael (also called Meshach)

3. Shadrach determined (along with his three friends) not to defile his body with the king's food and wine, but instead requested a special, simple diet (Dan. 1:8-14).

B. His reward

1. God honored Shadrach's decision, and gave him great ability to master all the literature and science he

was taught in Nebuchadnezzar's school (Dan. 1:17).

2. Upon completion of his three-year training program, Shadrach was found by the king to possess 10 times the knowledge and wisdom of those who had remained on the royal diet (Dan. 1:18-20). (See earlier note in Meshach.)

II. Shadrach and the king's frustration (Dan. 2:1-19)

A. Nebuchadnezzar had dreamed a dream which he could not understand.

B. Shadrach joined Daniel and his friends in asking God to reveal the content and meaning of Nebuchadnezzar's dream.

C. God answered their request that very night.

III. Shadrach and the king's furnace (Dan. 3:1-30)

A. His resolve

1. Shadrach, along with Abednego and Meshach, refused to bow down and worship a golden pagan statue Nebuchadnezzar had built.

2. After rejecting the king's final offer (who had given them a second chance), the three Hebrew youths were bound and cast into a fiery furnace.

B. His reward

1. Christ himself joined his three faithful servants in the fire, protecting them from all harm.

2. The three men stepped from the fire without even the smell of smoke upon them.

3. Shadrach received a promotion from Nebuchadnezzar and prospered greatly.

STATISTICS

First mention: Daniel 1:7 (His Jewish name was Hananiah.)

Final mention: Daniel 3:30

Meaning of his name: "Command of Aku, the moon god"

Frequency of his name: Referred to 20 times

Biblical books mentioning him: One book (Daniel)

Occupation: Political leader (Dan. 3:30)

Place of birth: Judah (Dan. 1:1-6)

Place of death: Babylon

Important fact about his life: He was preserved in the fiery furnace by Christ himself (Dan. 3:23-25).

✐Shallum

CHRONOLOGICAL SUMMARY

I. Shallum, the murderer

A. He was the fifteenth ruler of Northern Israel.

B. He reigned but one month (2 Kings 15:13).

C. He murdered King Zechariah to obtain the throne (2 Kings 15:10).

II. Shallum, the murdered—He was murdered in Samaria by Menahem, an especially brutal man (2 Kings 15:14).

STATISTICS

Father: Jabesh (2 Kings 15:10)

First mention: 2 Kings 15:10

Final mention: 2 Kings 15:15

Meaning of his name: "Recompenser"

Frequency of his name: Referred to three times

Biblical books mentioning him: One book (2 Kings)

Occupation: King of Northern Israel (2 Kings 15:13)

Place of death: Samaria (2 Kings 15:14)

Circumstances of death: He was murdered by Menahem (2 Kings 15:14).

Important fact about his life: He reigned only one month (2 Kings 15:13).

✐Shalmaneser V

CHRONOLOGICAL SUMMARY

I. He bound the king of Northern Israel.

A. Shalmaneser siezed the throne when Tiglath-pileser III died and became king over Assyria.

B. He then invaded Israel, deposed Hoshea, and forced him to pay heavy annual taxes (2 Kings 17:3).

C. When Hoshea conspired against him, Shalmaneser put him in chains (2 Kings 17:4).

II. He besieged the capital of Northern Israel.

A. Shalmaneser surrounded the capital city of Samaria, which held out for three years (2 Kings 18:9-10).

B. He died during the final part of this siege and was succeeded by Sargon II.

STATISTICS

First mention: 2 Kings 17:3
Final mention: 2 Kings 18:9
Meaning of his name: "Sulman is leader"
Frequency of his name: Referred to two times
Biblical books mentioning him: One book (2 Kings)
Place of death: Outside the city of Samaria
Important fact about his life: He invaded Northern Israel and carried off the people into Assyria (2 Kings 17:6).

Shamgar

CHRONOLOGICAL SUMMARY

I. Shamgar was the third judge mentioned in the book of Judges (Judg. 3:31).

II. He killed 600 Philistines with an ox goad and delivered Israel (Judg. 3:31).

III. He was mentioned later by Deborah and Barak in their victory song (Judg. 5:6).

STATISTICS

Father: Anath (Judg. 3:31)
First mention: Judges 3:31
Final mention: Judges 5:6
Meaning of his name: "Sword"
Frequency of his name: Referred to two times
Biblical books mentioning him: One book (Judges)
Occupation: Soldier (Judg. 3:31)

Important fact about his life: He killed 600 Philistines with an ox goad (Judg. 3:31).

Sheba

CHRONOLOGICAL SUMMARY

I. The foolish act of Sheba

A. He was a troublemaker from the tribe of Benjamin (2 Sam. 20:1).

B. He instigated a second revolt against David immediately after the king had put down the rebellion led by Absalom (2 Sam. 20:1-2).

C. Of all the tribes, only the tribe of Judah remained true to David (2 Sam. 20:2).

D. David ordered his commander-in-chief Joab to crush Sheba's revolt (2 Sam. 20:6-7).

II. The fatal act of Sheba

A. He took refuge in the city of Abel, located north of the Galilean Sea at the base of Mt. Hermon. This city was famous for the wisdom its citizens possessed (2 Sam. 20:14, 18).

B. Joab and his troops surrounded Abel, but upon conferring with a wise old woman within its walls, he agreed to withdraw if the city would deliver up the head of Sheba (2 Sam. 20:15-21).

C. This was done and the city was saved (2 Sam. 20:22).

STATISTICS

Father: Bichri (2 Sam. 20:1)
First mention: 2 Samuel 20:1
Final mention: 2 Samuel 20:22
Meaning of his name: "Oath, covenant"
Frequency of his name: Referred to seven times
Biblical books mentioning him: One book (2 Samuel)
Place of death: City of Abel (2 Sam. 20:15-22)
Circumstances of death: His head was chopped off (2 Sam. 15:22).
Important fact about his life: He led a revolt against David (2 Sam. 15:1-2).

✍Shebna

CHRONOLOGICAL SUMMARY

I. Reasoning with Rab-shakeh
   A. Shebna was the scribe and secretary for King Hezekiah (2 Kings 18:18).
   B. He attempted in vain to negotiate with Rab-shakeh, field commander under King Sennacherib when the Assyrians had surrounded the city of Jerusalem (2 Kings 18:26).

II. Reporting to Isaiah—Shebna, along with the palace administrator and the royal recorder, broke the bad news to both Hezekiah and Isaiah (2 Kings 18:37; 19:2).

STATISTICS

First mention: 2 Kings 18:18
Final mention: Isaiah 37:2
Meaning of his name: "Youthfulness"
Frequency of his name: Referred to eight times
Biblical books mentioning him: Two books (2 Kings, Isaiah)
Occupation: Scribe (2 Kings 18:18)
Important fact about his life: He was Hezekiah's scribe (Isa. 37:1-2).

✍Shechem

CHRONOLOGICAL SUMMARY

I. The transaction from Shechem
   A. Shechem was a Canaanite chief whose father, Hamor, sold Jacob the patriarch a plot of ground for 100 pieces of silver (Gen. 33:19).
   B. Centuries later, when Joshua entered Canaan, he buried the bones of Joseph (Jacob's son) which Israel had carried out of Egypt, on this very spot of ground (Josh. 24:32).

II. The transgression of Shechem
   A. Shechem sexually violated Dinah, Jacob's daughter (Gen. 34:1-2).
   B. He then requested that Hamor seek her for his wife (Gen. 34:3-4).

III. The treachery against Shechem
   A. Shechem and his men were tricked by Jacob's sons into circumcising themselves before this marriage could be allowed (Gen. 34:11-24).
   B. Three days later, when he and his men were swollen and helpless to defend themselves, two of Jacob's sons, Simeon and Levi, walked in and slaughtered them like wild animals (Gen. 34:25-29).

STATISTICS

Father: Hamor (Gen. 34:2)
First mention: Genesis 33:19
Final mention: Judges 9:28
Meaning of his name: "Shoulder"
Frequency of his name: Referred to 15 times
Biblical books mentioning him: Two books (Genesis, Judges)
Occupation: Hivite tribal leader (Gen. 34:2)
Place of death: In the city later named Shechem
Circumstances of death: He was murdered by Simeon and Levi (Gen. 34:25-26).
Important fact about his life: He seduced Dinah, Jacob's daughter (Gen. 34:1-3).

✍Shem

CHRONOLOGICAL SUMMARY

I. Shem and his father
   A. He was Noah's first son, born when his father was 500 years old (Gen. 5:32).
   B. He was one of eight human beings saved from the great flood by being on board the ark (Gen. 7:13).
   C. He was 97 when he boarded the ark.
   D. He was 100 when his final son, Arphaxad, was born, two years after the Great Flood (Gen. 11:10).
   E. He helped his brother Japheth cover the nakedness of Noah after their father had become drunk (Gen. 9:20-23).

II. Shem and his future (Gen. 9:24-27)
   A. After Noah had sobered up, he made
      the following prophecy concerning
      Shem:
      1. God would personally bless and
         prosper him.
      2. The Canaanites would be the ser-
         vants of his descendants.
      3. The descendants of Japheth
         would share in his prosperity.
   B. Shem thus became one of the three
      ancestors of all men living today, par-
      ticularly the Jewish race (Gen. 9:18-19;
      11:10-27).

STATISTICS
Father: Noah (Gen. 5:32)
Sons: Elam, Asshur, Arphaxad, Lud, and
   Aram (Gen. 9:26)
Brothers: Ham and Japheth (Gen. 5:32)
First mention: Genesis 5:32
Final mention: 1 Chronicles 1:24
Meaning of his name: "Renown"
Frequency of his name: Referred to 16 times
Biblical books mentioning him: Two books
   (Genesis, 1 Chronicles)
Age at death: 600 (Gen. 11:10-11)
Important fact about his life: He was one of
   Noah's three sons from whose line the
   Jewish people came (1 Chron. 1:24-
   27).

Shemaiah (1)

CHRONOLOGICAL SUMMARY
   I. The reprimand from Shemaiah—He was
      a prophet of God who warned Judean
      King Rehoboam not to wage war
      against Northern Israelite King Jero-
      boam I (2 Chron. 11:1-4).
  II. The repentance brought about by She-
      maiah
      A. He later explained that the Egyptian
         siege against Jerusalem was a divine
         warning and also punishment, be-
         cause both Rehoboam and his people
         had forsaken God (2 Chron. 12:1-5).

   B. His preaching brought about a tempo-
      rary repentance and respite for Jeru-
      salem (2 Chron. 12:6-12).
 III. The record by Shemaiah—He wrote a
      book about the reign of Rehoboam
      (2 Chron. 12:15).

STATISTICS
First mention: 1 Kings 12:22
Final mention: 2 Chronicles 12:15
Meaning of his name: "God is fame"
Frequency of his name: Referred to five times
Biblical books mentioning him: Two books
   (1 Kings, 2 Chronicles)
Occupation: Prophet (2 Chron. 12:15)
Important fact about his life: He was God's
   chief prophet to Rehoboam the king
   (1 Kings 12:22-24).

Shemaiah (2)

CHRONOLOGICAL SUMMARY
   I. Shemaiah, the corrupt prophet
      A. He was a false prophet of Judah who
         was taken into captivity in the days
         of Jeremiah, the true prophet (Jer.
         29:24).
      B. He wrote a lying message from Bab-
         ylon to the Jewish high priest Zepha-
         niah, and other priests (Jer. 29:24-
         28).
         1. He said God had set aside Jere-
            miah and wanted Zephaniah to
            become the chief prophet.
         2. He said Jeremiah should be
            thrown in prison.
         3. He said the Babylonian Captivity
            would be very short.
  II. Shemaiah, the condemned prophet—
      God instructed Jeremiah to respond by
      writing a letter to those Jews already in
      the Babylonian Captivity (Jer. 29:29-32):
      A. Informing them that Shemaiah was a
         false and lying prophet
      B. Predicting both Shemaiah and his
         seed would be cut off for teaching
         rebellion against God

STATISTICS

First mention: Jeremiah 29:24
Final mention: Jeremiah 29:32
Meaning of his name: "God is fame"
Frequency of his name: Referred to four times
Biblical books mentioning him: One book (Jeremiah)
Occupation: False prophet (Jer. 29:31)
Place of birth: Judah
Place of death: Babylon
Important fact about his life: He was a false prophet who predicted the Babylonian captivity would last only two years.

Shimei

CHRONOLOGICAL SUMMARY

I. Shimei under the reign of David
   A. The malice he displayed against David
      1. He was a relative of King Saul (2 Sam. 16:5).
      2. He cursed David and threw rocks at him as the king was fleeing from the rebellion led by Absalom (2 Sam. 16:5-6, 13).
      3. He falsely accused David of bloodletting against the house of Saul and claimed Absalom's revolt was in reality a punishment sent by God (2 Sam. 16:7-8).
   B. The mercy he received from David
      1. David refused the requests of his soldiers to kill Shimei at this time (2 Sam. 16:9-12).
      2. After the king had crushed Absalom's revolt he was met once again by Shimei, who now begged for his life (2 Sam. 19:16-20).
      3. Once again, over the objection of his men, David spared the life of Shimei (2 Sam. 19:22-23).
      4. Later, however, on his deathbed, David warned Solomon his son

concerning Shimei's treachery (1 Kings 2:8-9).
II. Shimei under the reign of Solomon
   A. His disobedience
      1. Solomon warned Shimei not to leave Jerusalem upon pain of death. Shimei agreed (1 Kings 2:36-38).
      2. Three years later, however, Shimei disregarded this command and went to Philistia to bring back some runaway servants (1 Kings 2:39-40).
   B. His destruction—Upon his return, Shimei was put to death by order of King Solomon (1 Kings 2:41-46).

STATISTICS

Father: Gera (2 Sam. 16:5)
Significant ancestor: Saul (2 Sam. 16:5)
First mention: 2 Samuel 16:5
Final mention: 1 Kings 2:44
Meaning of his name: "God is fame"
Frequency of his name: Referred to 18 times
Biblical books mentioning him: Two books (2 Samuel, 1 Kings)
Place of death: Jerusalem (1 Kings 2:41-46)
Circumstances of death: He was executed by order of King Solomon (1 Kings 2:46).
Important fact about his life: He cursed David during the king's retreat from Absalom's rebellion (2 Sam. 16:5-13).

Shiphrah

CHRONOLOGICAL SUMMARY

I. Shiphrah and Puah (Exod. 1:15-16)—These two courageous women were the chief midwives who were ordered by the Egyptian pharaoh to kill all Hebrew baby boys at birth.
II. Shiphrah and God (Exod. 1:17-21)
   A. Her resolve—She feared God and refused to carry out Pharaoh's command.
   B. Her reward—God blessed her greatly, giving her children of her own.

STATISTICS

First mention: Exodus 1:15
Final mention: Exodus 1:15
Meaning of her name: "Handsome"
Frequency of her name: Referred to one time
Biblical books mentioning her: One book (Exodus)
Occupation: Midwife (Exod. 1:15)
Important fact about her life: She feared God and refused to kill the male Hebrew babies in Egypt (Exod. 1:17).

# Sihon

CHRONOLOGICAL SUMMARY

I. The foolish attack of Sihon
  A. The request
    1. Sihon was an Amorite king who occupied the land area north of Moab on the eastern side of the Jordan River during the time of the Exodus march (Num. 21:21, 26).
    2. Joshua approached him, saying: "Let me pass through thy land: we will not turn into the fields, or into the vineyards; we will not drink of the waters of the well: but we will go along by the king's high way, until we be past thy borders" (Num. 21:22).
  B. The refusal—"Sihon would not suffer Israel to pass through his border: but . . . gathered all his people . . . and went out against Israel" (Num. 21:23).
II. The fatal attack on Sihon
  A. Israel counterattacked and totally defeated Sihon, occupying Heshbon, the capital city, and his entire kingdom (Num. 21:24-26).
  B. This utter destruction wrought upon Sihon by Israel gave birth to an ancient proverb (Num. 21:27-28).
  C. Moses then gave Sihon's land to

the tribes of Gad, Reuben, and the half tribe of Manasseh (Num. 32:33).

THEOLOGICAL SUMMARY

I. This event had far-reaching influence upon Israel and the surrounding nations.
  A. Moses referred to it during his final address, reminding the Israelite leaders that "Sihon . . . would not let us pass by him: for the LORD thy God hardened his spirit, and made his heart obstinate, that he might deliver him into thy hand" (Deut. 2:30).
  B. Rahab the harlot had heard of it (Josh. 2:10).
  C. The pagan Gibeonites referred to it (Josh. 9:10).
  D. Jephthah the judge mentioned it (Judg. 11:19).
II. The event was still a significant memory centuries later.
  A. The Levites spoke of it in their prayer during the days of Nehemiah (Neh. 9:22).
  B. The psalmist called it to our attention (Pss. 135:11; 136:19).
  C. Jeremiah wrote about it (Jer. 48:45).

STATISTICS

First mention: Numbers 21:21
Final mention: Jeremiah 48:45
Meaning of his name: "Great, bold"
Frequency of his name: Referred to 37 times
Biblical books mentioning him: Eight books (Numbers, Deuteronomy, Joshua, Judges, 1 Kings, Nehemiah, Psalms, Jeremiah)
Occupation: Amorite king (Num. 21:21)
Important fact about his life: He refused Israel's request to pass through his land during the Exodus march (Num. 21:23).

✍*Simeon*

CHRONOLOGICAL SUMMARY
I. Simeon, the heartless
   A. His retaliation
      1. He was the second son of Jacob and Leah (Gen. 29:33).
      2. He married a Canaanite woman (Gen. 46:10).
      3. He and a younger brother, Levi, slaughtered some helpless pagans, whom they had tricked into being circumcised, to avenge the sexual seduction of their sister (Gen. 34:25).
   B. His rebuke
      1. Jacob, their father, later severely rebuked Simeon and Levi for this brutal act (Gen. 34:30).
      2. On his deathbed years later, Jacob reminded both men of their cruel action (Gen. 49:5).
II. Simeon, the hostage—He was kept as a hostage by Joseph during the first trip the 10 brothers made to buy food in Egypt (Gen. 42:24).

STATISTICS
Father: Jacob (Gen. 35:22-23)
Mother: Leah (Gen. 35:22-23)
Spouse: A Canaanite woman (Gen. 46:10)
Sons: Jemuel, Jamin, Ohad, Jachin, Zohar, and Shaul (Gen. 46:10)
Brothers: Full brothers: Reuben, Levi, Judah, Issachar, and Zebulun (Gen. 35:22-23). Half brothers: Joseph, Benjamin, Dan, Naphtali, Gad, and Asher (Gen. 35:24).
Sister: Dinah (Gen. 30:21)
First mention: Genesis 29:33
Final mention: Exodus 6:15
Meaning of his name: "Hearing"
Frequency of his name: Referred to 13 times
Biblical books mentioning him: Two books (Genesis, Exodus)
Place of birth: Mesopotamia
Important fact about his life: He was Jacob's second son, who helped butcher some circumcised pagans (Gen. 34:25-29).

✍*Sisera*

CHRONOLOGICAL SUMMARY
I. He was defeated by Barak the soldier.
   A. Sisera was commander of the army of Jabin, a Canaanite king (Judg. 4:2).
   B. He had at his disposal 900 iron chariots (Judg. 4:3).
   C. His troops had oppressed Israel for 20 years (Judg. 4:3).
   D. Sisera was lured into battle with Barak the Israelite commander who had 10,000 soldiers (Judg. 4:6-10).
   E. He was then totally routed by Barak at the base of Mt. Tabor (Judg. 4:15).
II. He was destroyed by Jael, a housewife.
   A. Sisera escaped the battle on foot and took refuge in a tent of a Kenite woman named Jael (Judg. 4:17-18).
   B. After feeding him and waiting for him to fall asleep, Jael killed Sisera by driving a tent peg through his temple (Judg. 4:21).
   C. Following this, Barak and Deborah the prophetess composed and sang a song of praise to God which depicted both Sisera's defeat and death (Judg. 5:20-30).

THEOLOGICAL SUMMARY
I. Samuel the prophet made mention of this event during his farewell speech to the nation of Israel (1 Sam. 12:9).
II. The psalmist Asaph referred to this event (Ps. 83:9).

STATISTICS
First mention: Judges 4:2
Final mention: Psalms 83:9
Meaning of his name: "Mediation"
Frequency of his name: Referred to 19 times
Biblical books mentioning him: Three books (Judges, 1 Samuel, Psalms)
Occupation: Canaanite military commander (Judg. 4:2)
Place of death: In a tent (Judg. 4:21-22)
Circumstances of death: He had a tent peg driven through his head (Judg. 4:21-22).
Important fact about his life: He was attacked

and defeated by Barak and Deborah
(Judg. 4:14-16).

✍Solomon

CHRONOLOGICAL SUMMARY
I. The tender years of Solomon
   A. Chosen by God
      1. He was the second son born to
         David and Bath-sheba (2 Sam.
         12:24).
      2. Their first son (unnamed) had
         died in infancy as a punishment
         for their sin of adultery (2 Sam.
         12:15-18).
      3. Solomon was also called Jedidiah,
         meaning "beloved of the LORD"
         (2 Sam. 12:25).
      4. Even before David met and mar-
         ried Bath-sheba, God had already
         revealed to the king several
         prophecies concerning his yet-to-
         be-born son (2 Sam. 7:12-16).
         a. He (and not David) would
            build the temple of God.
         b. There would be a father and
            son relationship between God
            and Solomon.
         c. God's mercy would not depart
            from Solomon as it had from
            Saul.
         d. Through Solomon, David's
            kingdom would be established
            forever.
   B. Challenged by David
      1. The king's words to his subjects—
         David ordered the entire nation to
         help Solomon.
         a. The sojourners in Israel
            (1 Chron. 22:2, 5)
         b. The key princes in Israel
            (1 Chron. 22:17-19)
         c. The religious, military, political,
            and financial leaders in Israel
            (1 Chron. 28:1-8)
      2. The king's words to his son
         a. 1 Chronicles. 22:11-13—"The
            LORD be with thee; and prosper

thou, and build the house of
the LORD thy God, as he hath
said of thee. Only the LORD
give thee wisdom and understanding, and give thee charge
concerning Israel, that thou
mayest keep the law of the
LORD thy God. Then shalt thou
prosper, if thou takest heed to
fulfil the statutes and judgments which the LORD charged
Moses with concerning Israel:
be strong, and of good courage;
dread not, nor be dismayed."
         b. 1 Chron. 28:9— "Know thou
            the God of thy father, and
            serve him with a perfect heart
            and with a willing mind: for the
            LORD searcheth all hearts, and
            understandeth all the imagina-
            tions of the thoughts: if thou
            seek him, he will be found of
            thee: but if thou forsake him,
            he will cast thee off for ever."
         c. 1 Chron. 28:20—"Be strong and
            of good courage, and do it: fear
            not, nor be dismayed: for the
            LORD God, even my God, will
            be with thee; he will not fail
            thee, nor forsake thee, until
            thou hast finished all the work
            for the service of the house of
            the LORD."
         d. 1 Kings 2:2—"I go the way of
            all the earth: be thou strong
            therefore, and shew thyself a
            man."
      3. Along with these challenging
         words to Solomon, David made a
         presentation and offered up a
         prayer.
         a. The presentation—He gave Sol-
            omon the blueprints for the
            temple which God had given
            him (1 Chron. 28:11-19).
         b. The prayer—"Give unto Solo-
            mon my son a perfect heart, to
            keep thy commandments, thy
            testimonies, and thy statutes,
            and to do all these things, and

to build the palace, for the which I have made provision" (1 Chron. 29:19).

II. The triumph of Solomon
  A. His two anointings
    1. The first anointing (1 Chron. 23:1)
    2. The second anointing (1 Chron. 29:22; 1 Kings 1:39)—This second anointing, ordered by the dying David, and carried out by Zadok the high priest and Nathan the prophet, was done to counteract the attempted coup by Adonijah (Solomon's half brother) to steal the throne.
  B. His four adversaries—After Solomon's reign was firmly established, he found it necessary to punish four enemies who had continued to demonstrate a rebellious spirit.
    1. Adonijah—He was executed for his attempt to marry Abishag, David's final concubine. This was viewed by Solomon as Adonijah's first attempt to secure the throne (1 Kings 2:13-25).
    2. Abiathar—He was banished from the priesthood for joining in with Adonijah's original revolt (1 Kings 2:26-27).
    3. Joab—David's former military leader was executed for his part in the rebellion and for past crimes (1 Kings 2:28-34).
    4. Shimei—This rebel, who had once cursed David, was executed for disobeying the conditions of his parole (1 Kings 2:36-46).

III. The talent of Solomon
  A. Requesting this talent from God (1 Kings 3:4-9; 2 Chron. 1:3-10)
    1. At the beginning of his reign, Solomon went to the city of Gibeon, where the tabernacle was located, to sacrifice.
    2. He offered up 1,000 burnt sacrifices on the brazen altar and spoke to Israel's assembled leaders.
    3. It was at Gibeon that God spoke

to Solomon, promising to give the king anything he wanted.
    4. Solomon responded by asking God for a wise and understanding heart—"To judge thy people, that I may discern between good and bad: for who is able to judge this thy so great a people?" (1 Kings 3:9).
  B. Receiving this talent from God (1 Kings 3:10-15; 2 Chron. 1:11-12)— "The speech pleased the Lord, that Solomon had asked this thing" (1 Kings 3:10).
    1. God promised Solomon his request for wisdom would be granted. In fact, he would become the wisest man that ever lived.
    2. God would also give the king honor and riches.
  C. Revealing this talent from God (1 Kings 3:16-28)
    1. Solomon soon had the opportunity to reveal his gift of wisdom when two harlots appeared before him.
    2. Both harlots lived in the same house and both had recently given birth to infant sons, one of which had just died.
    3. Each harlot claimed the living infant was her son.
    4. Solomon proposed to divide the living baby by a sword and give half to each woman.
    5. One harlot agreed, but the other was so horrified at this suggestion that she was willing to give up her claim as the mother so the baby might be saved.
    6. Solomon quickly awarded the baby to this woman, correctly concluding that she was the true mother.
    7. The king's fame quickly grew following this court decision.

IV. The total and tranquil reign of Solomon
  A. The source of this reign (1 Kings 2:12; 1 Chron. 29:25; 2 Chron. 1:1)—"The Lord magnified Solomon exceedingly

in the sight of all Israel, and bestowed upon him such royal majesty as had not been on any king before him in Israel" (1 Chron. 29:25).

B. The extent of this reign—He reigned from the Euphrates River on the east to the Mediterranean on the west, the borders of Egypt on the south to the Lebanon border on the north (1 Kings 4:21, 24).

C. The nature of this reign—"Judah and Israel were many, as the sand which is by the sea in multitude, eating and drinking, and making merry" (1 Kings 4:20). "He had peace on all sides round about him. . . . Judah and Israel dwelt safely, every man under his vine and under his fig tree, from Dan even to Beer-sheba, all the days of Solomon" (1 Kings 4:24-25).

D. The appointed officials during this reign
   1. Eleven chief cabinet members over political matters (1 Kings 4:1-6)
   2. Twelve key men, one from each tribe, to be responsible for food supplies (1 Kings 4:7-19)
   3. Jeroboam, to govern over the tribes of Ephraim and Manasseh (1 Kings 11:28)

V. The temple of Solomon
   A. The preparation
      1. The co-contractor for the temple— Solomon appointed two men to supervise the overall construction of the temple. Both men had the same name, Hiram. One was a king, while the other was a craftsman.
         a. Hiram the king (1 Kings 5:1-12; 2 Chron. 2:1-10)
            (1) He was the ruler of Tyre.
            (2) He provided the cedar and fir trees from Lebanon.
            (3) In return for his services, Solomon sent him an annual payment of 125,000 bushels of wheat and 96 gallons of pure oil.
            (4) Hiram also helped build a home for Solomon.
            (5) Seven years after the construction of both the temple and the royal palace, Solomon gave 20 cities in the land of Galilee to King Hiram as final payment for all the cedar, cypress lumber, and gold which had been furnished for these two houses (1 Kings 9:10-11).
            (6) Hiram, however, for some reason was not satisfied with these cities, calling them Cabul, meaning "the wasteland" (1 Kings 9:12-14).
         b. Hiram the craftsman (1 Kings 7:13-14; 2 Chron. 2:14)
            (1) He also was from Tyre.
            (2) He was half Jewish, the son of a widow from the tribe of Naphtali.
            (3) This Hiram was "filled with wisdom, and understanding" (1 Kings 7:14).
            (4) He was highly skilled in working with gold, silver, bronze, iron, stone, wood, and linen.
      2. The location of the temple—It was constructed atop Mt. Moriah, on the threshing floor once purchased by David from a Jebusite named Ornan (2 Chron. 3:1).
      3. The time involved in building the temple
         a. It was begun on the second day of the second month of the fourth year of Solomon's reign (2 Chron. 3:2).
         b. This was 480 years after Israel's Exodus from Egypt (1 Kings 6:1).
         c. It was completed seven and a half years later (1 Kings 6:37-38).

4. The workers assigned to the temple
   a. Solomon indentured many non-Jewish Canaanites living in the land (2 Chron. 2:17-18): 70,000 common laborers, 80,000 loggers, and 3,600 foremen.
   b. In addition to these, he drafted 30,000 Israelite laborers (1 Kings 5:15-16).
B. The dedication
   1. Solomon brought into the temple all the gold and silver objects his father David had previously given (1 Kings 7:51; 2 Chron. 5:1).
   2. He assembled the spiritual leaders of Israel and together they carried the Ark of the Covenant into the temple (1 Kings 8:1-11; 2 Chron. 5:2-14).
C. The explanation—Solomon reviewed before the people both the persons and purpose connected with the building of the temple (1 Kings 8:12-21; 2 Chron. 6:1-11).
   1. The persons involved
      a. David had desired to build the temple.
      b. Solomon, however, had been chosen to build it.
   2. The purpose involved—It was to serve as a shelter and dwelling place for the Ark of the Covenant.
D. The supplication—Solomon knelt before the altar on a seven-and-a-half-foot elevated bronze platform in full view of the crowd and raised his hands toward heaven. His prayer involved both a review and a request (1 Kings 8:22-53; 2 Chron. 6:12-42).
   1. The review—He acknowledged the faithfulness, mercy, and omnipresence of God.
   2. The request
      a. That the very presence of the temple would cause Israel to seek God's protection, justice, and forgiveness in the following areas:

(1) When an oath was made at the altar
(2) In times of defeat
(3) In times of drought, famine, and pestilence
(4) In showing kindness to the stranger
(5) In the hour of battle
(6) In time of captivity

E. The consecration—At the end of his prayer, the king consecrated to God a twofold offering.
   1. He offered up the people as a living sacrifice to God (1 Kings 8:55-61).
   2. He offered up some animals as burnt sacrifices to God. This consisted of 22,000 oxen and 120,000 sheep and goats (1 Kings 8:62-64).
F. The manifestation—At this point God supernaturally intervened, demonstrating his divine approval of Solomon's temple—"When Solomon had made an end of praying, the fire came down from heaven, and consumed the burnt offering and the sacrifices; and the glory of the LORD filled the house. And the priests could not enter into the house of the LORD, because the glory of the LORD had filled the LORD's house" (2 Chron. 7:1-2).
G. The celebration—"When all the children of Israel saw how the fire came down, and the glory of the LORD upon the house, they bowed themselves with their faces to the ground upon the pavement, and worshipped, and praised the LORD, saying, For he is good; for his mercy endureth for ever. . . . Also at the same time Solomon kept the feast seven days, and all Israel with him, a very great congregation, from the entering in of Hamath unto the river of Egypt. And in the eighth day they made a solemn assembly: for they kept the dedication of the altar seven days, and the feast seven days. And on the three and twentieth day of the

seventh month he sent the people away into their tents, glad and merry in heart for the goodness that the LORD had shewed unto David, and to Solomon, and to Israel his people" (2 Chron. 7:3, 8-10).

VI. The treasure of Solomon—"So king Solomon exceeded all the kings of the earth for riches" (1 Kings 10:23).

A. The nature of his wealth—Solomon, it would seem, possessed great quantities of virtually every precious object on earth. This included:

1. The purest silver and gold
   a. Gold (1 Kings 10:10-11, 22; 2 Chron. 9:10, 14, 21, 24)
   b. Silver (1 Kings 10:22; 2 Chron. 9:14, 21, 24)
2. Precious stones of all kinds (1 Kings 10:10-11; 2 Chron. 9:10)
3. Beautiful and fragrant sandalwood, from which were made harps and psalteries (1 Kings 10:11; 2 Chron. 9:10-11)
4. Rare spices (1 Kings 10:10-11, 25; 2 Chron. 9:24)
5. Ivory (1 Kings 10:22; 2 Chron. 9:21)
6. The finest of clothes and armor (1 Kings 10:25; 2 Chron. 9:24)
7. Linen (2 Chron. 1:15)
8. Abundant and exotic foods (1 Kings 4:22-23; 10:5)
9. Imported animals and birds
   a. Apes (1 Kings 10:22; 2 Chron. 9:21)
   b. Peacocks (1 Kings 10:22; 2 Chron. 9:21)
10. Horses
    a. Solomon owned 40,000 (or 4,000?) stalls of horses (1 Kings 4:26; 2 Chron. 9:25).
    b. He also commanded 1,400 chariots and 12,000 horsemen (1 Kings 10:26; 2 Chron. 1:14).
    c. Many of these horses were brought out of Egypt (1 Kings 10:28; 2 Chron. 1:16; 9:28).
11. Mules (1 Kings 10:25; 2 Chron. 9:24)

B. The source of his wealth—Solomon received his vast riches from at least six sources.

1. From King Hiram's navy of sailing ships (1 Kings 10:11, 22; 2 Chron. 9:10, 21)
2. From an annual Israelite income tax revenue (1 Kings 10:14; 2 Chron. 9:13)
3. From the queen of Sheba (1 Kings 10:2; 2 Chron. 9:1)
4. From various traders and merchants (1 Kings 10:15; 2 Chron. 9:14)
5. From various foreign kings (1 Kings 10:24-25; 2 Chron. 9:23-24)
6. From his sale of horses and chariots (1 Kings 10:29; 2 Chron. 1:17)

C. The employment of his wealth—On what and for what did Solomon use his vast wealth?

1. His palace usage
   a. The meals involved—Solomon's daily food requirements for his staff alone were staggering (1 Kings 4:22-23).
      (1) Fine flour: 195 bushels
      (2) Bushels of meal: 390
      (3) Ten oxen from the fattening pens; 20 oxen from the pasture; 100 sheep
      (4) Assorted game food including deer, gazelle, robuck, and plump fowl
   b. The majesty involved (1 Kings 10:16-21; 2 Chron. 9:15-19)
      (1) Solomon made 200 pieces of golden armor and 300 golden shields which he kept in his palace in the hall of the forest of Lebanon.
      (2) He constructed a huge ivory throne and overlaid it with pure gold. It had six steps, a rounded back with arm rests, and a lion standing on

each side. In addition, there were two lions on each individual step. His was thus the most splendid throne in the entire world.

(3) All of the king's cups and vessels were made of solid gold, as were all the furnishings in his forest of Lebanon room.

2. His public usage—During his 40-year reign, Solomon caused silver and gold to be as plentiful in Jerusalem as rocks on the road, and expensive cedar lumber was used like common sycamore (1 Kings 10:27; 2 Chron. 1:15; 9:20, 27).

VII. The testimony of Solomon—The king's brilliant employment of both his wealth and wisdom was universally known and acknowledged.

A. Publicly attested to—He excelled in the following ways:

1. Jurisprudence (1 Kings 3:16-28)
2. Administration (1 Kings 4:1-19; 11:27-28)
3. Architecture and engineering— This is seen by the temple and his own magnificent palace.
4. Construction
   a. He built the cities of Hazor, Megiddo, and Gezer (1 Kings 9:15).
   b. He also built cities for various reasons (1 Kings 9:19).
      (1) For grain storage
      (2) For keeping his chariots
      (3) For his cavalry and chariot drivers
      (4) For resort purposes
5. Commercial enterprises
   a. He had a shipyard in Ezion-geber near Eloth on the Red Sea in the land of Edom, where he built a fleet of ships (1 Kings 9:26-28).
   b. His merchant fleet was in partnership with King Hiram's ships (1 Kings 10:22).

6. Forestry (1 Kings 4:33)—"He spake of trees, from the cedar tree that is in Lebanon even unto the hyssop that springeth out of the wall."
7. Zoology (1 Kings 4:33)—"He spake also of beasts, and of fowl, and of creeping things, and of fishes."
8. Music and poetry (1 Kings 4:32)— "His songs were a thousand and five."
9. Literature (1 Kings 4:32)—"He spake three thousand proverbs."
10. Drama and play-writing—Song of Solomon
11. Philosophy—Ecclesiastes
12. Counseling and psychology— Proverbs

B. Privately attested to—Solomon was visited by the queen of Sheba (1 Kings 10:1-13; 2 Chron. 9:1-12).

1. The reason for her visit—She came to find out if Solomon was indeed as great as she had heard. The queen would test him with hard questions.
2. The revelation during her visit
   a. She listened to the wisdom of Solomon.
   b. She looked upon the wealth of Solomon.
3. The results of her visit—The queen concluded that the actual greatness of Solomon far exceeded anything she had previously heard.

VIII. The transgressions of Solomon

A. The caution against his sins—God himself had previously appeared to the king with a promise and a warning (1 Kings 9:2-9).

1. The promise
   a. God would honor the temple.
   b. He would establish the kingdom.
   c. He would forgive confessed sin.
2. The warning

a. For unconfessed sins, he would destroy the temple of Israel.

b. For unconfessed sins, he would deport the people of Israel.

B. The cause of his sins—"When Solomon was old . . . his wives turned away his heart after other gods" (1 Kings 11:4).

1. The polygamy involved

a. He had 700 wives and 300 concubines (1 Kings 11:3).

b. These women were taken from Moab, Ammon, Edom, Sidon, and from the land of the Hittites (1 Kings 11:1-2).

2. The paganism involved

a. His first marriage was to the daughter of Pharaoh (1 Kings 3:1).

b. It was apparently a politically arranged marriage.

c. The girl was not a believer, for Solomon later built a separate house for her, away from the temple area, lest she defile it (1 Kings 9:24; 2 Chron. 8:11).

d. He also built various temples for his pagan wives to use for burning incense and sacrificing to their gods (1 Kings 11:8).

e. Finally, Solomon committed the ultimate transgression when he himself sought out those horrible idols. The king worshiped the following (1 Kings 11:5, 7):

(1) Ashtoreth, the goddess of the Sidonians

(2) Milcom, the vicious and vile gods of the Amorites

(3) Chemosh, the depraved god of Moab (Solomon even built a temple on the Mount of Olives for this idol)

(4) Molech, the god of the children of Ammon

C. The consequences following his sins

1. God predicted a coming civil war (1 Kings 11:9-13).

a. Much of Solomon's kingdom would be torn away from his successor and given to another.

b. Only the tribes of Judah and Benjamin would be left for his family to rule over.

c. For David's sake, however, this would not occur until after the death of Solomon.

2. God permitted a current civil unrest (1 Kings 11:14-40), allowing three adversaries to trouble Solomon.

a. Hadad the Edomite—He was a member of the royal family of Edom who had previously fled to Egypt to escape death at the hands of David during a war between the two nations.

b. Rezon—He was the leader of a gang of bandits and made his headquarters in Damascus.

c. Jeroboam

(1) He had been Solomon's former governor over Ephraim and Manasseh and had also fled to Egypt.

(2) The king had attempted to kill Jeroboam upon learning that this was the man to whom God would later give over much of Solomon's kingdom.

(3) Jeroboam continued to exert influence over 10 of Israel's 12 tribes even from Egypt.

THEOLOGICAL SUMMARY

I. Josiah referred to Solomon during his great Passover celebration (2 Chron. 35:3-4).

II. Nehemiah rebuked some Jewish men of his day who had married pagan wives, reminding them of how Solomon had once allowed this terrible sin to wreck his testimony for God (Neh. 13:25-27).

III. Matthew included Solomon's name in his royal genealogy leading to Christ (Matt. 1:6-7).

IV. Jesus referred to Solomon on two important occasions.
  A. To emphasize the faithfulness of God—"Why take ye thought for raiment? Consider the lilies of the field, how they grow; they toil not, neither do they spin: And yet I say unto you, That even Solomon in all his glory was not arrayed like one of these. Wherefore, if God so clothe the grass of the field, which to day is, and to-morrow is cast into the oven, shall he not much more clothe you, O ye of little faith?" (Matt. 6:28-30).
  B. To emphasize the faithlessness of Israel—"The queen of the south shall rise up in the judgment with this generation, and shall condemn it: for she came from the uttermost parts of the earth to hear the wisdom of Solomon; and, behold, a greater than Solomon is here" (Matt. 12:42).
V. Stephen referred to Solomon during his defense before the Sanhedrin (Acts 7:47).

STATISTICS

Father: David (2 Sam. 12:24)
Mother: Bath-sheba (2 Sam. 12:24)
Spouse: Naamah (among the many) (1 Kings 11:3; 14:21)
Son: Rehoboam (1 Kings 14:21)
Brothers: Full brothers: Shammua, Shobab, and Nathan (1 Chron. 3:5). Half brothers: Amnon, Daniel (also called Chileab), Absalom, Adonijah, Shephatiah, Ithream, Ibhar, Elishua, Eliphelet, Nogah, Nepheg, Japhia, Elishama, Eliada, and Eliphelet (2 Sam. 3:2-5; 5:13-16; 1 Chron. 3:1-8; 14:3-5).
Sister: Half sister, Tamar (2 Sam. 13:1)
First mention: 2 Samuel 5:14
Final mention: Acts 7:47
Meaning of his name: "Peace"
Frequency of his name: Referred to 297 times
Biblical books mentioning him: 14 books (2 Samuel, 1 Kings, 2 Kings, 1 Chronicles, 2 Chronicles, Nehemiah, Psalms, Proverbs, Song of Solomon, Jeremiah, Matthew, Luke, John, Acts)
Occupation: King of Israel
Place of birth: Jerusalem (2 Sam. 5:14)
Place of death: Jerusalem (1 Kings 11:43)
Important fact about his life: He was the world's wisest man (1 Kings 3:11-12).

Tamar (1)

CHRONOLOGICAL SUMMARY

I. Her distress
  A. She was left a widow by her two husbands.
    1. The first husband—Tamar married Er, the eldest son of Judah, and became a widow when God killed him for his wickedness (Gen. 38:6-7).
    2. The second husband—She was widowed the second time when Onan, younger brother of Er, whom she had married, was also killed by God (Gen. 38:8-10).
  B. She was lied to by her father-in-law, Judah, who promised her that, upon coming of age, his third son Shelah would become her husband (Gen. 38:11-13).
II. Her disguise
  A. However, upon realizing Judah would not keep his word, Tamar disguised herself as a common harlot and lured him into her tent for sexual immorality (Gen. 38:12-16).
  B. For payment she secured Judah's seal with its cord and his staff (Gen. 38:17-18).
  C. Three months later, upon learning of her pregnancy, an indignant Judah ordered her to be burned to death (Gen. 38:24).
III. Her defense—After she displayed the seal and staff belonging to the father of her unborn child, an embarrassed and repentant Judah confessed his sin and

set aside her punishment (Gen. 38:25-26).

IV. Her delivery—Tamar gave birth to twin boys, Pharez and Zarah (Gen. 38:27-30).

THEOLOGICAL SUMMARY

I. Tamar became an ancestress of Achan (possibly through her son Zarah), the troublemaker in the days of Joshua (1 Chron. 2:7; 4:1).

II. Through her firstborn son Pharez, she became an ancestress of both David and Christ.
A. An ancestress of David (Ruth 4:18)
B. An ancestress of Christ (Matt. 1:3)

STATISTICS

Spouses: Er and Onan (Gen. 38:6-10)
Sons: Pharez and Zarah (Gen. 38:27-30)
First mention: Genesis 38:6
Final mention: Matthew 1:3
Meaning of her name: "Palm"
Frequency of her name: Referred to seven times
Biblical books mentioning her: Four books (Genesis, Ruth, 1 Chronicles, Matthew)
Important fact about her life: She was Judah's daughter-in-law who bore him twins (Gen. 38:12-30).

✍Tamar (2)

CHRONOLOGICAL SUMMARY

I. She was attacked by Amnon, her half brother.
A. Tamar was the beautiful daughter of King David (2 Sam. 13:1).
B. She was Absalom's sister (2 Sam. 13:22).
C. She was raped and then rejected by her half brother Amnon (2 Sam. 13:6-18).

II. She was avenged by Absalom, her full brother.
A. Absalom later killed Amnon for his crimes against Tamar (2 Sam. 13:28-29).

B. Tamar became a broken and desolate woman (2 Sam. 13:20).

STATISTICS

Father: David (2 Sam. 13:1)
Mother: Maacah (2 Sam. 3:3; 13:1)
Brothers: Full brother, Absalom (2 Sam. 13:1). Half brother, Amnon (2 Sam. 3:2).
First mention: 2 Samuel 13:1
Final mention: 1 Chronicles 3:9
Meaning of her name: "Palm"
Frequency of her name: Referred to 14 times
Biblical books mentioning her: Two books (2 Samuel, 1 Chronicles)
Important fact about her life: She was David's daughter, who was raped by her half brother Amnon (2 Sam. 13:1-19).

Terah

CHRONOLOGICAL SUMMARY

I. Terah, the parent
A. He fathered three sons and one daughter through two wives (Gen. 11:26; 20:12).
B. Abraham was born of his first wife and Sarah of his second, thus making them half brother and sister (Gen. 20:12).
C. Rebekah was his great-granddaughter (Gen. 22:23).

II. Terah, the pagan—At one time, he worshiped idols in Mesopotamia (Josh. 24:2).

III. Terah, the pilgrim
A. Terah left Ur of the Chaldeans, taking with him Abraham, Sarah, and Lot (his grandson), and moved to the city of Haran. There he lived out his life and died at age 205 (Gen. 11:31-32).
B. He is mentioned in the genealogy leading to Christ (Luke 3:34).

STATISTICS

Father: Nahor (Gen. 11:24)
Spouses: Two wives (Gen. 11:26; 20:12)

Sons: Abraham, Nahor, and Haran (Gen. 11:26)

Daughter: Sarah (Gen. 20:12)

First mention: Genesis 11:24

Final mention: Luke 3:34

Meaning of his name: "Turning, duration"

Frequency of his name: Referred to 10 times

Biblical books mentioning him: Four books (Genesis, Joshua, 1 Chronicles, Luke)

Place of death: Haran (Gen. 11:32)

Age at death: 250 (Gen. 11:32)

Important fact about his life: He was the father of Abraham and Sarah (Gen. 11:26; 20:12).

☞Tiglath-Pileser III

CHRONOLOGICAL SUMMARY

I. Tiglath-pileser and Judean King Ahaz (2 Kings 16:7-10)
   A. The message from Ahaz (2 Kings 16:7-9)
      1. This powerful Assyrian king was also known as Pul (2 Kings 15:19; 1 Chron. 5:26).
      2. Ahaz sent messengers to Tiglath, begging the Assyrian king to help him against the attacking Syrian army.
   B. The meeting with Ahaz—After the battle, Ahaz hurried to Damascus and met with Tiglath.
II. Tiglath-pileser and Northern Israelite King Menahem—He invaded Israel during Menahem's reign but was bought off with a bribe of some two million dollars (2 Kings 15:18-19).
III. Tiglath-pileser and Northern Israelite King Pekah (2 Kings 15:28-29)
   A. During his reign Tiglath attacked and carried off many citizens of the 10 tribes into Assyrian captivity.
   B. Tiglath was succeeded at death by Shalmaneser V.

STATISTICS

First mention: 2 Kings 15:19

Final mention: 2 Chronicles 28:20

Meaning of his name: "My confidence is the son of Esarra"

Frequency of his name: Referred to nine times

Biblical books mentioning him: Three books (2 Kings, 1 Chronicles, 2 Chronicles)

Occupation: King of Assyria (2 Kings 15:19)

Important fact about his life: He was the first of several Assyrian kings to invade Israel.

☞Tobiah

CHRONOLOGICAL SUMMARY

I. His hatred for Nehemiah the prophet— He was an Ammonite who, along with Sanballat and Geshem, hated and opposed Nehemiah in his project to rebuild the fallen walls of Jerusalem (Neh. 2:10, 19).
II. His harassment of Nehemiah the prophet
   A. He began by ridiculing the prophet, saying his wall was so weak that a fox climbing up on it would break down the stones (Neh. 2:19; 4:1-3).
   B. He then became very angry as the work progressed (Neh. 4:7).
   C. He joined in a plot to attack the workers (Neh. 4:8).
   D. He and his associates attempted to assassinate Nehemiah by tricking him into a meeting (Neh. 6:1-9).
   E. He then, along with Sanballat, hired a friend of Nehemiah by the name of Shemiah to betray him, but the prophet saw through their plot (Neh. 6:10-14).
   F. Because of Tobiah's great wealth, prominence, and influence, many of the rich people of Judah displayed a loyalty to him (Neh. 6:17-19).
      1. He wrote letters to them and received letters from them.

2. They kept telling Nehemiah what a wonderful man he was.
3. Tobiah continuously sent threatening letters to Nehemiah.

III. His handling by Nehemiah the prophet

A. Eliashib, the high priest, was a personal friend of Tobiah and had actually provided this troublemaker with living quarters in the courts of the house of God itself (Neh. 13:4-5).

B. Upon returning from a trip and learning of this, Nehemiah ordered Tobiah to clear out immediately. In fact, the great wall builder personally threw all of Tobiah's household goods into the street and purified the room (Neh. 13:6-9).

STATISTICS

First mention: Nehemiah 2:10
Final mention: Nehemiah 13:8
Meaning of his name: "God is good"
Frequency of his name: Referred to 12 times
Biblical books mentioning him: One book (Nehemiah)
Important fact about his life: He was one of three troublemakers who opposed Nehemiah (Neh. 2:10; 4:3-8).

Uriah

CHRONOLOGICAL SUMMARY

I. Uriah, the soldier

A. He was a Hittite and the husband of Bath-sheba (2 Sam. 11:3).

B. He was numbered among 39 (2 Sam. 23:39) especially loyal and courageous soldiers of David who fought for him during those difficult and dangerous days when Saul sought his life (see 23:24-39).

II. Uriah, the sacrifice

A. He lost his wife—Uriah was sent for and brought home by David from the front lines when Israel was fighting the Ammonites (2 Sam. 11:1-13).

1. The review—David had slept with

Uriah's wife, Bath-sheba, and made her pregnant.

2. The reason—David had hoped that Uriah would sleep with Bath-sheba, that he might be deceived into assuming the unborn child was his.

3. The results—Uriah, probably suspecting the situation, refused to do this.

B. He lost his life.

1. In desperation, David sent Uriah back to the front lines with a letter ordering Joab, the Israelite commander, to put him in a place where he would be killed (2 Sam. 11:14-15).

2. This cruel order was carried out, and Uriah fell in battle (2 Sam. 11:16-17).

STATISTICS

Spouse: Bath-sheba (2 Sam. 11:3)
First mention: 2 Samuel 11:3
Final mention: Matthew 1:6
Meaning of his name: "God is Light"
Frequency of his name: Referred to 25 times
Biblical books mentioning him: Four books (2 Samuel, 1 Kings, 1 Chronicles, Matthew)
Occupation: Soldier (2 Sam. 23:8, 39)
Place of death: On a battlefield near the Ammonite city of Rabbah (2 Sam. 11:1, 17)
Circumstances of death: He was ordered killed by David (2 Sam. 11:14-15).
Important fact about his life: He was Bath-sheba's husband, whom David betrayed (2 Sam. 11).

Urijah

CHRONOLOGICAL SUMMARY

I. Constructing a false altar

A. Urijah was a priest in the days of Judean King Ahaz (2 Kings 16:10).

B. He was ordered to build an altar after the pattern the wicked king had seen

while visiting a pagan temple in Damascus (2 Kings 16:10).
II. Changing the true altar—Urijah, without any protest, removed the regular
bronze altar to the north side of the
room (2 Kings 16:14, 16).

STATISTICS

First mention: 2 Kings 16:10
Final mention: 2 Kings 16:16
Meaning of his name: "God is Light"
Frequency of his name: Referred to 25 times
Biblical books mentioning him: One book
(2 Kings)
Occupation: Priest (2 Kings 16:10)
Important fact about his life: He built a pagan
altar for King Ahaz (2 Kings 16:10-16).

✍Uzziah

CHRONOLOGICAL SUMMARY

I. The proficiency of Uzziah
  A. The builder
    1. He was also called Azariah
       (2 Kings 14:21).
    2. He was the tenth ruler of Judah.
    3. He ruled for 52 years (2 Kings
       15:2).
    4. He began to rule when he was 16
       (2 Kings 14:21).
    5. He was basically a good king, but
       he did not remove the pagan high
       places (2 Kings 15:3-4).
    6. He was instructed in the fear of
       the Lord by a godly prophet
       named Zechariah (2 Chron. 26:5).
    7. He built towers in Jerusalem at
       the corner gate and valley gate
       (2 Chron. 26:9).
    8. He built towers in the desert and
       dug many cisterns (2 Chron.
       26:10).
    9. He rebuilt Elath and returned it to
       Judah (2 Kings 14:22).
  B. The military leader
    1. He had a well-trained army
       (2 Chron. 26:11).

    a. The army numbered 307,500
       troops (2 Chron. 26:13).
    b. The leaders numbered 2,600
       (2 Chron. 26:12).
    2. He equipped them with shields,
       spears, helmets, coats of armor,
       bows, and slings (2 Chron.
       26:14).
    3. He placed machines on the towers
       in Jerusalem (2 Chron. 26:15).
  C. The rancher—He had much livestock
     in the foothills and in the plains
     (2 Chron. 26:10).
  D. The farmer—He had people working
     his fields and vineyards and was a
     lover of the soil (2 Chron. 26:10).
II. The pride of Uzziah
  A. Uzziah, the lawless (2 Chron. 26:16)
    1. After he became powerful, his
       pride led to his downfall.
    2. He intruded into the office of the
       priesthood by entering the temple
       to burn incense on the altar of
       incense.
  B. Uzziah, the leper
    1. He was confronted and con-
       demned for this by the high priest
       Azariah along with 80 other cou-
       rageous priests (2 Chron. 26:17-
       18).
    2. Uzziah, with the censer still in his
       hand, became furious and began
       raging at the priests (2 Chron.
       26:19).
    3. Even as he spoke, a leprosy
       plague from God broke out on his
       forehead (2 Chron. 26:19).
    4. He was hurriedly escorted out of
       the temple by Azariah (2 Chron.
       26:20).
  C. Uzziah, the lonely—From that day
     until the day he died, Uzziah lived
     alone in a separate house, excluded
     from the temple of the Lord
     (2 Chron. 26:21).

THEOLOGICAL SUMMARY

I. Isaiah prophesied during the reign of
Uzziah. In fact, when the king died,
Isaiah saw a vision of God's glory and

the angelic seraphs in heaven (Isa. 6:1-13).

II. Hosea prophesied during the reign of Uzziah (Hos. 1:1).

III. Amos also prophesied and stated that a tremendous earthquake occurred during the reign of Uzziah (Amos 1:1).

IV. Zechariah the prophet referred to this earthquake centuries after it happened, comparing it to the great earthquake which will split the Mount of Olives from east to west at the second coming of Christ (Zech. 14:3-5).

STATISTICS

Father: Amaziah (2 Kings 14:21)
Mother: Jecholiah (2 Kings 15:2)
Spouse: Jerusha (2 Kings 15:33)
Son: Jotham (2 Chron. 26:23-27:1-2)
First mention: 2 Kings 14:21
Final mention: Matthew 1:9
Meaning of his name: "God is strong"
Frequency of his name: Referred to 34 times
Biblical books mentioning him: Eight books (2 Kings, 1 Chronicles, 2 Chronicles, Isaiah, Hosea, Amos, Zechariah, Matthew)
Occupation: King of Judah (2 Chron. 26:1)
Place of birth: Jerusalem
Place of death: Jerusalem (2 Kings. 15:7)
Circumstances of death: He died of leprosy (2 Kings 15:5).
Important fact about his life: He attempted to intrude into the office of the priesthood (2 Chron. 26:16-21).

✒️*Vashti*

CHRONOLOGICAL SUMMARY

I. Her refusal of the king

A. She was the beautiful Persian queen married to King Ahasuerus (Esther 1:9, 11).

B. She hosted a banquet for the women in the royal palace during an important state dinner given by the king (Esther 1:5-9).

C. She refused to obey the king's command to display and parade her

beauty before his drunken crony friends (Esther 1:10-12).

II. Her refusal by the king

A. The furious king was then advised by his officials to divorce Vashti for her insubordination, which action he followed (Esther 1:13-22).

B. Upon sobering up, however, Ahasuerus reconsidered this hasty decision, but was bound by it according to Persian law (Esther 2:1).

C. Vashti was later succeeded by Esther as queen (Esther 2:17).

STATISTICS

Spouse: Ahasuerus (Esther 1:9, 11)
First mention: Esther 1:9
Final mention: Esther 2:17
Meaning of her name: "Beautiful"
Frequency of her name: Referred to 10 times
Biblical books mentioning her: One book (Esther)
Occupation: Queen of the Medo-Persian empire (Esther 1:1-3, 9)
Important fact about her life: She was the deposed queen of Persian king Ahasuerus (Esther 2:17).

✒️*Zachariah*

CHRONOLOGICAL SUMMARY

I. The apostate king

A. He was the fourteenth ruler of Northern Israel.

B. He ruled for six months (2 Kings 15:8).

C. He was an evil king (2 Kings 15:9).

II. The assassinated king—He was conspired against and murdered by a rebel named Shallum (2 Kings 15:10).

STATISTICS

Father: Jeroboam II (2 Kings 14:29)
First mention: 2 Kings 14:29
Final mention: 2 Kings 15:11
Meaning of his name: "God is renowned"
Frequency of his name: Referred to three times

Biblical books mentioning him: One book
(2 Kings)
Occupation: King of Northern Israel (2 Kings
15:8)
Place of death: Probably in the city of Samaria
Circumstances of death: He was murdered by
Shallum (2 Kings 15:10).
Important fact about his life: His death fulfilled
the prophecy against Jehu (2 Kings 15:12).

Zadok

CHRONOLOGICAL SUMMARY

I. Zadok under the reign of David
   A. His assignment by David
      1. Zadok was high priest along with
         Abiathar in the days of David
         (2 Sam. 8:17; 20:25).
      2. He helped David bring the Ark
         into the king's new capital, Jeru-
         salem (1 Chron. 15:11-15).
      3. Both men ministered to David in
         the wilderness when the king was
         driven from Jerusalem by Absa-
         lom's rebellion (2 Sam. 15:24).
      4. He was ordered by David to re-
         turn to Jerusalem the Ark of the
         Covenant that the two priests had
         brought to the king (2 Sam. 15:25-
         29).
   B. His assistance to David—After Absa-
      lom's revolt was crushed, Zadok
      helped restore the broken union be-
      tween David and the leaders of Judah
      (2 Sam. 19:11).
II. Zadok under the reign of Solomon
   A. The anointing
      1. Zadok supported Solomon during
         the attempted coup led by the
         king's half brother Adonijah
         (1 Kings 1:8).
      2. On his deathbed, David ordered
         Zadok to publicly anoint Solomon
         (1 Kings 1:34, 38-39).
   B. The appointing
      1. Zadok was then appointed by Sol-
         omon as the sole high priest, set-

ting aside Abiathar, who had
joined Adonijah's revolt (1 Kings
1:7; 2:35).
   2. He was also appointed to offer
      daily sacrifices to God (1 Chron.
      16:39-40).
   3. As a reward for his faithfulness,
      God promised that Zadok's
      descendants would serve as
      priests in the millennial temple
      (Ezek. 44:15; 48:11).
   4. One of Zadok's descendants was
      Ezra (Ezra 7:1-2).

STATISTICS
Father: Ahitub (1 Chron. 6:8)
Son: Ahimaaz (2 Sam. 15:27)
Significant ancestor: Aaron (1 Chron. 6:3-8)
Significant descendant: Ezra (Ezra 7:1-2)
First mention: 2 Samuel 8:17
Final mention: Ezekiel 48:11
Meaning of his name: "Righteous"
Frequency of his name: Referred to 40 times
Biblical books mentioning him: Six books
(2 Samuel, 1 Kings, 1 Chronicles,
2 Chronicles, Ezra, Ezekiel)
Occupation: High priest
Important fact about his life: He was co-high
priest in David's time and high priest in
the days of Solomon (2 Sam. 8:17; 1 Kings
2:35).

Zechariah (1)

CHRONOLOGICAL SUMMARY

I. Zechariah, the minister—He was the
   high priest in the days of Judean King
   Joash, who fearlessly preached against
   the sin of the people (2 Chron. 24:20).
II. Zechariah, the martyr
   A. For this he was stoned to death by
      his own people at Joash's command,
      despite the fact that his father, Jehoi-
      ada, had saved Joash's life (2 Chron.
      24:21-22).
   B. Jesus referred to this terrible event
      when rebuking the wicked Pharisees,

reminding them of their murderous ancestry (Matt. 23:35).

STATISTICS
Father: Jehoiada (2 Chron. 24:20)
Mother: Jehosheba (2 Chron. 22:11)
First mention: 2 Chronicles 24:20
Final mention: 2 Chronicles 24:20
Meaning of his name: "God has remembered"
Frequency of his name: Referred to one time
Biblical books mentioning him: One book
(2 Chronicles)
Occupation: High priest (2 Chron. 24:15-20)
Place of death: In the Jerusalem temple courtyard (2 Chron. 24:21)
Circumstances of death: He was stoned to death (2 Chron. 24:21).
Important fact about his life: He was the fearless high priest in the days of King Joash (2 Chron. 24:20-22).

✍Zechariah (2)

CHRONOLOGICAL SUMMARY
I. The visions of the prophet—Zechariah received 10 visions, all apparently during the same night (1–6).
  A. The rider on the red horse (1:7-17)
    1. Zechariah saw a heavenly rider on a red horse, surrounded by other riders, all mounted also upon various colored horses.
    2. This special rider on the red horse was probably Christ.
    3. The other riders were angels who had been sent by God to "Walk to and fro through the earth" (1:10).
    4. The angel of the Lord (Jesus) then prayed over the troubled state of Jerusalem and was reassured by the Father that "The LORD shall yet comfort Zion, and shall yet choose Jerusalem" (1:17).
      a. The question by the Son—"O LORD of hosts, how long wilt thou not have mercy on Jerusalem and on the cities of Judah, against which thou hast had

indignation these threescore and ten years?" (1:12).
      b. The answer by the Father—"I am returned to Jerusalem with mercies: my house shall be built in it, saith the LORD of hosts, and a line shall be stretched forth upon Jerusalem" (1:16).
  B. The four horns—Zechariah saw four animal horns and was told they represented the four world powers that had scattered Judah, Israel, and Jerusalem. These powers are probably Assyria, Egypt, Babylon, and Medo-Persia (1:18-19).
  C. The four artisans (an artisan is a worker in wood, stone, or metal) (1:20-21)
    1. The identity of these artisans—These may refer to the four judgments spoken of by both Ezekiel (Ezek. 14:21) and John (Rev. 6:1-8). These judgments are war, famine, wild animals, and pestilence.
    2. The purpose of the artisans—"These are come to fray them, to cast out the horns of the Gentiles, which lifted up their horn over the land of Judah to scatter it" (1:21). This will happen during the great tribulation (see especially Rev. 6:15-17).
  D. The man with a measuring line (2:1-13)
    1. Zechariah saw a man carrying a yardstick in his hand en route to measure Jerusalem.
    2. Zechariah was assured of the following thrilling facts concerning the millennial Jerusalem.
      a. Jerusalem would someday be so full of people that some would have to live outside its city walls, yet they would dwell in perfect safety.
      b. God himself would be a wall of fire protecting them.
      c. He would be the glory of the city (2:10-12).
      d. The one who harmed them

touched the apple of his eye. (See also Deut. 32:7-10; Ps. 17:8.)

E. The clothing of Joshua, the high priest—This is undoubtedly the greatest single chapter on the subject of salvation in all the Old Testament. In this vision Zechariah saw Joshua, the high priest, dressed in filthy clothing, and standing before God in heaven. He was being accused by Satan because of this soiled clothing. Christ, however, rebuked Satan, removed Joshua's dirty clothing, and dressed him in clean apparel. Joshua then was challenged to serve God with his whole heart. He was promised that someday God's Branch would appear to cleanse the land of its sin (3:1-10). The following facts concerning salvation are brought out here:

1. The enemy of salvation—Satan (3:1)
2. The person of salvation—He is, of course, the Savior. Here in verse two we have evidence of the truth of the trinity, for the Lord (Jesus) calls upon the Lord (the Father) to rebuke Satan.
   a. His name
      (1) The Branch (3:8)
      (2) The Cornerstone (3:9)
   b. His ministry
      (1) To clothe all believers in robes of righteousness
      (2) To make intercession for the believers against Satan's lies
      (3) To bring in and rule over the Millennium
3. The purpose of salvation (3:6-7)— These verses may be paraphrased as follows: "If you will walk in my ways and keep my charge, you [Joshua] shall not only have the honor of judging my house, and keeping my courts, but when your work on earth is done, you shall be transplanted to higher service in heaven, and have places to walk among these pure

angelic beings who stand by me harkening unto the voice of my word." (See also Ps. 103:20-21; Eph. 2:4-10.)

F. The golden lampstand and the two olive trees—Here Zechariah saw a seven-branched golden lampstand, supplied by a reservoir of olive oil. On either side of the lampstand was an olive tree (4:1-14).

1. A lampstand in the Bible represents God's witnesses in this world.
2. The olive oil is, of course, a symbol for the Holy Spirit (see Luke 4:18; Acts 10:38; Heb. 1:9; 1 John 2:20). Note the words of God: "Not by might, nor by power, but by my spirit, saith the LORD of hosts" (4:6). "The hands of Zerubbabel have laid the foundation of this house; his hands shall also finish it; and thou shalt know that the LORD of hosts hath sent me unto you" (4:9). The context here means that the unfinished temple will be completed by the power of the Holy Spirit.
3. The olive trees may refer to two famous teams—"Then said he, These are the two anointed ones, that stand by the LORD of the whole earth" (4:14).
   a. The historical team of Zerubbabel and Joshua
   b. The prophetical team of Elijah and Moses (See Revelation 11) (It is being assumed here that the two witnesses are definitely Elijah and Moses.) "I will give power unto my two witnesses, and they shall prophesy a thousand two hundred and threescore days, clothed in sackcloth. These are the two olive trees, and the two candlesticks standing before the God of the earth" (Rev. 11:3-4).

G. The flying scroll—Zechariah saw a flying scroll, 15 feet wide by 30 feet long. This represented the words of God's curse going out over the entire land of Israel (5:1-4).

   1. The scope of this judgment— Although only two of the original commandments are mentioned here, that of swearing (the third, Exod. 20:7) and stealing (the eighth, Exod. 20:15), they nevertheless covered the entire moral code of God.
   2. The accused at this judgment—All unsaved Israelites throughout history (Ezek. 11:21; 20:38; Matt. 23; Rom. 9:6; 1 Thess. 2:15-16)
   3. The time of this judgment—After the tribulation and just prior to the Millennium (Matt. 25:1-30)
   4. The penalty of this judgment—It will apparently include both physical and spiritual death.
H. The woman in the ephah—The prophet viewed a flying bushel basket (ephah) covered by a heavy lead top piece. When the lid was lifted he saw a woman inside (5:5-11). He was then told:
   1. The woman inside represented sin and wickedness. Often in the Bible iniquity is symbolized by a woman (see Matt. 13:33; Rev. 2:20; 17:1-7).
   2. The heavy lead cover probably symbolized the restraining power of God over evil.
   3. The destination was said to be Babylon, where evil and wickedness would "Be established, and set there upon her own base" (5:11). Thus, this is where it officially began (Gen. 11:1-9) and where it will end (Rev. 18).
I. The four chariots—Zechariah saw four chariots driven by four heavenly spirits proceeding from two brass mountains. Each chariot was pulled by a different colored team of horses. These colors were red, black, white,

and gray (6:1-8). The various symbols here would seem to be as follows:
   1. The two brass mountains speak of God's judgment.
   2. The angelic-driven chariots represent God's agents to effect various judgments upon Gentile nations.
J. The crowning of Joshua (6:9-15)
   1. Zechariah was told that three Jewish exiles would soon return to Jerusalem from Babylon, carrying gifts of silver and gold from the remnant there. Zechariah was instructed to make a golden crown from these gifts and place it upon Joshua, explaining to him that he (Joshua) would then represent the future Branch of Israel, the Messiah himself.
   2. This blessed Messiah would someday function both as priest and king. He would also build the temple of God (6:12-13).
   3. Zechariah was told the three returning exiles represented many others who would someday come from distant lands back to Palestine (6:15).
II. The vanities of the people
A. A group of Jews had come to Jerusalem from Bethel to ask the priests there if they could set aside their traditional custom of fasting and mourning each year during the month of August (7:3). The full question was: "Now that the temple is being rebuilt, is it necessary to keep that fast (in August) which commemorated the burning of the first temple by Nebuchadnezzar in 586 B.C.?"
B. God told them through the priests that it didn't really make much difference what they did, for their hearts were insincere. He admonished them to be honest in their dealings with both their God and their neighbors. Besides, some of their fast days were man-made and not God-appointed.
C. He promised that, because of his

grace, their fast days would someday be feast days, and their sorrow turned into singing (8:3-23).

III. The victories of the Greeks and Jews
A. The success of Alexander the Great over Tyre (9:1-8)
B. The success of the Maccabean Jews over the Syrians (9:13-17)
IV. The visitations of the Prince
A. The first coming of the Prince
1. He came to feed the flock as his Father had instructed him to do (11:7).
2. The false shepherds of Israel, however, rejected him (11:8)— "Their soul also abhorred me."
3. He thus broke one of his two staffs and set Israel aside for awhile (11:10; see also Matt. 21:19, 42-46; 23:37-39).
4. He finished his ministry by the triumphal entry into Jerusalem. "Rejoice greatly, O daughter of Zion; shout, O daughter of Jerusalem: behold, thy King cometh unto thee: he is just, and having salvation; lowly, and riding upon an ass, and upon a colt the foal of an ass" (9:9).
5. He was sold for 30 pieces of silver (11:12), the price of a slave which had been gored by an ox.
6. This price, contemptuously given, was then cast aside with additional contempt (the word "cast" used here is a gesture of disgust) (11:13).
7. He then broke his second staff, signifying perhaps the destruction of Jerusalem by Titus in A.D. 70 (11:14).
8. He was finally crucified—"They shall look upon me whom they have pierced" (12:10).
B. The second coming of the Prince:
1. The bloodletting of the false shepherd
a. Because they rejected their Good Shepherd at his first com-

ing, Israel will be given over for awhile to the cruel Antichrist shepherd just prior to the second appearing of their glorious Shepherd (11:15-17).
b. Two out of three will die in this horrible purge (13:8).
c. However, the one third shall be saved (13:9).
2. The bereavement of Israel—When Christ comes again, Israel will finally recognize him and mourn over their heinous national crime of rexicide, the killing of one's own king (12:10-14). "And they shall look upon Me whom they have pierced, and they shall mourn for him, as one mourneth for his only son" (12:10; see also 12:12-14).
3. The battle of Armageddon (12:1-9; 14:1-3, 12-15)
a. Jerusalem will be surrounded and occupied by the Antichrist (12:2-3; 14:2).
b. Christ will touch down upon the Mount of Olives to personally lead the battle against his enemies. "Then shall the LORD go forth, and fight against those nations, as when he fought in the day of battle. And his feet shall stand in that day upon the mount of Olives, which is before Jerusalem on the east, and the mount of Olives shall cleave in the midst thereof toward the east and toward the west, and there shall be a very great valley; and half of the mountain shall remove toward the north, and half of it toward the south" (14:3-4).
c. He will smite them with a divine plague (12:4, 9, 12)— "This shall be the plague wherewith the LORD will smite all the people that have fought against Jerusalem; Their flesh shall con-

sume away while they stand upon their feet, and their eyes shall consume away in their holes, and their tongue shall consume away in their mouth" (14:12).

4. The bow of victory (10:4)—The bow is, of course, the Son of God. We are assured of his deity because of the Father's statement in 13:7. "The man that is my fellow, saith the LORD of hosts." This is literally translated, "the man who is my equal." From the bow of God this Avenging Arrow comes to earth.

5. The blessings of God
   a. Israel will be regathered (10:6-8).
   b. God himself will become Jerusalem's defender (12:8).
   c. Israel will be purified (13:1).
   d. Christ will rule over all the earth (14:9).
   e. All nations will worship him (14:16).
   f. Living waters will flow from the Mediterranean to the Dead Sea (14:8).
   g. Every object will be holy (14:20-21).

THEOLOGICAL SUMMARY

I. Zechariah was a contemporary of Haggai the prophet (Ezra 5:1).
II. He had joined the Jewish remnant (along with Haggai, Zerubbabel, the political leader, and Joshua, the religious leader) during the return from Persia to Jerusalem in 536 B.C. to rebuild the temple (Ezra 5:1-2; 6:14).
III. Zechariah's book provides much information about both angels and Satan.
   A. The activities of angels
      1. He likens them to:
         a. Horsemen riding upon various colored horses (Zech 1:8)
         b. Chariots being pulled by various colored horses (6:1-7)

2. They are seen as those who patrol the earth (1:11).
3. They prophesy to men (2:3-4).
4. They minister to believers (3:4).
5. They execute judgment (6:8).
   B. The activities of Satan
      1. He has access to God's throne (3:1).
      2. He accuses believers before God's throne (3:1).
      3. He is rebuked from God's throne (3:2).
IV. Genesis 11 and Zechariah 5 may be compared.
   A. Genesis 11 states the land of Shinar (ancient Babylon) was Satan's original headquarters.
   B. Zechariah 5 suggests the land of Shinar may once again become Satan's headquarters.
V. Jewish tradition says Zechariah was a member of the great synagogue that collected and preserved the Old Testament books.
VI. Nehemiah said he became an important priestly leader (Neh. 12:16).
VII. Jesus said Zechariah was murdered by his own countrymen in the temple, between the altar and the sanctuary (Matt. 23:35).
VIII. His book is the longest of the 12 minor prophets.
IX. For its size, Zechariah is quoted from or alluded to more times in the New Testament than any other Old Testament book.
X. Zechariah may be contrasted to Daniel and Ezekiel.
   A. Daniel and Ezekiel were born in Judah, but wrote their books in Babylon/Persia.
   B. Zechariah was born in Babylon/Persia, but wrote his book in Judah.
XI. Zechariah received the greatest number of visions in the shortest space of time (10, apparently in one night) than any other Old Testament prophet (1–6).
XII. His is the only biblical book referring to Palestine as the Holy Land (2:12).

XIII. His book is, in essence, a summary of Jesus and Jerusalem, i.e., the Son of God and the city of God.

A. Facts about the Son of God
1. His commission from the Father (2:8-11)
2. His present-day work (3:1-2)
3. His concern over Jerusalem (1:2)
4. His title (6:12)
5. His millennial temple (6:13)
6. His triumphal entry (9:9)
7. His betrayal (11:12)
8. His crucifixion (12:10; 13:7)
9. His eventual recognition by Israel (12:10)
10. His appearance on the Mount of Olives (14:4)
11. His supernatural canal connecting the Great Sea to the Salt Sea (14:4, 8)
12. His worship by all nations (14:16)
13. His victory at Armageddon (14:3)

B. Facts about the city of God
1. To be called the city of truth (8:3)
2. To be surrounded by a protective wall of fire of God's glory (2:5)
3. To be filled with boys and girls playing (8:5)
4. To be visited by all nations (8:20-23)
5. To be besieged one final time by its enemies (12:2; 14:2)
6. To see its enemies destroyed forever (12:9; 14:12-14)
7. To have its citizens (the Jewish people) recognize their Messiah (12:10)
8. To be filled with God's holiness (14:20-21)

STATISTICS

Father: Berechiah (Zech. 1:1)
First mention: Ezra 5:1
Final mention: Matthew 23:35
Meaning of his name: "God hath remembered"
Frequency of his name: Referred to six times
Biblical books mentioning him: Four books (Ezra, Zechariah, Nehemiah, Matthew)

Occupation: Prophet (Ezra 5:1)
Important fact about his life: His book, for its size, has more to say about both Christ's first and second coming than any other Old Testament book.

✍Zedekiah

CHRONOLOGICAL SUMMARY

I. Zedekiah and the king of Babylon—Nebuchadnezzar

A. His appointment by the king
1. He was the twentieth and final ruler of Judah.
2. He ruled for 11 years (2 Kings 24:18).
3. He was 21 when he began to rule (2 Kings 24:18).
4. He was an evil king (2 Kings 24:19).
5. He was also known as Mattaniah (2 Kings 24:17).
6. He was appointed king by Nebuchadnezzar (Jer. 37:1).

B. His activities against the king
1. The revolt
   a. Zedekiah rebelled against Nebuchadnezzar during the ninth year of his reign in Judah (2 Kings 24:20—25:1).
   b. After a two-year siege, and being abandoned by his own army, Zedekiah fled the starving city of Jerusalem but was overtaken and captured at Jericho (2 Kings 25:2, 5-6; Jer. 39:2, 4-5).
2. The retaliation—Zedekiah's sons were then killed, and he was blinded, bound, and taken to Babylon (2 Kings 25:7; Jer. 39:6-8).

II. Zedekiah and the prophet of Judah—Jeremiah

A. The rebuke by Jeremiah—Prior to the terrible fate of the Judean king, God had attempted to reach him through Jeremiah.

1. God said he had not humbled himself (2 Chron. 36:12).
2. The king had become stiff necked and hardened his heart (2 Chron. 36:13).
3. Zedekiah sent two false prophets named Pashur and Zephaniah to Jeremiah, attempting to pressure him into offering a positive prophecy concerning the outcome of the Babylonian threat (Jer. 21:1-2).
4. Jeremiah refused, and predicted Zedekiah would be handed over to the Babylonians (Jer. 21:3-7).
5. He warned the king to submit to the Babylonian captivity as a punishment from God. If he did this, he would live (Jer. 27:12; 38:17-18).
6. Both the prophets Jeremiah and Ezekiel spoke punishment against the unrepentant Zedekiah.
   a. Jeremiah said he would be forced to look into the eyes of Nebuchadnezzar (Jer. 32:4-5).
   b. Ezekiel said he would not see the land of Babylon even though he would be carried there (Ezek. 12:13).
7. These two prophecies were, of course, tragically fulfilled at the blinding of Zedekiah after he had gazed into Nebuchadnezzar's eyes, but before he reached Babylon (Jer. 39:7).

B. The response by Zedekiah—How did the wicked and weak Judean king react to all of God's warnings?
   1. His immediate response was to imprison Jeremiah (Jer. 32:3).
   2. He commanded all those living in Jerusalem to free their slaves (Jer. 34:8-9).
   3. He asked Jeremiah to pray for Judah (Jer. 37:3).
   4. He then removed the prophet from a vaulted cell in a dungeon where he had been confined (Jer. 37:16-17).
   5. Zedekiah placed Jeremiah in the courtyard of the guard and ordered that he be fed sufficiently until the food in the city was gone (Jer. 37:21).
   6. Later, however, he submitted to the pressure from those who hated Jeremiah and allowed the prophet to be placed in a cistern, where the suffering servant sank down into the mud (Jer. 38:1-6).
   7. But another court official, friendly to Jeremiah, convinced the indecisive king to remove the prophet from the cistern back to the courtyard (Jer. 38:7-13).
   8. During the last recorded conversation between the two men, Zedekiah shared his terrible fear to Jeremiah that he, the king, would be turned over to his Jewish enemies (Jer. 38:19-20).

STATISTICS

Father: Josiah (1 Chron. 3:15)
Mother: Hamutal (2 Kings 24:18)
Brothers: Johanan, Jehoiachin, and Shallum (or Jehoahaz) (1 Chron. 3:15)
First mention: 2 Kings 24:17
Final mention: Jeremiah 52:11
Meaning of his name: "God is Might"
Frequency of his name: Referred to 55 times
Biblical books mentioning him: Four books (2 Kings, 1 Chronicles, 2 Chronicles, Jeremiah)
Occupation: King of Judah (2 Kings 24:18).
Place of birth: Jerusalem
Place of death: Babylon (Jer. 52:11)
Important fact about his life: He was the final king of Judah (2 Kings 25:1-7).

✍ *Zephaniah*

CHRONOLOGICAL SUMMARY

I. A bad day—The prophet pronounced judgment
   A. Upon the land of God
      1. The fact of this judgment—God would sweep away everything in the land and destroy it to the

ground. This would include man, birds, and even fish (Zeph. 1:2-4).

2. The reason for this judgment— Judah had worshiped Baal (the great god of the Canaanite pantheon), and Milcom (the chief Ammonite deity), thus ignoring the only true God (1:4-6). The city's leaders were like roaring lions and ravenous wolves devouring any and all victims (3:3).

3. The name of this judgment—The prophet called it "the day of the LORD." This term is used no less than seven times (1:7-8, 14, 18; 2:2-3).

   a. The immediate historical meaning of this term referred to the Babylonian Captivity under Nebuchadnezzar.

   b. The end times prophetical meaning of this term refers to the battle of Armageddon under the Antichrist.

4. The results of this judgment (1:14-18)

   a. God's wrath will be poured out upon Israel because of its sin.

   b. The nation will be as helpless as a blind man searching for a path.

B. Upon the enemies of God

   1. The Philistine cities, Israel's western enemies (2:4-7)

   2. Moab and Ammon, Israel's eastern enemies (2:8-11)

   3. Ethiopia, Israel's southern enemy (2:12)

   4. Assyria and its capital Nineveh, Israel's northern enemy (2:13-15)

C. Upon the city of God

   1. A cry of alarm would begin at the northern fish gate in Jerusalem. It would be heard from gate to gate until it reached the highest part of the city (1:10).

   2. God planned to search with lanterns in Jerusalem's darkest corners to find and destroy all sinners (1:12-13).

   3. He urged the godly remnant to hide themselves (2:3).

II. A glad day—The prophet announced justice

A. Upon the former enemies of God (3:9-10)—"Then will I turn to the people a pure language, that they may all call upon the name of the LORD, to serve him with one consent" (3:9).

B. Upon the land of God—"The remnant of Israel shall not do iniquity, nor speak lies; neither shall a deceitful tongue be found in their mouth: for they shall feed and lie down, and none shall make them afraid" (3:13).

C. Upon the city of God (3:14-20)

   1. Jerusalem will once again be filled with singing, for the theme of their songs, the King of Israel, will be there (3:14-15).

   2. God himself will lead this happy song (3:17).

THEOLOGICAL SUMMARY

I. Zephaniah was of royal blood, being the great-great-grandson of King Hezekiah (1:1).

II. He was thus a prince as well as a prophet.

III. He ministered during the reign of Josiah (1:1).

IV. He used the phrase "the day of the LORD" (a reference to the coming great tribulation) more times than any other biblical writer.

V. Zephaniah 3:8 is the only Old Testament verse which includes every one of the 22 letters in the Hebrew alphabet.

VI. His name, meaning "he whom God hath hidden," may indicate he was hidden during the bloody reign of King Manasseh.

VII. He predicted God will someday "rest" again after completing his final work of redemption as he once did after completing his first great work of creation.

A. Moses wrote: "On the seventh day God ended his work which he had made; and he rested on the seventh day from all his work which he had made" (Gen. 2:2).

B. Zephaniah wrote: "The LORD thy God in the midst of thee is mighty; he will save, he will rejoice over thee with joy; he will rest in his love, he will joy over thee with singing" (3:17).

VIII. The title "king of Israel" in referring to God is found but twice in the Bible.

A. Zephaniah used it—"The LORD hath taken away thy judgments, he hath cast out thine enemy: the king of Israel, even the LORD, is in the midst of thee: thou shalt not see evil any more" (3:15).

B. Nathanael used it—"Rabbi, thou art the Son of God; thou art the King of Israel" (John 1:49).

STATISTICS

Significant ancestor: Hezekiah (Zeph. 1:1)
First mention: Zephaniah 1:1
Final mention: Zephaniah 1:1
Meaning of his name: "He whom God hath hidden"
Frequency of his name: Referred to one time
Biblical books mentioning him: One book (Zephaniah)
Occupation: Prophet (Zeph. 1:1)
Important fact about his life: He used the term "the Day of the Lord" more often than any other Old Testament prophet.

✒️Zeresh

CHRONOLOGICAL SUMMARY

I. Her foolish advice to Haman

A. She was the wife of Haman, the wicked prime minister of Persia who plotted to kill all the Jews in the days of Esther (Esther 5:9).

B. She unwisely advised Haman to build a 75-foot high gallows upon which to hang Mordecai the Jew (Esther 5:14).

II. Her final advice to Haman—She correctly advised Haman at a later time

that he would come to ruin for plotting against Mordecai and the Jewish people (Esther 6:13).

STATISTICS

Spouse: Haman (Esther 5:10)
First mention: Esther 5:10
Final mention: Esther 6:13
Meaning of her name: "Gold"
Frequency of her name: Referred to four times
Biblical books mentioning her: One book (Esther)
Important fact about her life: She was Haman's wife, who suggested he hang Mordecai (Esther 5:14).

✒️Zerubbabel

CHRONOLOGICAL SUMMARY

I. Zerubbabel and the return

A. He was also called Sheshbazzar (Ezra 1:8, 11; 5:14, 16).

B. He was the grandson of Judean King Jehoiachin (1 Chron. 3:17-19).

C. He was the political leader who directed the first return of the Jews from Persia back to Jerusalem (Ezra 2:1-2).

D. He was appointed by King Cyrus himself (Ezra 5:13-15).

E. He carried back with him the gold and silver articles Nebuchadnezzar had once taken from the temple of Solomon (Ezra 1:11).

II. Zerubbabel and the rebuilding

A. He helped build the brazen altar upon reaching Jerusalem (Ezra 3:2).

B. He then started the work of rebuilding the second temple (Ezra 3:8-9).

III. Zerubbabel and the resolution

A. He refused to compromise his testimony by allowing the pagan Samaritans to aid in the building of the temple (Ezra 4:2-3).

B. He was assisted and encouraged in his work by Joshua the high priest, and two key prophets, Haggai and Zechariah (Ezra 5:1-2; Hag. 2:2-9).

IV. Zerubbabel and the reward—Haggai and Zechariah revealed the following information to Zerubbabel:

A. Haggai

1. God's presence and blessing would be upon him (Hag. 2:4-5).
2. A great tribulation would someday come (Hag. 2:21-22).
3. After this the "desire of all nations" (a reference to Christ) would return (Hag. 2:6-8).
4. God had chosen Zerubbabel for a glorious ministry in the Millennium (Hag. 2:23).

B. Zechariah

1. The battle is the Lord's (Zech. 4:6).
2. He, Zerubbabel, would be allowed to complete the second temple (Zech. 4:8-9).

STATISTICS

Father: Shealtiel (Ezra 3:2; Hag. 2:2)
Sons: Meshullam, Hananiah, Hashubah, Ohel, Berechiah, Hasadiah, Jushab-hesed (1 Chron. 3:19-20)
Daughter: Shelomith (1 Chron. 3:19)
Brother: Shimei (1 Chron. 3:19)
Significant ancestors: His grandfather was King Jehoiachin (1 Chron. 3:17-19).
First mention: 1 Chronicles 3:19
Final mention: Zechariah 4:10
Meaning of his name: "Seed, shoot of Babylon"
Frequency of his name: Referred to 26 times
Biblical books mentioning him: Five books (1 Chronicles, Ezra, Nehemiah, Haggai, Zechariah)
Occupation: Political leader (Hag. 1:1)
Place of birth: Persia (Ezra 2:2)
Place of death: Probably Jerusalem
Important fact about his life: He led the first return back to Jerusalem following the Babylonian Captivity (Ezra 2:2).

Ziba

CHRONOLOGICAL SUMMARY

I. Serving his master Mephibosheth

A. Ziba was a chief servant from the household of Saul (2 Sam. 9:2).
B. He had 15 sons and 20 underservants (2 Sam. 9:10).
C. At David's request, he located Mephibosheth, the lame son of Jonathan, beloved friend of the king who had died in battle (2 Sam. 9:2-8).
D. Ziba was then appointed by David to become the servant of Mephibosheth (2 Sam. 9:9-10).

II. Slandering his master Mephibosheth

A. During Absalom's rebellion, Ziba met David in the wilderness and lied to the king, accusing his master Mephibosheth of treason (2 Sam. 16:1-3).
B. Apparently believing him at first, David awarded Mephibosheth's estate to Ziba (2 Sam. 16:4).
C. After the revolt was crushed, Ziba again went out to meet David, this time by the Jordan River (2 Sam. 19:17).
D. Later, when Mephibosheth had the opportunity to defend himself to David, the king apparently had second thoughts concerning Ziba's accusations, for he ordered the estate to be divided up between the two men (2 Sam. 19:29).

STATISTICS

Sons: 15 sons (2 Sam. 9:10)
First mention: 2 Samuel 9:2
Final mention: 2 Samuel 19:29
Meaning of his name: "Plantation"
Frequency of his name: Referred to 16 times
Biblical books mentioning him: One book (2 Samuel)
Occupation: Chief steward (2 Sam. 9:10)
Important fact about his life: He was Mephibosheth's servant, who slandered his master before King David (2 Sam. 19:26-27).

◀Zilpah

CHRONOLOGICAL SUMMARY
I. Zilpah and Leah
   A. She was handmaid to Laban's oldest daughter, Leah (Gen. 29:24).
   B. Leah presented Zilpah to Jacob for childbearing purposes (Gen. 30:9).
II. Zilpah and Jacob—She bore Jacob two sons, Gad and Asher (Gen. 30:10-13).

STATISTICS
Spouse: Jacob (Gen. 30:9)
Sons: Gad and Asher (Gen. 30:10-13)
First mention: Genesis 29:24
Final mention: Genesis 46:18
Meaning of her name: "Myrrh, dropping"
Frequency of her name: Referred to six times
Biblical books mentioning her: One book (Genesis)
Place of birth: Mesopotamia
Important fact about her life: She was Leah's handmaid who bore Jacob two sons (Gen. 30:9-13).

◀Zimri (1)

CHRONOLOGICAL SUMMARY
I. The perversion of Zimri
   A. He was an Israelite leader from the tribe of Simeon (Num. 25:14).
   B. He was guilty of unabashed immorality with a Midianite woman named Cozbi, bringing her into his tent "In the sight of Moses, and in the sight of all the congregation of . . . Israel" (Num. 25:6).
II. The punishment of Zimri—"When Phinehas, the son of Eleazar, the son of Aaron the priest, saw it, he rose up from among the congregation, and took a javelin in his hand; And he went after the man of Israel into the tent, and thrust both of them through, the man of Israel, and the woman through her belly. So the plague was stayed from the children of Israel. And those that

died in the plague were twenty and four thousand" (Num. 25:7-9).

STATISTICS
Father: Salu (Num. 25:14)
Mistress: Cozbi (Num. 25:15)
First mention: Numbers 25:14
Final mention: Numbers 25:14
Meaning of his name: "Singer, celebrated"
Frequency of his name: Referred to one time
Biblical books mentioning him: One book (Numbers)
Occupation: Leader from the tribe of Simeon (Num. 25:14)
Place of death: In the Sinai Desert (Shittim—Num. 25:1)
Circumstances of death: He was executed by Eleazar's son, Phinehas (Num. 25:7-8).
Important fact about his life: His sin helped lead to the death of 24,000 people (Num. 25:9).

◀Zimri (2)

CHRONOLOGICAL SUMMARY
I. He killed his king.
   A. He was the fifth king of Northern Israel.
   B. He ruled only seven days (1 Kings 16:15).
   C. He was co-commander of the royal chariots under King Elah (1 Kings 16:8-9).
   D. He killed Elah while the king lay in a drunken stupor, and took over the throne (1 Kings 16:9-10).
II. He killed himself
   A. Shortly after, the Israelite troops rejected Zimri and proclaimed Omri, the main commander of the army, as their king (1 Kings 16:16).
   B. When Zimri realized the capital city of Tirzah had been taken by Omri, he went into the citadel of the royal palace and committed suicide by setting the palace on fire (1 Kings 16:18).
   C. Years later, the doomed Jezebel ridi-

culed King Jehu, comparing him to the treacherous Zimri (2 Kings 9:31).

STATISTICS
First mention: 1 Kings 16:9
Final mention: 2 Kings 9:31
Meaning of his name: "Celebrated"
Frequency of his name: Referred to eight times
Biblical books mentioning him: Two books (1 Kings, 2 Kings)
Occupation: King of Northern Israel (1 Kings 16:8-9)
Place of death: In his home at Tirzah (1 Kings 16:18)
Circumstances of death: He committed suicide (1 Kings 16:18)
Important fact about his life: He ruled only seven days as king, the shortest reign in the Bible (1 Kings 16:15).

✍Zipporah

CHRONOLOGICAL SUMMARY
I. She first saw her husband by a well.
  A. She and her six sisters had been driven away from this well in the desert by some shepherds, but "Moses stood up and helped them, and watered their flock" (Exod. 2:17).
  B. Zipporah was later given by her father to Moses in marriage (Exod. 2:18-21).
  C. Both Moses and Zipporah were descendants of Abraham.
    1. Moses was a descendant through Sarah, Abraham's first wife.
    2. Zipporah was a descendant through Keturah, Abraham's final wife (compare Gen. 25:1-2 with Exod. 2:16).
II. She later saved her husband by an inn.
  A. As Moses began his trip from the Sinai to Egypt we are told: "It came to pass by the way in the inn, that the LORD met him, and sought to kill him" (Exod. 4:24).
  B. By quickly circumcising their eldest son Gershom (Exod. 2:22), Zipporah

saved the life of her husband (Exod. 4:25-26).
  C. For some undisclosed reason Moses had previously either neglected or refused to perform this ceremony required by God himself.

STATISTICS
Father: Jethro (Exod. 2:21; 3:1)
Sons: Gershom and Eliezer (Exod. 18:2-4)
Significant ancestor: Keturah (Gen. 25:1; Exod. 2:16-21)
First mention: Exodus 2:21
Final mention: Exodus 18:2
Meaning of her name: "Little bird"
Frequency of her name: Referred to three times
Biblical books mentioning her: One book (Exodus)
Place of birth: Land of Midian (Exod. 2:16-21)
Important fact about her life: She was Moses' wife (Exod. 2:21).

✍Zophar

CHRONOLOGICAL SUMMARY
I. The concern of Zophar—"When Job's three friends heard of all this evil that was come upon him, they came every one from his own place: Eliphaz the Temanite, and Bildad the Shuhite, and Zophar the Naamathite; for they had made an appointment together to come to mourn with him and to comfort him. And when they lifted up their eyes afar off, and knew him not, they lifted up their voice, and wept; and they rent every one his mantle, and sprinkled dust upon their heads toward heaven. So they sat down with him upon the ground seven days and seven nights, and none spake a word unto him: for they saw that his grief was very great" (Job 2:11-13).
II. The criticism of Zophar—It wasn't long before the compassion of Zophar, as he

viewed the suffering Job, turned to hostile and unfair criticism (Job 11, 20). Zophar was in error on two counts:

A. His assumption was wrong—Like his 2 friends, Eliphaz and Bildad, Zophar assumed Job was suffering because of some terrible unconfessed sin. "For thou hast said, My doctrine is pure, and I am clean in thine eyes. But oh that God would speak, and open his lips against thee" (Job 11:4-5). NOTE: Zophar based his assumption on sheer dogmatism (see Job 11:6; 20:4).

B. His advice was wrong—Zophar's counsel was simple: Repent of your secret sin.

III. The chastisement of Zophar

A. Zophar was later rebuked by God along with his two friends for their unkind and untrue opinion of God (Job 42:7).

B. He was then required to offer up seven bulls and seven rams as burnt sacrifices for his sin of slander (Job 42:8-9).

STATISTICS

First mention: Job 2:11
Final mention: Job 42:9
Meaning of his name: "Hairy, rough"
Frequency of his name: Referred to four times
Biblical books mentioning him: One book (Job)
Important fact about his life: He was one of Job's critical "friends" (Job 11:1-6).

✐Unnamed Old Testament Individuals

1. Cain's wife (Gen 4:17)

A. Her father and mother were no doubt Adam and Eve (Gen. 5:4).

B. Her brothers were Cain (whom she married), Abel, and Seth (Gen. 4:1-2, 25).

C. Her son was Enoch (Gen. 4:17).

D. She thus became history's second recorded wife and mother.

2. The pharaoh whom Abraham met in Egypt (Gen. 12:10-20)

A. Pharoah and Sarai—Believing Abraham's lie that Sarai was his sister, Pharaoh gave him a dowry and planned to marry her.

B. Pharaoh and God—He and his household were judged by a plague from God for his actions concerning Sarai.

C. Pharaoh and Abraham—Realizing the reason for the plague and learning the truth, Pharaoh rebuked Abraham and sent him out of the land.

3. Lot's two unmarried daughters (Gen. 19:8, 15-16, 30-38)

A. Sinned against by their father in a home
1. Lot and his daughters were visited by two angels from God.
2. Soon their house was surrounded by some vile Sodomites who demanded to possess the angels for sexual purposes.
3. Unwilling to surrender the angels, Lot offered instead to hand over his two daughters to these perverts.

B. Sinning against their father in a cave
1. After Sodom's destruction, Lot and his daughters took refuge in a cave.
2. Fearing they would remain childless, the daughters got Lot drunk and had sex with him.
3. Each had a son through this union.
   a. The older girl named her baby Moab.
   b. The younger girl named her baby Ben-ammi.

4. Lot's wife (Gen. 19:26; Luke 17:32)

A. She looked back upon the burning city of Sodom and became a pillar of salt.

B. She was used by Jesus to illustrate the sin of materialism.

5. Potiphar's wife (Gen. 39:7-18)

A. Lusting after Joseph—She attempted

daily to involve Joseph in sexual immorality.

B. Lying about Joseph—After enduring constant refusal by Joseph, she lied about him, accusing the young man of rape.

6. **Joseph's prison keeper** (Gen. 39:21-23)— God granted Joseph favor with the chief jailor, who soon handed over to him the entire prison administration.

7. **An imprisoned butler who had a dream** (Gen. 40:1-13, 21)
   A. The information in his dream
      1. He saw a vine with three branches and some clusters of ripe grapes.
      2. He squeezed the juice into Pharaoh's cup and gave it to him.
   B. The interpretation of the dream— Joseph told the butler his dream meant that within three days Pharaoh would restore him as his chief butler. This happened as Joseph predicted.

8. **An imprisoned baker who had a dream** (Gen. 40:1-8, 16-19, 22)
   A. The information in his dream—He saw himself carrying three baskets of pastries on his head for the pharaoh.
   B. The interpretation of the dream— Joseph told him the dream meant Pharaoh would take off his head in three days and the birds would consume his flesh. This happened as Joseph predicted.

9. **The pharaoh who elevated Joseph** (Gen. 41:1-45: 45:17-20; 47:1-10; 50:6)
   A. Pharaoh and Joseph
      1. The dreams of the king
         a. He saw seven fat cows being consumed by seven lean ones.
         b. He saw seven plump heads of grain being consumed by seven lean ones.
      2. The decree of the king
         a. Joseph told Pharaoh his dreams meant there would be seven years of abundant crops followed by a seven-year famine and drought.

      b. The king was so impressed that he placed Joseph directly under him, over all Egypt.
      c. He then suggested Joseph move his entire family from Canaan to Egypt.
   B. Pharaoh and Jacob—He met Jacob and was blessed by the old patriarch.

10. **The pharaoh who "knew not Joseph"** (thought to be Thutmose I) (Exod. 1:8-22)
   A. The concern of Pharaoh—He felt something had to be done to curb the rapid growth of the Israelite people in Egypt.
   B. The cruelty of Pharaoh—The king issued a twofold command concerning the Israelites in Egypt.
      1. Mistreat them—The Egyptians subjected the Jews to cruel slavery. In spite of this, their number continued to grow.
      2. Murder them—Pharaoh ordered the death (by drowning) of all male Hebrew babies.

11. **The daughter of Pharaoh** (thought to be Hatshepsut) (Exod. 2:5-10)
   A. She rescued Moses from the Nile.
   B. She raised Moses as her son.

12. **The pharaoh who sought Moses' life** (thought to be Thutmose III) (Exod. 2:15)

13. **An ungrateful Hebrew slave** (Exod. 2:11-14)
   A. He was championed by Moses— Moses delivered this slave by killing an Egyptian soldier who was beating him.
   B. He was critical of Moses—Later, when Moses rebuked this slave for fighting with another Hebrew, the ungrateful servant accused him of trying to be a prince and judge.

14. **The pharaoh of the 10 plagues** (thought to be Amenhotep II) (Exodus 5, 7–10, 12, 14)
   A. The contempt of the king (5:1-18)

1. He ridiculed God and refused Moses' demand to let Israel go.
2. Instead, he added to the Israelites' work burden.
B. The chastisement of the king—God poured out 10 plagues upon the king.
   1. Water turned to blood (7:20)
   2. A frog invasion (8:6)
   3. Lice (8:17)
   4. Flies (8:24)
   5. Cattle disease (9:6)
   6. Boils (9:10)
   7. Hail mixed with fire (9:24)
   8. Locusts (10:13)
   9. A three-day darkness (10:22)
   10. Death of the firstborn (12:29)
C. The compromises of the king—During these 10 terrible plagues, Pharaoh suggested four compromises to Moses.
   1. Worship your God, but stay in Egypt (8:25).
   2. Leave Egypt, but don't go too far (8:28).
   3. Leave Egypt without your children (10:10).
   4. Leave Egypt without your flocks and herds (10:24).
D. The confessions of the king—On two occasions he admitted his sin, but was insincere in his confessions.
   1. First confession (9:27)
   2. Second confession (10:16)
E. The callous heart of the king—He is said to have hardened his heart on seven occasions: 7:13-14; 7:22; 8:19; 8:32; 9:7; 9:12; 9:34
F. The command of the king—After the Passover death plague, Pharaoh summoned Moses and ordered him to leave Egypt immediately, taking all Israel with him (12:31-33).
G. The conspiracy of the king (14:5-9, 21-28)
   1. After three days, he changed his mind and sent out an army, led by 600 chariots, to bring Israel back.
   2. His army was drowned in the waters of the Red Sea by God.

15. **The Sabbath breaker in the wilderness** (Num. 15:32-36)
    A. His disobedience—Totally ignoring the clear command of God concerning the Sabbath, this man was caught gathering wood.
    B. His death—At God's order, he was taken outside the camp and stoned to death.

16. **The unreasonable king of Edom** (Num. 20:14-22)
    A. The request of Moses
       1. He asked that Israel be allowed to go through Edom.
       2. He promised to stay on the main road and not to take as much as a grain of wheat from the fields or a cup of water from the wells.
    B. The refusal of the king
       1. He warned Moses Israel would be attacked by an army if he dared to step foot in Edom.
       2. His refusal caused Israel to backtrack and travel many unnecessary miles through hot and hostile land.

17. **The king of Arad** (Num. 21:1-3)
    A. Mistaking Moses and his leaders for spies, the king attacked Israel during the Exodus march and took some men as prisoners.
    B. Israel asked God for victory over Arad, which request was immediately granted, resulting in the total destruction of that nation.

18. **Two Israelite spies sent out by Joshua** (Joshua 2)
    A. Their mission to Jericho—Joshua sent them to spy out the strengths and weaknesses of Jericho before the Israelite attack.
    B. Their meeting in Jericho
       1. In the city they met a harlot named Rahab, who placed her faith in the Lord God.
       2. She hid the two men from a search party sent out by the king of Jericho.

3. Before leaving the city, the spies promised Rahab both she and her family would be spared when Israel attacked.
4. The spies then escaped, being let down by a scarlet rope from the city wall.

19. A prophet in Gideon's day (Judg. 6:1-10)
A. The problems of the people—Israel had suffered grievous oppression from the cruel Midianites who had stripped and devastated the land.
B. The pronouncement by the prophet—Upon hearing their cries for help, God spoke through this prophet, reminding them they were suffering for their sin of idolatry.

20. Two Midianite soldiers (Judg. 7:12-14)—
One of these soldiers had related a dream he had, which was interpreted by the other soldier.
A. The nature of the dream—The first soldier saw a huge loaf of barley bread come tumbling down into their camp, hitting them and knocking them flat.
B. The meaning of the dream—The second soldier said the dream meant Gideon the Israelite would attack and crush the Midianite army.
C. The reason for the dream—God allowed the dream to occur that he might use it to encourage a timid Gideon, who was hiding nearby, listening to every word.

21. A woman on a roof (Judg. 9:50-54)
A. What she did—She killed Abimelech, the murderous son of Gideon.
B. How she did it—She crushed his skull by hitting him with a millstone thrown from the roof.

22. The king of Ammon whom Jephthah confronted (Judg. 11:12-33)
A. The attack—This king attacked Israel, claiming some of its land had been stolen from Ammon.
B. The argument—Jephthah attempted to

show him from history this simply was not the case.
C. The annihilation—Ignoring Jephthah's message, the king pursued his attack, only to suffer total destruction from the Israelite army.

23. Jephthah's daughter (Judg. 11:30-32, 34-40)
A. Her song—She greeted her father by playing on a tambourine and dancing for joy when he returned from defeating the Ammonites.
B. Her sorrow—Her joy soon turned to despair upon learning of Jephthah's vow to offer up as a sacrifice the first person coming out of his house to meet him if God gave him the victory.
C. Her submission—She submitted to the will of her father, but requested a period of two months during which she could bewail her virginity.

24. Samson's mother (Judg. 13:2-24)
A. Her first meeting with the angel of the Lord
1. His revelation—The angel informed her of two things.
a. Even though previously barren, she would give birth to a son.
b. This son would be raised as a Nazarite.
2. Her reaction—She ran home and told her husband, Manoah, about the angel and his message.
B. Her second meeting with the angel of the Lord—This time she brought her husband and introduced him to the angel.

25. Samson's wife (Judg. 14:2, 15-17)
A. The pressure she experienced—Some Philistine wedding guests threatened her with death if she did not find out and reveal the answer to a riddle Samson had given them.
B. The pressure she exerted—For seven days she pressured Samson with tears, claiming he did not love her

unless he told her the answer to the riddle. Upon learning the answer, she quickly informed the Philistines.

26. **The boy who helped the blinded Samson** (Judg. 16:26)—At Samson's request, this lad (who had led him into the Philistine temple of Dagon) placed the strong man's hands against the two pillars supporting the building.

27. **The mother of Micah** (Judg. 17:1-6)— This story of a mother and her son is a classic and tragic example of the period of the judges when there was no king in Israel and everyone did that which was right in his own eyes.
   A. Her son was guilty of dishonesty— Micah stole 1,100 ($1,000) shekels of silver from his mother, then confessed and returned the money to her.
   B. She was guilty of idolatry—Instead of pointing out his problem, she decided to reward him by using the money to purchase a silver-plated idol which was given to Micah.

28. **A Levite from Mt. Ephraim** (Judg. 19:1— 20:7)
   A. The Levite and his concubine
      1. In a fit of anger, she left him and returned to her home in Bethlehem.
      2. He visited her there, hoping to win her back.
   B. The Levite and the concubine's father
      1. The two men met, liked each other, and became friends.
      2. The father probably convinced his daughter to return with the Levite.
   C. The Levite and an old man living in the Benjamite city of Gibeah
      1. En route to Mt. Ephraim, the Levite and his concubine were invited to spend the night in the home of the old man.
      2. Soon the house was surrounded by some sexual perverts who de-

manded the old man send out the Levite so they could rape him.
      3. In vain the old man attempted to offer his own virgin daughter in place of the Levite.
   D. The Levite and the sexual perverts
      1. In a cowardly act, he delivered his concubine to the perverts.
      2. They raped her to death.
   E. The Levite and the various tribes of Israel
      1. He cut his concubine's body into 12 parts and sent one piece to each tribe along with an explanation of what had happened.
      2. He then appeared before 450,000 troops which had assembled at Mizpeh and demanded that justice be done.
      3. This resulted in a civil war, pitting 11 tribes against the tribe of Benjamin.

29. **The relative of Elimelech called "such a one"** (Ruth 4:1-8)
   A. His rights as a kinsman redeemer reviewed
      1. Boaz reminded the man that, as a close relative of Elimelech, he had first choice in buying the dead man's property.
      2. "Such a one" at first agreed to buy it.
   B. His rights as a kinsman redeemer refused
      1. Upon learning he would also be required to take care of the widow Ruth, he renounced his right.
      2. Boaz, next in line, immediately exercised his right by purchasing the property and marrying the widow.

30. **A prophet in Eli's day** (1 Sam. 2:27-36)
   A. Proclaiming the particulars of Eli's sin
      1. Israel's high priest, Eli, had allowed greed to corrupt him.
      2. He also honored his wicked sons

more than God, refusing to rebuke them for their sin.
B. Prophesying the punishment for Eli's sin
   1. The family priesthood would die with him.
   2. His family members would die at an early age.
   3. His two wicked sons, Hophni and Phinehas, would die on the same day.
   4. A faithful priest (Zadok) and his descendants would replace Eli.

31. The wife of Phinehas (1 Sam. 4:19-22)
   A. The tragic news—This poor woman, already dying in childbirth, learned four horrible things.
      1. Israel had been defeated in battle by the Philistines.
      2. The sacred Ark of the Covenant had been captured.
      3. Her father-in-law, Eli, had broken his neck in a fall and was dead.
      4. Her husband, Phinehas, had been killed in battle.
   B. The tragic name—Her final act was to name her son Ichabod, meaning "the glory of the LORD has departed."

32. Jonathan's armor bearer (1 Sam. 14:1, 6-16)
   A. The commitment of this young man
      1. Jonathan's request—"Come, and let us go over unto the garrison of these uncircumcised [Philistines]: it may be that the LORD will work for us: for there is no restraint to the LORD to save by many or by few" (1 Sam. 14:6).
      2. His reply—"Do all that is in thine heart: turn thee; behold, I am with thee according to thy heart" (1 Sam. 14:7).
   B. The courage of the young man—Jonathan and his armor bearer attacked and killed 20 enemy soldiers, causing the entire Philistine army to panic and run.

33. The lad who gathered Jonathan's arrows (1 Sam. 20:35-40)—Without this boy being aware of it, Jonathan used him to warn David (who was hiding in a field) concerning Saul's murderous plans.

34. The witch at En-dor (1 Sam. 28:7-25)
   A. This woman and Saul the king—first reaction
      1. Disguising himself, Saul visited her one night, requesting that she put him in contact with the dead.
      2. She was reluctant at first but then agreed.
   B. This woman and Samuel the prophet
      1. To her horror she suddenly realized her client was Saul.
      2. Her fear was intensified when she saw Samuel rising from the heart of the earth.
      3. She described his appearance to Saul, who then conversed with the prophet.
   C. This woman and Saul the king—second reaction. After Samuel had departed, she cooked a meal for the desperate king and demanded that he eat it.

35. The Amalekite soldier who (probably) lied to David (2 Sam. 1:1-16)
   A. The particulars of his lie—He attempted to win favor with David by claiming he had killed Saul on the battlefield.
   B. The punishment for his lie—David ordered him to be executed by the sword for claiming to have killed the Lord's anointed.

36. The woman who hid Ahimaaz and Jonathan (2 Sam. 17:19-20)
   A. These two young men were the sons of the chief priests, Zadok and Abiathar, close friends of David.
   B. They were sent by their fathers with a message for the king, who was forced out of Jerusalem during Absalom's rebellion.
   C. After being spotted en route, this

woman hid them in a well over which she had placed a cloth and some grain to dry.

D. Upon being asked if she had seen them, the woman replied they had already crossed a brook and were gone.

37. **A wise woman from Abel** (2 Sam. 20:16-22).
    A. The problem stated
       1. The what of the matter—Her city of Abel was besieged by the troops of Joab, David's military commander.
       2. The why of the matter—They were attempting to capture a rebel named Sheba who had taken refuge inside.
    B. The problem solved—At the woman's advice, Sheba's head was cut off and presented to Joab, thus saving the city from destruction.

38. **Solomon's Egyptian princess wife** (1 Kings 3:1; 7:8; 9:24; 11:1; 2 Chron. 8:11)
    A. She may have been his first wife.
    B. She was the daughter of Pharaoh.
    C. It was a political marriage, meant to unite Israel and Egypt.
    D. The account suggests she remained a pagan, for Solomon built a special house for her away from his own palace and the sacred Ark of the Covenant.
    E. She, like his other foreign wives, probably helped turn Solomon's heart away from God.

39. **The harlot mother who stood before Solomon** (1 Kings 3:16-27)
    A. The situation
       1. Two harlot mothers living in the same house had both recently given birth to a baby, one of which had died.
       2. Both mothers claimed the living one as their baby.
    B. The solution
       1. Solomon proposed that the live

baby be cut in half with each mother receiving a part.
       2. One harlot agreed; the other was horrified and was willing to allow the first to take the child.
       3. Solomon awarded the baby to the second harlot, the true mother.

40. **The queen of Sheba** (1 Kings 10:1-13; 2 Chron. 9:1-12; Matt. 12:42; Luke 11:31)
    A. The testing by the queen
       1. Hearing of Solomon's greatness, she visited him to determine its extent for herself.
       2. She tested him with some hard problems and difficult questions.
    B. The testimony of the queen
       1. She was amazed at the wealth of Solomon.
       2. She was amazed at the wisdom of Solomon, for he answered all her questions.
       3. After presenting him with a large gift, consisting of gold, spices, and precious gems, she departed, concluding that his greatness was more than twice what she had heard.
       4. Jesus referred to her testimony in the New Testament—"The queen of the south shall rise up in the judgment with this generation, and shall condemn it: for she came from the uttermost parts of the earth to hear the wisdom of Solomon; and, behold, a greater than Solomon is here" (Matt. 12:42).

41. **A prophet from Judah** (1 Kings 13:1-32)
    A. This prophet and an evil potentate— King Jeroboam I
       1. The prediction
          a. The prophet watched the king as he approached an altar in Beth-el to burn incense to a golden idol.
          b. He predicted someday a son named Josiah would be born from the line of David, who would burn the bones of those false

priests who serviced the very altar Jeroboam was approaching.

2. The proof—To validate his message, the prophet said the altar would immediately split apart and spill its ashes upon the ground. This happened as the prophet had said.

3. The punishment—A furious Jeroboam shook his fist at the prophet, ordering his arrest, only to discover his arm had suddenly become paralyzed.

4. The prayer—Granting Jeroboam's tearful plea for healing, the prophet prayed and the arm was restored.

B. This prophet and an evil peer—A false prophet from Beth-el

1. He was compromised by a liar.
   a. The prophet had been previously instructed by God to return home immediately upon his confrontation with Jeroboam.
   b. He was persuaded, however, by the lying prophet that God had changed his mind.
   c. The true prophet accepted the invitation of the lying one, and visited his home in Beth-el.
   d. Here he learned, however, that he would lose his life from this act of disobedience.

2. He was killed by a lion.
   a. En route home, the prophet was attacked and killed by a lion.
   b. The old prophet, apparently suffering remorse, lamented over his body and saw that it was properly buried.

42. A lying prophet from Beth-el (1 Kings 13:11-23, 26-32). See the information under #41.

43. The wife of Jeroboam (1 Kings 14:1-18)
A. The deceit of her husband
1. Jeroboam commanded that she disguise herself and visit the home of Ahijah the prophet.
2. The purpose was to discover from

him whether their sick child would recover.
B. The death of her son—God revealed to Ahijah her identity along with a twofold prediction.
1. The ruling dynasty of her husband would be cut off because of his sin.
2. Her ailing son would die.

44. The woman at Zarephath (1 Kings 17:8-24)—This Gentile widow was ministered to by Elijah the prophet as she experienced two terrible crises.
A. First crisis—Drought
1. Elijah and the widow first met during a severe drought.
2. She was preparing a scant meal for her son and herself with the remaining food in the house.
3. At Elijah's command, however, she gave him their food, believing his promise that the remaining meal and oil would be supernaturally increased, which did happen.
B. Second crisis—Death
1. Her son became sick and died.
2. She wondered if this had happened as punishment for her sins.
3. Elijah raised the boy back to life.
4. She affirmed her belief that Elijah was indeed a prophet of God.
C. Jesus referred to the widow and Elijah during his sermon in the synagogue at Nazareth. "No prophet is accepted in his own country. But I tell you of a truth, many widows were in Israel in the days of Elias, when the heaven was shut up three years and six months, when great famine was throughout all the land; But unto none of them was Elias sent, save [but only] unto Sarepta, a city of Sidon, unto a woman that was a widow" (Luke 4:24-26).

45. A prophet who ministered to King Ahab (1 Kings 20:13-43)
A. He reassured him on several occasions

that he should attack Syria, promising God would give Israel the victory.

B. He rebuked him on one occasion for sparing the life of Ben-hadad, the enemy Syrian king.

46. A Syrian who unknowingly killed King Ahab (1 Kings 22:34)—"A certain man drew a bow at a venture, and smote the king of Israel between the joints of the harness."

47. An Israelite captain who begged Elijah for mercy (2 Kings 1:13-15)

A. The reason behind his plea
  1. Israelite King Ahaziah had previously dispatched two separate army captains with 50 soldiers each to arrest Elijah.
  2. Elijah had called down fire from heaven, destroying both groups.

B. The results of his plea—Both the captain and his men were spared, as Elijah agreed to go with them to confront the king.

48. A poor woman provided for by Elisha (2 Kings 4:1-7)

A. The problem
  1. A widow of a Bible student was threatened by her dead husband's creditors.
  2. They were planning to take her two sons as slaves if the bills could not be paid.

B. The provision
  1. At Elisha's command, the widow borrowed as many empty vessels as possible from her friends.
  2. These vessels were supernaturally filled with olive oil, thus allowing her debts to be paid.

49. A prominent woman living at Shunem (2 Kings 4:8-37; 8:1-6)

A. The kindness she showed to Elisha— She befriended Elisha the prophet by providing for him a guest room in her house.

B. The kindness she reaped from Elisha
  1. To reward her, Elisha predicted God

would allow her to give birth to a son, even though her husband was an old man.
  2. Her son, upon reaching his teens, became sick and died.
  3. The grief-stricken woman found Elisha at the base of Mt. Carmel and urged him to return with her.
  4. Elisha did so and restored the lad to life again.
  5. Later, at Elisha's advice, she and her family moved so as to avoid a future seven-year famine.
  6. Upon the family's return, the Israelite king (because of Elisha's influence) treated them kindly and restored the land they had vacated.

50. The little Israelite maid who served in Naaman's home (2 Kings 5:2-3)

A. The testing of her faith—This young girl had been captured by a band of roving Syrian slave runners and eventually given to Naaman's wife as a maid.

B. The triumph of her faith
  1. In spite of this terrible ordeal, she retained her faith in God.
  2. Upon learning of her master's leprosy, she offered the only real solution: "Would God my lord were with the prophet that is in Samaria! for he would recover him of his leprosy" (2 Kings 5:3).
  3. Thus, based solely upon her testimony, mighty Naaman traveled to Israel where he was healed by Elisha of his leprosy.

51. A Bible student for whom Elisha recovered a lost ax head (2 Kings 6:1-7)

A. How the axhead was lost
  1. The student was chopping down a tree to be used in a new building for their school.
  2. His ax head suddenly came off and sank in the Jordan River.

B. How the ax head was recovered
  1. Elisha threw a stick in the water where it had fallen.

2. The ax head floated to the top and was grabbed by the student.

52. A king's officer who was judged by Elisha in Samaria (2 Kings 7:1-2, 17-20)
A. His derision
   1. The city of Samaria was suffering great famine, being surrounded by enemy Syrian troops.
   2. In spite of this, Elisha had promised that within 24 hours food would be abundant in the city.
   3. The officer ridiculed this, concluding that even God himself could not perform such a miracle.
   4. Elisha told the officer he would nevertheless see this food but would not taste of it.
B. His death
   1. The following day when God did provide the food, the king appointed his officer to control the traffic at the gate.
   2. In the ensuing rush by the crowd, he was trampled to death.

53. Four lepers from Samaria (2 Kings 7:3-10)
A. Their desperation—They suffered not only from leprosy, but were starving to death just outside the walls of Samaria.
B. Their decision—Realizing the hopelessness of the situation, they decided to surrender to the enemy Syrian soldiers.
C. Their discovery
   1. Upon entering the Syrian camp, they found no one there.
   2. God had caused their approaching footsteps to resemble those of an attacking army, thus throwing the Syrians into utter panic.
D. Their delight—Before them lay vast supplies of food, wine, silver, gold, and clothing.
E. Their duty
   1. In the midst of the celebration, they suddenly remembered the starving citizens in Samaria.

2. They realized what their duty was—"We do not well: this day is a day of good tidings, and we hold our peace . . . therefore come, that we may go and tell the king's household" (2 Kings 7:9).

54. The prophet who ministered to Jehu (2 Kings 9:1-10)
A. His mission from Elisha—He was sent by Elisha to Jehu in the city of Ramoth-gilead.
B. His message to Jehu
   1. The prophet anointed Jehu with oil, proclaiming him as the new king of Israel.
   2. He then instructed him to destroy the descendants of King Ahab, including his wicked wife Jezebel.

55. A dead man raised by Elisha (2 Kings 13:20-21)
A. Where this miracle occurred—It happened within the actual tomb where the prophet was buried.
B. How this miracle happened
   1. Some men were burying a friend when they were threatened by a gang of hostile Moabites.
   2. In fear, they hastily threw his body into Elisha's tomb and fled.
   3. When the body touched Elisha's bones, the dead man revived and jumped to his feet.

56. The prophet who rebuked Judean King Amaziah on two occasions (2 Chron. 25:7-16)
A. First occasion—The king was warned to dismiss the 100,000 mercenary soldiers he had hired to strengthen Judah's army.
B. Second occasion
   1. The prophet rebuked the king for worshiping some Edomite idols he had captured in battle.
   2. The prophet predicted God would destroy him for this act of idolatry.

57. Job's wife (Job 2:9-10)
A. Her criticism of Job—Instead of at-

tempting to comfort her suffering husband, she offered carnal advice. "Dost thou still retain thine integrity? curse God, and die" (Job 2:9).

B. Her chastening by Job—"Thou speakest as one of the foolish women speaketh" (Job 2:10).

58. Isaiah's wife (Isa. 7:3; 8:3)

A. Her ministry as a mother—She bore Isaiah two sons.
  1. The oldest was Shear-jashub.
  2. The younger was Maher-shalal-hash-baz.
B. Her ministry as a messenger—She functioned as a prophetess.

59. Ezekiel's wife (Ezek. 24:16-24)

A. The suddenness of her death
  1. God warned Ezekiel one morning she would suddenly be removed by death.
  2. She died that very night.
B. The significance of her death
  1. Ezekiel was commanded to show no sorrow over her death.
  2. This illustrated how God would show no sorrow at the funeral of his "wife," Judah and Jerusalem, whose people would soon die at the hands of the Babylonians.

60. The prince of Tyre (Ezek. 28:1-10)

A. The pride of this prince
  1. He had used his considerable natural wisdom to accumulate great riches.
  2. He then looked upon himself as a god.
B. The punishment of this prince
  1. His island kingdom would be invaded by an enemy army.
  2. He would be pierced with many wounds and die.

61. The queen who advised King Belshazzar (Dan. 5:10-12)

A. The need for her advice
  1. Belshazzar had just witnessed a man's hand (minus an arm) writing a message on the wall above him.
  2. None of his wise men could interpret its meaning.
B. The nature of her advice
  1. She reminded him of Daniel, who had displayed vast wisdom and ability during the reign of King Nebuchadnezzar.
  2. She urged him to bring in the prophet that he might explain the mysterious writing.

62. The "he goat" king in Daniel (Dan. 8:5-8, 20-21)

A. Daniel predicted the rise of Alexander the Great.
B. He described the victory Alexander would win over the Medes and Persians.
C. He said Alexander would, however, be struck down and die at the height of his power.
D. His kingdom would then be divided into four parts.

63. The "little horn" and "vile person" king in Daniel (Dan. 8:9-14; 11:21-35)

A. The who of the matter
  1. In these passages, Daniel predicted the activities of a man known as Antiochus Epiphanes.
  2. He was a cruel, Jew-hating Syrian king, ruling over Judah from 175-164 B.C.
  3. He was the most pronounced type and foreshadow of the coming Antichrist in the entire Bible.
B. The when of the matter
  1. On September 6, 171 B.C., he began his blasphemy against the temple.
  2. On December 15, 168 B.C., he sacrificed a huge sow on the Jewish temple altar.
  3. On December 25, 165 B.C. (2,300 days after the September 16, 171 B.C. date), the Maccabees captured Jerusalem, ending the Syrian occupation (see Dan. 8:13-14).

C. The what of the matter—In chapters 8 and 11, the prophet described the activities of Antiochus Epiphanes as follows:

1. He would war against Israel.
2. He would fight against the people of God, defeating some of their leaders.
3. He would even challenge God by canceling the daily sacrifices and by defiling his holy temple. Jesus referred to this several centuries later (see Matt 24:15).
4. He would be allowed by God to continue for awhile.
5. He would possess great shrewdness and intelligence and be energized by Satan.
6. He would prosper for awhile and be allowed to destroy all who opposed him.
7. He would devastate God's people.
8. A master of deception, he would defeat many by catching them off guard as they basked in false security.
9. Then, without warning, he would destroy them.
10. He would use flattery and intrigue in obtaining his kingdom.
11. He would pretend to be a "Robin Hood" by taking the wealth from the rich and giving it to the poor.
12. He would be defeated by Rome and take out his fury on the city of Jerusalem.
13. He would then appoint godless Jews to rule over Judah.
14. He would eventually be destroyed by God.

64. **Amaziah's wife** (Amos 7:17)—Amos predicted the wife of this false priest from Bethel would become a prostitute in the city.

65. **The king of Nineveh in the days of Jonah** (Jon. 3:6-9)
   A. His works of repentance
      1. Upon hearing Jonah's message of repentance, he stepped down from his throne.
      2. He then laid aside his royal robes, put on sackcloth, and sat in ashes.
   B. His words of repentance
      1. He imposed a strict fast upon all his citizens.
      2. He commanded them to wear sackcloth, pray, and turn from their evil ways.

NOTES

NOTES

NOTES

NOTES

NOTES

NOTES

NOTES

NOTES

NOTES

NOTES

NOTES

NOTES

NOTES